Word 2002:
The Complete Reference

About the Authors

Peter Weverka is the author more than 30 computer books, including *Word 2002 for Dummies Quick Reference* and *ICQ for Dummies*. His articles and stories have appeared in *Harper's* and *Spy*.

Diane Poremsky is a consultant who specializes in Microsoft Windows, Office, and Outlook training and development. She is the co-author of *Beginning Visual Basic 6 Application Development* (WROX Press, Jan. 2000) and an upcoming book on Outlook programming. She is a Microsoft Outlook MVP (Most Valuable Professional) in recognition for her technical support of Microsoft Outlook. She's a technical reviewer for a number of computer books and is a columnist and technical reviewer for *Exchange and Outlook* magazine. Diane currently resides in eastern Tennessee with her family.

Word 2002:
The Complete Reference

Peter Weverka
Diane Poremsky

Osborne/**McGraw-Hill**

New York   Chicago   San Francisco
Lisbon   London   Madrid   Mexico City
Milan   New Delhi   San Juan
Seoul   Singapore   Sydney   Toronto

Osborne/**McGraw-Hill**
2600 Tenth Street
Berkeley, California 94710
U.S.A.

To arrange bulk purchase discounts for sales promotions, premiums, or fund-raisers, please contact Osborne/**McGraw-Hill** at the above address. For information on translations or book distributors outside the U.S.A., please see the International Contact Information page immediately following the index of this book.

Word 2002: The Complete Reference

1234567890 CUS CUS 01987654321

ISBN 0-07-213244-2

Publisher	**Copy Editor**
Brandon A. Nordin	Michael Dietsch
Vice President & Associate Publisher	**Indexer**
Scott Rogers	Irv Hershman
Acquisitions Editor	**Computer Designers**
Megg Bonar	Jean Butterfield, Carie Malnekoff, Lauren McCarthy
Project Editor	**Illustrators**
Pamela Woolf	Michael Mueller, Lyssa Sieben-Wald, Beth E. Young
Acquisitions Coordinator	
Alissa Larson	**Series Design**
	Peter F. Hancik
Technical Editor	**Cover Production Artist**
Bill Rodgers	Will Chan

This book was composed with Corel VENTURA™ Publisher.

For Sofia
—Peter Weverka

To my long-time online friend, Roy Lehrer, who was killed
in an automobile crash on February 15, 2000.
Your passing has left a huge hole in everyone's heart and
your expertise is missed by many.
—Diane Poremsky

Contents

Part I
Learning the Ropes

Part II

Formatting Text and Pages

Part IV

Using Word at the Office

Part V

Getting More Out of Word

Part VI

Visual Basic in Word 2002

Part VII
Appendixes

Acknowledgments

This book owes a lot to many hard-working people at Osborne/McGraw-Hill. I would especially like to thank acquisitions editor Megg Bonar for giving me the opportunity to write this book and for moving the project forward.

My co-author, Diane Poremsky, wrote Part VI, and for that I am very grateful. I would also like to thank Will Kelly for writing the latter half of Chapter 17.

Pamela Woolf served as project editor and part-time copy editor on this book, and she did a great job. I would also like to thank Alissa Larson for keeping everything on track and Michael Dietsch for helping with the copy edit.

Technical editor Bill Rodgers dogged me every step of the way to make sure that all the instructions in this book are indeed correct. He offered many suggestions for improving the book and his attention to detail was phenomenal. I would also like to thank Irv Hershman for writing the index.

These people at the offices of Osborne/McGraw-Hill went the extra mile for this book, and I am grateful to all of them: Jean Butterfield, Carie Malnekoff, Lauren McCarthy, Michael Mueller, Lyssa Sieben-Wald, and Beth E. Young.

I would be remiss if I didn't thank the people who worked so hard on the previous edition of this book, so many thanks to David Reid, Betsy Manini, Claire Splan, and Stephane Thomas.

Finally, I would like to thank my family—Sofia, Henry, and Addie—for accommodating my vampire-like writing schedule and eerie demeanor at daybreak.

Peter Weverka
San Francisco
April, 2001

Love and thanks to my husband, Phil and my daughters Liz, Jessie, and Cecilia for all the suppers they've cooked while I spent many long hours on the computer. Yes, it's finally finished and no, you can't go shopping for new clothes now. Love to my older children, Chris and Becky who missed all the fun this time around. I can't forget the rest of my family, Mom and Dad, Carol, Kate, and Kay for your encouragement now that I'm finally writing a book you will actually understand.

Thanks always to my friends and colleagues in the MVP communities, including Ken Slovak for knowing when I needed a laugh. To Steve Moede, Milly Staples, Sig Weber, Vince Averallo, Jessie Louise McClennan, Russ Valentine, Hollis Paul, Jay Harlow, Ben Schorr, Sue Mosher, Randy Byrne and Bill Rodgers for putting up with me.

Diane Poremsky
April, 2001

Introduction

This book presents instructions for completing every task that can be undertaken in Word 2002. This book is your key to understanding how Word 2002 works and how you can use the program to the best advantage. Whether you don't know how to complete a task or you want to learn a better way, look to the pages of this book. Here you will discover how to make Word work for you instead of the other way around.

How This Book Differs from Other Books About Word

You are holding in your hands a first of its kind—a computer book designed to make learning Word as easy and comfortable as possible. This book is decidedly different from other books about Word for the following reasons:

A Task-Oriented Approach   Most computer books describe how to use the software, but this book explains how to complete tasks. I assume you came to this book because you want to know how to *do* something—print form letters, run text in columns, generate an index. You came to the right place.

Information in this book is presented by topic, not according to where it is found on the Word menus. Nothing infuriates me more in a Word book than an exhaustive table that describes, for example, all the options on the Save tab in the Options dialog box (choose Tools | Options to get there). Just because all those options are found in the same place doesn't mean they have a lot in common or should be described in the same place in a book. No, the options on the Save tab pertain to many different tasks. In this book, you will find a description of each Save tab option in the appropriate place—as part of instructions for completing a task.

Accessibility of Information   This book is a reference, and that means you have to be able to find instructions quickly. To that end, the editors and I took great pains to make sure that the material in this book is well organized. You are invited to turn to a chapter, thumb through the pages, and find out by reading the headings which strategies are available for completing a task. The descriptive headings help you find information quickly. The bulleted and numbered lists make following instructions simpler. The tables make options easier to understand. I want you to be able to look down the page and see in a heading or list the name of the topic that concerns you. Computer books are famous for their long, dreary, ponderous paragraphs, but if you look for a long, dreary, ponderous paragraph in this book, you will look in vain. You don't have to slog through a morass of commentary to find the information you need in this book.

Top Ten Lists   At the end of every chapter in this book is a Top Ten List—a list of ten tips, tricks, or problem-solving techniques. Rather than distribute these valuable nuggets of knowledge throughout a chapter, I put them all at the end so you can find them easily. Be sure to look at the end of the chapters to find out strategies for doing it well, doing it right, and doing it quickly.

Annotated Figures   Most of the figures (not the illustrations) in this book are annotated. They are thoroughly annotated, in fact. A savvy Word user can simply look at the figures to find out how to complete tasks.

Easy-to-Understand Screen Shots   Look closely at the screen shots in this book and you will see that all of them show only what you need to see to understand a Word feature. When instructions refer to one part of the screen, only that part of the screen is shown. In most computer books, you see the entire Word screen whether you need to see the whole screen or a corner of it. I took great care to make sure that the figures and illustrations in this book serve to help you understand Word and know how to make the best use of the program.

Instructions For "Undoing It"   Every computer book tells you how to do tasks, but when you complete a task at the computer, half the time you discover that you shouldn't have completed it. In other words, you want to undo what you just did. In this book, wherever instructions for completing a task are given, instructions for undoing it follow. You are entitled to change your mind, and if you change your mind about doing a task for which I give instructions, all you have to do is follow the instructions for "undoing it."

Cross-References   This book is filled to the brim with cross-references. Word 2002 is even more complicated than its predecessor, and most features are linked to other features. You have to know about styles to create a Web page. You have to know about bookmarks to insert a cross-reference. Most books refer you vaguely to another chapter, but the cross-references in this book point to specific headings in other chapters. In this book, you know by name exactly where to go to get the background information you need to complete a task.

What's in This Book, Anyway?

This book is organized to help you find the information you need quickly. Your best bet for finding instructions is to turn to the table of contents or index, but you are also invited to turn the pages at leisure. Find a chapter whose topic interests you and thumb through its pages—you will discover tips and tricks you didn't know before.

The topics in this book are too numerous to describe in an introduction, but here are the bare outlines of what you will find in Parts I–VII:

- **Part I: Learning the Ropes**   Shows how to create, open, and edit documents. You also discover how to use the Help program and print documents.

- **Part II: Formatting Text and Pages**   Demonstrates how to take advantage of speed techniques for using Word. You learn how to format text, paragraphs, pages, and documents. You also find out how to handle lists and proof your work.

- **Part III: Professional-Looking Documents with Word**   Takes you beyond simple layouts. You find out how to handle and create styles, develop your own templates, and embellish documents with artwork and text boxes. Part III also gives instructions for creating newsletters and brochures. This part of the book offers the most comprehensive coverage of the drawing tools found in any computer book.

- **Part IV: Using Word at the Office**   Explores the many features that help when writing reports, manuals, and scholarly papers, including tables of contents, indexes, and cross-references. You learn the many ways that Word tools can help you collaborate with others. You find out how to generate form letters and labels as well.

- **Part V: Getting More Out of Word**   Explains how to manage documents and customize the program. Included is a chapter about creating Web pages with Word and the new speech-recognition software.

- **Part VI: Visual Basic in Word 2002**   Describes how to create, run, and manage macros, as well as the basics of VBA.

- **Part VII: Appendixes**   Includes three appendixes that explain how to install Word, run the Microsoft Clip Organizer program, and take advantage of the opportunities this book presents for getting a MOUS certificate.

Help for MOUS Exam Candidates

The Microsoft Office User Specialist (MOUS) program is a program whereby candidates can be certified to use Word 2002. Appendix C describes in detail how MOUS candidates can use this book to prepare for the MOUS exams. However, this book is by no means strictly for MOUS exam candidates. This book is for everybody who toils happily or unhappily in Word 2002.

 # Conventions Used in This Book

To make this book more useful and a pleasure to read, I joined heads with the publisher to create several conventions. Following are descriptions of the conventions in this book.

Icons

To alert you to an important bit of advice, a shortcut, or a pitfall, you see a Note, Tip, or Caution icon and a few important words in the text.

 Notes refer you to other parts of the book, offer background information, and occasionally define terms.

 Tips give you shortcuts and handy pieces of advice to make you a better user of Word. Take a tip from me and read the Tips carefully.

 When you see a Caution, prick up your ears. Cautions appear when you have to make a crucial choice or when you are about to undertake something you might regret later.

Sidebars

From time to time you will find sidebars in this book. Sidebars present information that is tangential to the main discussion. Sidebars appear in boxes—boxes like this one.

Command Names

In this book, the pipe (|) symbol is used in menu command sequences. For example, you can choose File | New to open a new Word document. The | is just a shorthand way of saying, "Choose New from the File menu." "Choose Tools | Language | Thesaurus" is a shorthand way of saying, "Open the Tools menu, choose the Language command, and choose Thesaurus from the Language submenu."

The Complete Reference

Word 2002

Part I

Learning the Ropes

The
Complete
Reference

Word 2002

Chapter 1

Getting Acquainted
with Word

3

n this chapter, you learn a handful of things that you will do nearly every time you run Word. This chapter explains the ins and outs of starting and closing Word and opening and closing documents. It describes the various parts of the Word screen and how to manipulate the toolbars and ruler. In this chapter are numerous shortcuts for opening files and managing files better. My word: There is a lot of good stuff in this chapter!

Fast Ways to Start Word

It goes without saying, but you can't begin writing a masterpiece on your word processor until you start Word. The standard way to start Word is to click the Start button and choose Programs | Microsoft Word, as shown in Figure 1-1. Everybody, or nearly everybody, knows how to start a program the standard way. The following pages explain how to open a document and Word at the same time, start Word with a shortcut icon, or start Word whenever you turn on your computer.

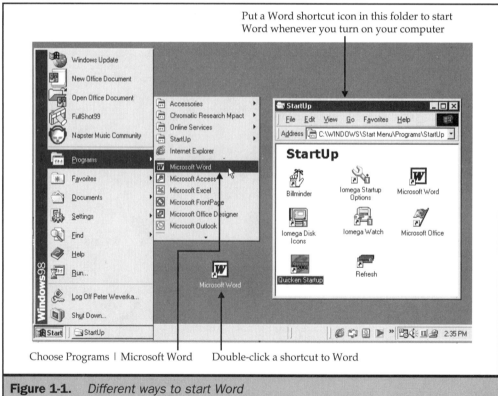

Figure 1-1. *Different ways to start Word*

A file you create with Word is called a document. For practical purposes, "file" and "document" mean the same thing when you are working in Microsoft Word.

Opening a Document and Word at the Same Time

Clicking the Start button and choosing Programs | Microsoft Word to start Word takes but a second, but suppose you are speed demon. In that case, you can open a Word document and start Word at the same time with one of these techniques:

- **Windows Documents Menu**   Click the Start button, choose Documents, and click the name of a Word document on the Documents menu. This menu lists the last 15 files you opened.

- **My Documents Folder**   Click the Start button and choose Documents | My Documents. The My Computer program opens and you see the contents of the My Documents folder. Double-click a document icon in this folder. "Opening Documents," later in this chapter, explains the My Documents folder.

- **Document in My Computer or Windows Explorer**   Open My Computer or Windows Explorer, find the folder that the document you want to open is located in, and double-click the document. My Computer and Windows Explorer are file-management programs that come with Windows.

Starting Word with a Shortcut Icon

Perhaps the fastest way to start Word is to create a *shortcut icon* (refer to Figure 1-1). After you create a Word shortcut icon, it sits on the Windows desktop where you can double-click it and start Word instantly. Probably one or two shortcut icons are on your desktop already. To find one, look for an icon with an arrow in the lower-left corner. Users running Windows on their computers can create a shortcut icon simply by right-clicking a program name on a menu.

Follow these steps to create a shortcut icon for Word if you are running Windows 98:

1. Click the Start button, choose Programs, and right-click Microsoft Word on the Programs menu. As shown in Figure 1-2, a shortcut menu appears.

2. Choose Create Shortcut on the menu. As shown in Figure 1-2, a new name appears at the bottom of the Programs menu: Microsoft Word (2).

3. Drag Microsoft Word (2) onto the desktop. That's right—simply click the name, hold down the mouse button, and drag the menu name off the menu. A Word shortcut icon appears on the desktop.

4. Right-click the Word shortcut icon, choose Rename, type **Word**, and press ENTER.

Right-click and choose Create Shortcut

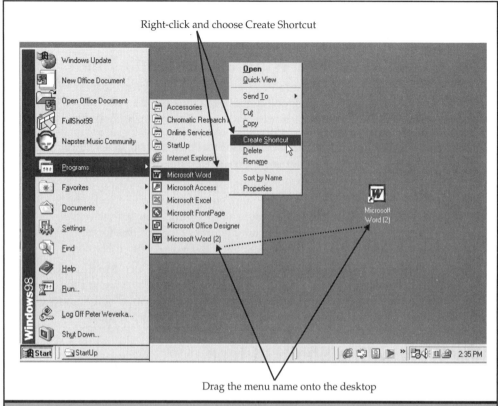

Drag the menu name onto the desktop

Figure 1-2. *Users of Windows 98 and Windows Me can create a shortcut icon for Word by right-clicking Microsoft Word and choosing Create Shortcut*

Starting Word from the Quick Launch Toolbar

Users whose machines run Windows can also start Word by clicking its shortcut icon on the Quick Launch toolbar, the toolbar on the Taskbar. Wherever your work takes you, you can see the Quick Launch toolbar and click its shortcut icons to open programs. To put a Word shortcut icon on the Quick Launch toolbar, create a Word shortcut for the desktop, and then copy the shortcut icon onto the Quick Launch toolbar. To do so, hold down the CTRL key and drag the Word shortcut icon onto the Quick Launch toolbar:

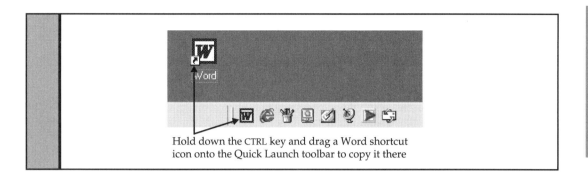

Hold down the CTRL key and drag a Word shortcut
icon onto the Quick Launch toolbar to copy it there

Making Word Start When You Turn on Your Computer

Instead of going to the trouble to start Word each time you sit at your desk, you can kill
two birds with one stone and make Word start automatically whenever you turn on your
computer. To do so, put a shortcut to Word in the C:\Windows\Start Menu\Programs\
StartUp folder. Windows offers a special set of commands for doing just that.

*The fastest way to make Word start automatically is to simply make a Word shortcut
icon and copy it in the C:\Windows\Start Menu\Programs\StartUp folder (refer to
Figure 1-1).*

Follow these steps to start Word whenever you turn on your computer:

1. Click the Start button and choose Settings | Taskbar & Start Menu.

2. Select the Start Menu Programs tab in the Taskbar Properties dialog box
   (in Windows Me, select the Advanced tab in the Taskbar and Start Menu
   Properties dialog box).

3. Click the Add button. You see the Create Shortcut dialog box.

4. Type **"C:\Program Files\Microsoft Office\Office\winword.exe"** in the
   Command Line text box, as shown in Figure 1-3. You can also click the Browse
   button and locate the winword file in the Browse dialog box. You will find it in
   the C:\Program Files\Microsoft Office\Office folder.

5. Click the Next button. You see the Select Program Folder dialog box.

6. Select the StartUp folder and click Next. You have to scroll to the bottom of the
   dialog box to find the StartUp folder.

7. Type **Word** in the Select a Title dialog box and then click Finish.

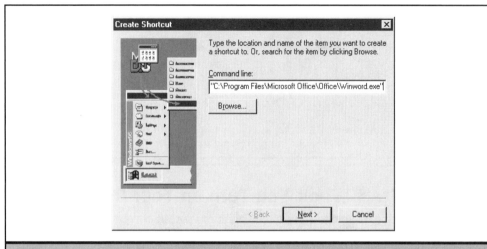

Figure 1-3.   *Creating a shortcut icon to Word so the program opens automatically when you turn on your computer*

Starting Word whenever you start you computer can slow you down a bit. If you decide against opening Word automatically, remove the Word shortcut icon from the C:\Windows\Start Menu\Programs\StartUp folder. To do so, open that folder in My Computer or Windows Explorer, right-click the shortcut icon, choose Delete from the shortcut menu, and click Yes when you are asked if you really want to delete the shortcut.

Finding Your Way Around the Screen

Learning your way around a new computer program is like the first day of junior high school—it's intimidating. Your palms sweat. You feel agitated. To keep you from being intimidated, the following pages explain what the different parts of the Word screen are, how to read the status bar at the bottom of the screen, and how to handle the ruler and toolbars.

The Different Parts of the Screen

Figure 1-4 shows the different parts of the Word screen. Fold down the corner of this page so you can return here if screen terminology confuses you. Here are brief descriptions of the parts of the screen:

- **Title Bar**   The stripe along the top of the screen. It lists the document's name.
- **Window Buttons**   These buttons are for shrinking, enlarging, and closing the window that you are working in. See "Working in Two Places or Documents at Once" in Chapter 6.

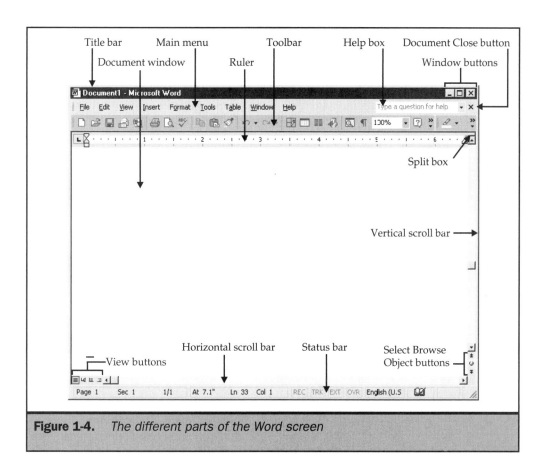

Figure 1-4.   *The different parts of the Word screen*

■ **Main Menu**   The menus you can open and choose commands from. "A Word About Menu Commands."

■ **Help Box**   Type a question in the box, choose a question from the drop-down list to open the Help program, and, with luck, get the answer to your question.

■ **Document Close Button**   Click this button when you want to quit working on a document.

■ **Document Window**   Where you process words but not cheese.

■ **Toolbar**   Click a button on a toolbar to give a command.

■ **Ruler**   Helps show where items are laid out on the page.

■ **Split Box**   For dividing the screen in two so you can work in more than one place in the same document. See "Working in Two Places or Documents at Once" in Chapter 6.

■ **Scroll Bars**   For moving up and down and side to side onscreen. The scroll bar along the right side of the screen is called the *vertical scroll bar*; the one along the bottom is the *horizontal scroll bar*.

■ **Select Browse Object Buttons**   Click the round button and you see a menu for moving to different places in a document. Click the arrows to move from place to place. See "Using the Select Browse Object Button to Get Around" in Chapter 2.

■ **View Buttons**   Changes your view of a document. Some views are better than others for doing different tasks. See "Getting a Better View of Your Work" in Chapter 2.

■ **Status Bar**   Shows what page the cursor is in, which section it is in, which page it is in, and where it is on the page.

Reading the Status Bar

Glance at the status bar along the bottom of the screen when you want to know where the cursor is in a document. In this illustration, for example, the status bar tells you that the cursor is

■ On page 22; in section 2; and on page 22 of a 32-page document.

■ At a position 1.7 vertical inches from the top of the page; on the fifth line of the page; and in a position 4 spaces, characters, or tab spaces from the left margin. Don't let the letters "Col" on the status bar fool you—the Col designation has nothing to do with columns, but with the location of the cursor onscreen.

■ The four sets of letters on the right side of the status bar are buttons. Double-click REC to record a macro; TRK to track revisions to documents; EXT to select text; and OVR to overwrite, or cover, characters that are already there as you type in new characters.

■ The Language box tells you what language the cursor is in. If you write in more than one language, you can always glance at this box to see which language Word thinks it is dealing with.

■ The Spelling box tells you when Word is checking for spelling errors. When a pencil appears over the book, Word is checking your spelling.

| Page 22 | Sec 2 | 22/32 | At 1.7" | Ln 5 | Col 4 | REC TRK EXT OVR | English (U.S |

If you are desperate for space onscreen, you can remove the status bar, horizontal scroll bar, and vertical scroll bar. To do so, choose Tools | Options, select the View tab in the Options dialog box, and, under Show, uncheck the Status Bar, Horizontal Scroll bar, and Vertical Scroll bar check boxes.

Displaying and Removing the Ruler

As shown in Figure 1-5, use the ruler when you are laying out a page and you want to see where text falls and pictures lie. The gray areas on either side of the horizontal ruler shown along the top of the screen show where the left and right margins are. By dragging indent markers on the ruler, you can indent text. Besides the horizontal ruler along the top of the document window, a vertical ruler appears along the left side in Print Layout view (choose View | Print Layout to switch to Print Layout view).

Throughout this book I describe different ways to use the ruler. For now, you need to know that displaying the ruler isn't always necessary. When you want more room onscreen or you are writing and you want to focus on the words, you might as well remove the ruler. To remove or display the ruler, choose View | Ruler.

When the ruler isn't displayed, you can still make it appear briefly by sliding the pointer to the top of the window where the ruler normally is.

Figure 1-5.   *Choose View | Ruler when you want to display or remove the ruler*

Changing the Ruler Measurements

President Gerald Ford, I believe it was, set the goal of converting the United States to the metric system by 1981. Today, standard measurements are still the norm, but that doesn't mean you can't display millimeters or centimeters on the ruler if you are metric-minded. You can display points or picas as well.

To change the unit of measurement on the ruler, choose Tools | Options and select the General tab in the Options dialog box. Then make a choice from the Measurement Units drop-down menu. Here are five rulers, one for each option—Inches, Centimeters, Millimeters, Points, and Picas—on the Measurement Units drop-down menu:

1 · · · 2 · · · 3	Inches
1·2·3·4·5·6·7·8·9	Centimeters
20 · 40 · 60 · 80	Millimeters
36·72·108·144·180·216·252	Points
6 · 12 · 18	Picas

By the way, when you choose a new unit of measurement for the ruler, you also change the unit of measurement in many of the dialog boxes in which measurements are entered. For example, the Paragraph dialog box (choose Format | Paragraph to get there) offers text boxes for indenting paragraphs. If you choose centimeters instead of inches as the unit of measurement, the Paragraph dialog box asks for centimeter instead of inch measurements when you indent text.

Getting to Know the Toolbars

A *toolbar* is an assortment of buttons for completing tasks. Two toolbars appear onscreen when you start Word—the Standard toolbar and the Formatting toolbar—but those are by no means the only toolbars. Word offers more than 25 toolbars, and you can create your own as well (a subject of Chapter 21). Click a button on a toolbar instead of choosing a command and you can usually get things done faster.

Throughout this book, I explain when to display various toolbars and click different buttons. These pages are devoted to manipulating toolbars. They explain how to learn what toolbar buttons do, display and hide toolbars, and arrange toolbars onscreen. You also learn about a strange but highly useful variation on the toolbar—the floating toolbar.

To start with, the Standard and Formatting toolbars appear in one long row, which makes it hard to get to the buttons on the Formatting toolbar. To display the toolbars in two rows, click the Toolbar Options button and choose Show Buttons on Two Rows on the drop-down menu. The Toolbar Options button is the narrow button with the little arrow on it.

Finding Out What Buttons Do

To find out what clicking a button on a toolbar does, gently slide the mouse pointer over the button. You see the button's name, which gives some idea of its purpose. Another way to find out what a button does is to press SHIFT-F1 (or choose Help | What's This?), click a button, and read the button's name and description:

If toolbar button names don't appear when you move the pointer over them, choose View | Toolbars | Customize, select the Options tab in the Customize dialog box, and check the Show ScreenTips On Toolbars check box. Click the Show Shortcut Keys In ScreenTips check box as well to see the shortcut key equivalent of clicking buttons when you move the mouse pointer over buttons.

Displaying and Hiding Toolbars

I suggest that you get used to hiding and displaying toolbars. Keeping a toolbar onscreen when you no longer need it wastes screen space. And displaying or hiding a toolbar takes but a second. Word offers two ways to display or hide a toolbar:

- Choose View | Toolbars and select the name of the toolbar on the submenu.
- Right-click a toolbar or the menu bar and select the name of the toolbar on the shortcut menu, as shown in Figure 1-6.

The Drawing toolbar and Tables and Borders toolbar get special treatment. To hide or display them, click the Drawing button or the Tables and Borders button on the Standard toolbar.

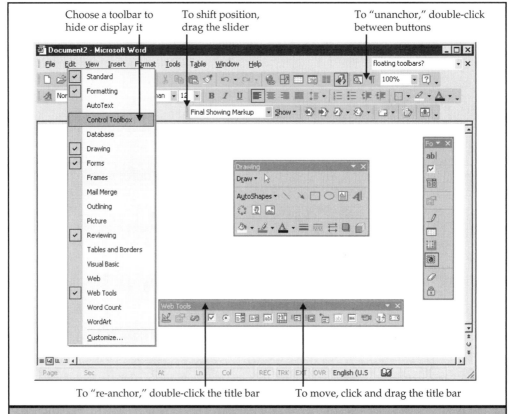

Figure 1-6. *Learn to manipulate toolbars and you are well on your way to becoming a speedy user of Word*

Arranging Toolbars Onscreen

Most toolbars are "anchored" to the top or bottom of the screen when you display them. However, as Figure 1-6 shows, you can move a toolbar away from the top or bottom of the screen. You can change its shape, too. Tuck a toolbar in the corner of the screen to move it out of the way but still be able to click its buttons. Here are instructions for manipulating toolbars:

- **"Unanchoring"** To move a toolbar away from its home port at the top or bottom of the screen, double-click between toolbar buttons. You can also move the pointer to the left side of the toolbar, and, when you see the four-headed arrow, click and start dragging. Soon the toolbar appears in the middle of the screen and you can see its title bar, the stripe along the top with the toolbar's name on it.

- **Shifting**   On the left side of toolbars is a slider. Drag the slider to move an anchored toolbar from side to side.

- **Moving**   Drag the title bar to move a toolbar onscreen.

- **Changing Shape**   Gently move the mouse pointer over the perimeter of the toolbar. When you see the double arrows, click and drag.

- **"Re-anchoring"**   Double-click the title bar to move a toolbar back to its home port at the top or bottom of the screen.

The Strange Case of the Floating Toolbar

Notice the four-headed arrow and the stripe at the top of the submenu in the illustration shown here. As the tip in the illustration says, you can drag the stripe to make the menu float. Here, I have dragged the strip to turn the Order submenu into a floating toolbar:

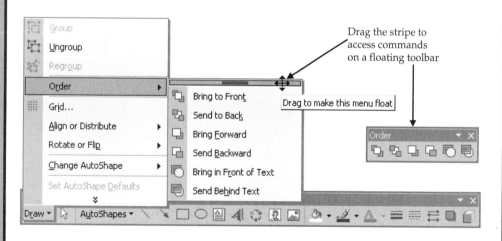

Throughout this book, I will show you why the buttons on floating toolbars are so useful. For now, all you need to know is that a four-headed arrow and a stripe at the top of a submenu means you can turn the submenu into a floating toolbar by dragging it. Commands on floating toolbars are much easier to get at than commands on submenus.

Handling the Task Pane

Choose certain commands and the *task pane,* a separate window on the right side of the screen, appears. Choose File | New, for example, and you see the New Document task pane. Click the Styles and Formatting button and you see the Styles and Formatting task pane. Click the Search button and the Basic Search task pane appears, as shown in Figure 1-7.

The different task panes are described throughout this book. For now, all you need to know about them is the following:

- **Close the task pane**   Click the Close button or choose View | Task Pane.

- **Enlarge or shrink the task pane**   Move the pointer over the border between the task pane and the window. When you see the double-arrow, click and drag.

- **Go from task pane to task pane**   Click the Other Task Panes button (it's beside the Close button) and choose a task pane name on the drop-down menu.

- **Choose View | Task Pane**   If you get lonely and want to see the task pane but aren't sure how to open it, use this option.

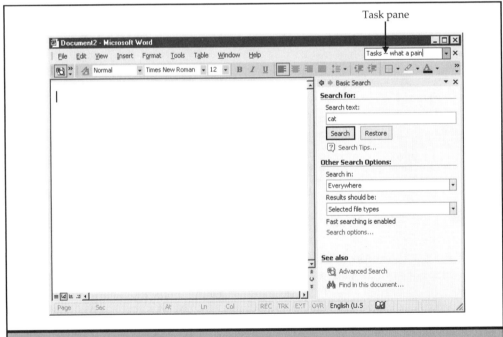

Figure 1-7.   *The task pane is designed to help you work faster and better*

The New Document task pane opens when you start Word. If you prefer not to see it, choose Tools | Options, select the View tab, and, under Show, uncheck the Startup Task Pane check box.

All About Documents

Word files are called "documents," a highfalutin name if there ever was one. A document is nothing more than a file you create with Word. This section explains everything you need to know about documents: how to create new ones, save and name them, open and close them, and delete and rename them. Along the way, you learn what templates are and how you can use templates to create fancy layouts without having to go to a lot of trouble.

Creating New Documents

When you start Word, you also create a brand-new document. As a glance at the title bar shows, the document is called "Document1" until you save and give it a name. To create a document on your own, you can either create another normal document like the one you see when you start Word or create a document with the help of a template or wizard.

Figure 1-8 shows a document that was created with the Contemporary Letter template (squint at the page and you can see the document behind the dialog box). A *template* is a set of styles, or formats. When you create a document with a template, your document is laid out and decorated for you. All you have to do is enter the text. A *wizard* is similar to a template in that you also get a laid-out, formatted document. To create a document with a wizard, however, you answer questions in dialog boxes about how you want to lay out the document before Word creates it.

 If you want any degree of sophistication in a document, create it with a template or wizard. You'll save time that way and impress others with your desktop-publishing prowess.

Follow these steps to create a new document:

- **Normal Document**   Click the New Blank Document button on the Standard toolbar or press CTRL-N. You can also choose File | New and double-click the Blank Document link under "New" in the New Document task pane.

- **General Template or Wizard Document**   Choose File | New to open the New Document task pane. Then, under "New from Template," click the General Templates link. You see the Templates dialog box shown in Figure 1-8. Select a tab—Legal Pleadings, Letters & Faxes, and so on—and select a template or wizard icon. As long as you loaded the template when you installed Word, the

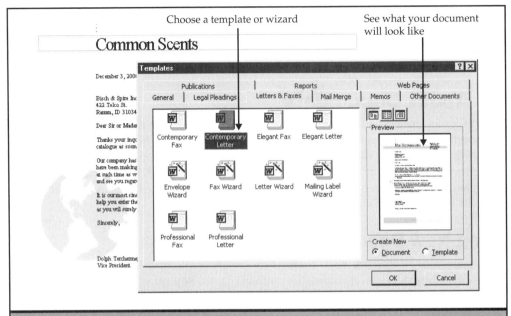

Figure 1-8.   *Creating a document with a template or wizard saves you the trouble of laying out and designing the document on your own*

Preview box shows what your document will look like. Click OK to create your document. In the case of a wizard, answer the questions as they are presented in dialog boxes.

If you try to create a document with a template that hasn't been installed on your computer, Word will ask whether you want to install the template. Insert the installation disk in your computer and click OK. You can tell if a template has been installed by selecting it in the Templates dialog box and glancing at the Preview box. If you see a template in the Preview box, the template has been installed.

- **Microsoft Template**   In the New Document task pane (choose File | New to get there), click Templates on Microsoft.com. Your browser opens and you go to the Microsoft Office Template Gallery. From here you can choose from a number of templates and boilerplate documents. Be careful, because not all of them are meant for Word (some were designed for other Office applications). When you find a template you like, click Edit in Microsoft Word to download it to your computer and make your new document appear onscreen.

- **Template on Your Web Site**   If you keep templates on a network, Web, FTP, or Exchange 2000 server, click Templates on My Web sites in the New Document task pane (choose File | New to see it). Then select the folder where the templates are kept, go to the folder, and select a template. (To tell Word where your Web folders are located, click the Add Web Folder link and negotiate the dialog boxes in the Add Web Folder Wizard.)

  When you create a normal document by clicking the New button or pressing CTRL-N, *you also create a document with a template—the Normal template. Unlike the other templates, however, Normal is a bare-bones template with only a few formats. Chapter 12 takes up the subject of templates, including how to create your own. For now, all you need to know is that every Word document is based on a template, either the Normal template or another, more sophisticated one.*

Saving and Naming Documents

Soon after you create a new document, be sure to save it. And save your document from time to time as you work on it as well. Until you save your work, it rests in the computer's electronic memory (RAM), a precarious location. If a power outage occurs, your computer crashes, or someone trips over the computer's power cord, you lose all the work you did since the last time you saved your document. Make it a habit to save files every ten minutes or so or when you complete an important task.

To save a document

1. Click the Save button.
2. Press CTRL-S.
3. Choose File | Save.

Chapter 20 explains how to save a document under a new name, save a document for use in an earlier version of Word or another word processor, save different versions of the same document, and other file-saving esoterica.

The first time you save a document, Word opens the Save As dialog box shown in Figure 1-9 and invites you to give the document a name and choose the folder in which to store it. As explained in "Ten Techniques for Managing Files Better" at the end of this chapter, creating a folder for each project you are working on and saving documents in those folders saves time because you always know where to find a document when you want to open it. When you save a document, be sure to save it where you can find it again.

The next part of this chapter explains the tools you can use to locate folders—on your computer, a network, or a Web folder—in the Save As or Open dialog box.

Make sure the name of the folder where you want to store your document shows in the Save In box. Then enter a name for your document and click the Save button. Document names can be 255 characters long and can include spaces, but cannot include these characters: / ? : * " < > and | .

Folder where the document is saved

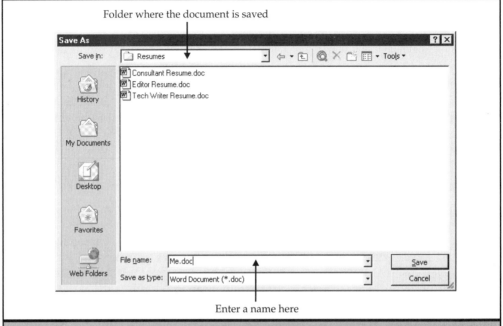

Enter a name here

Figure 1-9. *When you save a document for the first time, you give it a name and choose where to save it in the Save As dialog box*

Choosing a Default File Format

Unless you tinker with the default settings, documents you save are given the Word Document (.doc) format. That's fine and dandy, except if you prefer to save them in the Rich Text Format (.rtf), as a Web Page (.htm, .html), or in another format.

To tell Word how you want to save documents by default, choose Tools | Options and select the Save tab in the Options dialog box. Then choose a format from the Save Word Files As drop-down list and click OK. In Chapter 20, "Strategies for Saving Documents" describes different ways to save documents.

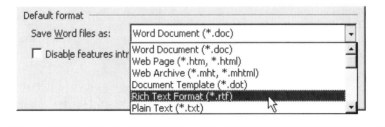

Opening Documents

Word and Windows offer many shortcuts for opening documents. To open a document, you can either take the standard route or take advantage of the numerous ways to open documents quickly. Better read on.

How would you like to be able to open a document and move the cursor to the spot you were working in when you closed it? It can be done. After you open the document, press SHIFT-F5 *or* ALT-CTRL-Z. *Word scrolls to the last place where you made an editorial change.*

The Slow, Standard Way to Open a Document

If you can't open a file by any other means, you have to resort to the Open dialog box:

1. Click the Open button, choose File | Open, or press CTRL-O. You see the Open dialog box shown in Figure 1-10. If you've opened a document already, the dialog box opens to the folder where the last document you opened is kept. Otherwise, the dialog box opens to the My Documents folder. You can tell which folder you are looking at by glancing at the folder name in the Look In text box.

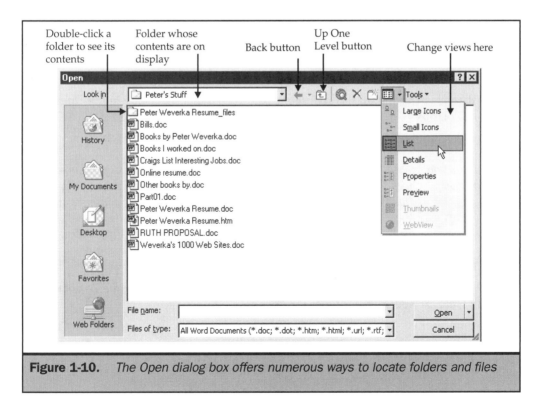

Figure 1-10.   *The Open dialog box offers numerous ways to locate folders and files*

2. Find the folder in which the document you want to open is located. The Open dialog box offers these tools to help you do so:

- **Look In Drop-Down Menu**   To look for folders or documents on a different drive, network location, or disk, open the Look In drop-down menu and make a selection. Choose Network Neighborhood if you want to open a document that is saved on the network to which your computer is connected.

- **Back Button**   Click the Back button to revisit folders you saw before in the course of your search. In other words, click this button to backtrack.

- **Up One Level Button**   Moves up the folder hierarchy to show the contents of the folder one level above the one you are looking at.

- **Views Drop-Down Menu**   Lets you display folder contents differently in the Open dialog box. Click the down arrow and select a new view (see Figure 1-10). Details view can be very helpful when you have trouble finding a file. In Details view, you see how large files are and when they were last edited.

- **Folders**   Double-click a folder to see its contents in the Open dialog box. If you chose Network Neighborhood on the Look In drop-down menu, double-click the name of the computer where the document you want to open is stored.

Note   *The next part of this chapter, "Fast Ways to Open a Document," explains what the buttons on the left side of the Open dialog box do.*

3. Keep searching until the document you want to open appears in the Open dialog box.

4. Either double-click the document or select it and click the Open button.

Tip   *To find out what is in a document without having to open it, right-click the document and choose Quick View on the shortcut menu. As long as Quick View is a part of your operating system (it's not a part of Windows Me or Windows 2000), the document appears in the Quick View screen. To open the document from there without having to return to the Open dialog box, choose File | Open File for Editing in the Quick View screen.*

Fast Ways to Open a Document

Next, the shortcuts. If you can use one of the following techniques to open a document, go for it! Here are speedy techniques for opening documents.

Windows Documents Menu The Windows Documents menu lists the last 15 files you opened. If the Word document you want to open is one of the lucky 15, click the Start button, choose Documents, and click the name of the document to open it.

File Menu and New Document Task Pane Names of the last four documents you opened are listed on the bottom of the File menu and the top of the New Document task pane. Perhaps the document you want to open is listed. Either click it on the task pane or open it from the File menu.

You can make more than four document names appear on the New Document task pane and the bottom of the File menu. To do so, choose Tools | Options and select the General tab in the Options dialog box. Then enter a number greater than 4 in the Recently Used File List text box. I suggest making eight or more document names appear on the File menu and task pane. Why not? You save time opening files that way.

Favorites Folder Put a shortcut to the documents and folders you use often in the Favorites folder. That way, you can get to your favorite documents and folders quickly. Word offers a special command in the Open dialog box for creating Favorites folder shortcuts. After you have created the shortcut, all you have to do to open a folder or document is click the Favorites button in the Open dialog box to open the Favorites folder and then double-click a document or folder name.

Follow these steps to put a shortcut to a folder or document in the Favorites folder:

1. Choose File | Open to see the Open dialog box.

2. Find the folder or document that needs a shortcut and click to select it.

3. Click the Tools button and choose Add to Favorites on the drop-down menu.

4. Click the Favorites button. Do you see your folder or document? All you have to do to open it now is double-click it.

In versions of Windows previous to Windows Me, you can also click the Start button, choose Favorites, and make a selection to open a folder or document that you are keeping in your Favorites folder.

My Documents Folder One way to open files quickly is to keep the documents on which you are currently working in the My Documents folder where you can get at them. That way, all you have to do to open a document is choose File | Open, click the My Documents button in the Open dialog box to see the contents of the My Documents folder, and double-click a document name. When you finish with a document and don't need to open it often, move it from the My Documents folder to a permanent home.

Choosing a New Default Folder for Storing Documents

Unless you tell it otherwise, Word assumes that you want to keep documents in the My Documents folder. The first time you try to open a file after you start Word, you see the contents of the My Documents folder in the Open dialog box. However, you can make another folder appear by default in the Open dialog box (and the Save As dialog box, too). Perhaps you keep the documents you use most often in another folder and you want to see it by default when you choose File | Open. Follow these steps to tell Word which folder to display by default in the Open and Save As dialog boxes:

1. Choose Tools | Options to open the Options dialog box.

2. Select the File Locations tab.

3. Under File Types, select Documents, and then click the Modify button.

4. In the Modify Location dialog box, find and select the folder that you want to see by default in the Open and Save As dialog boxes.

5. Click OK. The location and name of the folder you chose appears in the Location column of Options dialog box.

6. Click the Close button.

History Folder   The Open and Save As dialog boxes might also offer the History button. Click it and you see an exhaustive list of the last hundred or so files you opened with Office programs. Double-click a file to open it.

Web Folders   Click the Web Folders button in the Open and Save As dialog boxes to access folders and files that are stored on your intranet or Web site. (Depending on your version of Windows, you might not see the Web Folders button.)

To change the size of the buttons on the left side of the Open or Save As dialog box, right-click a button and choose Small Icons or Large Icons. You can also choose commands for removing buttons or moving them up and down the ladder.

Opening Documents by Way of Shortcut Icons

Create shortcut icons to the documents you open very, very often and put the shortcut icons on the desktop. That way, you can open documents quickly by double-clicking their shortcut icons on the Windows desktop. Or, if you are in the Open dialog box, you can click the Desktop button and then double-click a shortcut icon.

To create a shortcut icon to a document, choose File | Open and find the file to which you want to create a shortcut in the Open dialog box. Then right-click the file, choose Send To on the shortcut menu, and choose Desktop (Create Shortcut) on the submenu.

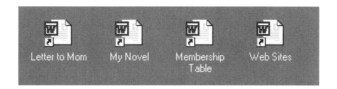

Closing Documents

Closing documents is certainly easier than opening them. To close a document, save your file and then choose File | Close or click the Close Window button. To close documents and shut down Word at the same time, click the Close button. It is located in the upper-right corner of the Word window, right above the Close Window button.

 To close several documents at once, hold down the SHIFT *key and choose File | Close All. The Close All command appears on the File menu when the* SHIFT *key is pressed.*

If you forget to save a file before you close it, the Office Assistant or a dialog box asks whether you want to save the changes you recently made to the document. Click Yes, or else click No if you made changes but regret making them. Next time you open the document, the changes you regret making won't show. Instead, you will see an earlier version of the document, the one that you saved on-disk before you made the changes you so regret.

 Sometimes closing a document without saving the changes you made to it is worthwhile. Suppose you make a bunch of editorial mistakes and want to start over. To do so, close the file without saving the changes you made. Next time you open the file, you will see the version that you had before you made all those mistakes.

Deleting and Renaming Documents

Deleting and renaming documents is easier to do in My Computer and Windows Explorer, the Windows programs that handle files, but you can delete and rename documents in Word. To do so, choose File | Open as though you were opening the document you want to rename or delete, locate the document in the Open dialog box, and follow these instructions:

- **Renaming**   Right-click the document and choose Rename on the shortcut menu. Then type a new name and press ENTER.

- **Deleting**   Right-click the document and choose Delete on the shortcut menu. Then click Yes when Word asks if you really want to delete the file. To delete several documents at once, CTRL-click each one, then right-click one of the files and choose Delete.

If you regret deleting a document, you can resuscitate it. Go to the Windows desktop and double-click the Recycle Bin icon. The Recycle Bin opens with a list of the files you deleted. Click the one you regret deleting and choose File | Restore in the Recycle Bin.

A Word About Menu Commands

To make choosing commands simpler, only commands that you chose recently appear on menus. Don't worry if you pull down a menu but don't see the command you want—you haven't chosen the command lately, that's all. Click the double arrows at the bottom of the menu to make all the commands appear, and then click the one you want:

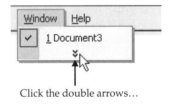

Click the double arrows…

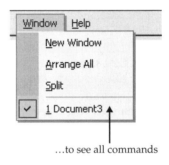

…to see all commands

 If you don't like how Word offers menu commands and you want to see all the commands at once, choose View | Toolbars | Customize. Then select the Options tab in the Customize dialog box and check the Always Show Full Menus check box.

Exiting Word

Word offers no fewer than four ways to shut down the program:

- Click the Close button (the X) in the upper-right corner of the Word screen.
- Choose File | Exit.
- Press ALT-F4.
- Double-click the Control menu icon—the W in the upper-left corner of the screen next to the name of the document you are working on.

Be sure to save your documents before closing Word. Anyhow, if you forget to do that, a dialog box or the Office Assistant appears and asks if you want to save your work before you shut down Word.

MOUS Exam Objectives Explored in Chapter 1

Objective	Heading
Creating a Document from a Template	"Creating New Documents"

Ten Techniques for Managing Files Better

You can save a lot of time and grief by managing files well. Here are ten tips for managing files so that you never lose them and you can find them quickly.

1. Create Folders and Subfolders for New Projects   As soon as you begin a new project, create a folder or perhaps a folder and subfolders to store the documents you will create. While you're at it, name the folder after the project. By keeping documents that pertain to the same project in the same place, you make it easier to find and open documents.

The easiest and probably the best way to create new folders is to do so with My Computer or Windows Explorer in the Windows operating system. However, you can follow these steps to create a folder without leaving Word:

1. Choose File | Open or File | Save As to see the Open or Save As dialog box.
2. In the dialog box, find and select the folder that you want your new folder to be subordinate to. See "Opening Documents" earlier in this chapter if you need help finding your way around the Open dialog box.
3. Click the Create New Folder button. You see the New Folder dialog box.
4. Enter a descriptive name for the folder and click OK. Your new folder appears in the Look In box.
5. Click Cancel to close the Open or Save As dialog box.

2. Keep All Your Personal Folders in One Place   Many people mistakenly believe that documents created with Word have to be stored on disk deep in the folder hierarchy where the Word program files are. Nothing could be further from the truth. You can store the Word files you create yourself anywhere you want. And you should store them in a convenient place where you can find them easily.

This user keeps all her documents in a folder at the top of the C drive called "AAA My Stuff." The letters *AAA* ensure that the folder will be the first in the list of folders in the Open dialog box. Devise a strategy like this one for storing your work on disk where you can find it quickly.

3. Know Which Documents Need Backing Up—And Back Them Up   Be sure to back up important documents. *Backing up* means to make a second copy of a document, put it on a floppy disk, Zip disk, CD-R, or CD-RW, and store the disk in a safe place where nothing can harm it. Not all documents need to be backed up, but if losing a document would cause undo grief or require too much time to restore, back it up. Unless you back up important files, you are doomed if your computer breaks down, your computer is stolen, or your computer is ruined by a virus. See "Backing Up Your Work" in Chapter 20.

4. Periodically Delete Documents You No Longer Need   Finding the document you want to open is difficult when the folder in which you are looking is crowded with documents. To prevent overcrowding, periodically delete the documents you no longer need. See "Deleting and Renaming Documents" earlier in this chapter.

5. Archive Documents You Don't Use Often   Another way to prevent overcrowding in folders is to archive documents. *Archive* means to store documents in a special folder meant for documents that you need but don't need very often. By keeping documents in an archive folder, you prevent them from crowding the folders you go to often.

6. Keep Current Documents in the My Documents Folder   As explained in "Fast Ways to Open a Document" earlier in this chapter, you can open documents quickly by keeping current documents in the My Documents folder. All you have to do to see the contents of this folder is click the My Documents button in the Open dialog box. When you finish working on a document, move it from the My Documents folder to a more permanent folder.

7. Put Shortcuts to Important Folders in the My Favorites Folder   "Fast Ways to Open a Document" also explained that you can open documents quickly by putting shortcuts to the folders that hold them in the My Favorites folder. Click the My Favorites button in the Open dialog box to see and double-click the shortcuts in the Favorites folder.

8. Open Documents Quickly from the File Menu and Task Pane   At the top of the New Document task pane and the bottom of the File menu is a list of the last four documents you opened. Opening the File menu or task pane and clicking the name of a document is perhaps the fastest way to open a document in Word. And you can list more than four documents: Choose Tools | Options, click the General tab in the Options dialog box, and enter a number larger than 4 in the Recently Used File List text box. I highly recommend putting more than four document names on the File menu and task pane. My File menu and task pane list eight documents.

9. Use the Windows Documents Menu to Open Documents Quickly   As explained in "Opening a Document and Word at the Same Time" at the start of this chapter, you can open Word and a document in one swoop by clicking the Start button, choosing Documents, and clicking a document name. The Windows Documents menu lists the last 15 files you opened, be they Word documents or other files.

10. Decide How to Save Documents   On the Save tab of the Options dialog box (choose Tools | Options to get there), Word offers several options for saving documents, saving documents quickly, and recovering documents in the event of a computer crash. "Telling Word How to Save Files" in Chapter 20 explains what these options are. Sooner or later, decide on a strategy for saving documents and backup copies of documents in Word.

Chapter 2

Writing and Editing a Document

This chapter explains everything you need to know to write the first draft of your masterpiece. It describes how to enter and edit text, get quickly from place to place in a document, and change views. Along the way, you find out many excellent shortcuts for getting your work done quickly and thoroughly.

Entering the Text

To type a document, you wiggle your fingers over the keyboard. That's all there is to it, although Word provides a few shortcuts to help you along the way. In the following pages, you find out how to fix mistakes; enter foreign characters and symbols; enter capital letters quickly; and start a new paragraph, line, or page. Readers new to word processing who were born before 1973 are encouraged to read the following section of this book. All others can skip ahead to "Typing Text and Erasing Mistakes."

Note *In Chapter 6, "Ways to Enter Text Quickly" offers more techniques for entering text in a hurry.*

Word Processing Advice for People Born Before 1973

If you were born before 1973, you are old enough to remember the pop-top can, curb-feelers, 8-track tapes, and the typewriter. Chances are, in fact, you learned how to type on a typewriter, and that means you have to unlearn a few habits:

- Do not press the ENTER key to end one line and start another. Word starts a new line for you when you come to the end of a line. Only press the ENTER key to begin a new paragraph.

- Do not press the SPACEBAR to move text around or align text. For example, don't press the SPACEBAR to move a heading to the center of a page. Word has special tools for aligning and centering text.

- Do not press the ENTER key over and over again to move to the next page. Simply press CTRL-ENTER to start a new, blank page.

- Do not rest your hands on the keyboard.

Typing Text and Erasing Mistakes

When you type, text appears at the *insertion point*, the blinking vertical line shown in Figure 2-1. Suppose you want to enter a word or two in the middle of a sentence. To move the insertion point elsewhere, either press arrow keys or move the *text cursor* (the large egotistical *I*) to a new location and click. To move it onscreen, roll your mouse across your desk.

When you type, text that is already there moves to the right to accommodate the new text. However, you can type over text that is already there by pressing the INS key or double-clicking the OVR button on the Status bar, as shown in Figure 2-1.

LEARNING THE ROPES

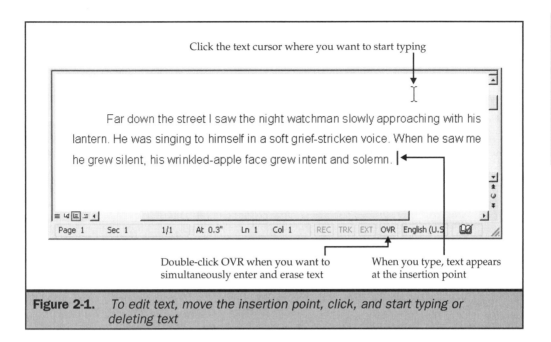

Click the text cursor where you want to start typing

Far down the street I saw the night watchman slowly approaching with his lantern. He was singing to himself in a soft grief-stricken voice. When he saw me he grew silent, his wrinkled-apple face grew intent and solemn.

Page 1   Sec 1   1/1   At 0.3"   Ln 1   Col 1   REC   TRK   EXT   OVR   English (U.S

Double-click OVR when you want to simultaneously enter and erase text

When you type, text appears at the insertion point

Figure 2-1.   *To edit text, move the insertion point, click, and start typing or deleting text*

Double-click OVR when you want to simultaneously enter and erase text—and be sure to double-click OVR or press the INS key again to go back to inserting text, not overtyping it. Simultaneously entering and erasing text is called *Overtype mode.*

Word offers a command for people who are fans of Overtype mode. To put yourself permanently in Overtype mode, choose Tools | Options, select the Edit tab in the Options dialog box, and check the Overtype Mode check box.

Everybody makes typing errors. To erase an error, click to move the insertion point to the left or right of the error, and then press the BACKSPACE key to erase the character to the left of the insertion point or the DELETE key to erase the character to the right of the insertion. In Chapter 3, "Deleting Chunks of Text" explains how you can select text—a word, a paragraph, several paragraphs, or even a whole document—and erase it all at once by pressing the DELETE key. Meanwhile, for people who like keyboard shortcuts, here are the keyboard techniques for erasing text:

Pressing	Deletes
BACKSPACE	The character to the left of the insertion point
DELETE	The character to the right of the insertion point
CTRL-BACKSPACE	The word to the left of the insertion point
CTRL-DELETE	The word to the right of the insertion point

Suppose you are editing a document and you realize to your dismay that the last edit you made was done incorrectly. If the edit was made in the middle of a document, finding the error can be difficult. To locate the last three places where you entered or edited text, press SHIFT-F5 once, twice, or three times.

UPPERCASE to lowercase and Back Again

"Case" refers to whether letters are capitalized or not. In the old days when type was set by hand, typesetters kept capital letters in the upper tray, which is why these letters are called *uppercase* letters, and they kept *lowercase* letters in—you guessed it—the lower tray.

Everybody knows that you hold down the SHIFT key and press a letter on the keyboard to enter an uppercase letter. And everybody knows that you press the CAPS LOCK key to enter many uppercase letters at once. What most people don't know is that Word offers a keyboard shortcut for changing letters from upper- to lowercase and vice versa. Select text and keep pressing SHIFT-F3 to change words to sentence case, lowercase, uppercase, or title case. Or choose Format | Change Case and make a selection in the Change Case dialog box, as shown in Figure 2-2.

Figure 2-2 demonstrates what the choices are. Some choices are suitable for headings, others for plain text. The tOGGLE cASE option is for correcting text that you entered accidentally while CAPS LOCK was turned on. Pressing SHIFT-F3 to change the case of letters is one of the best shortcuts I know of in Word.

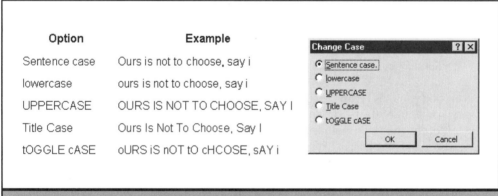

Figure 2-2. *To change the case of text, select it and keep pressing SHIFT-F3, or else choose Format | Change Case and choose an option in the Change Case dialog box*

You can also press CTRL-SHIFT-A *to capitalize letters directly without seeing them in title case, lowercase, or sentence case.*

Entering Symbols and Foreign Characters

Don't panic if you need to enter an umlaut, a grave accent, or a cedilla in a document, because you can do it by way of one of the shortcut keys shown in Table 2-1 or the Symbol dialog box shown in Figure 2-3. And Word offers other means of entering symbols and foreign characters as well.

To Enter*	Type This...	...and Then This
à, è, ì, ò, *or* ù	CTRL-`	a, e, i, o, *or* u
á, é, í, ó, ú, *or* ý	CTRL-'	a, e, i, o, u, *or* y
â, ê, î, ô, *or* û	CTRL-SHIFT-^	a, e, i, o, *or* u
ä, ë, ï, ö, ü, *or* ÿ	CTRL-SHIFT-:	a, e, i, o, u, *or* y
ã, ñ, *or* õ	CTRL-SHIFT-~	a, n, *or* o
Å	CTRL-SHIFT-@	a
Æ	CTRL-SHIFT-&	a
Œ	CTRL-SHIFT-&	o
Ç	CTRL-,	c
Ø	CTRL-/	o
ß	CTRL-SHIFT-&	s
¿ *or* ¡	ALT-CTRL-SHIFT	? *or* !

* This table only lists lowercase foreign characters, but you can enter uppercase characters by substituting the lowercase characters in column three with uppercase characters.

Table 2-1. *Keyboard Shortcuts for Entering Foreign Characters*

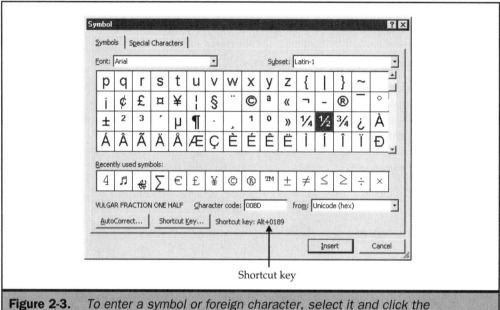

Shortcut key

Figure 2-3.   *To enter a symbol or foreign character, select it and click the Insert button*

The Symbol dialog box offers symbols as well as foreign characters. To enter one, place the insertion point where you want the symbol to stand in your document and follow these steps:

1. Choose Insert | Symbol to open the Symbol dialog box.

2. Choose a font and subset, if necessary, from the drop-down menus. (If the Subset menu doesn't appear, choose Unicode (Hex) in the From drop-down list. You'll find this list in the lower-right corner of the Symbol dialog box.)

3. Select a symbol or foreign character.

4. Click the Insert button to enter the symbol and click Close to close the dialog box.

The Symbol dialog box (see Figure 2-3) also offers these amenities:

■ **AutoCorrect Button**   Choose a symbol and click this button to devise an AutoCorrect shortcut for entering the symbol you chose. See "Entering Text and Graphics Quickly with the AutoCorrect Command" in Chapter 6.

■ **Shortcut Key Button**   Choose a symbol you enter often and click this button to create a shortcut key for entering it (if the shortcut key isn't already listed in Table 2-1). See "Designating Your Own Keyboard Shortcuts" in Chapter 21.

> **Note** *Chapter 11 explains how to use Word to write in more than one language. There, you will also find information about other ways to enter foreign text.*

In Figure 2-3, notice the shortcut key ALT+0189 in the bottom of the Symbol dialog box. You can also enter symbols and foreign characters by pressing keyboard shortcuts. If you are a translator who often has to enter foreign characters, learn the characters' keyboard shortcuts from the Symbol dialog box and try your hand at entering characters this way.

Keyboard shortcuts come in three varieties:

- **Word shortcuts**   Table 2-1 lists Word keyboard shortcuts for entering foreign characters.

- **ALT+the character code**   When you see "ALT+*a code*" (as in Figure 2-3), hold down the ALT key and enter the numbers by way of the numeric keypad. You can't enter the numbers by pressing the numbered keys on the keyboard itself with this technique, so make sure NUM LOCK is turned on (and press the NUM LOCK key if it isn't).

- **The character code, Alt+X**   When you see a code followed by "ALT+X," enter the code and then press ALT-X. You can enter the numbers by pressing keys along the top of the keyboard or keys on the numeric keypad. Again for what it's worth, this is the technique for entering Unicode characters.

Starting a New Paragraph, Line, or Page

Press the ENTER key to start a new paragraph. Suppose, however, that you want to start a new line, or *break a line,* without starting a new paragraph. For example, consider the heading in Figure 2-4 and the lines of text below the heading. The first heading is top-heavy, so I broke it after the word "Sucker" to make the heading easier to read. In the lines of text, I broke the second line after the word "Kiwanis" to make the words break more evenly along the right margin. To break a line and thereby make text easier to read, click where you want the break to occur and press SHIFT-ENTER.

> **Note** *"Viewing the Hidden Format Symbols" later in this chapter explains how to find out where line breaks are. To delete a line break, click the Show/Hide ¶ button and backspace over the line break symbol.*

When you come to the bottom of one page, Word starts a new page for you, but if you want to start a new page immediately, press CTRL-ENTER to enter a *hard page break,* also known as a *forced page break* or *manual page break.* You can also start a new page by choosing Insert | Break and selecting the Page Break option in the Break dialog box. Break the page after you enter the text on a title page, for example. Whatever you do, don't press ENTER over and over to reach the bottom of a page.

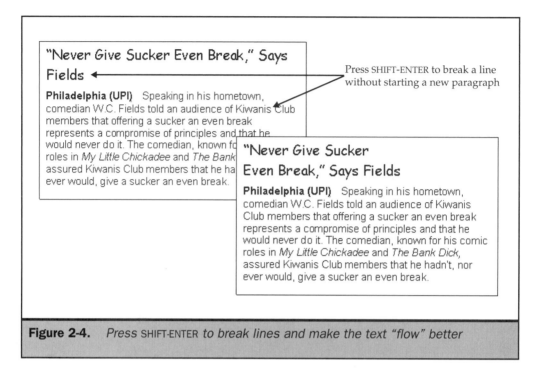

Figure 2-4. *Press* SHIFT-ENTER *to break lines and make the text "flow" better*

Recognizing a hard page break in Normal view is easy because the words "Page Break" and a dotted line appear onscreen, where normally you see a dotted line to mark the end of the page. In Print Layout view, however, hard page breaks look exactly like the soft page breaks that Word introduces when you reach the end of a page: You see the bottom of one page and the top of the next. To erase a page break, switch to Normal view, double-click the words "Page Break," and press the DELETE key. Later in this chapter, "Getting a Better View of Your Work" explains the different views.

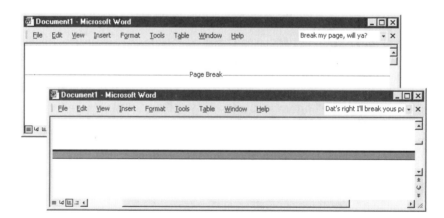

How Word Handles Paragraphs

All the formatting—the indentations, character fonts, and formats—are carried to the next paragraph when you press ENTER. When you start formatting paragraphs, you will learn how critical paragraphs are to formatting. In Word, formatting commands affect the paragraph that the cursor is in, or, if you selected several paragraphs, formatting commands affect the paragraphs you selected. A heading, single line of text, and blank line are all considered paragraphs. In Word, a paragraph is simply what you put onscreen before you press the ENTER key.

Tricks for Editing Text

Following are some tried-and-true techniques for editing faster and better. On these pages, you find out how to take some of the drudgery out of repetitive work, fix errors, fit text on the screen, and view format symbols so you can tell why text lies where it does on the page.

Repeating a Command or Text Entry

Repeat is my favorite command. For especially repetitive word-processing tasks—and there are many—see if you can make the Repeat command do the work for you. To give the Repeat command, press F4, choose Edit | Repeat, or press CTRL-Y. The command repeats the last command or keyboard entry you made.

Suppose you have to indent 12 different paragraphs throughout a document. Instead of attacking the 12 paragraphs one at a time and repeating the burdensome indentation command, indent the first paragraph. Then put your left index finger on the F4 key, click the next paragraph that needs indenting, and press F4. The paragraph is indented—not only that, you can rest assured that it and the remaining 10 paragraphs will be indented the same way.

In Chapter 6, "Entering Text and Graphics Quickly with the AutoCorrect Command" explains another way to quickly enter your address, company name, or other item you have to enter often.

Undoing a Mistake—and Redoing What You Undid

Suppose you give a command or enter text and realize immediately that you shouldn't have done that. Don't despair—you can undo your mistake by clicking the Undo button, pressing CTRL-Z, or choosing Edit | Undo. The Undo command reverses your last action, whatever it happened to be. And if you regret undoing your last action, you can "redo" it by clicking the Redo button. The Redo command is an antidote to the Undo command— it redoes what you undid.

Not only can you undo your most recent editorial change or command with the Undo command, you can undo as many as all the actions you completed since you opened the document you are working on. To undo a mistake you made some time ago, click the down arrow beside the Undo button. You see a drop-down menu of your last six actions, but you can scroll down the list and see many more. When you have found the action you want to undo, select it on the drop-down menu:

Click Undo or choose an action on the menu to reverse mistakes

Click Redo to "redo" what you undid

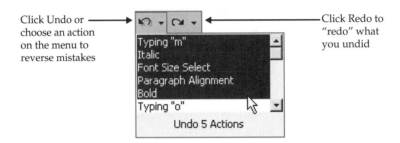

When you close a document, all records of the edits you made are lost. The Undo menu is emptied out. Sorry, you can't undo an edit you made last time you opened your document.

The only drawback to choosing an action on the Undo drop-down menu is that you also undo all the actions that took place before it. For example, if you undo the 97th action on the list, you undo the 96 before it, too. Besides the Undo command, another way to fix monstrous errors is to close the document and click No when Word asks if you want to save the changes you made. As long as you didn't save your document after you made the monstrous error, the error won't be in your document when you reopen it.

"Wrapping" Text So It Stays Onscreen

As you write the first draft of a document, work in Normal view and Outline view. In those views, you can exclude the fancy stuff and concentrate on the words. In Normal view and Outline view, however, the text is prone to stray off the right side of the screen, as shown in Figure 2-5, but you can prevent that from happening by choosing the Wrap To Window option in the Options dialog box. In Figure 2-5, text strays outside the window in the first document, but in the second it wraps to, or stays inside, the window so you can see and work on it.

To make text stay inside the window in Normal view and Outline view, choose Tools | Options, select View tab in the Options dialog box, and check the Wrap To Window check box.

Wrapping text inside the window gives an unrealistic picture of where lines end on the page. When you are laying out text or working on tables, be sure to turn off the Wrap To Window mechanism or else do your work in Print Layout view or Web Layout view. Those views show precisely where lines break on the page.

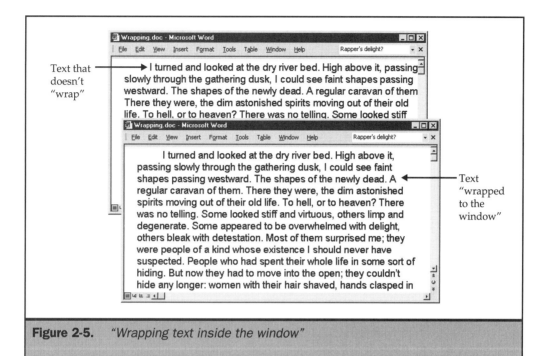

Figure 2-5.   *"Wrapping text inside the window"*

Viewing the Hidden Format Symbols

Sometimes it pays to see the hidden format symbols when you are editing and laying out a document. The symbols show where lines break, where tab spaces are, where one paragraph starts and another ends, and whether two spaces instead of one appear between words. To see the hidden format symbols, click the Show/Hide ¶ button. Click the button again to hide the symbols. This illustration shows what the hidden symbols are, how to enter them, and what they look like onscreen:

Symbol	Name	How to Enter
↵	Line break	Press SHIFT-ENTER
¬	Optional hyphen	Press CTRL-HYPHEN
¶	Paragraph	Press ENTER
·	Space	Press SPACEBAR
→	Tab	Press TAB

→ The·show·features· an·all-star·cast·and·is· sure·to·be·a·hit.··Al¬ready· ticket·sales·are·brisk·and· the·Orpheum·box·office·↵ is·predicting·a·block¬ buster·of·a·show.¶

To permanently unhide the formatting symbols and see them whether or not you clicked the Show/Hide ¶ button, choose Tools | Options, select the View tab in the Options dialog box, and check boxes under Formatting Marks. Why would you want to see format symbols now and forever? To get a very good look at how your document was formatted, that's why.

Moving Around in Long Documents

Documents have a habit of getting longer, and as they do, getting from place to place gets harder and harder. These pages explain the numerous ways to go here and there in documents. You can press keys, use the scroll bar, use the Document Map, place bookmarks in documents, or click the Select Object Browse button. Pick your poison. You will discover one or two favorite techniques after you have experimented a bit.

In a pinch, you can also use the Find command to get around. Press CTRL-F *or choose Edit | Find, enter a target word in the Find and Replace dialog box, and click the Find Next button. In Chapter 6, the "Finding and Replacing Text and Other Things" section explains the nuances of the Find command.*

Keyboard Techniques for Getting Around

Even if, like me, you are a fan of the mouse and prefer clicking the scrollbar to get around, one or two keyboard shortcuts are worth using. I especially like CTRL-HOME, which moves the insertion point to the top of the document, and CTRL-END, which moves it to the bottom. Table 2-2 lists the keyboard shortcuts that are indispensable to everyone.

To Move Here	Press
Top of document	CTRL-HOME
Bottom of document	CTRL-END
Up one screen	PAGE UP
Down one screen	PAGE DOWN
Start of paragraph	CTRL-↑
End of paragraph	CTRL-↓
Start of line	HOME
End of line	END
Previous edit	SHIFT-F5 OR ALT-CTRL-Z

Table 2-2.   *Essential Keyboard Shortcuts for Moving Around*

LEARNING THE ROPES

To Move Here	Press
Top of window	CTRL-PAGE UP
Bottom of window	CTRL-PAGE DOWN
Next page	ALT-CTRL-PAGE DOWN
Previous page	ALT-CTRL-PAGE UP
Next paragraph	CTRL-↓
Previous paragraph	CTRL-↑
Next window	CTRL-F6
Previous window	CTRL-SHIFT-F6
Beginning of column	ALT-PAGE UP
End of column	ALT-PAGE DOWN

Table 2-2.   *Essential Keyboard Shortcuts for Moving Around* (continued)

Scroll Bar Methods for Getting Around

For the mouse-inclined, the best way to go here and there in a document is to use the scroll bars. Figure 2-6 shows how the scroll bars work. Use the vertical scroll bar on the right side of the window to move backward and forward in a document. When you drag the scroll box on the vertical scroll bar, you see which page you are scrolling to. And if you assigned heading styles to the headings in your document, you also see heading names.

By scrolling, you don't move the insertion point—all you do is put a different page onscreen. To move the insertion point to the page to which you scrolled, click on the page.

 To scroll long distances very quickly, hold down the SHIFT *key as you drag the scroll box.*

Using the Select Browse Object Button to Get Around

In the lower-right corner of the Word screen is an obscure but very useful button called Select Browse Object. Why the ugly name? Because computer people are very fond of the word "object," by which they mean just about anything, and the word "browse," by which they mean "to go to." Click the Select Browse Object button and you see 12

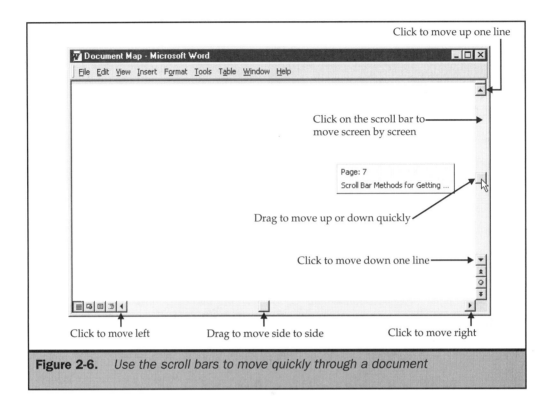

Figure 2-6.   *Use the scroll bars to move quickly through a document*

"Browse By" buttons. Click a button and you go immediately to the thing whose button you clicked—the next heading, graphic, table, or whatever.

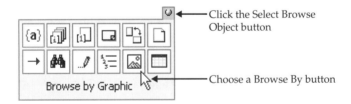

What makes the Select Browse Object so useful is that you can skip merrily from thing to thing after you click a Browse By button. After you click a button, the double arrows on either side of the Select Browse Object turn blue. To go to the previous or next heading, graphic, table, or whatever, click one of the blue double arrows (or press CTRL-PAGE UP or CTRL-PAGE DOWN).

When the double arrows on either side of the Select Browse Object button are black, clicking the double arrows takes you to the previous or next page. Choose the Browse By Page button to turn the double arrows black again and be able to click the double arrows to skip from page to page.

Going from Place to Place with the Go To Command

Yet another way to get from place to place is to use the Go To command. The Go To command works much like the Select Browse Object button. After you choose the item you want to "go to," the double arrows on either side of the Select Browse Object button turn blue, and you can click the blue double arrows to go to the item you chose without having to open a dialog box.

To use the Go To command, choose Edit | Go To, press CTRL-G, press F5, or double-click the left side of the Status bar. You see the Go To tab of the Find and Replace dialog box. Choose what you are seeking in the Go To What box and then do either of the following:

■ Click the Previous or Next button to go to the previous or next instance of the thing you chose.

■ Make an entry or a choice in the Enter Field Name box and click the Go To button. For that matter, you can enter a plus (+) or minus (–) sign and a number to skip forward or backward by several instances of the thing you are going to. The Enter Field name box changes names, depending on what you chose in the Go To What box.

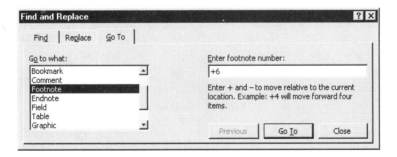

Bookmarks for Getting Around

One of the fastest ways to get from place to place is to mark the places in your document that you will return to time and time again with a bookmark. When you want to return to an important place, all you have to do is choose Insert | Bookmark, double-click a bookmark name in the Bookmark dialog box, and click Close. True to the craft, the mystery writer whose bookmarks are shown in Figure 2-7 wrote the end

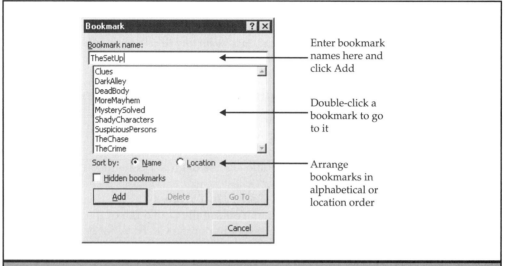

Figure 2-7.   *Bookmark important places in long documents and be able to go to those places very quickly*

of the story first and used bookmarks to jump back and forth between the beginning and end to make all the clues fit.

Besides bookmarking a place, you can also select text and bookmark the text you selected. Bookmark a lengthy table, for example, and you'll be able to select it merely by choosing its bookmark instead of going to the trouble of using the selection commands. As "Indexing a Document" in Chapter 16 explains, you have to bookmark a text selection to include a page range ("California, economy 92–97") in an index entry. Bookmarks are also used to make hyperlinks between two places in the same document or Web page.

Choose Insert | Bookmark (or press CTRL-SHIFT-F5) and do the following in the Bookmark dialog box to create bookmarks or go to them in a document:

- **Create a Bookmark**   Make sure the insertion point or text selection is where you want the bookmark to be before you choose Insert | Bookmark. In the Bookmark dialog box, enter a name in the Bookmark Name text box and click the Add button or press ENTER. Bookmark names cannot include blank spaces. The first character must be a letter, not a number.

- **Go to a Bookmark**   Double-click a bookmark name in the Bookmark dialog box. To find names, use the scroll bar if necessary. You can also choose a Sort By option to arrange the names in alphabetical or location order.

If you want to see where bookmarks are located in your document, choose Tools |
Options, select the View tab in the Options dialog box, and check the Bookmarks
check box. Gray I-beam characters show you where the bookmarks are located.

Using the Document Map to Get Around

Last but not least, you can use the document map to jump from heading to heading
in a document. To use the document map, however, you must have assigned heading
styles—Heading 1, Heading 2, and so on—to the headings in your document. By clicking
the Document Map button or choosing View | Document Map, you can see the names of
headings in the document map on the left side of the screen, as shown in Figure 2-8. To
move to a heading, all you have to do is click its name in the document map.

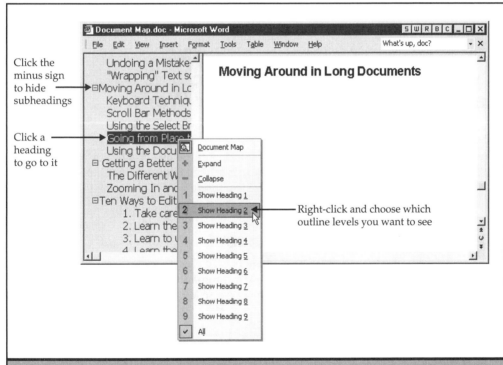

Figure 2-8.   *As long as you applied heading styles to the headings in your document,*
you can move from place to place by clicking heading names in the
document map

Note *Chapter 12 explains styles, why they are so useful, and how you can apply them from the Style menu on the Formatting toolbar.*

To help you find the headings you want to go to, the document map offers these amenities:

- **Read Headings** Place the pointer over a heading to be able to read it in its entirety. You can also drag the bar that separates the document map from the document to the left or right to make the document map narrower or wider.

- **Choose Which Outline Levels You Want to See** Right-click the document map and choose an outline level option to tell Word which headings to display. See "Choosing an Outline Level for Paragraphs" in Chapter 8 to learn more about outline levels.

- **See or Hide Subheadings** Click the minus sign next to a heading to remove its subheadings from the document map and make more headings appear in the Document Map. Click the plus sign next to a heading to see its subheadings.

Getting a Better View of Your Work

Wherever you go in Word, make sure you get a good view. The program offers four different ways to view documents, plus two more if you count Print Preview and Full Screen as views. Depending on the task at hand, some views are better than others. Throughout this book, I mention which view is best for doing which task. For now, these pages explain the different views, how to change views, and how to zoom in and zoom out to keep yourself from going blind at the computer screen.

Changing Your View of a Document

Figure 2-9 shows the six ways to view documents. To change views, click a View button in the lower-left corner of the screen or choose a command from the View menu. In the case of Print Preview, choose File | Print Preview or click the Print Preview button on the Standard toolbar to see it.

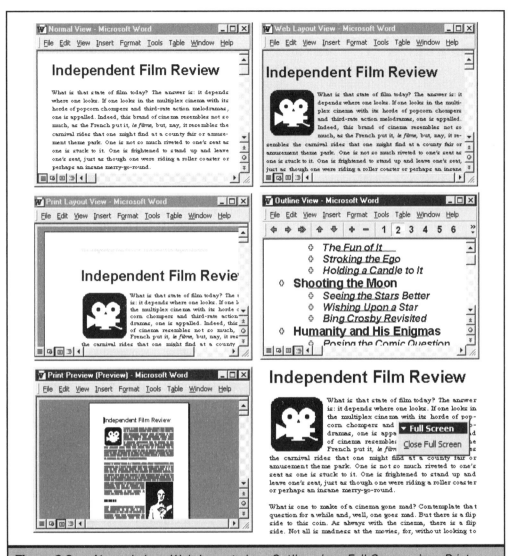

Figure 2-9.   *Normal view, Web Layout view, Outline view, Full Screen view, Print Preview, and Print Layout view*

Here are brief descriptions of the six views and when to use them:

Normal
For writing first drafts and basic editing. In Normal view, you can focus on writing. Sophisticated layouts, including graphics and columns, do not appear in this view.

Web Layout
For laying out Web pages to be displayed on an intranet or the Internet. Color backgrounds only appear in this view. By switching to Web Layout view, you can see what Web pages will look like online in the Internet Explorer Web browser (choose File | Web Page Preview to see what I mean—the page in Word and Internet Explorer looks the same).

Print Layout
For laying out documents. In this view, you can see where graphics, columns, and the page itself begin and end. Headers and footers also appear, however faintly, in Print Layout view.

Outline
For organizing papers and reports. In Outline view, you can move headings (and the text underneath them) around quite easily. See the section "Organizing Your Work with Outlines" in Chapter 17.

Print Preview
For seeing what entire pages look like. Use this view to see the big picture and find out whether documents are laid out correctly. See "Previewing a Document Before You Print It" in Chapter 5.

Full Screen
For focusing on the task at hand. In this view, the toolbars, menu bar, Status bar—everything, in fact—is removed from the screen except the page you are working on. Full Screen view gives the best idea of what a document will look like after you print it. To give commands, use keyboard shortcuts, right-click to see shortcut menus, or slide the mouse pointer to the top of the screen to make the menu bar appear. You can also right-click the menu bar and choose a toolbar name to display a toolbar onscreen. Press ESC or click Close Full Screen to leave Full Screen view.

Zooming In and Zooming Out

No matter which view you are in—Normal, Web Layout, Print Layout, or Outline—you can zoom in or zoom out to make the onscreen page look larger or smaller. Zoom in when you are proofreading to get a better look at the letters; zoom out to shrink pages and see whether they were laid out correctly.

As Figure 2-10 shows, Word offers two ways of zooming—with the Zoom menu on the Standard toolbar or the Zoom dialog box. To open the Zoom dialog box, choose View | Zoom. The Zoom settings are

- **By Percentage**   Either choose a percentage or enter one of your own. At 100%, the letters and page are the same size they will be when you print them; below 100%, they are smaller; above 100%, they are bigger. To choose your own percent setting, enter it in the Zoom text box and press ENTER.

- **By Width**   Makes the widest line of text or the entire page fit snugly across the screen.

- **By Page**   Fits one, two, or several pages on the screen. In the Zoom dialog box, click the down arrow beside the computer monitor and choose how many pages to display, as shown in Figure 2-10.

The Two Pages option on the Zoom menu is very handy when you want to see a page spread—that is, two facing pages as they will look when they are laid flat on the table.

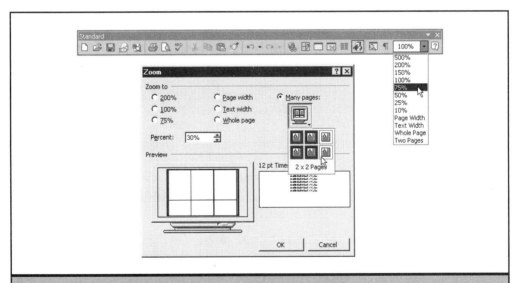

Figure 2-10.   *Use the Zoom command to enlarge or shrink the text onscreen*

MOUS Exam Objectives Explored in Chapter 2

Objective	Heading
Insert, modify, and move text and symbols	"Typing Text and Erasing Mistakes" and "Entering Symbols and Foreign Characters"
Modify document layout and Page Setup options	"Starting a New Paragraph, Line, or Page" (Press CTRL-ENTER to break a page)
Modify text flow options	"Starting a New Paragraph, Line, or Page Break" (Press SHIFT-ENTER to break a line)
Navigate within documents	"Moving Around in Long Documents"

Ten Ways to Edit Faster

Half the time you spend at the keyboard is spent editing, but I want you to spend a fourth of the time, not half the time. To that end, here are ten editing techniques that every Word user should know.

1. Take Care of the Text First, and then Do the Layout   Write the first draft of a document before you attempt to lay out the pages or text. Editing text after it has been squeezed into columns, rammed into text boxes, or pressed into tables is difficult. Write the clean copy first and you will spare yourself the trouble of having to edit with one hand tied behind your back.

2. Learn the Techniques to Select, Copy, and Move Text   Much of editing requires copying and moving text. And as the next chapter explains, you can't copy or move text until you select it. Therefore, knowing all the shortcuts for selecting, copying, and moving text is worthwhile. Well worthwhile, in fact. Chapter 3 explains selecting, copying, and moving text.

3. Make Use of the Undo and Repeat Commands   In "Tricks for Editing Text," earlier in this chapter, I explained how valuable the Undo and Repeat commands are. Instead of cursing when you make a mistake, click the Undo button to redeem it. And opportunities to use the Repeat command are many. After a while, you start to recognize them and you get used to using the Repeat command to cut down on the amount of work you have to do.

4. Learn the Capitalization Keypress   Few things are easier than selecting text and pressing SHIFT-F3. That's all it takes to correct a capitalization error, as this chapter explains.

5. Take Advantage of the Window Menu Commands   As "Working in Two Places or Documents at Once" in Chapter 6 explains, the New Window and Split commands on the Window menu can be very useful when you are editing a document. Choose the New Window command to simultaneously work in two different places in a document without having to scroll between the two places. Choose the Split command to put two parts of the same document onscreen at the same time.

6. Choose a Good View and Zoom Setting   Get used to switching views and choosing new zoom settings. Depending on the task at hand, some views and zoom settings are better than others. Fortunately, between the convenient View buttons and just-as-convenient Zoom drop-down menu, getting a better view is easy. The previous part of this chapter explains views.

7. Learn How to Move Quickly Through Documents   In this chapter, "Moving Around in Long Documents" offers several techniques for getting around quickly: keyboard shortcuts, the scroll bar, the Select Browse Object button, the Go To command, bookmarking, and the document map. Explore all the techniques to find the ones that work best for you.

8. For First Drafts, Choose a Font that Is Easy to Read   In Chapter 7, "Changing the Way Characters Look on the Page" explains how to change fonts. A *font* is a typeface style. When you write the first draft, choose a font that is easy on the eyes. Most people prefer the Courier New, Times Roman, or Arial font.

9. "Wrap" Text So It Stays Onscreen   If, like me, you treasure your eyesight and you like to gaze at large letters onscreen, you run into the problem of not being able to see all the text because the letters are too large and get pushed off screen. You can solve that problem by "wrapping" text to the screen, as explained in the section "Wrapping Text So It Stays Onscreen," in this chapter.

10. Learn How to Use the Autotext and Autocorrect Commands   Some words and names get typed over and over again—your name and address, for example. And if you work in, say, a scientific field, you might have to type long scientific names all day long. To spare yourself from having to do that, you can let the AutoText and AutoCorrect commands do the work for you. See "Ways to Enter Text Quickly" in Chapter 6.

The Complete Reference

Chapter 3

Copying, Moving, and Deleting Text

This short but important chapter describes the many techniques for selecting, deleting, copying, and moving text. I'm afraid you will find an inordinate number of "tips" in this chapter because there are so many shortcuts for selecting, deleting, copying, and moving text. Learn the many shortcuts and techniques and you will considerably cut down the time you spend editing.

Selecting Blocks of Text

Many word-processing tasks require you to select text first. Before you can delete text, you have to select it. Before you can move or copy text, you have to select it. You can't change fonts or font sizes until you select the text first. To make selecting text easy, Word offers nearly a dozen ways to do it. These pages explain how to select text with the mouse and how to do it with precision by double-clicking the EXT button on the Status bar.

"Selecting Objects So You Can Manipulate Them" in Chapter 13 explains how to select clip art images, graphics, text boxes, a drawing canvas, autoshapes, and other so-called objects.

Basic Mouse Techniques for Selecting Text

Table 3-1 describes the nearly dozen ways to select text with the mouse. The trick to selecting more than one word or several words at a time is to click (or double-click) in the margin to the left of the words and do so when the mouse pointer is pointing to the right, not the left. In this illustration, I selected an entire paragraph by double-clicking to its left, and the selected text is highlighted onscreen. Don't click or double-click until the pointer points to the right, as it does in this illustration.

Wait till the pointer looks like this…
…before clicking or double-clicking to select text

took over the immortality of Chiron and satisfied Zeus by letting Chiron die in his place.

We can only select a few of the many legends that became attached to the name of Heracles. He fought and killed a number of monstrous beings; one of these was Cycnus,[5] son of Ares, who used to rob men passing on their way through Thessaly to Delphi of the victims that they were taking to sacrifice to Apollo.[6]

In one version of the story the fight ended when Zeus threw a thunderbolt between Cycnus and Heracles, but in the commoner

To Select This	Do This
A word	Double-click the word.
A few words	Drag over the words.
A line	Click to the left of the line.*
Several lines	Drag up or down to the left of the lines.*
A sentence	Hold down the CTRL key and click in the sentence.
A paragraph	Double-click to the left of the paragraph* (or triple-click inside the paragraph).
A block of text	Click at the start of the text you want to select, hold down the SHIFT key, and click at the end of the text.
Several paragraphs	Double-click to the left of a paragraph and then drag up or down.*
Different blocks of text	Hold down the CTRL key as you select.
A table	Choose Table	Select	Table or hold down the ALT key and double-click in the table.
The whole document	Press CTRL-A or choose Edit	Select All (or triple-click to the left of the text*).

* *Make sure the pointer points to the right before clicking, double-clicking, or triple-clicking to the left of the text.*

Table 3-1.   *Mouse Techniques for Selecting Text*

The program selects one word at a time when you drag over words to select them. Some people find that a bother. If you are good with the mouse and used to selecting text, you can tell Word not to jump ahead and select entire words when you drag over them. To do so, choose Tools | Options, select the Edit tab in the Options dialog box, and uncheck the box called When Selecting, Automatically Select Entire Word.

Word offers a special command for selecting all the text in a document that was formatted the same way. Click the Styles and Formatting button to open the Styles and Formatting task pane, which opens on the right side of the window. Then click text that was formatted a certain way and click the Select All button in the task bar. Throughout your document, text that was formatted identically is highlighted. Now you can give a command to format all highlighted text at the same time.

Selecting Blocks of Text with Precision

Word offers a special technique for selecting large or unwieldy blocks of text with precision. Suppose you want to select everything from the middle of page 2 to the middle of page 4, including a table and graphic on page 3. In that case, the selection techniques in Table 3-1 won't do any good, because they are designed for selecting units of text—a line, a paragraph, and so on. However, you can select a large or unwieldy block of text by following these steps:

1. Click at the start or end of the text you want to select.
2. Either double-click the EXT button on the Status bar or press F8. The dark letters EXT on the Status bar tell you that you can start selecting text:

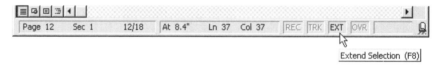

3. Scroll to or move to the other end of the text you want to select and click. The text is highlighted to show it has been selected.

All the keyboard shortcuts for moving around in documents also work for selecting text after you press F8 or double-click EXT. For example, press CTRL-HOME to select all text to the beginning of the document. See "Keyboard Techniques for Getting Around" in Chapter 2 for a list of keyboard shortcuts.

What Happens to Formats When You Copy Text

When you select text for the purpose of copying it, whether you select the paragraph format symbol at the end of the paragraph determines whether you copy the paragraph's formats as well as the text. Besides marking the end of a paragraph, the all-important paragraph format symbol holds the formatting for the paragraph. As a general rule, clicking or double-clicking to the left of the text selects the paragraph symbol as well as the text itself. Press the Show/Hide ¶ button to see the format symbols. "Viewing the Hidden Format Symbols" in Chapter 2 explains what the symbols are.

In·this·paragraph,·the·paragraph·formatting·symbol·has·been·selected.¶

As long as EXT is highlighted on the Status bar, you can click elsewhere in your document to change the size of the text block you selected. Perhaps you didn't select enough text; click again to select more words and letters. But after you give a command—you change fonts or copy the block of text, for example—EXT is no longer highlighted on the Status bar and you can't click elsewhere to select more text or less text.

Press ESC or double-click EXT on the Status bar if a bunch of highlighted text is onscreen but you don't want to do anything with it. Pressing ESC or double-clicking EXT tells Word that you want to quit trying to select text.

  To select successively larger blocks of text, click in the text and start pressing F8. The second key press selects a word, the third a sentence, the fourth a paragraph, the fifth a section, and the sixth the entire document.

Special Keyboard Shortcuts for Selecting Text

Finally, for fans of the keyboard, Table 3-2 lists keyboard shortcuts for selecting text. (If you came here from the index, be sure to turn back a couple of pages to Table 3-1, which describes mouse techniques for selecting text.)

To Select This	Press
A character	SHIFT-→ *or* SHIFT-←
A word	F8, F8
Word at a time	CTRL-SHIFT-→ *or* CTRL-SHIFT-←
Start of line	SHIFT-HOME
End of line	SHIFT-END
Up one line	SHIFT-↑
Down one line	SHIFT-↓
A sentence	F8, F8, F8
Paragraph at a time	CTRL-SHIFT-↑ *or* CTRL-SHIFT-↓
To top or bottom of page	SHIFT-PAGE UP *or* SHIFT-PAGE DOWN
To the start or end of the document	CTRL-SHIFT-HOME *or* CTRL-SHIFT-END
The whole document	CTRL-A

Table 3-2. *Keyboard Techniques for Selecting Text*

Deleting Chunks of Text

Deleting chunks of text is simple as long as you know how to select text. To delete chunks of text, all you have to do is select the text and press the DELETE key (or choose Edit | Clear | Contents). Remember: The Undo button is ready and waiting to be clicked in case you accidentally delete the wrong text.

Chapter 1 explained how to press DELETE or BACKSPACE to delete one character at a time. Here are a couple of keyboard shortcuts for deleting one word at a time:

- **CTRL-BACKSPACE**   Deletes the word to the left of the insertion point.

- **CTRL-DELETE**   Deletes the word to the right of the insertion point.

You can delete text without pressing the DELETE key. After you select the text you want to delete, start typing. The words you selected are replaced instantly by the words you type. (If you prefer not to be able to delete text this way, choose Tools | Options, select the Edit tab in the Options dialog box, and uncheck the Typing Replaces Selection check box.)

Moving and Copying Text Between Word Documents

In my opinion, one of the best things going in Word is being able to copy and move text. A paragraph from the company report, with a few changes, can be included in a letter. The summary paragraph at the end of an academic paper can be moved to the start of the paper and be made into the introduction. Copying and moving text are valuable word-processing tasks, so knowing the different techniques for copying and moving text is worthwhile.

On the following pages are numerous tip and tricks for moving and copying text quickly. Here are instructions for copying and moving with the Clipboard, dragging to copy and move, and assembling "scraps" from different documents in a single document.

Copying and Moving Text with the Clipboard

Copy and move text with the Clipboard when you want to copy or move text long distances or to other documents. The *Clipboard* is a sort of electronic holding tank for storing text. The last 24 items you cut or copied—in Word or in another program—are stored on the Clipboard. Follow these steps to move or copy text with the Clipboard:

1. Select the text you want to move or copy.

2. Move or copy the text to the Clipboard:

    - **Moving**   Choose Edit | Cut, press CTRL-X, click the Cut button, or right-click the text and Cut from the shortcut menu. The text is removed from the document.

- **Copying** Choose Edit | Copy, press CTRL-C, click the Copy button, or right-click and choose Copy.

3. Open a second document, if necessary, and click where you want to move or copy the text.

4. Paste the text in your document:

- **Item You Just Cut or Copied** Choose Edit | Paste, press CTRL-V, click the Paste button, or right-click and choose Paste.

- **Item You Cut or Copied Earlier** Display the Clipboard task pane, as shown in Figure 3-1, by choosing Edit | Office Clipboard, pressing CTRL-C twice, or double-clicking the Office Clipboard icon on the taskbar. Then locate the item you want to move or copy and click to select it in the task pane.

After you copy or move an item, the Paste Options button appears (see Figure 3-1). The button and its drop-down menu are meant to help you format text that has been moved or copied. Normally when you cut or copy text, it keeps its formatting, but you

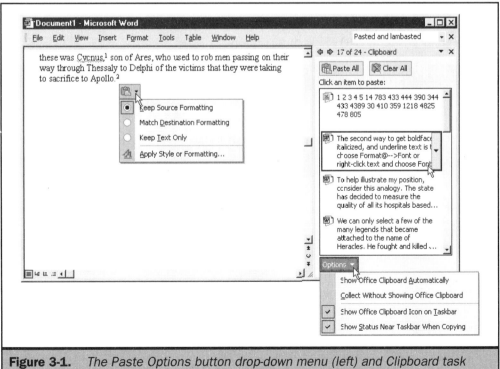

Figure 3-1. *The Paste Options button drop-down menu (left) and Clipboard task pane (right) make moving and copying items easier*

can click the Paste Options button and choose an option on the drop-down menu to format the text a different way:

- **Keep Source Formatting**   The text retains its formatting (what normally occurs if you don't choose an option from the drop-down menu).

- **Match Destination Formatting**   The text adopts the formatting of the surrounding text.

- **Keep Text Only**   The text adopts the formatting of the surrounding text. Moreover, it is stripped of text effects, such as boldfacing and italics.

- **Apply Style or Formatting**   Word opens the Styles and Formatting task pane so you can choose a new style or format for the text.

Managing the Clipboard Task Pane

The Clipboard task pane is a piece of work. It can hold 24 items. To dump all 24 in a document, click the Paste All button. Click the Clear All button to empty the Clipboard task pane of all items. To remove a single item, open its drop-down menu and choose Delete.

Meanwhile, the Options drop-down menu at the bottom of the Clipboard task pane (refer to Figure 3-1) offers these options:

- **Show Office Clipboard Automatically**   Under some circumstances, the Clipboard task pane can open automatically (when you cut or copy two items consecutively, copy an item twice, or copy and paste and then copy again). If you want it to open automatically, choose this option.

- **Collect Without Showing Office Clipboard**   When this option is selected, you can tell when an item has been cut or copied to the Clipboard without the Clipboard task pane being open. However, to be notified, you must have selected either or both of the following two options.

- **Show Office Clipboard Icon on Taskbar**   Places a Clipboard icon in the *system tray*, the part of the Windows taskbar by the clock (the icon appears after you cut or copy the first item to the Clipboard). You can double-click the icon to open the Clipboard task pane. When an item is cut or copied to the Clipboard, a tiny page glides across the icon.

- **Show Status Near Taskbar When Copying**   When you cut or copy an item to the Clipboard, a pop-up notice appears in the lower-right corner of the screen. It tells you how many items have been "collected" on the Clipboard. Uncheck this option if the notice bothers you.

Some people think that the Paste Options button is a bother. If you are one of those people, choose Tools | Options, select the Edit tab in the Options dialog box, and uncheck the Show Paste Options buttons check box. The Edit tab also offers a check box called Use the INS key for Paste. Check it and you can paste the last item you cut or copied to the Clipboard by pressing the INS key.

Copying and Moving Text Short Distances with Drag-and-Drop

The most convenient way to move or copy text short distances is to use the drag-and-drop method. By "short distances" I mean two places in the same document when you can see both places onscreen. You can also drag text from one open window to another or across a split window, but to do so you must be more dexterous with the mouse than I am. Text isn't copied or cut to the Clipboard when you copy or move it with the drag-and-drop method.

Follow these steps to copy or move text with the drag-and-drop method:

1. Make sure both the text you want to copy or move and the place to which you will copy or move it appear onscreen.

2. Select the text.

3. As shown in Figure 3-2, either move or copy the text. As you move or copy the text, a vertical line shows where the text will go and a box appears below the pointer. If you are copying the text, a small cross appears in the box.

   ■ **Moving** Drag the text where you want to move it.

   ■ **Copying** Hold down the CTRL key as you drag the text where you want to copy it.

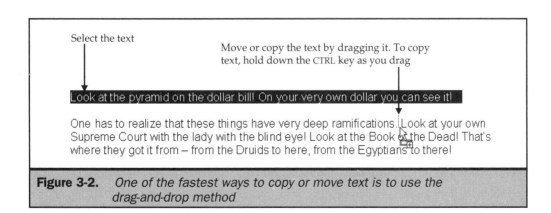

Figure 3-2. *One of the fastest ways to copy or move text is to use the drag-and-drop method*

If you find yourself unable to copy or move text this way, somebody disabled drag-and-drop text editing in your copy of Word. Choose Tools | Options, select the Edit tab in the Options dialog box, and check the Drag-and-Drop Text Editing check box.

As if there aren't enough copying and moving techniques to remember, you can also drag the text while holding down the right mouse button. Release the right mouse button when the text is where you want to move or copy it. You see a shortcut menu. Click either Move Here or Copy Here to move or copy the text:

Look at the pyramid on the dollar bill! On your very own dollar you can see it!

One has to realize that these things have very deep ramifications. Look at your own Supreme Court with the lady with the blind eye! Look at the Book o Move Here where they got it from – from the Druids to here, from the Egyptian: Copy Here

Link Here

Create Hyperlink Here

Cancel

Another way to move text is to do it in Outline view. In Chapter 17, "Moving Headings—and Text—in a Document" explains how you can move headings and the text below headings backward and forward in a document very quickly in Outline view.

More Techniques for Copying and Moving Text

Because this book has the word *complete* in its title and it endeavors to cover every nook and cranny of Word, here are more techniques for copying and moving text. Except for the "copy it to the Clipboard and then dump it" technique, text is not stored on the Clipboard with any of the techniques described here:

- **Copying**   Select the text and press SHIFT-F2. The Status bar asks, "Copy to where?" Click where you want to copy the text and press ENTER. This technique does not work for copying text to another document.

- **Moving a Paragraph at a Time**   Click a paragraph you want to move and then press ALT-SHIFT-↑ or ALT-SHIFT-↓ as many times as necessary to move the paragraph up or down the page.

- **Copy Text to the Clipboard and Dump It**   As you know if you have been reading this chapter closely (see "Copying and Moving Text with the Clipboard"), the Clipboard can hold 24 items. To assemble that many text scraps in one place, copy them one at a time to the Clipboard. Then open the Clipboard task pane and click the Paste All button.

- **Using the Spike to Move Text from Many Different Places**   The *Spike* can hold as many items as you want it to hold. Use the Spike to move text and graphics from many different places to a single place. When you empty the

Spike, the items you moved are deposited in the order in which you cut them from a document or documents. Start by selecting each piece of text or graphic you want to move and pressing CTRL-F3. Then click the insertion point where you want to dump the material and press CTRL-SHIFT-F3 to empty the contents of the Spike. (To copy the contents of the Spike so you can paste them more than once, choose Insert | AutoText | AutoText, select the AutoText tab in the AutoCorrect dialog box, select the word "Spike" in the Enter AutoText Entries Here box, and click the Insert button.)

■ **Copying and Moving Text with the "Scraps" Method**   Select text and drag it onto the Windows desktop. To copy the text, simply drag it out of the Word window; to move the text, hold down the SHIFT key while you drag. After text arrives on the desktop, it takes the form of a scrap, as shown in Figure 3-3. When you have assembled all the scraps on the desktop, drag them one by one into a document to move them there. Scraps remain on the desktop after you drag them into a new document. To keep scraps from littering the desktop, hold down the CTRL key and click each scrap to select it. Then right-click a scrap and choose Delete from the shortcut menu.

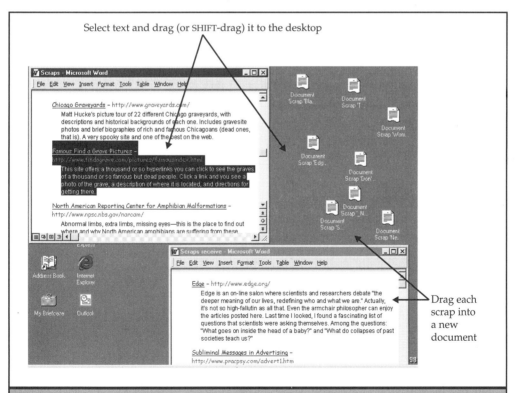

Figure 3-3.   *One way to assemble text from many different documents is to move or copy text onto the desktop and then drag the scraps one at a time into a document*

Saving What Is on the Clipboard in a File

You can see the last item that was copied or cut to the Clipboard and even save the contents of the Clipboard in a file. To do so, click the Start button and choose Programs | Accessories | System Tools | Clipboard Viewer. The Clipboard Viewer window appears and you see what is on the Clipboard, as shown in the illustration (you might have to choose Display | Text or Display | Picture to see anything). To save the contents of the Clipboard in a file, choose File | Save As, choose a folder, enter a name for the file, and click OK in the Save As dialog box.

Choose File | Save As to save the Clipboard contents in a file

Copying Documents

Copying text isn't enough? You want to copy an entire document? It can be done. Word offers commands for inserting one document into another, opening a second copy of a document, and copying an entire document to the Clipboard:

- **Inserting One Document into Another**   You can recycle documents by inserting one into another. Perhaps the essay about Thomas Jefferson, with a change here and there, can be put to use in the term paper about Colonial America. To insert one document into another, choose Insert | File to open the Insert File dialog box. Then find and select the document you want to insert and click the Insert button.

- **Copying a Document to the Clipboard**   To copy an entire document to the Clipboard, choose File | Open and find the name of the document you want to copy in the Open dialog box. Then right-click the name of the document and choose Copy from the shortcut menu. Click the Cancel button to close the Open dialog box.

- ■ **Opening a Second Copy of a Document**   Choose File | New to open the New Document task pane, and, under "New from Existing Document" in the task pane, click the Choose Document link. You see the New from Existing Document dialog box. Select a document and click the Create New button.

"Saving (and Opening) Different Versions of a Document" in Chapter 20 explains how, as you work on a document, you can retain copies of it in various stages of completion. Chapter 20 also explains how to save a document so it can be opened in another word processor or earlier version of Word.

Linking Word Documents So That Text Is Copied Automatically

Besides conventional ways of copying text, you can also link documents so that changes made to text in the source of the copy are made automatically to the copy as well. A telephone list that is updated regularly, for example, can be linked to other documents so that changes made to the master telephone list are made automatically to all documents that include the telephone list. These pages explain how to establish a link so that copies can be made automatically, as well as how to update and alter a link.

Links are broken when documents are renamed or moved to different folders. If you are disciplined and can plan ahead, make links between documents. But linking documents is more trouble than it's worth if you often move or rename documents. Very carefully create or choose folders for storing linked documents so you don't have to move them.

Establishing the Link

For the purposes of linking documents, the original document from which the copy is made is called the *server*. Its cousin, which gets updated when the copied text in the server document changes, is called the *client*.

Follow these steps to establish a link so that copied text in the client document is updated when text in the server document changes:

1. Open the server document with the text that you will copy to the client document.

2. Select and copy the text (choose Edit | Copy, press CTRL-C, or click the Copy button).

3. Open or switch to the client document and click where you want the copy to go.

4. Choose Edit | Paste Special. You see the Paste Special dialog box, as shown in Figure 3-4.

5. Click the Paste Link option button.

6. Click OK.

By the way, did you notice in the Paste Special dialog box that HTML Format is chosen in the As box (refer to Figure 3-4)? Seems weird, doesn't it? However, HTML is now the default format for transferring Clipboard data. Word, like the other Office programs, uses HTML tags as a way to make sure that fonts, text formats, and other formats are translated correctly.

 You can tell where a link is located because it is highlighted onscreen when you click it. Don't edit the highlighted text—your edits will be erased next time the link is updated.

Updating a Link

Unless you change the default settings, links are updated automatically and the text in the client document is updated from the server document under these circumstances:

- When you open the client document. (If the server copy isn't updated automatically when you open the client document, choose Tools | Options, select the General tab in the Options dialog box, and check the Update Automatic Links At Open check box.)

- When you click the link and press F9 or right-click it and choose Update Link.

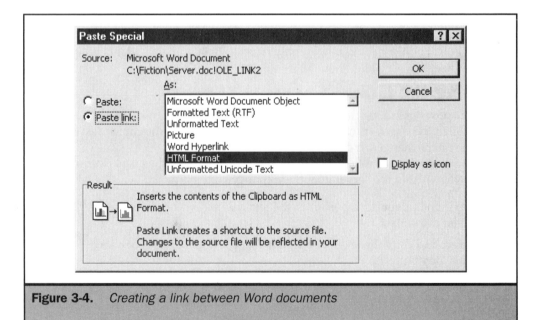

Figure 3-4.   *Creating a link between Word documents*

While you are working in the client document, you can open the server document and perhaps make changes there. To do so, right-click the copied text in the client document and choose Linked Document Object | Edit Link.

However, you can decide for yourself how and when changes made in the server document show up in the client document. To do so, open the client document and choose Edit | Links. As shown in Figure 3-5, the Links dialog box appears. This dialog box lists all the links in the client document and gives you opportunities for updating links and deciding how links should be updated.

Unlike automatic links, manual links are updated only when you tell Word to update them. To change an automatic link to a manual link, select a link in the Links dialog box and select the Manual Update option button. To update the manual links in the client document, choose Edit | Links to open the Links dialog box, select the link you want to update (or CTRL-click to select several links), and click the Update Now button.

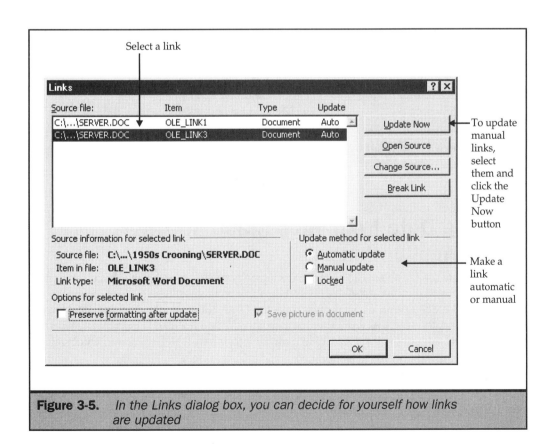

Figure 3-5.   *In the Links dialog box, you can decide for yourself how links are updated*

To make sure all links are updated before you print the client document, choose Tools | Options, select the Print tab in the Options dialog box, and check the Update Links check box.

Breaking, Locking, and Unlocking Links

The Links dialog box (see Figure 3-5) offers many options for handling links. Select a link and do one of the following to break it, lock it, or unlock it:

- **Breaking Links**   Break a link when you want the copied material to stay the same no matter what happens to the source material in the server document. To break a link, click the Break Link button. After you break the link, you can't reestablish it.

- **Locking and Unlocking Links**   Lock a link to make the copied material stay the same and not be updated from the server document. To lock a link, check the Locked check box. Unlike the Break Link option, however, a locked link keeps its relationship with the server document. You can still update the link by unchecking the Locked check box.

- **Reestablishing a Link When the Server Document Has Changed Locations**   Reestablish a link after you move the server document to a different folder, rendering its link to the client document invalid. To reestablish a link, click the Change Source button, find and select the server document in the Change Source dialog box, and click the Open button.

- **Opening the Server Document**   Click the Open Source button to open the server document and perhaps edit the original data there. (You can also open the server document by right-clicking the link and choosing Linked Document Object | Open Link.)

Copying Data from Files Made in Other Office Applications

When you use the Clipboard to copy an item from an Office program—Excel, Access, PowerPoint, and so on—into Word, Word decides on its own how to format the material in the document. Copy Access data to Word, for example, and the data turns into a Word table. An Excel worksheet is also turned into a Word table when you copy it into a Word document. An Excel chart, on the other hand, is turned into an object (Chapter 13 explains what those are).

You can, however, decide on your own how data is to be formatted when it is copied from another Office program to Word. You might do that, for example, to strip the formats from the data that is being copied. Perhaps you are copying very fancy text from a Web page and you want it to look plain as day when it lands in your Word document.

Nine times out of ten, Word makes the right decision about formatting data from other Office programs, but if Word doesn't do it right, you can follow these steps to copy the data and choose for yourself how it is formatted:

1. In the other Office program, copy the data to the Clipboard with the standard Copy commands (choose Edit | Copy, press CTRL-C, or click the Copy button).

2. In your Word document, click where you want the data to appear.

3. Choose Edit | Paste Special. You see the Paste Special dialog box, as shown in Figure 3-6.

4. Under As, choose which format you want for the text. Table 3-2 explains the different formats. Which options appear in the As box depends on which kind of data you are trying to copy.

5. Click the OK button.

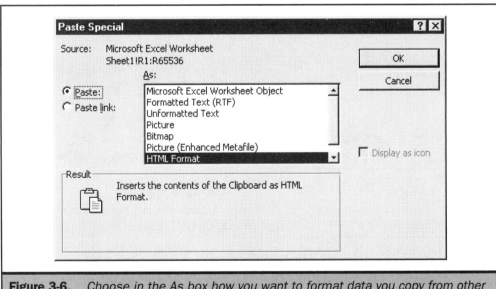

Figure 3-6.   *Choose in the As box how you want to format data you copy from other Office programs*

Paste Link Option	How the Copy Is Made
Object	The data is pasted in Word as an embedded object, with the formats the same as those in the source file (the next section in this chapter explains embedded objects). Because it's an object, you can drag it to different places onscreen or wrap text around it. (This option changes names, depending on where the copied material came from. For example, the option is called Excel Worksheet Object if the data came from an Excel worksheet.)
Formatted Text (RTF)	The data retains formats—boldfacing, shading, backgrounds, color, and so on.
Unformatted Text	Formats are stripped from the data when it is pasted in the client document. The data adopts the formats of surrounding text.
Picture	Copies the data as a picture object. You can use resize commands to change its size.
Bitmap	Copies the data as a bitmap graphic. Only use this option to copy bitmap images, as other data gets blurred when you copy it in bitmap form.
Picture (Enhanced Metafile)	Also copies the data as a picture object that you can resize and move on the page.
HTML Format	Text is pasted in HTML format. This is the default format. The data retains all its formats.
Unformatted Unicode Text	Copies multilingual text such as Japanese or Chinese characters into the document and displays the characters correctly.

Table 3-3.   *Format Options for Copying Data with the Paste Special Command*

Compound Documents: Embedding Data from Other Programs in a Word Document

By embedding data in a Word document, you can edit it in your document without leaving Word. Excel worksheets, for example, can be embedded in the middle of Word documents. So can charts and bitmap graphics and any number of other things. Word documents that include data that was made in other programs are called *compound documents.*

The data appears in the Word document in the form of an object. When you double-click an embedded object, the computer program with which you created it opens so you can edit the object. Figure 3-7 shows an embedded object, in this case a bitmap image. As you can see in the figure, Paint, a program for editing bitmap images, appears in the Word window when the embedded object is double-clicked. To return to Word, all you have to do is click outside the embedded object—on the text in your Word document, for example.

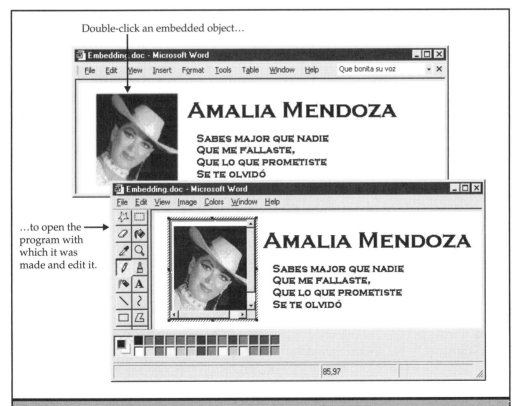

Figure 3-7.   *Amalia Mendoza, mariachi torch singer and embedded Paint object*

To Link or to Embed, That Is the Question

Earlier in this chapter, "Linking Word Documents So That Text Is Copied Automatically" explains how to link documents so that updates made to the source are made as well in the copy. Besides linking Word documents, you can link data from an Office file to a Word document, so that updates to an Excel table, for example, are made automatically to a Word document. To link this way, follow the procedures in "Linking Word Documents So That Text Is Copied Automatically," but start by selecting data in Excel, Access, PowerPoint, or another Office program.

Here are the relative advantages of linking and embedding:

- **File Size**   Embedding objects in a Word document, especially graphics, makes a document grow in size. These days, hard disk space isn't the issue it used to be, but a large document can still be unwieldy and hard to store. By linking, you solve the file-size problem, because the item only has to be stored once—in its original location.

- **Carrying Charges**   Linking documents and files poses a problem: what to do if documents and files need moving. A Word document that is linked to other documents can't be sent over the Internet or copied to a laptop without the links being broken. Linking is out of the question in the case of Word documents that will travel to other computers.

- **Updating**   The great advantage of linking is that documents are always up to date. When the source document or file is altered, so is the linked copy. Telephone lists and other documents that are only useful if they are up to date are ideal candidates for linking.

Word keeps track of which programs were used to create embedded objects, and when you double-click an embedded object, Word opens its parent program. Nevertheless, the data in the object is kept right in the Word document. Contrary to what happens when objects are linked, data for embedded objects is not kept in a different document or file. (Earlier in this chapter, "Linking Word Documents So That Text Is Copied Automatically" explains links. The sidebar, "To Link or to Embed, That Is the Question" compares linking and embedding.)

Here are the three ways to implant an embedded object in a Word document:

- **Create It**   Choose Insert | Object. On the Create New tab of the Object dialog box, select the name of the computer program with which you will create the object, and click OK. The computer program opens, as does an object box. Create the embedded object inside the box. Click outside the object box to return to your Word document.

- **Copy It from the Clipboard**   Copy the object to the Clipboard and choose Edit | Paste Special. In the Paste Special dialog box, select the Object option in the As box and click OK. See "Copying Data from Files Made in Other Office Applications" earlier in this chapter for details.

■ **Copy It from a File**   Choose Insert | Object and select the Create from File tab in the Object dialog box. Then either enter the path to the file where the object is kept or click the Browse button to open the Browse dialog box and select the file. When you click OK, the object appears in your document.

Note *In Chapter 13, "Manipulating Art, Text Boxes, Shapes, and Other So-Called Objects" explains how to handle objects on the page.*

MOUS Exam Objectives Explored in Chapter 3

Objective	Heading
Insert, modify, and move text and symbols	"Moving and Copying Text Between Documents" and "Linking Documents So That Text Is Copied Automatically"

Ten Ways to Prevent Eyestrain

People who spend many working hours in front of a computer screen owe it to themselves to look after their health. Computers are dangerous to the lower back, the wrists, and the eyes—especially the eyes. Here are ten Windows and Word techniques to help prevent eyestrain.

Note *Some of the techniques listed here only work on latter-day versions of the Windows operating system. If you want to try a technique but you can't on your computer, blame it on Windows, not me.*

1. Keep Your Monitor In the Proper Light   Glare on a monitor screen causes eyestrain. Keep the monitor out of direct light to reduce glare and use an adjustable light to illuminate whatever it is you are working with besides your computer and monitor. If you are using a laptop, put the monitor in direct light. Laptops are sidelit or backlit, and they work better in full lighting.

2. Play with the Knobs on Your Monitor   Those funny knobs on the monitor can be useful indeed. Twist them, turn them, and experiment until you find a look that is comfortable for your eyes.

3. Opt for Smaller Screen Resolution   With a smaller screen resolution, or area, everything looks bigger, although things can get cramped, too. To get a smaller resolution, right-click on the Windows desktop and choose Properties. In the Display

Properties dialog box, select the Settings tab. Then drag the Screen Area slider to the left, so the setting reads 640 by 480 pixels, and click OK. Try this setting on for size. If you don't like it, return to the Settings tab and drag the screen slider to the right. If you can't see the OK button because the screen is too small, just press the ENTER key instead of clicking OK.

4. Put Large Icons on the Desktop and in Folders   To make the icons on the Windows desktop and in folders larger, right-click on the desktop and choose Properties. In the Display Properties dialog box, select the Effects tab, check the Use Large Icons check box, and click OK.

5. Make the Icons on the Start Menu Larger   To make the icons on the Start menu larger, right-click the Taskbar and choose Properties. Then, in the Taskbar Properties dialog box, uncheck the Show Small Icons In Start menu check box, and click OK.

6. Use Large Icons to Display Fonts   Large display fonts make menu choices and icon names easier to read. To see if you like them, right-click the Windows desktop and choose Properties to open the Display Properties dialog box, and select the Settings tab. Then click the Advanced button. On the Font Size drop-down menu, choose Large Fonts. Windows says that the large fonts can only take effect after you restart the computer. Restart the computer and see how you like large fonts.

7. Make the Mouse Pointers Larger   Another way to make your eyes last longer is to make the mouse pointers larger. Click the Start button and choose Settings | Control Panel. Then double-click the Mouse icon, select the Pointers tab in the Mouse Properties dialog box, and choose Windows Standard (extra large) or Windows Standard (large) from the Scheme drop-down menu.

8. For Laptop Users: Use Mouse Pointer Trails   Pointer trails can help laptop users find the mouse pointer onscreen. To tell Windows to display pointer trails, click the Start button and choose Settings | Control Panel. Then double-click the Mouse icon, select the Motion tab (or the Visibility tab or Pointer Options tab in some editions of Windows), and check the Show (or Display) Pointer Trails check box in the Mouse Properties dialog box.

9. Use a Blue Background with White Text   As a drastic measure, you can see if you like seeing a blue background on the screen and white text. In Word, choose Tools | Options, and select the General tab in the Options dialog box. Then check the Blue Background, White Text check box and click OK.

10. Gaze at the Horizon   Every so often, leave your desk, step to the window, part the curtains, and stare. Stare at the most faraway point you can see. Stare and dream. Then blink a few times and marvel at how good the world looks when you're not staring at a computer screen.

Chapter 4

Getting the Help You Need

As soul singers say, "Everybody needs a little help sometime, baby." This chapter explains how to seek help for using Word. Here you will find instructions for using the Help programs as well as looking to outside sources such as the Internet. Personally, I think the best way to get help with Word is to look in the Index or Table of Contents in this book, find the topic you need help with, and turn to the page that the Index or Table of Contents refers to.

Surveying the Ways to Get Help

Before you start flailing your arms and screaming for help, consider your options, all of which are described in the pages that follow:

- **Office Assistant**   This cartoon character offers advice, some of it unwanted.

- **Help Program**   The Help program is the surest but also the slowest way to seek help.

- **What's This? Command**   You can choose the Help | What's This? command and click text or a paragraph to see how it was formatted.

- **Help Button in Dialog Boxes**   Click the Help button in a dialog box and then click an option to find out what the option does.

- **WordPerfect Help**   Word offers a special Help program for people who have quit WordPerfect and embraced Word.

- **By Telephone**   You can call Microsoft and get help that way.

- **On the Internet**   This chapter explains how to get help on the Internet from Microsoft and from other sources.

The Office Assistant and What You Can Do About It

As you must have noticed by now, an animated figure called the Office Assistant appears onscreen from time to time whether you like it or not. Type **Dear Jane:** and press the ENTER key, for example, and the Office Assistant leaps onscreen. "It looks like you're writing a letter," the Assistant says. "Would you like help?" Close a document without saving the changes you made to it and the Office Assistant rears its ugly head again. "Do you want to save the changes?" the Assistant asks.

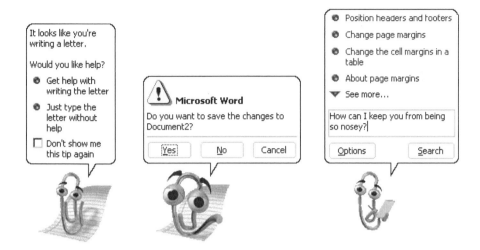

The Office Assistant is programmed like the Lone Ranger to appear out of the blue when you need help or assistance. And if you press F1 or choose Help | Microsoft Word Help, the Office Assistant appears onscreen, not the Help program. In my experience, the Office Assistant is more of a nuisance than anything else, so the following pages explain how to keep the Office Assistant from appearing as well as how to tell Word that you want to go straight to the Help program when you press F1 or choose Help | Microsoft Word Help. You will also find instructions for fine-tuning the Office Assistant so you can make it work your way.

To temporarily remove the Office Assistant from the screen, choose Help | Hide the Office Assistant, or right-click the Office Assistant and choose Hide on the shortcut menu. You can also shove the Office Assistant out of the way by dragging it to a corner of the screen.

Seeking Help with the Office Assistant

Follow these steps to find instructions for doing a task with the Office Assistant:

1. Press F1, click the Microsoft Word Help button, or choose Help | Show the Office Assistant. The Office Assistant appears onscreen.

2. Click the Office Assistant. As shown in Figure 4-1, a bubble caption appears with a "What would you like to do?" list of topics. At the bottom of the list is

a box for entering a topic of your own. Word notes which activities you have performed lately and lists topics that have to do with those activities.

3. If the topic for which you need help is listed, double-click the topic. You might have to click See More at the bottom of the list to see all the topics. If your topic isn't listed, enter a topic name in the box, click the Search button, examine the new list of topics, and double-click a topic.

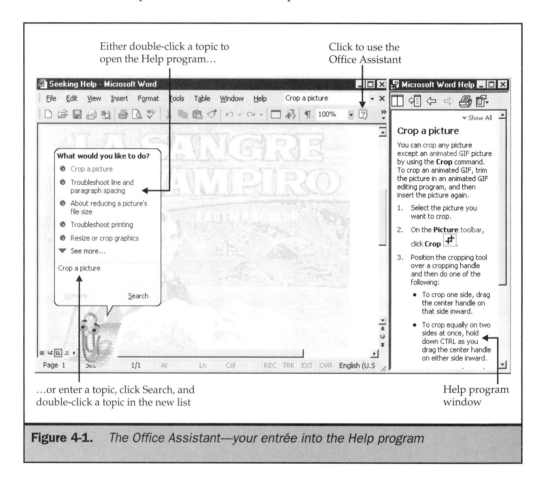

Either double-click a topic to open the Help program…

Click to use the Office Assistant

…or enter a topic, click Search, and double-click a topic in the new list

Help program window

Figure 4-1. *The Office Assistant—your entrée into the Help program*

Getting Rid of the Office Assistant

To my way of thinking, the Office Assistant is nothing but a hurdle you have to leap over to get to the Help program. After you press F1, click the Microsoft Word Help button, or choose Help | Microsoft Word Help, the Office Assistant appears. Then you double-click a topic, wait for the Help program window to appear, and hope that the right Help screen or right set of questions appears in the Help window.

How would you like to bypass the Office Assistant and go straight to the Help program when you press F1 or click the Microsoft Word Help button? It can be done. For that matter, you can keep the Office Assistant from appearing at all. Follow these steps to retire the Office Assistant and keep it from bothering you again:

1. Choose Help | Show the Office Assistant if the Office Assistant isn't already onscreen.

2. Click the Options button in the bubble caption above the Office Assistant, or, if you don't see the bubble caption, right-click the Office Assistant and choose Options on the shortcut menu. You see the Options tab of the Office Assistant dialog box.

3. Uncheck the Use The Office Assistant check box and click OK.

Next time you press F1, click the Microsoft Word Help button, or choose Help | Microsoft Word Help, the Help program opens right away. Suppose you miss the Office Assistant and you want the lovable animated figure to start distracting you again. To breath life back into the Office Assistant, choose Help | Show the Office Assistant. The Office Assistant appears and you are back where you started.

The Help program opens on the right side of the screen. See "Using the Word Help Program" later in this chapter to learn how to rummage for advice in the Help program.

Note   *The last topic in the bubble caption is called "None of the above, look for more help on the Web." Open your Web browser and click that topic to visit a Microsoft Web site where, theoretically, your question will be answered.*

Fine-Tuning the Office Assistant

Instead of ditching the Office Assistant altogether, you can visit the Options tab of the Office Assistant dialog box and fiddle with the options to make the thing work better. To do so, click the Microsoft Word Help button or press F1 to see the Office Assistant (choose Help | Show the Office Assistant first, if necessary), and then click the Options button in the bubble caption (right-click and choose Options if you don't see the bubble caption). The Office Assistant dialog box appears.

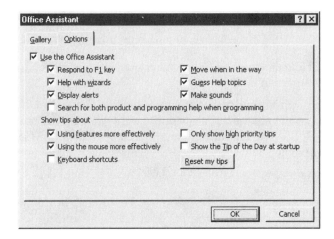

Caution *Changes made to the Office Assistant settings apply to all the Office programs, not just Word.*

Check or uncheck these options to make the Office Assistant work your way:

- **Respond to F1 Key**   This option opens the Office Assistant instead of the Help program when you press F1. Uncheck this box if you want to go straight to the Help program by pressing F1.

- **Help with Wizards**   When you use a wizard to create a Web page or document, for example, the Office Assistant occasionally jumps aboard to offer advice. Uncheck this box if you find that annoying.

- **Display Alerts**   Alerts are timely messages like the one that appears if you try to close a file without saving the changes you made to it. Uncheck this check box to make alerts appear in message boxes instead of the Office Assistant's bubble caption.

- **Search for Both Product and Programming Help When Programming**   This option offers help advice for Word as well as Visual Basic when you are programming with Visual Basic.

- **Move When In The Way**   With this option enabled the Office Assistant moves to the other side of the screen when you work beside its present location. Leave the check mark here.

- **Guess Help Topics**   This option makes Help topics appear in the bubble caption when you click the Office Assistant.

- **Make Sounds**   As you might have noticed, some Office Assistants are noisy. Uncheck this option to shut them up.

A tiny light bulb appears on the Microsoft Word Help button when the Assistant wants to offer you a tip. The light bulb appears above the Office Assistant as well. The options at the bottom of the Office Assistant dialog box pertain to which kinds of tips you want to receive:

- **Light Bulb Tips**   Check the first four boxes—Using Features Effectively, Using the Mouse More Effectively, Keyboard Shortcuts, and Only Show High Priority Tips—to tell Word how often you want the light bulb to appear and what kind of tips you want to see, if any.

- **Startup Tips**   Click the Show The Tip of the Day at Startup check box to make the Office Assistant appear and offer a tip whenever you start Word. The Reset My Tips button is for telling Word to start at the beginning of the list of tips it shows you when you start the program.

Choosing an Office Assistant Animated Figure

Because the word "complete" appears in the title of this book, I am obliged to tell you how to choose an animated figure for the Office Assistant. You have eight choices, including a bug-eyed paperclip rendition of Jimmy Durante and a robot. To choose a new animated figure for the Office Assistant:

1. Press F1 or click the Microsoft Word Help button to display the Office Assistant.

2. Right-click the Office Assistant and select the Choose Assistant option on the shortcut menu. You see the Gallery tab of the Office Assistant dialog box.

3. Click the Next or Back button to examine the different choices.

4. Click OK when you have found the Office Assistant you want.

Using the Word Help Program

The Help program is a program unto itself and is completely separate from Word. The program appears in a window on the right side of the screen so you can refer to help instructions as you do your work (see Figure 4-1). Read on to find out how to open the Help program, find the instructions you need, and handle the Help window.

Starting and Closing the Help Program

Earlier in this chapter, "Seeking Help with the Office Assistant" explains how to open the Help program by way of the Office Assistant. Unless you tinker with default settings, the only way to start the Help program, apart from entering a question in the Help box, is to invoke the Office Assistant first. However, "Getting Rid of the Office Assistant" and "Fine-Tuning the Office Assistant," also found earlier in this chapter, explain two strategies for opening the Help program without having to see the Office Assistant first. If you're serious about using the Help program, I suggest learning how to bypass the Office Assistant by reading the earlier sections in this chapter.

   You can open the Help program without seeing the Office Assistant first by typing a question in the Help box, pressing ENTER, and selecting a help topic on the drop-down menu.

The Help program window is like any program window. Click its Minimize button to shrink it to nothing. Click its Maximize button to make it fill the screen. To close the Help program, click the Close button (the X) in the upper-right corner of the Help program window.

Managing the Help Window

The Help program is designed so you can open its window on one side of the screen and keep the Word window open on the other. By clicking buttons on the top of the Help program window, you can see as much of the window as you need to see to get your work done in Word and still be able to read Help instructions.

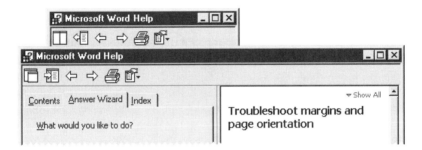

Take advantage of these buttons to help find the instructions you need:

■ **Auto Tile/Untile**   Click the Auto Tile button to make the Word window fit snugly against the Help window. When you click Untile, the Help window is allowed to overlap the Word window.

■ **Show/Hide Button**   Click the Show button to see the three tabs—Contents, Answer Wizard, and Index—and turn your search for help in another direction (see "Three Ways to Look for Help," later in this chapter). Click the Hide button to remove the three tabs and focus on the instructions on the Help screen.

■ **Back and Forward Buttons**   The Help program remembers all the instruction screens you visit in the course of a search. Click the Back button to revisit a help screen; click the Forward button to move ahead to a screen from which you retreated.

■ **Print Button**   Click the Print button to print Help instructions and be able to refer to them later.

■ **Options**   Opens a drop-down menu for doing the things you can do by clicking buttons in the Help window.

To make the Help program window wider or narrower, move the mouse pointer over the left border of the window. When you see the double-headed arrows, click and start dragging.

Three Ways to Look for Help

When the Help window opens, you see a Help screen with instructions for doing this, that, or the other thing. But suppose the Help screen doesn't present the instructions you need. In that case, click the Show button at the top of the Help program window to enlarge the window. You see three tabs—Contents, Answer Wizard, and Index— for turning your search for help in another direction. Use the Contents tab like the table of contents in a book to find instructions, the Answer Wizard tab to query the Help program, and the Index tab to search the Help files for instructions.

Starting from the Contents Tab

As shown in Figure 4-2, the Contents tab offers a list of topics similar to a table of contents in a book. Follow these steps to find help on the Contents tab:

1. Scour the list of topics until you find the one you are looking for.

2. When you've found the topic that interests you, double-click its book icon. The book "opens" and you see subtopics, each with a question mark icon beside its name, and sometimes more book icons as well.

3. Click the question mark beside the name of the subtopic that interests you. Instructions pertaining to the topic appear on the right side of the screen.

By the way, you can double-click an open book to close it and keep its subtopics from cluttering the Help window.

Double-click a book to see its subtopics

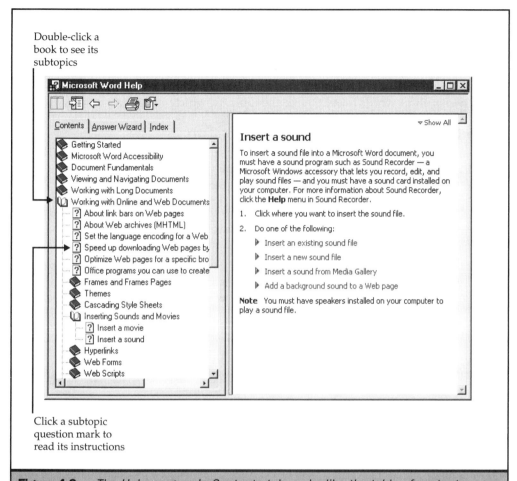

Click a subtopic question mark to read its instructions

Figure 4-2.   *The Help program's Contents tab works like the table of contents in a book*

Asking Questions of the Answer Wizard

The Answer Wizard works exactly like the Help box, and, for that matter, like the Office Assistant. In fact, as Figure 4-3 demonstrates, all three work the same. Enter the topic for which you need assistance in the text box, press ENTER, and click a topic on the list that appears. By the way, you don't really have to enter a question. Just enter one or two or three words that describe the topic for which you need instructions.

Searching by Keyword on the Index Tab

Searching for instructions on the Index tab is like searching the Internet. To search, you enter *keywords*—words that describe what you want to know. Follow these steps to search for Help program instructions on the Index tab:

1. In box 1, type a keyword that describes the topic you want to know about. As shown in Figure 4-4, the list of words in box 2 scrolls to the word you entered. You must enter one of the keywords listed in box 2 to conduct the search.

2. Press the SPACEBAR or the ENTER key. As shown in Figure 4-4, a list of Help topics appears in box 3. These are topics whose instructions mention the keyword you entered in step 1. The top of box 3 says how many Help topics were found.

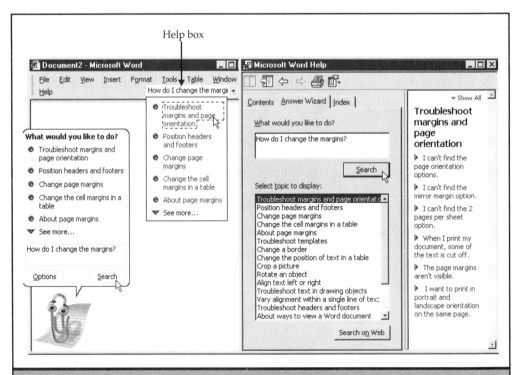

Figure 4-3. *Entering a question in the Help box is tantamount to entering a question in the Answer Wizard or Office Assistant text box*

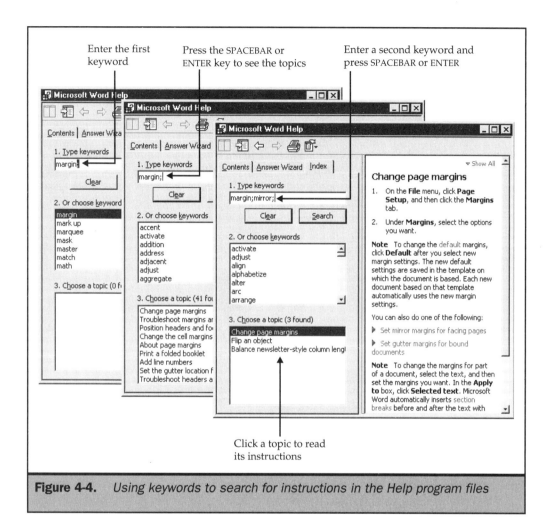

Figure 4-4.   *Using keywords to search for instructions in the Help program files*

At this point, you can either scroll through the list of Help topics in box 3 and click a topic to read its instructions on the right side of the program window, or you can enter another keyword to decrease the number of topics in box 3 and thereby narrow the search to fewer topics.

3. Type another keyword in box 1 and press the SPACEBAR or the ENTER key. The list of topics in box 3 is narrowed, as shown in Figure 4-4. Now only topics whose instructions mention both keywords appear.

4. Click a topic in box 3 to see its instructions on the right side of the Help program window.

Of course, you can enter as many keywords as you want, but the list in box 3 shrinks pretty quickly, and I've never had to enter more than two.

Be sure to click the Clear button before you conduct a new search. Clicking the Clear button empties box 3 of topics so you can start all over.

The What's This? Button for Finding Out What's What

With the idea that the fastest way to find out anything is to ask, Word offers the What's This? command. Choose Help | What's This? or press SHIFT-F1 and the pointer changes into an arrow with a question mark beside it. Click the quizzical pointer on the thing you want to know more about and you see a box with an explanation, a box with rudimentary instructions for completing a task, or the Reveal Formatting task pane, which tells you how text was formatted. The What's This? command is great for finding out what menu commands do. Choose Help | What's This? and then click the command as though you were choosing it.

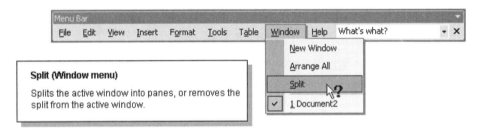

Learning What Dialog Box Options Are

In the upper-right corner of most dialog boxes is a question mark. Click the question mark and then click a dialog box option, text box, check box, or spinner box to find out what you are supposed to do with or enter in the thing you clicked. Some dialog box options are hard to decipher. Get used to clicking the question mark in dialog boxes to find out what's what, as shown in Figure 4-5.

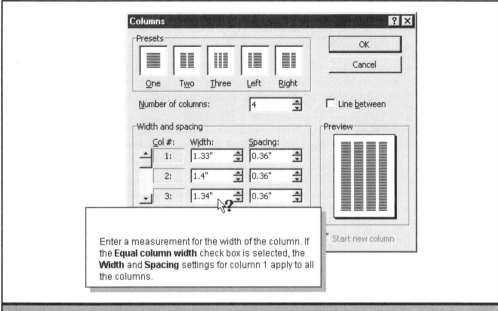

Figure 4-5. *Click the question mark in dialog boxes and then click an option to see what the option does*

Help for WordPerfect Turncoats

As part of its plan to entice WordPerfect users, Word offers a special Help program for people who have made the switch to Word from WordPerfect. To check it out, choose Help | WordPerfect Help. You see a Help window with topics that concern WordPerfect users.

 Converts from WordPerfect who prefer the WordPerfect keypresses for getting from place to place in a document can use the WordPerfect keypresses in Microsoft Word. Choose Tools | Options, select the General tab in the Options dialog box, and check the Navigation Keys For WordPerfect Users check box.

Detecting and Repairing Word Installation Errors

Use the Help | Detect and Repair command to make sure that Word program files are intact. Files are sometimes overwritten or replaced when you install new software.

A WordPerfect User's Lament: "Where Are the Reveal Codes?"

Reveal codes are to WordPerfect what water is to Niagara Falls. In WordPerfect, you press F11 and reveal codes show precisely how text is formatted. Most WordPerfect users love their reveal codes. When they switch to Word, the first question they ask is, "Where are the reveal codes?"

Sorry, but there are none. To see how text is formatted, look at the text, the rulers, the Font menu, and the Style menu. If you are desperate, choose Format | Reveal Formatting. You will see the Reveal Formatting task pane, which shows how the text where the cursor is was formatted.

Don't worry, you will soon learn to live without reveal codes. After a while, you learn to tell by looking how text is formatted. You learn to stand on your own two feet and not look at reveal codes when you want to know what is on the screen.

And sometimes files get damaged. The Help | Detect and Repair command checks the health of Word program files and reinstalls files if that proves necessary.

The Help | Detect and Repair command takes a good 30 minutes to run. Don't detect and repair if you are in a hurry.

Appendix A offers advice for reinstalling Word and for installing patches, the fix-it files that repair bugs in computer programs.

Getting Technical Support from Microsoft

Besides getting help from Microsoft on the Internet (see the next section in this chapter), you can also use that ancient device, the telephone, to seek help. Call 425-462-9673 to speak to a Microsoft technician. The cost for this service is a whopping $35 per call if your copy of Word came preinstalled on your computer. If you bought your copy of Word over the counter, the call is free. Hours are 5 A.M. to 9 P.M. Pacific Standard Time on weekdays, and 9 A.M. to 3 P.M. on Saturdays.

The Microsoft telephone number listed here is for people calling inside the United States. Others are advised to go to this Web site to find out what number to call and how much Microsoft charges for technical support: http://support.microsoft.com/support.

You can also e-mail a request for help to Microsoft. In the Subject line of the message, enter the topic for which you need help. Send the message to mshelp@microsoft.com.

Seeking Help from Microsoft on the Internet

Table 4-1 describes the different ways to go on the Internet and get help for using Word from the Microsoft Corporation.

Tip
Be sure to visit the Word home page (www.microsoft.com/word/) from time to time. Inevitably, bugs appear in software programs. The Word home page describes Word bugs and offers repair files called patches that you can download to your computer to fix the bugs.

Ten Places on the Internet to Get Help with Word

Microsoft isn't the only place on the Internet that offers advice for using Microsoft Word. A lot of people want to get into the act. Following is a list of ten Web sites where you can seek help for using Word.

Note
The Web site addresses listed here were valid as of spring 2001. Web sites, however, come and go. If you can't locate a site listed here, try using an Internet search engine to find more current addresses.

Web Site	What You Will Find There
Contact Microsoft	Tell Microsoft what you think of Word and how Word could be improved. Address: register.microsoft.com/regwiz/regwiz.asp
Office Home Page	Information about Office, Word's older brother. Address: www.microsoft.com/office/default.htm
Support Page	For getting information about how to use Word. Search for and download "KnowledgeBase" articles from this site. Address: support.microsoft.com/support/
Word Home Page	Offers patches and other software fixes for Word. Address: www.microsoft.com/word/

Table 4-1. *Ways to Seek Help from Microsoft on the Internet*

1. America Online's Help Desk   Starting here, you can find support channels that pertain to Microsoft Word. For AOL subscribers only. Keyword: **Help Desk**

2. Bug Net   Bug Net is the self-proclaimed "world's leading supplier of PC bug fixes." Click the Search button, enter **word** in the Search For text box, and see how many, how various, and how disagreeable the bugs are in Word. Address: www.bugnet.com

3. CNet Help.com   CNet's famous help desk also offers advice about using Microsoft Word, although you have to do a bit of searching to find it. Enter **word** in the Search text box to look for advice about using Microsoft Word. Address: www.help.com

4. ElementK Journals   This online journal takes on all kinds of Word esoterica—formatting fractions, table cell dimensions, and useful macros. It's well worth a look. Address: www.elementkjournals.com/msw

5. Helptalk Online   This Web site offers a discussion forum where you can post questions. Come back a day later, and your question may be answered. Questions on the MS Word forum range from high-tech to low-tech. All questions are welcome. Address: www.helptalk.net/officeapps

6 My Helpdesk.com   You have to register to make use of this Web site, but after you do that, you can ask questions at the Microsoft Office forum, read questions that others asked, and maybe find answers to your questions. Address: www.myhelpdesk.com

7. Roadside America   No, this isn't a place on the Internet where you can get help with Microsoft Word, but it is, at least in my opinion, the best Web site on the Internet. From here, you can view strange roadside attractions—the Uniroyal Giantess, the Hindenburg Crash Site. Click a state on the Electric Map to visit roadside attractions in your state. Maybe one is just around the corner from you. Address: www.roadsideamerica.com

8. Woody's Office Portal   Woody Leonhard, the "Woody" of this Web site, is a bit too enamored of Office minutiae. However, if you can get past his opinions concerning how Office software *should* work and get to his advice concerning how Office software *does* work, you will be a wiser user of Word. Woody offers a free weekly newsletter for Office power users. Address: www.wopr.com

9. Wordinfo   Say the creators of this site: "Our mission is simple: To help Microsoft Word users create attractive, well-written documents as painlessly as possible." Includes a good list of links to other sites that pertain to Word and a list of online magazine articles as well. Address: www.wordinfo.com

10. ZD Help   From this site, run by Ziff-Davis, publisher of *PC Magazine* and other glossy computer tomes, you can search for articles about Word. This site is a very useful resource, although I should warn you that the *PC Magazine* set is in love with computers and sometimes the authors gush when they should clarify. Address: www.zdnet.com/zdhelp

Chapter 5

All About Printing

In spite of predictions to the contrary, the paperless office is still a pipe dream. The day when Johnny is at his computer, totally digitized and communicating with his colleagues without having to commit anything to paper, has yet to materialize. Johnny still has to print letters, contracts, prospectuses, and other material. As for Jane, she can hardly go a day without printing reports, legal briefs, and brochures. The office is still awash in paper, and all Jane and Johnny can do for consolation is try their best to recycle.

This chapter explains everything you need to know to print documents in Word. You learn how to acquaint Word with your printer, preview documents so you can see what they look like before you print them, and make small editorial changes on the Preview screen. This chapter explains the numerous ways to print documents and how to print different parts of a document—the odd pages, a section, or a handful of pages in the middle. In this chapter you will also find instructions for printing envelopes and labels. At the end, for the weary and frustrated, are instructions for solving printer problems.

Introducing Word to Your Printer

Word and your printer need to be on speaking terms before you can print documents flawlessly. These pages explain how to make the introduction. Read on to find out how to tell Word which printer you will use (if your computer is connected to more than one printer) and which paper tray you get paper from when you print documents (if your printer has more than one paper tray).

Telling Word Which Printer You Will Use

If you can send files to more than one printer, perhaps a color printer and a black-and-white job, you need to tell Word which printers you will print your files on. Do this long before you actually print your file. In fact, choose the printer shortly after you create your document. Different printers have different capabilities, and Word changes layouts, however slightly, to accommodate the printer on which you will print your file. Therefore, Word needs to know which printer you intend to use.

To tell Word on which printer you will print your document, choose File | Print (or press CTRL-P). Then, in the Print dialog box, open the Name drop-down list and choose a printer.

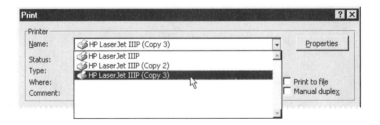

Telling Word Which Paper Tray to Use

Some people are fortunate enough to have two paper trays in their printers. Perhaps you are one of those lucky people, and you keep 8.5 × 11-inch paper in the upper tray and legal-size or color paper in the lower tray. If your printer has two trays, printing on different kinds of paper is easier for you, but you also have to tell Word from which tray to get the paper when you print a document.

Word offers a two-pronged strategy for choosing a paper tray. As shown in Figure 5-1, you can go to the Printer Properties dialog box (choose File | Print and click the Properties button) to choose a default paper tray, the paper tray where Word goes first to get paper for printing documents. You can also go to the Page Setup dialog box (choose File | Page Setup) to tell Word to print certain documents or certain pages with paper from a tray other than the default tray.

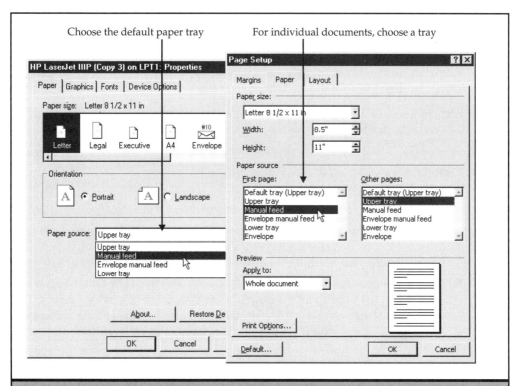

Figure 5-1. *Choose the default paper tray in the Printer Properties dialog box (left); to override the default paper tray setting, go to the Page Setup dialog box (right)*

The choice of paper trays that you make in the Print dialog box applies to all your documents. In other words, it becomes the default tray, the one that all your print jobs grab paper from. When you choose a tray in the Page Setup dialog box, however, your choice applies only to the document that is open onscreen.

Choosing the Default Paper Tray

The default paper tray is Word's first choice for printing documents. Unless you tell Word otherwise, paper is taken from the default tray. For the default tray, choose the tray with the paper on which you will print most often. To choose the default paper tray:

1. Choose File | Print and select a printer, if necessary, in the Print dialog box.

2. Click the Properties button and choose a default tray from the Paper Source drop-down list in the Printer Properties dialog box (see Figure 5-1).

Telling Word to Print from a Tray Other Than the Default Tray

Occasionally you have to go against the default choice and print certain pages or even a whole document with paper in a tray that isn't the default. Word offers options for printing all pages or just the first page of a document or section, perhaps a letterhead page, with paper from a different tray. Follow these steps to tell Word to get paper from a tray other than the default tray where you normally get paper:

1. Click in a section if you want to print a particular section on different paper; otherwise, it doesn't matter where you start.

2. Choose File | Page Setup to open the Page Setup dialog box.

3. Click the Paper Source tab (see Figure 5-1).

4. Choose a tray:

   ■ **Different Paper for the First Page** From the First Page list, choose a tray other than the default tray to print the first page of a document or section on different paper. If you want to print the first page of a section on different paper, choose This Section in the Apply To drop-down list.

   ■ **Different Paper for All the Pages** Choose a tray from the Other Pages drop-down list to print all the pages in the document or section (except perhaps the first page) on different paper. Be sure to choose This Section in the Apply To drop-down list to print the pages in a section differently.

5. Click OK.

 In order to include paper of a different size in a document and be able to print on it, you have to create a new section for the different-size paper. See "Section Breaks for Changing Layouts" in Chapter 9.

Precautions to Avoid Printing Problems

Printing problems are like soccer goals. As any soccer mom can tell you, the goalie gets the blame when the other team scores, but the problem is usually caused upfield by poor defending on the part of the fullbacks. Similarly, printing problems get noticed when documents are printed, but the origin of most printing problems can be traced to faulty decision-making on the part of the person who created the document. To keep printing errors to a minimum, take these precautions:

- **Fix the Margins Early On**   When the margins are too wide, text doesn't fall in the right places and lines don't break correctly. Moreover, if you change margin sizes after you are well into a project, you are asking for it. Text is indented from the margins, not from the edge of the page, so changing the margins changes all the text indents and can create a mess. Decide on the size of the margins early on to avoid line-break and other layout problems.

- **Know What Paper Size the Document Was Made For**   Make sure you know which size paper you are printing on. If you are trying to print a document that you got from a foreigner, chances are the document was formatted for paper other than the standard 8.5 × 11 that North Americans love so well. Chances are, too, that your margins and other layout settings are askew. See "Ten Printing Problems and How to Solve Them" at the end of this chapter (see item number 2) to learn how to format an A4 210 × 297 mm document for an American printer.

- **Tell Word Which Printer You Intend to Use**   As you make layout settings, Word takes note of which printer you intend to use and adjusts the layout settings accordingly. Therefore, if you are lucky enough or wealthy enough to have two printers, or you intend to print your document at a print shop, you should tell Word right away which printer you intend to print your document on. See "Telling Word Which Printer You Will Use" earlier in this chapter.

- **Use TrueType Fonts**   Some printers cannot print all the fonts whose names appear on the Font menu. However, all printers can print TrueType fonts, the fonts with "*TT*" next to their names on the Font menu. To make sure letters look the same onscreen as they will look when you print them, stick to TrueType fonts.

Previewing a Document Before You Print It

Before you print a document, examine it closely to see if a last-minute error needs correcting. That way, you save yourself from printing two, three, or twenty pages before you realize that the document needs more work. Word offers a special screen for previewing documents. These pages explain how to preview documents before you print them and make layout changes in the Print Preview window.

Examining a Document in the Print Preview Window

As "Getting a Better View of Your Work" in Chapter 2 explains, the Print Preview window is a great place to see what documents will look like on the printed page. And the window also offers a number of tools for finding and fixing errors. To see a document in the Print Preview window, either click the Print Preview button on the Standard toolbar or choose File | Print Preview. The Print Preview window appears, as shown in Figure 5-2.

On the Print Preview toolbar are buttons and menus for examining documents, fixing errors, and printing. Here are instructions for examining a document in the

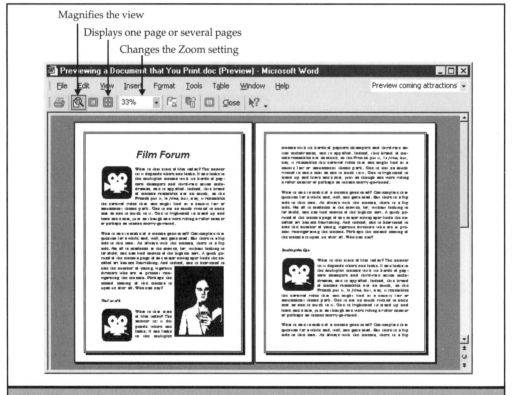

Figure 5-2. *Examine documents on the Print Preview window to get a better look at your work and to catch errors before you commit them to paper*

Print Preview window (the next part of this chapter explains how to make editorial and layout changes):

■ **Looking Closely at Part of a Document**   If part of a document looks odd and needs investigating, examine it with the Magnifier. If necessary, click the Magnifier button so it is "pressed down," and then move the pointer onto the part of the document you want to examine. When the pointer changes to a magnifying glass with a cross inside it, click your document. The document is enlarged to its real size—that is, to 100 percent—so you can read it. To shrink the document onscreen, click it a second time.

■ **Enlarging the Pages**   To make pages look larger, either change the Zoom setting or click the Full Screen button. "Getting a Better View of Your Work" in Chapter 2 explains the Zoom menu and Full Screen view.

■ **Hiding and Displaying the Rulers**   Click the View Ruler button to hide or display the rulers. You need to see the rulers if you want to adjust margin sizes or indentations in the Print Preview window.

■ **Viewing One or Several Pages**   Click the Multiple Pages button and drag the pointer to tell Word how many pages to display. To display a single page, click the One Page button.

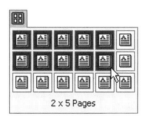

2 x 5 Pages

To get from page to page, press PAGE UP or PAGE DOWN, or else click the Previous Page or Next Page button (the double arrows) in the lower-right corner of the Print Preview window.

Making Editorial and Layout Changes in Print Preview

You can make editorial changes, change the size of margins, or indent text in the Print Preview window (see Figure 5-2), although doing any kind of work in the window can be difficult, because text is hard to read and pages are hard to examine when two or more appear. Before you attempt to edit a document in the Print Preview window, click the Magnifier button, if necessary, to turn off the Magnifier, and click the One Page button, if more than one page is shown, to display only one page. Then do the following:

■ **Editorial Changes**   Click where you want to enter or erase text, and go to it. Remember: You can use the Zoom menu to enlarge the text. See "Zooming In and Zooming Out" in Chapter 2.

■ **Changing the Size of Margins** Drag the Left Margin, Right Margin, Top Margin, or Bottom Margin marker on the rulers, as shown in Figure 5-3. The pointer changes to a double-headed arrow when you move it over a marker. Click the View Ruler button if you don't see the rulers. Changes to the margins affect the entire document or, if the document has been divided into sections, the section that the cursor is in. See "Setting the Margins" in Chapter 9 to learn more about margins.

■ **Indenting Text** Drag an indent marker on the ruler—Left Indent, Right Indent, or First Line Indent—to change indents in the paragraph that the cursor is in. To indent several paragraphs at once, drag the pointer onscreen to select them before you start dragging the indent markers. "Indenting Text on the Page" in Chapter 8 explains indent markers.

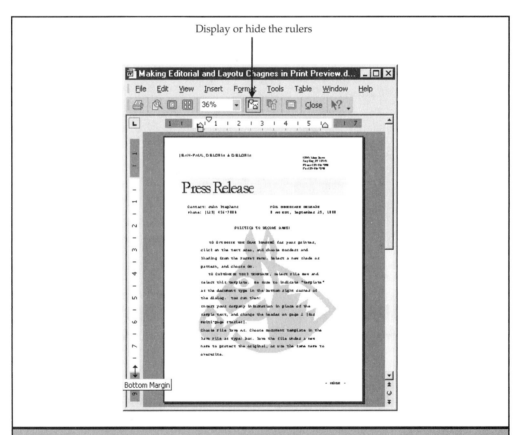

Figure 5-3.   *You can indent text and change margin settings in the Print Preview window*

Making Faxes, Letters, and Résumés Fit on One Page

Strange how faxes, résumés, and business letters always stray onto the second page. No matter how hard you try to fit them on a single page, one or two lines always creep onto page 2. Here are a couple of techniques for shrinking a document so it fits squarely on one, two, or however many pages it needs to fit on:

- Click the Shrink to Fit button on the Print Preview toolbar. Word endeavors to shrink your document. To do so, it reduces font sizes, margins sizes, and line spacing ever so slightly. After you shrink a document this way, examine it to see whether it shrunk too much in the wash. You can do that by clicking parts of the document with the Magnifier. If you don't like the shrunken document, choose Edit | Undo (or press CTRL-Z) to get the old document back. And do it before you click the Close button to leave the Print Preview screen. After you close the Print Preview screen, you can't "unshrink" your document if you regret shrinking it.

- Fool with the line-spacing options, and this time, instead of entering round numbers, open the Paragraph dialog box and enter fractions in the Line Spacing box. For example, if your document is double-spaced, enter **1.85** instead of 2 to shrink the document ever so slightly. In Chapter 8, "Adjusting the Space Between Lines and Paragraphs" explains line spacing.

 Unless you are working on a one-page document—an announcement or invitation, for example—don't change margin settings in the Print Preview window. Margin settings affect many different paragraphs, far more than can be seen well in the Print Preview window, so changing margins in the window can have unforeseen consequences.

Printing Documents

How do you print a document in Word? Let me count the ways. You can "quick-print" a document, print parts of documents, print many copies, print on both sides of the paper, print to a file, print an outline, or cancel a print job before you waste five or ten pages. Better start reading.

"Quick Printing" Documents

To print a document in its entirety, open it and either click the Print button on the Standard toolbar or choose File | Print and immediately click OK in the Print dialog box. Try this technique to print a document or several documents without opening them first:

1. Choose File | Open (or press CTRL-O) to see the Open dialog box.

2. Find and open the folder with the document or documents you want to print.

3. CTRL-click the names of documents that need to be printed. In other words, hold down the CTRL key and click the names.

4. Right-click a document you selected and choose Print from the shortcut menu, as shown in Figure 5-4.

5. Click Cancel or press ESC to close the Open dialog box.

Printing Parts or Copies of a Document

When you want to print part of a document, print more than one copy, print thumbnail pages, or print to a file, choose File | Print (or press CTRL-P). You see the Print dialog box shown in Figure 5-5. This dialog box offers numerous options for printing this, that, and the other thing, as the following pages so eloquently demonstrate.

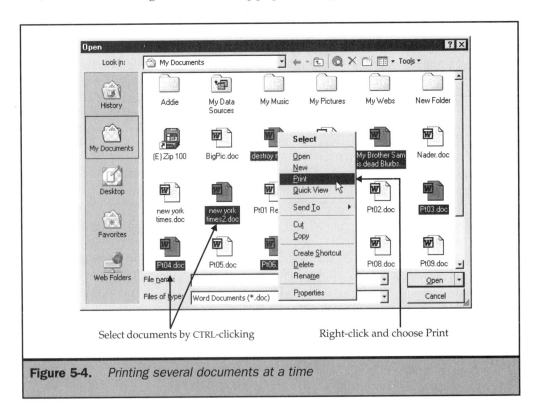

Select documents by CTRL-clicking

Right-click and choose Print

Figure 5-4. *Printing several documents at a time*

Dragging to Print a Document

The fastest way to print a document is to create a shortcut icon to your printer, open My Computer or Windows Explorer, find the document you want to print, and drag its icon over the printer shortcut icon, as shown here:

Find and select the document you want to print

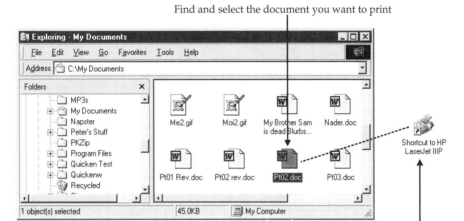

Drag it over the printer shortcut icon

Follow these steps to create a shortcut icon for your printer:

1. Click the Start button and choose Settings | Printers. You see the contents of the Printers folder in the My Computer window. In this folder are icons for each printer that is installed on your system.

2. Right-click the printer you print with and choose Create Shortcut from the menu. A message box tells you that Windows can't place the shortcut icon in the folder but you can place it on the Windows desktop.

3. Click Yes in the message box.

4. Find your new shortcut on the Windows desktop, right-click it, choose Rename from the shortcut menu, and type a descriptive name for the printer shortcut icon.

Choose which part of the document to print

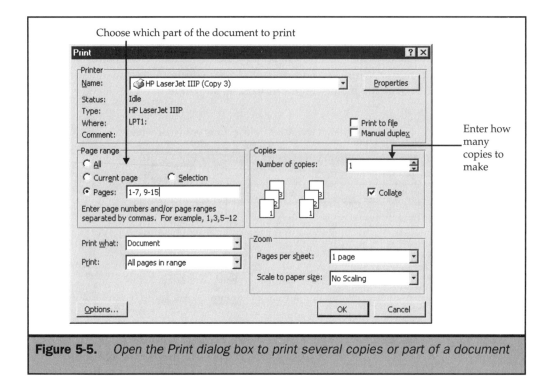

Enter how many copies to make

Figure 5-5.   *Open the Print dialog box to print several copies or part of a document*

Printing Particular Pages or Text

Herewith are instructions for printing a single page, several pages, parts of pages, even and odd pages, and document sections.

Printing a Page or Range of Pages   Click the Current Page option button to print the page that the cursor is on. To print certain pages only, enter their page numbers in the Pages text box. You can print a range of pages by entering hyphens between the page numbers, and even enter commas and hyphens to print several different pages or page ranges. For example, the following entry in the Pages text box tells Word to print page 4, 7–10, 13, 15, and 18–21.

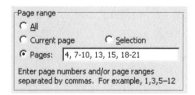

Printing Part of a Page   To print part of a page, select it before choosing File | Print to open the Print dialog box. Then click the Selection option button and click OK.

Printing On Both Sides of the Paper   To print on both sides of the paper, you print the odd pages first, then turn the pages over, feed them into your printer, and then print the even pages. Word offers two ways to do that:

- **Manual Duplex Printing**   Select the Manual Duplex check box in the Print dialog box and click OK. Word prints the odd-numbered pages, and a message box appears onscreen: "Please remove the printout of the first side from tray and place it in the output bin. Then press OK to continue printing." Do just that—turn the pages over after you have printed them, feed the pages to your printer, and click OK.

- **Printing the Odd-, Then the Even-Numbered Pages**   The Print drop-down list at the bottom of the Print dialog box offers options for printing odd or even pages. Choose Odd Pages to print the odd-numbered pages first. Then turn the pages over, feed them to your printer, and choose the Even Pages option to print on the opposite side of the paper.

Printing Sections and Pages in Sections   When a document has been divided into sections, you can print it the usual way by entering page numbers and page ranges, or you can print documents a section at a time:

- **Printing Whole Sections**   Choose File | Print to open the Print dialog box, and enter an **s** and then the section number in the Pages text box. For example, entering **s4** tells Word to print section 4; entering **s4-s6** tells Word to print sections 4 through 6.

- **Printing Pages in Sections**   In the Print text box, enter a **p**, a page number, and then an **s** and the section number. For example, entering **p8s6** in the Pages text box tells Word to print page 8 in section 6. Entering **p1s6-p4s6** tells Word to print pages 1 through 4 in section 6.

Printing Copies of Documents

To print more than one copy of a document, enter a number in the Number of Copies text box. Normally, pages are collated when you print more than one copy. For example, three three-page documents come out of the printer like so: 1-2-3, 1-2-3, 1-2-3. But if you uncheck the Collate check box, the pages arrive this way: 1-1-1, 2-2-2, 3-3-3. Most printers can print uncollated pages faster. However, the time you gain by printing a document this way is lost when you have to put the pages in the right order by hand.

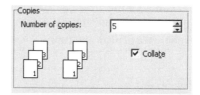

If for whatever reason you need to print a file backward, you can do it. Click the Options button in the Print dialog box (see Figure 5-5). Then, in the next Print dialog box, check the Reverse Print Order check box.

Printing Thumbnail Pages

One way to review a document to make sure all is well is to print thumbnail copies of the pages. Follow these steps to print thumbnail copies of all the pages in a document:

1. Choose File | Print or press CTRL-P to open the Print dialog box (see Figure 5-5).

2. Under Zoom in the lower-right corner of the Print dialog box, open the Scale To Paper Size drop-down list and select the size of the paper you will print on.

3. From the Pages Per Sheet drop-down list, choose how many thumbnail pages to print on each piece of paper and click OK:

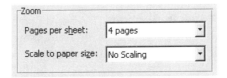

To print thumbnail copies of some of the pages in a document, select them. Then choose File | Print, click the Selection option button under Page Range in the Print dialog box, choose a Pages Per Sheet and Scale to Paper Size option, and click OK.

Printing to a File

Printing to a file means to make a copy of a document with text but also with the instructions that printers need to print documents. You can take the file to a print shop and print it on an expensive laser printer without having to open Microsoft Word. Or, if someone is hogging the printer, you can print the file later on simply by right-clicking its name in Windows Explorer or My Computer and choosing Print on the shortcut menu, or by dragging its icon over the Printer icon (see "Dragging to Print a Document" earlier in this chapter).

That's what is good about printing to a file. Here's the bad news: To make it work, you have to install a printer driver for the printer you intend to use. In other words, if you intend to print the file on a FancyPrinter XIVs at the local print shop, you must have installed a driver for the FancyPrinter XIVs printer on your computer.

To print to a file, choose File | Print. In the Print dialog box, select the printer on which you will print the document from the Name drop-down list, and select the Print to File check box.

Printing an Outline

As "Organizing Your Work with Outlines" in Chapter 17 explains, you can see in Outline view whether your manual, treatise, or report is well organized, and if it isn't well organized, you can rearrange the headings and the text below headings in Outline view. What Chapter 17 doesn't say is that you can print an outline.

Note   *See "Getting the Right View of Your Outline" in Chapter 17 to learn the different ways to display a document in Outline view.*

When you click the Print button in Outline view, Word prints whatever is displayed onscreen. If only first-level headings are displayed, they are printed; if all the headings appear, all the headings are printed. Use the buttons on the Outlining toolbar to display the parts of the Outline that you want to print and then give the Print command to print your outline. Remember: You can click the Show Formatting button on the Outlining toolbar to display fonts in headings.

Canceling and Postponing Print Jobs

Suppose you give the command to print a document or a bunch of documents but then you realize that one or two documents shouldn't be printed or one needs to be printed before the rest. You can control how documents are printed by following these steps:

1. Either double-click the Printer icon next to the clock on the Taskbar, or click the Start button, choose Settings | Printers, and double-click the icon of the printer you are using to print the documents. You see a Printer window similar to the one in Figure 5-6. Documents in the window are shown in the order they will be printed.

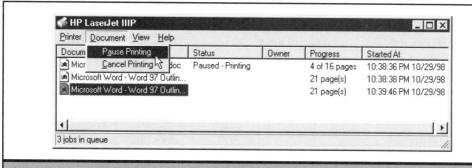

Figure 5-6.   *In the Printer window, you can keep documents from being printed or postpone printing a document*

2. Do the following to postpone or stop printing a document:

- ■ **Stop Printing a Document**   Click the document and choose Document |
  Cancel Printing. The document is removed from the list.

- ■ **Stop Printing All Documents**   Choose Printer | Purge Print Documents.

- ■ **Postpone Printing a Document**   Click a document and choose Document |
  Pause Printing. The words "Paused - Printing" appear in the Status column
  (see Figure 5-6), and the document is not printed. To print it, click it and
  choose Document | Pause Printing again.

Separator Pages for Keeping Your Printed Material Separate from Others'

In a crowded office in which many people share the same printer, digging into a
stack of printed material to find your printed pages is a hassle. However, you can
make finding your pages easier by creating a *separator page,* a page that appears
between each printed document in a stack of printed documents. Separator pages
announce the name of the printed document, who printed it, and when it was
printed. Follow these steps to create a separator page and make finding your
documents easier:

1. Click the Start button and choose Settings | Printers. The contents of
   the Printers folder appear in a My Computer.

2. Right-click the icon of the printer with which you print your files
   and choose Properties from the shortcut menu. You see the Properties
   dialog box.

3. Select the General tab, if necessary.widow

4. From the Separator Page drop-down list, choose Simple to print a
   plain-text separator page or Full to print a page with large type
   and the words "Separator Page" across the top.

5. Click OK.

Next time you print a document, you will be able to find it by looking for your
separator page.

Printing Addresses and Return Addresses on Envelopes

Yes, you can print addresses and return addresses on envelopes. Still, depending on how good your printer is at handling envelopes, sometimes writing addresses by hand is easier. Envelopes sometimes get stuck in printers. And setting up a printer so it can print envelopes can be difficult. Still, printing addresses on envelopes has one advantage: Delivery point bar codes and facing identification marks appear on the envelope to help the postal service deliver your letter faster:

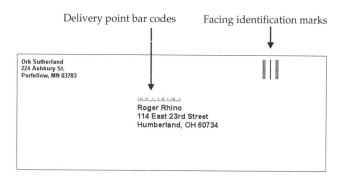

Tip *One way to get around the problem of putting addresses on envelopes is to print an address label and paste it on the envelope. The next part of this chapter explains how to print address labels. If you send a lot of letters to clients and customers, try using window envelopes to get around the problem of how to print addresses.*

Follow these steps to print an address and a return address on an envelope:

1. Open the document with the letter you want to send and select the recipient's name and address. If you didn't type the recipient's name and address in the letter, go straight to step 2.

2. Choose Tools | Letters and Mailings | Envelopes and Labels. As shown in Figure 5-7, you see the Envelopes and Labels dialog box.

3. Enter the recipient's address in the Delivery Address box if the address isn't listed already. If you are using Outlook, Outlook Express, or Schedule+, you can click the Address Book button to get the recipient's name from the address list. In the Select Name dialog box, select the name and click OK. For that matter, you can click the New button to add the addressee's name to your Contact List.

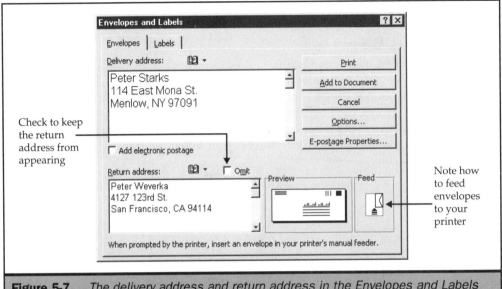

Check to keep
the return
address from
appearing

Note how
to feed
envelopes
to your
printer

Figure 5-7. *The delivery address and return address in the Envelopes and Labels dialog box are printed on the envelope*

4. If no name or address or the wrong name and address appear in the Return Address box, enter the correct name and address. Or check the Omit check box to keep a name and return address from appearing on the envelope.

Tip *Word gets the name and address in the Return Address box from the User Information tab in the Options dialog box. Make sure your name and address appear on this tab. To get to the User Information tab and enter your name and address there, choose Tools | Options and select the User Information tab in the Options dialog box. Be sure to enter your name and address in the Mailing Address box. What appears in that box is what goes on the envelopes.*

5. Feed an envelope to your printer and click the Print button. The envelope in the lower-right corner of the Envelopes and Labels dialog box shows how to feed envelopes to your printer. Keep reading if your envelope didn't print correctly, you want to print on an envelope other than the standard 4¾ × 11-inch legal envelope, or you want to tinker with fonts.

With a little bit of luck, your envelope prints correctly and all is well after you click the Print button in the Envelopes and Labels dialog box. But maybe you need to tinker a bit, in which case you should follow these instructions:

■ **Making the Envelope Part of the Document**   Click the Add To Document button to make the envelope page 1 of the document. Choose File | Page Setup, select the Paper tab in the Page Setup dialog box, and, on the First Page drop-down list, choose the option that describes how you feed envelopes to your printer.

■ **Printing on a Different-Size Envelope**   To tell Word which size envelope to print on, click the Options button in the Envelopes and Labels dialog box. Then, in the Envelope Options dialog box shown in Figure 5-8, choose an envelope from the Envelope Size drop-down list.

■ **Changing Fonts and Address Positions**   Click the Options button in the Envelopes and Labels dialog box and, in the Envelope Options dialog box (see Figure 5-8), click a Font button and then choose a new font. You can also change the position of the addresses on the envelope by playing with the From Left and From Top options.

■ **Telling Word How Your Printer Accepts Envelopes**   As long as Word knows what kind of printer you have (see "Introducing Word to Your Printer" at the start of this chapter), the program probably knows how envelopes are fed to

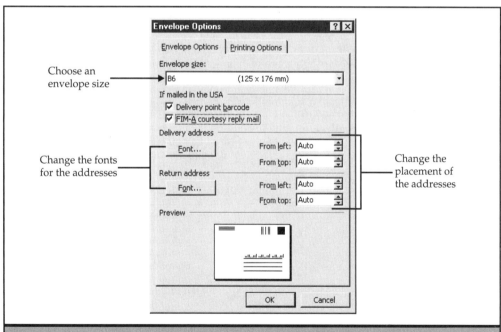

Figure 5-8.   *Go to the Envelope Options dialog box to print on a different-size letter, change fonts, or tell Word how envelopes are fed to the printer*

your printer. But if you try to print an address and it comes out on the wrong part of the envelope, visit the Printing Options tab of the Envelope Options dialog box and select an option or options to tell Word how your printer accepts envelopes:

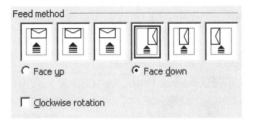

 "Generating Form Letters for Mass-Mailings" in Chapter 18 explains how you can print many envelopes at once.

Decorating an Envelope with a Graphic or Logo

For a professional look, you can place a logo or clip art image on an envelope. To do so, click the Add To Document button in the Envelopes and Labels dialog box (see Figure 5-7) to make the envelope page 1 of the document. Then go to page 1 and place a clip art image or logo there (Chapter 13 explains how to handle graphics). For that matter, you can make your return address and logo or graphic an AutoText entry to make entering return addresses and graphics on envelopes very, very easy (see "Creating and Inserting AutoText Entries" in Chapter 6).

To print the address, place an envelope in the printer tray and click the Print button in the Envelopes and Labels dialog box. After Word prints the address on the envelope, put paper in the tray to commence printing the rest of the letter.

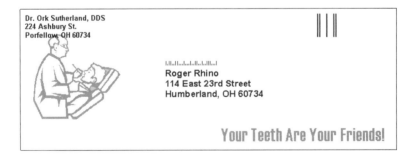

Printing a Single Label or Sheet of Labels with the Same Address

Printing on envelopes can be a hassle. You may as well print labels and paste labels on the letters you want to send. You can save time that way. Before you print labels, take note of what brand of labels you have and what size your labels are. Word needs that information to print labels.

Note   *See "Printing Labels for Mass-Mailings" in Chapter 18 if you want to print labels addressed to many different people.*

Follow these steps to print a single label or a sheet of labels with the same address:

1. Select the name and address for the label if it is in a document you are working on; otherwise, go straight to step 2.
2. Choose Tools | Letters and Mailings | Envelopes and Labels and select the Labels tab in the Envelopes and Labels dialog box. Figure 5-9 shows the Labels tab.

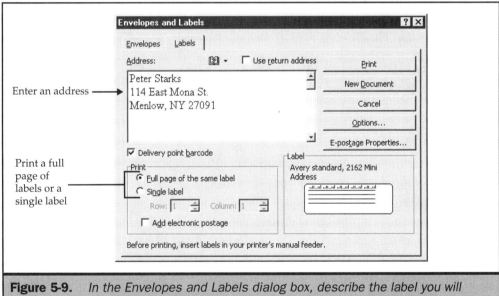

Figure 5-9.   *In the Envelopes and Labels dialog box, describe the label you will print on and tell Word whether you are printing a single label or a sheet of labels*

3. Enter an address in the Address box, if necessary.

4. Glance at the label brand in the lower-right corner of the dialog box, and if the brand and label size shown there aren't what you intend to use, click the Options button. In the Label Options dialog box, choose options from the Label Products and Product Number drop-down lists to describe the labels you will print on. The Label Information box clearly shows what size label you are choosing. Click OK to return to the Envelopes and Labels dialog box.

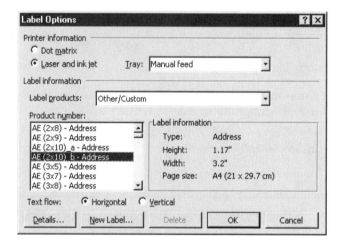

 If you can't find your label brand, choose Other on the Label Products drop-down list and try to find a product number that matches the labels you have. If you are desperate, you can click the New Label button and describe your labels in the New Custom dialog box. Be sure to enter a name for the label you describe. The name will appear at the top of the Product Number drop-down list.

5. Under Print, click the Full Page option or the Single Label option.

6. Print your label or labels:

   ■ **Full Page of the Same Label**   Click the New Document button. You see your labels in a Word document. Save and name the document so you can use it over and over again to print labels. To print the labels, insert a sheet of labels in the printer and then print the document you created.

   ■ **Single Label**   Insert the sheet of labels in your printer and enter the row and column where the label is. Then click the Print button to print the label.

MOUS Exam Objectives Explored in Chapter 5

Objective	Heading
Preview and print documents, envelopes, and labels	"Previewing a Document Before You Print It," "Printing Documents," "Printing Addresses and Return Addresses on Envelopes," and "Printing a Single Label or Sheet of Labels with the Same Address"

Ten Printing Problems and How to Solve Them

Few things are more frustrating than not being able to print a document. To keep you from gnashing your teeth or tearing your hair out, here are ten common printing problems and the steps you can take to solve them.

1. Nothing Happens When I Try to Print   Not being able to print anything is the most common printing problem of all. Usually, the problem can be fixed by plugging in the printer, turning on the printer, or making sure that the computer is indeed connected to the printer.

2. The Margins and Line Breaks on My Pages Are All Goofy   Either your margins are too wide or you are printing on the wrong size paper. If you inherited your document from a European, Latin American, African, Asian, or Australian, choose File | Page Setup, select the Paper tab in the Page Setup dialog box, and look in the Paper Size box to see what kind of paper Word wants to print on. If the Paper Size box says "A4 210 × 297 mm," you are dealing with a foreign paper size standard. Click Cancel in the Page Setup dialog box and follow these steps to solve the problem:

1. Choose Tools | Options to open the Options dialog box.
2. Select the Print tab.
3. Check the Allow A4/Letter Paper Resizing check box, if it is not already checked, and click OK.
4. Print your document.

 Don't choose a new paper size in the Paper Size dialog box to solve the problem of handling a foreign paper size standard. Doing so can cause margin settings and other page layout elements to go haywire.

3. I'm Having Trouble Printing a Long Document That I Divided into

Sections   Printing documents that have been divided into sections is problematic, especially if each section has its own page-numbering scheme. For example, if pages in the first section are not numbered, perhaps because a table of contents or title page is found in the first section, and page numbering begins at the start of section 2, knowing what page you are looking at and which pages to print can be difficult. The Status bar tells you that you are on page 8, for example, because you are on the eighth page in the document, but the header on page 8 tells you that you are on page 5, because you are on the fifth page in section 2.

To solve the problem of printing a document that has been divided into sections, print the sections one at a time. See "Printing Parts or Copies of a Document," earlier in this chapter, to learn how to print sections.

4. My Fonts Don't Look Right   First, make sure you are in Print Layout view so

you can see the fonts properly. If they still don't look right, your document probably includes fonts that your printer can't reproduce. Replace the fonts that didn't come out right with TrueType fonts. These fonts, which have the letters "*TT*" next to their names on the Font menu, look the same onscreen and on paper when they are printed.

"Conducting a Find-and-Replace Operation" in Chapter 6 explains how you can use the Find and Replace command to replace one font with another throughout a document.

5. My Graphics Aren't Being Printed   Your machine could be running low on

memory. Try shutting down, restarting your computer, and printing again. If that doesn't work, investigate these possibilities:

- Choose File | Print and click the Options button in the Print dialog box. In the second Print dialog box, make sure that the Drawing Objects check box is selected.

- Also in the second Print dialog box, make sure that the Draft Output check box is *not* selected. Checking the Draft Output option tells Word to print documents with very few formats. The option is for working with documents in the proofreading stage. Graphics are not printed as part of draft output.

6. A Blank Page Is Printed at the End of My Document   This one is easy to

solve. The blank page gets printed because you left a few blank paragraphs at the end of your document. Press CTRL-END to go to the end of the document, click the Show/Hide ¶ button to see the paragraph formatting symbols (¶), and delete the symbols.

7. My Headers and Footers Didn't Come Out Right   If your headers and footers

don't fit on the page, there isn't enough room in the margin for the header or footer or else the header or footer lies in a nonprinting part of the page. To make more room for headers and footer, choose File | Page Setup, select the Margins tab in the Page Setup dialog box, and enlarge the top and bottom margins. Go to the Layout tab as well and increase the From Edge distances to make sure headers and footers aren't being pushed into the nonprinting part of the page.

8. Word Won't Let Me Choose the File | Print Command   If File | Print is grayed out on your computer and you can't choose the command, your computer doesn't know that it is attached to a printer. Reinstall the printer.

9. I Can't Print Page Borders   Most printers cannot print text or graphics that are too close to the edge of the page. By definition, borders fall close to the edge of the page, which is why your printer can't handle them. Follow these steps to solve the problem:

1. Choose Format | Borders and Shading. You see the Borders and Shading dialog box.
2. Select the Page Border tab.
3. Click the Options button to open the Border and Shading Options dialog box.
4. Under Margin, enter larger point sizes in the Top, Bottom, Left, and Right boxes to move the borders farther from the edge of the page.
5. Click OK twice.

10. My Printer Prints Too Slowly   Welcome to the club! Unfortunately, how fast a printer can do its job depends mostly on how fast it can process requests to print documents. However, if you are growing very impatient with your printer, you can take this drastic measure to increase its speed: Disable background printing.

"Printing in the background" means that Word can print files while you do other tasks—format a document or type text, for example. By disabling the background printing mechanism, you tell Word to devote all its resources to printing, and consequently documents get printed faster. The drawback, however, is that you can do nothing else while your documents are being printed. Until the printer spits out the last page, you have to twiddle your thumbs. You can't format a document or enter text.

Follow these steps if you want to take the drastic measure of turning off the background printing mechanism:

1. Choose Tools | Options.
2. Select the Print tab in the Options dialog box.
3. Uncheck the Background Printing check box and click OK.

The
Complete
Reference

Word
2002

Part II

Formatting Text and Pages

The
Complete
Reference

Word
2002

Chapter 6

Speed Techniques for Using Word

This chapter is dedicated to the proposition that there is a faster way. In this chapter, you learn how to do things fast. I want you to be done with your work at lunchtime and catch the afternoon matinee. I want you to run back to the office when the movie is over and arrive in a sweat so that everyone thinks you had to hurry to get it done, when really you just had to hurry back from the movie theater.

In this chapter, you learn how to work with several documents at once, work in two places in the same document, and rearrange windows onscreen. You also discover techniques for searching for and replacing text. The Search and Replace commands are very powerful. This chapter delves into a handful of ways to enter text quickly, including the AutoText and AutoCorrect mechanisms. Finally, you learn ten tried-and-true techniques for working faster in Word.

 Chapter 21 offers more techniques for working faster. Believe me, creating toolbars for your favorite commands, rearranging the Word menus, creating new menus, and designating your own keyboard shortcuts is a lot easier than most people think and can save lots of time.

Working in Two Places or Documents at Once

Who wouldn't like to be in two places at once? In Word, you can be in two documents or two places in the same document at the same time. These pages explain how to split the screen so that you can see two different places in the same document and open a second window on a document so you can work in two places at once. You will also find instructions here for working on several documents and manipulating the windows that Word documents appear in.

Splitting the Screen

Figure 6-1 shows a screen that has been split across the middle. Notice the scroll bars on each half of the screen. By using the scroll bars or pressing keyboard shortcuts, you can go wherever you please on either side of the screen. Splitting the screen is invaluable when you want to refer to one part of a document while you work on another part. And you can copy or move text with the drag-and-drop method by dragging the text across the divide from one side of the screen to another.

Do the following to split the screen:

1. Choose Window | Split (or press CTRL-ALT-S). The pointer changes to a double-headed arrow and a line appears across the middle of the screen.

2. Move the pointer up or down onscreen to adjust the position of the line and click when the line is where you want the screen to be split. If the ruler is on display, a second ruler appears across the middle of the screen.

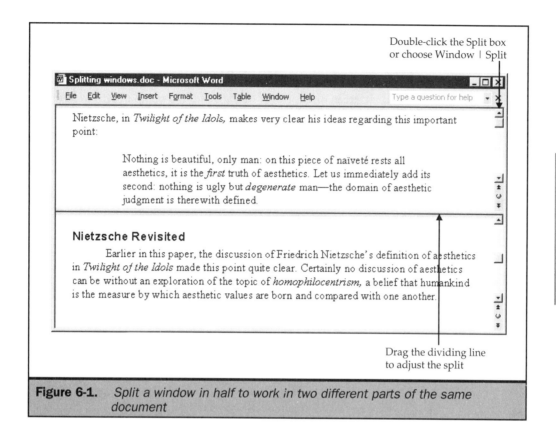

Figure 6-1. *Split a window in half to work in two different parts of the same document*

Drag the line across the middle of the screen to adjust the split and give more room to the top or bottom portion of the screen. Click in one side or the other to move the cursor there.

The fastest way to split the screen is to double-click the Split box, the tiny box at the top of the vertical scroll bar. You can tell when you have moved the pointer over the Split box because it changes into double arrows.

When you get tired of the schizophrenic split-screen arrangement, do any of the following to unsplit the screen:

■ Choose Window | Remove Split.

■ Double-click the dividing line between the screen halves.

■ Press ALT-SHIFT-C.

■ Press CTRL-ALT-S.

Viewing the Same Page Two Different Ways

Another advantage of splitting the screen is being able to view the same document in different ways. All you have to do is click in one half of the screen and click a View button. In this illustration, the top half of the screen appears in Outline view and the bottom half in Print Layout view. Besides changing views on either side of the dividing line, you can change Zoom settings. Being able to view the same document in two different ways is mighty convenient, as this illustration shows:

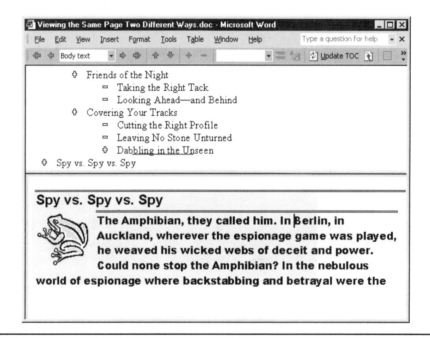

Opening Two or More Windows on the Same Document

Besides splitting the screen, another way to be two places at once is to open a second window on the same document. For that matter, you can open a third, fourth, or fifth window—you can open as many new windows as you want. In the following illustration, I have opened four windows on the same document. The Window menu lists the four different windows, and to go from one place to another in my document I have only to click a button on the Taskbar or make a choice on the Window menu:

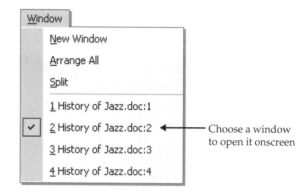

Choose a window
to open it onscreen

Follow these instructions to work with more than one window:

- **Opening a New Window**   Choose Window | New Window.

- **Going from Window to Window**   Open the Window menu and choose another window, click a button on the Taskbar, or keep pressing CTRL-F6 until your window appears onscreen.

- **Closing a Window**   Click the Close button (the X) in the upper-right corner of the window or press ALT-F4.

- **Returning to a Window**   To return to the Word window you were viewing before, press ALT-F6.

To keep the Taskbar from getting crowded with too many buttons, you can tell Word not to place a button on the Taskbar for each document you have opened. To do so, choose Tools | Options, select the View tab in the Options dialog box, and uncheck the Windows in Taskbar check box.

Working on Several Documents at Once

Yes, you can work on several Word documents at once. The names of documents that are open appear on buttons on the Taskbar and in alphabetical order on the Window menu. To start working on a different document, either click its button on the Taskbar or open the Window menu and click its name. You can also keep pressing CTRL-F6 until the document you are looking for appears onscreen.

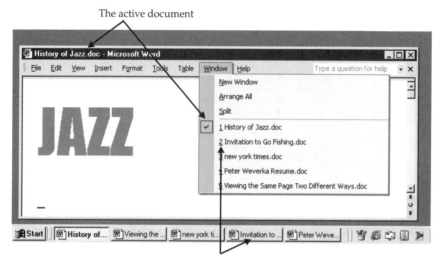

The active document

Choose a name or click a button to switch documents

> **Note**   *To tell which document you are working on, glance at the name on the title bar. On the Window menu, a check mark appears beside the active document, the one in which you are currently working.*

Changing the Size and Position of Windows

Windows are so important, Microsoft named an operating system after them. (Microsoft thought of naming the operating system "Buttons," since many buttons appear in the Windows operating system, but "Buttons" sounded too much like a kitten or clown's name and, besides, the name "Windows" appeals to voyeurs.) If you can learn how to manipulate the windows that Word documents appear in, you can work much, much faster. Read on to learn how to minimize and maximize windows, arrange windows onscreen, move windows, and change the size of windows.

Minimizing, Maximizing, and Closing Windows

When you open a Word document, it appears in its own window and fills the entire screen. However, you can *minimize* the window to remove a document from the screen without closing it, and when you want to see the document again, you can *maximize* its window. Minimizing, maximizing, and closing windows is accomplished with the three square buttons in the upper-right corner of windows—the Minimize, Maximize (or Restore), and Close buttons. Table 6-1 explains what the window buttons do.

Button	Button Name	What It Does
	Minimize	Collapses the window and makes it disappear. However, clicking this button does not close a document. To see a window after it has been minimized, click its button on the Taskbar.
	Restore	Shrinks the window to the size it was before you maximized it last time. After you click the Restore button, it changes names (and appearances) and becomes the Maximize button. You can also double-click the title bar to restore a window.
	Maximize	Enlarges the window to full-screen size. After you click the Maximize button, it changes names (and appearances) and becomes the Restore button. You can also double-click the title bar to maximize a window.
	Close Window	Closes the document. Don't confuse this button with the Close button found right above it. Clicking the Close button closes Word, not the document you are working with.

Table 6-1. *The Window Buttons*

FORMATTING TEXT
AND PAGES

Changing the Shape and Position of Windows

Sometimes minimizing and maximizing windows is not enough and you have to change a window's size and position on your own. Use these techniques to move and change the size of windows:

■ **Moving a Window**   As shown in Figure 6-2, click the window's title bar and start dragging. When the window is where you want it to be, release the mouse button.

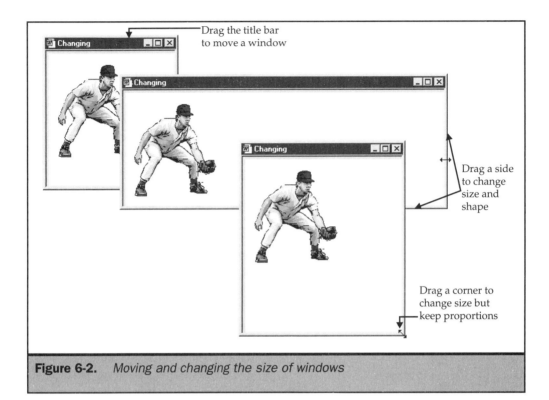

Figure 6-2. *Moving and changing the size of windows*

- **Changing a Window's Size** Move the mouse pointer over a border of the window and start dragging when the pointer changes into double-arrows. Release the mouse button when the window is the right size.

Drag a corner of a window to change its size but keep its proportions.

Finding and Replacing Text and Other Things

The Find and Replace commands in Word are two of the most powerful commands in the program. Use them wisely and you can quickly find passages in documents, correct mistakes *en masse,* change words and phrases throughout a document, and reformat a document without having to visit all the pages that need reformatting. To give you an idea how powerful these commands are, suppose you wrote an 800-page Russian novel and realized on page 799 that the main character's name should be Oblomov, not Oblonsky. Using the Find and Replace command, you could change all *Oblonsky*s to *Oblomov*s throughout the document in about ten seconds.

Note *Another way to find items in a Word document—a footnote, endnote, field, graphic, comment, section, table, bookmark, or heading—is to take advantage of the Select Browse Object button or the Edit | Go To command. See "Using the Select Browse Object Button to Get Around" and "Going from Place to Place with the Go To Command" in Chapter 2.*

Find Basics: Searching for Text

When you conduct a search with the Edit | Find command, Word starts searching where the cursor is, searches to the end of the document, and then searches from the beginning of the document to the place where the search began. You can search part of a document by selecting it before you give the Edit | Find command.

Follow these steps to search for a word, name, or phrase in a document:

1. Press CTRL-F, choose Edit | Find, or click the Select Browse Object button and choose Find on the menu. You see the Find and Replace dialog box shown in Figure 6-3. (In the figure, I clicked the More button so you can see all the Find options.)

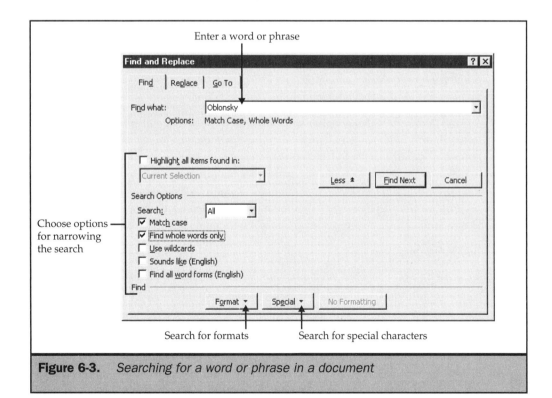

Figure 6-3.   *Searching for a word or phrase in a document*

2. Type the word or phrase that you seek in the Find What box.

Tip   *On the Find What drop-down list are the words and phrases, if any, that you looked for since you started Word. Open the list and make a choice to repeat a search you made earlier.*

3. Click the More button if you want to see and take advantage of the advanced search options (they are explained shortly).

4. Click the Find Next button. If Word finds the text, it is highlighted onscreen. You can click outside the Find and Replace dialog box and edit the text.

5. Either click Find Next again to keep searching or click the Cancel button to close the Find and Replace dialog box.

Tip   *You can leave the Find and Replace dialog box onscreen while you edit a document, but an easier way to handle searches is to close the dialog box and click the double-arrows in the lower-right corner of the screen to go from search item to search item. After you give the Find command, the double arrows turn blue. Click a blue double arrow (or press* CTRL-PAGE UP *or* CTRL-PAGE DOWN*) to conduct a search without having to see the bulky Find and Replace dialog box.*

The Find and Replace dialog box offers numerous options for making searches faster and more accurate. Use these options or a combination of these options to find exactly what you are looking for:

- **Highlight All Items Found In**   Rather than search for items one at a time, you can tell Word to highlight all instances of an item by checking the Highlight All Items Found In check box. And, by making a choice in the drop-down menu, you can highlight items in headers and footers, footnotes, endnotes, or comments instead of the main text.

- **Search**   Tells Word in which direction to search: All searches the entire document; Up searches from the cursor position to the start of the document; Down searches from the cursor position to the end of the document.

Caution   *When you search with the Up or Down option, Word does not look at these items in the course of the search: headers, footers, comments, footnotes, and endnotes. With the All option, however, Word searches in every nook and cranny of the document.*

- **Match Case**   Finds words with upper- and lowercase letters that exactly match those of the word or phrase in the Find What box. For example, a search for **Bow** finds "Bow" but not "bow" or "BOW".

- **Find Whole Words Only**   Finds the word in the Find What box, but ignores the word if it is part of another word. For example, a search for **bow** finds "bow" but not "bows," "elbow," "bowler," or "rainbow." Unless you are looking for a proper name or other one-of-a-kind word, be sure to check this option. Your search will go faster and be more accurate.

■ **Use Wildcards**   Check this check box, click the Special button, and choose a search operator to use wildcards in searches. See "Searching for Formats and Special Characters," the next topic in this chapter.

■ **Sounds Like**   Searches for words that sound like the word in the Find What box. For example, a search for **bow** also finds "beau"; a search for "metal" also finds "medal," "middle," and "muddle."

■ **Find All Word Forms**   Takes into account plurals, verb endings, and tenses in searches. For example, a search for **bow** also finds "bows," "bowed," and "bowing."

As you choose search options, they are listed below the Find What text box. Be sure to double-check the list before you click the Find Next button to start searching.

Find what:	Paradise	▾
Options:	Search Up, Match Case, Whole Words	

Searching for Formats and Special Characters

By way of the Format and Special buttons at the bottom of the Find and Replace dialog box, you can conduct searches for formats and what Word calls "special characters"—paragraph marks, tab characters, page breaks, and the like. These pages explain how to search for formats and special characters.

Searching for Formats and Text That Was Formatted a Certain Way

Suppose you want to find a certain kind of formatting in your document, perhaps because it needs changing, or you want to find text that was formatted a certain way. Press CTRL-F (or choose Edit | Find) to open the Find and Replace dialog box and follow these steps to find formats or formatted text:

1. Enter the text in the Find What box if you are looking for text that was formatted a certain way (go straight to step 2 if you are merely searching for a format).

2. Click the Format button. As shown in Figure 6-4, you see a menu with seven format types on it.

3. Choose a format type—Font, Paragraph, Tabs, Language, Frame, Style, or Highlight. The Find dialog box opens, as shown in Figure 6-4, so you can describe the format you are looking for. Which dialog box you see depends

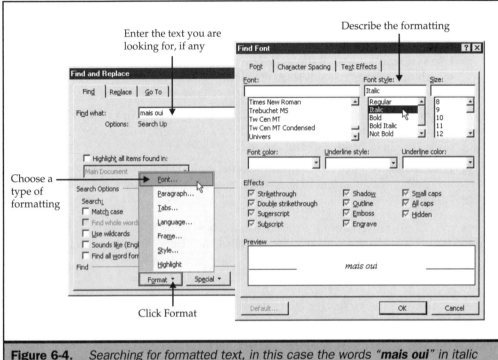

Figure 6-4. *Searching for formatted text, in this case the words "**mais oui**" in italic*

on which format command you chose. In Figure 6-4, I chose the Font command, so the Find Font dialog box appears. The Find dialog boxes are identical to the dialog boxes that are used to create the different formats.

4. In the dialog box, choose options to describe the format. In Figure 6-4, I am looking for italicized text, so Italic has been chosen in the Font Style box. Look in the Preview box to see what your choices amount to in real terms.

5. Click OK to close the Find dialog box. In the Find and Replace dialog box, the word "Format" and a description of the formats you are looking for appears below the Find What text box:

6. Click Find Next to conduct the search.

Be sure to click the No Formatting button in the Find and Replace dialog box when you are finished looking for formats and you want to search for plain text again or start all over and search for another type of format. Clicking the No Formatting button tells Word that you no longer want to look for formats or you want to search for a different set of formats.

By the way, you can search for formats for which there are keyboard shortcuts without clicking the Format button in the Find and Replace dialog box (see Figure 6-4). To do so, click to move the cursor into the Find What text box and then type a keyboard shortcut. In this illustration, I pressed CTRL-B (Bold), CTRL-I (Italic), and CTRL-E (Centered):

Fi_n_d what:

Format: Font: Bold, Italic, Centered

Searching for Special Characters

Table 6-2 describes the special characters you can look for in Word documents. To look for the special characters listed in Table 6-2, either enter the character directly into the Find What text box, as shown in Figure 6-5, or click the Special button in the Find and Replace dialog box and choose a special character from the menu. Be sure to enter lowercase letters. For example, you must enter **^n**, not **^N**, to look for a column break. And take note: A caret (^) precedes special characters.

To Find/Replace	Enter
Manual Formats That Users Insert	
Column break	^n
Manual line break (↵)	^l
Paragraph break (¶)	^p
Section break[1]	^b
Tab space (→)	^t
Carets, Hyphens, Dashes, and Spaces	
Caret (^)	^^
Em dash (—)	^+

Table 6-2. *Searching and Replacing with Special Characters, Format Characters, and Foreign Characters*

FORMATTING TEXT AND PAGES

To Find/Replace	Enter
Carets, Hyphens, Dashes, and Spaces	
En dash (–)	^=
Nonbreaking hyphen	^~
Optional hyphen	^-
Characters and Symbols	
Foreign character	You can type foreign characters in the Find What and Replace With text boxes (see Table 2-1 in Chapter 2).
Clipboard contents[2]	^c
Contents of the Find What box[2]	^&
Elements of Reports and Scholarly Papers	
Endnote mark[1]	^e
Footnote mark[1]	^f
Graphic[1]	^g

[1] *For use in search operations; can only be entered in the Find What text box*

[2] *For use in replace operations; can only be entered in the Replace With text box*

Table 6-2.   *Searching and Replacing with Special Characters, Format Characters, and Foreign Characters* (continued)

 Before you search for special characters, click the Show/Hide ¶ button. That way, you will see the special characters—also known as the hidden format symbols—onscreen when Word finds them. See "Tricks for Editing Text" in Chapter 2 if you need to know how the hidden format symbols work.

If you are creative, you can find many uses for the special characters. For example, the easiest way to find section breaks, column breaks, and manual line breaks in a document

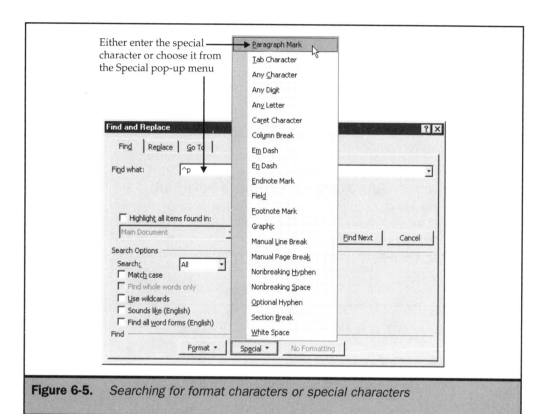

Figure 6-5.   *Searching for format characters or special characters*

is to enter ^b, ^n, or ^l, respectively, in the Find What text box and start searching. By combining special characters with text, you can make search operations more productive. Consider how special characters and text are used in this illustration. This search operation finds all paragraphs that begin with a tab space and the word "This":

> Find what: ^p^tThis
> Options: Match Case

Special characters are especially useful in find-and-replace operations (a subject you will learn about shortly). This find-and-replace operation finds all double hyphens in a document and replaces them with em dashes. I find this kind of find-and-replace operation especially useful for cleaning up text-only documents and other kinds of documents that I have imported into Word.

| Find what: | -- | ▼ |
| Replace with: | ^+ | ▼ |

Using Wildcard Operators to Refine Searches

A *wildcard operator* is a character that represents characters in a search expression. Wildcards aren't for everybody, since using them requires a certain amount of expertise, but once you know how to use them, wildcards can be very valuable in searches and macros. Table 6-3 explains the wildcard operators you can use in searches.

Operator	What It Finds	Example
?	Any single character	**b?t** finds "bat," "bet," "bit," and "but."
*	Zero or more characters	**t*o** finds "to," "two," and "tattoo."
[xyz]	A specific character, x, y, or z	**t[aeiou]pper** finds "tapper," "tipper," and "topper."
[x-z]	A range of characters, x through z	**[1-4]000** finds "1000," "2000," "3000," and "4000," but not "5000."
[!xy]	Not the specific character or characters, xy	**p[!io]t** finds "pat" and "pet," but not "pit" or "pot."
<	Characters at the beginning of words	**<info** finds "information," "infomaniac," and "infomercial."
>	Characters at the end of words	**ese>** finds "these," "journalese," and "legalese."

Table 6-3.   *Wildcard Search Operators*

Operator	What It Finds	Example
@	One or more instances of the previous character	**sho@t** finds "shot," "shoat," and "shoot."
{n}	Exactly *n* instances of the previous character	**sho{2}t** finds "shoot" but not "shot."
{n,}	At least *n* instances of the previous character	**^p{3,}** finds three or more paragraph breaks in a row, but not a single paragraph break or two paragraph breaks in a row.
{n,m}	From *n* to *m* instances of the previous character	**10{2,4}** finds "100," "1000," and "10000," but not "10" or "100000."

Table 6-3.   *Wildcard Search Operators* (continued)

Check the Use Wildcards check box in the Find and Replace dialog box to use wildcard operators in searches. To enter a wildcard operator in the Find What text box, either type it yourself or click the Special button and choose a wildcard from the top of the menu (see Figure 6-5).

You can't conduct a whole-word-only search with a wildcard. For example, a search for **f*s** *not only finds "fads" and "fits," it also finds all text strings that begin with f and end with s, such as "for the birds" and "fire my bos" (in "fire my boss"). Wildcard searches can yield many, many results and are sometimes useless.*

To search for an asterisk (*), question mark (?), or other character that serves as a wildcard search operator, place a backslash before it in the Find What text box. For example, /*{2,} tells Word to look for two or more asterisks in a row.

Conducting a Find-and-Replace Operation

Conducting a find-and-replace operation is the spitting image of conducting a find operation. Figure 6-6 shows the Replace tab in the Find and Replace dialog box, the place where you tell Word what to find and what to replace. Do the options and buttons look familiar? They do if you read the past several pages about searching, because the settings on the Replace tab are the same as those on the Find tab, except the Replace tab offers Replace and Replace All buttons.

Enter the text to be replaced   Enter the replacement text

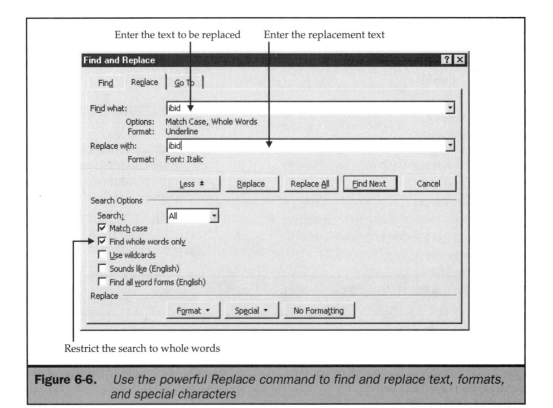

Figure 6-6.   *Use the powerful Replace command to find and replace text, formats, and special characters*

Caution
Be sure to examine your document after you conduct a find-and-replace operation. You never now what the powerful Replace command will do. If the command makes a hash of your file, click the Undo button or choose Edit | Undo.

The next few pages explain the nuances of finding and replacing text, formats, and special characters. Follow these basic steps to conduct a find-and-replace operation:

1. Choose Edit | Replace, press CTRL-H, or click the Replace tab in the Find and Replace dialog box. The Replace tab of the Find and Replace dialog box appears (see Figure 6-6).

Tip
The key to a successful find-and-replace operation is making sure you find exactly what you want to find and replace. One way to make sure you find the right text or formatting is to start by choosing Edit | Find (or press CTRL-F). Choose options on the Find tab in the Find and Replace dialog box (see Figure 6-3) and click the Find Next button. If Word scrolls to precisely the text or formatting you wanted to find, you're in business. Click the Replace tab in the Find and Replace dialog box. On that tab, the Find What options and text are already entered. All you have to do is enter the Replace With options and text.

2. If necessary, click the More button to see the advanced search options, the Format button, the Special button, and the No Formatting button.

3. Enter the text, formats, or special characters you are searching for in the Find What text box.

Note   *If necessary, click the No Formatting button if you searched for formats before and formats are still listed below the Find What or Replace With text box. Clicking the No Formatting button tells Word to strip the formats from the Find and Replace dialog box so you can search for new formats.*

4. Enter the replacement text, formats, or special characters in the Replace With text box.

5. Click the Find Next button. If Word finds the text, formats, or special characters that you seek, the text, formats, or special characters are highlighted in the document.

6. Click the Find Next, Replace, or Replace All button:

   ■ **Find Next**   Bypasses the text, format, or special character that has been found and does not replace it with what is in the Replace With text box.

   ■ **Replace**   Makes the replacement. What is in the Replace With text box is entered in the document and Word scrolls to the next instance of the thing you want to find and replace. Click the Replace button to review each occasion in which Word wants to make a replacement.

   ■ **Replace All**   Makes all replacements throughout the document immediately.

Caution   *Only click the Replace All button if you are very, very confident that the thing Word has found is the thing you want to replace throughout the document. If you click Replace All but regret doing so, click the Undo button to undo all the replacements.*

Replacing Text with Text

To replace text with text, choose Edit | Replace to open the Find and Replace dialog box, enter the word or words you want to find in the Find What text box and the replacement word or words in the Replace With text box. Following are a couple of things to know about replacing text with text.

Be Sure to Check the Find Whole Words Only Check Box   The Find Whole Words Only check box tells Word to look for whole words, not character strings. Forgetting to select the check box can have disastrous consequences in a find-and-replace operation that involves words. To see why, suppose you are editing a sexist author who

insists on using "man" where "humankind" or "humanity" would be more appropriate. To solve the problem, you run a find-and-replace operation like this one:

| Find what: | man |
| Replace with: | humanity |

   If you forget to check the Find Whole Words Only check box, your search will find the letters "man" wherever they are found and replace them with the letters "humanity." A sentence like "Man, the manifest measure of all things, the talisman of nature, wears the mantle of God," is turned into "Humanity, the humanityifest measure of all things, the talishumanity of nature, wears the humanitytle of God."

Find-and-Replace Operations Take Account of Upper- and Lowercase Letters

Don't worry about case when you conduct a find-and-replace operation. If a word you want to replace happens to appear at the start of a sentence and is capitalized, its replacement word will be capitalized as well. However, if you want to change the case of a word or words in a document, you can do so by entering different upper- or lowercase letters in the Replace With text box, as shown here:

| Find what: | nearly dead poets society |
| Replace with: | Nearly Dead Poets Society |

You Can Replace Formatted Text with Formatted Text   By entering text in the Find What and Replace With dialog boxes, and by choosing formats for the Find What text and Replace With text (read the next part of this chapter), you can replace formatted text with formatted text. For example, this find-and-replace operation searches for a company name that has been formatted a certain way and replaces it with a different company name with an entirely different format:

Find what:	Johnathon Freemon Technology, Inc.
Format:	Font: Impact, 16 pt
Replace with:	Cyberinfo Management, Inc.
Format:	Font: Haettenschweiler, 16 pt, Bold, Font color: Blue

Replacing Formats with Formats

One of the fastest ways to reformat a document is to search for one kind of format and replace it with another. Earlier in this chapter, "Searching for Formats and Special Characters" explains how you can click the Format button in the Find and Replace dialog box to search for formats in documents. The procedure for entering a replacement format is the same (see Figure 6-5)—click the Format button, choose a format from the pop-up menu, and describe the format in the Replace dialog box.

This find-and replace operation looks for 16-point text that has been formatted in Tahoma font and changes it to 18-point text formatted in Comic Sans MS font:

Find what:	
Format:	Font: Tahoma, 16 pt
Replace with:	
Format:	Font: Comic Sans MS, 18 pt

 Another way to replace formats is to select a format you want to change, open the Styles and Formatting task pane, and click the Select All button. Then, with formats selected throughout your document, you can change formats in one place and simultaneously change them elsewhere as well.

Finding and Replacing with the Special Characters

Finding and replacing with the special characters can be very helpful for cleaning up a document, especially one that you imported from another word processing program. To enter special characters in the Replace With text box, either enter them yourself or click the Special button and choose them from the menu. Earlier in this chapter, Table 6-2 describes the special characters and "Searching for Formats and Special Characters" describes how they work.

In this illustration, the paragraph break special character (^{p}) and white space special character (^{w}) are used in a find-and-replace operation to strip blank spaces from the ends of paragraphs:

Find what:	^w^p
Replace with:	^p

Here, the paragraph break special character (^p) and tab character (^t) are used to strip tab-space indents from the first line of paragraphs:

Find what:	^p^t^p
Replace with:	^p^p

The Two Replace with Special Characters

If you look closely at Table 6-2, which describes the special characters you can use in find and find-and-replace operations, you may notice that two special characters can't be entered in the Find What text box and are strictly for use as replacement text: ^c, which places the Clipboard contents in the Replace With text box, and ^&, which places what is in the Find What text box in the Replace With text box.

Use the Clipboard contents special character (^c) to insert large blocks of text in documents or to insert text that has been formatted in various ways:

■ **Large Blocks of Text**   Entering a lot of text in the Replace With box is difficult, so if you have to do that, enter the text in Word and copy it to the Clipboard (by pressing CTRL-C or choosing Edit | Copy). Then choose Edit | Replace, enter the text you want to search for in the Find What box, and enter **^c** in the Replace With box to make the large block of text the replacement text.

■ **Text with Different Formats**   As you know, you can click the Format button in the Find and Replace dialog box to search for formats and replace one format with another. Suppose, however, that the replacement text includes more than one format. For example, if a company changed its motto from "We do it better" to "We *really* do it better," you couldn't find-and-replace the motto by clicking the Format button, because only one word in the new motto is italicized, and the Format commands apply to all the words in the Find What and Replace With text boxes. To solve this problem, you could copy the new motto—italicized word and all—to the Clipboard and enter **^c** in the Replace With box.

Find what:	We do it better
Replace with:	^c

Use the contents of the Find What box special character (^&) to enter whatever is in the Find What box in the Replace With box as well. This special character is really just a means of making sure that text is replaced correctly. In the find-and-replace operation shown here, for example, *Esq.* is being attached to the name McClannahan Skejellifetti throughout a long document. Because the name is so hard to type, you would run a risk of misspelling it by typing it in the Replace With box. If you spelled the name incorrectly, you would introduce errors throughout the document. Rather than do that, you can enter the ^& special character and be absolutely certain that the text you find is also used in the replacement text:

Find what:	McClannahan Skejellifetti
Replace with:	^&, Esq.

Ways to Enter Text Quickly

This section presents two nifty techniques for entering text and graphics quickly: AutoText and AutoCorrect. As well as entering text and graphics, the AutoCorrect mechanism corrects typos on the fly. Addresses, letterheads, boilerplate text of all shapes and sizes—anything that you have to enter frequently—is a candidate for an AutoText or AutoCorrect entry. These pages explain the AutoText and AutoCorrect mechanisms.

 "Correcting Typos with the AutoCorrect Command" in Chapter 11 explains how AutoCorrect can help you fix the typing errors you frequently make. Here, I explain how AutoCorrect can help you enter text and graphics quickly.

Creating and Inserting AutoText Entries

An *AutoText entry* is a word, a few words, or a graphic that you can enter merely by making a selection from a menu. To see how the AutoText entries work, choose Insert | AutoText | Salutation | Dear Sir or Madam:. The salutation "Dear Sir or Madam:" is entered immediately in your document.

Word provides a dozen or two AutoText entries on 11 or more submenus, and you can create your own AutoText entries as well. As shown in Figure 6-7, the submenus are Attention Line, Closing, Header/Footer, and so on. In most cases, AutoText entries that you create yourself are placed on the Normal submenu (see the sidebar "A Tedious Digression About AutoText Entries You Create Yourself" for details). These pages explain how to insert, create, and manage AutoText entries.

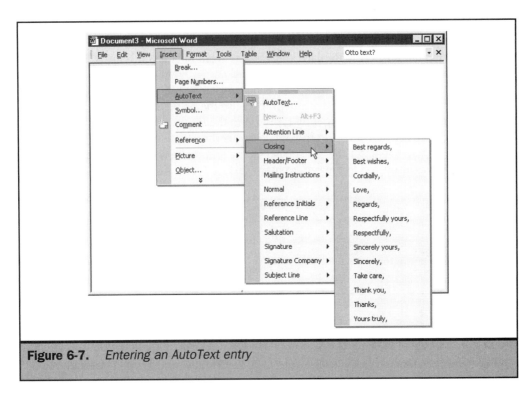

Figure 6-7.   *Entering an AutoText entry*

Note   *AutoText entries, like styles, toolbars, and macro project items, can be copied from template to template. See "Building Your Own Templates" in Chapter 12.*

Inserting an AutoText Entry in a Document

Carefully place the cursor where you want to insert the AutoText and insert it with one of these techniques:

- Choose Insert | AutoText, a submenu name, and the name of an AutoText entry (see Figure 6-7).

- Type the first few letters of the AutoText entry, and when you see the complete entry in the bubble, press ENTER (this technique works only with entries kept on the AutoText tab of the AutoCorrect dialog box):

  The Flying Weverkas (Press ENTER to Insert)

  Everyone knows that the best circus is The F

- Type the name of the AutoText entry and press F3. This technique works best when you want to enter a paragraph or two of boilerplate text or a graphic as an AutoText entry.

■ Open the AutoText toolbar, click the All Entries button, choose a submenu, and select the name of the AutoText entry.

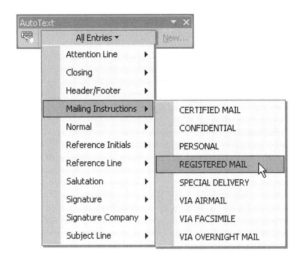

By the way, the AutoText entries on the All Entries and Insert | AutoText menus are not the only entries that Word attempts to make on your behalf. Word also enters months, days of the week, and today's date.

Some people find the AutoText bubbles annoying. If you are one of those people, you can keep them from appearing. Choose Insert | AutoText | AutoText. On the AutoText tab of the AutoCorrect dialog box, uncheck the Show AutoComplete Suggestions check box.

Creating Your Own AutoText Entries

The name "AutoText" is a little misleading because you can create an AutoText entry for graphics as well as text. In fact, you can create an AutoText entry for anything whatsoever that can be selected in a Word document. Follow these steps to create an AutoText entry:

1. Select the text or graphic that you want to enter in a hurry. If you are making a text entry, select a blank space on one side of the text. That way, the AutoText entry will fit nicely in the middle of a sentence when you insert it there.

When you insert an AutoText entry, it adopts the formatting of the text around it. However, if you want your entry to have a specific format, click the Show/Hide¶ button to see hidden format characters, and select the paragraph symbol that follows the text as well as the text itself. As "How Word Handles Paragraphs" explains in Chapter 2, the paragraph symbol that appears at the end of every paragraph holds formatting information. By selecting it, you will make formats a part of your AutoText entry.

2. Choose Insert | AutoText | New, click the New button on the AutoText toolbar, or press ALT-F3. You see the tiny Create AutoText dialog box. If you selected text in step 1, the text appears in the dialog box:

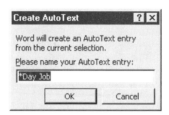

3. Enter a name for the AutoText entry, if necessary. Enter a short and to-the-point name so you'll be able to enter your AutoText entry with the F3 keyboard shortcut (typing the entry's name and pressing F3).

4. Click OK to close the Create AutoText dialog box.

A Tedious Digression About AutoText Entries You Create Yourself

For the most part, all you need to know about the AutoText entries you create is that they are usually available on the Normal submenu. Choose Insert | AutoText | Normal or click the All Entries button on the AutoText toolbar and choose Normal to enter an AutoText entry you created.

Sometimes, however, you head to the Normal submenu to enter an AutoText entry and it isn't there. Why's that?

To understand why, you have to understand that AutoText entries are linked to the template that is in use when you create them. Because most documents are created with the Normal template or are created with templates that are based on the Normal template (Chapter 12 explains templates), most AutoText entries that you create are available on the Normal submenu. If you can't find an AutoText entry you created on the Normal submenu, you can't find it for one of these reasons:

■ You are working in a document that wasn't created with the Normal template or a template based on the Normal template. To find the AutoText entry you are looking for, either click the AutoText button on the AutoText toolbar or choose Insert | AutoText | AutoText. Then, on the AutoText tab of the AutoCorrect dialog box, open the Look In drop-down menu and choose All Active Templates or Normal.dot (global template), select the AutoText entry you want in the scroll list, and click OK. Henceforward, when you open the AutoText menus, you will find AutoText entries from all active templates or from the Normal template, depending on which option you chose in the AutoCorrect dialog box.

■ When you created the AutoText entry, you did so with text that was assigned a custom-made style that you created yourself. This one is really weird. When you create an AutoText entry with a self-made style, Word adds a new submenu option to the All Entries drop-down menu on the AutoText toolbar and a new submenu to the Insert | AutoText menu. And that new submenu is named after the style in which you created the AutoText entry! For example, if you create a style called "Big Indent" and you create an AutoText entry in the "Big Indent" style, you will find a "Big Indent" submenu. Choose the AutoText entry you want from the submenu. (Big fans of AutoText create their own submenus for AutoText entries by using this technique.)

Remember: If you can't find the AutoText entry that you are looking for, you can always find it on the AutoText tab of the AutoCorrect dialog box (choose a new option from the Look In drop-down menu, if necessary). What's more, you can copy the AutoText entries you are fond of into the templates you use most often (see "Building Your Own Templates" in Chapter 12).

Deleting, Renaming, and Editing AutoText Entries

Go to the AutoText tab of the AutoCorrect dialog box to delete, rename, or edit an AutoText entry. To get there, either choose Insert | AutoText | AutoText or click the AutoText button on the AutoText toolbar. You see the dialog box shown in Figure 6-8.

Follow these instructions to delete, rename, or edit an AutoText entry:

■ **Deleting**   Select the entry and click the Delete button in the AutoCorrect dialog box.

■ **Renaming**   Insert the entry, select it, and click the AutoText button or choose Insert | AutoText | AutoText. In the AutoCorrect dialog box, enter a new name in the Enter AutoText Entries Here text box and click the Add button. Then delete the old name.

■ **Editing**   Insert the AutoText entry, edit it, and select it. Then click the New button on the AutoText toolbar or press ALT-F3. In the Create AutoText dialog box, enter the entry's name and click OK. Word asks if you want to redefine the AutoText entry. Click Yes.

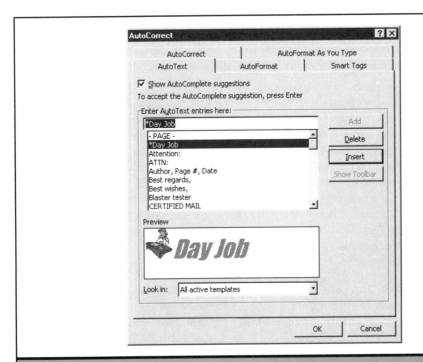

Figure 6-8.   *The AutoText tab of the AutoCorrect dialog box is where you delete, rename, and edit AutoText entries*

Quickly Entering the Date and Time

On the subject of entering text quickly, nothing could be faster than entering the date or time with the Insert | Date and Time command. Choose the command and you see the Date and Time dialog box. Click a date format, time format, or date-and-time format to enter the date or time in your document:

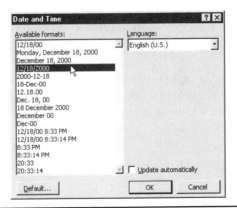

The Date and Time dialog box also offers these amenities:

■ **Default Button** Choose a format and click this button to change the default date or time—the date or time that appears in the bubble box as you type. When you see the bubble, you can press ENTER to insert the date or time without having to type the whole enchilada.

■ **Update Automatically Check Box** Check this check box to enter a date or time field—a date or time entry that always stays up to date with the clock in your computer. To make the date or time field show the current date or time, select the field and press F9. To make sure printed documents list the date or time they were printed, choose Tools | Options, select the Print tab in the Options dialog box, and check the Update Fields check box.

Entering Text and Graphics Quickly with the AutoCorrect Command

The AutoCorrect command was invented to help correct typing errors, but with a little cunning you can also use it to insert text and graphics quickly. To see how AutoCorrect works, choose Tools | AutoCorrect Options. You see the AutoCorrect dialog box shown in Figure 6-9. In the Replace column on the AutoCorrect tab are hundreds of common typing errors that Word corrects automatically. The program corrects the errors by entering text in the With column whenever you mistakenly type the letters in the Replace column.

Note *See "Correcting Typos with the AutoCorrect Command" in Chapter 11 for an explanation of how the AutoCorrect command can help you fix typing errors.*

To make AutoCorrect work as a means of entering text or a graphic, you tell Word to enter the text or graphic whenever you type three or four specific characters. In Figure 6-9, for example, Word is being instructed to insert a graphic and the words "Day Job" whenever I enter the characters **/dayj** (and press the SPACEBAR) in a document. Follow these steps to use AutoCorrect to enter text, a graphic, or text and a graphic:

1. Enter the text, graphic, or text and graphic in a document and select it. Format the text if you want the AutoCorrect mechanism to insert formatted text.

2. Choose Tools | AutoCorrect Options. The AutoCorrect dialog box appears (see Figure 6-9). The item you selected in step 1 appears in the With box.

3. In the Replace text box, enter the three or four characters that will trigger the AutoCorrect mechanism and make it enter your text or graphic.

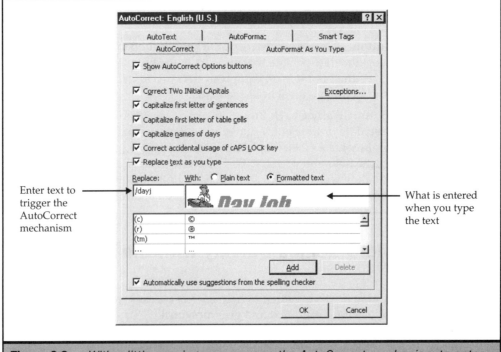

Enter text to trigger the AutoCorrect mechanism

What is entered when you type the text

Figure 6-9.   *With a little cunning, you can use the AutoCorrect mechanism to enter text and graphics quickly*

Caution   *Don't enter a word in the Replace box or characters that you might really type someday. If you do, the AutoCorrect mechanism might kick in when you least expect it. Enter three or four characters that never appear together. And start all AutoCorrect entries with a slash (/). You might forget which characters trigger the AutoText entry or decide to delete your AutoCorrect entry someday. By starting it with a slash, you can find it easily in the AutoCorrect dialog box at the top of the Replace list.*

    4. Click the Formatted Text option button if your entry includes a graphic or you want a text entry to keep its formatting when it is inserted in a document.

    5. Click the Add button and click OK to close the AutoCorrect dialog box.

    Test your AutoCorrect entry by typing the Replace text you entered in step 3 and pressing the SPACEBAR. AutoCorrect doesn't do its work until you press the SPACEBAR. To delete an AutoCorrect entry, open the AutoCorrect dialog box, select the entry, and click the Delete button.

Making Your Own Letterhead

Why spend money on stationery when you can make your own letterhead with the AutoText or AutoCorrect command? You can even include the date—a date that stays current, no matter when you print letters—in the letterhead (see "Quickly Entering the Date and Time" earlier in this chapter). Being able to enter a fancy letterhead with the AutoText or AutoCorrect command beats having to enter text and a graphic whenever you begin a letter:

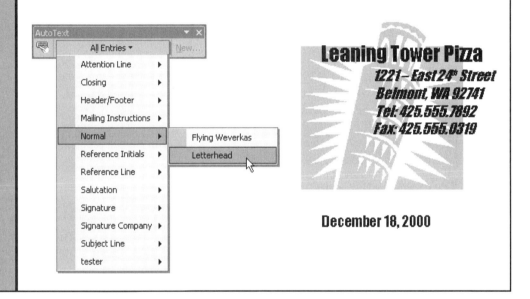

FORMATTING TEXT AND PAGES

MOUS Exam Objectives Explored in Chapter 6

Objective	Heading
Insert, modify, and move text and symbols	"Finding and Replacing Text and Other Things," "Creating and Inserting AutoText Entries," and "Entering Text and Graphics Quickly with the AutoCorrect Command"
Enter and format data and time	"Quickly Entering the Data and Time"

Ten Ways to Work Faster in Word

Following are ten suggestions for working faster in Word. Being a speed demon myself, I am very interested in how tasks can be done faster, and you will find tips and tricks throughout this book for working faster. These ten tips, however, represent the ten best ways to get it done—or get it over with, depending on your point of view—in Microsoft Word.

1. Learn to Use Styles   Nothing makes formatting easier than using styles. A *style* is a collection of commands and formats that have been bundled under one name. By using styles, you free yourself from having to visit and revisit numerous dialog boxes whenever you want to change the formatting of a paragraph. Chapter 12 of this book is devoted to learning about styles.

2. Use a Template or Wizard if You Can   Why waste time formatting a document when you can create it with one of Word's templates or wizards? Your document is laid out for you when you create a document with a template. All you have to do is enter the text. "Creating New Documents" in Chapter 1 explains how to create a document with a Word template. You can create your own templates as well. See "Building Your Own Templates" in Chapter 12.

3. Take Advantage of the AutoText and AutoCorrect Commands   This chapter describes the very speedy AutoText and AutoCorrect commands and how you can use them to enter addresses and other kinds of boilerplate text that has to be entered frequently. You can also stick a graphic in a document very easily with the AutoText or AutoCorrect command. I suggest learning how to use these valuable commands forthwith.

4. Learn All the Ways to Open Documents Quickly   The Open dialog box offers many ways to open documents. And you can open documents from the Windows Document menu or Favorites menu as well. "Opening Documents" in Chapter 1 explains the numerous ways to open documents. Learn them all or at least a handful of good ones and you can get your work done faster.

5. Move and Copy Text with the Drag-and-Drop Method   If you can manage it, the fastest way to copy or move text is to drag and drop it. However, dragging and dropping takes practice, since you have to be good with the mouse to drag and drop. I suggest taking the time to learn to drag and drop and using the method to copy and move text whenever you can. "Copying and Moving Text Short Distances with Drag and Drop" in Chapter 3 explains the drag-and-drop method.

 Don't confuse the drag-and-drop method of copying or moving text with the drop-and-drag method of hunting deer. The two are completely different and have nothing in common.

6. Get in the Habit of Right-Clicking to Select Menu Commands   You can tell
who the experienced word processors are because they rely on shortcut menus more
than they do toolbar buttons and menu commands. Chances are you can right-click
whatever you happen to be working on and see, on a shortcut menu, the command
you need. Check it out. Get in the habit of right-clicking to access commands faster.

7. Create a Toolbar with Your Favorite Buttons on It   Creating a toolbar is much,
much easier than most Word users know. In fact, it's downright easy. You can create a
toolbar for your favorite commands or remove the buttons you never use from toolbars.
See "Creating Your Own Toolbars and Toolbar Buttons" in Chapter 21.

8. Use the Repeat Command as Often as You Possibly Can   The Edit | Repeat
command (press F4) may be the most valuable of all. You can make the command do
repetitive tasks for you. Instead of choosing the same style over and over again from
the unwieldy Style menu, for example, you can select the style once and then give the
Repeat command many times to reformat several paragraphs. See "Repeating a Command
or Text Entry" in Chapter 2.

9. Remember the Undo Command When You Make a Mistake   Word invented
the Undo button and Undo command for the mistake-prone—I should know, I'm one
of them. "Undoing a Mistake—and Redoing What You Undid" in Chapter 2 explains
the Undo command in detail. Suffice it to say you can click the Undo button on the
Standard toolbar to correct a mistake as soon as you make it or open the Undo menu
and choose an action to undo several different mistakes.

10. Learn a Task's Keyboard Shortcut—or Create Your Own Shortcut
Especially if you are a laptop user and you have to rely on keyboard shortcuts, you
owe it to yourself to learn keyboard shortcuts for the commands you often use. One
way to do that is to make keyboard shortcuts appear next to button names when you
move the pointer over a button. After you click the button a few times, you will learn
its keyboard shortcut and start relying on it. Follow these steps to make the keyboard
shortcuts appear when you move the pointer over a toolbar button:

1. Choose View | Toolbars | Customize.
2. Select the Options tab in the Customize dialog box.
3. Check the Show Shortcut Keys In ScreenTips check box.

Note   *"Designing Your Own Keyboard Shortcuts" in Chapter 21 explains how to create your
own keyboard shortcuts.*

FORMATTING TEXT
AND PAGES

Chapter 7

Formatting Text on the Page

This and the next two chapters are hereby dedicated to Oscar Wilde, who said, "Appearances are everything." A well-formatted document says a lot about how much thought and effort was put into the work. Appearances count in word processing. In this chapter, you discover how to make text look "just so" on the page.

This chapter explains how to change the look of characters, draw borders around paragraphs, and place a shaded background behind a paragraph. You also learn all the subtleties of punctuation—how to handle hyphens, dashes, and quotation marks, for example. This chapter describes WordArt, a feature for bending, spindling, and mutilating text, as well as how to make "hanging headings" and do other strange things to headings in documents.

Changing the Way Characters Look on the Page

The first part of this chapter explores the various and sundry ways to decorate text. You learn how to change fonts and font sizes, boldface and underline text, and experiment with text effects. You also learn to do to text what Ted Turner and his crayons did to classic black-and-white movies: colorize it. I suggest reading the following pages with a pencil in hand so you can underline the numerous shortcuts, tips, and tricks.

No matter what you want to do to decorate text, however, you can do it by way of the Font dialog box shown in Figure 7-1. And you can decorate text several ways at once in the Font dialog box. In Figure 7-1, I've chosen the Impact font, the Italic font style, a font size of 36 points, an underline, and the Shadow text effect. The Preview box shows the cumulative effect of all my choices so I know what the text will look like when I return to my document.

You will be hearing a lot about the Font dialog box in the next few pages. To open this dialog box, do one of the following:

- Choose Format | Font.
- Right-click and choose Font from the shortcut menu.
- Press CTRL-D.

By the way, you can choose text formats before you type text or after you've typed it. To apply formats to text you have typed already, select the text and choose a text format command. Otherwise, choose the text formats and start typing—your letters will appear in the text formats you chose.

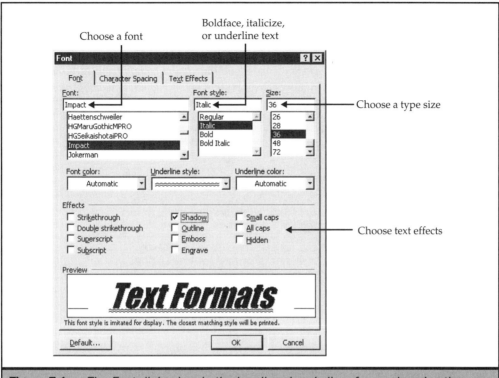

Choose a font

Boldface, italicize,
or underline text

Choose a type size

Choose text effects

Figure 7-1. *The Font dialog box is the be-all and end-all as far as changing the appearance of text is concerned*

FORMATTING TEXT AND PAGES

Tip   *Suppose you format characters a certain way and you regret doing so or you want to start all over. To remove all formats, select the text and press* CTRL-SPACEBAR *or open the Styles and Formatting task pane and choose Clear Formatting, the first option in the Pick Formatting to Apply box.*

Tip   *As Chapter 12 explains, a style is a collection of commands that have been assembled under one name. A character style can include font, font size, text effect, font color, and language settings. To save time and heartache, create a character style if you find yourself giving the same text-formatting commands over and over and over again.*

Boldfacing, Italicizing, and Underlining Text

Probably the three most common character formats are boldface, italics, and underlines. To boldface, italicize, or underline text, go to the Font dialog box and choose an option from the Font Style and Underline Style lists (see Figure 7-1); click the Bold, Italic, or Underline button on the Formatting toolbar; or press CTRL-B, CTRL-I, or CTRL-U, respectively.

> **Boldface text appears in a heavier type so it looks darker and stands out on the page. When readers see a page, their eyes travel first to the boldface words, which is why headings are almost always boldfaced.**
>
> *Italicized letters slant upward and to the right. Foreign words and expressions are usually set in italics. Conventional wisdom says to italicize words for emphasis, but only one or two words should be italicized at a time. Otherwise, you get the impression that the author is screaming at you!*
>
> <u>Underlines are also used for emphasis. Like boldface text, readers' eyes travel first to underlined text. I have noticed that a lot of junk mail solicitations include underlined words where italics might be used. Why's that?</u>

Why anyone needs them all I don't know, but Word offers no less than 17 different ways to underline letters. Press CTRL-U to underline text, as you know already; press CTRL-SHIFT-W to underline words only; or press CTRL-SHIFT-D to double underline text. And when you have exhausted all possibilities of underlining text with keyboard shortcuts, choose Format | Font to open the Font dialog box (see Figure 7-1) and make a choice from the Underline Style drop-down list. For what it's worth, here are the 17 ways to underline text:

> One little piggy went to market.
> Two little piggies went to market.
> Three little piggies went to market.
> Four little piggies went to market.
> Five little piggies went to market.
> Six little piggies went to market.
> Seven little piggies went to market.
> Eight little piggies went to market.
> Nine little piggies went to market.
>
> Ten little piggies went to market.
> Eleven little piggies went to market.
> Twelve little piggies went to market.
> Thirteen little piggies went to market.
> Fourteen little piggies went to market.
> Fifteen little piggies went to market.
> Sixteen little piggies went to market.
> Seventeen little piggies went to market.

To add wealth to riches, the Font dialog box also offers a drop-down list called Underline Color for changing the color of underlines.

In Chapter 8, "Learning How Paragraphs or Text Was Formatted" explains how to open the Reveal Formatting task pane and use it to learn more about text formats.

Choosing a Font and Font Size for Text

A *font* is a typeface design of a particular type. Usually, headings and text are in different fonts. It may or may not interest you to know that the headings in this book are in 18-, 16-, 14-, and 11-point Franklin Gothic bold font and the body text is in 10-point Palatino font. Font size is measured in *points*; a point is 1/72 of an inch. The larger the point size, the larger the letters. At 72 points, text is one inch high. Most people prefer to read type between 10 and 14 points high; headings are usually larger.

 To start all over and remove all font and text formatting from text, select the text and press CTRL-SPACEBAR *or choose Clear Formatting on the Styles and Formatting task pane. Doing so also removes any character styles that were applied to the text.*

Choosing a Font

Follow these instructions to choose a new font for text:

- **Font Menu on the Formatting Toolbar**   Click the down arrow to open the Font menu and then click a font name. As Figure 7-2 shows, you can tell what fonts look like by studying their names on the Font menu. You might have to scroll down the list to find the font you are looking for. Fonts you chose in the course of your work appear at the top of the Font menu in case you want to choose them again. (If you see font names but not fonts on the Font menu, Word isn't displaying names in their font. To fix that, choose Tools | Customize, select the Options tab on the Customize dialog box, and check the List Font Names in Their Font check box.)

   If yours is a long list of fonts and you know the name of the font you need, try clicking in the Font menu box and typing the first one or two letters of the font's name. The list scrolls to the font whose name you started to enter.

TrueType Fonts for Making Sure Fonts Are Printed Correctly

Choose TrueType fonts if you intend to print your documents. TrueType fonts look the same onscreen as they do when printed. You can tell a TrueType font because the letters *TT* appear beside its name on the Font menu on the Formatting toolbar. Choose TrueType fonts and you will never be surprised by strange text formats when you print a document.

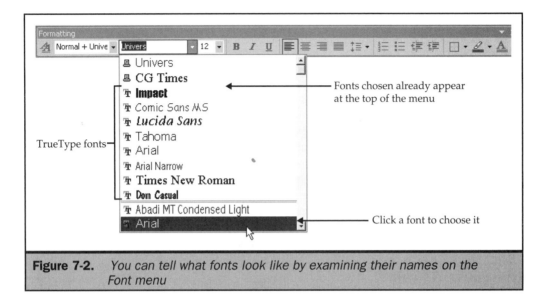

Figure 7-2.   *You can tell what fonts look like by examining their names on the Font menu*

Laptop users: You can also press CTRL-SHIFT-F and start pressing the ↓ key. The names of fonts appear one after the other in the Font menu box. When the name of the font you want appears, press ENTER.

■ **Font Dialog Box**   Choose Format | Font or press CTRL-D to open the Font dialog box (see Figure 7-1). Then choose a font from the Font list, glance at the Preview box to see what your font looks like, and click OK.

■ **Styles and Formatting Task Pane**   Open the Styles and Formatting task pane (click the Styles and Formatting button to do so) and then choose a font in the Pick Formatting to Apply box. Note, however, that you may apply a font size as well as a font with this technique.

Changing the Font Size

Follow these instructions to change the size of letters:

■ **Font Size Menu on the Formatting Toolbar**   As shown in Figure 7-3, click the down arrow to open the Font Size menu and choose a point size. To choose a point size that isn't on the menu, click in the Font Size menu box, enter a point size, and press the ENTER key. (Laptop users: Press CTRL-SHIFT-P to move the cursor into the Font Size menu box. Then either press the ↓ key until you see the point size you want or enter the point size you want, and then press the ENTER key.)

- **Size List in the Font Dialog Box**   Choose Format | Font or press CTRL-D to open the Font dialog box (refer to Figure 7-1). Then either choose a point size from the Size list or enter a point size in the Size box, glance at the Preview box to see how large the letters will be, and click OK.

- **Pressing CTRL-SHIFT-> or CTRL-SHIFT-<**   Press either key to increase or decrease the point size by the next interval on the Font Size menu on the Formatting toolbar. Watch the Font Size menu or your text and note how the text changes size. This is an excellent technique when you want to "eyeball it" and you don't care to fool with the Font Size menu or Font dialog box.

- **Pressing CTRL-] or CTRL-[**   Press either key to increase or decrease the point size by 1 point. Use this technique to make subtle changes to the font size of letters.

Tip   *Use the CTRL-] or CTRL-[shortcut keys when you are dealing with fonts of different sizes and you want to change the size of all the letters at once but still retain their size differences relative to one another.*

Tip   *Here's a little trick for finding out what all the characters in a font look like: Choose Insert | Symbol, select the Symbols tab in the Symbol dialog box, and choose a font name from the Font drop-down menu. You see all the letters in the font, as well as many of the symbols.*

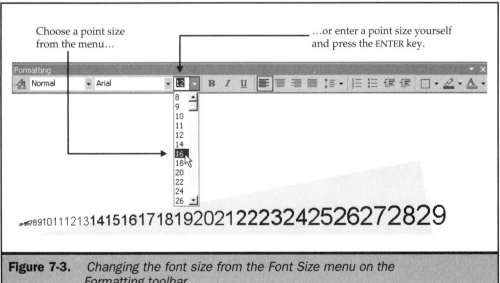

Figure 7-3.   *Changing the font size from the Font Size menu on the Formatting toolbar*

FORMATTING TEXT AND PAGES

Changing the Color of Text

The Font dialog box offers a Font Color drop-down list for choosing colors, but the easiest way to do it is to select the text and choose a color from the Font Color menu on the Formatting toolbar. What's more, the Font Color menu is a "floater," so you can drag it off the toolbar and start clicking buttons until the text you selected looks just right. See "The Strange Case of the Floating Toolbar" in Chapter 1 if your Font Color menu sinks instead of floating like the one in this illustration:

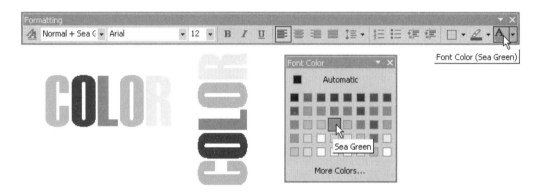

Tip   *Two commands come in especially handy when you are changing fonts and font sizes: Edit | Repeat and Apply Formatting to Original Selection. Change fonts once in the Font dialog box (choose Format | Font), and all you have to do to change them elsewhere in the same way is keep selecting text and pressing* F4 *(the Repeat command shortcut key). To change font formats in many different places at once, select text with a font you want to apply elsewhere and choose Format | Reveal Formatting. Then click the Compare to Another Selection check box in the task pane, select the text whose formats you want to copy, open the drop-down list in the second box under Selected Text in the task pane, and choose the Apply Formatting of Original Selection command.*

Playing with Word's "Text Effects"

Dead center in the Font dialog box (choose Format | Font to get there) are the Effects options. These options have various uses, some utilitarian and some strictly for yucks. They are described on the following pages.

Effects
- ☐ Stri<u>k</u>ethrough
- ☐ Do<u>u</u>ble strikethrough
- ☐ S<u>u</u>perscript
- ☐ Su<u>b</u>script
- ☐ Sh<u>a</u>dow
- ☐ <u>O</u>utline
- ☐ <u>E</u>mboss
- ☐ En<u>g</u>rave
- ☐ <u>S</u>mall caps
- ☐ <u>A</u>ll caps
- ☐ H<u>i</u>dden

Strikethrough and Double Strikethrough   Strikethrough is used to show where passages have been struck from a contract or other important document. Double strikethrough, for all I know, is used to shows where passages have been struck out forcefully. Click the Strikethrough or Double Strikethrough check box to draw lines through text:

~~Upon orders from above, this text is hereby struck from our contract.~~
~~And, look here I say, this text is hereby struck out twice as hard.~~

If you see strikethrough text colored red, blue, or another color, you are very likely looking at revised text, not strikethrough text. Word offers a Revision Marks feature whereby deleted text is not removed from the page but struck out instead. See "Keeping Track of Revisions to Documents" in Chapter 17.

Superscript and Subscript   A superscripted letter or number is one that has been raised in the text. Superscript is used in mathematical and scientific formulas, in ordinal numbers (1st, 2nd, 3rd), and to mark footnotes (but if you need to enter footnotes, use Word's Insert | Reference | Footnote command, which is explained in Chapter 16). In the theory of relativity, the 2 is superscripted: $E = mc^2$.

Word enters ordinal numbers in superscript automatically. If you prefer to write ordinal numbers that are not superscripted, choose Tools | AutoCorrect Options, select the AutoFormat As You Type tab in the AutoCorrect dialog box, and uncheck the Ordinals (1st) With Superscript check box.

A subscripted letter has been lowered in the text. In this chemistry equation, the 2 has been lowered to show that two atoms of hydrogen are needed along with one atom of oxygen to form a molecule of water: H_2O.

To superscript or subscript a number or letter, select it and do the following:

- **Superscript**   Check the Superscript check box in the Font dialog box (choose Format | Font or press CTRL-D to get there) or press CTRL-SHIFT-=.
- **Subscript**   Check the Subscript check box or press CTRL-=.

In Chapter 16, "Writing Equations with the Equation Editor" describes the Equation Editor, a special tool for entering equations—including superscripted and subscripted characters and numbers—in documents.

Shadow   The Shadow check box in the Font dialog box is for use in desktop publishing to make headlines cast a faint shadow on the page. To make the Shadow option work, however, you have to choose a heavy font so the characters are wide enough to cast a shadow:

Outline   The Outline option presents letters in outline form. This option, like Shadow, Emboss, and Engrave, is for use in desktop publishing. To use it successfully, the letters have to be heavy enough and tall enough to be seen as outlines:

Emboss and Engrave   Clicking the Emboss or Engrave check box turns the text white. Embossed text looks as though it has been raised from the paper; engraved text is meant to look as though it has been chiseled into the paper like words on a gravestone. With either option, be sure to choose a *serif font*, a font like the Times Roman font shown here with short, ornamental strokes called *serifs* on the ends of letters. The serifs help make the embossing or engraving stand out.

Embassy Boss

Engraved and Buried

Note *Hidden text is used for critiquing others' work and communicating secretly across interstate boundaries. It does not appear on the page unless you click the Show/Hide¶ button. See "Making Notes with Hidden Text" in Chapter 17.*

Small Caps A *small cap* is a small capital letter. To give you an idea how small caps are used, Table 7-1 describes how the *Chicago Manual of Style,* the copy editor's Bible, instructs editors and typesetters to use small caps. In this book, you may have noticed, small caps are used to describe keys on the keyboard ("press CTRL-SHIFT-K"). In newspapers, small capital letters are often used in the dateline at the start of the article ("Key West, FL Nov. 8 [UPI]"). To enter a small cap, type the letter in lowercase, select it, and do either of the following:

- Open the Font dialog box, and check the Small Caps check box (or open the Font dialog box first, check the Small Caps check box, close the dialog box, and then start typing).
- Press CTRL-SHIFT-K.

Small Cap	Meaning	Explanation	Example
A.M.	*ante meridian*	Before noon	4:00 A.M.
P.M.	*post meridian*	Afternoon	5:30 P.M.
A.D.	*anno Domini*	In the year of the Lord	A.D. 1066*
A.H.	*anno Hebraico;* also *anno Hegirae*	In the Hebrew year; in the year of (Mohammed's) Hegira (i.e., his flight from Mecca in A.D. 622)	A.H .1378*
A.U.C.	*ab urbe condita*	From the founding of the city (i.e., Rome, in 753 B.C.)	2753 A.U.C.
B.C.	"before Christ"	Before the birth of Jesus Christ	540 B.C.
B.C.E.	"before the common era"	Religiously neutral equivalent to B.C.	540 B.C.E.
B.P.	"before the present"	Before the present year	1 B.P.
C.E.	"of the common era"	Religiously neutral equivalent to A.D.	1066 C.E.

* *The small cap abbreviations A.D. and A.H. precede the year.*

Table 7-1.   Chicago Manual of Style *Uses for Small Capital Letters*

Be sure to type lowercase letters in order to create small caps. Type an uppercase letter and Word refuses to turn it into a small cap. Not all fonts can produce small capital letters.

Putting Borders, Shading, and Color on Paragraphs

Word offers a command for putting borders around paragraphs and color or gray shades behind paragraphs. Before you know anything about the Format | Borders and Shading command, however, you should know that the command is not necessarily the best way to draw lines around paragraphs or put color or a gray shade behind them.

Figure 7-4 shows a document in which borders and gray shades have been placed on several paragraphs with the Format | Borders and Shading command. Notice what is wrong with the borders and gray shades in the figure:

- **Borders and Shades Don't Line Up**   With the Format | Borders and Shading command, borders are drawn along the left and right margins, unless the paragraph is indented, in which case the borders are drawn at the indentation. In Figure 7-4, several paragraphs are indented, so the left and right borderlines don't line up and you get an ugly, blocky-looking couple of pages. Without digging around in the Border and Shading Options dialog box (I'll show you how), you can't decide for yourself where the borders lie or how much of the page to fill with color or a gray shade.

- **No Border at Page Break**   The last paragraph breaks across two pages, so no borderline appears along the bottom of the first page or the top of the second.

What is the Format | Borders and Shading command good for, seeing that you can't decide where the borders fall or keep a paragraph with borders and shading from breaking across the bottom of a page? The command *is* good for putting borders,

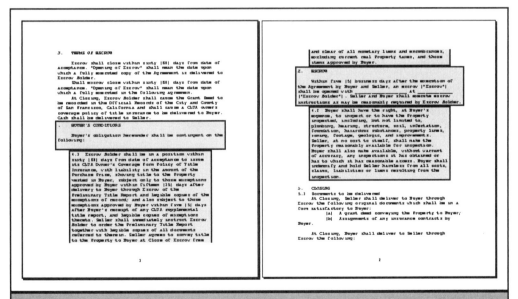

Figure 7-4.   *With the Format | Borders and Shading command, borders are placed on the margin or where paragraphs are indented*

Alternatives to the Format I Borders and Shading Command

Consider these alternatives to the Format I Borders and Shading command before you draw borders around a paragraph or place a gray shade or color behind it:

- **Text Boxes**   A *text box* is a box in which you can enter text. Text boxes can be shaded, filled with color, and given borders. You can move them wherever you want on the page. Text boxes do not break across pages—they slide to the next page if they are pushed too close to the bottom of the previous one. See "Putting a Text Box on the Page" in Chapter 13.

- **Rectangles**   Click the Rectangle button on the Drawing toolbar to draw a rectangle onscreen. You can fill a rectangle with color or a gray shade, put borders on it, and make text show through it. See "Drawing Lines and Shapes" in Chapter 13.

shading, and color on a single paragraph. And, as shown in this illustration, you can use it to draw borderlines across the top and bottom of paragraphs:

It is only shallow people who do not judge by appearances. The true mystery of the world is the visible, not the invisible. — Oscar Wilde

 You can also draw borders along the sides of the page. See "Decorating a Page with a Border" in Chapter 9.

Putting Borderlines Around a Paragraph

To put borders around a paragraph, start by clicking the paragraph. Then follow these instructions:

- **Simple Lines**   As shown in Figure 7-5, go to the Formatting toolbar and click the down arrow next to the Border button to open the Border menu. Then click a Border button or click two or three buttons to put borders on two or three sides of the paragraph.

- **Box, Shadow, 3-D, and Custom Borders**   Choose Format I Borders and Shading and select the Borders tab in the Borders and Shading dialog box, shown in Figure 7-5, to draw fancy borders. Click a Setting button—Box, Shadow, 3-D, and so on—to create an unusual border. From the Style, Color, and Width drop-down lists, choose what the lines will look like. Under Preview, either click the buttons or click sides of the square to tell Word on which sides of the paragraph to draw borderlines.

- ■ **Tables and Borders Toolbar**   Display the Tables and Borders toolbar, as shown in Figure 7-5. The Line Style, Line Width, and Border Color menus offer the same kinds of lines and colors as the Borders and Shading dialog box.

Removing borderlines is a lot easier than drawing them. Click anywhere inside the border, click the down arrow beside the Borders button on the Formatting toolbar, and click the No Border button to remove all the borders. To remove one or two of them, click buttons that are "pressed down" on the Border drop-down menu.

Note   *You can control how close text comes to the border around a paragraph. To do so, choose Format | Borders and Shading, select the Borders tab, and click the Options button. In the Border and Shading Options dialog box, change the measurements in the Top, Bottom, Left, and Right boxes to move text closer or farther away from the borders.*

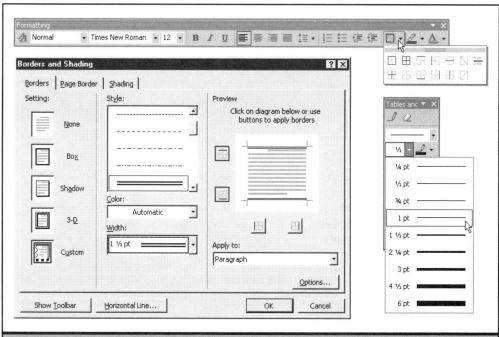

Figure 7-5.   *The Borders and Shading dialog box offers many options for drawing borders, and you can also use the Border buttons or the Tables and Borders toolbar*

FORMATTING TEXT
AND PAGES

Shading or Coloring a Paragraph

To shade or put a color background on a paragraph, click it and display the Tables and Borders toolbar. Then open the Shading Color drop-down menu and choose a color or gray shade. That's all there is to it. If you decide to remove the color or shading, open the Shading Color menu again and choose No Fill.

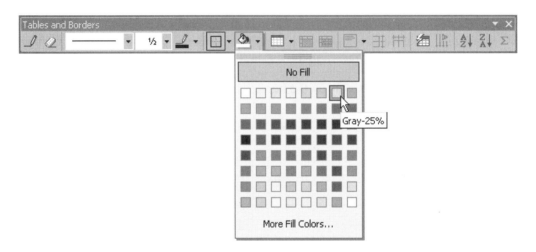

A better way to shade or color a paragraph is to put a rectangle or other shape behind it and then fill the rectangle or shape with a light color or shade of gray. See "Putting Borders and 'Fills' on Objects" in Chapter 13.

Exciting Ways to Format Heading Text

Everybody knows that heading text is larger than other text and that headings are boldfaced. Suppose you want headings to really stand out? These pages explain how to make jazzy headings that get readers' attention. Read on to learn about WordArt, a means of stretching and teasing words into different shapes, and hanging heads, headings that hang into the margin. You also learn how to raise and lower letters from the baseline and fix letter-spacing problems in headings.

WordArt for Bending, Spindling, and Mutilating Text

A *WordArt image* is a word or two that has been stretched, crumpled, or squeezed into an odd shape. Figure 7-6 shows the WordArt Gallery, where WordArt images are made, and an example of a WordArt image. After you insert a WordArt image, you can fool

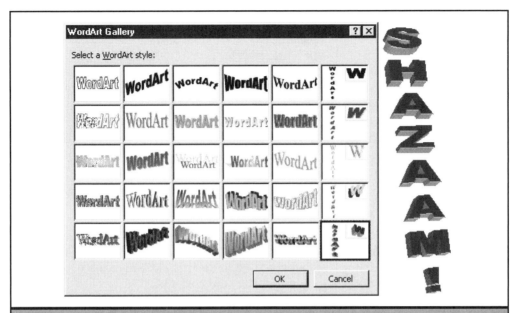

Figure 7-6.   *To create a WordArt image like the one shown here, start by selecting a style in the WordArt Gallery*

with the buttons on the WordArt toolbar and torture the word or phrase even further. Read on.

Creating a WordArt Image

You can get a head start creating a WordArt image by selecting the text you want in the image. Anyhow, follow these steps to insert a WordArt image in a document:

1. Click the page where you want the WordArt image to go and either choose Insert | Picture | WordArt or click the Insert WordArt button on the Drawing toolbar. You see the WordArt Gallery dialog box shown in Figure 7-6.

2. Select a WordArt style and click OK. Don't worry about selecting the right style—you can choose a different one later on. You see the Edit WordArt Text dialog box.

3. Enter the text for the image (if you didn't select it to begin with), choose a font and font size, and boldface or italicize the letters if you want. As I explain shortly, returning to the Edit WordArt Text dialog box later is easy, so don't worry about choosing the right font and font size.

4. Click OK.

The next section in this chapter explains how to change the appearance and words in a WordArt image. See "Manipulating Art, Text Boxes, Shapes, and Other So-Called Objects" in Chapter 13 to learn how to move a WordArt image on the page or wrap text around it. A WordArt image, like clip art and text boxes, is an object. As far as Word is concerned, the same commands apply to WordArt images, text boxes, and clip art when it comes to manipulating objects.

Editing a WordArt Image

Usually, you have to wrestle with a WordArt image before it comes out right. By clicking buttons on the WordArt toolbar, you can win the wrestling match. (The WordArt toolbar is displayed when you click a WordArt image, but if for some reason you don't see it, choose View | Toolbars | WordArt.)

Changing the Text, Font, and Font Size   To change the text or font of an image, click the Edit Text button on the WordArt toolbar or double-click the image. You see the Edit WordArt Text dialog box that you used in the first place to create your image. Type new words, choose a new font or font size, and click OK.

Changing the Style of the Image   You don't like the WordArt style you chose when you created the image? You can choose a new one by clicking the WordArt Gallery button on the WordArt toolbar. In the WordArt Gallery dialog box (see Figure 7-6), select a new style and click OK.

Changing the Color of the Letters   Click the Format WordArt button and choose new colors on the Colors and Lines tab of the Format dialog box. As this illustration shows, the dialog box offers two Color drop-down lists if your WordArt image has two colors. Experiment with the Fill Color list and the Line Color list, not to mention the Transparency slider, until your WordArt image is just so. Increase or decrease the weight of lines to make the letters in the image thicker or spindlier.

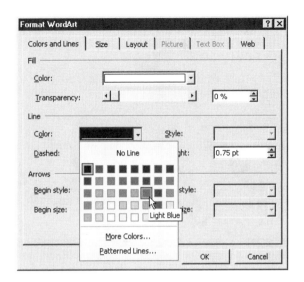

Stretching and Skewing Images To change the shape of an image, do one or all three of the following:

- Click and drag the diamond to stretch or scrunch the image. (If you don't see the diamond, select the image, click the Text Wrapping button on the WordArt toolbar, and choose any option from the drop-down menu except In Line With Text.)

- Drag a selection handle.

- Click the WordArt Shape button on the WordArt toolbar and choose a new shape from the menu.

Click the WordArt Vertical Text button on the WordArt toolbar to flip an image so that letters appear one below the other, like the word "Crack" in this illustration.

Rotating an Image   To turn an image on its back or side, click to select it, and then drag the rotate handle, a small green circle.

 If you don't see the rotate handle, your WordArt image is in line with the text. Click the Text Wrapping button on the WordArt toolbar and choose any option on the pop-up menu except In Line With Text.

Playing with the Letters   The final three buttons on the WordArt toolbar are for fooling with the letters in the image:

- **WordArt Same Letter Heights**   Click this button to make all the letters, upper- or lowercase, the same height.

- **WordArt Alignment**   To begin with, WordArt images are centered, but you can click this button and make a choice from the drop-down list to change that. The Stretch Justify option stretches the letters so they fill the frame that the WordArt image resides in; the Letter Justify option puts enough space between letters so the letters fill the frame; and the Word Justify option puts spaces between words so that the words fill the frame.

- **WordArt Character Spacing**   Click this button and choose an option from the drop-down list to make the letters looser or tighter.

 To make WordArt images look especially strange, try clicking the Shadow or 3-D button on the Drawing toolbar and choosing a Shadow setting or 3-D setting for your WordArt image. You could amuse yourself for hours this way.

Raising and Lowering Letters from the Baseline

Contrary to what tennis players and referees know, the *baseline* is the imaginary line that letters sit on in a line of text. Word offers commands for raising and lowering letters from the baseline. These commands are supposed to be for adjusting the distance that superscripted letters are raised above and subscripted letters are lowered below the baseline, but you can also use them to good effect in headings. In this wacky-looking heading, for example, letters are raised and lowered from the baseline and different fonts are used. A heading like this is sure to attract readers' attention.

Follow these steps to raise or lower letters from the baseline:

1. Select the letter or letters that you want to raise or lower.
2. Choose Format | Font.
3. Select the Character Spacing tab in the Font dialog box.
4. From the Position drop-down list, choose Raised or Lowered.
5. In the By box beside the Position box, enter how many points above or below the baseline you want to raise or lower the letters.
6. Click OK.

Raising and lowering letters from the baseline is one of those tasks in which the Repeat command comes in especially handy. After you've raised or lowered one letter from the baseline, select another and press F4 or choose Edit | Repeat Font Formatting to raise or lower the other letter as well.

Making Headings Fit Across Pages and Columns

Suppose you want a heading to fit across an entire page or column but the heading only goes partway across or, worse yet, it breaks onto another line. In Figure 7-7, for example, the heading on the left side of the first set of headings breaks onto another line. How can you fix that? Meanwhile, the heading on the right does not stretch across the column. Suppose you want it to fit across the column. The Font dialog box offers commands for shrinking and stretching headings in cases like these.

Follow these steps to make a heading fit snugly atop a page or column:

1. Select the heading.
2. Choose Format | Font.
3. Select the Character Spacing tab in the Font dialog box.

4. Enter a percentage in the Scale box by clicking an arrow or typing a number. Numbers above 100% stretch headings; numbers below 100% shrink them. Look in the Preview box to see how much you are stretching or shrinking your heading.

5. Click OK.

 See "Starting a New Paragraph, Line, or Page" in Chapter 2 to learn how to deliberately break a heading across two lines (Hint: Press SHIFT-ENTER).

Kerning to Fix Spacing Problems in Headings

Occasionally when you increase the size of letters for a heading, certain letter pairs stand too far apart. The letter pairs "YO," "WA," "AV," "Tw," and "To" are notorious in this regard. In the first heading in Figure 7-8, notice how far apart the "YO," "WA," and "AV" letter pairs are. I fixed this problem in the second heading by kerning the letter pairs. *Kerning* means to push two letters closer together or farther apart to make words easier to read. You can only kern TrueType fonts and Adobe Type Manager fonts.

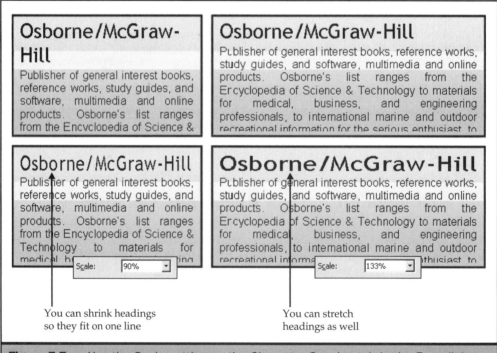

Figure 7-7. *Use the Scale setting on the Character Spacing tab in the Font dialog box to shrink or stretch headings so they fit across pages or columns*

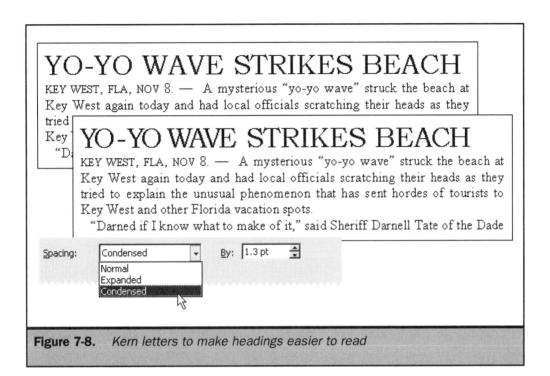

Figure 7-8. *Kern letters to make headings easier to read*

Follow these steps to kern a pair of letters in a word to make a heading easier to read:

1. Select the letter pair in the heading.
2. Choose Format | Font.
3. Select the Character Spacing tab in the Font dialog box.
4. On the Spacing drop-down list, choose Condensed to draw the letters closer together or Expanded to push them farther apart.
5. In the By box, click the up or down arrow as many times as necessary to tell Word by how many points to move the letters. Watch the Preview box to see how close or far apart your letter pair will be.
6. Click OK.

While you are visiting the Character Spacing tab in the Font dialog box, you can check the Kerning For Fonts check box and enter a point size measurement in the Points And Above text box to tell Word to automatically kern letter pairs above a certain font size. Word, however, cannot kern all fonts.

Another way to handle characters that are too close together is to insert a wee bit of space between them. To do so, place the cursor between the characters, choose Insert | Symbol, select the Special Characters tab in the Symbol dialog box, and choose 1/4 Em Space to insert a space that is a fourth of the width of the letter M.

Creating a "Hanging Heading"

A so-called *hanging heading* is one that appears to hang, or stick, into the left margin of the page. Look in this book at the heading directly above this paragraph to see what a hanging heading is. Notice how the first few letters of the word "Creating" stick into the left margin. Hanging headings work very nicely in reference books like this one because they permit readers to look up headings quickly. The headings hang in the margin, which makes finding them easier.

Here are two strategies for creating hanging headings in documents:

- **Indent the Text Below Headings**   By indenting the text below headings, you make headings appear to hang in the margin.

- **Use a Negative Left Indent for the Heading**   Create a negative indent for the heading so it sticks in the margin, as shown in this illustration. To do so, either drag the Left Indent marker on the ruler into the left margin or open the Paragraph dialog box (choose Format | Paragraph) and enter a negative number in the Left text box under Indentation. See "Indenting Text on the Page" in Chapter 8 to learn all the indenting details. If you go this route, be sure to make the left margin wider to account for hanging headings. See "Setting the Margins" in Chapter 9.

Negative indent

Finding the Instructions You Need

Many argue that finding information is easier in a book in which the headings hang in the left margin. Suppose a reader goes to the table of contents, finds a chapter that he or she is interested in, and decides to take a closer look at the chapter. Upon arriving at the chapter, the reader skims the pages, reading heading after heading after heading. If the headings "hang," the reader can find and read them faster. Hanging headings, you see, stick in the margin where you can't miss 'em.

Hanging headings are a prefect candidate for a style. If you want to use hanging headings in your report or manual, see Chapter 12 to learn how to create a style for them. Or else create a style to indent the text in the document and make the headings above the text appear to hang in the left margin.

Handling Hyphens, Dashes, and Other Punctuation

The next several pages take on what many people consider the dreariest topic in the human lexicon: punctuation. Before you start yawning, however, consider the fact that hyphenating words makes text fit better on the page. In narrow columns, hyphenating is a must, since only by hyphenating can you squeeze all the words in. As for em dashes, en dashes, ellipses, and the other esoterica you will find on the following pages, read on only if you are interested in creating professional documents that meet the high standards of magazine and book publishers.

Hyphenating Text

Hyphenating text isn't always necessary. Hyphenated text is harder to read, which is why the words in this book, for example, are not hyphenated. Only hyphenate when you have to squeeze text into narrow columns, you are dealing with justified text and you have to pack more letters on each line to keep empty spaces from appearing in lines, or a word is simply crying out to be hyphenated. The beauty of hyphenating in Word is that the hyphens only appear where words break at the end of lines. When a hyphenated word gets shunted to the next line, the hyphens disappear.

Note *Don't confuse hyphens with two similar-looking punctuation marks: the em dash and en dash. Dashes are used to indicate inclusive numbers or to introduce a new thought in the middle of the sentence—know what I mean? Later in this chapter, "Handling Dashes, Quotation Marks, Ellipses, and Other Tricky Punctuation" explains dashes.*

Word offers no less than three strategies for hyphenating words. These strategies are explained in the pages that follow and are outlined here:

- ■ **Automatic Hyphenation** Word hyphenates the entire document for you. With this technique, you have to hyphenate the entire document at once (although you can mark paragraphs beforehand and tell Word not to hyphenate them). If you change your mind about hyphenating, however, removing all the automatic hyphens is simple.

FORMATTING TEXT AND PAGES

- **Manual Hyphenation**   Word suggests putting hyphens in various words and you say Yes or No to each suggestion. The only way to remove hyphens that were entered manually is to delete them one at a time, which can be time-consuming if you change your mind about hyphenating a document.

- **Optional Hyphens**   If a single word is crying out to be hyphenated, you can enter an *optional hyphen*—a hyphen that breaks the word but disappears if the word doesn't break across two lines.

Don't enter a plain hyphen to solve a line-break problem. If the word you hyphenated gets pushed to the next line, the hyphen will remain. Use an optional hyphen instead, since optional hyphens only appear when words break at the end of lines.

When you hyphenate, be sure to switch to Print Layout view. That way, you can see precisely where the hyphens fall.

Inserting an Optional Hyphen on Your Own

Even in a document that you don't intend to hyphenate, occasionally a word begs for a hyphen. In this illustration, the word "tintinnabulation" (it means "a jingling or tinkling sound") needs to be hyphenated to keep the large empty space from appearing below it on the second line. Optional hyphens, also known as *soft hyphens*, only appear when words break on the line; the rest of the time they stay hidden.

As she strolled, she heard the tintinnabulation of the bells in distant and dreadful Minneapolis, and she sighed.

As she strolled, she heard the tintinnabul- ation of the bells in distant and dreadful Minneapolis, and she sighed.

To insert an optional hyphen:

1. Click where you want the hyphen to appear.
2. Press CTRL-hyphen or choose Insert | Symbol, select the Special Characters tab in the Symbol dialog box, select Optional Hyphen, click the Insert button, and click Close.

To enter an optional hyphen, press CTRL and the hyphen key to the right of the 0 on the keyboard, not the minus sign on the numeric keypad. Press CTRL and the minus key enters an en dash, not a hyphen.

As you know, optional hyphens don't appear unless they break words on the right sides of lines, but if you want to see them, click the Show/Hide ¶ button. For that matter, if you need to see optional hyphens all the time, choose Tools | Options, select the View tab in the Options dialog box, and check the Optional Hyphens check box (look for it under "Formatting Marks"). You can also search for optional hyphens in documents by choosing Edit | Find, clicking the Special button in the Find and Replace dialog box, and choosing Optional Hyphen. Be sure to click the Show/Hide ¶ button so you can see the hyphens as Word finds them. Boy, this book *is* a complete reference, isn't it?

Hyphenating Words Automatically

Follow these steps to make Word hyphenate your entire document automatically:

1. Choose Tools | Language | Hyphenation.

2. In the Hyphenation dialog box, check the Automatically Hyphenate Document check box.

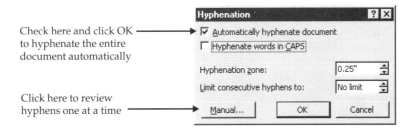

Check here and click OK to hyphenate the entire document automatically

Click here to review hyphens one at a time

3. Uncheck Hyphenate Words in CAPS if you don't care to hyphenate words in uppercase.

4. The Hyphenation Zone text box is for hyphenating left-aligned text. The *hyphenation zone* is the maximum amount of space that Word permits on the right side of lines. A large zone makes for fewer hyphens, since Word allows more white space, but allows more gaps to appear on the right side of lines. A narrow zone makes for more hyphens and breaks lines more often. However, seeing many hyphens down the side of a column or page is a little disconcerting.

5. In book publishing, the convention is not to allow more than two consecutive hyphens in a row, so enter **2** in the Limit Consecutive Hyphens To box if you are bookish.

6. Click OK.

FORMATTING TEXT
AND PAGES

Keeping Text from Being Hyphenated

As a rule, headings are not hyphenated. Neither are indented paragraphs where quotations are found. To keep Word from hyphenating parts of a document, select them and choose Format | Paragraph, select the Line and Page Breaks tab in the Paragraph dialog box, and check the Don't Hyphenate check box. If you devise a style for headings, be sure to visit the Page Break tab and check the Don't Hyphenate box. Styles are explained in Chapter 12.

To "unhyphenate" a document you hyphenated automatically, choose Tools | Language | Hyphenation, uncheck the Automatically Hyphenate Document check box, and click OK.

Manually Hyphenating Words

As I noted earlier in this chapter, you can't unhyphenate words very easily after you hyphenate them by using the manual method. To remove manual hyphens, you have to do so one at a time or start clicking the Undo button like a madman. You've been warned! Follow these steps to pick and choose where words are hyphenated:

1. Click where you want to start hyphenating and choose Tools | Language | Hyphenation. You see the Hyphenation dialog box.

2. Change the Hyphenation Zone and Limit Consecutive Hyphens To settings if you so desire (the previous set of instructions explains how to do so).

3. Click the Manual button. The Manual Hyphenation dialog box appears and you see a blinking cursor where Word suggests putting a hyphen:

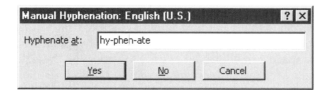

4. Click Yes or No, and keep clicking Yes or No until Word informs you that "Hyphenation is complete."

Nonbreaking Hyphens and Nonbreaking Spaces

Some hyphenated compound words and verbs that include a hyphen are hard to read when they break on the right side of a line. Consider the illustration shown here. Words such as *e-mail* and *yo-yo* are jarring when they break across two lines.

> It's about time you showed a little self-
> restraint. Your very disturbing habit of e-
> mailing me all the time about the Vice-
> President's fixation with that comic strip X-
> Men is making me buggy. You're just a yo-
> yo.

To keep these words from breaking, press CTRL-SHIFT-hyphen to enter a *nonbreaking hyphen* where normally you would enter a hyphen (you can also choose Insert | Symbol, select the Special Characters tab, and choose Nonbreaking Hyphen). Even where nonbreaking hyphens appear at the end of a line, Word does not shunt the second word to the next line.

Certain kinds of compound phrases should stay on the same line, too. Consider the ones shown in this illustration. Lines should not break after an ampersand (&), for example, or before a number if the number is attached to something else (Act 1, Psalm 22).

> I understand from my sources that Sen.
> Jones intends to write the book for Harper &
> Row. But just surely as Act 2 follows Act
> 1, and as surely as Psalm 23 follows Psalm
> 22, you can bet that the senator will forget.

To keep compounds like these from breaking at the end of a line, press CTRL-SHIFT-SPACEBAR to enter a *nonbreaking space* where normally you would press the SPACEBAR to enter a space. You can also choose Insert | Symbol, select the Special Characters tab in the Symbol dialog box, and choose Nonbreaking Space.

FORMATTING TEXT
AND PAGES

Handling Dashes, Quotation Marks, Ellipses, and Other Tricky Punctuation

The last part of this longwinded chapter takes on a couple of mundane subjects. Read on to learn how to enter em and en dashes, em and en spaces, smart quotes or straight quotes, ellipses, and accent marks over capital letters in French words.

Entering Em and En Dashes

What most people know as the "dash" is really two types of punctuation mark, the *em dash* and the *en dash*. The em dash, which is the width of the letter M, is used to show an abrupt change of thought in a sentence. The en dash indicates inclusive numbers. It is also used instead of a hyphen in a compound adjective if one or both parts of the adjective consists of two words ("San Francisco–Seattle shuttle"). Not surprisingly, the en dash is the width of the letter N. Note the use of en dashes on the left side of this illustration and em dashes on the right side.

1941–1945	"Would you—could you—with a goat?"
John Doe (1958–)	The patient—he had suffered all night—finally succumbed.
Exodus 16:11–16:18	She completed the job—a job well done.
pp. 54–58	The four boys—Jim, Tad, Bill, and Donny—finally arrived.
July–August 1863	Picasso, Matisse—they are the 20th Century masters.
New York–Caracas flight	"What the—?" gasped Lt. Jones.

Follow these instructions to insert dashes:

- **Em Dash (—)**   Press ALT-CTRL-minus key on the numeric keypad or choose Insert | Symbol, click the Special Characters tab in the Symbol dialog box, and select Em Dash.

- **En Dash (–)**   Press CTRL-minus key on the numeric keypad or choose Insert | Symbol and select En Dash on the Special Characters tab of the Symbol dialog box. You can also press two hyphens in a row (—) to enter an en dash. As soon as you press the SPACEBAR, Word inserts the en dash for you.

Tip *If you prefer to enter en dashes in your manuscript with two hyphens (—) instead of an en dash (–), you can tell Word to let the two hyphens stand when you enter them. To do so, choose Tools | AutoCorrect Options, select the AutoFormat As You Type tab in the AutoCorrect dialog box, and uncheck the Hyphens (—) With Dash (—) check box.*

Besides em and en dashes, you can enter em and en spaces. Em and en spaces, like em and en dashes, are the width of an *M* or *N*. Em dashes are used in this book, for example, to separate the boldfaced part of an item in a bulleted list from the rest of the item. Choose Insert | Symbol, select the Special Characters tab, and choose Em Space or En Space to insert an em or en space.

Choosing Which Kind of Quotation Mark You Want

Unless you change the default settings, Word inserts "smart" quotation marks when you press the single quote (') or double quote (") key on the keyboard. A smart quote is one that curls, either to the left if it appears at the start of a word or phrase in quotations, or to the right if it appears after the word or phrase. You can, however, enter straight-up quotation marks that don't curl. This illustration shows the difference between smart quotation marks and straight quotation marks.

"These are 'dumb' quotation marks," she said.

"These are 'smart' quotation marks," he said.

If you prefer straight quotes to smart quotes, follow these steps to enter straight quotes:

1. Choose Tools | AutoCorrect Options.
2. Select the AutoFormat As You Type tab in the AutoCorrect dialog box.
3. Uncheck the "Straight Quotes" With "Smart Quotes" check box.
4. Click OK.

Suppose you opted for straight quotes, but you need to insert a single smart quote (a curly quote) in a document. In that case, choose Insert | Symbol, select the Special Characters tab in the Symbol dialog box, choose a quote option (Single Opening, Single Closing, Double Opening, or Double Closing), and click the Insert button. Take note of the shortcut keys in the dialog box and use the shortcut keys if you find yourself having to enter curly quotes often.

To change all the smart quotes to straight quotes or vice versa, choose Edit | Replace, and, in the Find and Replace dialog box, enter a quotation mark in both the Find What and Replace With text boxes.

Handling Ellipses and Accents on Uppercase Letters

Finally, to end this chapter with a whimper and not a bang, here are two more slices of punctuation esoterica:

- **Ellipses (...)**   When you type three periods in a row to enter an ellipsis, Word automatically spreads the periods out a bit to make the ellipsis easier to see on the page. If for some reason you don't want Word to do that, choose Tools | AutoCorrect Options, select the AutoCorrect tab in the dialog box that appears, click the ellipsis (...) in the Replace list, and click the Delete button.

- **Accents on Uppercase Letters**   Word does not print accent marks over uppercase letters in French words. *Quel damage!* If you want the accent marks to appear, choose Tools | Options, select the Edit tab in the Options dialog box, and check the Allow Accented Uppercase In French check box.

MOUS Exam Objectives Explored in Chapter 7

Objective	Heading
Apply and modify text formats	"Changing the Way Characters Look on the Page" and "Choosing a Font and Font Size for Text"
Apply character effects and highlights	"Playing with Word's 'Text Effects'"
Modify format, alignment, and layout of paragraphs	"Putting Borders, Shading, and Color on Paragraphs"

Ten Tips for Handling Fonts

Not that I claim to be a font of wisdom when it comes to using fonts in Word documents, but here are ten tips to help you with fonts.

1. Know the Standard Rules for Using Fonts   Rules, of course, were made to be broken, but in the interest of serving convention, here are the standard rules for applying fonts in documents:

- Don't overdo it. A document with too many fonts (and too many boldfaced, italicized, and underlined characters) resembles a ransom note and is difficult to read.

- Decorative fonts are fine but sometimes hard to read. Reserve them for headings.

- Sans-serif fonts are used in headings; serif fonts, which are easier on the eyes, are used in the main text. A *serif font* has short, ornamental strokes on the ends of letters. Times New Roman is an example of a serif font. A *sans-serif font* is a plain font in which the characters do not have short ornamental lines (serifs) at the end.

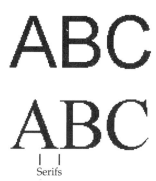

Serifs

2. Use TrueType Fonts   TrueType fonts look the same onscreen as they do when you print them. By using TrueType fonts, you can rest assured that the fonts in your documents will print correctly. TrueType fonts are marked on the Font drop-down menu with the letters *TT*.

3. Create a Character Style for Unusual Font Formats   By creating a character style, you save yourself from having to dig into the Font and Font Size menu whenever you want to format characters a certain way. Instead, all you have to do is choose an option in the Styles menu or Styles and Formatting task pane. See "Creating Your Own Styles" in Chapter 12.

4. Use AutoText to Enter Fancy Format Text   To make an AutoText entry, all you have to do is choose a command from an AutoText menu. Logos, letterheads, and similar items that require a fancy font are ideal candidates for AutoText entries.

5. Choose a Default Font You Really Like   What's your favorite font? Which font do you find easiest to work in? You can make your favorite font and font size the default font, the one that Word uses to begin with when you create a new document based on a particular template. See "Choosing Default Settings for the Normal Template" in Chapter 21.

6. Create a Toolbar or Menu for Your Favorite Fonts   If you do a fair amount of desktop publishing in Word, you need to know that commands and buttons aren't the only items you can place on toolbars and menus. You can also place font names on toolbars and menus. To apply the font, all you have to do is select its button or click its command. See "Customizing the Menus, Toolbars, and Keyboard Shortcuts" in Chapter 21.

7. Substitute for Fonts You Don't Have   If you get a document from someone else and it includes fonts that aren't loaded on your computer or aren't embedded in the document, Word substitutes fonts you don't have for fonts you do have, and in some cases, Word makes a poor substitution. Sometimes, for example, you get Courier New or another plain font where something fancier would do the job better.

To choose for yourself which font to substitute for a font you don't have, choose Tools | Options, select the Compatibility tab in the Options dialog box, and click the Font Substitution button. You see a list of the fonts that are substituted. From the drop-down menu, choose your own set of substitutes.

8. Embed Fonts in Documents You Will Give to Others   Embedding fonts in a document means to save the fonts in the document along with the document itself. By embedding fonts, the fonts that are installed on your computer need not be installed on other computers for the document to be printed correctly. If the document you are passing to your friend includes fancy fonts that are not likely to be on your friend's computer, embed the fonts so your friend can see and print the fonts as well as you can see and print them. Only TrueType fonts can be embedded in a document.

 Embedding TrueType fonts in a document makes it grow in size exponentially. You might have trouble fitting your document on a floppy disk. Sending it over a network or the Internet could take an age.

To embed fonts, choose Tools | Options and select the Save tab in the Options dialog box. Then check the Embed TrueType Fonts check box. The Save tab also offers these check boxes, which are meant to trim the size of a document with embedded fonts:

- **Embed Characters in Use Only**   Saves instructions for printing and displaying specific characters, not whole fonts, when 32 or fewer characters appear in the same font. Normally when you embed a font, Word stores all the information that is needed to display all the characters in the font.

- **Do Not Embed Common System Fonts**   Saves instructions for printing fancy fonts, but not the popular fonts that are found on most people's computers.

9. Install More Fonts on Your Computer   These days, getting new fonts is as easy as falling off a log. Try searching the Internet for fonts—you'll find about a million Web sites that offer them. If the selection of fonts on your computer is on the skimpy side, download a few fonts from the Internet. Then follow these instructions to load a font that you downloaded:

1. Click the Start button and choose Settings | Control Panel.

2. In the Control Panel, double-click the Fonts icon. You see the Fonts window (C:\Windows\Fonts), which lists the fonts that are loaded on your computer. (Want to get a good look at a font? Double-click its name in the Fonts window.)

3. Choose File | Install New Font. The Add Fonts dialog box appears.

4. Under Folders, locate the folder where you are storing the font file you downloaded.

5. In the List of Fonts box, CTRL-click to select the fonts you want to install.

6. Click OK.

10. Remove Fonts You Don't Need from the Font Menu   Scrolling through the Font drop-down menu or Font dialog box to find a font when hundreds of fonts are loaded on your computer can be a drag. If too many fonts are on your Font menu, remove the ones you don't need anymore. To do so, open the C:\Windows\Fonts folder in My Computer or Windows Explorer and move the fonts you no longer need to a different folder (I suggest creating a folder called "My Old Fonts" for that very purpose so you can reinstall the fonts if you need them later). Next time you start your computer and open Word, the names of the fonts you moved to a different folder are no longer on the Font menu.

By the way, you can't move all the fonts out of the C:\Windows\Fonts folder. Windows needs some of them to display menu names, screen names, and the like.

FORMATTING TEXT
AND PAGES

Chapter 8

Aligning and Controlling Text

195

The last chapter looked into the question of how to format text on the page. In this chapter, you lean away from the page a bit and examine the question of how to format paragraphs. You learn how to arrange text on the page by aligning, centering, or justifying it, and how to manage hanging indents and other indentation tricks. This chapter takes on the difficult matter of how to handle tab stops in a document. You also learn how to adjust the space between lines and paragraphs and how to make sure that paragraphs stay on the same page. First, however, a little background....

Everything You Need to Know About Formatting Paragraphs

Before you start giving paragraph-formatting commands, you need to know how Word handles paragraphs, the essential element of a Word document. The following pages explain what Word thinks a paragraph is, which commands pertain to paragraphs, the Golden Rules of paragraph formatting, and how to tell how a paragraph has been formatted.

What Paragraphs Mean to Formatting

Back in English class, your teacher probably told you that a paragraph is a part of a longer composition that presents one idea, or, in the case of dialogue, the words of one speaker. And your teacher was right, too. But in Microsoft Word a paragraph is much less than that. In Word, a paragraph is simply what you put onscreen before you press the ENTER key.

A blank line is considered a paragraph. So are 40 rambling Faulkneresque sentences without a paragraph break. So is a heading.

Knowing what a paragraph is in Word is especially important when you are formatting paragraphs because the formatting commands apply to entire paragraphs, not to words or lines of text. And you can change the formatting of several paragraphs at once by selecting them before you give a paragraph-formatting command.

Giving Commands from the Paragraph Dialog Box and Formatting Toolbar

Apart from pressing shortcut keys, the chief means of formatting paragraphs are the Paragraph dialog box and the Formatting toolbar, both of which are shown in Figure 8-1. The options in the Paragraph dialog box and the buttons on the Formatting toolbar are explained throughout this chapter. Do either of the following to open the Paragraph dialog box:

- Choose Format | Paragraph.
- Right-click and choose Paragraph from the shortcut menu.

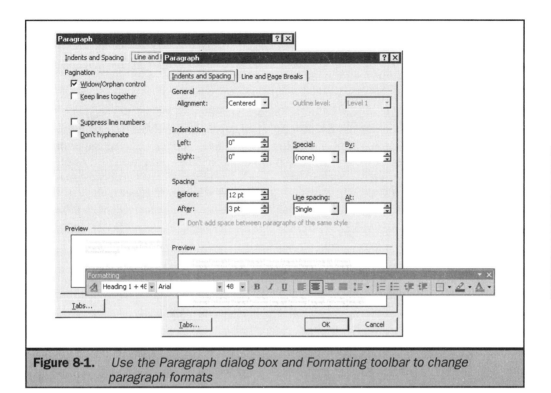

Figure 8-1.   *Use the Paragraph dialog box and Formatting toolbar to change paragraph formats*

In the Paragraph dialog box, you can give many paragraph-formatting commands at once. The dialog box offers commands for aligning text, assigning outline levels to text, indenting text, changing the line spacing, and controlling where text breaks across pages. On the other hand, it's hard to beat the Formatting toolbar for formatting paragraphs. All you have to do is click a button or two and see what happens.

"Changing the Ruler Measurements" in Chapter 1 explains how to change the unit of measurement on the ruler. When you choose a new unit of measurement, you do so as well in most parts of the Paragraph dialog box and other dialog boxes where measurements are entered. If you prefer centimeters, millimeters, points, or picas to inches, choose Tools | Options, click the General tab in the Options dialog box, and choose a new unit of measurement.

The Golden Rules of Paragraph Formatting

Remember these Golden Rules of paragraph formatting:

- When you press the ENTER key, all formats from the paragraph you finished entering are carried to the next paragraph.

■ To change the formatting of a paragraph, all you have to do is click it and give a formatting command. Because paragraph-formatting commands apply to entire paragraphs, you don't have to select an entire paragraph as you do, for example, to change the font of all the letters in a paragraph.

■ To change the formatting of adjacent paragraphs, you can select part of each one instead of all of them at once. In fact, as shown in Figure 8-2, you can simply swipe the pointer over a part of each paragraph to select part of each and then give a paragraph-formatting command. Your command will work on all the paragraphs. In Figure 8-2, the three middle paragraphs—a quotation from a book—have been justified and indented from the left and right margins. If you notice, only part of each paragraph was selected before I changed paragraph formats, yet all three paragraphs have been reformatted in toto. (By the way, you can CTRL-click in the left margin to select disparate paragraphs.)

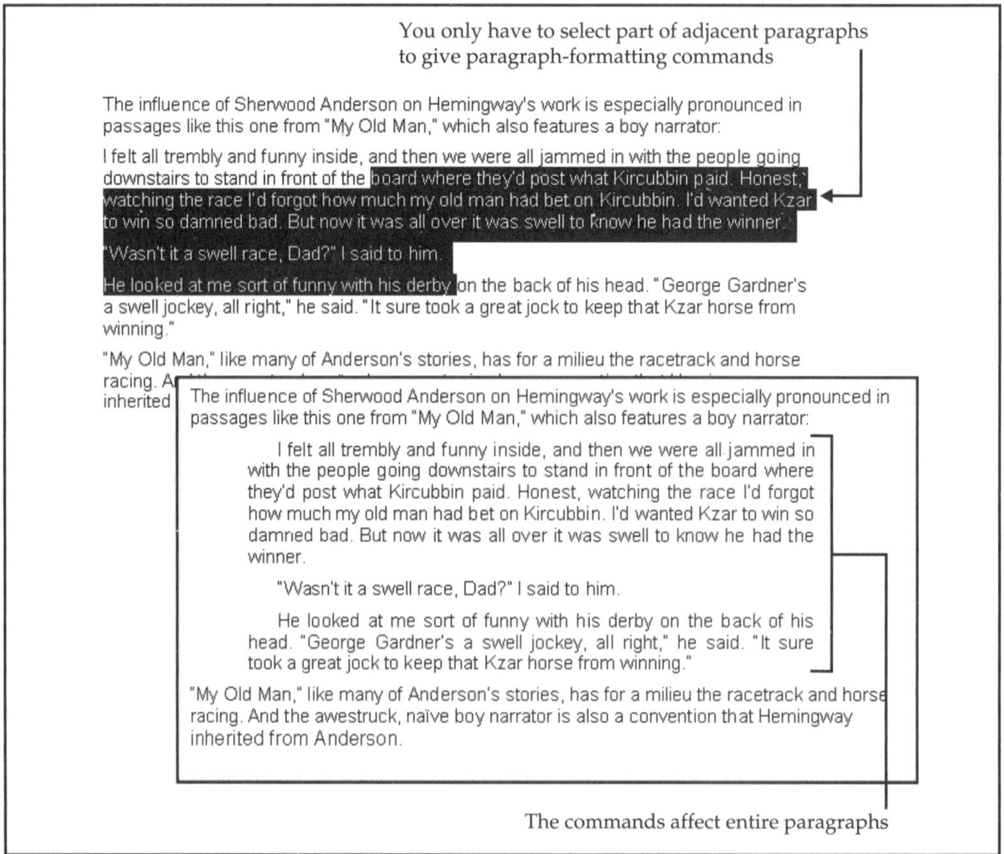

You only have to select part of adjacent paragraphs
to give paragraph-formatting commands

The influence of Sherwood Anderson on Hemingway's work is especially pronounced in passages like this one from "My Old Man," which also features a boy narrator:

I felt all trembly and funny inside, and then we were all jammed in with the people going downstairs to stand in front of the board where they'd post what Kircubbin paid. Honest, watching the race I'd forgot how much my old man had bet on Kircubbin. I'd wanted Kzar to win so damned bad. But now it was all over it was swell to know he had the winner.

"Wasn't it a swell race, Dad?" I said to him.

He looked at me sort of funny with his derby on the back of his head. "George Gardner's a swell jockey, all right," he said. "It sure took a great jock to keep that Kzar horse from winning."

"My Old Man," like many of Anderson's stories, has for a milieu the racetrack and horse racing. A ... inherited

The influence of Sherwood Anderson on Hemingway's work is especially pronounced in passages like this one from "My Old Man," which also features a boy narrator:

I felt all trembly and funny inside, and then we were all jammed in with the people going downstairs to stand in front of the board where they'd post what Kircubbin paid. Honest, watching the race I'd forgot how much my old man had bet on Kircubbin. I'd wanted Kzar to win so damned bad. But now it was all over it was swell to know he had the winner.

"Wasn't it a swell race, Dad?" I said to him.

He looked at me sort of funny with his derby on the back of his head. "George Gardner's a swell jockey, all right," he said. "It sure took a great jock to keep that Kzar horse from winning."

"My Old Man," like many of Anderson's stories, has for a milieu the racetrack and horse racing. And the awestruck, naïve boy narrator is also a convention that Hemingway inherited from Anderson.

The commands affect entire paragraphs

Figure 8-2. *Paragraph-formatting commands affect entire paragraphs, so you only have to click a paragraph or select part of several paragraphs to change their formats*

■ Each paragraph is assigned a set of formatting commands called a *style*. You can tell which style has been assigned to a paragraph by clicking the paragraph and reading the name in the *Style menu*, the leftmost box on the Formatting toolbar, or the Styles and Formatting task pane, where its name appears at the top. The fastest way to change paragraph formats is to assign a new style to a paragraph. Styles are the subject of Chapter 12.

■ If you can't tell where one paragraph ends and the next begins, click the Show/Hide¶ button (or press CTRL-SHIFT-*). Paragraph symbols (¶) appear where you pressed ENTER to end a paragraph. In this illustration, Word thinks I have entered seven paragraphs, when really I have entered the title and chorus of a Cole Porter song:

Anything·Goes¶

¶
In·olden·days·a·glimpse·of·stocking¶
Was·looked·on·as·something·shocking¶
But·now,·God·knows,¶
Anything·goes.¶
¶

  See "Viewing the Hidden Format Symbols" in Chapter 2 to learn what all the hidden format symbols are.

Learning How Paragraphs or Text Was Formatted

Sometimes you have to tell how a paragraph or text was formatted to decide whether it needs reformatting. Click the paragraph in question and look for these clues to see which formats are at work:

■ **Bold, Italic, and Underline Buttons**   Look at these buttons. If one is selected, you know that text is boldfaced, italicized, or underlined.

■ **Alignment**   Look at the Alignment buttons on the Formatting toolbar. Whichever is pressed down—Align Left, Center, Align Right, or Justify— tells you how the paragraph is aligned.

■ **Indent Marks on the Ruler**   The indent marks on the ruler show whether the first line of the paragraph was indented and if the paragraph was indented from the left and right margins. Later in this chapter, "Indenting Text on the Page" explains how to read the indent markers. Choose View | Ruler to see the ruler, if necessary.

■ **Style Menu**   The Style menu tells you which style was assigned to the paragraph.

FORMATTING TEXT AND PAGES

If these clues still don't tell you what you want to know, you can always open the Reveal Formatting task pane and take a look. As Figure 8-3 shows, the task pane tells you very plainly which font is in use, how a paragraph was aligned, and how a section was aligned.

To open the Reveal Formatting task pane, do one of the following:

- Choose Help | What's This? (or press SHIFT-F1) and click the part of your document whose formatting you want to learn about.

- Choose Format | Reveal Formatting and click a part of your document.

With the Reveal Formatting task pane open, you can learn a bit more about your document:

- **Compare One Part of a Document to Another**   Click the Compare to Another Section check box and click the part of your document that needs comparing. The Formatting Differences box tells you how the two parts differ.

- **See Which Style Is in Play**   Click the Distinguish Style Source check box. The task pane lists style assignments as well as the usual stuff.

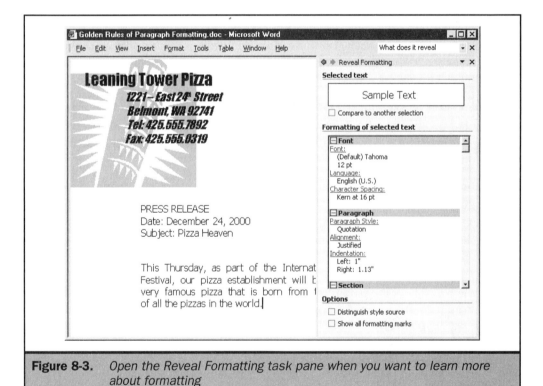

Figure 8-3.   *Open the Reveal Formatting task pane when you want to learn more about formatting*

- **View Formatting Marks**   Click the Show All Formatting Marks check box. Clicking this box is tantamount to clicking the Show/Hide¶ button. You see the hidden format symbols (see "Viewing the Hidden Format Symbols" in Chapter 2).

You can press CTRL-Q or select Clear Formatting in the Styles and Formatting task pane (click the Styles and Formatting button to get there) to strip a paragraph of all formats except the ones that belong to the style that was assigned to the paragraph.

Arranging Text on the Page

Now that you know the details about paragraph formatting, you can get down to work. These pages explain how to align, center, and justify text on the page. You also learn how to indent text from the left and right margins, indent the first line of paragraphs, and create a hanging indent.

Aligning, Centering, and Justifying Text

Figure 8-4 demonstrates the four ways that you can align text on the page. You are invited to try out the different ways of aligning text. By using more than one alignment

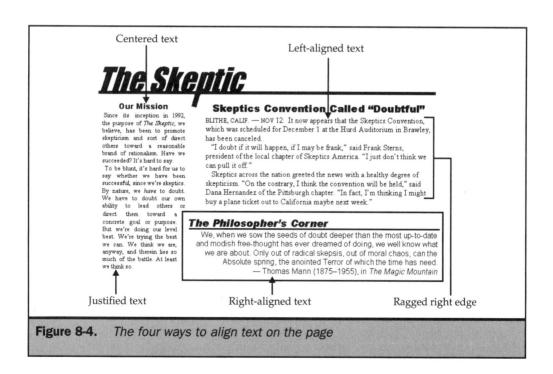

Figure 8-4. *The four ways to align text on the page*

on the same page, you can create interesting effects. To align text, select it if necessary and then do the following:

- **Formatting Toolbar**   Click an Alignment button on the Formatting toolbar: Align Left, Center, Align Right, or Justify.

- **Keyboard Shortcut**   Press a keyboard shortcut: CTRL-L (align left), CTRL-E (center), CTRL-R (align right), or CTRL-J (justify).

- **Paragraph Dialog Box**   Choose Format | Paragraph. In the Paragraph dialog box on the Indents and Spacing tab (refer to Figure 8-1), open the Alignment menu and choose Left, Centered, Right, or Justified.

Notice that two of the four alignment methods produce what typesetters call a *ragged edge*—a paragraph in which words do not line up flush on the left or right side. Ragged text is thought to be easier to read and is why the text in the book you are reading, for example, has a ragged right edge. Justify text in formal documents or when you want to squeeze words into columns. Remember: Left-aligned text with a ragged right edge is considered easiest for reading.

   To justify text, Word has to put extra space between the words on a line. However, you can keep the ugly white spaces to a minimum by hyphenating text that has been justified. See "Handling Hyphens, Dashes, and Other Punctuation" in Chapter 7.

Indenting Text on the Page

By indenting text, you make a paragraph or paragraphs stand out on the page. Figure 8-5 shows the different ways to indent text in a Word document. In the figure, everything outside the gray box is in the margin. As you can see, text is indented with respect to the left and right margins, not the sides of the page. A .5-inch indent, for example, places text 1.5 inches from the edge of the page if the left and right margins are 1 inch wide.

Word offers two ways to indent text—make that three ways. You can drag indent markers on the ruler, choose Format | Paragraph and tinker with the Indentation settings in the Paragraph dialog box (see Figure 8-1), or click the Increase Indent or Decrease Indent button on the Formatting toolbar.

Indenting Text from the Left and Right Margins

To indent text from the left and right margins, choose your weapon:

- **Increase Indent and Decrease Indent Buttons (Left Indent Only)**   Click the Increase Indent button (or press CTRL-M) to indent the paragraph rightward by one tab stop (tab stops are set at half-inch intervals, but you can change tab-stop settings, as "Aligning Text with Tab Stops" explains later in this chapter). Click the button as many times as you want to indent the left side of the paragraph. To move the paragraph toward the left margin and "unindent" it, click the Decrease Indent button (or press CTRL-SHIFT-M).

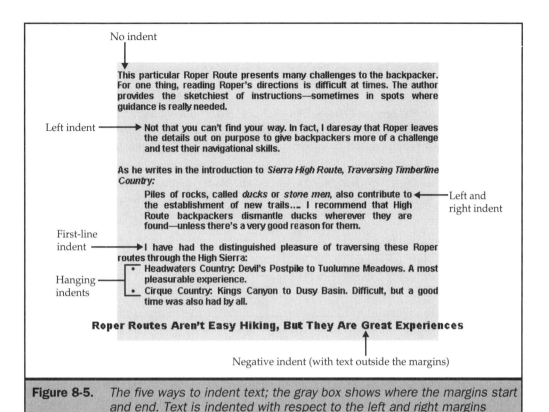

No indent

Left indent

First-line indent

Hanging indents

Left and right indent

Negative indent (with text outside the margins)

Figure 8-5. *The five ways to indent text; the gray box shows where the margins start and end. Text is indented with respect to the left and right margins*

■ **Paragraph Dialog Box**   Choose Format | Paragraph or right-click and choose Paragraph. Under Indentation in the dialog box, enter measurements in the Left and Right boxes. Watch the Preview box to see how far you indent text.

■ **Indent Markers on the Ruler**   Drag the Left Indent and Right Indent markers on the ruler. The gray areas on the ruler show where the left and right margins are. Drag the Indent markers toward the center of the page to indent text. Choose View | Ruler if the ruler isn't displayed onscreen.

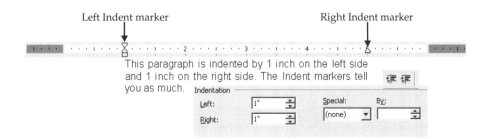

Left Indent marker

Right Indent marker

Indenting the First Line of a Paragraph or Paragraphs

A first-line indent moves the first line of the paragraph away from the left margin and saves you the trouble of pressing the TAB key to indent the first line. To indent the first line of paragraphs:

- **Using the Paragraph Dialog Box**   Choose Format | Paragraph or right-click and choose Paragraph. Under Indentation, open the Special menu and choose First Line. Then enter a measurement in the By box to tell Word how far to indent first lines.

- **Using the First Line Indent Marker on the Ruler**   Drag the First Line Indent marker to the right. You can also click the box on the left side of the ruler as many times as necessary to see the First Line Indent marker, and then click on the ruler where you want the first line to be indented.

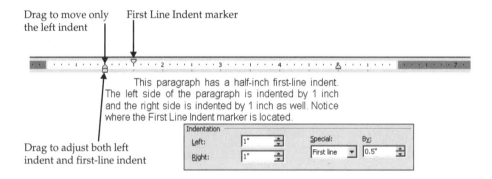

Drag to move only the left indent

First Line Indent marker

This paragraph has a half-inch first-line indent. The left side of the paragraph is indented by 1 inch and the right side is indented by 1 inch as well. Notice where the First Line Indent marker is located.

Drag to adjust both left indent and first-line indent

After you move the First Line Indent marker, changing the left margin becomes slightly problematic. Drag the square at the base of the Left Indent marker to simultaneously adjust both the left margin and the first-line indent. Drag the triangle at the top of the Left Indent marker to adjust the left margin, but leave the first-line indent where it stands.

Creating a Hanging Indent

A *hanging indent* is the opposite of a first-line indent. Instead of the first line being shorter than subsequent lines in the paragraph, the first line is longer because subsequent lines are indented by one tab stop. Because the first line is longer, it appears to jut into the margin, which accounts for the name "hanging indent." A hanging indent is also known as an *outdent*.

Use hanging indents in lists when you want the first word or two in each list item to stand out. Word creates hanging indents for you when you click the Numbering or Bullets button on the Formatting toolbar to create a numbered or bulleted list. Notice where the First Line Indent marker is in this illustration and how the bullets stick out in the list:

- Mary, the lonely country lass who dared to make her dreams come true in the Silicon Valley.
- Tom, "Mr. Ambition" to his friends, who struck out to become a millionaire software developer but who, alas, struck out.
- Jimmy, the tireless programmer, who loved them all and bore a terrible, ill fated secret.

Do the following to create a list in which each item begins with a hanging indent:

1. Enter the text for the list.

2. In each line in the list, press TAB after the part of the list that you want to "stick out." For the list in Figure 8-6, for example, I pressed the TAB key after the names Mary, Tom, and Jimmy. When you create a hanging indent, you indent the second and subsequent lines in paragraphs by one tab stop. By pressing TAB after the part of the list that is to stick out, you indent part of the first line so that it will line up with the second and subsequent lines.

3. Select the list and do either of the following:

   ■ **Paragraph Dialog Box**   Choose Format | Paragraph or right-click and choose Paragraph. Under Indentation, open the Special menu and choose Hanging. Then enter a measurement in the By box to tell Word how far to indent the second and subsequent lines in the paragraph or paragraphs. Be sure to watch the Preview box to make sure the hanging indent is wide enough.

   ■ **Hanging Indent Marker on the Ruler**   Drag the Hanging Indent marker—the triangle directly above the Left Indent marker—toward the right. You

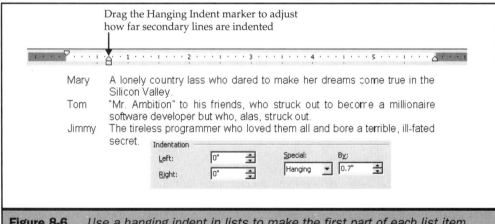

Figure 8-6.   *Use a hanging indent in lists to make the first part of each list item stand out; to adjust the hanging indent, drag the Hanging Indent marker on the ruler*

can also click the box on the left side of the ruler as many times as necessary to see the Hanging Indent marker and then click on the ruler where you want subsequent lines in the paragraph to be indented.

■ **Shortcut Keys** Press CTRL-T to create the hanging indent and then adjust it by dragging the Hanging Indent marker. You can also press CTRL-SHIFT-T to move the secondary lines to the previous tab stop.

A layout like the one in Figure 8-6 is far easier to achieve by creating a table than by creating hanging indents. (Chapter 14 explains tables.) What's more, if you want to adjust how far bulleted and numbered lists are indented, don't fool with the hanging indent commands. Word offers special dialog boxes for adjusting bulleted and numbered lists. See "Adjusting How Far Bullets and Numbers Are Indented" in Chapter 10.

Negative Indents for Making Headlines Fit on One Line

One way to make headings fit on one line, or make them really stand out, is to create a negative indent (also called an *outdent*) and allow the heading to trespass on the left and right margins. However, if you find yourself fooling with negative indents throughout a document, chances are you need to make the margins narrower. Follow these steps to create a negative indent:

■ **Paragraph Dialog Box** Choose Format | Paragraph or right-click and choose Paragraph. Under Indentation, enter a negative number in the Left and Right boxes. The numbers indicate how far to let text drift into the left and right margins.

■ **Hanging Indent Marker on the Ruler** Drag the Left Indent marker and Right Indent marker into the gray areas of the ruler. The gray areas show where the margins are. Notice where the Left Indent and Right Indent markers are in this illustration.

Read these and other tales of Silicon Valley romance from the HEARTSICK PRESS!

"Making Headings Fit Across Pages and Columns" in Chapter 7 explains another way to make headings fit on one line—shrinking them.

Choosing an Outline Level for Paragraphs

As shown in Figure 8-7, which outline level has been assigned to a paragraph matters in Outline view, in the Document Map, and in tables of contents. Word offers nine levels as well as Body Text, the lowest level on the totem pole. Headings are given outline level assignments automatically, the idea being that everyone wants to see headings in the Document Map, Outline view, and tables of contents. A heading assigned the Heading 1 style from the Style menu, for example, is assigned outline level 1. What about captions, sidebar titles, table headings, and other unusual elements? Do you want to see them in the Document Map, Outline view, and tables of contents?

Note

Outline levels are primarily for use with styles. When you create a new style, be sure to assign it an outline level so that Word knows how to handle it in Outline view, in the Document Map, and in tables of contents. Chapter 12 explains how to create styles and also how to modify styles in case you want to give a style a different outline level.

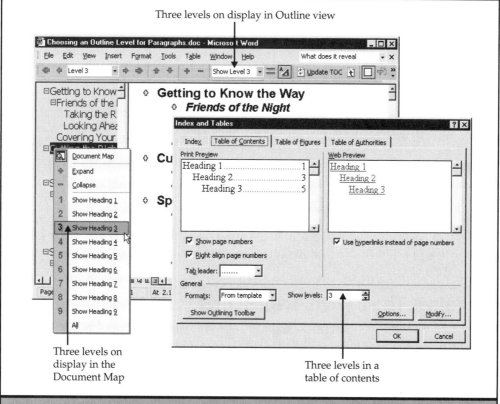

Figure 8-7. *Whether or how a paragraph appears in the Document Map, Outline view, and tables of contents depends on which outline level you assign it*

FORMATTING TEXT AND PAGES

Follow these steps to assign an outline level to a paragraph or paragraph style:

1. With the cursor in the paragraph whose outline level needs assigning, choose Format | Paragraph or right-click and choose Paragraph from the shortcut menu. You see the Paragraph dialog box (see Figure 8-1).

2. Open the Outline Level menu and choose an option.

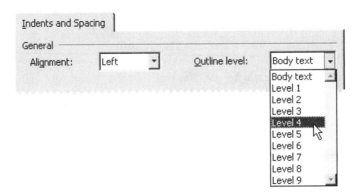

By choosing an outline level from the Outline Level menu in the Paragraph dialog box, you can tell Word whether or how to make a paragraph appear in Outline view, the Document Map, and tables of contents:

- **Outline View**   Choose an option from the Show Level drop-down menu to display or not display text to which you've assigned outline levels 1 through 9. See "Organizing Your Work with Outlines" in Chapter 17.

- **Document Map**   Right-click the Document Map and choose a Show Heading option to tell Word which outline levels to display. See "Using the Document Map to Get Around" in Chapter 2.

- **Tables of Contents**   Open the Index and Tables dialog box and enter a number in the Show Levels text box to tell Word which outline levels to include in the table of contents. See "Generating a Table of Contents" in Chapter 16.

Aligning Text with Tab Stops

A *tab stop* is a position on the page against or around which text is aligned. In a new document, tab stops are set at half-inch intervals and are left-aligned. However, Word offers five different kinds of tab stops and four tab-stop alignments. Use the tabs to align text in different ways—or else skip tab stops and use the Table commands instead. These pages explain why Table commands are usually superior to tab stops, the different kinds of tab stops, how to set tabs with the ruler and the Tabs dialog box, and how to create a leader with options in the Tabs dialog box.

Why You Should Use the Table Commands Instead of Tabs

Tab stops are a means of aligning text on the page, but not *the* means. Before you know anything about tab stops, you should know that aligning text in table columns is far, far easier than aligning text with tab stops. Tabs are really a throwback to the days of the typewriter when you needed tabs to align text. You don't need tab stops anymore. The only reason to use them is to align numbers along a decimal point or to enter a leader.

To see why Table commands are superior to tab stops, look at this illustration. The top half shows text aligned with tab stops; the bottom shows the same text in a table. When these documents are printed, they will look exactly alike (the gridlines in the table are for formatting purposes only and do not appear when tables are printed). The difference between the two is that it took me, the Word expert, five minutes to enter and align the data with tab stops; it took me only a minute to create the table and enter the data in it.

Moreover, if I need to edit the data or realign it, I can do so far more easily in the table:

- To add another column of figures to the tabbed data, I have to drag three different tab stops on the ruler, press the TAB key several times to make room for another column, pray that everything lines up correctly, and enter the numbers. In the table all I have to do is choose an Insert Column command and start entering numbers.

- To indent the tabbed data, I drag three tab stops sideways on the ruler and hope for the best. In the table, I choose Table | Properties and give an indent command. I can indent the table from the left margin or right margin, or I can center the table on the page. I can even wrap text around the table.

FORMATTING TEXT AND PAGES

■ To change the alignment of the tabbed data, I have to remove one tab stop on the ruler and very carefully enter another in its place. In the table, I simply click an alignment button. Moreover, the Tables and Borders toolbar offers nine ways to align data, not three.

Chapter 14 is devoted to the subject of tables. If you came to this chapter because you want to align data on the page, I strongly suggest turning to Chapter 14 before going any further.

The Five Kinds of Tab Stops

Figure 8-8 shows the five kinds of tab stops. They work similarly to the Align buttons on the Formatting toolbar, except for the Decimal tab, which aligns text along a decimal point or period, and the Bar tab, which draws a line down the page. Use the Bar tab to distinguish one set of figures from another, as was done on the right side of Figure 8-8, where someone's bar tab has been recorded. You can tell which tab stops are in effect by glancing at the tab stop markers on the ruler. Notice the six tab stop markers in Figure 8-8.

By default, tab stops are left-aligned and are set at half-inch intervals. Until or if you change the tab settings, pressing the TAB key moves the cursor by a half-inch to the next tab stop—a left-aligned tab stop.

Sometimes it is hard to tell where the TAB *key was pressed and text was moved to the next tab stop. To find out, click the Shows/Hide¶ button (or press* CTRL-*) *to see the format symbols. "Viewing the Hidden Format Symbols" in Chapter 2 explains what all the symbols are.*

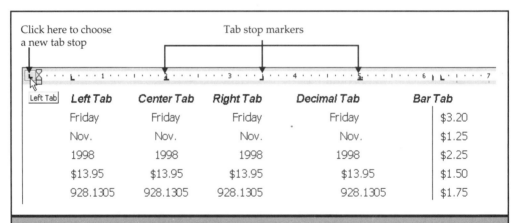

Figure 8-8.   *The five kinds of tab stops. You can tell which tab stops are in effect by looking on the ruler*

Changing the Tab Settings

Continuing a theme that has been developing throughout this chapter, you can change tab settings in two different ways: using a dialog box or the ruler. Choose View | Ruler if the ruler doesn't appear onscreen and you want to use it to change tab settings. As for the Tabs dialog box, using it to change tab settings is kind of difficult, being as you can't see on the page where you are creating your tab stops. But you can use the dialog box to draw leaders between tab stops.

  Tab settings belong to the paragraphs in which they are found. When you press ENTER and start typing a new paragraph, you carry tab settings from one paragraph to the next. Before you change tab settings, make sure the cursor is in the right paragraph—the one for which you want to change the settings. Make sure as well that you have selected the paragraphs whose tab settings you want to change if you want to change settings in several paragraphs.

Changing Tab Settings with the Ruler

Follow these instructions to change the tab settings with the ruler:

1. Click the box on the left side of the ruler as many times as necessary to see the symbol of the kind of tab stop you want (the last two symbols you encounter are for first-line indents and hanging indents).

2. Click on the ruler where you want the tab stop to be. The symbol on the ruler tells you which kind of tab stop you created.

You can put as many tab stops on the ruler as you want this way. When you place a new tab stop on the ruler, all default tab stops to the left of the one you created are removed. You can tell where default tab stops are by leaning into the computer monitor, squinting, and looking for the tiny gray lines on the ruler's bottom stripe. On this ruler, a left tab stop is located at the 1-inch mark, and a right tab stop is located at the 3-inch mark. The default, left-aligned tab stops located to the right of the 3-inch tab stop are still intact.

Changing Tab Settings with the Tabs Dialog Box

Follow these steps to change tab settings with the Tabs dialog box:

1. Choose Format | Tabs (you can also click the Tabs button in the Paragraph dialog box). You see the Tabs dialog box shown in Figure 8-9.

2. Enter a position for the first new tab stop in the Tab Stop Position box.

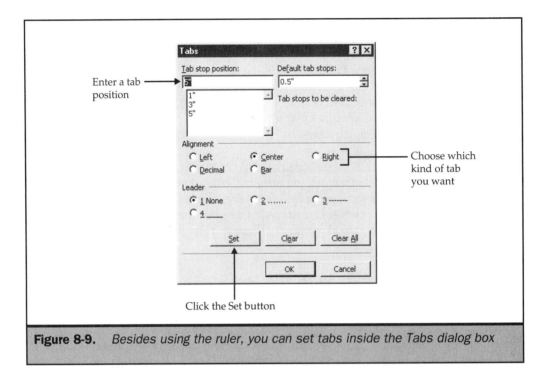

Figure 8-9.   *Besides using the ruler, you can set tabs inside the Tabs dialog box*

3. Choose an Alignment option to declare what kind of tab you want.

4. Click the Set button.

5. Repeat steps 2–4 to create other tab stops and click OK.

To remove a tab stop, select it in the Tab Stop Position list and click the Clear button. Click the Clear All button to remove all the tab stops if you get tangled up and need to start over.

Adjusting and Removing Tab Stops

Before you adjust or remove a tab stop, carefully select the paragraph or paragraphs whose tab settings you want to change, and then glance at the ruler. Do you see black tab symbols or gray tab symbols on the ruler? If you see gray symbols, you have selected paragraphs whose tab settings are different, and the adjustments you make are likely to have unexpected consequences, because you are working on two sets of tab settings at once. Before you adjust or remove tab stops, make sure you are working with one set of tab settings and that the tab symbols on the ruler are black.

Follow these instructions to adjust or remove tab stops:

■ **Adjusting Tab Stop Positions**   On the ruler, drag the tab marker left or right. Text that is aligned to the tab stop moves as well. In the Tabs dialog box (see Figure 8-9), delete the tab stop by selecting it and clicking the Clear button, and then enter a new tab stop position.

■ **Removing Tab Stops** Drag the tab marker off the ruler. In the Tabs dialog box, select the tab stop and click the Clear button. When you remove a tab stop, text that is aligned to that tab stop is aligned to the next tab stop on the ruler instead.

Using Tab Stops to Create a Leader

A *leader* is a series of identical characters, usually periods, that lead the reader's eye from one place on the page to another. In tables of contents, leaders are often used to connect table of contents entries to the page numbers they refer to. ("Generating a Table of Contents" in Chapter 16 explains how you can fashion a table of contents, with leaders, from headings in a document.) Leaders look very elegant and are the best reason to fool with tab settings. In this illustration, dashed-line, underline, and period leaders are used in playbills so you can see which actor plays which role in Tennessee Williams's *A Streetcar Named Desire*:

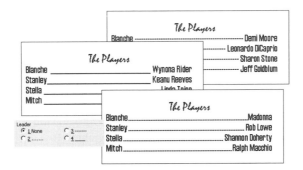

To create a leader, follow these steps:

1. Choose Format | Tabs to open the Tabs dialog box (see Figure 8-9).

2. Enter the first tab position by entering a measurement in the Tab Stop Position box, clicking an Alignment option button, and clicking the Set button. The first tab position determines how far the items on the left side of the list (the role names in the previous illustration) are indented from the left margin.

3. Enter the second tab position, but this time click an option button under Leader before you click the Set button. The choices are periods, dashes, or underlines (the None option is for removing leaders). Leaders appear between tab stops. When you set leader tabs, attach the leader to the second tab stop—the one on the right side of the periods, dashes, or underlines.

4. Click OK to close the Tabs dialog box.

5. Enter the text. When you press the TAB key after entering the text at the first tab stop, the periods, dashes, or underlines appear.

To adjust the position of text on the sides of the leader, select the text and drag tab markers on the ruler. Choose View | Ruler to display the ruler.

Click and Type to Make Formatting Easier (Sort Of)

Word offers a special feature called *click and type* that is supposed to help you format text, graphics, and tables quickly. Click and type is one of those "I'll do the thinking for you" features. To see how it works, open a blank document, switch to Print Layout view, and move the pointer around the screen. As you do so, notice how alignment symbols appears to the side of the pointer. If you double-click and start typing when the Align Right symbol appears, for example, your text is right-aligned. Double-click in the middle of a blank page and you can type a centered title whether you want one or not.

Double-click and start typing in a blank area of a document to use click and type. Like most of Word 's features that do the thinking for you, click and type is more trouble than it is worth (at least in my opinion). However, you are invited to keep your eyes peeled for symbols beside the pointer and double-click when you see a format symbol to use the click and type feature.

 If you don't see formatting symbols on the side of the cursor when you move it to a blank area of a document, either you are not in Print Layout view, you are not in Web Layout view, or click and type has not been activated. To activate the feature, choose Tools | Options, select the Edit tab in the Options dialog box, and check the Enable Click and Type check box.

Adjusting the Space Between Lines and Paragraphs

This section has to do with space—not outer space, but the amount of space between lines of text and between different paragraphs. No longer do you have to tremble for fear that a professor or supervisor will tell you to double-space it or single-space it. Changing the amount of space between lines is simply a matter of clicking the Line Spacing button or choosing options in the Paragraph dialog box. Adjusting the amount of space between paragraphs is also easy, but the task isn't one to undertake lightly, either.

Adjusting the Space Between Lines

Unless you tell Word to measure the distance between lines in points, the amount of space between lines is measured in lines. In a single-spaced paragraph in which a 12-point font is used, for example, lines are slightly more than 12 points apart. Word throws in a bit of extra space to keep the low-slung letters, called *descenders*, on one line ("y" and "g", for example) from touching high-and-mighty letters, called *ascenders*, on the following line ("h" and "k"). In a double-spaced paragraph in which a 12-point font is used, lines are exactly 24 points, or two lines, apart.

However, when Word encounters a tall character, superscripted character, subscripted character, handful of words in a larger font, or formula that is too tall to fit between lines, the program automatically puts more space between lines to accommodate the tall characters. It does that unless you change the line-spacing settings and tell Word to place a specific amount of space between lines with the Exactly option in the Paragraph dialog box.

If you're in a hurry to change the amount of space between lines, try one of these shortcuts: press CTRL-1 *for single-spacing,* CTRL-5 *for 1.5-line spacing, or* CTRL-2 *for double-spacing.*

Now that you know how Word spaces lines, you can go about doing it. Start either by clicking in a single paragraph or selecting part of several paragraphs whose line spacing you want to change. Then change line spacing with the Line Spacing button or Paragraph dialog box:

- **Line Spacing button** Click the Line Spacing button on the Formatting toolbar or open its drop-down menu and choose a line multiple.

- **Paragraph dialog box** To open the dialog box, choose Format | Paragraph, right-click, and choose Paragraph on the shortcut menu, or open the drop-down menu on the Line Spacing button and choose More. Then open the Line Spacing menu and make one of the choices described in Table 8-1. Keep your eye on the Preview box to see what your choices mean in real terms.

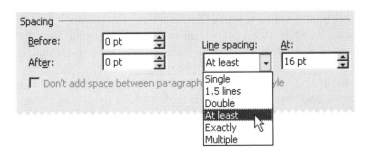

Option	Places This Much Space Between Lines
Single-spacing	The amount of space in the font plus a bit more to accommodate ascending and descending letters. Word increases the amount of space to accommodate tall characters.
1.5-spacing	One-and-a-half times the font size. Spacing is increased to accommodate tall characters.
Double-spacing	Two times the font size, with spacing increased to accommodate tall characters.
At Least	The amount of space, in points, that you enter in the At box. Line spacing is increased to accommodate tall characters.
Exactly	The amount of space, in points, that you enter in the At box. Space between lines is *not* increased to accommodate tall characters with this option. Characters taller than the Exactly amount get their heads chopped off.
Multiple	Three, four, or another multiple of the font size. Enter the multiple in the At box. For example, entering **3** when a 12-point font is in use places 36 points between lines. However, Word increases the line spacing to accommodate tall characters.

Table 8-1.   *Line-Spacing Options in the Paragraph Dialog Box*

Besides single-, 1.5-, and double-spacing, you can place other line multiples between lines of type. For example, choose Multiple and enter **1.75** *in the At box to place one and three-quarters lines between lines of type.*

Adjusting the Space Between Paragraphs

Rather than press ENTER to put a blank line between paragraphs, you can open the Paragraph dialog box and enter a point-size measurement in the Before or After text box. The Before and After options, adjuncts to the line-spacing commands, place a specific amount of space before and after paragraphs.

Truth be told, the Before and After options are for use with styles (a subject of Chapter 12). When you create a style, you can tell Word to always follow a paragraph in a certain style with a paragraph in another style. For example, a paragraph in the

Chapter Title style might always be followed by a paragraph in the Chapter Intro style. In cases like those when you know that paragraphs assigned to one type of style will always follow paragraphs assigned to another style, you can confidently put space before and after paragraphs. But if you use the Before and After styles indiscriminately, you can end up with large blank spaces between paragraphs. Suppose you call for one paragraph to be followed by 12 points of empty space and the next paragraph to be preceded by 12 points of empty space. You end up with 24 points of empty space—a gaping hole—between paragraphs.

Tip   *Word ignores space tacked to the top of a paragraph with the Before option if the paragraph falls at the top of a page. However, if the paragraph is the first in a document, is the first in a section, or follows a hard page break, the Before space is acknowledged and it appears above the paragraph. Press* CTRL-0 *(zero) to remove (or add) a line's worth of space before a paragraph.*

Follow these steps to make a specific amount of space precede or follow a paragraph or paragraphs assigned to a style:

1. Select the paragraphs that need changing.

2. Choose Format | Paragraph or right-click and choose Paragraph from the shortcut menu. The Paragraph dialog box appears.

3. Under Spacing, make an entry in the Before box to tell Word how many points of empty space to put before the paragraph.

4. Make an entry in the After box to tell Word how much empty space to put below the paragraph, and click OK. Be sure to watch the Preview box, since it shows better than anything what your choices do to the space before and after paragraphs.

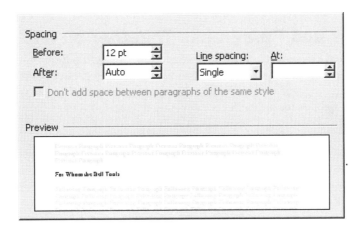

FORMATTING TEXT AND PAGES

Tip *Click the down arrow once in the Before or After text box to choose the Auto option. The Auto option enters one blank line between paragraphs in whatever the line-spacing choice happens to be. For example, if the Line Spacing menu calls for double-spacing between paragraphs and you choose Auto in the After box, two blank lines appear after the paragraph.*

Controlling Where Text Falls on the Page

The Line and Page Breaks tab in the Paragraph dialog box offers commands for controlling where text falls on the page. These commands are useful for making sure that lines of text and paragraphs that should be on the same page stay on the same page. A bulleted or numbered list with only three items, for example, is easier to read when all three items are on the same page. A heading that stands by itself at the bottom of a page without any text below it is an embarrassment that should be avoided.

Follow these steps to go to the Line and Page Breaks tab of the Paragraph dialog box and give commands for controlling where text falls on the page:

1. Choose Format | Paragraph or right-click and choose Paragraph from the shortcut menu.
2. Select the Line and Page Breaks tab in the Paragraph dialog box.

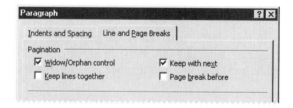

Keeping Lines and Paragraphs Together on a Page

As you know, text creeps up and down pages when you edit a document. Enter a new paragraph at the start of a document and all the text below gets pushed into a new position. Snip a paragraph out of the middle of page 1 and text on subsequent pages creeps upward. One of the side effects of editing is that sometimes page breaks occur in awkward places after text is added to or removed from a document. The shaded paragraph that looked fine when you entered it in the middle of a page gets broken across two pages. A figure gets separated from its caption, so that the figure is on the bottom of one page and the caption is on the top of the next.

To make sure paragraphs and lines stay on the same page, you can use the Keep With Next and Keep Lines Together commands in the Paragraph dialog box:

- **Keep With Next**   Makes sure a paragraph and at least the first line of the paragraph below it appear on the same page. This command is especially valuable for headings, since a heading should not appear by itself at the bottom of a page but should be followed by at least one line of text.

  To keep a page break from occurring between two paragraphs, click the topmost paragraph of the two you want to keep together, choose Format | Paragraph, select the Line and Page Breaks tab, and check the Keep With Next check box.

- **Keep Lines Together**   Tells Word not to break a paragraph (or more than one paragraph if you select more than one) across two pages. Use this command to keep short lists and announcements on the same page.

  To keep a page break from interfering with one or more paragraphs, click the paragraph or select all of them if you are dealing with more than one, choose Format | Paragraph, select the Line and Page Breaks tab, and check the Keep Lines Together check box.

When you choose the Keep Lines Together command, Word usually has to push the entire paragraph or all the paragraphs to the top of the next page to keep text together. Consequently, a huge blank space can appear at the bottom of the page from which the paragraph or paragraphs were pushed. Before choosing the Keep Lines Together command, see whether using a text box might do the job better. Text boxes are not broken across pages. They can be locked to one place on the page. And you can make text flow around the sides of a text box. See "Putting a Text Box on the Page" in Chapter 13.

Making Sure Text Appears at the Top of a Page

Certain kinds of paragraphs beg to appear at the top of pages. A chapter title, for example, belongs at the top of a page. So might a figure or a table. Follow these steps to make sure a paragraph appears at the top of a page:

1. Click the paragraph.
2. Choose Format | Paragraph or right-click and choose Paragraph.
3. Select the Line and Page Breaks tab in the Paragraph dialog box.
4. Check the Page Break Before check box and click OK.

Be careful about using the Page Break Before command. Word usually has to end one page in the middle in order to make a paragraph appear at the top of the next page, so the command has a habit of introducing half-empty pages in documents.

If you came here to learn how to make chapter titles appear on the top of pages, be sure to investigate section breaks before you go any further. As "Section Breaks for Changing Layouts" in Chapter 9 explains, you can also begin a chapter on a new page by introducing a section break.

Preventing Widows and Orphans

The Widow/Orphan Control check box in the Paragraph dialog box is checked for you. Don't uncheck it except under unusual circumstances (keep reading to see what those circumstances are). The command prevents what typesetters call *widows* and *orphans* from appearing in documents:

■ **Widow**   A single line, the last in a paragraph, which appears by itself at the top of a page. Especially on a page where empty space appears between paragraphs, a widow sticks out like a sore thumb. To prevent widows, Word automatically places at least two lines of a paragraph at the top of the page when a paragraph breaks across pages.

■ **Orphan**   A single line, the first in a paragraph, that appears by itself at the bottom of a page. Orphans are also considered eyesores. Not only that, they are thought to cheat readers, since the reader doesn't know that a single line on the bottom of a page isn't a paragraph unto itself until he or she turns the page and finds the rest of the paragraph missing. To prevent orphans, Word puts the first two lines of paragraphs at the bottom of the page when paragraphs break across two pages.

And suppose a paragraph is only three lines long? How does Word prevent a widow or orphan from occurring, seeing that the program can't place two lines at the bottom of one page and two lines at the top of the next? In a three-line paragraph, all three lines are moved to the top of the next page—and therein lies the only reason why you would uncheck the Widow/Orphan Control check box.

If you are using a very large font and your paragraph is three-lines long, moving all three lines to the next page to prevent a widow or orphan from occurring creates a big empty space at the bottom of the first page. Uncheck the Widow/Orphan Control box to prevent the empty space from occurring. With large fonts, a widow or orphan isn't an eyesore, since the letters take up so much space at the top or bottom of the page.

The Format Painter for Quickly Changing Formats

I've reserved the Format Painter for the last topic in this chapter because, frankly, I don't think it's worth using. Unless you are in a hurry to reformat paragraphs and text or you want to do a superficial job of it, don't use the Format Painter. Change paragraph styles instead. Or find and replace formats.

To use the Format Painter, start by clicking a place in your document whose paragraph and text formats you want to copy elsewhere, and then double-click the Format Painter button on the Standard toolbar (or press CTRL-SHIFT-C). The pointer changes into a paintbrush. Next, drag the pointer across each part of your document to which you want to copy the formats. When you're finished copying, click the Format Painter button.

MOUS Exam Objectives Explored in Chapter 8

FORMATTING TEXT AND PAGES

Objective	Heading
Modify format, alignment, and layout of paragraphs	"Everything You Need to Know About Formatting Paragraphs," "Aligning, Centering, and Justifying Text," and "Indenting Text on the Page"
Set and modify tabs	"Aligning Text with Tab Stops"
Modify text flow options*	"Preventing Widows and Orphans"
Create and format document sections*	"Learning How Paragraphs or Text Was Formatted"

Denotes an Expert, not a Core, exam objective.

Ten Ways to Format Paragraphs Faster

Formatting paragraphs does not rank high on the list of fun things to do. To make the irksome task go faster, here are ten tidbits of advice to help you along.

1. Use Styles to Format Paragraphs   A style is a bunch of different paragraph-formatting commands that have been bundled under one name. To keep from having to choose numerous formatting commands, you can simply construct a new style with the formatting commands you want and choose the style from the Style menu to apply the formats. That's all there is to it. Chapter 12 explains styles.

2. Learn the Ways to Select Text   Being able to select text quickly and in a variety of ways helps a lot when you are formatting text. "Selecting Blocks of Text" in Chapter 3 explains the numerous ways to select text. Experiment with a half-dozen text-selection techniques, find the four or five you like best, and make them part of your repertoire as you format paragraphs.

3. Understand What Paragraphs Are in Word   "What Paragraphs Mean to Formatting" near the start of this chapter explains what Word thinks a paragraph is. To Word, a paragraph is simply what appears onscreen before you press the ENTER key. A heading, a blank line, as well as what is normally considered a paragraph are all paragraphs in Word. Make sure you understand what paragraphs are before you start formatting paragraphs.

4. Use the Find-and-Replace Command to Replace Formats   Did you know that you can replace paragraph formats with the Edit | Replace command? Follow these steps to do so:

1. Click the Save button (or press CTRL-S) to save your document.

 Always save your document before a find-and-replace operation. That way, if finding and replacing turns your document into guacamole, you can close the document without saving the changes you made to it, reopen the document, and get the original back.

2. Choose Edit | Replace (or press CTRL-H). You see the Replace tab of the Find and Replace dialog box.

3. Click the More button to see all of the find-and-replace options.

4. Click the Format button and choose Paragraph from the pop-up menu. You see the Find Paragraph dialog box. Not coincidentally, it looks like and offers the same options as the Paragraph dialog box.

5. By choosing options in the Find Paragraph dialog box, describe the paragraph formats that need replacing; then click OK. Back in the Find and Replace dialog box, a description of the paragraph formats you want to replace appears under the Find What box.

6. Click in the Replace With box.

7. Click the Format button and choose Paragraph from the pop-up menu. You see the now familiar Replace Paragraph dialog box.

8. Carefully enter the paragraph formats that you want to replace the formats you entered in the Find Paragraph dialog box; then click OK.

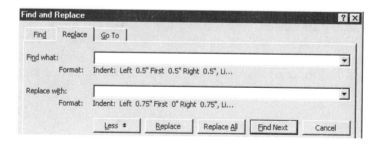

9. Click the Find Next button. If Word finds a paragraph whose paragraph formatting matches the description under the Find What box, the paragraph is highlighted onscreen.

10. Click the Replace button to change the paragraph's formats. Word scrolls to the next paragraph that matches your description.

11. Click the Replace button again, or else click the Replace All button to change paragraph formats throughout your document without reviewing them one at a time.

Next time you choose Edit | Find or Edit | Replace, the Find and Replace dialog box will list the formats you entered. To look for plain text instead of formats, click the No Formatting button. "Finding and Replacing Text and Other Things" in Chapter 6 explains everything a mortal would care to know about the Edit | Replace command.

5. Learn All the Ways to Get from Place to Place Quickly   When you are formatting documents, you need to know how to get from place to place quickly. When you are doing anything whatsoever in Word, you need to know how to get there fast. See "Moving Around in Long Documents" in Chapter 2.

6. Use the Repeat Command When You Format Paragraphs   The Repeat command comes in especially handy when you are formatting paragraphs. After you format one paragraph in the Paragraph dialog box, all you have to do is click another and press F4 or choose Edit | Repeat Paragraph Formatting to format another paragraph the same way. The Repeat command repeats the last command you gave, whatever it happened to be.

7. Know the Remove Format Shortcut   Word offers a special keyboard shortcut— CTRL-Q—for stripping a paragraph of all formats except the ones that belong to the style that was assigned to the paragraph. On occasion, the average Word user goes overboard with paragraph formats and wants to return to the original, bare-bones paragraph formatting. On those occasions, press CTRL-Q or select Clear Formatting in the Styles and Formatting task pane (click the Styles and Formatting button to get there).

8. Learn How to Create Numbered and Bulleted Lists Automatically   Earlier in this chapter, "Indenting Text on the Page" explained how to create a hanging indent, a paragraph whose first line appears to hang into the left margin. Word creates hanging indents automatically when you click the Numbering or Bullets button on the Formatting toolbar. Chapter 10 explains how to create numbered and bulleted lists.

9. Use Tables Instead of Tabs   As "Why You Should Use the Table Commands Instead of Tabs " pointed out so vehemently earlier in this chapter, aligning text with tab stops is a monumental waste of time when the task can be done so much faster with commands on the Table menu. Tabs are really a holdover from the typewriter. Except for creating leaders, you are wasting your time by using the Format | Tabs command.

10. Apply One Format to Another in the Reveal Formatting Pane   Follow these steps to change formats in many different places at once:

1. Select the text whose formats you want to apply elsewhere.

2. Choose Format | Reveal Formatting to open the Reveal Formatting task pane.

3. Click the Compare to Another Selection check box.

4. Select the text that you want to reformat.

5. In the task pane, open the drop-down list in the second box under Selected Text and choose the Apply Formatting of Original Selection.

The Complete Reference

Word 2002

Chapter 9

Framing and Laying Out the Pages

The last chapter looked at how to lay out text on the page, and the one before that took on the subject of formatting text. In this chapter, you discover how to format pages. A well-laid-out page says a lot about how much time and thought was put into a document. This chapter presents tips, tricks, and techniques for making pages look just right.

In this chapter, you learn how to change the size of page margins, and, just as importantly, when to change the margins. This chapter describes what section breaks are and when to introduce a section break, how to create headers and footers for all occasions, and how to number pages. You learn how to change the orientation of pages, print on paper of various sizes, decorate a page with a border, and align text on the page with respect to the top and bottom of the page. At the end of this chapter is a list of ten tasks to complete right away when you start a complex document.

Setting the Margins

Margins are the empty spaces that appear along the sides of the page. Figure 9-1 shows where the left, right, top, and bottom margins are. Notice the header and footer in Figure 9-1. Headers and footers fall, respectively, in the top and bottom margins. And you can put graphics, text boxes, and page numbers in the margins as well. Margins serve to frame the text and make it easier to read.

Caution   *If you came here to indent text, you came to the wrong place. See "Indenting Text on the Page" in Chapter 8. Text is indented from the margins. Don't change margin settings to indent text.*

When you start a new document, give a moment's thought to the margins. Changing the size of margins after you have entered the text, clip art, graphics, and whatnot can be disastrous. Text is indented from the left and right margins. Pages break on the bottom margin. If you change margin settings, indents and page breaks change for good or bad throughout your document. By setting the margins carefully from the beginning, you can rest assured that text will land on the page where you want it to land.

Word offers two ways to change the size of margins. Besides explaining the two ways, these pages explain how to create mirror margins for double-sided pages, adjust margins to make room for binding, and change the default margins that are in effect when you create a new document by clicking the New button or pressing CTRL-N.

Note   *"Creating a Side Heading or Margin Note" in Chapter 15 explains how you can create a side heading or put artwork in the margins of a document.*

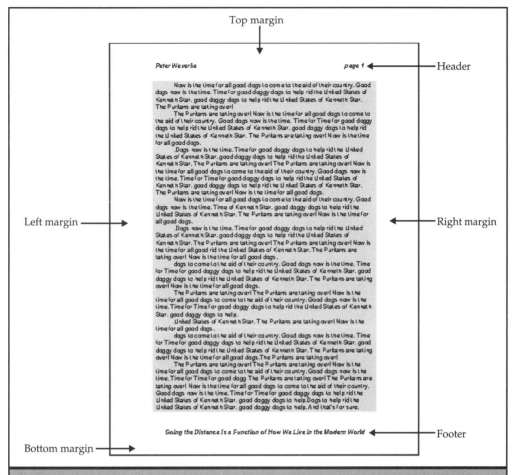

FORMATTING TEXT
AND PAGES

Figure 9-1.   *One of your first tasks when you open a new document is to decide on the size of the margins*

Getting a Better Look at Page Layouts

When you are laying out a page, knowing where the margins are can help immensely, especially when you are dealing with graphics, text boxes, autoshapes, and other unwieldy objects. To help you lay out pages, Word offers a command called Text Boundaries. After you choose the command, dotted lines appear around page margins, columns, clip art images, and other objects so you can see precisely where they are. The dotted lines appear, I should say, when you are in Print Layout view or Web Layout view. To test-drive the Text Boundaries command, choose Tools | Options, select the View tab in the Options dialog box, and check the Text Boundaries check box.

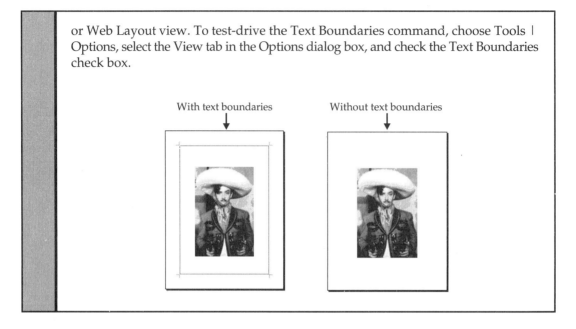

With text boundaries   Without text boundaries

The Two Ways to Change Margin Sizes

Change the size of margins either by going to the Page Setup dialog box or by dragging the margin markers on the rulers. The Page Setup dialog box offers many more options for changing margin sizes. Only use the margin markers on the rulers to make last-minute adjustments to one-page documents such as announcements and invitations.

In order to change margin settings in the middle of a document, you have to create a new section. In fact, Word creates a new section for you if you change margin settings in the middle of a document. Later in this chapter, "Section Breaks for Changing Layouts" explains what sections are.

Changing Margin Sizes in the Page Setup Dialog Box

Follow these steps to change margin settings by way of the Page Setup dialog box:

1. Place the cursor in the section whose margins you want to change; if you want to change margin settings throughout a document, it doesn't matter where the cursor is.

2. Either double-click the ruler or choose File | Page Setup. You see the Page Setup dialog box.

3. Select the Margins tab, as shown in Figure 9-2.

4. In the Top, Bottom, Left, and Right boxes, enter margin measurements. You can see what your measurements mean in real terms by glancing at the sample page in the Preview box.

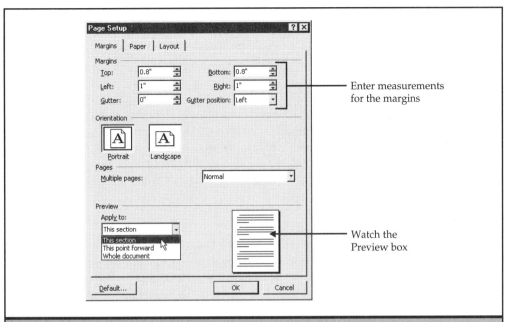

Enter measurements
for the margins

Watch the
Preview box

Figure 9-2. *The Preview box shows roughly what the margins will look like after you enter margin measurements*

5. If necessary, open the Apply To drop-down menu and choose in which part of your document you want to change margins.

6. Click OK.

If you prefer to work with a unit of measurement other than inches in the Page Setup dialog box, you can do so. Choose Tools | Options, select the General tab in the Options dialog box, and choose Centimeters, Millimeters, Points, or Picas from the Measurement Units menu.

Changing Margin Sizes with the Rulers

The other way to change margin sizes is to drag markers on the rulers. Only use the ruler method to make slight adjustments to a one- or maybe a two-page document. Adjusting the margins across page after page by dragging markers on the rulers is an invitation to trouble, since you can't see all the pages whose margins are being changed. Follow these steps to change the size of margins with the rulers:

1. Switch to Print Layout view or Print Preview view. "Getting a Better View of Your Work" in Chapter 2 explains how to change views of a document.

2. Choose View | Ruler if the rulers aren't showing on your screen. If you still can't see the vertical ruler on the left side of the screen after choosing View | Ruler, choose Tools | Options, select the View tab in the Options dialog box, and check the Vertical Ruler (Print View Only) check box.

3. Change the size of margins by dragging the margin markers:

■ **Left or Right Margin** Move the pointer over the ruler along the top of the screen, to the left or right side where the ruler changes from gray to white. When the pointer changes into double arrows, click and drag to adjust the size of the margin. If you have trouble finding the gray zone, open the Zoom menu and choose 75% to get a better look at margins.

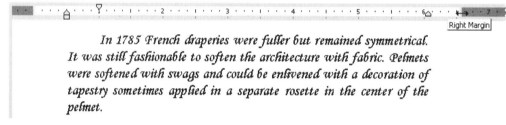

In 1785 French draperies were fuller but remained symmetrical. It was still fashionable to soften the architecture with fabric. Pelmets were softened with swags and could be enlivened with a decoration of tapestry sometimes applied in a separate rosette in the center of the pelmet.

■ **Top or Bottom Margin** Move the pointer to the ruler along the left side of the screen, to the point at the top or bottom where the ruler changes color. Then click and drag when the pointer changes into double arrows.

Notice how, when you drag a Right or Left margin marker, all indent markers on the ruler move as well. There is your irrefutable proof that text is indented from the margins, not from the page edge.

Adjusting Margins for Bound Documents

When documents are bound with fat plastic bindings, the bindings eat into the page margins. To accommodate bindings and make them part of your calculations when you decide what size to make the margins, Word provides the Gutter box in the Page Setup dialog box (see Figure 9-2). In a bound document, the *gutter* is the part of the paper that the binding eats into.

To see how bindings will affect the layout of a document's pages, choose File | Page Setup, select the Margins tab in the Page Setup dialog box, and click the up arrow in the Gutter box. As you do so, bindings appear on the sample page in the Preview box. Changing the gutter size doesn't do anything to margin sizes, but it does give you a sense of how wide or narrow to make the margins. After you have found the right gutter size, you can change the margins to accommodate bindings.

You can also bind pages from the top instead of the side. To do so, select the Top option on the Gutter Position drop-down menu in the Page Setup dialog box. Bindings at the top of pages can interfere with headers.

"Mirror Margins" for Bound, Two-Sided Pages

When the pages of a document are bound together, readers see two pages at a time instead of one. Take the book you are reading at this very moment, for example. You can see two pages, this and its opposite. In typesetter's terms, you can see a *page spread* like the one in Figure 9-3. Even-numbered pages appear on the left side of the page spread; odd-numbered pages appear on the right side.

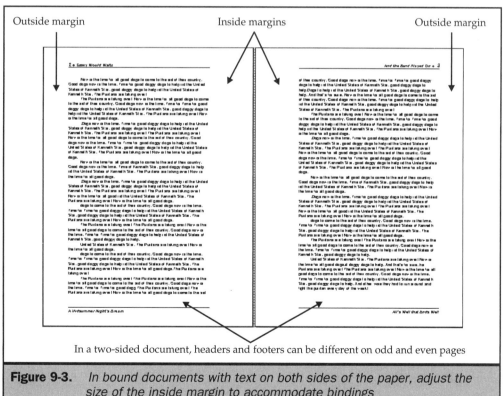

Figure 9-3.   *In bound documents with text on both sides of the paper, adjust the size of the inside margin to accommodate bindings*

FORMATTING TEXT AND PAGES

In a bound document with text on both sides of the pages, the terms "left margin" and "right margin" are meaningless. What matters instead is in the *inside margin*, the margin in the middle of the page spread next to the bindings, and the *outside margin*, the margin on the outside of the page spread that isn't affected by the bindings. The inside margin has to absorb the bindings. Especially if the document is a thick one that requires fat plastic bindings, words can get lost in bindings if the inside margin is too narrow.

Follow these steps to adjust the inside and outside margins to accommodate bindings in a two-sided Word document that you intend to bind:

1. Choose File | Page Setup.

2. Select the Margins tab in the Page Setup dialog box.

3. In the Multiple Pages drop-down menu, choose the Mirror Margins. When you do so, the Left box for changing the size of the left margin changes names—it becomes the Inside box. The Right box also changes names and becomes the Outside box.

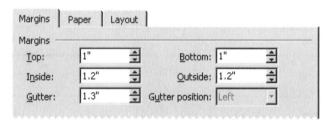

4. Click the up arrow in the Gutter box and watch bindings appear on the sample page in the Preview box.

5. Enter measurements in the Inside box and Outside box to adjust the size of the inside and outside margins (see Figure 9-3).

6. Click OK.

  As shown in Figure 9-3, the custom in books and two-sided, bound documents is to put a different header and footer on odd- and even-numbered pages. See "Headers and Footers for Different Pages and Sections," later in this chapter.

Choosing Page Setup Default Settings

Unless you change the default settings, Word gives you a generic document with these margin settings when you click the New Blank Document button or press CTRL-N to create a new document:

- Top and bottom margin: 1 inch
- Left and right margin: 1 inch
- Header and footer from edge of page: .5 inch

Suppose you want to change these margin settings so that you get margins that you like whenever you open a new document. To do so, choose File | Page Setup, enter your favorite margin settings in the Page Setup dialog box, and click the Default button. A message box appears and tells you what you knew already—that the new settings will go into effect whenever you open a new document based on the Normal template. Click Yes in the message box. The Normal template is the standard template that is used to create documents when you click the New Blank Document button or press CTRL-N. "Choosing Default Settings for the Normal Template" in Chapter 21 explains how to change other default settings in the Normal template.

Section Breaks for Changing Layouts

In order to put text in columns, change the margins, change page-numbering schemes, or change headers and footers in the middle of a document, you have to create a new section. A *section* is a formal break in a document where certain kinds of formats are introduced or a different paper size is used. Word is very touchy about sections. If you try to change margin settings or introduce columns without creating a section, Word takes over and creates a section for you.

To be thorough, you need a new section under these circumstances:

- Changing headers and footers or page-numbering schemes in headers and footers
- Inserting newspaper-style columns
- Changing the orientation of pages (from portrait to landscape or vice versa)
- Changing margin sizes
- Changing page alignments with respect to the top and bottom margin
- Using endnotes instead of footnotes or vice versa
- Printing on different-size paper in the middle of a document
- Changing paper sources during printing (changing the printer tray in which paper or envelopes are kept)

You can tell if a document has been divided into sections and which section the cursor is in by glancing at the Status bar along the bottom of the screen. Next to the page number are the letters "Sec" followed by the section the cursor is in:

Follow these steps to introduce a section break in a document:

1. Choose Insert | Break. You see the Break dialog box shown in Figure 9-4.

2. Under Section Break Types, choose which kind of section break you want:

   ■ **Next Page**   Introduces a section break and a page break to start a new section immediately on the next page.

   ■ **Continuous**   Introduces the section break starting in the middle of the page. Choose Continuous, for example, to put text in columns in the middle of a page.

   ■ **Even Page**   Creates the section break on the next even-numbered page.

   ■ **Odd Page**   Creates the break on the next odd-numbered page. In conventional publishing, a new chapter always begins on an odd page. Choose this kind of section break when headers and footers change from chapter to chapter and you want to start a new chapter in your document on an odd-numbered page.

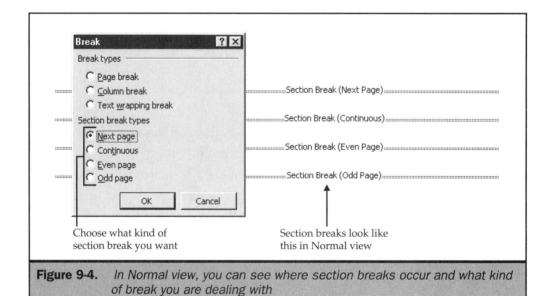

Figure 9-4.   *In Normal view, you can see where section breaks occur and what kind of break you are dealing with*

3. Click OK. If you are in Normal view, dotted lines and the words "Section Break" followed by the kind of break you chose appear onscreen.

The best way to see where section breaks are located is to switch to Normal view. As Figure 9-4 shows, you can see where the break starts and even what kind of section break you are dealing with in Normal view. In Print Layout view, Outline view, and Web Layout view, you have to click the Show/Hide ¶ button to see the dotted lines, the word "Section Break," and the variety of section break.

You can use the Find command to locate section breaks. Choose Edit | Find and, in the Find and Replace dialog box, enter ^b in the Find What box. You can also click the More button, click the Special button, and choose Section Break.

To delete a section break, click it and then press the DELETE key. Think twice about deleting a section break in a document with several different sections. Because a section break, like a paragraph break, stores formats for the text that precedes it, deleting a section break effectively makes the section adopt the formats of the section that comes *after* it. Suppose you want the section whose break you are deleting to adopt the formats of the section that comes *before* it? In that case, go to the previous section break, copy it (the following Tip explains how), and paste it after the break that you want to delete. Next, delete the section break. It will adopt the formats of the section break you recently copied.

You can copy a section break, paste it elsewhere, and in so doing create a new section with the same formats as another section. All the formats in a section are recorded in the section break that follows it, much the same way that paragraph formats are stored in the paragraph symbol at the end of each paragraph. To copy a section's formats, go to the end of the section, click in the left margin beside the section break to select it, and click the Copy button. Then scroll to the tail-end of the part of the document you want to copy the formats to, click there, and click the Paste button. By doing so, you create a new section with the same formats as the section whose section break you copied.

Putting Headers and Footers on Pages

A *header* is a line of text in the top margin of the page that tells readers what is in the document. In the book you are reading, for example, headers on the left-hand page list the title of the book and headers on the right-hand page list the chapter number and chapter title. In Word documents, headers often list the author's name, the title of the work, and sometimes a page number. A *footer* is a line of text in the bottom margin. Footers do what headers do, except they do it along the bottom of the page instead of the top.

These pages explain everything a body cares or needs to know about headers and footers. You learn how to enter headers and footers and how to take advantage of the buttons on the Header and Footer toolbar as you enter a header or footer. These pages explain how to include page numbers in headers and footers, as well as dates, times, and other document information that can be updated automatically. Read on to find out how to change the header or footer in the middle of a document, remove a header or footer from the first page of a document or section, and create different headers for odd-numbered and even-numbered pages. You also learn how to draw a line beneath a header or above a footer to help separate headers and footers from the main text.

Entering a Header or Footer

Entering a header or footer in a document is simple enough. After you get to the Header or Footer box, all you have to do is start typing. Follow these steps:

1. Choose View | Header and Footer. You see the Header and Footer toolbar, and, on the top of the page, the Header box:

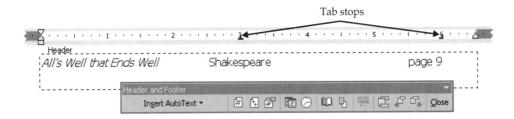

2. Type the header. As you do so, you can call on most of Word's formatting commands. Boldface or italicize the header, for example. Click an Align button on the Formatting toolbar to center text or align it with the left or right margin. You can even include a clip art image in a header or footer.

As the previous illustration shows, Word places two tab stops, a center tab and a right tab, in headers and footers. Use them to center or right-align text. See "Aligning Text with Tab Stops" in Chapter 8 if you need help with aligning text by way of tab stops.

3. Click the Switch Between Header and Footer button on the toolbar to enter a footer, if you so desire. You see the Footer box along the bottom of the page. Click the Switch Between Header and Footer button to go back and forth between the header and footer.

4. Enter the text of the footer. Again, you can call upon most of Word's formatting commands to decorate the footer.

5. Click the Close button on the Header and Footer toolbar to return to the document proper.

To edit a header or footer, choose View | Header and Footer to open the Header box, and go to it. If necessary, click the Switch Between Header and Footer button on the Header and Footer toolbar to get to the Footer box.

After you enter a header and footer, it appears, however faintly, at the top and bottom of pages in Print Layout view. To edit a header or footer in that view, simply double-click the header or footer. You see the Header or Footer box without having to choose View | Header and Footer.

In the Introduction of this book, I promised not to include exhaustive lists of toolbar buttons or dialog box options. I said that such lists are useless for the most part because wading through an exhaustive list of buttons or option names in hopes of finding the one button or option that will do the trick is a waste of time. I promised a book that shows how to complete tasks, not a description of the Word software.

However, because every rule requires an exception, following are descriptions of the buttons on the Header and Footer toolbar. These buttons are hard to figure at first. And most of the buttons on the Header and Footer toolbar do not have equivalents on the command menus. A quick survey of the buttons will help you understand all the things you can do with headers and footers:

- **Insert AutoText**   Opens a drop-down list so you can include document information—the filename or author's name, for example—in a header or footer. You can also include your own AutoText entries. See "Creating and Inserting AutoText Entries" in Chapter 6 to learn what AutoText entries are.

- **Insert Page Number**   Puts the page number in the header or footer. Page numbers are updated automatically. See "Numbering the Pages" later in this chapter.

- **Insert Number of Pages**   Lists the total number of pages in the document. The number is updated automatically. By typing **page**, clicking the Insert Page Number button, typing **of**, and clicking this button, you can include an up-to-date report on the page number and number of pages in the document in a header and footer. If Word doesn't list the total page count right away, choose Tools | Word Count.

- **Format Page Number**   Opens the Page Number Format dialog box so you can change page-numbering schemes. See "Numbering the Pages" later in this chapter.

- **Insert Date**   Lists the date the document was opened. When you print the document, it lists the date it was printed.

- **Insert Time**   Lists the time the document was opened, or, when you print the document, the time it was printed.

The date and time appear in the default date and time format, whatever it happens to be, when you click the Insert Date or Insert Time button. To enter the date or time in a different format, choose Insert | Date and Time, select a date or time format in the Date and Time dialog box, and click OK. "Quickly Entering the Date and Time" in Chapter 6 explains how to change the default date and time formats. Hint: Click the Default button in the Date and Time dialog box.

■ **Page Setup**   Opens the Layout tab of the Page Setup dialog box so you can make different headers and footers for odd and even pages, change the header or footer on the first page of a document or section, or draw lines below or above headers and footers. See "Numbering the Pages" and "Drawling a Line Below a Header or Above a Footer," later in this chapter.

■ **Show/Hide Document Text**   Hides or shows the text in the document so you can see what it looks like in relation to the header or footer text.

■ **Same as Previous**   Allows you to create different headers or footers for different sections in a document or make the headers and footers in one section the same as the those in the previous section. See "Headers and Footers for Different Pages and Sections," later in this chapter.

■ **Switch Between Header and Footer**   Shows the Header box at the top of the page or the Footer box at the bottom so you can enter or edit a header or footer.

■ **Show Previous**   Shows the header or footer in the previous section of a document that has been divided into sections. Click this button to see what the previous section's header or footer is.

■ **Show Next**   Shows the header or footer in the next section.

■ **Close**   Closes the Header and Footer toolbar.

Deciding How Close to Put Headers and Footers to the Page

Unless you change the settings, Word allows a half-inch at the top of the page for headers and a half-inch at the bottom of the page for footers. Suppose you want to change the position of headers or footers. To do so, click in the section where you want to change them (if your document is divided into sections) and choose File | Page Setup or click the Page Setup button on the Header and Footer toolbar. In the Page Setup dialog box, select the Layout tab. Then, in the Header and Footer boxes, enter measurements to tell Word how close to put the header and footer to the top or bottom of the page.

> The smaller the measurement in these boxes, the closer headers and footers will be to the page edge. Be careful not to enter too large or small a measurement. A large measurement pushes headers and footers too close to the text on the page; a small measurement moves them perilously close to the page edge, where your printer might not be able to print them.

Numbering the Pages

Page numbers are probably the most common items found in headers and footers. Everybody wants to know what page they are currently reading. Everybody wants the sense of accomplishment that comes from glancing at the page number and finding out that you are now on page 10 or 23 or 57. Read on to find out how to put simple page numbers in headers and footers, change the page-numbering scheme so that pages are numbered with Roman numerals or letters, make chapter numbers part of the page number, and put page numbers in the left or right margin instead of the header or footer.

Later in this chapter, "Headers and Footers for Different Pages and Sections" describes how to remove the page number from the first page of a document but keep page numbers on subsequent pages.

The Quick, No-Frills Way to Number Pages

As you know if you read the last page or two, you can click the Insert Page Number button on the Header and Footer toolbar (or press ALT-SHIFT-P) to insert the page number in a header or footer. Word offers a second, no-frills way to enter page numbers: the Insert | Page Numbers command. This command places a page number and nothing more in the header or footer. You get to decide where in the header or footer the page number goes.

Choose Insert | Page Numbers if all you want is a simple number on each page. However, if you intend to include headers or footers in your document, enter page numbers in the header or footer. A page number entered with the Insert | Page Numbers command does not fit beside text entered in a header or footer. The Insert | Page Numbers and View | Header and Footer commands do not work harmoniously.

Follow these steps to place a simple page number in the header or footer:

1. Choose Insert | Page Numbers. You see the Page Numbers dialog box shown in Figure 9-5.

2. From the Position menu, choose whether to place the page number in the header or footer.

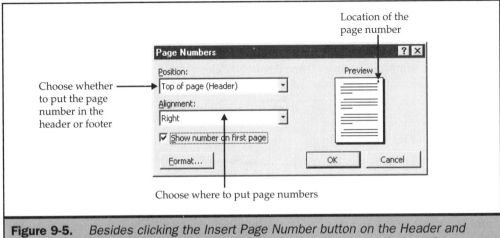

Location of the
page number

Choose whether
to put the page
number in the
header or footer

Choose where to put page numbers

Figure 9-5.   *Besides clicking the Insert Page Number button on the Header and
Footer toolbar, you can insert page numbers with the Insert | Page
Numbers command*

3. From the Alignment menu, choose to place the page number on the left side,
middle, or right side of the header or footer; or, in the case of two-sided
documents that will be bound, choose Inside to place page numbers near the
binding (not recommended) or Outside to place them away from the binding.
The sample page in the Preview box shows precisely where your page numbers
will land.

4. Click OK.

As shown in Figure 9-6, page numbers entered with the Insert | Page Numbers
command appear in frames. A *frame*, like a text box, is a container for text. Frames are kind
of problematic, because when you delete page numbers, change their fonts, or change their
positions, you have to select either the text inside the frame or the frame itself.

To remove page numbers, change their fonts, or adjust their positions on the page,
start by going to the Header box or Footer box where the page number is: Either
double-click the page number in Print Layout view, or choose View | Header and
Footer to see the Header box. (If necessary, click the Switch Between Header and
Footer button on the toolbar to see the page number in the Footer box.) Then follow
these instructions:

■ **Deleting Page Numbers**   Click the page number to make its frame appear,
and then gently move the pointer over the frame border. When you see the
four-headed arrow, click again. Eight black selection handles appear on the
frame to show it has been selected (see Figure 9-6). Click the DELETE button.

■ **Changing the Font of Page Numbers**   Click the page number to see the frame,
and then carefully drag the mouse over the page number to select it. With the
page number highlighted and selected (see Figure 9-6), choose a new font and

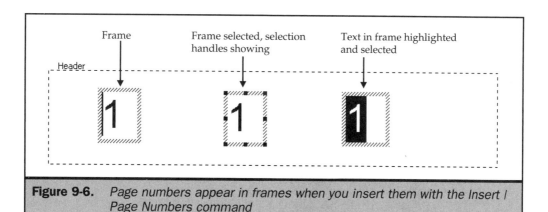

Figure 9-6. *Page numbers appear in frames when you insert them with the Insert | Page Numbers command*

font size from the Font and Font Size menus on the Formatting toolbar. If you need to enlarge the frame, select it and move the mouse pointer over a corner. When you see the double-headed arrow, click and start dragging.

■ **Adjusting the Page Number Position** Click the page number to see its frame, and then gently move the pointer over the frame border. When you see the four-headed arrow, click and drag the frame to a new position in the Header or Footer box.

Note *Page numbers are field codes. If you see field codes such as {PAGE} or {NUMPAGES} in the Header or Footer box instead of bona fide page numbers, you or someone else told Word to display field codes instead of field code results. To remedy the problem, press ALT-F9 or choose Tools | Options, select the View tab in the Options dialog box, and uncheck the Field Codes check box.*

Changing the Page-Numbering Scheme

The Arabic number system has been in use in Western culture since the thirteenth century, but that doesn't mean you can't forsake Arabic numerals and number pages as the Romans used to when Word VI came out in A.D. 6. Besides Roman numerals, you can number pages from A–Z with letters. Follow these steps to change the page-numbering scheme:

1. Either click the Format Page Number button on the Header and Footer toolbar (choose View | Header and Footer to see the toolbar) or click the Format button in the Page Numbers dialog box (choose Insert | Page Numbers to see the dialog box). The Page Number Format dialog box shown in Figure 9-7 appears.

2. From the Number Format menu, choose a page-numbering scheme.

3. Click OK.

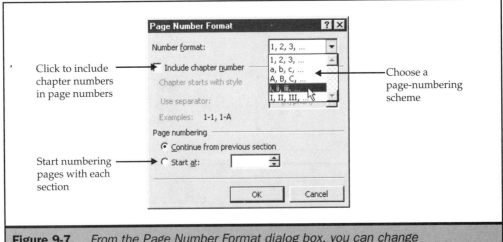

Figure 9-7.   *From the Page Number Format dialog box, you can change page-numbering schemes, put chapter numbers in page numbers, and start numbering pages anew in a section*

Including Chapter Numbers in Page Numbers

In manuals and scholarly papers, the chapter number is sometimes made part of the page number. For example, the pages in Chapter 1 are numbered 1-1, 1-2, 1-3, and so on; the pages in Chapter 2 are numbered 2-1, 2-2, 2-3, and so on. The idea behind numbering pages this way is that including the chapter number in the page number helps readers find the material they are looking for.

You must do or have done the following to your document in order to make the chapter number part of the page number:

- Divide the document into sections so that each section comprises one chapter. Be sure to start each new break on an odd page (by choosing Odd Page in the Break dialog box). See "Section Breaks for Changing Layouts," earlier in this chapter.

- Tell Word to start numbering each section beginning with page 1. See "Headers and Footers for Different Pages and Sections," later in this chapter (specifically, see "Numbering Pages Section by Section" under that heading).

- Use the Format | Bullets and Numbering command to assign chapter numbers to the headings throughout your document. Be sure to assign chapter numbers and not outline numbers and letters. The chapter number schemes are found on the bottom half of the Outline Numbered tab in the Bullets and Numbering dialog box. See "Numbering the Headings and Chapters in a Document" in Chapter 10.

■ Make sure that each section begins with a heading assigned the same Heading 1 style and that subsequent headings in the section are assigned subordinate styles. Chapter 12 explains how to assign and modify styles. Word gets the chapter number part of the page number from headings assigned the Heading 1 style, so if more than one heading in a chapter is assigned the Heading 1 style, the page-numbering scheme will go awry in the middle of the chapter. For example, pages in Chapter 2 would be numbered 2-1, 2-2, 3-3, 3-4 if a second heading assigned the Heading 1 style appeared on page 3.

After the ground has been tilled and you are ready to include chapter numbers in page numbers, visit the first page of each section and do the following:

1. Either double-click the header or footer in Page Layout view or choose View | Header and Footer to see the Header or Footer box (click the Switch Between Header and Footer button on the Formatting toolbar, if necessary, to see the Footer box).

2. Click where you want the page number to appear. If a page number has already been entered, select it by dragging the pointer across it.

3. Click the Format Page Number button on the Header and Footer toolbar. The Page Number Format dialog box appears.

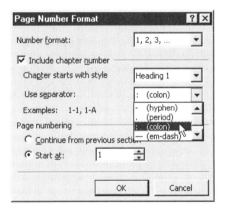

4. Check the Include Chapter Number check box.

5. In the Use Separator menu, choose a punctuation mark to separate the chapter number from the page number.

6. Click the Start At option button to make 1 appear in the Start At box.

7. Click OK.

Putting Page Numbers in the Left or Right Margin

The top and bottom margins aren't the only places you can put page numbers. You can also put them in the left or right margin. A page number in the left or right margin looks kind of elegant and is a good way to impress your impressionable friends. Word offers two strategies for putting page numbers in the margin, the hard way and the easy way:

- **Easy way**   Insert the page number with the Insert | Page Numbers command and then drag the frame that the page number is in to the left or right margin. Earlier in this chapter, "The Quick, No-Frills Way to Number Pages" explains how to change the size of frames, drag them to new positions, and change the font and font size of text inside a frame.

- **Hard way**   Create a text box for the page number, drag the text box into the left or right margin, click in the text box, and click the Insert Page Number button on the Header and Footer toolbar (or press ALT-SHIFT-P). Go this route only if you want to include a bit of text with the page number.

To do this successfully, you have to choose View | Header and Footer and insert the text box while the Header box or Footer box is showing. And, more problematically, you also have to wrestle with the drawing canvas after you create the text box. After you have dragged the text box safely into the margin, remove the drawing canvas by selecting it and pressing DELETE. Technically, the text box is part of the header or footer, even though it has been dragged into the left or right margin. Because the text box is part of the header or footer, it appears on every page, and the page number inside it is updated as you add pages to or remove pages from the document. Chapter 13 explains text boxes, the drawing canvas, and how to manipulate them.

In Print Layout view, you can see page numbers that you moved to the left or right margin. To edit a page number that is dangling out there, choose View | Headers and Footers to open the Header or Footer box where the page number is lodged, and then start hacking away.

2

12:30 — Luncheon

"Lovely Italy's Magliano Region"
Mr. Ickles Bowdoin

"Whither the Whooping Crane"
Prof. Bertron Rainder

1:30 — Seminars

"In Search of the Birdwatcher's Paradise"
Prof. Harlin Quatley

Headers and Footers for Different Pages and Sections

The same header and footer does not have to appear on every page of a document. No way. You can change headers and footer in the middle of a document, keep headers and footers from appearing on page 1, create different headers and footers for odd-numbered and even-numbered pages, and number pages starting with 1 in each section of a document that has been divided into sections. Better read on.

Changing Headers and Footers in the Middle of a Document

In order to introduce a new header or footer in the middle of a document, you have to create a new section where you want the new header and footer to start appearing. (Earlier in this chapter, "Section Breaks for Changing Layouts" explains how to insert a section break.) Word assumes that you want to keep the same header and footer throughout, and it runs the headers and footers from the previous section into the new section as well.

Follow these steps to introduce a new header or footer after you have created a new section:

1. Choose View | Header and Footer (and click the Switch Between Header and Footer button if you want to enter a new footer). The Header or Footer box tells you which section you are in and informs you that the header or footer in this section is the same as that in the previous section. Notice as well that the Same as Previous button on the Header and Footer toolbar is pressed down.

2. Click the Same as Previous button to disconnect the header and footer in the section you are in from the header and footer in the previous section. Now the Header or Footer box no longer reads "Same as Previous."

3. Delete the header or footer in the Header or Footer box and enter a new header or footer.

4. Click the Close button on the Header and Footer toolbar.

On the Header and Footer toolbar are buttons called Show Previous and Show Next. You can click these buttons to read and perhaps change the header or footer in the next or previous section in your document.

Removing or Changing Headers and Footers on Page 1

Usually, a header and footer does not appear on the first page, or title page, of a document. Sometimes the header and footer are different on the first page. Follow these steps to remove or change the header and footer on the first page of a document or the first page of a section in a document:

1. Put the cursor in the section if you want to change the header and footer on its first page; it doesn't matter where the cursor is if you want to change the header and footer on the first page of a document.

2. Choose File | Page Setup or click the Page Setup button on the Header and Footer toolbar. You see the Page Setup dialog box.

3. Select the Layout tab, if necessary. Figure 9-8 shows the Layout tab.

4. Check the Different First Page check box.

5. In the Apply To menu, choose This Section to change the header and footer on the first page of the section, or Whole Document to change the first page of your document.

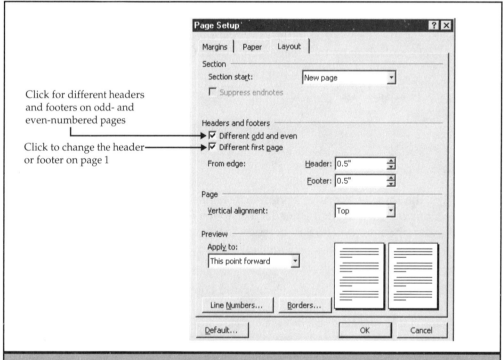

Figure 9-8. *The Layout tab of the Page Setup dialog box is where you tell Word to put different headers and footers on different pages*

6. Click OK. No header or footer appears on the first page, and the Header or Footer box reads, "First Page Header (or Footer)."

7. Enter a new header or footer if your purpose is to change the header or footer, not remove it.

 You can click the Show Next button on the Header and Footer toolbar to leap from the first page header or footer to the header or footer on the following page. Click the Show Previous button to return to the first page.

Headers and Footers for Odd- and Even-Numbered Pages

Earlier in this chapter, "'Mirror Margins, for Bound, Two-Sided Pages" explained how readers see two pages instead of one when documents are bound and printed on both sides of the paper. Instead of a single page, readers see a page spread, with the odd-numbered page on the left and the even-numbered page on the right.

Usually, a different header and footer appear on either side of the page spread when a book or document is printed on both sides of the paper. In the book you are reading, for example, headers on even-numbered pages on the left side of the page-spread list the title of this book; headers on odd-numbered pages on the right side of the page spread list which chapter you are reading. In two-sided documents, even-numbered pages always appear on the left side of the page spread and odd-numbered pages appear on the right side—they do, at least, if the document is printed and bound correctly.

If you opted for "mirror margins" because you intend to print your document on both sides of the paper and bind it, you owe it to yourself to create different headers and footers for odd- and even-numbered pages. Do it even if the text in headers and footers is the same on odd- and even-numbered pages to keep text from getting too close to the binding where it is hard to read. In the following document, for example, the text in the headers is the same, but I created a left-aligned header for even-numbered pages and a right-aligned header for odd-numbered pages to keep the headers from falling in the gutter, the place where the binding eats into pages.

Left-aligned header on even-numbered page   Right-aligned header on odd-numbered page

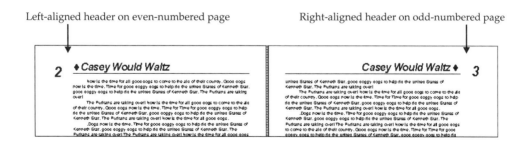

Follow these steps to create different headers and footers for odd- and even-numbered pages:

1. Choose File | Page Setup or click the Page Setup button on the Header and Footer toolbar. You see the Page Setup dialog box.

2. Click the Layout tab, if necessary (see Figure 9-8).

3. Check the Different Odd And Even Check box.

4. Click OK.

5. In your document, visit an odd-numbered page and enter headers and footers there; do the same on an even-numbered page.

Remember to right-align headers and footers on odd-numbered pages to keep headers and footers on those pages away from the bindings. To right-align text, click the Align Right button on the Formatting toolbar.

Numbering Pages Section by Section

Word offers a command for numbering pages starting at the beginning of a section. Use this command, for example, if your document begins with a title page, table of contents, preface, or other "front matter" material. Usually, front matter material is numbered in Roman numerals (as it is in this book), whereas the rest of the document is numbered, beginning with the first chapter or first heading, in Arabic numerals. If yours is a long document with a table of contents and other front matter, create a section for the front matter and start numbering pages anew in Arabic numerals where the document really begins, in section 2.

Follow these steps to number the pages of a section beginning with 1 (or a, A, I, i, I—whatever numbering scheme you choose):

1. Place the cursor in the section you want to start numbering at page 1.

2. Either click the Format Page Number button on the Header and Footer toolbar (choose View | Header and Footer to see the toolbar) or click the Format button in the Page Numbers dialog box (choose Insert | Page Numbers to see the dialog box). The Page Number Format dialog box appears (see Figure 9-7).

3. Under Page Numbering, click the Start At option button. The number 1 (or a, A, i, or I) appears in the text box.

4. Click OK.

Pages throughout a document are numbered consecutively. When you start numbering a section at page 1, the following sections are renumbered. If your document has many sections and you want each to be numbered starting at 1, visit each section and give the command to number it starting with 1.

Drawing a Line Below a Header or Above a Footer

One of the easiest ways to spruce up a document is to draw a line below headers and above footers. The line separates the header or footer from the main text in the document. In Word, you can choose from many different lines, as this illustration shows:

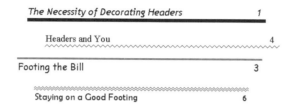

Follow these steps to place a line—that is, a border line—below a header or above a footer:

1. Either double-click a header or footer in Print Layout view or choose View | Header and Footer to see your header. If you want to draw a line above a footer, click the Switch Between Header and Footer button on the Header and Footer toolbar.

2. Choose Format | Borders and Shading and select the Borders tab in the Borders and Shading dialog box, if necessary.

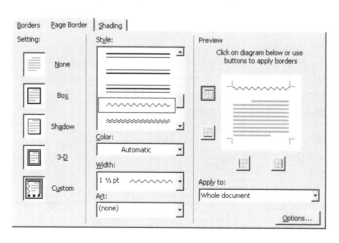

3. On the Style menu, find and click the kind of line you want. The lines get more exotic the farther you travel down the menu.

4. Choose a width for the line from the Width drop-down menu.

5. Make sure Paragraph is selected in the Apply To menu.

6. Click all four buttons in the Preview box to remove all lines in the Preview box.

7. Make a line appear below the header or above the footer by clicking in the Preview box:

   ■ **Below a Header**   Click the bottom of the box to make a line appear, or else click the button with the line along the bottom.

   ■ **Above a Footer**   Click the top of the box, or else click the button with the line long the top.

8. Click OK.

You can click the Options button in the Borders and Shading dialog box and enter measurements in the Border and Shading Options dialog box if you want to be specific about how close the line can come to the header or footer.

Changing the Size and Orientation of Pages

One of the surest ways to make a document stand out is to print it on unusual-size paper or change orientation and print the document in landscape view instead of portrait view. A 'zine printed on oblong paper or a chapbook printed on half-size pages sticks out in a crowd. Read on to find out how to change the orientation of a page and print on unusual-size paper.

Creating a Landscape Document

A *landscape* document is wider than it is long, like a painting of a landscape. Most documents, like the pages of the book you are reading, are printed in the *portrait* style, with the short sides of the page on the top and bottom. Figure 9-9 demonstrates the difference between the portrait and landscape orientations. The figure shows the same page—more or less—in portrait and landscape style.

To change the orientation of one or two pages in the middle of a document, you have to create a new section for the pages. See "Section Breaks for Changing Layouts" earlier in this chapter.

If you are changing page orientations in a section, put the cursor there. Follow these steps to change the orientation of the pages in a document:

1. Choose File | Page Setup to open the Page Setup dialog box.

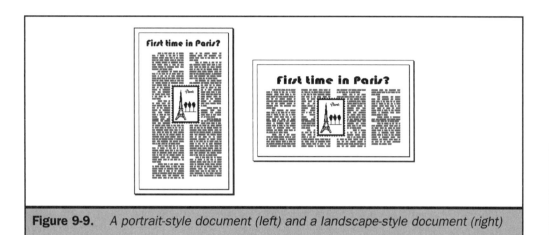

Figure 9-9.   *A portrait-style document (left) and a landscape-style document (right)*

FORMATTING TEXT
AND PAGES

2. Select the Margins tab.

3. Click the Landscape option button.

4. If you are changing the orientation of pages in a section, choose This Section from the Apply To menu.

5. Click OK.

Laying Out a Document on Legal- or Unusual-Size Paper

As long as your printer can handle it, you can print on unusual-size paper. Does legal-size paper (8.5 × 14 inches) count as unusual? Well, you can print pages on legal-size paper, too, as well as the A4 European standard (210 × 297 millimeters). To tell Word what size paper you want to print on:

1. Choose File | Page Setup.

2. Select the Paper tab in the Page Setup dialog box.

3. Either choose a size from the Paper Size menu or choose the Custom Size option and then enter the dimension of the paper you want to print on in the Width and Height text box.

4. Click OK.

Decorating a Page with a Border

A border around a page is mighty handsome. And page borders tell readers that the page is an important one. Often the title page of a document has a page border around it. Certificates, menus, and invitations all deserve page borders. You can place borders on all four sides of the page, or on three sides, two sides, or one side. Word offers many kinds of page borders. You can even put artwork around the sides of the page. This illustration shows examples of page borders.

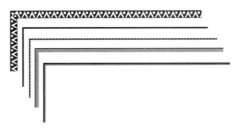

You're ready to go if you want to put borders around the first page in a document or section. But if you want to put borders around a certain page or certain pages in the middle of a document, create a section for that page or those pages (see "Section Breaks for Changing Layouts" earlier in this chapter). Word offers commands for putting borders around all the pages in the document, an entire section, the first page in a section, and all pages in a section except the first page.

Putting page borders on pages with headers and footers is not recommended because the page borders usually run too close to the header and footer. Besides, on a page without borders, it is easy to see that the header and footer are in the margin, but on a page with borders, the header and footer appear to be part of the main text. Remove the header and footer from the first page of a document or section before you put borders on a first page. Earlier in this chapter, "Headers and Footers for Different Pages and Sections" explains how to remove headers and footers from first pages.

Follow these steps to put a border around pages:

1. Click in the section whose first page or subsequent pages you want to place borders on. If your document is not divided into sections, where the cursor is doesn't matter.

2. Choose Format | Borders and Shading to open the Borders and Shading dialog box. If you happen to be in the Page Setup dialog box (choose File | Page Setup or click the Page Setup button on the Header and Footer toolbar to get there), you can also click the Borders button on the Layout tab.

3. Select the Page Border tab, as shown in Figure 9-10. Be prepared to wrestle with the options on the Page Border tab. The Preview box shows what your page borders will look like as you choose a setting, style, color, and line width.

4. Under Setting, choose which kind of border you want. The None option is for removing borders. The Custom option is for drawing or removing borderlines on different sides of the page.

5. On the Style menu, choose what kind of line you want.

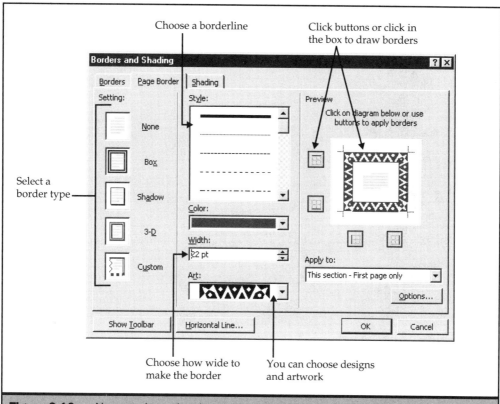

Figure 9-10.   *You can be quite the artist when it comes to drawing borders around the edge of a page*

6. From the Art menu, you can choose a design instead of a line.

7. If you so desire, choose a color for borderlines from the Color menu. The Automatic option removes colors.

8. In the Width menu, enter a point-size setting to tell Word how fat to make the borderlines or artwork.

9. Either click the Border buttons or click on the sides of the Preview box to draw the borders on the sides of the sample page.

10. Choose an Apply To option to tell Word on which pages to put borders. Choose This Section – First Page Only to put the borders around the first page of a document even if it isn't divided into sections.

11. Click OK.

To remove borders from a page, choose Format | Borders and Shading, select the Page Border tab, choose the None setting, and click OK.

Certain kinds of printers can't print text that falls too close to the edge of the page. If your printer is one of them, click the Options button on the Page Border tab (see Figure 9-10). In the Border and Shading Options dialog box, increase the measurements in the Top, Bottom, Left, and Right text boxes to move page borders farther away from the edge of the page.

Aligning Text with Respect to the Top and Bottom of the Page

For title pages and other marquee pages in a document, Word offers commands for aligning text with respect to the top and bottom of the page. Figure 9-11 shows the four ways to align text on a page. You can align text in these ways:

- **Top-Aligned**   Pushes text to the top of the page. Normally, text on pages is top-aligned.
- **Centered**   Centers the text so that the same amount of empty space appears above and below the text.
- **Justified**   Spreads the text evenly across the length of the page.
- **Bottom-Aligned**   Pushes text to the bottom of the page.

 Word doesn't offer a means of realigning the first page of a document or section but not the other pages. To center, justify, or bottom-align a page, you must create a section for it. See "Section Breaks for Changing Layouts" earlier in this chapter.

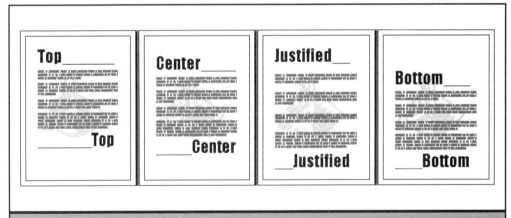

Figure 9-11.   *The four ways to align text with respect to the top and bottom of the page: Top, Center, Justified, and Bottom*

Follow these steps to align a page with respect to the top and bottom margins:

1. Put the cursor in the page you want to realign. Unless you want to realign all the pages in the document, you should have created a section for the page.
2. Choose File | Page Setup.
3. Select the Layout tab in the Page Setup dialog box.
4. In the Apply To menu, choose This Section.
5. Choose an option from the Vertical Alignment menu and click OK.

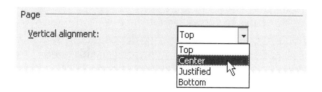

MOUS Exam Objectives Explored in Chapter 9

Objective	Heading
Create and format document sections	"Section Breaks for Changing Layouts"
Create and modify a header and footer*	"Putting Headers and Footers on Pages"
Modify document layout and Page Setup properties*	"Numbering the Pages," "Setting the Margins," and "Creating a Landscape Document"

Denotes an Expert, not a Core, exam objective.

Ten Tasks to Do Right Away When You Start a Complex Document

You can spare yourself heartache and perhaps a headache by doing these important tasks straightaway when you start work on a complex document, such as a long report, manual, or white paper.

1. See If You Can Use One of Word's Templates   Half the work of formatting a document is done already if you create it with a template. Choose File | New, click the General Templates link in the New Document task pane, select the Publications or Reports tab in the Templates dialog box, and see if you can find a template to help you on your way. The Publications tab offers templates called Manual and Thesis, and the Reports tab presents three different report templates. Check 'em out.

2. Decide How Many Styles You Need—and Create the Styles   Chapter 12 explains how you can save hours and hours of formatting time by thoughtfully creating the styles you need for a document. Choosing styles from the Style menu on the Formatting toolbar or the Styles and Formatting task pane is by far the easiest way to format a document. Especially if others will work on the complex document you are creating, nail down the styles from the start and tell others to use your styles, not invent their own, as they format the document.

3. Use the Outline Feature to Draw an Outline   For long documents, the Outline feature is invaluable. You can use it to stay organized, see how the different parts of a document fit together, promote and demote headings, and even get quickly from place to place. If your document needs organizing, you can move headings and subheadings from one place to another. Chapter 17 explains how the Outline feature works.

4. Create the Sections You Need—if You Need Sections   Dividing a document into sections after it has been written is hard because you have to go through the business of disconnecting each section from the previous one when you enter the headers and footers. Create sections from the get-go if you happen to know that your document requires sections. You'll save time that way.

5. Set the Margins   Changing margins after a document has been written and formatted is asking for trouble. All indentations are made from the left and right margins, so if you change margin settings, indentations change as well. And pages break in unexpected places. Give a moment's consideration to margins as soon as you create a new document.

6. Create the Headers and Footers   The purpose of a header or footer is to tell the reader what he or she is reading. Headers and footers can also help writers by showing them what they are supposed to write. If you enter the headers and footers early on, you will never get lost in a document. All you have to do is look at the header and footer to see where you are and what you are supposed to be writing.

7. Decide How to Number the Pages   As "Putting Headers and Footers on Pages" in this chapter pointed out, there are about 15 different ways to number the pages in a Word document. You can opt for no-frills page numbers by putting the numbers in frames. You can start numbering pages anew in each section. You can remove page numbers from the first page of a section or document. You can choose among different numbering schemes. Decide how to number the pages early on, while you are entering the headers and footers, to get the irksome chore out of the way.

8. Choose a Paper Size and Orientation   Like margin sizes, page size and orientation settings should be made from the start. Changing the page size or orientation after you have written and formatted a document causes nothing but trouble because lines break in new places and you have to do much of the formatting all over again. "Changing the Size and Orientation of Pages" in this chapter explains how to choose a page size and orientation.

9. Turn Off Background Pagination   "Background pagination" is a feature whereby Word redraws page breaks as you edit text. In other words, when you remove a paragraph or add a paragraph, all page breaks in the document are redrawn. Redrawing the page breaks is fine and dandy except when you are working on a very long document with graphics, charts, and other memory-hungry items. Redrawing pages around those items can take a long time. You have to twiddle your thumbs while Word draws the page breaks.

To turn off the background pagination, choose Tools | Options, select the General tab, and uncheck the Background Repagination check box. Be sure to turn the feature back on again when you are finished editing and you want to see where the page breaks will occur in your document.

10. Create a Master Document—Maybe   The Master Document feature takes outlines a step further and lets you create a master document—a document made of subdocuments that you can bring in or out of the master document at will. Chapter 17 explains master documents, their pitfalls, and how you can use them to stay organized in really big jobs if you have enough foresight and cunning.

FORMATTING TEXT AND PAGES

The
Complete
Reference

Word
2002

Chapter 10

Handling Lists and Numbered Items

This chapter looks at lists and numbered items. What is a word-processed document without a list or two? It's like an emperor without any clothes on. This chapter explains how to alphabetize a list, make bulleted and numbered lists, and give the chapters and appendixes numbers so that you can use the numbers in page-numbering schemes, for example.

Numbered and bulleted lists can be as simple or complex as you want them to be. Word offers a bunch of different ways to format lists, but if you are in a hurry or you don't care whether your Word documents look like everyone else's, you may as well take advantage of the Numbering and Bullets buttons on the Formatting toolbar. Click either of those buttons and you get a generic numbered or bulleted list. Nonconformists and people with nothing else to do, however, can try their hand at making a fancy list. This chapter covers that topic, too.

"Numbering the Lines in a Document" in Chapter 19 explains that particular aspect of numbering in Word. Chapter 19 also describes how to number the paragraphs in a document.

Alphabetizing and Sorting Lists

Alphabetizing a list, especially a long one, is one of those tasks that makes most people wince. Besides the tediousness of it, deciding whether certain words come before or after others can be difficult. In a list of cities, for example, which comes first, San Jose, California or San José, Costa Rica? What does the accented "e" do to alphabetical order? And how do you account for blank spaces? Does Sandia or San Diego come first in a list?

Fortunately for you, Word offers the Table | Sort command for alphabetizing and sorting lists. As demonstrated in Figure 10-1, *sorting* means to arrange text alphabetically from A to Z (or Z to A), numbers in order from smallest to largest (or largest to smallest), and dates in order from past to future (or future to past). When you use the Table | Sort command, Word makes all the little decisions about alphabetizing or sorting for you. Best of all, Word rearranges the list in the right order, so you don't have to cut and paste names, dates, or numbers to put the list in order.

The Table | Sort command is meant for sorting data in tables, but you can use it on plain lists as long as the list entries are entered the same way. For example, if you are alphabetizing a list by last name, make sure each entry starts with a last name. If by accident an entry reads "John Smith" instead of "Smith, John," Word places John Smith with the J's although he belongs with the S's. Before you sort a list, read it over to make sure the entries were made correctly and consistently.

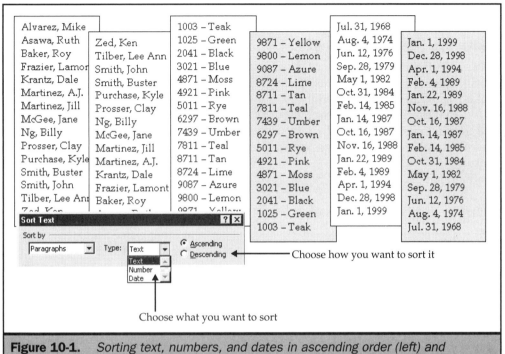

Figure 10-1.   *Sorting text, numbers, and dates in ascending order (left) and descending order (right)*

Follow these steps to sort a list:

1. Select the list.

2. Choose Table | Sort. The Sort Text dialog box appears (see Figure 10-1).

3. In the Type drop-down list, make sure the correct data type—Text, Number, or Date—appears, and choose the right data type if necessary.

4. Click the Ascending or Descending option button:

   ■ **Ascending**   Arranges text from A to Z, numbers from smallest to largest, and dates from earliest in time to latest in time.

   ■ **Descending**   Arranges text from Z to A, numbers from largest to smallest, and dates from latest in time to earliest.

5. Click OK.

Note   *The Then By options in the Sort Text dialog box are for use with tables. See "Sorting, or Reordering, a Table" in Chapter 14.*

The Bare-Bones Basics: Bulleted and Numbered Lists

Look no further if you are new to Word and you want to know how to make a bulleted or numbered list the conventional way. As I mentioned at the start of this chapter, making a bulleted or numbered list is simple if you use the generic numbers and bullets that Word provides. Throughout this chapter, I explain how to twist, tweak, and torture bulleted and numbered lists to make them your own. For now, here are the basics of creating a bulleted or numbered list according to Word's specifications. You will also find instructions here for telling Word not to generate numbered and bulleted lists automatically.

Making a Generic Bulleted List

In typesetting terms, a *bullet* is a black, filled-in circle or other character that marks an item on a list. As Figure 10-2 shows, bulleted lists are useful when you want to present the reader with alternatives or present a list in which the items are not ranked in any order. Follow these steps to create a bulleted list:

1. Click the Bullets button on the Formatting toolbar. The standard round bullet appears.

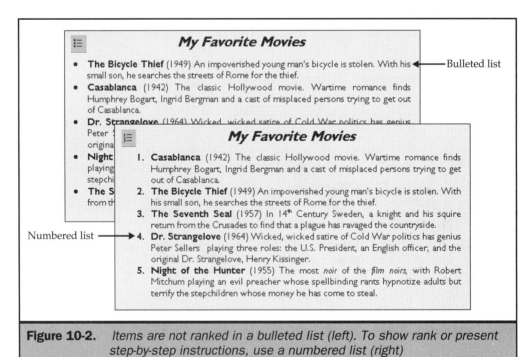

Figure 10-2.   *Items are not ranked in a bulleted list (left). To show rank or present step-by-step instructions, use a numbered list (right)*

If you don't see the standard bullet character when you click the Bullets button, you or someone else has been tinkering with the bullet character settings. Later in this chapter, "Creating Your Own Numbering Scheme for Lists" explains how to mark bulleted lists with different characters and how to start using the standard bullet character again.

2. Type the first entry in the list and press ENTER. A bullet appears on the next line as well.

3. Type the next and subsequent entries.

4. Either backspace over the last bullet or press the ENTER key twice to end the list and keep bullets from appearing at the start of each line.

Tip

The easiest way to create a bulleted list is to type it first without clicking the Bullets button. Type all the list entries, select them, and then click the Bullets button.

Making a Generic Numbered List

Numbered lists are invaluable in manuals and books like this one for presenting step-by-step instructions. You can also rank the items in a list by making the list a numbered list (see Figure 10-2). Lists are numbered sequentially. When you remove an item from a list or stick a new item in the middle of the list, Word renumbers the list for you.

Follow these steps to create a generic numbered list:

1. Click the Numbering button on the Formatting toolbar. You see the number 1.

2. Type the first entry in the list and press ENTER. The number 2 appears on the next line.

3. Type the rest of the list.

4. To end the list and prevent Word from putting numbers at the start of lines, either press BACKSPACE to remove the last number or press ENTER twice.

Tip

Numbering a list after you've typed it makes typing the list a little easier. Try typing the list entries, selecting the list, and clicking the Numbering button to create a numbered list.

Removing the Bullets or Numbers from a List

Removing the bullets or numbers from a list is quite simple:

1. Select the list.

2. Click the Bullets or Numbering button. The bullets or numbers are removed instantly, and you are left with several paragraphs where a list used to be.

FORMATTING TEXT AND PAGES

The other way to remove bullets or numbers is to select the list, choose Format | Bullets and Numbering, and click the None button in the Bullets and Numbering dialog box.

To turn a numbered list into a bulleted list or a bulleted list into a numbered list, select the list and click the Numbering button or Bullets button on the Formatting toolbar.

Preventing Word from Generating Numbered and Bulleted Lists

Word numbers lists automatically when you type **1.** (or **A.**, **a.**, **I.**, or **i.**), press the SPACEBAR or the TAB key, type a line, and press ENTER. Do that and the number 2 (or B, b, II, or ii) followed by a period appears on the next line. Similarly, the program creates a bulleted list automatically if you start a line with an asterisk (*) or one of several other characters or character combinations ("Using Symbols and Pictures for Bullets," later in this chapter, describes them all), press the SPACEBAR or TAB key, type a line, and press ENTER.

Many Word users, however, think that automatic numbered and bulleted lists are a nuisance. These users would like to create lists on their own without the invisible hand of Word butting in.

If automatic numbered and bulleted lists annoy you, try one of these techniques to keep from being annoyed:

- Click the AutoCorrect Options button and choose Stop Automatically Creating Numbered Lists or Stop Automatically Creating Bulleted Lists on the drop-down menu. The AutoCorrect Options button appears when Word takes formatting matters into its own hands.

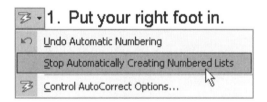

- Either choose Tools | AutoCorrect and select the AutoFormat As You Type tab in the AutoCorrect dialog box, or click the AutoCorrect Options button and choose Control AutoCorrect Options. Then, under Apply As You Type, uncheck the Automatic Bulleted Lists and Automatic Numbered Lists check boxes and click OK.

Resuming and Restarting Lists

Suppose you write a numbered or bulleted list, stop the list at the fourth entry, type a paragraph or two of commentary, and decide to resume the list. In the case of a bulleted list, resuming the list is easy. All you have to do is click the Bullets button on the Formatting toolbar and start typing. But resuming a numbered list is more complicated. If you stopped the list at step 4 and want to resume it later at step 5, for example, you have to tell Word to pick up the list at step 5.

Follow these steps to resume a numbered list:

1. Either click where you want to resume the list or, if you have already typed the next entry or entries in the list, select the next entry or entries.

2. Click the Numbering button on the Formatting toolbar. Word numbers the list beginning with 1. Now you tell Word to resume numbering the list.

3. Do either of the following to resume the numbered list:

   ■ Right-click and choose Continue Numbering on the shortcut menu.

Another Way to Interrupt and Resume Numbered Lists

Another way to interrupt a numbered list with a paragraph or two of commentary is to press SHIFT-ENTER instead of ENTER after you type a list entry. As you know if you read "Starting a New Paragraph, Line, or Page" in Chapter 2, pressing SHIFT-ENTER breaks the line without starting a new paragraph. When you press SHIFT-ENTER at the end of a numbered line, the next line is not numbered because it is officially part of the previous line. Instead of getting a number, the line following the numbered line is indented.

Press SHIFT-ENTER, not ENTER, to keep the
next line from being numbered

3. Vigorously swing the baseball bat around, "cracking your wrists" as you do
so, and continue with the follow through.
As the bat swings round the body, the hips move parallel to home plate in
swivel-like motion.
Moreover, bodyweight is transferred from the back leg to the front leg as the
bat travels its course.

4. Transfer the weight of the bat from the arm farthest from the pitcher to the
arm closest to the pitcher.

Keep pressing SHIFT-ENTER to end paragraphs until you reach what you want to be the next numbered line. When get there, press ENTER. The next line is numbered.

- Choose Format | Bullets and Numbering, and, on the Numbered tab of the Bullets and Numbering dialog box, click the Continue Previous List option button.

- Click the AutoCorrect Options button and choose Continue Numbering on the drop-down menu.

Once in a while you attempt to start a numbered list and Word mistakenly thinks you want to resume a list. When that happens, the numbered list you want to start at 1 starts at 3, 4, 5, or another number. To remedy the problem, either right-click and choose Restart Numbering, or choose Format | Bullets and Numbering and click the Restart Numbering button in the Bullets and Numbering dialog box.

Fancy Formats for Bulleted and Numbered Lists

Word makes it fairly easy to do fancy things to lists. As shown in Figure 10-3, you can start by choosing Format | Bullets and Numbering to open the Bullets and Numbering dialog box and choosing a different bullet character or numbering scheme. And if you

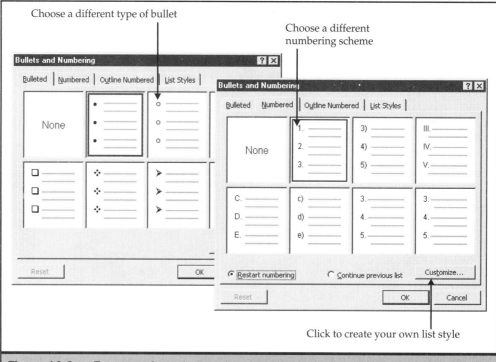

Figure 10-3.   *To create fancy bulleted and numbered lists, start by choosing Format | Bullets and Numbering to visit the Bullets and Numbering dialog box*

are daring and want to get very fancy, you can click the Customize button in the Bullets and Numbering dialog box, visit the Customize dialog box, and really go to town. These pages explain how to choose a new numbering scheme for numbered lists, change the look of bullets and numbers, and change the indentation and alignment of bulleted and numbered lists. First, however, a word about what happens in the Bullets and Numbering dialog box when you do fancy things to list.

 The fastest way to open the Bullets and Numbering dialog box is to double-click a number or bullet in a list.

FORMATTING TEXT
AND PAGES

What Changing List Formats Does to the Bullets and Numbering Dialog Box

After you create a new format for a bulleted or numbered list, your new format appears as a choice in the Bullets and Numbering dialog box (see Figure 10-3). This card shark, for example, created formats in which clubs, diamonds, hearts, and spades are used as bullet characters. Now the Bulleted tab of the Bullets and Numbering dialog box offers the four bulleted list formats that she created:

Being able to choose a fancy format you created yourself in the Bullets and Numbering dialog box is convenient. All you have to do to apply your fancy format to a list is choose it in the dialog box. In fact, after you have applied the fancy format, you can apply it again simply by clicking the Numbering or Bullets button on the Formatting toolbar. Clicking the Numbering or Bullets button applies the last numbering or bulleted list format that you selected in the Bullets and Numbering dialog box, whatever that format happened to be.

As convenient as choosing fancy formats in the Bullets and Numbering dialog box is, however, sooner or later you might want the original bullets and numbers back. To make one of the default bullets and numbers shown in Figure 10-3 appear again in the Bullets and Numbering dialog box, select a format and click the Reset button. A message box asks if you want to "reset this gallery position to the default setting?" Click Yes.

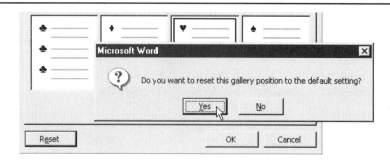

By the way, if you try to click the Reset button but you can't because it is grayed out, you are dealing with a default format already. You can't change it back because, to paraphrase James Brown, "it is what it is."

   If you go to the trouble to create a new format for a bulleted or numbered list, you might as well create a list style for your new format. After you create the style, you can copy the bulleted or numbered list format to other documents and templates and use it there. What's more, applying a style is the fastest way to reformat a bulleted or numbered list. Instead of visiting the Bullets and Numbering dialog box, all you have to do is choose your bulleted or numbered list style from the Style menu or the Styles and Formatting task pane. Chapter 12 explains styles and how to copy them from document to document and template to template.

Choosing a New Numbering Scheme

As Figure 10-4 shows, Word offers a bunch of different ways to number lists. The program also gives you the opportunity to decide for yourself which character comes after the letter or number—a period, for example, or a parenthesis or hyphen. Follow these steps to choose a numbering scheme for a list:

1. Click the first item in the list if your intent is to change the style of a numbered list you already entered.

2. Choose Format | Bullets and Numbering to open the Bullets and Numbering dialog box (see Figure 10-3).

3. Select the Numbered tab, if necessary.

4. Choose a numbering scheme, if the scheme you want appears on the Numbered tab, and click OK.

To choose a scheme that doesn't appear on the Numbered tab or select a punctuation character for your numbered list, select the numbering scheme in the Bullets and Numbering dialog box that most resembles the scheme you want, and then click the

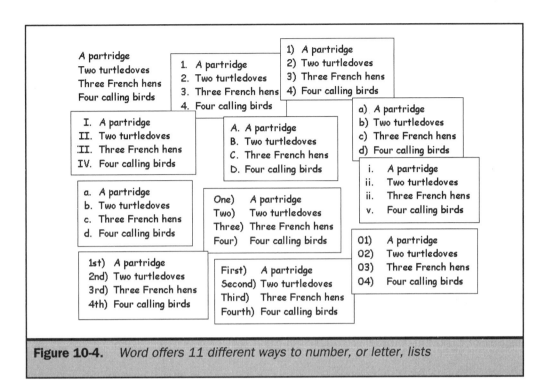

Figure 10-4.   *Word offers 11 different ways to number, or letter, lists*

Customize button. You see the Customize Numbered List dialog box. Follow these instructions and click OK twice to fashion a numbering scheme:

- **Number Format**   In the Number Format text box, enter the character that you want to appear after the number or letter. Enter a hyphen, for example, or a bracket (]). Or else delete the character after the number to remove punctuation from numbers.

- **Number Style**   Choose a numbering method from the drop-down list.

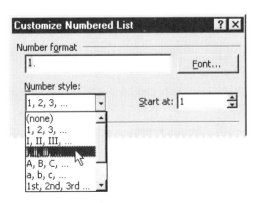

After you choose or fashion a new numbering scheme, all you have to do to apply it a second time is click the Numbering button on the Formatting toolbar. Clicking this button applies the numbering format you last chose, whatever that format happens to be.

Using Symbols and Pictures for Bullets

The black, filled-in circle seems to be everyone's first choice for a bullet symbol, but that doesn't mean you can't stray from the herd and use another symbol to decorate your bulleted lists. Every character in the Symbol dialog box can be used to mark entries in a bulleted list. And you can also use bullets from the Picture dialog box and even use clip art images for bullets. Better read on.

Choosing a Bullet Symbol of Your Own

Follow these steps to choose a symbol for bulleted lists apart from the black, filled-in circle that you get when you click the Bullets button on the Formatting toolbar:

1. Choose Format | Bullets and Numbering to open the Bullets and Numbering dialog box.
2. Select the Bulleted tab, if necessary.
3. Choose a new bullet style and click OK.

After you choose a new bullet, it becomes the default bullet that gets entered when you click the Bullets button on the Formatting toolbar.

	• John	○ John	▪ John
John	• Paul	○ Paul	▪ Paul
Paul	• George	○ George	▪ George
George	• Ringo	○ Ringo	▪ Ringo
Ringo			

❑ John	❖ John	➢ John	✓ John
❑ Paul	❖ Paul	➢ Paul	✓ Paul
❑ George	❖ George	➢ George	✓ George
❑ Ringo	❖ Ringo	➢ Ringo	✓ Ringo

As the illustration shows, the seven bullets in the Bullets and Numbering dialog box are pretty, but they are by no means the only symbols you can use in bulleted lists. Any symbol in the Symbol dialog box can be made a symbol in a bulleted list. Follow these steps to mark a bulleted list with an exotic symbol:

1. Choose Format | Bullets and Numbering to open the Bullets and Numbering dialog box.
2. Choose the bullet style on the Bulleted tab that you like the least.

3. Click the Customize button. As shown in Figure 10-5, you see the Customize Bulleted List dialog box, which lists symbols you already chose for bulleted lists. If the symbol you want is one of the six in the dialog box, select it and click OK.

4. Click the Character button to open the Symbol dialog box.

5. Find and select a symbol. You'll find a lot of good ones in the Wingdings font. "Entering Symbols and Foreign Characters" in Chapter 2 explains the Symbol dialog box in detail.

6. Click OK twice to return to your document and see your new bullet in all its glory.

Tip   *Click the Picture button in the Customize Bulleted List dialog box to open the Picture Bullet dialog box. There you will find many Web-style bullets for HTML documents.*

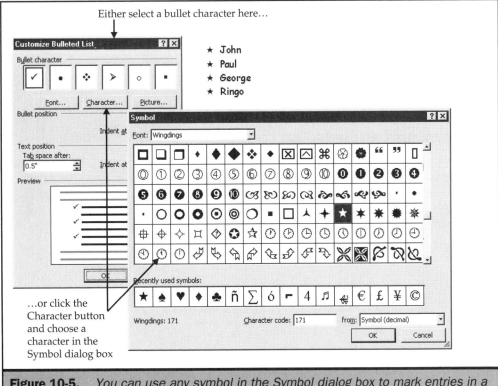

Figure 10-5.   *You can use any symbol in the Symbol dialog box to mark entries in a bulleted list*

Keyboard Shortcuts for Entering Bullet Symbols

Besides entering bullet symbols by way of the Bullets and Numbering dialog box, you can enter them by typing keyboard shortcuts. To do so, type the character or characters shown in the left-hand column of the following illustration, press the SPACEBAR or the TAB key, write the first entry on the list, and press ENTER. In place of the character or characters you typed, Word enters the bullet symbol shown in the illustration. See "Preventing Word from Generating Numbered and Bulleted Lists " earlier in this chapter if you prefer that Word not generate bulleted lists like the ones shown here.

*	•	• Minneapolis, the largest city in Minnesota • St. Paul, the capital of Minnesota
-	-	- Hibbing, birthplace of Kevin McHale - Duluth, birthplace of Blanche McPhee
--	■	■ Meeker County, home of Land O' Lakes Butter ■ Rochester, home of the Mayo Clinic
>	➤	➤ Hastings, gravesite of Plantina Chaffee Hayford ➤ Hastings, birthplace of Mauce Hayford
->	➔	➔ Boundary Waters Canoe Area ➔ 55 persons per square mile population density
=>	⇨	⇨ The Sioux once roamed Minnesota ⇨ The Chippewa (Ojibway) roamed the state, too

Changing the Font, Font Size, and Color of Numbers and Bullets

Unless you give instructions otherwise, bullets and numbers are the same font size as the text in the rest of the list; numbers appear in the same font as well. As this illustration shows, however, a few larger-than-life bullets or numbers perched on the side of a list looks elegant. In numbered lists, you can make the numbers stand out even more by giving them a different font as well as a different font size. You can even give bullets or numbers a different color.

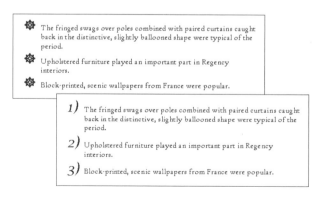

Follow these steps to change the font, font size, and color of the bullets or numbers in a list:

1. Select the list if you have already written it. Be sure to select the entire list. If you select part of it, Word thinks you want to change the font and font size of the list entries, not the numbers or bullets.

2. Double-click a bullet or number or choose Format | Bullets and Numbering to open the Bullets and Numbering dialog box (see Figure 10-3).

3. As necessary, click the Bulleted or Numbered tab.

4. Select a bullet or numbering style and click the Customize button. As shown in Figure 10-6, you see the Customize Bulleted List dialog box or the Customize Numbered List dialog box.

5. Click the Font button. You see the Font dialog box.

6. Choose a new font size and perhaps a different color. For numbers, choose a new font and perhaps a font style as well. "Choosing a Font and Font Size for Text" in Chapter 7 explains the ins and outs of the Font dialog box.

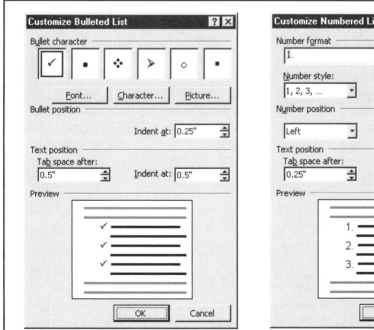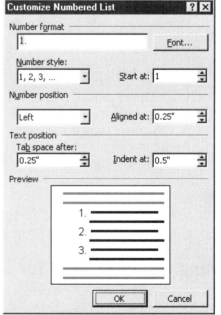

Figure 10-6. *In the Customize Bulleted List and Customize Numbered List dialog boxes, you can create your own style of bulleted and numbered lists*

7. Click OK to return to the Customize dialog box.

8. If you chose a large font size, you probably have to adjust the Indent At and Aligned At measurements to make the entries in the list line up correctly. The next section in this chapter explains how to indent lists. Keep your eye on the Preview box. It shows how text lines up in the list.

9. Click OK twice to return to your document and see what your bullets or numbers look like.

Adjusting How Far Bullets and Numbers Are Indented

Continuing the crusade to deviate from the standard bulleted or numbered list, you can also change the distance that list entries are indented from the left margin. In a standard bulleted or numbered list, the number or bullet is indented from the left margin by .2 inch, and the text in the list is indented from the left margin by .45 inch. However, you can change that by following these steps:

1. Either double-click a number in the list or choose Format | Bullets and Numbering to open the Bullets and Numbering dialog box, and then click either the Bulleted or Numbered tab.

2. Select the bullet or numbering style whose indentation you want to change, and click the Customize button. The Customize Bulleted List or Customize Numbered List dialog box appears (see Figure 10-6).

3. Under Bullet Position or Number Position, change the measurements in the Indent At or Aligned At box to alter the distance by which the bullets or numbers in the list are indented from the left margin.

4. Under Text Position, change the distance that the text in the list is indented from the left margin. Watch the Preview box as you change the settings—the box shows where the bullets or numbers and text will appear in relation to the left margin.

5. Click OK twice to return to your document.

To indent an entire list by one tab stop from the left margin, select the list and click the Increase Indent button on the Formatting toolbar. You can also right-click and choose Increase Indent from the shortcut menu.

Choosing an Alignment for the Numbers in Lists

In the two default numbering schemes in which plain Arabic numbers are used, the numbers are left-aligned. In other words, the numbers in lists are aligned under the first, or left-hand, character. In lists that do not reach double-digits, left-aligned numbers are not a problem, but left-aligned numbers look odd when lists go beyond the number 10 because the text entries come too close to the numbers, as shown in this illustration.

Maids a-milking	8. Maids a-milking	8) Maids a-milking
Ladies dancing	9. Ladies dancing	9) Ladies dancing
Swans a-swimming	10. Swans a-swimming	10) Swans a-swimming
Lords a-leaping	11. Lords a-leaping	11) Lords a-leaping
Drummers drumming	12. Drummers drumming	12) Drummers drumming

You can, however, right-align or center-align the numbers in a list to solve the problem of text running too close to the numbers. For that matter, you can left-align, right-align, or center-align the numbers and letters in any list for the sheer aesthetic enjoyment of it or to amuse yourself on a rainy day. Follow these steps:

1. If you have already entered the list, either double-click a number in the list or select it and choose Format | Bullets and Numbering.

2. Click the Customize button on the Numbered tab in the Bullets and Numbering dialog box. The Customize Numbered List dialog box appears (see Figure 10-6).

3. Under Number Position, choose Left, Centered, or Right from the drop-down list; adjust the Aligned At and Indent At measurements, if necessary; and click OK twice to return to your document.

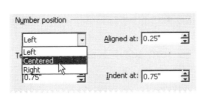

8)	Maids a-milking
9)	Ladies dancing
10)	Swans a-swimming
11)	Lords a-leaping
12)	Drummers drumming

8.	Maids a-milking
9.	Ladies dancing
10.	Swans a-swimming
11.	Lords a-leaping
12.	Drummers drumming

Making Sublists or Nested Lists

A *sublist*, also known as a *nested list*, is a list that is found inside another list. On the left side of Figure 10-7 is a common type of sublist, a bulleted sublist inside a numbered list. The numbered sublist on the right side of Figure 10-7 is not as common. Still, you see numbered sublists inside of numbered lists from time to time.

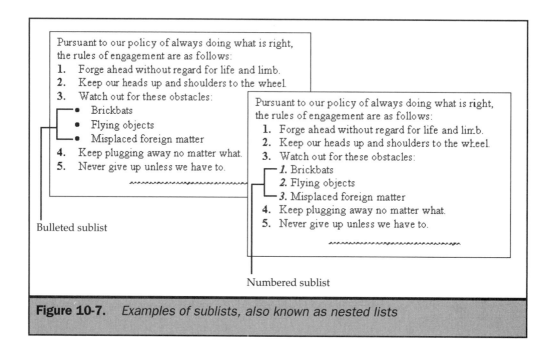

Figure 10-7. *Examples of sublists, also known as nested lists*

Creating a bulleted sublist is simple: Type the entire list without regard for sublists, and click the Numbering or Bullets button to make the entire list a bulleted or numbered list. Then select the items that you want for the sublist and do either of the following:

- **Bulleted Sublist Inside a Numbered List**   Click the Bullets button. The list is renumbered, and the items you selected are given bullets. If you want, click the Increase Indent button to indent the bulleted sublist or else choose Format | Bullets and Numbering to format the sublist.

- **Bulleted Sublist Inside a Bulleted List**   Click the Increase Indent button to indent the sublist and set it apart from the bulleted list. Word assigns a new bullet character to the sublist entries. Choose Format | Bullets and Numbering if you want to change the bullet character or indentation of the sublist.

To create a numbered sublist, type the entire list and click the Bullets or Numbering button to make the list a bulleted or numbered list. Then select the items for the numbered sublist and do the following:

- **Numbered Sublist Inside a Bulleted List**   Click the Numbering button on the Formatting toolbar. That's all there is to it, unless you want to click the Increase Indent button or choose Format | Bullets and Numbering to set the sublist apart somehow.

■ **Numbered Sublist Inside a Numbered List**   Click the Increase Indent button on the Formatting toolbar to indent the list and make it a sublist. Word assigns a new numbering scheme to the items in the sublist. If you want, choose Format | Bullets and Numbering to choose a different numbering scheme or to format the sublist. However, do not choose the same numbering scheme as you chose for the numbered list. If you do, Word does not indent the sublist and you can hardly distinguish it from the numbered list.

The following illustration shows another kind of sublist—a series of numbered clauses inside a paragraph. Normally in a list like this, you have to retype the numbers if you add or remove a numbered item. For this list, however, I used the ListNum field to enter the numbers automatically. When I remove or add a clause, Word renumbers the list. Because I used a field code to number the clauses in the paragraph, I can choose a new numbering scheme for all the clauses instantaneously without having to retype anything.

Pursuant to the terms of the contract the author shall 1) turn in the work in a timely fashion, 2) provide all artwork, 3) address all manuscript changes, 4) review tech editor comments, 5) review copy editor comments, 6) incorporate said comments in the work, 7) review the galley changes, 8) review the index, 9) review the cover copy, 10) review the catalog copy, 11) provide necessary promotional materials, 12) keep backup copies of the work, 13) assist the wondrous acquisitions editor.

Field codes are explained in detail in Part VI. For now, here are basic instructions for numbering items in the same paragraph with the ListNum field code:

1. Type all the text for the paragraph, excluding the numbers and punctuation marks (such as close parentheses) that distinguish one clause from another. Word will insert the punctuation marks for you.

2. Click in the paragraph before the first clause you want to number.

3. Choose Insert | Field. You see the Field dialog box.

4. Select Numbering in the Categories drop-down menu, as shown in Figure 10-8, and select the ListNum field name.

5. In the List Name list, choose NumberDefault.

6. Under Field Options, enter a number in the Level in the List text box to tell word what kind of numbering scheme you want:

   ■ **1** 1), 2), 3),…

   ■ **2** a), b), c),…

   ■ **3** i), ii), iii),…

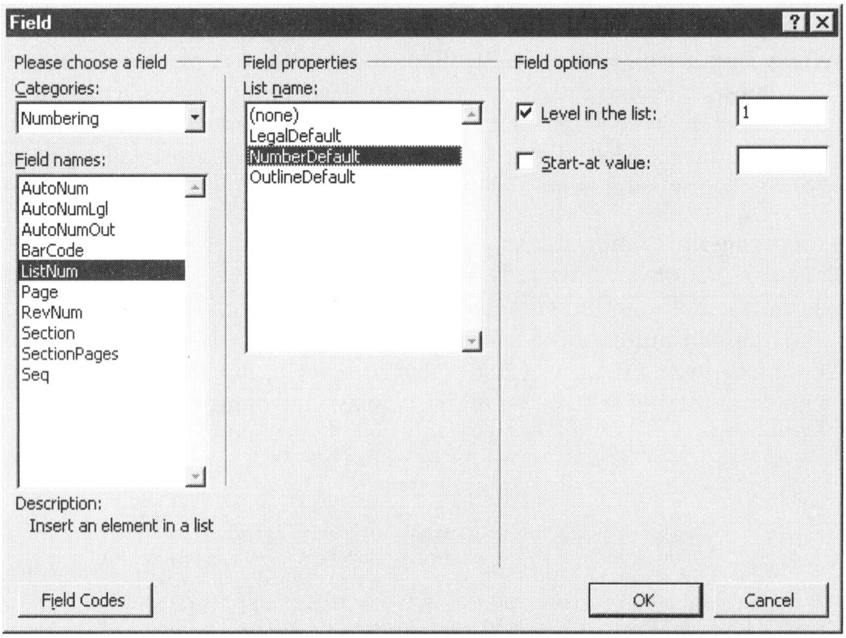

Figure 10-8.   *You can use the ListNum field code to number items in a paragraph*

- ■ 4 (1), (2), (3),...
- ■ 5 (A), (B), (C),...
- ■ 6 (i), (ii), (iii),...
- ■ 7 1., 2., 3.,...
- ■ 8 a., b., c.,...

Caution   *If your document already includes one list that was numbered by way of the NumList field, enter 1 in the Start-At Value text box (see Figure 10-8). Unless you enter 1 there, Word will resume numbering from the previous list. What's more, to enter the second and subsequent numbers in the list, click where you want the second number to go, and then start over and follow steps 3–9 of this instruction list after you complete step 7.*

7. Click OK to close the Field dialog box. A number appears in your document.

8. Click where you want the second number to be and press F4 (or choose Edit | Repeat). The second number is entered.

9. Keep pressing F4 until you have entered all the numbers.

Don't worry about the gray shades in your numbered paragraph. Gray shades show where field code results are located. They don't appear on the page when you print a document. You can press ALT-F9 to toggle them on and off.

Making an Outline-Style List

Figure 10-9 shows examples of *outline-style lists*. The lists are hierarchical and are meant to help readers grasp items' rank or order of importance. Normally, knowing how to number the items in a list and deciding how far to indent items is a big chore. But Word can do the work for you by way of the Bullets and Numbering dialog box.

To construct a list, choose a list style, make the entries, and give Indent commands to tell Word where to place items in the hierarchy:

- **Choosing a List Style**   Choose Format | Bullets and Numbering. Then, on the Outline Numbered or List Styles tab of the Bullets and Numbering dialog box, choose a style. (The bottom four styles on the Outline Numbered tab are for numbering headings, not lists, as are some items on the List Styles tab.)

- **Making the List Entries**   Either make the list entries as you go along or start by typing the list and choosing a list style later.

- **Placing Items in the Hierarchy**   Click a list entry, and, to tell Word where to place it in the hierarchy, give Indent commands. Click the Increase Indent button (or press the TAB key) to knock an item down a rung or the Decrease Indent button to raise its rank. Lists have nine different rankings, or levels. To place an item on the lowest rank, click the Increase Indent button nine times.

Note   *The next section in this chapter explains how to devise your own numbering schemes, if you are bold enough to try it.*

1. King	❖ King	1) King
2. Queen	❖ Queen	2) Queen
2.1. Lady in Waiting	➢ Lady in Waiting	a) Lady in Waiting
2.2. Handmaid	➢ Handmaid	b) Handmaid
3. Knave	❖ Knave	3) Knave
3.1. Squire	➢ Squire	a) Squire
3.2. Page	➢ Page	b) Page
4. Prime Minister	❖ Prime Minister	4) Prime Minister
4.1. Cabinet Sect'y	➢ Cabinet Sect'y	a) Cabinet Sect'y
4.2. Special Counselor	➢ Special Counselor	b) Special Counselor

Figure 10-9.   *Examples of outline-style lists*

Creating Your Own Numbering Scheme for Lists

Perhaps you want to change the way headings are numbered, change the punctuation of numbering schemes, or change the distance that a heading is indented. Personally, I think Word is wrong to put a blank space after the chapter number where a colon (:) and a blank space would do the job better. Maybe you want to include a style in the numbering scheme apart from the heading styles that Word includes.

If you want to change the numbering scheme in lists, you can do so by customizing a numbering scheme, modifying a list style, or creating your own list style. Whatever method you choose, creating a numbering scheme for lists is a tough, tedious job. I suggest doing it by creating or modifying a list style. That way, you can copy the style to other documents and templates if you decide you need it elsewhere. When you customize a numbering scheme, the scheme is only good in the document in which you are working.

 Chapter 12 explains styles in detail, including how to copy styles from document to document and template to template.

Creating and Modifying Number Schemes for List Styles

To create or modify a list style, start by choosing Format | Bullets and Numbering and selecting the List Styles tab in the Bullets and Numbering dialog box. The tab tells you the names of list styles that are available in the template from which your document was made. Create or modify a style:

- **Creating a Style**   Click the Add button. You see the New Style dialog box shown in Figure 10-10. Enter a name for the style in the Name text box.

- **Modifying a Style**   Select a style and click the Modify button. You see the Modify Style dialog box. It looks and works exactly like the New Style dialog box shown in Figure 10-10.

List styles govern the behavior of nine different lines, one for each level, or rank, in the nine-level hierarchy. So when you create or modify a numbering scheme, you tell Word how to treat nine different lines.

For each line you will modify or shape, open the Apply Formatting To drop-down menu and choose a level. The level is highlighted in the Preview box so you can tell which level, or rank, you are dealing with. For each level, do the following in the dialog box to tell Word how to number, indent, and format its lines:

- **Choose to mark the line with a number or bullet**   Click the Numbering button or the Bullets button.

- **If you chose a number, choose a number scheme and starting number**   Open the Scheme drop-down menu (it's to the right of the Bullets button) and choose a scheme for the line. Then click arrows in the Start At box to tell Word which number to mark the line with. Likely, you will choose 1 if you are dealing with the first line, 2 if you are dealing with the second, and so on.

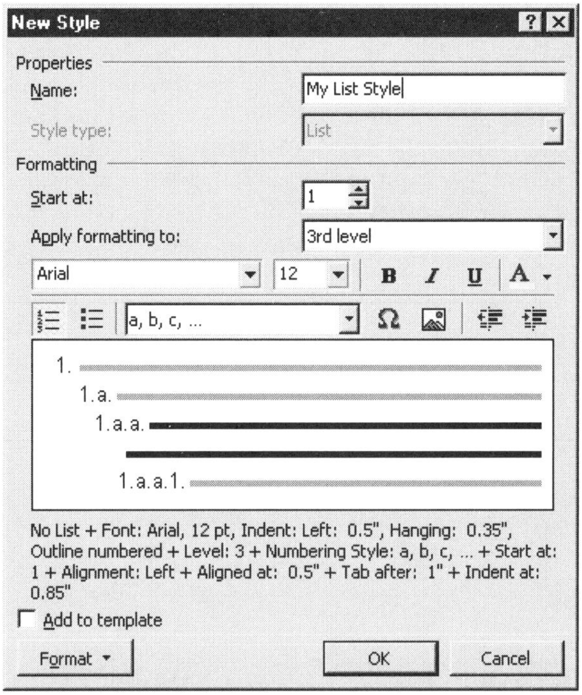

Figure 10-10.   *Creating a new numbering scheme for a list*

- **If you chose a bullet, choose a bullet character**   Either open the Scheme drop-down menu and choose a bullet on the list, or click the Insert Symbol button and select a symbol in the Symbol dialog box. You can also click the Insert Picture button to choose a Web-style picture bullet. You can also make use of the drop-down list to choose a new picture or symbol.

- **Format the bullet or number**   Open the Font menu and choose a font. To make the bullet or number a different size than the text, choose an option from the Font Size drop-down menu. You can also boldface, italicize, underline, and change the color of the bullet or number with the buttons in the dialog box.

- **Indent the bullet or number**   Click the Increase Indent and Decrease Indent buttons as many times as necessary to indent the line the proper distance from the margin. Remember: Indentation determines rank. The further down the hierarchy, the more lines should be indented.

- **Decide whether to add the style to the template**   Click the Add to Template check box.

Customizing a Numbering Scheme

Choose Format | Bullets and Numbering and select the Outline Numbered tab to customize a numbering scheme. On the tab, the top three choices are for imposing a numbering scheme on a list; the bottom four choices are for numbering the headings and chapters in a document (as the next section in this book explains).

Select the scheme that you want to alter and click the Customize button. You see the unduly complicated Customize Outline Numbered List dialog box shown in Figure 10-11. Following are explanations of the options in the dialog box. Watch the Number

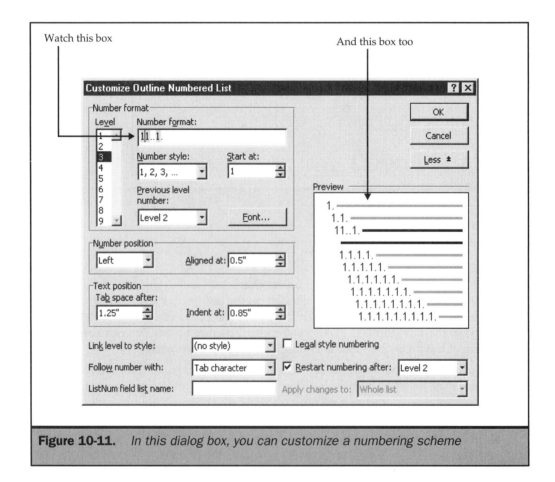

Figure 10-11. *In this dialog box, you can customize a numbering scheme*

Format box and Preview box as you construct your number format. Those boxes show exactly what your choices will do to numbers.

- **Level**   Choose which level of heading you want to alter. If you are dealing with a heading, choose 3 if you want to change the number formats of headings assigned the Heading 3 style in your document. If you want to change the third-level list formats, choose 3.
- **Number Style**   Choose which style of numbering you want.
- **Number Format**   Enter a punctuation mark—a colon, hyphen, or blank space, for example—after the number or letter. In the case of headings, enter a word— **Section**, **Title**, or **Instruction**, for example—before the number or letter if you want to label headings as well as number them.
- **Start At**   Choose a number or letter other than 1, I, A, or a, if for some reason you want heading numbers not to start at the beginning.
- **Previous Level Number**   For levels 2–9, make a choice from the drop-down menu to incorporate the numbering scheme from the previous level in the level you are currently dealing with. For example, if the level 1 number is *I* and the level 2 number is *A*, the first second-level number will be number I.A. The number appears in the Number Format box after you select it.
- **Font Button**   Click this button to open the Font dialog box and choose a new font or font size for your number and perhaps heading label as well.
- **Number Position**   Change the alignment of the number. The choices are left-aligned, center-aligned, or right-aligned.
- **Aligned At**   Adjust the distance between the number and the left margin.
- **Tab Space After**   Adjust the distance between the number and the beginning of the line. By entering a measurement in this box, you create a left-aligned tab space.
- **Indent At**   Adjust the distance at which text in the list is indented from the left margin. This option applies to list items longer than one line. When text wraps to the following line, it is indented by the measurement you enter here.

Click the More button to see and negotiate these options:

- **Link Level to Style**   Choose a style if you want to format text in the list in a different style.
- **Legal Style Numbering**   Changes Roman numerals throughout a numbering scheme to their Arabic numeral equivalents.

- **Follow Number With**   If you didn't enter a blank space after the number in the Number Format text box or enter a tab setting in the Tab Space After box, you can choose Space or Tab Character from the drop-down list and enter it now.

- **Restart Numbering After**   Uncheck this check box on the outside chance that you do not want to restart the numbers after a certain level heading. For example, suppose you want third-level headings to continue incrementing throughout the chapter and not be reset to number 1 after another, higher-level heading. In that case, uncheck this check box.

- **ListNum Field List Name**   If you intend to write detailed lists with ListNum field codes, enter the word or two that introduces those lists. (This option is for numbering items in paragraphs. See "Making Sublists or Nested Lists" earlier in this chapter.)

- **Apply Changes To**   Make sure Whole Document appears here.

Suppose you modify a numbering scheme but realize to your dismay that you want one of Word's original schemes back. To get it back, open the Bullets and Numbering dialog box, select the scheme you altered, and click the Reset button. Then click Yes when Word asks if you want the default setting.

Numbering the Headings and Chapters in a Document

In formal documents, scholarly papers, and legal briefs, headings are sometimes numbered so that commentary and cross-references can refer to headings by number as well as by name. Numbering the headings has other advantages, too. For example, you can include chapter numbers in page numbers if you number the chapters in your document.

The commands for numbering the headings in a document are found in the Bullets and Numbering dialog box. Word renumbers headings automatically if you delete a heading or add a new one. To use the heading-numbering commands, however, you must have assigned heading styles to the headings in your document (Chapter 12 describes styles).

Figure 10-12 shows, in Outline view, the four ways to number the headings in a document. Notice in some heading-number schemes that words—"Article," "Section," "Chapter"—as well as numbers and letters are attached to headings. One scheme is strictly for numbering the chapters in a document. In that scheme, Heading1 headings are given the prefix "Chapter 1," "Chapter 2," and so on, but other headings are not numbered or lettered.

```
Article I.    Lower Paleolithic              1   Lower Paleolithic
      Section 1.01  Australopithecine                1.1  Australopithecine
            (a)  Choppers                                    1.1.1       Choppers
            (b)  Hand Axes                                   1.1.2       Hand Axes
      Section 1.02  Sinathropus                       1.2  Sinathropus
Article II.   Middle Paleolithic            2   Middle Paleolithic
      Section 2.01  Steinheim                         2.1  Steinheim
      Section 2.02  Neanderthal                       2.2  Neanderthal
            (a)  Flake Tools                                 2.2.1       Flake Tools
            (b)  Fire                                        2.2.2       Fire
Article III.  Upper Paleolithic             3   Upper Paleolithic
      Section 3.01  Cro-Magnon                         3.1  Cro-Magnon
            (a)  Sewing                                      3.1.1       Sewing
            (b)  Spear Throwers                              3.1.2       Spear Throwers
      Section 3.02  Grimaldi                           3.2  Grimaldi


   I.   Lower Paleolithic                   Chapter 1 Lower Paleolithic
         A.   Australopithecine                      Australopithecine
               1.   Choppers                              Choppers
               2.   Hand Axes                             Hand Axes
         B.   Sinathropus                           Sinathropus
   II.  Middle Paleolithic                  Chapter 2 Middle Paleolithic
         A.   Steinheim                             Steinheim
         B.   Neanderthal                           Neanderthal
               1.   Flake Tools                          Flake Tools
               2.   Fire                                 Fire
   III. Upper Paleolithic                   Chapter 3 Upper Paleolithic
         A.   Cro-Magnon                            Cro-Magnon
               1.   Sewing                               Sewing
               2.   Spear Throwers                       Spear Throwers
         B.   Grimaldi                             Grimaldi
```

Figure 10-12.   *The four ways to number headings in a document, shown in Outline view*

Before you number headings, understand that only headings assigned the Heading 1 through Heading 9 styles are given heading numbers, unless you assign heading styles to other elements in your document (see "Choosing an Outline Level for Paragraphs" in Chapter 8).

Follow these steps to number all the headings in a document:

1. Switch to Outline view by clicking the Outline View button in the lower-left corner of the screen. In Outline view, you can see headings more easily. Choose a Show Heading option from the Show Level menu on the Outlining toolbar to see only the headings in the document. Chapter 17 explains how to work in Outline view.

2. Select the headings you want to number, if you don't want to number all of them.

3. Choose Format | Bullets and Numbering.

4. Select the Outline Numbered tab.

5. Choose one of the four heading numbering options in the bottom half of the dialog box.

6. Click OK.

If I were you, I would scroll through the document, look at the headings, and see if you like them. Click the Undo button if you regret numbering the headings. Follow these instructions in Outline view to fiddle with heading numbers:

- **Removing Numbers from Headings**   Select the headings whose numbers you want to remove and click the Numbering button on the Formatting toolbar.

- **Resuming the Numbers**   Suppose you number a few headings at the top of a document and you want to resume the numbers at a point midway through. Simply select the headings in Outline view and click the Numbering button on the Formatting toolbar.

- **Restarting the Numbers**   Suppose you want to restart the heading numbers at 1. In Outline view, click the heading that you want to be given the first number. Then choose Format | Bullets and Numbering, select the Outline Numbered tab, and click the Restart Numbering option button.

MOUS Exam Objectives Explored in Chapter 10

Objective	Heading
Apply bullet, outline, and numbering format to paragraphs	"The Bare-Bones Basics: Bulleted and Numbered Lists"

Ten Tricks for Handling Lists

Throughout this chapter are a number of tips and tricks for handling lists. However, most people will not read this chapter all the way through. Most people have better things to do than read computer books. For those people, here is a list of ten tricks for handling lists.

1. Press SHIFT-ENTER to Break Paragraphs in Lists   Occasionally a numbered line or bulleted paragraph grows too long, and you want to break it in half so that the reader doesn't have to labor through a long paragraph. If you press the ENTER key to break the paragraph, however, Word attaches a number or bullet to the next line, and the next line might not deserve a number or bullet. To break a bulleted or numbered paragraph without numbering or bulleting the next paragraph, press SHIFT-ENTER instead of ENTER.

2. You Can Turn a List into a Style   The newest edition of Word offers list and table styles as well as paragraph and character styles. You can now create your own list style, as "Creating and Modifying Number Schemes for List Styles" explains earlier in this chapter.

3. Press the Increase Indent Button to Indent Lists   Apart from altering a style, you can indent a list by selecting it and clicking the Increase Indent button on the Formatting toolbar. Wouldn't you know it, you can also click the Decrease Indent button to move a list closer to the left margin.

4. Word Can Create Bulleted Lists Automatically   Word creates bulleted lists automatically. If you enter the following characters or character combinations, press the SPACEBAR or TAB key, enter the first line in the list, and press ENTER, Word places a bullet on the first and subsequent lines in the list: *, -, —, >, ->, =>.

5. Word Also Creates Numbered Lists Automatically   Word also creates numbered lists automatically, whether you like it or not. If you enter a **1**, enter a period, press the SPACEBAR or TAB key, enter a line of text, and press ENTER, Word places numbers on the first and subsequent lines in the list.

6. You Can Turn Off Word's Automatic Lists   Some people think that Word's automatic lists are a bother. If you are one of those people, you can prevent Word from making lists on its own with these techniques:

- Choose Tools | AutoCorrect Options, select the AutoFormat As You Type tab in the AutoCorrect dialog box, and uncheck the Automatic Bulleted Lists and Automatic Numbered Lists check boxes.
- Click the AutoCorrect Options button and choose Stop Automatically Creating Numbered Lists or Stop Automatically Creating Bulleted Lists on the drop-down menu.

7. You Can Restart a List by Right-Clicking   Suppose you want to restart a list in the middle. Let's say Word attaches the number 5 to a line, but you want that line to be given the number 1. To restart a list, right-click the entry that you want to be first in the

FORMATTING TEXT AND PAGES

new list and choose Restart Numbering on the shortcut menu. You can also choose Format | Bullets and numbering, select the Numbered tab in the dialog box, and select the Restart Numbering option button.

8. You Can Resume a List from Earlier in a Document   It so happens now and then that you want to interrupt a list with a few paragraphs of commentary and then resume the list further down the page. To resume a list, create the list as you normally would. Then click where you want to resume your new list from the previous list and do one of the following:

- Right-click and choose Continue Numbering on the shortcut menu.
- Choose Format | Bullets and Numbering, select the Numbered tab in the Bullets and Numbering dialog box, and select the Continue Previous List option button.

9. Besides the Standard Bullet, You Can Use Symbols   Some people think that the standard bullet—the round black dot—is too conventional. To decorate a bulleted list with a different symbol, select the list, choose Formats | Bullets and Numbering, select the Bulleted tab, and choose a different symbol. You can also click the Customize button in the Bullets and Numbering dialog box, click the Character button in the Customize Bulleted List dialog box, and choose just about any symbol imaginable in the Symbol dialog box.

10. You Can Use Web-Style Picture Bullets   When you are working on an HTML document that will be viewed by way of a Web browser, consider using Web-style picture bullets for your bulleted lists. To select one of the colorful bullets, choose Formats | Bullets and Numbering, select the Bulleted tab, click the Customize button, click the Picture button in the Customize Bulleted List dialog box, and choose a bullet. Picture bullets are not recommended for normal documents, however, because they look kind of odd when they are printed on paper.

The Complete Reference

Chapter 11

Proofing Your Work

I was going to call this chapter "Foolproofing Your Work," but that seemed kind of presumptuous, since keeping every error from slipping into a document is impossible. Still, you can do a good job of proofing your work and eliminating errors by using the tools that Word provides for that purpose. This chapter describes those tools. Read on to find out how to correct typos and capitalization errors with the AutoCorrect command, correct spelling and grammatical errors, and improve your writing by taking advantage of the thesaurus. You will also find instructions in this chapter for handling text that was written in a foreign language.

Correcting Typos with the AutoCorrect Command

You may have noticed that the invisible hand of Word corrects certain misspellings and typos as you make them. For example, try typing "accomodate" with one "m"—Word corrects the misspelling and inserts the second "m" for you. Try typing "perminent" with an "i" instead of an "a"—the invisible hand of Word corrects the misspelling and you get "permanent." While you're at it, type a colon and a close parenthesis :)—you get a smiley face.

Word corrects common spelling errors and turns punctuation mark combinations into symbols as part of its AutoCorrect feature. To see which typos are corrected and which punctuation marks are turned into symbols, choose Tools | AutoCorrect Options. You see the AutoCorrect dialog box shown in Figure 11-1. Scroll down the Replace list in the middle of the dialog box to see the list of words and typos that are autocorrected.

As good as the AutoCorrect feature is, you can make it even better. And you can also add the typos and misspellings you often make to the list of words that are corrected automatically. These pages explain how to do that and also how to fix capitalization errors automatically.

Note *"Entering Text and Graphics Quickly with the AutoCorrect Command" in Chapter 6 explains how you can use the AutoCorrect command as a means of entering boilerplate text and graphics.*

Supposing You Don't Care to Be AutoCorrected...

What if Word "autocorrects" or capitalizes a word against your wishes? To reverse an autocorrection, move the pointer over the place where the correction occurred. You see a small blue line. Move the pointer over the line and you see the AutoCorrection Options button. Click the button and you can choose an option from the drop-down menu to handle autocorrections:

- **Reverse the Correction One Time Only** Choose the first option on the menu. The option is called Change Back To or Undo. Another way to reverse an autocorrection is to choose Edit | Undo (or press CTRL-Z) right after Word makes the autocorrection.

- **Tell Word not to Make the Correction in the Future**   Choose the second option on the menu. The option is called Stop Automatically Correcting or Stop Auto-Capitalizing.

- **Open the AutoCorrect Dialog Box**   Choose Control AutoCorrection options, the third option on the menu. Doing so opens the AutoCorrect dialog box (see Figure 11-1), where you pick and choose what gets autocorrected.

Some people think that the AutoCorrect Options button is annoying. If you are one of those people, you can keep it from appearing by choosing Tools | AutoCorrect options and unchecking the Show AutoCorrect Options Buttons check box in the AutoCorrect dialog box (see Figure 11-1).

FORMATTING TEXT AND PAGES

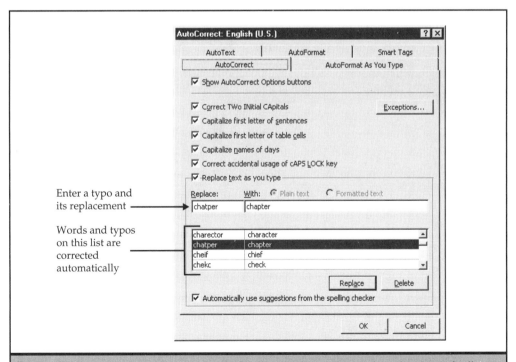

Figure 11-1.   *Words and typos in the Replace column are replaced automatically with the words in the With column*

Telling Word Which Typos and Misspellings to Correct

No doubt you make the same typing errors and spelling errors time and time again. The author of this book cannot type the word "chapter" without spelling it "chatper." Several years ago, a vice president of the United States named Dan Quayle made headlines when he spelled "potato" with an "e" on the end: "potatoe." To save time and to keep from looking foolish, you can add typos like "chatper" and misspellings like "potatoe" to the list of words that are corrected automatically.

The fastest and surest way to add misspellings and typos to the list is to do it while you are spell-checking a document. In Figure 11-2, the misspelling "Chatper" and its replacement "Chapter" are being added to the Replace With list in the AutoCorrect dialog box (see Figure 11-1). During a spell-check, add words to the list with these techniques:

- **By Clicking AutoCorrect in the Spelling and Grammar Dialog Box**   In the Spelling and Grammar dialog box, select the word that is to replace the typo or misspelling in the Suggestions list. Then click the AutoCorrect button. Later in this chapter, "Correcting Your Spelling Errors" explains all the options in the Spelling and Grammar dialog box.

- **By Choosing AutoCorrect on the Shortcut Menu**   Word draws squiggly red lines underneath words that are misspelled. Right-click a misspelling if you want to add it to the list of errors that are corrected automatically, choose AutoCorrect from the shortcut menu, and select the word that is to replace the typo or misspelling on the submenu.

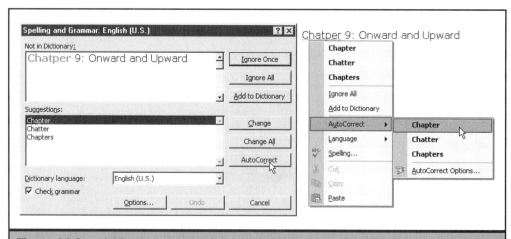

Figure 11-2.   *Adding a word to the list of misspellings and typos that are corrected automatically*

The other, roundabout way to add to the list of misspellings and typos that are corrected automatically is to choose Tools | AutoCorrect Options to open the AutoCorrect dialog box, enter the misspelling or typo in the Replace text box, enter the correctly spelled word in the With box, and click the Add button.

> **Tip** *You can remove misspellings and typos from the list of words that are corrected automatically. Perhaps you are working on a novel with gritty realistic dialogue and you want "should of," "themself," and other such words to stay in the text without being corrected. To remove a word from the list of corrected words, select it in the AutoCorrect dialog box and click the Delete button. Then backspace over the word and its replacement in the Replace and With text boxes.*

Preventing Capitalization Errors with AutoCorrect

Near the top of the AutoCorrect dialog box (choose Tools | AutoCorrect Options to get there) are five check boxes whose job is to prevent capitalization errors. These options do their jobs very well, sometimes to a fault:

- **Correct TWo INitial CApitals**   Prevents two capital letters from appearing in a row at the start of a word with more than two letters. Only the first letter is capitalized. This option is for people who can't lift their little fingers from the SHIFT key fast enough after typing the first capital letter at the start of a word.

- **Capitalize first letter of sentences**   Makes sure that the first letter in a sentence is capitalized.

> **Tip** *Don't forget the Capitalize first letter of sentences option when you enter computer code or other text that doesn't need to be capitalized. Unchecking the option can be very helpful on occasions like that.*

- **Capitalize first letter of table cells**   Makes sure that the first letter you enter in a table cell is a capital letter.

- **Capitalize names of days**   Makes sure the names of the days of the week are capitalized.

- **Correct accidental usage of cAPS LOCK key**   Changes capital letters to lowercase letters if you press the SHIFT key to start a sentence while Caps Lock is on. The idea here is that if you press down the SHIFT key while Caps Lock is on, you don't know that Caps Lock is on, since you don't need to hold down the SHIFT key to enter capital letters. Word turns the first letter into a capital letter and the following letters into lowercase letters and turns Caps Lock off.

Making Exceptions to the AutoCorrect Capitalization Controls

Except when certain abbreviations are used in sentences, you have to type the rare name that starts with two uppercase letters, or you want to enter an acronym that happens to be listed in the AutoCorrect dialog box, the AutoCorrect capitalization settings work fine. For those rare occasions when they don't work, click the Exceptions button in the AutoCorrect dialog box (see Figure 11-1).

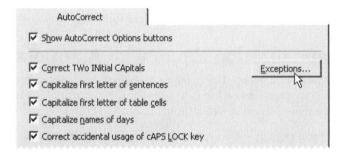

You see the AutoCorrect Exceptions dialog box. By making entries in the First Letter, INitial CAps, and Other Corrections tabs, you can eat your cake and have it too. In other words, you can continue to use AutoCorrect to correct typos and misspellings except under certain circumstances:

- **First Letter Tab**   When Word encounters an abbreviation that is listed on the First Letter tab, it allows the word following the abbreviation to start with a lowercase letter. However, if the abbreviation is not listed, Word assumes that the period at the end of the abbreviation marks the end of a sentence, so the program begins the next word incorrectly with a capital letter. If Word persists in capitalizing a word after an abbreviation you use, solve the problem by entering the abbreviation on the First Letter tab so that Word can recognize it as an abbreviation.

- **INitial CAps Tab**   Newfangled company names sometimes start with two capital letters: QUest Data Inc., DIgital DIngbats, Inc. Enter such names on the INitial CAps tab to keep Word from lowercasing the second capital letter.

- **Other Corrections Tab**   This one is for exceptions that don't fit on the First Letter or INitial CAps tabs. Enter them here.

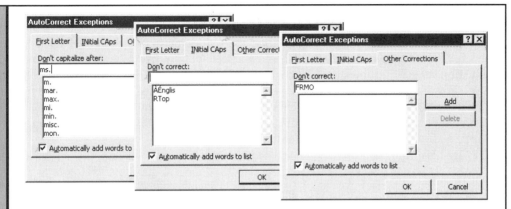

As long as the Automatically Add Words To List check boxes are selected in the AutoCorrect Exceptions dialog box, Word adds abbreviations and words with two initial capital letters to the Exceptions lists when you correct them with the AutoCorrect Options button or by backspacing. For example, suppose you enter **TEchnics**, the first word in a company name, and Word changes "TEchnics" to "Technics." To keep that from happening in the future, you can click the AutoCorrect Options button and choose the Stop Automatically Correcting "TEchnics" option. You can also backspace over "echnics" and type the rest of the company name again. Either way, you add "TEchnics" to the list of words on the INitial CAps tab that are not autocorrected. (Words aren't added to the Exceptions list when you choose the Undo command to reverse capitalizations.)

Correcting Your Spelling Errors

Word keeps a dictionary in its hip pocket. The program consults the dictionary as you enter text and draws lines in red underneath words that are misspelled and words that were entered twice in a row. To correct misspellings, you can either address them one at a time or start the spell-checker and proof many pages or an entire document at once. You can even create a dictionary of your own with the jargon and slang peculiar to your way of life and have Word check the spelling of jargon and slang. Better read on.

Caution
Don't trust the smell-checker to be accurate all of the time. It doesn't really locate misspelled words—it locates words that are not in its dictionary. For example, if you write, "Nero diddled while Rome burned," the spell-checker will not catch the error. Nero fiddled while Rome burned, but because "diddle" is a legitimate word in the spelling dictionary, the spell-checker overlooks the misspelling. The moral: Proofread your documents carefully and don't rely on the spell-checker to catch all your smelling errors.

Correcting Misspellings One at a Time

With the one-at-a-time method of spell-checking a document, you right-click each word that is underlined in red and choose a correct spelling from the shortcut menu. (If you don't see any suggestions for correct spellings, choose Tools | Options, select the Spelling & Grammar tab in the Options dialog box, and check the Check Spelling As You Type check box.) When you choose a word from the shortcut menu, it replaces the misspelling that you right-clicked. Click the Delete Repeated Word option to erase a duplicated word you entered accidentally.

The spell-checker finds words entered in duplicate duplicate. It also flags misspellings so you can corect them.

Tip *If you aren't sure but vaguely remember how to spell a word, you can use wildcards and the spell-checker to find out how to spell it. Enter the asterisk (*) or the question mark (?) wildcard in place of the letters or letter you aren't sure of and run the spell-checker on the word. This trick works especially well with place names. For example, entering **Timbuk*** finds the correct spelling of the ancient kingdom where the great Sundiata Keita ruled—Timbuktu.*

Getting Rid of the Squiggly Red Lines

More than a few users of Word think that the squiggly red lines that appear under misspelled words are annoying. To keep those lines from appearing, choose Tools | Options, select the Spelling & Grammar tab in the Options dialog box, and check the Hide Spelling Errors In This Document check box.

Even with the red lines gone, you can do a quick spell-check of a word that you suspect has been misspelled. To do so, select the word (by double-clicking it) and do one of the following:

- Either press F7 or choose Tools | Spelling and Grammar. The Spelling and Grammar dialog box appears if the word has indeed been misspelled. Click a word in the Suggestions box and then click the Change button.

- Double-click the Spelling and Grammar Status icon on the right side of the Status bar. A short list of alternative spellings appears if the word was misspelled. Click a word on the list to enter it in place of the misspelling. When you correct a word this way, however, the squiggly red lines soon begin appearing in your document because correcting a word this way also tells Word to start marking errors again.

Spell-Checking an Entire Document or Text Selection

Instead of correcting misspellings one at a time, you can spell-check a document or part of a document and address misspellings one after the other. To spell-check part of a document, select the part you want to spell-check. Start the spell-check by pressing F7, choosing Tools | Spelling and Grammar, or right-clicking a misspelled word and choosing Spelling from the shortcut menu. You see the Spelling and Grammar dialog box shown in Figure 11-3. Misspellings are highlighted in the document and appear in bright red in the Not In Dictionary box.

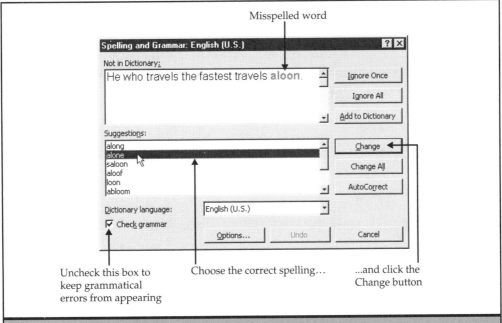

Figure 11-3. *Misspelled words appear in bright red in the Spelling and Grammar dialog box*

Table 11-1 describes the buttons and other items in the Spelling and Grammar dialog box. As Word encounters misspellings, do one of the following to correct them:

- Select the correct spelling in the Suggestions box and click the Change button.

- Delete the misspelled word in the Not In Dictionary box (by double-clicking to select it and pressing DELETE or BACKSPACE), type the correct spelling in the Not In Dictionary box, and click the Change button.

- Move the Spelling and Grammar dialog box aside, click outside the dialog box, correct the misspelled word in the document, and click the Resume button in the Spelling and Grammar dialog box (the Resume button appears where the Ignore button used to be).

Grammatical errors appear in green in the Spelling and Grammar dialog box. To ignore grammatical errors for the time being and focus on misspellings, uncheck the Check Grammar check box. Later in this chapter, "Correcting Grammatical Errors" explains how to address grammatical errors in a document.

Button	What It Does
Ignore Once	Ignores this instance of the misspelling but stops on it again if the same misspelling appears later in the document.
Ignore All	Ignores the misspelling throughout the document and in all other open documents. If you click this button but regret doing so, click the Recheck Document button on the Spelling & Grammar tab of the Options dialog box to stop ignoring the misspelling. To get to the Spelling & Grammar tab and see the Recheck Document button, click the Options button in the Spelling and Grammar dialog box (see Figure 11-3).
Add to Dictionary	Adds the misspelling to a spelling dictionary so that Word never stops on it again. By clicking the Add button, you tell Word that the misspelling is a legitimate word or name.
Suggestions	Lists words to replace the misspelling. (If you don't see words in this box, click the Options button to open the Spelling & Grammar tab of the Options dialog box, and then check the Always Suggest Corrections check box.)

Table 11-1.   *The Parts of the Spelling and Grammar Dialog Box*

Button	What It Does
Change/Delete	Enters the highlighted word in the Suggestions box in the document where the misspelling used to be. When the same word appears twice in a row, the Delete button appears where the Change button was. Click the Delete button to delete the second word in the pair.
Change All/ Delete All	Replaces all instances of the misspelled word with the word that is highlighted in the Suggestions box. Click the Change All button to correct a misspelling that occurs throughout a document. When two words appear in a row, this button is called Delete All. Click the Delete All button to delete the second word in the pair throughout your document.
AutoCorrect	Adds the spelling correction to the list of words that are corrected automatically. See "Correcting Typos with the AutoCorrect Command," earlier in this chapter.
Options	Opens the Spelling & Grammar tab of the Options dialog box so you can tell Word how to spell-check your document.
Undo	Reverses your previous action in the Spelling and Grammar dialog box. You can keep clicking Undo to reverse more than one action.

Table 11-1.   *The Parts of the Spelling and Grammar Dialog Box* (continued)

To skip ahead to the next spelling or grammatical error in a document, double-click the Spelling and Grammar Status icon (you'll find it on the right side of the status bar) or press ALT-F7.

In spell-checks, Word makes the following presumptions:

- Words in uppercase are acronyms and so should be ignored.
- Words with numbers in them should be ignored.
- Internet addresses and file addresses should be ignored. An Internet address is one with the letters *www* (www.runnersworld.com) or *http://* (http://mymachine.mydomain.com). A file address includes backslashes (\), as in C:\Windows\Temporary Internet Files. E-mail addresses with the @ sign are also ignored.

However, you can spell-check those items as well by clicking the Options button in the Spelling and Grammar dialog box (see Figure 11-3) or choosing Tools | Options and selecting the Spelling & Grammar tab in the Options dialog box. On the Spelling & Grammar tab are three Ignore check boxes. Uncheck them to spell-check uppercase words, words with numbers, and Internet and file addresses.

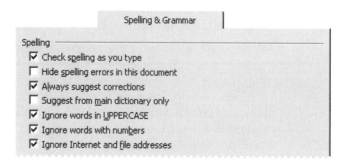

Keeping Words from Being Spell-Checked

Spell-checking address lists, lines of computer code, and foreign languages such as Spanglish for which Microsoft doesn't offer foreign-language dictionaries is a thorough waste of time. Follow these steps to tell the spell-checker to ignore text in a document:

1. Select the text.
2. Choose Tools | Language | Set Language. You see the Language dialog box.
3. Check the Do Not Check Spelling Or Grammar check box and click OK.

Create a character style for text that need not be spell-checked. That way, you can simply apply the style to the text instead of having to select it and choose the Tools | Language | Set Language command. *Hint:* Click the Format button in the New Style dialog box and choose Language. Chapter 12 explains styles.

Spell-Checking Text in Foreign Languages

Spanish and French dictionaries are included in the version of Word that is sold in the United States. That means you can spell-check Spanish and French words. And you can spell-check words in other languages, too, as long as you installed proofing tools for those languages and told Word which languages you intend to use (see "Working with Text Written in a Foreign Language" later in this chapter). Right-click a misspelled word or choose Tools | Spelling and Grammar, and Word proofs the word in the foreign language.

Employing Other Dictionaries to Help with Spell-Checking

To find spelling errors, Word compares each word on the page to the words in its main dictionary and a second dictionary called Custom.dic. If a word you type is not found in either dictionary, the program considers the word a misspelling. The main dictionary lists all known words in the English language. The Custom.dic dictionary lists words, proper names, and technical jargon that you deemed legitimate when you clicked the Add to Dictionary button in the course of a spell-check. In this illustration, for example, the word "gangsta" is being added to the Custom.dic dictionary. Never again will the spell-checker pause over this hybrid of the word "gangster" because I am adding it to the Custom.dic dictionary.

Taking the Rap for Gangsta Rap

 From Word's standpoint, a dictionary is merely a list of words, one word per line, that have been spelled correctly and saved as a .dic (dictionary) file. You can acquire dictionary files for use with Word from Microsoft and from professional associations.

Besides the Custom.dic dictionary, you can employ other dictionaries to help with spell-checking. People who work in specialized professions such as law or medicine can also use legal dictionaries and medical dictionaries to spell-check their work. You can create dictionaries of your own for slang words, colloquialisms, or special projects. Before you start spell-checking, you can tell Word which dictionaries to use. And you can edit dictionaries as well. All this magic is done by way of the Custom Dictionaries dialog box shown in Figure 11-4. Do either of the following to open this dialog box:

- Press F7 or choose Tools | Spelling and Grammar to open the Spelling and Grammar dialog box, and then click the Options button. In the Spelling & Grammar tab, click the Custom Dictionaries button.

- Choose Tools | Options, select the Spelling & Grammar tab in the Options dialog box, and click the Custom Dictionaries button.

Using Secondary Dictionaries for Spell-Checking

People who work in law offices, research facilities, and medical facilities type hundreds of arcane terms each day, none of which are in the main dictionary. One way to make sure that arcane terms are spelled correctly is to create or acquire a dictionary of legal, scientific, or medical terms and use it for spell-checking purposes.

Follow these steps to create a new spelling dictionary or tell Word that you want to use a secondary dictionary to check the spelling of words:

- **Create a New Spelling Dictionary** Click the New button in the Custom Dictionaries dialog box (see Figure 11-4). In the Create Custom Dictionary dialog box, enter a name for your new dictionary and click the Save button. See "Editing the Words in a Dictionary," later in this chapter, to learn how to enter terms in your new spelling dictionary.

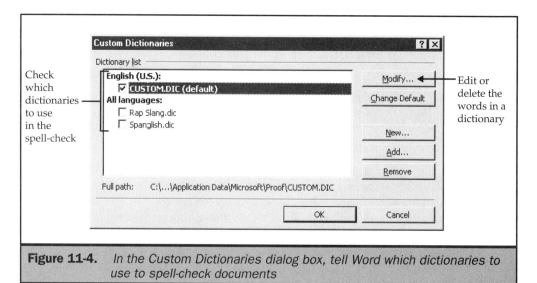

Figure 11-4. *In the Custom Dictionaries dialog box, tell Word which dictionaries to use to spell-check documents*

- **Use a Secondary Dictionary** Make note of where the dictionary file is located on your computer. It doesn't have to be in the C:\Windows\Application Data\Microsoft\Proof folder along with the other dictionaries for Word to use it. Click the Add button in the Custom Dictionaries dialog box (see Figure 11-4) to use a dictionary that you acquired elsewhere. The Add Custom Dictionary dialog box appears. Locate the dictionary on your computer, select it, and click OK. Its name appears in the Custom Dictionaries dialog box.

Note *Select a dictionary and click the Remove button to remove its name from the Custom Dictionaries dialog box. Removing a name in no way, shape, or form deletes the dictionary. You can click the Add button to place the dictionary's name in the dialog box again and use it for spell-checking. Only ten dictionaries total can appear in the Custom Dictionaries box.*

Editing the Words in a Dictionary

To edit the words in the Custom.dic dictionary or any other dictionary, select it in the Custom Dictionaries dialog box (see Figure 11-4) and click the Modify button. You see the Custom.dic dialog box shown in Figure 11-5. From there, you can delete words and even add words to the dictionary by clicking the Add button.

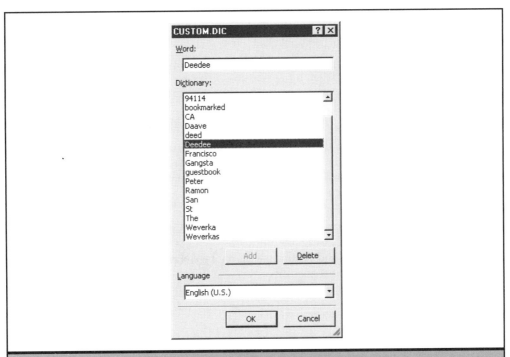

Figure 11-5. *Editing words in and adding words to the Custom dictionary*

To add a word to a secondary dictionary, open it in Notepad or Word. You can do that by finding the dictionary (.dic) file in My Computer or Windows Explorer and double-clicking it. Enter the new word and make sure it appears on its own line.

Telling Word Which Dictionaries to Use in a Spell-Check

Word checks for misspellings against the words in the main dictionary and each dictionary whose name is checked off in the Custom Dictionaries dialog box (see Figure 11-4). To make use of a dictionary in spell-checks, click the check box beside its name; uncheck the boxes beside the names of dictionaries you don't need.

On the Spelling & Grammar tab of the Options dialog box is a check box called Suggest From Main Dictionary Only; click it to exclude all secondary dictionaries from spell-checks. Choose Tools | Options and select the Spelling & Grammar tab in the Options dialog box to see and check this option.

Correcting Grammatical Errors

Much of what constitutes good grammar is, like beauty, in the eye of the beholder. Still, you can do your best to repair grammatical errors by getting the assistance of the grammar-checker. The grammar-checker identifies grammatical errors, explains what the errors are, and gives you the opportunity to correct the errors. These pages explain how to check for and repair grammatical errors, tell Word how scrupulously to look for errors, and turn off the grammar-checker.

Checking a Document for Grammatical Errors

By now you must have noticed the green lines that appear underneath words from time to time. (If you don't see the green lines, choose Tools | Options, select the Spelling & Grammar tab in the Options dialog box, check the Check Grammar As You Type check box, and make sure that no check mark appears in the Hide Grammatical Errors In This Document check box.) The green lines appear where Word thinks it has encountered a grammatical error.

Figure 11-6 shows the two ways to correct grammatical errors. You can correct them one at a time by right-clicking and choosing a correction from the shortcut menu, or you can open the Spelling and Grammar dialog box and correct grammatical errors one after the other throughout a document.

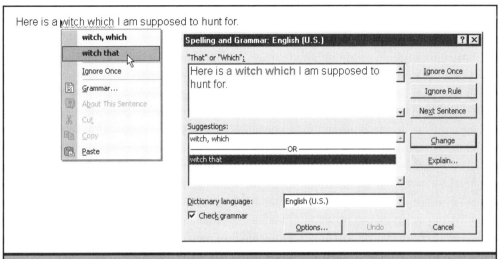

Figure 11-6. *Grammar is not an exact science, but you can try your best to fix grammatical errors with the grammar-checker*

FORMATTING TEXT
AND PAGES

 As long as the Office Assistant is turned on, you can get explanations of grammatical errors. To do so, right-click a grammatical error and choose About This Sentence from the shortcut menu. While the Spelling and Grammar dialog box is open, the Office Assistant appears automatically to clarify grammatical errors. In Chapter 4, "The Office Assistant and What You Can Do about It" describes the Office Assistant.

Press F7 or choose Tools | Spelling and Grammar to correct grammatical errors in the Spelling and Grammar dialog box. Sentences in which grammatical errors appear are highlighted in the document. The grammatical errors themselves appear in bright green in the box at the top of the dialog box (along with spelling errors, which are red). If the Office Assistant is running, the little rascal gives you an explanation of the grammar error. Table 11-2 describes the buttons in the Spelling and Grammar dialog box for correcting grammatical errors. When Word encounters an error, take one of these actions to correct it:

- Select a correction in the Suggestions box and click the Change button.

- Delete the grammatical errors or rephrase the sentence in the top of the dialog box, enter a correction, and click the Next Sentence button.

- Click outside the Spelling and Grammar dialog box, correct the grammatical error in the document, and click the Resume button (you will find it where the Ignore button used to be).

Button	What It Does
Ignore Once	Ignores the breach of grammar and proceeds to the next grammatical error.
Ignore Rule	Tells Word to ignore, throughout the document and in all open documents, the kind of grammatical error that is listed at the top of the Spelling and Grammar dialog box. For example, if the top of the dialog box reads "Passive Voice," all passive-voice errors are disregarded.
Next Sentence	Tells Word to move on to the next sentence. Click this button after you repair a grammatical error by editing words inside the Spelling and Grammar dialog box.
Change	Corrects the grammatical error by entering the selected word, phrase, or sentence in the Suggestions box in the document.
Explain	Offers an explanation as to why Word tagged the sentence as ungrammatical.
Options	Opens the Spelling & Grammar tab of the Options dialog box so you can tell Word how to check for grammatical errors in your document.
Undo	Reverses your previous action in the Spelling and Grammar dialog box. You can keep clicking Undo to reverse more than one action.

Table 11-2. *Buttons for Correcting Grammatical Errors in the Spelling and Grammar Dialog Box*

Strategies for Handling the Grammar-Checker

The grammar-checker isn't for everybody. Some people think that the green lines that the grammar-checker draws underneath grammatical errors are annoying. And if you have any degree of confidence in your writing, you probably don't need the grammar-checker. What's more, the grammar-checker occasionally offers up a ridiculous suggestion for correcting what it thinks is an error. This famous line from *Hamlet*, for example, would not make any sense if Shakespeare had corrected it with his grammar-checker.

Neither a borrower nor a lender be.

Choose Tools | Options, select the Spelling & Grammar tab in the Options dialog box, and take note of the check boxes under the word "Grammar." By checking or unchecking these boxes, you can impair the grammar-checker or make it work better:

- **Turn the Grammar-Checker Off**   Uncheck the Check Grammar As You Type check box to turn off the grammar-checker altogether.

- **Keep the Green Lines from Appearing**   Check the Hide Grammatical Errors In This Document check box. With this strategy, the green lines don't appear, but Word still looks out for grammatical errors. When you press F7 or choose Tools | Spelling and Grammar, the grammatical errors appear in the Spelling and Grammar dialog box (see Figure 11-6). You can also find grammatical errors by double-clicking the book icon on the Status bar.

- **Only Handle Spelling Errors in the Spelling and Grammar Dialog Box**   Uncheck the Check Grammar With Spelling check box if you want to keep grammatical errors from appearing in the Spelling and Grammar dialog box. You can still correct grammatical errors by right-clicking the error and making a choice on the drop-down menu.

Telling Word How to Check for Grammatical Errors

Not all documents are alike, so Word gives you a means of deciding how thoroughly and rigidly to check for grammatical errors. After all, a letter to Aunt Enid does not have to be as grammatically up to snuff as a letter to a bank examining board or a clemency plea addressed to the governor of Texas. Read on to learn how to change the standards by which good grammar is measured and choose for yourself what the rules of good grammar are.

Choosing a Standard for Judging Grammar

Follow these steps to tell Word how carefully to grammar-check a document:

1. Choose Tools | Options and select the Spelling & Grammar tab in the Options dialog box. You can also get to the Spelling & Grammar tab by clicking the Options button in the Spelling and Grammar dialog box (see Figure 11-6).

2. From the Writing Style drop-down menu, choose an option that describes your document and click OK.

   ■ **Grammar & Style** Enforces the grammar as well as the style rules. Table 11-3 explains what these rules are.

   ■ **Grammar Only** Enforces Word's grammar rules, but not its style rules. See Table 11-3.

Option	What It Checks For
Require	
Comma Required Before Last List Item	A comma before the word "and" or "or" when more than two nouns are strung together ("no, yes, or maybe," not "no, yes or maybe"). The options are Always, Never, and Don't Check.
Punctuation Required with Quotes	Whether punctuation marks such as commas and periods appear inside or outside quotation marks. In American usage, punctuation marks always appear inside quotation marks (He was "inconvenienced.") In British usage, punctuation marks sometimes appear outside quotation marks. (He was "inconvenienced".) The options are Inside, Outside, and Don't Check.

Table 11-3. *Grammatical Rules Used in Grammar-Checking*

Option	What It Checks For
Spaces Required Between Sentences	Whether one or two blank spaces appear after the periods at the end of sentences. The options are 1, 2, and Don't Check.
Grammar	
Capitalization	Capitalization errors in proper names ("Ms. gonzales") and titles ("president Wilson").
Fragments and Run-Ons	Sentences missing verbs ("This a big mess") and sentences with comma splices ("Nobody buys it, it's too expensive").
Misused Words	Misuse of adjectives, superlatives, and comparatives such as "like," "nor," and "whom."
Negation	Use of double negatives ("You don't have no reason to do that").
Noun Phrases	Number disagreement errors ("three boy") and the misuse of "a" and "an" ("a important time").
Possessives and Plurals	Misuse of possessives and plurals as regards the use of the apostrophe (') ("Janes' car," "the peoples' voice").
Punctuation	Incorrect use of commas, periods, and colons.
Questions	Failure to enter a question mark (?) at the end of a question.
Relative Clauses	Incorrect use of relative clauses ("which" for "that," "that's" for "whose").
Subject-Verb Agreement	Subjects and verbs that do not agree ("The country are big," "Dogs is tired").
Verb Phrases	Incorrect verb tenses ("they will smiled").
Style	
Clichés, Colloquialisms, and Jargon	Shopworn phrases ("each and every," "one and all"); words and phrases that belong in conversation, not writing ("how come," "awfully nice"); and words peculiar to a trade or technical profession.

Table 11-3. *Grammatical Rules Used in Grammar-Checking* (continued)

Option	What It Checks For
Contractions	Use of contractions that could be spelled out ("won't," "could've," "hadn't").
Fragment - Stylistic Suggestions	Sentence fragments that are not suitable for formal writing ("Cool, dude!" "Right-o!").
Gender-Specific Words	Words with the letters "man" that might also refer to women ("chairman," "workmanlike").
Hyphenated and Compound Words	Words that are hyphenated mistakenly ("pre-historic") and words that should be hyphenated but aren't ("self restraint").
Misused Words – Stylistic Suggestions	Words and phrases that are considered improper ("ain't," "where's it at?").
Numbers	The digits 1 through 10, which are often spelled out ("one," "ten").
Passive Sentences	Sentences in the passive voice ("He was tackled by me").
Possessive and Plurals – Stylistic Suggestions	Dubious uses of possessives ("My sense of loyalty is like a dog's").
Punctuation – Stylistic Suggestions	Unneeded or missing punctuation marks.
Relative Clauses – Stylistic Suggestions	Uses of "that" and "which."
Sentence Length (More than Sixty Words)	Sentences longer than 60 words.
Sentence Structure	Sentence fragments, run-on sentences, and sentences with too many conjunctions (that is, too many "ands" and "ors").
Sentences Beginning with And, But, and Hopefully	Sentences that begin with these three words.*
Successive Nouns (More than Three)	More than three nouns in a row ("The countryside market development fund is healthy").
Successive Prepositional Phrases	Three or more prepositions in a row ("The neighborhood on the hill in the city by the sea").

Table 11-3. *Grammatical Rules Used in Grammar-Checking* (continued)

Option	What It Checks For
Unclear Phrasing	Sentences with referents that are hard to locate ("All of the racers did not finish the race" instead of "Not all the racers finished the race").
Use of First Person	Use of the word "I" and "me," which is considered a *faux pas* in technical writing ("I must be right").
Verb Phrases – Stylistic Suggestions	Odd and split verb phrases ("I am able to sing").
Wordiness	Excessive use of modifiers ("necessarily," "certainly") and overuse of adverbs.
Words in Split Infinitives	Split infinitives ("They want to very thoroughly complete the job").

* There is nothing wrong with starting a sentence with "And" or "But." Strange that "Hopefully" is lumped with the other two words, because "hopefully," a dangling modifier, is grammatically wrong and should not be used under any circumstances, much less the start of a sentence.

Table 11-3. *Grammatical Rules Used in Grammar-Checking* (continued)

Click the Settings button on the Spelling & Grammar tab to open the Grammar Settings dialog box and read the rules for yourself.

Deciding for Yourself What the Rules of Good Grammar Are

Depending on which writing style is in use, some of the grammar rules described in Table 11-3 are enforced and some are not enforced. Follow these steps to tell Word which grammar rules to use during a grammar-check:

1. Go to the Spelling & Grammar tab of the Options dialog box. To get there, either choose Tools | Options and select the Spelling & Grammar tab, or, starting from the Spelling and Grammar dialog box (refer to Figure 11-6), click the Options button.

2. Click the Settings button. You see the Grammar Settings dialog box shown in Figure 11-7.

3. Choose options from the Require drop-down menus and check off boxes next to the rules that you want to apply. Table 11-3 describes these options.

4. Click OK twice to return to your document.

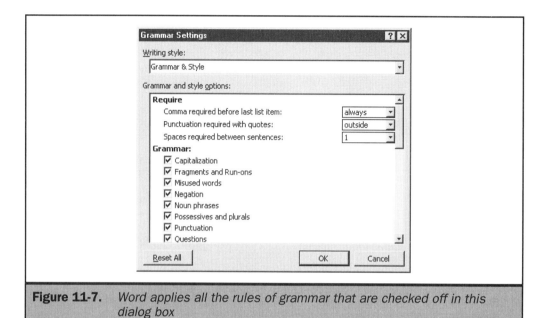

Figure 11-7. *Word applies all the rules of grammar that are checked off in this dialog box*

Click the Reset All button in the Grammar Settings dialog box if you get in a tangle and want the original set of Grammar & Style or Grammar Only grammatical rules to apply.

Checking Out Your Readability Statistics

For what it's worth, and I don't think it's worth a lot, you can obtain "readability statistics" that describe how easy or difficult reading a document is. Readability statistics include the average number of sentences per paragraph and what percentage of sentences in a document were written in the passive voice. You can also find out where your document stands on two scales, both of which take account of the average number of syllables per word and the average number of words per sentence:

- **Flesch Reading Ease Scale**   On a scale of 100, how easy it is to read a document. A score of 60–70 is considered average.

- **Flesch-Kincaid Grade Level**   At what grade level a document was written. Seventh to eighth grade is considered average.

To obtain these statistics of dubious value, check the Show Readability Statistics check box on the Spelling & Grammar tab of the Options dialog box before you grammar-check your entire document. To get to the Spelling & Grammar tab, click the Options button in the Spelling and Grammar dialog box (see Figure 11-6).

As an experiment, I obtained readability statistics for Martin Luther King Jr.'s "I Have a Dream" speech, one of the finest examples of oratory in the English language. The results of my experiment (see the following illustration) show that Dr. King barely passed the Flesch Reading Ease test and that his speech was written at a ninth-grade reading level. From my experiment we can conclude that the average number of syllables per word and the average number of words per sentence do not amount to a useful indication of the power or clarity of anyone's writing.

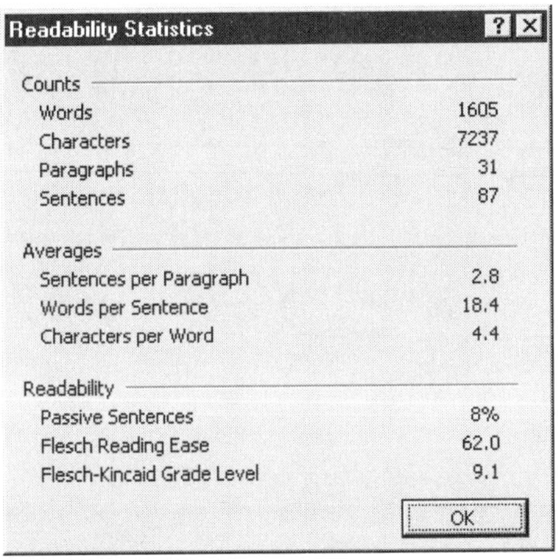

Readability Statistics	? X
Counts	
Words	1605
Characters	7237
Paragraphs	31
Sentences	87
Averages	
Sentences per Paragraph	2.8
Words per Sentence	18.4
Characters per Word	4.4
Readability	
Passive Sentences	8%
Flesch Reading Ease	62.0
Flesch-Kincaid Grade Level	9.1
	OK

Finding the Right Word with the Thesaurus

Choosing the right word is so important in writing, Microsoft included a thesaurus with its word processor. As you endeavor to describe your thoughts, use the thesaurus to find *synonyms*—words that have the same or a similar meaning. Do either of the following to find a synonym for a word:

■ Right-click the word, choose Synonyms on the shortcut menu, and choose a synonym from the shortcut menu, as shown in Figure 11-8.

■ Click the word and press SHIFT-F7 or choose Tools | Language | Thesaurus to open the Thesaurus dialog box shown in Figure 11-8. You can also open the dialog box by right-clicking and choosing Thesaurus on the Synonyms submenu. Open the Thesaurus dialog box when you want to conduct an intensive search for a synonym.

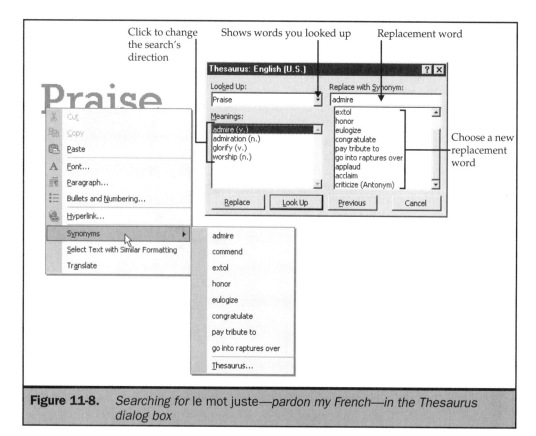

Figure 11-8.   *Searching for* le mot juste—*pardon my French—in the Thesaurus dialog box*

Use these boxes and buttons in the Thesaurus dialog box to find the synonym you so desperately seek:

■ **Looked Up**   Lists the words you investigated in your search for a synonym. Choose a word from the drop-down list to backtrack.

■ **Meanings**   Lists variations of the word you are looking up, including different word forms. Click a word to steer the search in a different direction.

■ **Replace With Synonym**   Lists what the program thinks is the best synonym for the word in the Looked Up box. Click a word in the box below to make it the replacement word—the word that goes in your document when you click the Replace button. You can type a word in this box.

■ **Replace Button**   Enters the word in the Replace With Synonym box in the document. Click this button when your search is done.

■ **Look Up Button**   Tells the program to find synonyms for the word in the Replace With Synonym box. Click to see a new batch of synonyms.

■ **Previous Button**   Lists synonyms for the last word you investigated. Click this button to backtrack.

Tip	*If you can't quite remember a word but you know its antonym (its opposite), enter its antonym in the Replace With Synonym text box and click the Look Up button. With any luck, the Replace With Synonym list shows the word you are looking for—the antonym of the antonym you entered. In Figure 11-8, for example, the antonym "criticize" appears in the Replace With Synonym list. If you were looking for a word that means the opposite of "praise," you could look up "praise" in the Thesaurus dialog box, look for an antonym of "praise," and find the word "criticize" that way.*

Working with Text Written in a Foreign Language

In the interest of being cosmopolitan, Word makes it possible to create documents in a foreign language or include foreign-language text in a document otherwise composed in English. To enter and edit text in a foreign language, start by installing proofing tools for the language on your computer. After you have done that, you can spell-check and grammar-check text written in the language.

The version of Word that is sold and distributed in the United States comes with a Spanish and French dictionary as well as an English one. That means you can spell-check and grammar-check words in Spanish and French. To spell- and grammar-check text written in Uzbek, Estonian, Afrikaans, and other languages apart from English, Spanish, and French, you have to obtain the additional proofing tools. In the United States, call Microsoft at 425-462-9673 to obtain the kit. Everyone can visit the Office Home Page (www.microsoft.com/office/default.htm) to learn more how to employ foreign languages in a Word document.

Microsoft's literature claims that Word can "detect" a language other than English when you enter text in another language. Without being asked, Microsoft says, the program can bring to bear its proofing tools on the other language. Before you can work in a foreign language, however, you have to tell Word which language or languages besides English you intend to use. Read on.

The Status bar lists which language the cursor is in if your document includes more than one language that Word recognizes. Look at the box directly to the right of the OVR button on the Status bar to see which language you are dealing with.

| Page 1 | Sec 1 | 1/1 | At 1.7" | Ln 5 | Col 27 | REC | TRK | EXT | OVR | Spanish (Sp | |

Telling Word Which Languages You Will Use

Follow these steps to inform Word that you will use a language or languages besides English in your documents:

1. Close all programs, if any are open.

2. Click the Start button and choose Programs | Office Tools | Microsoft Office Language Settings. You see the Microsoft Office Language Settings dialog box.

3. On the Enabled Languages tab, CTRL-click the names of languages you intend to use in your work and click the Add button.

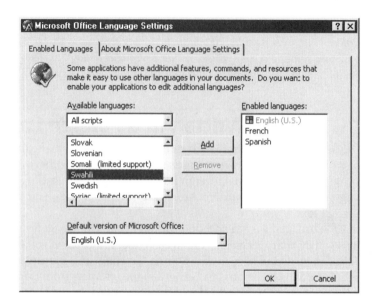

4. Click OK.

5. Insert the proper disk and follow the onscreen instructions to install the proofing tools.

6. Restart your computer, if necessary, to make the language settings take effect.

Telling Word When You Are Using a Foreign Language

As I mentioned earlier, Microsoft boasts that its software can "automatically detect" when a language besides English is in use. How does the software do it? In the first place, Word knows which languages to look for, since you told it which languages you will use in the Microsoft Office Language Settings dialog box. As for determining which language is on the page, "Word uses special language algorithms and statistics to analyze the letter combinations in every sentence," says a Help program screen. Huh? Sounds dubious to me. To be on the safe side, I suggest marking foreign language text in your documents as well as telling the program to "detect" the foreign words. After you mark the text as foreign language text, Word can spell-check and grammar-check it with the proper dictionaries.

Follow these steps to tell Word to keep a lookout for foreign languages and to mark text so Word knows in which language it was written:

1. Select the text that you wrote in a foreign language.

2. Choose Tools | Language | Set Language. You see the Language dialog box shown in Figure 11-9.

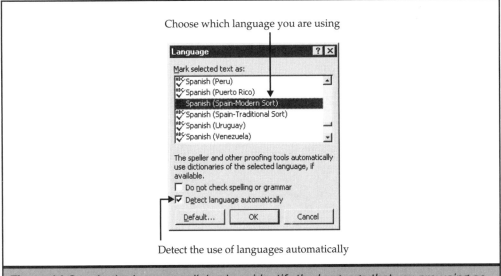

Choose which language you are using

Detect the use of languages automatically

Figure 11-9. *In the Language dialog box, identify the language that you are using so that Word can spell-check the words and grammar-check the sentences*

3. In the Mark Selected Text As list box, find the language and select it.

4. Check the Detect Language Automatically check box if you want Word to try on its own to find out when you are using the language.

5. Click OK.

 Create a character style for other languages. That way, you can simply select the foreign language text and choose a style from the Style menu to mark the text as foreign. Chapter 12 explains character styles.

Translating Foreign-Language Text

As long as you installed the proofing tools, you can translate text with Word. I should warn you, however, that the translation mechanism is only good for translating one word at a time. Word offers commands for translating a sentence or two or even an entire document, but the job is too difficult and the commands don't work, at least in my experiments.

Follow these steps to translate text:

1. Select the word or phrase that needs translating.

2. Either right-click and choose Translate or choose Tools | Language | Translate. The Translate task pane opens, as shown in Figure 11-10.

3. In the Dictionary drop-down list, choose an option that describes how you want the translation to be done.

FORMATTING TEXT
AND PAGES

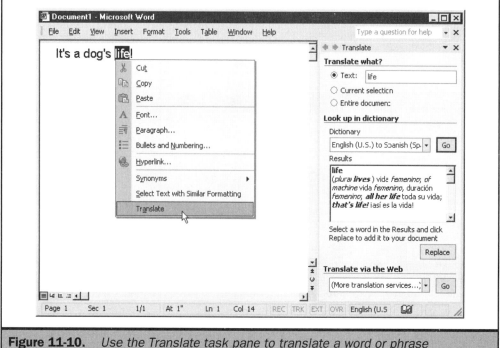

Figure 11-10. *Use the Translate task pane to translate a word or phrase*

4. Click the Go button. A translation appears in the Results box.

5. If you selected a word or phrase in step 1, you can enter its translation in your document by selecting a word or phrase in the Results box and clicking the Replace button.

While the Translate task pane is open, you can enter a word in the Text box and click the Go button to translate the word.

MOUS Exam Objectives Explored in Chapter 11

Objective	Heading
Correct grammar and spelling usage	"Correcting Your Spelling Errors" and "Finding the Right Word with the Thesaurus"

Ten Internet Resources for Writers and Researchers

"Proofing Your Work" is the title of this chapter, which leads me to believe that a lot of readers who come here will be writers and researchers. Here are ten Internet resources for writers and researchers. If you know a good resource that isn't listed here, please tell me about it by writing to peter@ionix.net.

1. AltaVista Translation Services   From here, you can translate sentences as well as words. Enter what needs translating in the Text box, choose an option in the Translate From drop-down list, and click the Translate button. Address: babel.altavista.com.

2. Babylon.com Translation Services   Enter a word that needs translating, choose a language from the drop-down list, and click the Go button to get the translation. Last time I looked, the service offered translations to 16 languages, including Turkish and Dutch. Address: www.babylon.com.

3. Bartlett's Familiar Quotations   When you need a good quotation to spice up an essay or the words of a master to bolster an unfounded opinion, go to this site. Starting here, you can also dig into many other references books, including dictionaries and histories, by making a choice from the Search menu. Address: www.bartleby.com/100.

4. Central Intelligence Agency World Factbook   Turns out the CIA is willing to share some of what it knows about its friends and foes. You will find maps and country profiles at this Web site, as well as some interesting tidbits about climate, literacy rates, natural hazards (tornadoes and such), and other subjects. The site includes information about the United States. Strange, I thought the FBI, not the CIA, is supposed to spy on us. Address: www.odci.gov/cia/publications/factbook.

5. Columbia Encyclopedia   This is the Sixth Edition of the *Columbia Encyclopedia*. Looking up a topic at a Web site is easier than lugging volumes from a library shelf. Address: www.bartleby.com/65.

6. Infoplease.com Almanacs   Starting here, you can find almanacs for the United States and various other countries. You can also research a bunch of other topics, including sports, business, and the sciences. Address: www.infoplease.com.

7. Merriam-Webster Collegiate Dictionary Online   The well-known dictionary is online and ready to provide definitions. You can also make use of the Merriam-Webster thesaurus from this Web site. Address: www.m-w.com.

8. Roget's Thesaurus   Mr. Roget has put his famous thesaurus on the Internet. If the Word thesaurus isn't doing the job, go to this site. You can also look up words in a dictionary and search for antonyms. Address: www.thesaurus.com.

9. Tommy's List of Live Cams   This site represents the next best thing to going there, I suppose. Tommy's List of Live Cams offers links to hundreds, if not thousands, of "cams"—live camera views that are updated regularly. Starting here, you can see what a part of the world you are interested in looks like. Address: chili.rt66.com/ozone/countries.htm.

10. WriteExpress Online Rhyming Dictionary   Who doesn't need a rhyming dictionary now and then? For balladeers, songwriters, poetasters, versifiers, and jingle-slingers, this site provides the means to find the word that rhymes. Enter a word and click—what else?—the Rhyme button. I got these results for the word *orange:* challenge, expunge, lozenge, lunge, plunge, scavenge, and sponge. Address: www.writeexpress.com/online.html.

The Complete Reference

Word 2002

Part III

Professional-Looking
Documents with Word

The Complete Reference

Word 2002

Chapter 12

Styles and Templates for Consistent and Easy Formatting

Welcome to what may be the most important chapter in this book. A *style* is a collection of commands and formats that have been bundled under one name. By using styles, you free yourself from having to visit and revisit numerous dialog boxes whenever you want to change the formatting of a paragraph, table, or list. Styles save a lot of time. When you want to reformat a paragraph or text, you simply choose a style name from the Styles and Formatting task pane or Style drop-down menu. The paragraph, text, table, or list is reformatted instantly. What's more, you can rest assured that all parts of the document that were assigned the same style are laid out and look the same. By using styles, you make sure that various parts of your document are consistent with one another and that your documents have a professional look.

Read on if styles interest you—and they should if you intend to do any serious work whatever in Microsoft Word. Styles can save a ridiculous amount of time you would otherwise spend formatting and wrestling with text. And many Word features rely on styles. You can't create a table of contents or use the Document Map unless each heading in your document was assigned a heading style. Nor can you take advantage of Outline view and the commands on the Outline toolbar. And you can't cross-reference headings or number the headings in a document. To create a table of figures or illustrations, you must have tagged their captions with the Caption style.

The advantages of using styles are many. Do yourself a big favor by learning how to work with and apply styles. This chapter explains how to create a style of your own, apply a style, and modify a style. You also learn the subtle and not-so-subtle ways to manage styles, how to copy styles between documents and templates, and how to create a template for styles that you created. At the end of this chapter is a list of ten style problems and how to solve them.

Styles: An Overview

Most people break into a yawn or a cold sweat when they hear the word "styles." But styles are essential in Word and are worth taking the trouble to learn. To help you get going, this section presents a brief overview of styles. Later, I describe all the things you can do with styles in detail.

Uniformity of Styles

By using styles, you make sure that the various parts of your document present a uniform appearance and are consistent with one another. All headings assigned the Heading 1 style look the same. Paragraphs assigned the Quotation style look alike, as shown in Figure 12-1. If you change your mind about a style's appearance, all you have to do is redefine it. The new, redefined style is applied instantly throughout your document. Paragraphs and text that were assigned the style are reformatted. You don't have to do the reformatting yourself by going from paragraph to paragraph and choosing commands.

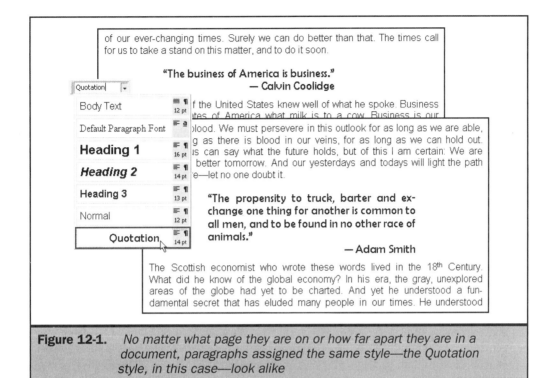

Figure 12-1. *No matter what page they are on or how far apart they are in a document, paragraphs assigned the same style—the Quotation style, in this case—look alike*

Styles are especially important in the business world. A company makes a good impression on customers and clients when its letters, faxes, and invoices present a uniform appearance. You can make sure your company's correspondence presents a uniform appearance by creating styles for use in letters, faxes, and invoices, and saving the styles in templates that employees can use when they create documents. Creating styles for company correspondence also saves time because employees can choose styles from the Styles and Formatting task pane or Style menu as they create documents instead of formatting the text themselves.

Styles and Templates

A *template* is a special kind of file that is used as the starting point for creating other files. All Word documents are created from templates. When you click the New Blank Document button or press CTRL-N to create a new document, Word uses the Normal template to create your file, but when you choose File | New and click General Templates, Templates on My Web Sites, or Templates on Microsoft.com in the New Document task pane to create a new document, you can choose among many exotic templates in the Templates dialog box.

Each template comes with a collection of styles that you can use to format documents. Figure 12-2, for example, shows a document that was created with the Elegant Report template. In the figure, the Styles and Formatting task pane is open and you can see the many styles that are available in documents created with the Elegant Report template. These are styles that the document in Figure 12-2 inherited from the template with which it was created.

However, the styles that a document inherits from a template are not the only ones you can use for formatting. You can fetch styles from other templates and also create your own styles. And if a style you create happens to be one you want to use again, you can add your new style to a template. That way, the style you created will be available when you create other documents with the template. You can even create a template of your own with styles that you know and love.

The Different Kinds of Styles

Word offers four kinds of styles, *paragraph styles, character styles, table styles,* and *list styles.* By far, the majority of styles are paragraph styles. Character styles apply to text

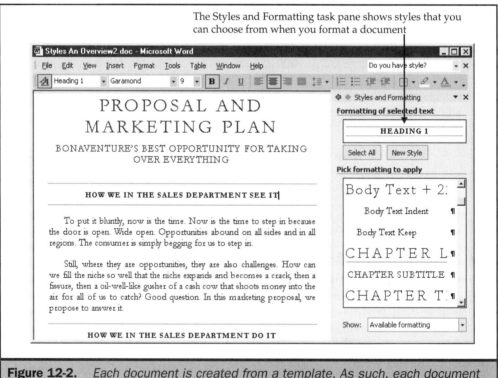

Figure 12-2. *Each document is created from a template. As such, each document comes with many predefined styles that you can use for formatting*

you select, whereas paragraph styles apply to entire paragraphs, including the text. As for table styles and list styles, they are for formatting tables and lists.

- Paragraph styles format paragraphs—they indent them, align them, and change their line spacing, for example. A paragraph style, like a character style, can include font and font size settings as well.

- Character styles are for hard-to-lay-out text such as small capital letters, for combinations of font and font size commands that are too troublesome to apply in conventional ways, and for foreign words that you want the spell-checker and grammar-checker to proof. Before you assign a character style, select text in the document. Character styles apply to selected text, not to all the text in a paragraph.

- Table styles are for advanced table layouts that you want to copy to and use in different templates.

- List styles are for complex bulleted or numbered lists whose entries and number schemes you want to copy to and use in different templates.

You can tell what kind of style you are dealing with by glancing at the names in the Style menu and Styles and Formatting task pane. Paragraph styles are marked with the paragraph symbol (¶); character styles marked with the letter a; table styles with a small table; and list styles with a tiny bulleted list.

Applying Styles in a Document

Word offers a bunch of different techniques for applying styles. Some of the techniques fall in the esoteric category and are not used very often, but knowing about them doesn't hurt a bit. Read on to find out how to apply styles one at a time and how to get Word's help in applying many styles at once.

Note *In most cases, the style from the previous paragraph is carried to the new one automatically when you press ENTER to start a new paragraph. After heading styles and certain other kinds of styles, however, Word applies a different style to the new paragraph. Later in this chapter, "Creating Your Own Styles" explains the benefits of making one style automatically follow another and how you can make a style follow another style automatically.*

Applying Styles One at a Time

The fastest and best way to apply a style is to do so from the Style menu on the Formatting toolbar or the Styles and Formatting task plane, but you can also apply a style by way of one or two keyboard shortcuts and the Format Painter. For that matter, sometimes Word applies styles on its own. Better read on.

The Repeat command comes in especially handy when you apply styles to paragraphs. Apply a style to a paragraph, click another paragraph, or select other paragraphs to which you want to apply the same style, and press F4 or choose Edit | Repeat.

Applying a Style from the Styles and Formatting Task Pane

The Styles and Formatting task pane lists styles that are available in the template you are using. Follow these steps to open the task pane and select a style:

1. Place the insertion point in the paragraph whose style you want to change, or select several paragraphs to apply a style to them. To apply a character style, select the text. To apply a table style, click the table. Select a list to select a list style.

2. Open the Styles and Formatting task pane by clicking the Styles and Formatting button or choosing Format | Styles and Formatting.

3. In the Styles and Formatting task pane (refer to Figure 12-2), click the name of the style you want to apply.

Unless you make a choice from the Show drop-down menu, the Styles and Formatting task pane lists formats you've applied as well as styles. Open the Show drop-down menu and choose one of these options to get a better look at which styles are available to you:

- **Available Styles**   Lists styles that are needed to format your document.
- **All Styles**   Lists all styles in the template, including esoteric ones for printing envelopes, entering pages numbers, and whatnot. Don't choose this one unless you really have to.

By the way, the choices you make on the Show drop-down menu determine how many style names appear on the Style drop-down menu as well. That menu is located on the Formatting toolbar.

Choosing What Appears on the Styles and Formatting Task Pane

You can decide for yourself which styles appear in the Styles and Formatting task pane when you choose Available Styles or All Styles on the Show drop-down menu. Follow these steps:

1. Open the Show drop-down menu at the bottom of the task pane and choose Custom. You see the Format Settings dialog box.

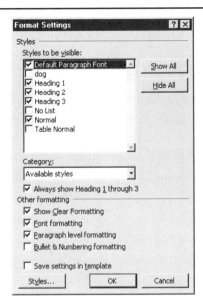

2. From the Category drop-down menu, choose Available Styles or Styles in Use.

3. In the Styles to Be Visible box, check the styles that you want to see when you click the Show option you chose in step 2.

4. Select or ignore these check boxes, which determine what besides styles appear on the task pane:

   - **Always Show Heading 1 through 3**   Lists Heading 1, Heading 2, and Heading 3 on the task pane

   - **Show Clear Formatting**   Places the Clear Formatting option on the task pane so you can click it to remove style assignments

   - **Font Formatting**   Lists font names after you choose a new font so you can choose the font again

   - **Paragraph Level Formatting**   Lists alignment commands and other Paragraph dialog box commands so you can choose them quickly

   - **Bullet & Numbering Formatting**   Lists Bulleted and Numbered list commands so you can make lists quickly

5. Click the Save Settings in Template check box if you want the customizations you make to apply to other documents based on the template you are working in.

6. Click the OK button.

Applying a Style by Way of the Style Menu

Follow these steps to apply a style from the Style drop-down menu:

1. Place the insertion point in the paragraph whose style you want to change, or select several paragraphs to apply a style to them. To apply a character style, select the text. To apply a table style, click the table. Select a list to select a list style.

2. Open the Style drop-down menu on the Formatting toolbar and choose a style.

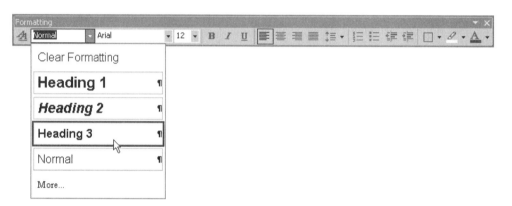

Keyboard fans can choose styles from the Style menu by pressing CTRL-SHIFT-S. Pressing that key combination moves the cursor into the Style menu. Either press the ↓ key repeatedly until the name of the style you want appears in the Style menu box, or press ALT-↓ to make the Style menu drop, and then press the ↓ key until you land on the style you want to apply. Press ENTER when the name of the style you want to apply appears in the Style menu box, or else press the first letter of the style's name to go straight to styles whose names begin with the letter you pressed.

To make all styles in the template appear on the Style menu, hold down the SHIFT key as you click to open the menu.

What Happens to Styles When You Format Documents

Formats that you make yourself take precedence over styles. Suppose, for example, that a style calls for a paragraph to be left-aligned, but you center the paragraph. Because manual formats take precedence, Word ignores the alignment portion of the style and centers the paragraph. Seems simple enough, doesn't it? The problem is, things get sticky when you are dealing with a style that updates automatically or text that has been formatted quite a bit.

■ **Style Updates Automatically** As "Creating Your Own Styles" explains later in this chapter, you can tell Word to modify a style each time you reformat a text or paragraph to which the style has been applied. If the style calls for text to be centered but you left-align it, for example, the style changes. Now the style left-aligns text, and all parts of your document that were assigned the style are left-aligned, not centered.

How can you tell if a style updates automatically? One way is to move the pointer over its name in the Styles and Formatting task pane. In the pop-up box that appears, that last entry reads "Automatically Update " if the style updates automatically. You can also open the style's drop-down menu in the Styles and Formatting task pane, choose Modify, and look at the Automatically Update check box in the lower-right corner of the Modify Style dialog box.

■ **Text Is Formatted Every Which Way** If you apply a bunch of different formats to text, telling which style has been assigned the text can be difficult. To tell, select the text, click the Styles and Formatting button (or choose Format | Styles and Formatting) and glance at the Formatting of Selected Text box in the task pane. It tells you which style is in effect and which formats were applied apart from the style. If you want to remove all extraneous formats from text and be left with the paragraph style only, select the text and press CTRL-SPACEBAR.

Formatting of selected text

Introduction + 16 pt, Centered

Keyboard Shortcuts for Applying Styles

For people who can type faster than they can click the mouse, here are some keyboard shortcuts for applying styles:

Apply This Style	By Pressing
Normal	CTRL-SHIFT-N
Heading 1	ALT-CTRL-1

Apply This Style	By Pressing
Heading 2	ALT-CTRL-2
Heading 3	ALT-CTRL-3
Next higher heading	ALT-SHIFT-→
Next lower heading	ALT-SHIFT-←
Bulleted list	CTRL-SHIFT-L

 "Designating Your Own Keyboard Shortcuts" in Chapter 21 explains how you can invent a keyboard shortcut of your own for applying a style.

The Style Gallery for Applying Styles from a Different Template

A slightly awkward but sometimes useful way to assign styles is to go to the Style Gallery and grab styles en masse from another template. Go this route if you created your document in the Templates dialog box with one of Word's templates and you suspect that you choose the wrong template. Say you chose the Elegant Memo template for your document but you find yourself pining away for the Professional Memo template. To solve the dilemma, you can open the Style Gallery and assign styles from the Professional Memo template to your document.

The Style Gallery gives you the opportunity to see what your document will look like after the styles have changed. Follow these steps to visit the Style Gallery:

1. Choose Format | Theme to open the Theme dialog box.

2. Click the Style Gallery button. You see the Style Gallery dialog box shown in Figure 12-3.

3. In the Template list, select the name of the template from which you want to pilfer styles. You can click the Example option button to see a sample document that shows what the template does to text. Click the Style Samples option button to see samples of the different styles found in the template.

4. Click OK. Styles from the new template are imposed on your document, and it looks brand new.

 Later in this chapter, "Assigning Documents to a Different Template" explains how to attach a document to a different template instead of borrowing another template's styles.

Styles That Word Applies on Its Own

Word applies certain styles automatically when you enter headers and footers and choose certain commands from the Insert menu. Don't be surprised when the Style menu gets loaded down with the names of styles that you didn't apply yourself. Table 12-1 lists styles that Word applies automatically. These styles start appearing on the Style menu after you choose the commands listed in the table.

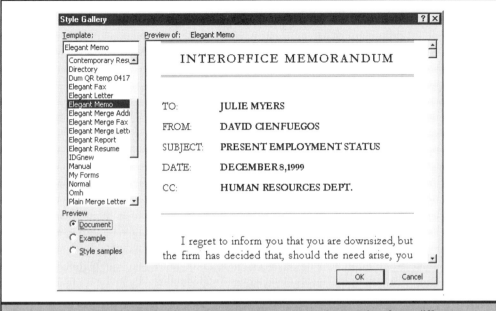

Figure 12-3. *The Style Gallery, where you can appropriate styles from different templates*

> **Tip** *Hold down the SHIFT key and click the down arrow in the Style menu on the Formatting toolbar to make the menu display all the styles that are available in a document.*

Style Name	Style Applied When You
Comment Text	Choose Insert | Comment and enter a comment.
Caption	Choose Insert | Reference | Caption and enter a caption.
Endnote Reference	Choose Insert | Reference | Footnote and enter an endnote. Marks the endnote reference.
Endnote Text	Choose Insert | Reference | Footnote and enter an endnote.
Footer	Choose View | Header and Footer and enter a footer.

Table 12-1. *Styles That Word Applies Automatically*

Style Name	Style Applied When You
Footnote Reference*	Choose | Reference | Insert Footnote. Marks the footnote reference.
Footnote Text	Choose Insert | Reference | Footnote.
Header	Choose View | Header and Footer and enter a header.
Index 1–9	Choose Insert | Reference | Index and Tables and generate an index.
Page Number*	Click the Insert Page Number button on the Header and Footer toolbar.
Table of Authorities	Choose Insert | Index and Tables and generate a table of authorities.
Table of Figures	Choose Insert | Reference | Index and Tables and generate a table of figures.
TOA Heading	Choose Insert | Reference | Index and Tables and generate a table of authorities.
TOC 1–9	Choose Insert | Reference | Index and Tables and generate a table of contents.

Character style, not a paragraph style

Table 12-1. *Styles That Word Applies Automatically* (continued)

Seeing Which Styles Are in Use

Sometimes distinguishing one style from another is hard when you are working on a complex document. And if the Style menu and Styles and Formatting toolbar are loaded down with a number of styles, remembering which style is which can be doubly hard. To help make style choices in complex documents, Word offers a special option in the Options dialog box called Style Area Width. When this option is turned on, style names appear on the screen to the left of the text.

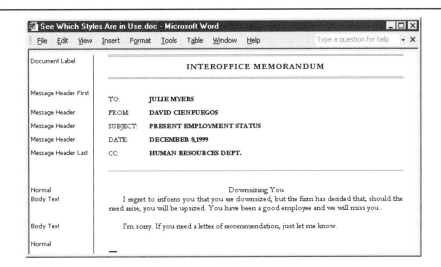

To see style names on the left side of the document window, follow these steps:

1. Choose Tools | Options to open the Options dialog box.
2. Select the View tab.
3. Under Outline and Normal Options at the bottom of the dialog box, enter **.5** or **.7** inches in the Style Area Width box and click OK.

You can only see the style names in Normal view and Outline view. If the style area is too wide or narrow, drag its boundary line to the left or right. To remove the style names, drag the boundary line all the way to the left. By the way, you can print descriptions of all the styles in a document. Choose File | Print, open the Print What drop-down menu in the Print dialog box, choose Styles, and click OK.

Assigning a Document to a Different Template

Occasionally you make a mistake and create a document with the wrong template. Or you get a document from someone else and realize to your dismay that the styles you thought would be there aren't there, and the person who gave you the document created it with the wrong template. For those occasions, Word offers the Tools | Templates and Add-Ins command. The command rips a document from its original template and gives it to a new template.

To find out which template is assigned to a document, choose File | Properties, select the Summary tab in the Properties dialog box, and look beside the word "Template" at the bottom of the tab.

To be specific, the Tools | Templates and Add-Ins command does and doesn't do the following to a document:

- Paragraphs assigned to a style whose name is found in the original template and the new template are reformatted. For example, if the original template includes a style called Body Text and the new template also has a style called Body Text, paragraphs assigned the Body Text style are reformatted according to the rules of the new template.

- Nothing happens to paragraphs assigned to a style whose name is not found in the new template. A paragraph tagged with the Quotation style, for example, looks the same under the new template if the new template doesn't include the Quotation style.

Usually, you have to assign a new style to paragraphs that didn't change or else modify a style to make paragraphs that didn't change fit the new, revamped document. Later in this chapter, "Finding and Replacing Styles" explains how you can use the Find and Replace command to exchange one style for another. "Modifying a Style" explains how to modify a style.

- Margin settings and page-orientation settings stay the same.

- Macros and AutoText entries, like styles, are part the template in which they are found, so they do not make the transition. Instead, you get the macros and AutoText entries in the new template.

Create a backup copy or second copy of a document before you attach it to a new template. You can't click the Undo button if you change your mind about which template belongs to which document. If attaching a new template makes hash of your document, you can use the backup copy.

Follow these steps to attach a new template to a document and in so doing apply new styles throughout:

1. Choose Tools | Templates and Add-Ins. You see the Templates and Add-ins dialog box shown in Figure 12-4. The Document Template box lists the template to which the document is currently attached.

2. Click the Attach button. You see the Attach Template dialog box. In this dialog box, you find the template that you want to impose on your file. Word templates are located in the C:\Windows\Application Data\Microsoft\Templates folder.

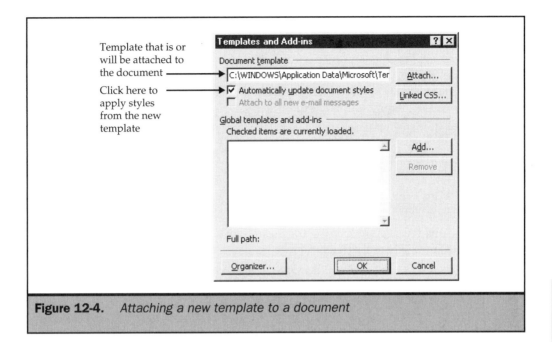

Template that is or will be attached to the document

Click here to apply styles from the new template

Figure 12-4.   *Attaching a new template to a document*

3. Find and select the template you want, and click the Open button. You return to the Templates and Add-ins dialog box, where the name of the template you chose appears in the Document Template box.

Caution *The original template and new template must be similar for the Tools | Templates and Add-Ins command to work. Changing a report to a letter or a letter to a report, for example, can turn a perfectly good document into guacamole.*

4. Click the Automatically Update Document Styles check box. Doing so tells Word to apply the styles from the new template to your document.

5. Click OK.

Tip *When you clicked the Attach button to attach a new template to a file, did the Attach Template dialog box open to the right folder? If it didn't, choose Tools | Options and click the File Locations tab in the Options dialog box. Then, under File Types, choose User Templates and click the Modify button. In the Modify Location dialog box, find the folder in which your templates are located and click OK.*

PROFESSIONAL-LOOKING DOCUMENTS WITH WORD 2002

Setting the Default File Location for Workgroup Templates

If you are using Word in an office and your machine is attached to a network workgroup, you can share templates over the network with other members of the workgroup. To do so, however, you have to tell your computer where the templates are located by following these steps:

1. Choose Tools | Options.
2. Select the File Locations tab in the Options dialog box.
3. Under File Types, select Workgroup Templates, and then click the Modify button. You see the Modify Location dialog box.
4. Find the folder on your network where the workgroup templates are located. You might have to ask the network administrator or someone in the know where that sacred place is.
5. Click OK and then click OK again in the Options dialog box.

 You can retrieve macros and AutoText entries from another template but not apply its styles to your document. To do that, don't check the Automatically Update Document Styles check box in the Templates and Add-Ins dialog box (see Figure 12-3).

Creating Your Own Styles

You are hereby invited to create a new style whenever you format a paragraph, text, table, or list and you suspect that sometime in the future you will have to format another paragraph, line of text, table, or list the same way. By creating a style, you only have to format the paragraph, text, table, or list once. After that, you can simply choose an option from the Style menu or Styles and Formatting task pane when the time comes to format.

What's more, you can copy styles from document to document or template to template. So the time you take to create a style can pay many dividends in the future. I know someone who has a whole library of Word styles and makes a living by recycling them. My friend designs Word templates for companies. Her clients don't know it, but most of her templates are stitched together from styles she created for projects she did years ago. (Later in this chapter, "Building Your Own Templates" explains how to bundle styles into a template.)

These pages explain how to create a style, redefine a style, copy styles from document to document, and find and replace styles. Better read on.

The Two Ways to Create a Style

Word offers two ways to create a style: the prototype method and the from-the-ground-up method:

- **Prototype Method**   You create a model paragraph for your new style, and the formats in the paragraph become the formats that are bundled in the style. The advantage of the prototype method is that you can tell precisely how your new style formats paragraphs—the prototype paragraph shows you. The disadvantages are that the style belongs to the document, not the template; it isn't available to other documents founded on the template you are working with (you can, however, modify the style after you create it so that it becomes available in the template). What's more, only paragraph styles can be created with the prototype method.

- **From-the-Ground-Up Method**   Creating a style this way takes longer, and you can't see what the style looks like onscreen, but you can do a more thorough job of creating a style. With this method, you visit different dialog boxes—the same dialog boxes you visit to format a paragraph—and pick and choose formats for your style. Moreover, this method offers some amenities that you can't get with the prototype method. For example, you can tell Word to update the style automatically as you make formatting changes and add the style to the template you are working in.

Creating a Paragraph Style from a Prototype

Start with a model paragraph to create a style with the prototype method. Indent the paragraph, align the paragraph, change the line spacing—do to your model paragraph what you want your style to do to text when your style is applied to text. Then follow these steps to create the style:

1. Click in the paragraph.
2. Click inside the Style menu box. The words in the Style menu box are highlighted.

Click in the Style menu box, type a style name, and press ENTER

3. Type a name for the new style and press ENTER.

Styles names can be 253 characters long, but choose a short, descriptive name. For that matter, choose a name that doesn't stretch the Style menu out of shape when you open it from the Formatting toolbar.

 One drawback of creating a style with the prototype method is that the style is based on the style that was in effect when you clicked inside the Style menu box to type a name. If the "based on" style changes—for example, if the font in the "based on" style changes— so does the style you created. See "Basing One Style on Another Style," later in this chapter, to learn about the pitfalls of basing one style on another.

Creating a Style from the Ground Up

To create a style from the ground up, follow these steps:

1. Click the paragraph or heading for which you want to create a new paragraph style; select the text for which you want to create a character style; select the table if you are creating a table style; or select the list if you desire a list style.

2. Click the Styles and Formatting button or choose Format | Styles and Formatting to open the Styles and Formatting task pane.

3. Click the New Style button in the task pane. You see the New Style dialog box shown in Figure 12-5.

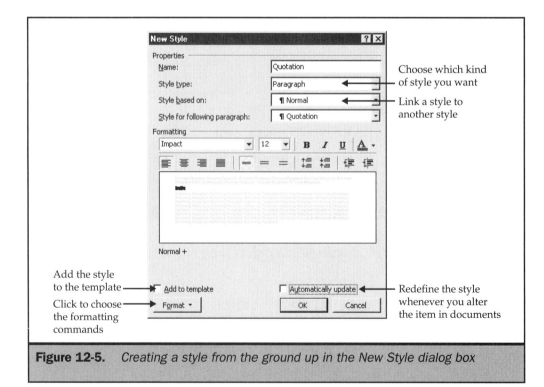

Figure 12-5. *Creating a style from the ground up in the New Style dialog box*

4. Enter a name in the Name box. The style name you enter will appear on the Style drop-down list and Styles and Formatting task pane. Names can be 253 characters long, but choose a short, descriptive name that will fit on the Style menu and task pane.

5. In the Style Type menu, choose which kind of style you want to create: Paragraph, Character, Table, or List. Earlier in this chapter, "The Different Kinds of Styles" explains the four styles.

6. Use the tools in the dialog box to fashion the style. If you are creating a paragraph style, for example, you can click Alignment buttons.

7. If your style is a complicated one, click the Format button. You see a pop-up menu of formatting choices for defining your style. Table 12-2 describes the options on the Format menu. Which options you see depends on what kind of style you are creating. Choose an option from the Format pop-up menu to open a dialog box and give formatting commands. For example, choosing Font opens the Font dialog box. In the dialog box that appears, choose formatting options for the new style and then click OK. Click the Format button and open as many dialog boxes as necessary to make your style just so.

Format Button Option	Defines These Formats
Font	Fonts, font styles, font sizes, font color, underlining, text effects, character spacing, kerning, animation *Menu equivalent:* Format | Font
Paragraph	Text alignment, outline level, indentation, before-and after-paragraph spacing, line spacing, widow and orphan control, pagination instructions, suppressing hyphenation, suppressing line numbers *Menu equivalent:* Format | Paragraph
Tabs	Tab stop settings, leader settings *Menu equivalent:* Format | Tabs
Border	Borderlines for paragraphs, shading for paragraphs *Menu equivalent:* Format | Borders and Shading
Table Properties	Width and height of rows and columns, table and cell alignment *Menu equivalent:* Table | Table Properties

Table 12-2.   *Format Commands for Building Styles*

Format Button Option	Defines These Formats
Borders and Shading	Borderlines and background shades for tables *Menu equivalent:* Format ∣ Borders and Shading
Language	Language for proofing documents *Menu equivalent:* Tools ∣ Language ∣ Set Language
Frame	Text wrapping around frames, frame size, horizontal and vertical position *Menu equivalent:* Format ∣ Frame (not to be confused with the Format ∣ Frames command)
Numbering	Bulleted lists, numbered lists, outline numbers, and heading numbers *Menu equivalent:* Format ∣ Bullets and Numbering

Table 12-2.   *Format Commands for Building Styles* (continued)

8. The other options in the New Style dialog box are optional. Choose them as you see fit:

- **Style Based On**   See "Basing One Style on Another," the next section in this chapter, to learn the ins and outs of building one style atop another.

- **Style For Following Paragraph**   Choose a style from the drop-down list if the style you are creating is always to be followed by an existing style. For example, a style called Chapter Head might always be followed by one called Chapter Intro. Someone who applies the style you are creating and presses ENTER finds the style you choose here on the next line of the document. Choosing a style for the following paragraph saves time when you enter text and helps make sure that styles are applied correctly.

- **Add To Template**   Click this check box if you want to add the style you are creating to the template with which you created the document you are working on. Unless this box is checked, new styles are available only in the document for which they were created. Click this box to save the style in the document *and* in the template. Anyone who creates a file with the template can draw upon the style you create if this box is checked.

- **Automatically Update**   Check this box to be able to modify the style simply by reformatting a paragraph to which the style has been applied. For example, indent a paragraph and all other paragraphs that were assigned the style are indented accordingly. Checking this box tells Word to redefine the style automatically whenever you format a single paragraph that was assigned the style.

9. Click OK to close the New Style dialog box and apply your style to a paragraph, text, a table, or a list.

> **Tip** *Click the Format button and choose Shortcut Key button if you care to create a shortcut key for applying the style. The Customize Keyboard dialog box appears. See "Designating Your Own Keyboard Shortcuts" in Chapter 21.*

Basing One Style on Another Style

When you create a style from a prototype paragraph, your new style is "based on" the style that was assigned to the prototype paragraph to begin with. For example, suppose a paragraph is assigned the Normal style when you fashion it into a prototype paragraph. After you create a style from the paragraph, your new style is "based on" the Normal style. Similarly, you can choose a "based on" style in the New Style dialog box (see Figure 12-5) when you create a style from the ground up.

The "based on" terminology that Word uses to describe the relationship between two styles is kind of misleading. Really, the new style isn't so much "based on" as it is "linked to" the other style, because when the "based on" style changes, so does the new style. For example, if you change the font in the Normal style, fonts change in all styles based on the Normal style as well. Change the line spacing or alignment of paragraphs in the Body Text style, and all styles that are based on the Body Text style change.

Unexpected changes brought about because someone modified the "based on" style are a chief cause of style problems. Therefore, you should be careful which "based on" style you choose. Choose one that isn't likely to be changed. Or choose the No Style option, the one at the top of the Based On menu in the New Style dialog box (later in this chapter, "Modifying a Style" explains how to change the particulars of a style, including which style it is based on). The point is to choose a "based on" style that won't wreak havoc on other styles if it is changed.

To be fair to the "based on" idea, however, basing one style on another can be a powerful way to make sure that the different parts of a document are consistent with one another. To see why, suppose you are designing a menu with many different elements—a title, subtitles ("Breakfast," "Lunch"), and descriptions of food. As you tinker with your design, you intend to experiment with many different font sizes and text alignments. Throughout the menu, however, all styles will share the same font. To make sure they share the same font, you create a Menu Font style and base all other styles on Menu Font. That way, if you change the font in the Menu Font style, fonts in all the other styles change as well, and you can rest assured that the same font appears in all parts of the menu.

Copying Paragraph Styles from Document to Document

All you have to do to copy a paragraph style from one document to another is copy a paragraph to which you've assigned the style from the first document to the second. Copying paragraph styles this way works fine as long as you copy an entire paragraph (including the paragraph symbol at the end). You can delete the text after you copy the paragraph. Although the text has been deleted, the paragraph style you copied to the second document remains and is available on the Style menu and Styles and Formatting task pane.

You can't copy a style from one document to another if the style you are copying has the same name as a style in the document to which the copy is being made. To copy a style, its name must be different from all the style names in the document that is receiving the copy. Rename the style being copied, if necessary.

Later in this chapter, "Assembling Styles (and Macros and AutoText) from Different Templates" describes how you can use the Organizer to copy styles from one document to another. The same techniques for assembling styles for a template work for copying styles between documents.

Finding and Replacing Styles

Sometimes when you change templates or copy text from another document, you discover paragraphs throughout a document that have the wrong style assignment. One way to fix this problem is to use the Find and Replace command to replace one style with another. The Find and Replace dialog box offers a special option for doing just that.

"Finding and Replacing Text and Other Things" in Chapter 6 explains the Find and Replace command in gruesome detail.

Follow these steps to find and replace a style throughout a document and thereby assign the right style to paragraphs:

1. Select part of your document if you want to find and replace styles on a handful of pages; to find and replace styles throughout, start at the top of the document.

2. Choose Edit | Find or press CTRL-F. You see the Find and Replace dialog box.

3. Click the More button to see all the options in the dialog box, as shown in Figure 12-6.

4. Make sure you are looking at the Find tab, and then click the Format button and choose Style from the pop-up menu.

5. In the Find Style dialog box, locate the style that needs replacing, select it, and click OK. The name of the style you selected appears next to the word "Format" under the Find What box (see Figure 12-6).

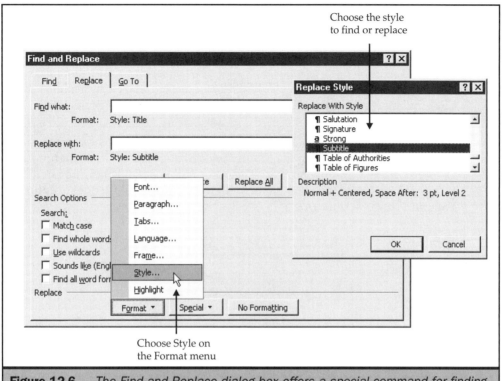

Figure 12-6.   *The Find and Replace dialog box offers a special command for finding and replacing styles*

> **Tip**   *On your keyboard, press the first letter of the name of the style you are looking for to scroll to the style in the Find or Replace Style dialog box.*

6. Click the Find Next button. Word scrolls to the first instance of the style you choose and selects the paragraph to which it was assigned. Examine the paragraph to make sure that Word has found the style that needs replacing.

7. Click the Replace tab in the Find and Replace dialog box (see Figure 12-6).

8. Click in the Replace With text box, click the Format button, and choose Style from the pop-up menu.

9. In the Replace Style dialog box (see Figure 12-6), select the style that will *replace* the style you chose in step 5, and click OK. On the Replace tab, the name of the replacement style appears next to the word "Format" under the Replace With text box.

10. Either click the Replace All button to replace all styles without reviewing them first, or click the Replace button and examine each paragraph before you assign the replacement style to it.

Modifying a Style

So a paragraph or text doesn't look quite right when you assign a style to it? You can fix that by modifying the style. Follow these steps:

1. Click an item whose style needs redefining.

2. Click the Styles and Formatting button to open the Styles and Formatting task pane.

3. In the task pane, find the style that needs redefining, open its drop-down menu, and choose Modify. You see the Modify Style dialog box shown in Figure 12-7. Does this dialog box look familiar? The options in this dialog box are identical to those in the New Style dialog box (refer to Figure 12-5) with one exception: You can't choose a style type.

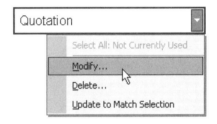

4. Modify the style in the Modify Style dialog box. Use the same techniques you use when creating a style (see "The Two Ways to Create a Style," earlier in this chapter).

5. Click OK.

A Word about Modifying the Normal Template

The Normal template is arguably the most important template of all. If you add a new style to the Normal template, or if you modify a style on the Normal template, you and others who use your computer have to live with it. ("Choosing Default Settings for the Normal Template" in Chapter 21 explains a quick way to modify the Normal template.)

Because changes to the Normal template affect so many documents, Word gives you the opportunity to decide when you shut down the program whether you want to keep changes that you made to the Normal template. You see the dialog box shown here, which asks whether the changes are worth keeping.

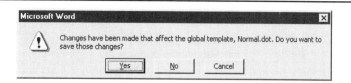

To see this dialog box when the Normal template is changed and you shut down, choose Tools | Options, select the Save tab in the Options dialog box, and check the Prompt to Save Normal Template check box.

By the way, suppose you modify the Normal template but regret doing so and you want the original Normal template. The easiest way to restore the Normal template to its original state is to delete it! That's right—delete the thing. When you try to open a document based on the Normal template and Word can't find the template, it creates a new one. And the new Normal template that Word creates includes the standard formats, menus, shortcuts, and whatnot that were there when you loaded Word on your computer. You will find the Normal template in this folder: C:\Windows\Application Data\Microsoft\Templates.

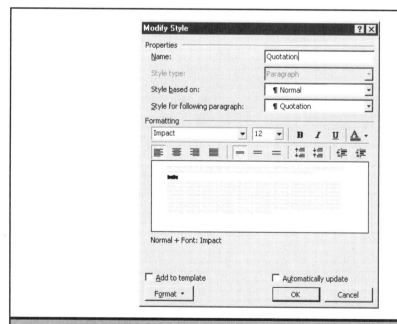

Figure 12-7. *The Modify Style dialog box is nearly identical to the New Style dialog box. The options and choices are nearly identical as well*

Renaming and Deleting Styles

Sometimes you have to rename a style in order to copy it to another document. As "Copying Paragraph Styles from Document to Document" explained earlier in this chapter, you can't copy a style from one document to another if a style in the receiving document has the same name as the style being copied. As for deleting styles, you might as well delete a style from a document if you don't need it to keep Style lists from growing too long.

Renaming a Style

Follow these steps to rename a style:

1. Find the style on the Styles and Formatting task pane. If necessary, open the Show drop-down menu and choose Available Styles or All Styles to find it.

2. Open the style's drop-down menu and choose Modify. You see the Modify Style dialog box (refer to Figure 12-7).

3. Enter a new name for the style in the Name box.

4. Click OK.

Paragraph, character, table, or list style assignments throughout the document are given the new name.

 If you rename one of Word's built-in styles, Word keeps the old name and merely attaches your name to it. Rename the Heading 1 style, for example, and you get "Heading 1, your style name."

Deleting a Style

You can't delete the built-in styles that come with every Word document (Normal and the Heading styles, for example), but you can delete styles you fashioned yourself. After you delete a style, paragraphs to which the style was assigned are assigned the Normal style.

 Think twice before deleting a style. If another style you created is based on the style you want to delete, deleting the style can cause untold damage. What's more, you can't tell by looking how many paragraphs in a long document were assigned a style, so there is no telling what deleting it will do.

Follow these steps to delete a style:

1. Find the style in the Styles and Formatting task pane.

2. Open the style's drop-down menu and choose Delete. Word asks if you really want to delete the style.

3. Click the Yes button.

 # Building Your Own Templates

After you create a template, you can use it as a launching pad for creating other documents. All Word documents are created from templates, as you know if you ever created a document by way of the Templates dialog box. Each template comes with many predefined styles, as well as AutoText entries and macros. In these pages, you learn how to create templates of your own. Read on to find out how to create a new template and assemble styles from different templates to create a new template.

Tip   *A template can include text and graphics. When you create a file with the template, the text and graphics appear, at which point you can delete them or keep them. Putting a company logo and address in a template is a great way to create stationery for a company. Anyone who wants to write a letter on company stationery has only to open a Word document based on the Company template.*

Creating a New Template

One way to create a template is to make one from a document you have been working on. With this technique, you choose File | Save As to save the document as a template, open the template, and delete the text. After you delete the text, the styles, AutoText entries, and macros you created remain in the template. Later, you can create a Word document from your new template and make use of all the styles, AutoText entries, and styles you so carefully created.

Follow these steps to create a template from a prototype document:

1. With the document open and staring you in the face, choose File | Save As. The Save As dialog box appears.

2. Open the Save As Type drop-down menu and choose Document Template. You see the Templates folder in the Save In list at the top of the dialog box. In the dialog box are the names of templates that appear on the General tab of the Templates dialog box, the dialog box you see when you click General templates in the New Document task pane to create a document with a template other than Normal.

3. Type a descriptive name for your template in the File Name box. Template names must observe all the Windows file-naming conventions.

4. Click the Save button to complete the operation and close the Save As dialog box. The document you see onscreen is not really a document—it's a template file.

PROFESSIONAL-LOOKING DOCUMENTS WITH WORD 2002

5. Delete everything in the template file except the stuff you want to see when you create a new document with the template. You may decide to keep an address, for example, or a watermark.

6. Click the Save button to save your changes to the template.

7. Choose File | Close to close the template.

As this illustration shows, templates you store in the Templates folder appear beside the Blank Document template on the General tab of the Templates dialog box. Here, I created a template called Personal Template and stored it in the Templates folder. To create a document with this template, I click the General Templates link in the New Document task pane, select the Personal Template template on the General tab of the Templates dialog box, and click OK.

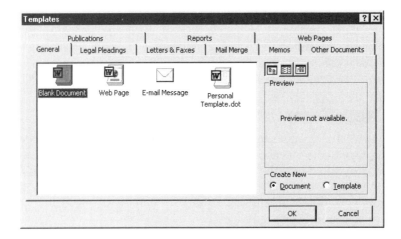

Deciding Where to Store Personal Templates

Unless you tamper with the default settings, templates you create yourself are kept in the C:\Windows\Application Data\Microsoft\Templates folder (Windows 2000 uses a path based on the current user logged in). You can keep them elsewhere, however, by choosing Tools | Options, selecting the File Locations tab in the Options dialog box, selecting User Templates, and clicking the Modify button. You see the Modify Location dialog box. Find and select a new folder there and click OK.

However, I strongly recommend keeping the templates you create in the C:\Windows\Application Data\Microsoft\Templates folder. If you move them elsewhere, you won't see them on the General tab of the Templates dialog box and you will have a hard time finding them when you want to create documents with them.

Assembling Styles (and Macros and AutoText) from Different Templates

Another way to create a template is to assemble styles from other templates and documents. Word offers a special gizmo called the Organizer for assembling styles from various places. Besides passing styles from template to template, you can also pass macros, AutoText entries, and toolbars with the Organizer. A template is a repository for macros, AutoText entries, and custom-made toolbars as well as styles.

To create a template with the Organizer, start by creating a new template (the previous page or two in this chapter explains how) or taking note of the name of the template to which you want to copy elements. Then follow these steps to copy elements from other documents or templates into a template:

1. Choose Tools | Templates and Add-Ins. You see the Templates and Add-Ins dialog box.

2. Click the Organizer button. The Organizer dialog box shown in Figure 12-8 appears. The Organizer dialog box is kind of confusing at first. When you open it, the Organizer is set up to copy styles and other elements. However, you can change that with a few clicks, as the next few steps demonstrate.

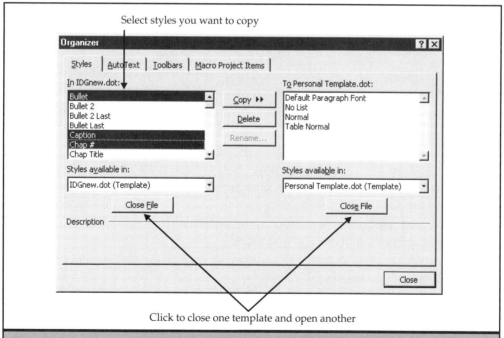

Select styles you want to copy

Click to close one template and open another

Figure 12-8. *Use the Organizer dialog box to copy styles and other elements from one template to another*

PROFESSIONAL-LOOKING DOCUMENTS WITH WORD 2002

3. Click the Close File button on the left side of the dialog box. When you do so, the button changes its name to Open File.

4. Click the Open File button, and, in the Open dialog box, find and select the template or document you want to copy styles *from*, and click the Open button. After you are done, elements of the template or document you selected appear on the left side of the Organizer dialog box. Remember: You can find Word templates in these folders:

   - C:\Program Files\Microsoft Office\Templates folder and its subfolders
   - C:\Windows\Application Data\Microsoft\Templates

5. On the right side of the Organizer dialog box, click the Close File button. The button changes names to Open File.

6. Click the Open File button, and, in the Open dialog box, find and select the template or document you want to copy styles *to,* and then click the Open button. When you are done, styles and other elements in the template you selected appear on the right side of the dialog box.

Tip *You can select an element in the Organizer dialog box and read its description at the bottom of the dialog box. If you have any doubts about which element you are copying, read its description.*

7. On the left side of the dialog box, CTRL-click to select items you want to copy to the template on the right side of the dialog box, and then click the Copy button.

Caution *If you try to copy a style with the same name from one template to another, Word warns you that you will delete the style in the template to which the copy is made. To keep from losing a style in the "copied to" template, rename the style. To do so, select its name and click the Rename button in the Organizer dialog box. Then type a new name in the Rename dialog box and click OK.*

8. If you want, click the Close File/Open File button on the left side of the Organizer dialog box to open another template or document and copy more elements from it.

9. Click the Close button in the Organizer when you are done assembling elements from templates and documents.

10. Click Yes when Word asks whether you want to save the changes to the template or document to which you copied elements.

MOUS Exam Objectives Explored in Chapter 12

Objective	Heading
Apply character styles	"The Different Kinds of Styles" and "Applying Styles in a Document"
Modify format, alignment, and layout of paragraphs	"Applying Styles in a Document"
Apply paragraph styles	"Applying Styles in a Document"
Create and apply character styles*	"Creating Your Own Styles" and "Applying Styles in a Document"

* Denotes an Expert, not a Core, exam objective.

Ten Style Problems and How to Solve Them

Especially when you copy text from other documents or work on documents that you got from other people, styles can be problematic. Sometimes Word changes style assignments without being asked to. Sometimes style formats get changed right under your nose and you can't do anything about it. Sometimes perfectly normal lines of text turn into headings. Here are ten common style problems and explanations for solving them.

1. My Styles Keep Changing on Me   It could be that your styles are supposed to change on you and you don't know it. As long as the Automatically Update check box is selected in the Modify Style dialog box, formats throughout a document change whenever you make a change to a single paragraph. Indent a paragraph that has been assigned the Quotation style, for example, and, if the Quotation style has set up to be updated automatically, all paragraphs in the document to which that style was assigned are indented accordingly.

To keep formats from being changed, go to the Styles and Formatting task pane, open the style's drop-down menu, and choose Modify. Then, in the Modify Style dialog box, uncheck the Automatically Update check box. See "Modifying a Style," earlier in this chapter for details.

2. My Styles Still Keep Changing on Me   You could have a "based on" problem. One style can be based on another, and if the "based on" style changes, all styles to which it is linked change as well. As I pointed out earlier in this chapter in "Basing One Style on Another Style," a style isn't so much based on another style as linked to it.

This problem is not easy to solve and may require some detective work. Did you change a style lately—a style that other styles are based upon? Pinpoint a style that has changed, open the Modify Style dialog box, and see whether the style is based on another. If the problem turns out to be that you changed a style, change it back. Otherwise, choose a new "based on" style for the styles that keep changing on you. See "Modifying a Style," earlier in this chapter.

3. Most of My Styles Changed on Me   When this happens, you can bet that your document is attached to the wrong template. To solve the problem, attach your document to another template to which it is more suitable. See "Assigning a Document to a Different Template."

To sever the tie between a document and the template with which it was created, choose Tools | Templates and Add-Ins and uncheck the Automatically Update Document Styles check box. As long as no check mark is in that check box, a document's styles remain the same no matter what happens to the template with which it was created.

4. Word Isn't Updating My Styles Automatically After I Make a Format Change   Being able to modify a style automatically merely by formatting a paragraph to which a style has been applied is a powerful way to update styles. However, styles are not updated automatically unless you tell Word to do so. "Modifying a Style," earlier in this chapter, explains how to design a style that is updated automatically. Here's a quick way make a style "automatically updateable":

1. In the Styles and Formatting task pane, open the style's drop-down menu and choose Modify.
2. In the Modify dialog box, check the Automatically Update check box and click OK.

5. When I Copy Text to Another Document My Styles Don't Hold Up   You can't copy text from one document to another and keep your style formats if the style you are copying has the same name as a style that is in the document to which the copy is being made. For example, if both documents have styles called Body Text but the Body Text formats are different, the copied text adopts the formats of the Body Text style in the document to which it is copied. To copy text assigned a particular style and keep the formatting, the style's name must be different from all the style names in the document that is receiving the copy. Change the style's name before you copy the text if you want the text to retain its formatting when it lands in the other document. See "Renaming a Style," earlier in this chapter.

To keep the source formatting if you are copying only one paragraph at a time, open the drop-down menu on the Paste Options button and choose Keep Source Formatting.

By the way, if you copy styles from one document to another with the Organizer, the style that is being copied takes precedence over the style that is already there when two styles have the same name. See "Assembling Styles from Different Templates," earlier in this chapter.

6. Sometimes I Get a New Style After I Press ENTER   Some styles—heading styles, for example—are designed so that a new style is assigned to the next line. Press ENTER after typing a Heading 1 heading and the next line is usually assigned either the Normal style or the Body Text style.

Automatically assigning a new style to the following paragraph is supposed to be a convenience. Instead of having to choose a style from the Style menu, the style you need is ready and waiting. Obviously, a different style needs to follow a heading style because two headings cannot appear one after the other.

However, sometimes template designers mistakenly design a style so that a different style follows one style when really no style should follow it. Sometimes the same style should carry to the next paragraph when you press ENTER. See "Modifying a Style," earlier in this chapter, to learn how to modify a style so that no style follows it. *Hint:* In the Modify Style dialog box, open the Style For Following Paragraph drop-down list and choose the name of the style you are modifying, not the name of a different style.

7. Word Keeps Assigning Heading Styles to My Paragraphs   Don't worry—it happens in the best of families. You type a line of text, press ENTER twice, and get a heading whether you like it or not. The heading appears because Word assigns a heading style to any line of text that begins with a capital letter, is not followed by a punctuation mark, and is followed by a blank line. Follow these steps to tell Word to stop turning innocent lines of text into headings:

1. Choose Tools | AutoCorrect Options.
2. Select the AutoFormat As You Type tab in the AutoCorrect dialog box.
3. Under Apply As You Type, uncheck the Built-In Heading Styles check box and click OK.

8. Word Keeps Assigning Styles Without My Permission   Sometimes, like a thing that goes bump in the night, Word assigns a paragraph style to text when you least expect it. Word follows various rules for assigning styles automatically. Many people like to merrily type along and let Word handle style assignments, but others resent Word's interference and prefer to assign styles on their own. Follow these steps to prevent Word from assigning styles automatically:

1. Choose Tools | AutoCorrect Options to open the AutoCorrect dialog box.
2. Select the AutoFormat As You Type tab.
3. Uncheck the Define Styles Based On Your Formatting check box and click OK.

Earlier in this chapter, Table 12-1 lists the styles that Word applies automatically when you choose commands on the Insert and View menus.

9. Two of My Paragraphs Look Different Even Though I Applied the Same Style to Each   Probably you formatted some of the text by conventional means—by boldfacing it, for example, or indenting it. When you format text or a paragraph to which you applied a style, your formats take precedence over the style's. Try one of these keyboard shortcuts to strip formats from a paragraph or text so that only style formats remain:

- Press CTRL-Q to remove all formats from a paragraph.
- Press CTRL-SPACEBAR to remove formats from characters. Be sure to select the characters first.
- Select Clear Formatting on the Styles and Formatting task pane to strip all formats and apply the Normal style.

10. Not All Styles Appear on the Styles and Formatting Task Pane   Maybe not. But you can make them appear by opening the Show drop-down list and choosing All Styles. To see all the styles on the Formatting toolbar's Style menu, hold down the SHIFT key and click the down arrow.

Chapter 13

Embellishing Documents with Artwork and Text Boxes

This chapter is meant to bring out the artist in you. In this chapter, you learn the many ways to decorate a document with artwork and text boxes. You will be pleasantly surprised to find that dropping a clip art image or text box in a document is easy. Word offers other kinds of art as well. The problems start when you try to make your clip art image, text box, or piece of artwork fit on the page.

The first half of this chapter is devoted to the different kinds of artwork you can place on the page, text boxes included. You will find instructions for inserting clip art images, graphics, watermarks, and text boxes in a document. You also learn how to draw lines and shapes with the tools on the Drawing toolbar. The second half of the chapter explains how to manipulate images, shapes, text boxes, and other so-called objects. The commands for selecting, positioning, changing the size of, applying borders to, filling, overlapping, and wrapping text around objects such as clip art images, shapes, and text boxes are the same no matter which kind of object you are dealing with.

"WordArt for Bending, Spindling, and Mutilating Text" in Chapter 7 explains how to decorate documents with WordArt images—words that have been stretched, crumpled, or squeezed into odd shapes.

Placing Graphics and Clip Art in Documents

Surely the easiest way to spruce up a document is to include a clip art image or two. Putting clip art images in documents is ridiculously easy. Word comes with many clip art images, as well as the Clip Organizer, a program to help you manage and insert clip art and other kinds of media (Appendix B explains the Clip Organizer). You can even go on the Internet, rummage for clip art, and insert it directly into a document.

These pages explain how to insert a clip art image or graphic in a document, whether you obtained the image from the Clip Organizer or elsewhere.

Searching by Keyword for Images in the Insert Clip Art Task Pane

To search by keyword in Microsoft Word for a clip art image in the Clip Organizer, start by choosing Insert | Picture | Clip Art or clicking the Insert Clip Art button on the Drawing toolbar. The Insert Clip Art task pane opens, as shown in Figure 13-1. Enter the following information and click the Search button:

- **Search Text** Enter a keyword that describes what kind of image you want. (If you happen to know the filename of the clip art image you want, enter it.) A handful of keywords is associated with each file in the Clip Organizer.

- **Search In** Choose which collection to search. Appendix B describes collections.

- **Results Should Be** Choose which kind of media file you are looking for. By clicking a plus sign to open the Clip Art or Photographs folder, you can search for different file types, as shown in Figure 13-1.

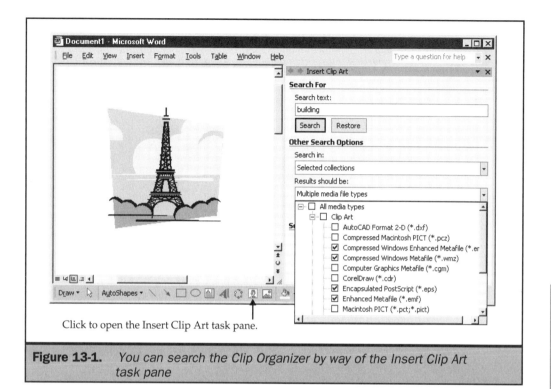

Click to open the Insert Clip Art task pane.

Figure 13-1.   *You can search the Clip Organizer by way of the Insert Clip Art task pane*

If your search is unsuccessful, you see the words "No Results Found." Click the Modify button to start all over in the task pane or click the Clip Organizer hyperlink to open the Clip Organizer and start searching there.

If your search is successful, a scroll box with images appears, as in Figure 13-2. (Click the Results button to see more images in the scroll box.) Scroll to the image you want and, to enter it, click it or open its drop-down menu and choose Insert.

Suppose you notice an image whose artistic style you like. You can see images designed by the same artist by opening the image's drop-down menu and choosing Find Similar Style.

Inserting a Graphic File in a Document on Your Own

For all I know, you have accumulated hundreds of graphic files and you want to use them in your documents in lieu of clip art from the Clip Organizer. Table 13-1 lists the graphic file formats that are compatible with Word. You can bring a graphic into a Word document as long as it is in one of the formats listed in the table. In some cases, however, you must have installed a graphics filter when you installed Word to import a graphic. Table 13-1 describes which graphic formats require a filter (look in the "Filter Required?" column). If necessary, reinstall Word, and install the graphics filter you need this time around.

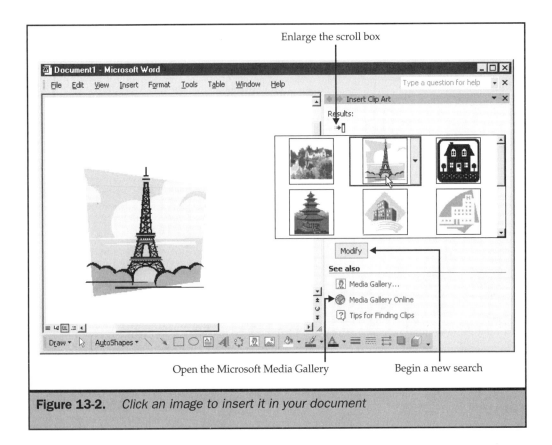

Figure 13-2. *Click an image to insert it in your document*

Note *Appendix A explains how to install and reinstall Word. To install graphics filters, Choose Add or Remove Features in the Setup dialog box. When you are asked which features to install, open the Office Shared Features folder, open the Converts and Filters folder, open the Graphics Filters folder, and select the filters you need.*

File Extension	Format	Bitmap/Vector	Filter Required?
BMP	Microsoft Windows Bitmap	Bitmap	No
CDR	CorelDRAW	Vector	Yes

Table 13-1. *Graphic File Formats You Can Use in Word Documents*

File Extension	Format	Bitmap/Vector	Filter Required?
CGM	Computer Graphics Metafile	Vector	Yes
DIB	Device Independent Bitmap	Bitmap	No
EMF	Enhanced Metafile	Vector	No
EPS	Encapsulated PostScript	Vector	No
FPX	FlashPix	Bitmap	Yes
GIF	Graphics Interchange Format	Bitmap	No
JPG	Interchange Format	Bitmap	No
PCD	Kodak Photo CD	Bitmap	Yes
PCT	Macintosh PICT	Vector	Yes
PCX	PC Paintbrush	Bitmap	Yes
PNG	Portable Network Graphics	Bitmap	No
RLE	Bitmap File in RLE Compression Scheme	Bitmap	No
TIF, TIFF	Tagged Image File Format	Bitmap	No
WMF	Windows Metafile	Vector	No
WPG	WordPerfect Graphics	Vector	Yes

Table 13-1.   *Graphic File Formats You Can Use in Word Documents* (continued)

Follow these steps to copy a graphic file directly into a Word document:

1. Choose Insert | Picture | From File or click the Insert Picture button on the Picture toolbar. You see the Insert Picture dialog box shown in Figure 13-3.

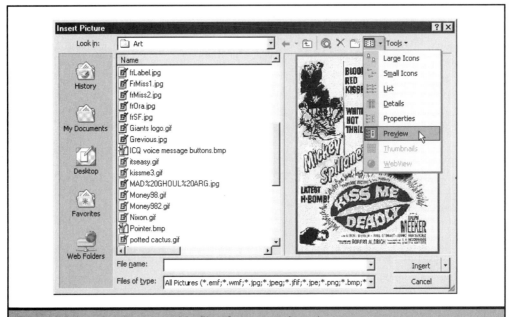

Figure 13-3. *Putting a graphic file of your own in a document*

2. Find and select the graphic you want. As Figure 13-3 shows, you can open the drop-down menu on the Views button and choose Preview to see what the graphic looks like before you import it. Thumbnails view can also be a help because it gives you a glimpse of several different files.

3. Click the Insert button.

When you import a graphic, it arrives as an inline graphic and can't be moved horizontally on the page. You can change that, however, by displaying the Picture toolbar, clicking the Text Wrapping button on the toolbar, and selecting an option besides In Line with Text. Later in this chapter, "Manipulating Art, Text Boxes, Shapes, and Other So-Called Objects" explains how to move graphics and position them on the page.

You can tell Word to go directly to the folder where you keep graphics whenever you click the Insert Picture button or choose Insert | Picture | From File. To do so, choose Tools | Options and select the File Locations tab in the Options dialog box. Then select Clipart Pictures on the File Types list, click the Modify button, and, in the Modify Location dialog box, find and select the folder where you keep art. After you click OK, the Location list in the Options dialog box shows the folder you chose.

Bitmap and Vector Graphics

All graphic images, including the ones listed in Table 13-1, fall into either the bitmap or vector category. A *bitmap graphic* is composed of thousands upon thousands of tiny dots called *pixels* that, taken together, form an image (the term "pixel" comes from "picture image"). A *vector graphic* is drawn with the aid of computer instructions that describe the shape and dimension of each line, curve, circle, and so on.

As far as Word documents are concerned, the difference between the two formats is that vector graphics do not distort when you enlarge or shrink them, whereas bitmap graphics lose resolution when their size is changed. Furthermore, vector images do not require near as much disk space as bitmap graphics. Drop a few bitmap graphics in a Word document and soon you are dealing with a document that is 500KB or 750KB in size.

Changing the Appearance of an Image or a Graphic

Every clip art image or graphic in a Word document can be a collaboration, not the work of a single artist. By clicking an image, displaying the Picture toolbar, and clicking the Image Control, More Contrast, Less Contrast, More Brightness, and Less Brightness buttons, you can collaborate with the original artist and create something new. You can also crop an image and use the cropping command to put more space between an image and its border. Better read on.

Changing an Image's Contrast and Brightness

Figure 13-4 shows an image that has been made over several times with tools on the Picture toolbar. Click an image and play with these buttons on the Picture toolbar to change an image's contrast and brightness:

- **Color Button** The Grayscale and Black & White options on the Color button menu are for rendering a color image in shades of gray or black and white. The Washout option creates a transparent image and is useful when creating watermarks ("Decorating Pages with Watermarks," later in this chapter, explains watermarks).

- **More Contrast and Less Contrast Buttons** Enhance or mute the difference between light and dark colors or shades.

- **More Brightness and Less Brightness Buttons** Make an image brighter or more somber.

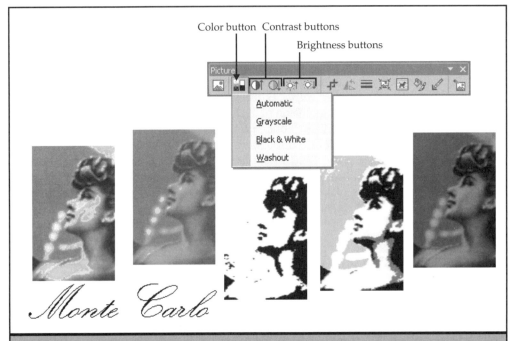

Figure 13-4.   *You are hereby encouraged to experiment with the buttons on the Picture toolbar to change the appearance of a graphic or clip art image*

Note   *See "Changing the Size and Shape of Objects," later in this chapter, to learn how to stretch, scrunch, or miniaturize a clip art image.*

The Format Picture dialog box also offers a Brightness command, Contrast command, and means of rendering a graphic as a black-and-white, grayscale, or watermark image. Either right-click the graphic and choose Format Picture from the shortcut menu or choose Format | Picture to open the Format Picture dialog box. Commands for changing the appearance of an image are found under Image Control on the Picture tab. It might interest you to know that clicking a Brightness or Contrast button on the Picture toolbar changes the Brightness or Contrast setting by 3%.

If you regret changing the appearance of a graphic and you want your original graphic back, select your graphic, click the Image Control button on the Picture toolbar, and choose Automatic from the drop-down menu.

Cropping Off Part of an Image

Cropping means to cut off part of a clip art image or graphic. I'm afraid you can't use Word's cropping tool like a pair of scissors or X-ACTO knife to cut zigzag around the edges of a graphic or clip art image or cut a hole in the middle. You can, however, cut strips from the side, top, or bottom. Here, the cropping tool was used to cut off all but the heads of different images, and then the heads were laid over another clip art image to make for a very strange group picture.

To crop off part of a graphic or clip art image, click the image to select it, and then click the Crop button on the Picture toolbar. Instead of selection handles, cropping handles appear around the graphic. Drag a handle to crop start cropping. Dashed lines show what will be left of your image when you finish cropping it. Release the mouse button when only the portion of the image that you want is inside the dashed lines. If you cropped too far, grab a cropping handle and drag away from the center of the image—what you cropped reappears.

Cropping handles

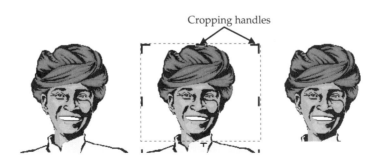

Depending on whether pictures in your document "snap to the grid," cropping a picture with precision can be difficult. As "Positioning Objects on the Page" explains later in this chapter, the grid is a set of invisible horizontal and vertical lines on which graphics and other objects are aligned. When objects snap to the grid, aligning them is easier because they always stick to the gridlines, but moving them and cropping them with precision is more difficult. If you need to shave off a small part of a picture but are having trouble doing it, hold down the ALT key as you drag the Cropping tool. By holding down the ALT key, you can crop off the parts of a picture that fall between gridlines.

You can also crop an image in the Format Picture dialog box, although the only reason to do that is to crop an image by the same amount on all sides or, better yet, increase the distance between the image and its border on all sides. By entering negative numbers in the Crop From boxes, you can increase the distance between an image and the border that surrounds it. To reach the Format Picture dialog box, double-click the image, click the image, and choose Format | Picture, or right-click and choose Format Picture. Go to the Picture tab to enter the negative numbers in the Crop From boxes.

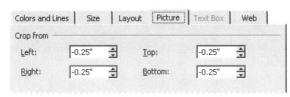

Suppose you regret cropping your graphic. Besides clicking the Undo button, you can restore it to its original condition by selecting it and clicking the Reset button on the Picture toolbar.

By the way, when you crop a graphic, you don't cut off a part of it, not as far as your computer is concerned. All you do is tell Word not to display part of a graphic. The graphic is still whole. You can, however, compress a graphic after you crop it and in so doing truly shave off a part of the graphic and thereby decrease the size of the document you are working with. Deleting the cropped areas of a document can greatly decrease the size of a file when you are working with bitmap images, which take up a lot of disk space.

To truly delete part of a graphic, select it and click the Compress Pictures button on the Picture toolbar. In the Compress Pictures dialog box, make sure the Delete Cropped Areas of Pictures check box is selected, uncheck the Compress Pictures check box, and choose the No Change option under Change Resolution.

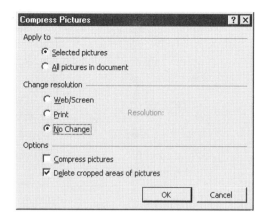

PROFESSIONAL-LOOKING
DOCUMENTS WITH
WORD 2002

> **Note**   *Near the end of this chapter, "To Compress or Not to Compress Graphics" explains compression issues in detail.*

Decorating Pages with Watermarks

According to the Microsoft Corporation, a *watermark* is a faint image, word, or phrase that appears behind the text in the same place on each page. As papermakers know, a watermark is really an image impressed in the paper that appears when you hold the paper to the light. A Word watermark is not impressed in the paper, but it's the closest thing to watermarks you can get in the debased digital world in which we live. Figure 13-5 shows an example of a watermark.

> **Note**   *Watermarks only appear in Print Layout view.*

To create a watermark that appears in the center of each page of your document, start by choosing Format | Background | Printed Watermark. The Printed Watermark dialog box appears. From there, click the Picture Watermark option button to use an image as the watermark or the Text Watermark option button to use a word or phrase:

■ **Picture Watermark**   Click the Select Picture button, and, in the Insert Picture dialog box, select the image that you want to use as a watermark and click the Insert button. In the Printed Watermark dialog box, choose an option from the Scale drop-down menu to select a size for the watermark image. If you uncheck the Washout check box, your image will be faint, but not completely so, and it may obscure text on the page.

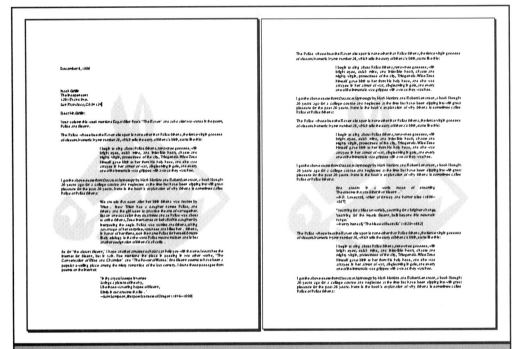

Figure 13-5.   *Watermarks appear behind the text and are very elegant-looking*

- ■ **Text Watermark**   In the Text box, either type words for the watermark or choose words from the drop-down menu. You can also select a font, size, color, and layout for the watermark. Be careful about unchecking the Semitransparent check box, as doing so might make the watermark text too dark on the page.

To tinker with or remove a watermark, choose Format | Background | Printed Watermark. In the Printed Watermark dialog box, change the settings or choose the No Watermark option button to remove the watermark.

Watermarks that you create with the Format | Background | Printed Watermark command appear on every page of the document. Suppose you want the watermark to appear on only a handful of pages. To do that, create a section for the pages on which the watermark is to appear and disconnect its header and footer from the other sections in the document (see "Section Breaks for Changing Layouts" and "Headers and Footers for Different Pages and Sections" in Chapter 9).

Why create a separate header and footer for the section in which the watermark will appear? Odd as it may seem, a watermark can be made a part of the page header. To create a watermark for a particular section, you can choose View | Header and Footer, click in the Header box, import the clip art image, and tell Word to place it behind the text. Because the clip art image is technically part of the header, it appears on every page in the section, as a header does.

Follow these steps to insert a watermark in one section of a document:

1. Click in the section.

2. Open the Zoom drop-down menu and choose 50%. At 50 percent, you can see how well an image fits on the page.

3. Choose View | Header and Footer. You see the Header box for entering headers.

4. Insert the clip art image or graphic. See "Placing Graphics and Clip Art in Documents" earlier in this chapter. Be sure to insert a dark image. Light-colored images can hardly be seen on the page as watermarks.

5. Select the image, click the Text Wrapping button on the Picture toolbar, and choose Behind Text from the drop-down menu. You can also right-click the image, choose Format Picture, select the Layout tab in the Format Picture dialog box, and choose Behind Text there.

6. Drag the image out of the Header box and into the middle of the page. Enlarge or shrink the image as need be. Later in this chapter, "Manipulating Art, Text Boxes, Shapes, and Other So-Called Objects" explains how to move and change the size of clip art images. Click the Close button in the Header and Footer toolbar.

Don't forget that to reposition the watermark or change its hue, you have to choose View | Header and Footer first. Without choosing that command, you can't get at the watermark. Earlier in this chapter, "Changing the Appearance of an Image or a Graphic" explains how to change the contrast or brightness of an image. Click the More Brightness button on the Picture toolbar to make a watermark less opaque. Click the Color button and choose Washout on the drop-down menu to make the image more opaque.

> **Tip** *To place a watermark in the very center of the pages in a section, choose View | Header and Footer, if necessary, to get at the watermark image, and double-click the image. On the Layout tab of the Format Picture dialog box, click the Advanced button, and then select the Picture Position tab in the Advanced Layout dialog box. Under Horizontal, choose the Alignment option button, and choose Centered and Page from the Relative To drop-down lists. Under Vertical, choose the Alignment button and choose Centered and Page again. Then click OK twice to return to your document.*

Putting a Text Box on the Page

Text boxes are one of the best things going in Word. Think of a text box as a page within a page. Almost everything that can be done to a page—putting borders around it, formatting text in different ways—can be done inside a text box. After you drop a text box on the page, you can move it very easily from place to place. Typically, text boxes are used to make boxed announcements like the one on the left side of Figure 13-6. However, with a little imagination you can use them in all kinds of interesting ways. That's a text

Figure 13-6. *A typical text box with borders and a color background (left) and a text box without borders superimposed on a clip art image (right)*

box on the right side of Figure 13-6, too, but I removed the border and the "fill"—the color inside the box—so that the clip art image of the frog can show through the text box.

These pages explain how to insert a text box, change the direction of text in a text box, and make text flow from text box to text box. Later in this chapter, "Manipulating Art, Text Boxes, Shapes, and Other So-Called Objects" explains how to change the borders of a text box, change its fill color, move it around on the page, wrap text around it, and change its size.

Inserting a Text Box

To put a text box on the page, either choose Insert | Text Box or click the Text Box button on the Drawing toolbar. The pointer turns into a cross, and you see the drawing canvas. Click where you want one corner of the text box to be and drag toward its opposite corner. Lines appear as you draw the box. Release the mouse button when the box is the right size.

Remember these little tricks when you draw text boxes:

- To make a perfect square, hold down the SHIFT key as you draw the text box.

- To draw a perfect square in an outward direction starting in the middle, hold down the CTRL and SHIFT keys as you draw the box.

- To dispense with the drawing canvas, either draw the text box starting at a point outside the canvas, or type the text that will go in the text box, select the text, and then click the Text Box button on the Drawing toolbar or choose Insert | Text Box. (Later in this chapter, "Drawing on the Canvas" explains the drawing canvas.)

After you have created your text box, click inside it and start typing to enter the text. Everything you ever learned about text formatting applies to the text in a text box as well. Click the Align Left or Align Center button on the Formatting toolbar to left-align or center text, for example. Or drag indent markers on the ruler to indent the text.

To remove a text box, select it by clicking its perimeter, and then press the DELETE key. Deleting a text box deletes all the text inside it as well. Copy the text inside the text box to the Clipboard before you delete the text box if you want to preserve the text.

Caution   *Selecting a text box can be problematic. See "Selecting Objects So You Can Manipulate Them," later in this chapter.*

Changing the Internal Margins of a Text Box

Unless you change the internal measurements, words in a text box lie .1 inch from the left and right sides, and .5 inch from the top and bottom. Suppose you want text to come closer to or move further from the sides of a text box. Follow these steps to change the internal margins of a text box:

1. Double-click the border of the text box, right-click the perimeter of the text box and choose Format | Text Box on the shortcut menu, or select the text box and choose Format | Text Box. You see the Format Text Box dialog box.

2. Select the Text Box tab.

3. Change the Internal Margin settings. The only way to change these settings is to visit the Format Text box dialog box. Drag the sides of a text box to change the internal margins and you drag in vain.

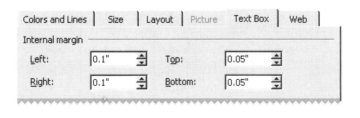

Changing the Direction of the Text

On the Text Box toolbar is a button called Change Text Direction. Select a text box, click the button, and all the words in the text box change direction, as shown in Figure 13-7. Keep clicking the button until the text turns in the direction you want it to turn. You don't have to select any words or letters before clicking the button. All you have to do is select the text box, choose View | Toolbars | Text Box if necessary, and start clicking the Change Text Direction button on the Text Box toolbar.

By the way, when you turn text on its side, the buttons on the Formatting toolbar that pertain to arranging text also turn on their sides. If you have trouble reading the buttons, lean far to the left or right, cock your head, and squint.

Linking Text Boxes So That Text Passes from Box to Box

With the right amount of foresight and planning, you can link text boxes so that text passes from box to box as each box is filled. You need to plan ahead, however, because you can't link text boxes into which text has already been typed. To link text boxes, write the text first, then insert each text box in the chain, pour the text in the first box, and tell Word where to make text go as each box is filled up.

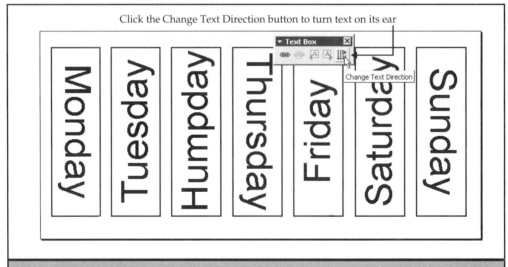

Figure 13-7. *By clicking the Change Text Direction button on the Text Box toolbar, you can make the words and letters in a text box land sideways*

Figure 13-8 shows an example of text boxes that have been linked. When you add a word or two to the first box, text is pushed into the second and subsequent text boxes. Delete words in a box and text is pulled from subsequent boxes. Linked text boxes are especially useful in newsletters and brochures when an article on page 1, for example, is continued on page 6. As long as the text boxes on page 1 and 6 are linked, text passes directly from page 1 to 6 as the box on page 1 fills up. Many people prefer to create columns by linking text boxes because the Format | Columns command, the usual way to lay out columns, doesn't permit text to jump long distances.

To make text pass between text boxes, click the sender text box to select it, click the Create Text Box Link button on the Text Box toolbar, and click inside the receiver text box. Here are the specifics of linking text boxes:

1. Type the text and proofread it. Editing text after it has been put in text boxes is difficult, so edit the text first.

2. Insert all the text boxes you will need (see "Inserting a Text Box," earlier in this chapter).

3. Cut or copy the text, click in the first text box, and click the Paste button or choose Edit | Paste. Now all the text is in the first text box. Don't worry about the text not fitting in the first text box—you will take care of that shortly.

4. Click the first text box in the chain to select it.

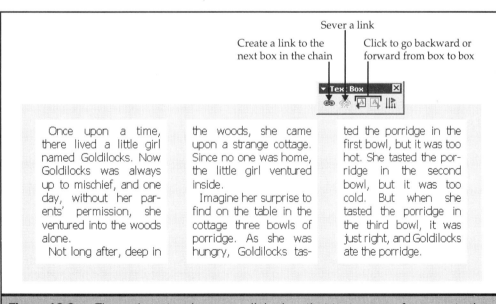

Figure 13-8.   *These three text boxes are linked so that text passes from one to the next as each is filled up*

5. Display the Text Box toolbar and click the Create Text Box Link button. The pointer changes into a pitcher with an arrow on it.

6. Move the pitcher over the next text box in the chain, and click when the pitcher turns into a pouring pitcher. Text passes into the text box.

Press the ESC key if you find yourself with a full pitcher but nowhere to pour it. In other words, if you click the Create Text Box Link button but forget which text box is next in the chain, press ESC so you can start all over.

7. Select the text box that you just poured text into and repeat steps 5 and 6 to enter text into the next and subsequent text boxes.

Don't forget these amenities as you work with linked text boxes:

- **Going from Text Box to Text Box**   To travel from box to box in the chain, click the Previous Text Box or Next Text Box button on the Text Box toolbar. By clicking these buttons, you don't have to scroll from page to page when far-flung text boxes are located on different pages.

- **Keeping Text from Passing to the Next Box**   To keep text from going to the next text box in the chain, select the text box and click the Break Forward Link button. Text boxes subsequent to the one you selected are made empty.

- **Selecting All the Text**   To select all the text in all the boxes in the chain, click in any box and press CTRL-A or choose Edit | Select All.

Introducing a New Text Box in the Middle of a Chain

Suppose you made a planning error and you realize after all the text boxes have been linked that a new text box needs to be inserted in the middle of the chain. Follow these steps to introduce a new text box:

1. Create the new text box.

2. Select the text box in the chain that is to go before the new text box and click the Break Forward Link button on the Text Box toolbar. All text is removed from text boxes that are subsequent to the text box you selected in this step.

3. With the text box you selected in step 2 still selected, click the Create Text Box Link button. The pointer turns into a pitcher.

4. Click inside the new text box you created in step 1. Now text passes to this text box. Your next task is to link the new text box to the rest of the chain.

5. Select your new text box, click the Create Text Link button, and click the text box that is to go after the one you created. By doing so, you connect your new text box to the boxes in the second half of the chain.

Using a Shape or an AutoShape as a Text Box

Here's a neat trick: Rather than use the conventional rectangle as a text box, you can use one of Word's shapes or autoshapes. As "Drawing Lines and Shapes" explains later in this chapter, an *autoshape* is a polygon of some kind—an arrow, a banner, or a star, for example. Click the AutoShape button on the Drawing toolbar and examine the different options on the submenus to see all the autoshapes that you can create.

Follow these steps to use an autoshape or a shape such as an oval as a text box:

1. Create the shape.

2. Right-click the shape and choose Add Text on the shortcut menu.

 Making text fit in a shape or autoshape can be difficult, but you can tell Word to enlarge the shape just enough to fit the text. Before you enter the text, double-click the border of the shape or choose Format | AutoShape, select the Text Box tab in the Format AutoShape dialog box, and check the Resize AutoShape to Fit Text check box.

3. Enter and format the text.

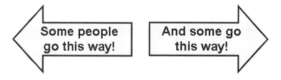

 You can turn a conventional text box into an autoshape text box. To do so, select the text box by clicking its perimeter, click the Draw button on the Drawing toolbar, choose Change AutoShape on the pop-up menu, and select an autoshape from a submenu.

Drawing on the Canvas

As shown in Figure 13-9, the *drawing canvas* appears onscreen when you put a text box, shape, or autoshape on the page. Similar to the Group command, the drawing canvas is a way to manipulate several objects at once. Instead of moving a text box and two autoshapes down the page, for example, all you have to do is drag the drawing canvas and everything along with it. Instead of scaling objects one at a time, you can scale them all at once.

 Strangely, you can't display the Drawing Canvas toolbar by choosing View | Toolbars or right-clicking a toolbar. If you lose sight of the Drawing Canvas toolbar or need to see it, right-click inside the canvas and choose Show Drawing Canvas Toolbar on the shortcut menu.

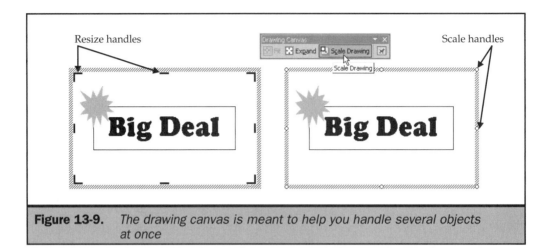

Figure 13-9. *The drawing canvas is meant to help you handle several objects at once*

Here are instructions for handling the drawing canvas:

- **Changing the Canvas's Size**   Drag a resize handle on the corner or side of the canvas or click the Expand button on the Drawing Canvas toolbar.

- **Making the Canvas Just Big Enough to Hold Objects**   Click the Fit button if the canvas holds more than one object and you want the canvas to be just large enough to hold all objects.

- **Scaling to Change the Size of all Objects on the Canvas**   Click the Scale Drawing button on the Drawing Canvas toolbar. Where resize handles used to be, you see scale handles (refer to Figure 13-9). You know the routine: Drag a corner handle to change the size of all objects in the drawing canvas but keep their proportions; drag a side handle to change the objects' size as well as their proportions.

- **Moving the Drawing Canvas**   Move the pointer over the perimeter of the canvas and start dragging when you see the four-headed arrow. If you can't drag the canvas, click the Text Wrapping button on the Drawing Canvas toolbar and choose an option apart from In Line with Text.

- **Dispensing with the Drawing Canvas**   The drawing canvas can be a help and a hindrance. To dispense with it, draw your text box or shape outside the canvas. When you are done drawing, the canvas disappears. Move your text box or shape where you want it to appear on the page. You can also drag objects off the canvas and then delete the canvas to remove the canvas but spare the objects.

- **Putting the Drawing Canvas Onscreen Before You Enter Objects**   Fans of the drawing canvas can choose Insert | Picture | New Drawing to create a drawing canvas from the get-go. Objects, including clip art images, that you place in the canvas are subject to the same commands that text boxes and shapes must submit to. For example, you can scale a clip art image after you place it on or drag it onto the drawing canvas.

Later in this chapter, "Grouping Objects to Make Working with Them Easier" explains another means of handling several different objects at once—the Group command.

The drawing canvas in and of itself is an object. Later in this chapter, "Manipulating Art, Text Boxes, Shapes, and Other So-Called Objects" explains how to move objects, including the drawing canvas, change their sizes, change their shapes, and wrap text around them, among other things.

Drawing Lines and Shapes

Whether you know it or not, Word comes with a drawing program with which you can create your own images. These pages explain how to use the drawing program to embellish a document with lines and shapes. For that matter, you can amuse yourself on a rainy afternoon with the drawing program. Read on to find out how you can use the tools on the Drawing toolbar to draw curved and straight lines, arrows, freeform lines, ovals, rectangles, and all manner of shapes. This illustration shows the various and sundry things you can draw.

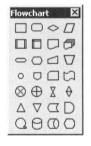

PROFESSIONAL-LOOKING DOCUMENTS WITH WORD 2002

Drawing Lines and Arrows

Drawing a line can be as easy or as difficult as you want it to be. To draw a straight line, all you have to do is click the Line button on the Drawing toolbar and start dragging. But you can also draw curves, freeform lines, and arrows. And you can choose a thickness for your line or a dashed or dotted line as well. Better read on.

Later in this chapter, "When Objects Overlap: Choosing Which Appears Above the Other" explains how to make a line appear in front of or behind text boxes, clip art images, and other so-called objects.

Drawing and Editing Straight Lines

To draw a straight line, click the Line button on the Drawing toolbar and drag onscreen where you want the line to appear. A selection handle appears on either end of the line after you draw it. By dragging the selection handles, you can change the length or angle of a line after you draw it.

 You can't change anything about a line until you select it. To select a line, gently move the pointer over it and click when you see the four-headed arrow. The selection handles appear after you select a line.

To move a line or adjust its length or angle, select it and do the following:

- **Change the Angle of a Line** Drag a selection handle up, down, or sideways. A dashed line shows where the line will be when you release the mouse button.

- **Change the Length** Drag a selection handle and release the mouse button when the dashed line is the right length.

- **Move a Line** Move the pointer over the line and click when you see the four-headed arrow. Then drag the line to a new location.

Choosing a Line Type, Width, and Color for Lines

To begin with, lines are .75 points wide, black, and not dotted or dashed, but you can change that by clicking buttons on the Drawing toolbar. Select a line and follow these instructions to change it to a dotted or dashed line, change its width, or change its color:

- **Line Type** Click the Dash Style button on the Drawing toolbar and choose a line type from the pop-up menu.

- **Width** Click the Line Style button and choose a point size for your line or a fancy line. To make the line wider than 6 points, click the More Lines option. You go to the Format AutoShape dialog box. In the Weight text box, enter a point size of your choice.

- **Color**   Open the drop-down menu on the Line Color button and choose a color from the pop-up menu. Choose Patterned Lines to open the Patterned Lines dialog box and choose a very fancy line.

 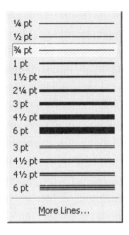 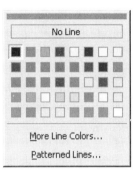

You can also double-click a line to open the Format AutoShape dialog box and do any number of things to lines while the dialog box is open.

Drawing an Arrow

The rules for drawing arrows and lines, changing their widths, and changing their colors and dash styles are the same. The only difference is you draw an arrow by clicking the Arrow button on the Drawing toolbar instead of the Line button.

Select the arrow and follow these instructions to change the style of the arrowhead, attach an arrowhead to both or either side of the arrow, or change the size of the arrowhead:

- **Changing the Style of the Arrowhead**   Click the Arrow Style button on the Drawing toolbar and choose a style from the pop-up menu.

- **Deciding Which End the Arrowheads Go On**   Click the Arrow Style button on the Drawing toolbar and choose an option to put arrowheads on both or either side of the arrow. If the arrow style you want isn't on the menu, choose the More Arrows option or double-click the arrow to open the Format AutoShape dialog box. Under Arrows, choose a Begin Style option and End Style option. Choose No Arrow to keep an arrowhead from appearing on either side of the line.

■ **Changing the Size of the Arrowheads**   Click the Arrow Style button on the Drawing toolbar and choose More Arrows or double-click the arrow. In the Format AutoShape dialog box, choose a Begin Size and End Size option.

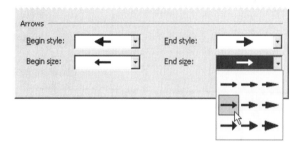

   To attach an arrowhead to a line you have already drawn, select the line, click the Arrow Style button on the Drawing toolbar, and choose an arrow option.

Drawing and Editing Arcs and Curved Lines

Before you attempt to draw curved lines or arcs, you should know that drawing curved lines falls in the "more trouble than it's worth" category. It can be done, but not very elegantly. You can spare yourself a lot of trouble by choosing an AutoShape and manipulating it instead of drawing curves and arcs on your own. Editing a curve or arc is especially difficult.

Creating the Curved Line or Arc   Click the Curve button to draw a curved line or arc. To find and select the Curved button, click the AutoShapes button on the Drawing toolbar, choose Lines on the pop-up menu, and click the Curve button on the submenu. Drag onscreen to draw a curved line. As you do so, take note of these important facts:

■ **Drawing Curves in the Line**   As you draw, click where you want to draw the apex of the curve. Word enters a *point* on the line each time you click. Very shortly, you will learn how to view the points on a line and edit a line by dragging or removing its points. This illustration shows where I clicked to draw a curved line. Each black square on the line is a point.

■ **Ending the Curved Line**   Double-click when you want to stop drawing. When you double-click, selection handles appear around the extremities of the line you drew. You see eight selection handles, not the two you get when you draw a straight line.

Note   *A curved line or an arc is an object. Techniques for moving objects, changing their sizes, and making them appear above or below other objects are explained in the second half of this chapter. See "Manipulating Art, Text Boxes, Shapes, and Other So-Called Objects."*

Drawing a Closed Shape   To draw a closed shape with no beginning or end, double-click to end the curved line. Then right-click immediately and choose Close Path from the shortcut menu. Word draws a straight line from the point you clicked to the start of the line.

Drawing an Arc   An arc is simply a line with one curve in it. To draw an arc, click the Curve button and draw a straight line. Then click the line to select it, right-click, and choose Edit Points on the menu. Next, move the pointer over the line where you want the apex of the arc to be, click, and drag to turn the line into an arc. Word places a point on the line at the apex of the arc. Drag the point, if necessary, to change the arc's appearance.

Editing Curved Lines and Arcs   To change the shape of a curved line or an arc, click to select it, and then right-click and choose Edit Points. Points appear on the line and show where each curve in the line is located. To make a curve sharper or smoother, drag its point.

If you have a lot of time on your hands, you can right-click a curved line while its points are on display and choose options from the shortcut menu to do the following to curved lines:

■ **Removing a Curve**   Right-click a point and choose Delete Point from the menu.

■ **Adding a Curve**   Right-click where you want the curve to go, choose Add Point from the menu, and drag the point on the line.

■ **Turning a Curve into a Straight Line**   Right-click between two points and choose Straight Segment from the menu. To turn a straight line into a curve, choose Curved Segment from the menu.

■ **Removing Part of a Line**   Right-click between two points and choose Delete Segment from the menu.

■ **Opening a Closed Shape**   Right-click a point and choose Open Path from the menu.

■ **Changing the Curve Type**   Right-click a point and choose Smooth Point, Straight Point, or Corner Point to make a curve steeper or smoother. A blue line appears across the point. Drag an end of the line to change the angle of the curve.

To select a curved line or any object for that matter, move the pointer over it and click when you see the four-headed arrow. You can tell when a curved line has been selected because its eight selection handles appear.

Freeform Drawing

So you want to play Etch-A-Sketch® on your computer? Bully for you. Here's how to do it:

1. Click the AutoShapes button on the Drawing toolbar, choose Lines on the pop-up menu, and click either the Freeform or Scribble button. The Freeform tool draws smoother lines than the Scribble tool.

2. Start drawing.

3. Double-click when you have finished drawing your line.

Eight selection handles instead of the usual two appear around a freeform line when you have finished drawing it. Your freeform line, for better or worse, is an object. Later in this chapter, "Manipulating Art, Text Boxes, Shapes, and Other So-Called Objects" explains how to move objects and change their sizes and shapes.

Another way to engage in freeform drawing is to use the Drawing Pad, a tool in Office's handwriting-recognition software. See "Handwriting to Enter Text" in Chapter 22.

Shapes, Shapes, and More Shapes

Besides drawing lines and arrows, you can draw shapes and what Word calls *autoshapes* with the tools on the Drawing toolbar. The Drawing toolbar offers about 60 different shapes and autoshapes. Apart from the rectangle and oval, you can draw octagons and various other "-agons," arrows, stars, and banners. Click the AutoShapes button on the Drawing toolbar and rest the pointer on the Basic Shapes, Block Arrows, Flowchart, Stars and Banners, and Callouts options on the menu to view the submenus and see all the autoshapes you can draw.

The drawing canvas appears when you create an autoshape, but if you prefer it not to appear, choose Tools | Options, select the General tab in the Options dialog box, and uncheck the Automatically Create Drawing Canvas when Inserting AutoShapes check box.

Follow these steps to draw a shape or an autoshape:

1. Click the Oval or Rectangle button on the Drawing toolbar to draw an oval or a rectangle; otherwise, click the AutoShapes button, click a menu name, and choose a shape from the submenu. The cursor changes into a cross.

2. Click onscreen and drag to draw the shape. It appears before your eyes.

Tip *Hold down the SHIFT key as you draw the autoshape if you want it to retain its symmetry.*

3. Release the mouse button. Selection handles appear around the shape or autoshape so you can move it or change its size. The next section in this chapter explains all the different ways to manipulate an object.

A yellow diamond, sometimes two or three, appears on some autoshapes. By dragging the diamond, you can change the symmetry of the autoshape. Figure 13-10, for example, shows the same autoshape—the Quad Arrow Callout on the Block Arrows submenu—twisted into four different shapes. Notice where the diamonds are. By dragging a diamond even a very short distance, you can do a lot to change the symmetry of an autoshape.

Tip *To exchange one autoshape for another, select it, click the Draw button on the Drawing toolbar, choose Change AutoShape on the menu, choose an AutoShape submenu, and select a substitute on the submenu.*

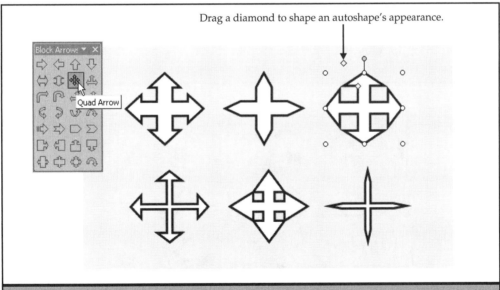

Figure 13-10.   *By dragging the diamonds on an autoshape, you can change its appearance slightly or not so slightly*

Manipulating Art, Text Boxes, Shapes, and Other So-Called Objects

After you insert a clip art image, graphic, autoshape, shape, line, text box, WordArt image, drawing canvas, or embed object in a document, it becomes what Word calls an "object." Figure 13-11 shows seven objects. The techniques for manipulating objects like these are the same whether you are dealing with a graphic, text box, line, or shape. To use objects successfully in a document, you have to know how to position them on the page. And you also have to know to make them fit beside other objects and text.

Including a few so-called objects on pages is probably the best way to make a document look more sophisticated. But manipulating objects can be troublesome if you don't know how Word handles objects or how to use the commands for working with objects. On the following pages are instructions for doing these tasks with objects:

- **Selecting**   Before you can do anything to objects, you have to select them.

- **Positioning**   Drag an object to move it on the page. However, positioning objects is not as simple as that because objects can move with the text to which they are attached or be "locked" so that they don't move on the page. Word offers many commands for positioning, aligning, and distributing objects on a page.

- **Changing Size and Shape**   You can enlarge, shrink, stretch, and scrunch objects.

- **Rotating and Flipping**   Readers turn their heads when they see an object that has been flipped or rotated. You can rotate and flip shapes, autoshapes, lines, and WordArt images.

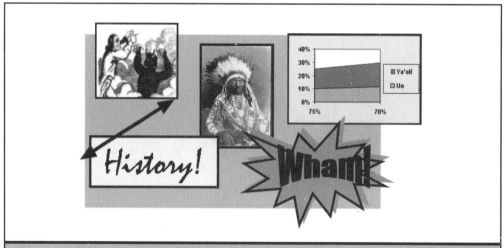

Figure 13-11.   *Examples of objects: clip art, a graphic, a chart, a text box, a line, an autoshape, and a WordArt image. Behind all these objects is yet another object—a rectangle*

- ■ **Applying Borders and Fills**   Putting borders on objects makes them stand out. You can also fill some kinds of objects with a color or pattern.

- ■ **Using a Shadow or Third Dimension**   On the Drawing toolbar are special commands for making an object cast a shadow or appear in three dimensions.

- ■ **Overlapping**   Making an object appear above or behind another object is a tricky task. In Figure 13-11, for example, a WordArt image, *Wham!*, overlaps an autoshape, which in turn overlaps a graphic. Word offers several confusing commands for "layering" objects on the page.

- ■ **Grouping**   To make working with several different objects at the same time easier, you can "group" them so that they become a single object. After objects have been grouped, manipulating them—manipulating it, I should say—is easier.

- ■ **Wrapping Text**   When text runs beside an object, the text can appear behind the object, appear in front of it, or be wrapped around it. Word offers many artful ways to wrap text.

Word only permits you to work on graphics, text boxes, and other objects in Print Layout and Web Layout views. In Normal view, you can't see objects. If the graphics in your document mysteriously disappear, don't panic. Click the Print Layout button or choose View | Print Layout instead.

By the way, if you spend any time whatsoever manipulating objects, you soon learn how important the Draw menu and its submenus are. As shown in Figure 13-12, to

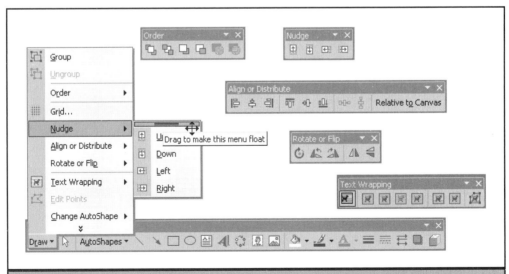

Figure 13-12.   *Commands on the Draw submenus are hard to get at; giving commands from the toolbars is much, much easier and gives you opportunities to experiment*

open the Draw menu, click the Draw button on the Drawing toolbar (if you don't see the Drawing toolbar, choose View | Toolbars | Drawing or click the Drawing button on the Formatting toolbar). On the Draw menu, the Order, Nudge, Align or Distribute, Rotate or Flip, and Text Wrapping submenus can be turned into floating toolbars, as Figure 13-12 shows. To turn a submenu into a toolbar and make options easier to choose, drag the gray line at the top of the submenu onto the screen. You often have to experiment with commands on the Draw submenus. You can save time by giving the commands from toolbars instead of submenus.

Selecting Objects So You Can Manipulate Them

Before you can move or change the border of a graphic, text box, or other object, you have to select it. To select an object, simply move the pointer over it, wait till you see the four-headed arrow, and click. Sometimes, to align or decorate several objects at once, you have to select more than one object at the same time. To select more than one object:

- ■ SHIFT-click them. In other words, hold down the SHIFT key as you click the objects.
- ■ Click the Select Objects button on the Drawing toolbar, click one side of the object you want to select, and drag the cursor across the objects. A box with dotted lines appears. All objects inside the dotted lines are selected when you release the mouse button.

You can tell when an object or objects have been selected because small round selection handles appear. As this illustration shows, objects have eight selection handles each; a line has two selection handles. On rectangular objects, the selection handles appear on the corners and sides. On irregularly shaped objects like the autoshape shown here, handles appear on the corners and sides of the object's outermost extremities. Use selection handles to change an object's shape.

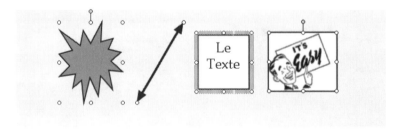

Selecting a text box can be tricky. When you click inside a text box, the selection handles appear but the box isn't really selected—you have simply clicked in the box and can start typing or editing text. To select a text box in order to manipulate it, move the pointer over the perimeter of the text box and click when you see a four-headed arrow. Instead of diagonal lines around the perimeter of the box, you see crosshatches when a text box has been selected.

Positioning Objects on the Page

Word offers about a dozen commands for positioning objects on the page. Get to know these commands and you can lay out pages quickly. Herewith are instructions for doing these tasks:

- **Moving Objects**   Move objects either by dragging them or by entering measurements in the Advanced Layout dialog box.

- **Aligning Objects**   Objects can be lined up with one another or with a page border.

- **Distributing Objects**   Distribute objects on the page so that the same amount of space appears between each one.

- **Snapping Objects to Word's Grid**   Snap objects to the grid to make aligning them easier.

- **Making Sure Objects Stay in the Right Place**   Lock an object so it stays in the same place on the page no matter where the paragraph to which it is attached moves.

Moving Objects

The easiest way to position an object is to simply drag it. To do so, move the pointer over the object and click when you see the four-headed arrow (click the perimeter of text boxes). Then hold down the mouse button and start dragging. Hold down the SHIFT key as you drag to move an object either horizontally or vertically in a straight line. As this illustration shows, the pointer changes into a four-headed arrow and a dot-and-dash outline appears where the object will move when you release the mouse button. Release it when you have moved the object to the right place:

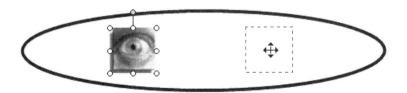

Tip   *When you insert or move an object, Word attaches it to the nearest paragraph. You can tell which paragraph an object is attached to by clicking the Show/Hide ¶ button. An anchor appears next to the paragraph to which the object is attached. Choose Tools | Options, select the View tab in the Options dialog box, and check the Object Anchors check box if you want to see the anchors at all times.*

Another, more complicated way to position objects is to enter measurements on the Picture Position tab of the Advanced Layout dialog box shown in Figure 13-13. If you

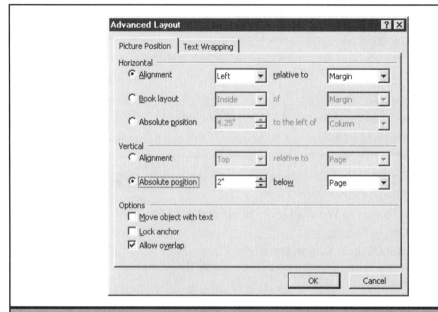

Figure 13-13. *The easiest way to position an object is to click and drag, but for precision settings you can also enter measurements in the Advanced Layout dialog box*

are dealing with the Alignment settings in the dialog box (not Absolute Position settings), the Horizontal and Vertical settings work like so:

- Horizontal settings determine the left-to-right position of the object with respect to the left or right edge of the page, left or right side of the margin, left or right side of the column (if the text runs in columns), or the left or right side of a character.

- Vertical settings determine the up-and-down position of the object with respect to the top or bottom of the page, the top or bottom margin, or the line that the object is on.

If you are dealing with Absolute Position settings in the Advanced Layout dialog box, the Horizontal and Vertical settings all work with respect to the top or left side of a part of the layout:

- Horizontal settings determine the exact position of the object from the left edge of the page, the left margin, the left side of the column (if the text runs in columns), or the left side of a character.

- Vertical settings determine the exact position of the object from the top of the page, the top margin, the top of the paragraph, or the top of a line.

The Book Layout options are for placing objects on or in the margin in double-sided, bound documents in which text will be printed on both sides of the page:

- **Inside Page**   Places the object in the inside margin next to the binding.
- **Outside Page**   Places the object in the margin furthest from the binding.
- **Inside Margin**   Places the object flush with the inside margin next to the binding.
- **Outside Margin**   Places the object flush with the outside margin furthest from the binding.

You can combine Alignment and Absolute Position settings. For example, suppose you are laying out a catalog with three graphics per page. You want the graphics to line up with the left margin and be, respectively, 2 inches, 4 inches, and 6 inches from the top of the page. In that case, you would choose the settings shown in Figure 13-13 for the first graphic on the page: Alignment Left Relative to Margin, Absolute Position 2" Below Page.

 Only use the Advanced Layout dialog box if you are working on a catalog or brochure in which objects such as graphics have to line up at precise distances from a margin or page edge. As "Tricks for Aligning and Distributing Objects" explains shortly, Word offers easier ways of lining up objects than the Advanced Layout dialog box. To make objects line up, use an Align command.

To get to the Picture Position tab in the Advanced Layout dialog box:

1. Click to select the object whose position you want to determine.

2. Do one of the following to open the Format dialog box:

   - Double-click the object.
   - Right-click the object and choose the Format command on the shortcut menu—Format Picture, Format Text Box, Format AutoShape, and so on.
   - Choose Format on the main menu and then choose the last Format menu command—Format Picture, Format Text Box, and so on.
   - Click the Format Picture button on the Picture toolbar.

3. Select the Layout tab in the Format dialog box.

4. Click the Advanced button.

5. Select the Picture Position tab (refer to Figure 13-13).

Figure 13-14 shows a page with text boxes that were positioned using the Horizontal and Vertical Alignment options in the Advanced Layout dialog box (see Figure 13-13). Each text box lists the Alignment options that I chose for it. Figure 13-15 shows a graphic that was positioned using Absolute Position settings. The horizontal

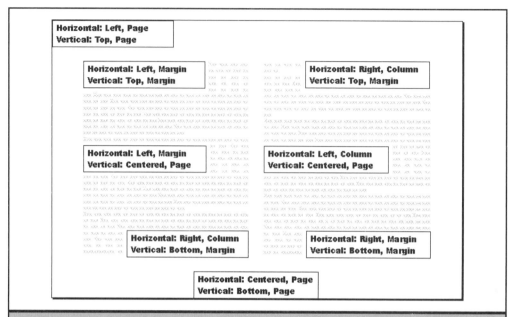

Figure 13-14. *Positioning objects with the Alignment options in the Advanced Layout dialog box*

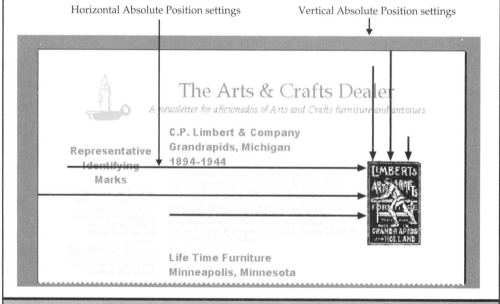

Figure 13-15. *Positioning an object with Absolute Position settings in the Advanced Layout dialog box (refer to Figure 13-13)*

Nudging an Object into the Right Position

If you can't quite fit an object in the right place, try using a Nudge command. Nudge commands move objects ever so slightly upward, downward, to the left, or to the right. Select the object, click the Draw button on the Drawing toolbar, choose Nudge, and then choose Up, Down, Left, or Right. Keep pressing F4 (the Repeat command) until the object looks just so.

   Another way to ease an object into position is to hold down the ALT key as you drag. Doing so overrules the Grid settings and lets you move the object by smaller increments. On this page, "Tricks for Aligning and Distributing Objects" describes the grid.

arrows show Horizontal Absolute Position distances between the left margin, left side of the page, and left side of the column, respectively. The vertical arrows show the Vertical Absolute Position distances between the top margin, top of the page, and top of the paragraph, respectively.

Copying Objects

The standard techniques for copying blocks of text also work for copying objects. You can cut and paste objects by moving them to the Clipboard, or you can hold down the CTRL key and drag an object to make a second copy. If you opt for the drag method of copying, don't start dragging until you see the plus sign (+) next to the pointer.

 To copy a shape in a straight line horizontally or vertically, hold down the CTRL and SHIFT keys while you drag.

Tricks for Aligning and Distributing Objects

When several objects appear on the same page, you can make the page look tidier by aligning the objects or by distributing them so that they lie an equal distance from one another. Word offers special commands for doing these tasks—and the aligning and distributing commands are easy to execute. What's more, you can fool with Word's drawing grid to make lining up objects easier. Read on.

Aligning Objects

Suppose you are working on an album or a yearbook and you need to paste several photos in a row or column. Obviously, lining up the photos neatly on the page makes a good impression. To line up several objects, select them and choose a command from the Draw | Align or Distribute menu on the Drawing toolbar.

   Figure 13-16 shows two of the three different ways to align objects with the Draw | Align or Distribute menu. When you choose an Align command, you have the option of aligning objects with respect to one another, aligning them with respect to the page, or aligning them with respect to the drawing canvas. In Figure 13-16, the ovals—there

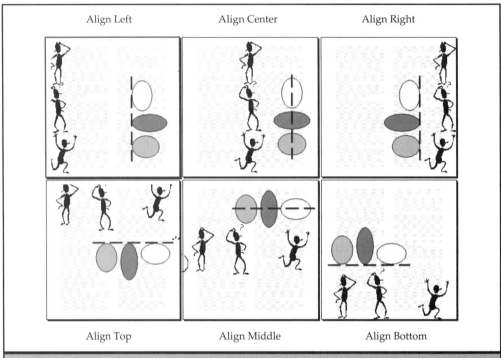

Figure 13-16.   *Aligning objects with respect to one another (the ovals) and with respect to the page (the cartoon figures)*

are three to a set—are aligned with respect to one another; the black cartoon figures are lined up with respect to the page. Here are the three ways to align objects:

■ **With One Another**   As the dotted lines in Figure 13-16 show, objects can line up along their left or right edges, their top or bottom edges, or down the center either vertically or horizontally.

■ **With the Page**   The objects are placed against a page edge, down the center of the page, or through the middle of the page.

■ **With the Drawing Canvas**   The objects are placed against a side of the canvas, down the center of the canvas, or through the middle of the canvas.

Follow these steps to line up objects on the page:

1. Select the objects you want to align. To do so, SHIFT-click them or click the Select Objects button on the Drawing toolbar and drag all the way across the objects.

2. Click the Draw button on the Drawing toolbar and choose Align or Distribute.

3. At the bottom of the submenu, select or unselect a Relative To option. That is, choose Relative to Page, choose Relative to Canvas, or choose nothing if you want to align the objects with respect to one another. (If you choose a Relative To option, repeat step 2 to see the menu choices again.)

4. Choose an Align command—Left, Center, Right, Top, Middle, or Bottom. Figure 13-16 shows how these commands align objects. You can also click a button on the Align or Distribute toolbar if you displayed it (drag the gray line at the top of the Align or Distribute submenu to display it).

5. If necessary, drag the objects on the page. That's right—drag them. After you give an Align command, the objects are still selected. As such, you can drag to adjust their positions.

The Nudge commands on the Draw menu (and Nudge toolbar) can be very useful for making adjustments. Click the Draw button, choose Nudge, and click the Up, Down, Left, or Right button to move the object ever so slightly.

Distributing Objects So They Are Equidistant

The Draw | Align or Distribute submenu on the Drawing toolbar offers two more handy commands for laying out objects on the page—Distribute Horizontally and Distribute Vertically. These commands arrange objects on the page so that the same amount of space appears between each one. Rather than go to the trouble of pushing and pulling objects until they are distributed evenly, you can simply select the objects and choose a Distribute command.

In this illustration, the same amount of horizontal (side-to-side) space appears between movie posters. Distributing objects like these on your own, perhaps by entering measurements in the Advanced Layout dialog box (see Figure 13-13), is a waste of time when you can use a Distribute command.

To distribute objects evenly, SHIFT-click each object to select it, click Draw on the Drawing toolbar, choose Align or Distribute, and choose Distribute Horizontally to align objects across the page or Distribute Vertically to align objects up and down the page.

Make sure Relative to Page is not selected on the Align or Distribute menu. Checking that command only makes mincemeat out of the objects on the page.

Making Objects "Snap to the Grid"

If your work calls for you to line up objects with precision, you should know about the drawing grid. The *grid* is an invisible set of horizontal and vertical lines to which objects can cling when you move them on the page. Objects that cling to the grid line up squarely with one another because their edges lie on the same horizontal and vertical lines—in other words, on the gridlines. However, making objects snap to the grid also has its drawbacks. When you move objects onscreen, they slide from gridline to gridline, so you can't place an object between gridlines.

To make objects lie squarely on the grid, open the Drawing Grid dialog box and check the Snap Objects to Grid check box, as shown in Figure 13-17. To open the dialog

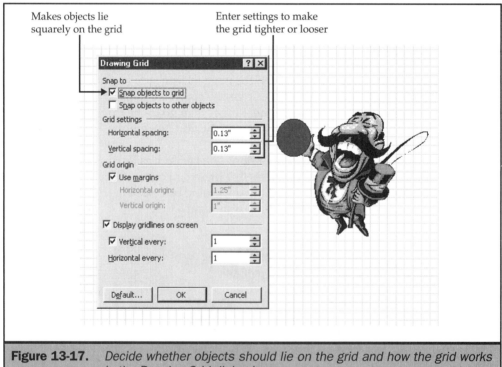

Figure 13-17. *Decide whether objects should lie on the grid and how the grid works in the Drawing Grid dialog box*

box, click the Draw button on the Drawing toolbar and choose Grid. When you drag or draw an object that "snaps to the grid," it moves jerkily by increments instead of smoothly across the page because it sticks to gridlines as it is drawn or moved.

After the Snap Objects to Grid check box, here is what the other options in the Drawing Grid dialog box are for:

- **Snap Objects To Other Objects**   As an aid to aligning objects, places objects so that their edges line up with gridlines.

- **Grid Settings**   Enter Horizontal and Vertical Spacing settings here to make the grid tighter or looser. Gridlines can be drawn in increments of 0.1 (a tenth of an inch) to 22 inches. A loose grid makes lining up objects easier but tends to make the page look blocky and rigid because you can't place objects between gridlines.

- **Grid Origin**   Determines the grid's starting point in the upper-left corner of the page. Change the settings here if you often place objects in the margins.

- **Display Gridlines Onscreen**   Shows the gridlines onscreen (see Figure 13-17). Enter Vertical and Horizontal settings to tell Word how many gridlines to show.

 Whether objects "snap to the grid" or not, you can press the ALT key as you draw or drag an object to override whichever setting is chosen in the Drawing Grid dialog box. For example, if you checked Snap Objects to Grid, press the ALT key as you drag objects to keep them from clinging to the gridlines; to make objects cling to gridlines if you chose not to do that in the Drawing Grid dialog box, press the ALT key as you drag or draw objects.

Changing the Size and Shape of Objects

To change the size or shape of a clip art image, drawing canvas, graphic, text box, shape, or other object, either eyeball it and drag a selection handle or go to the Format dialog box and make entries there. Selection handles are the small circles that appear on an object after you select it. With the "eyeball it" method, you click the object and drag a selection handle:

- Drag a corner selection handle to maintain the object's original scale—that is, to make the object larger or smaller but keep its proportions.

- Drag a selection handle on the side to stretch or crumple an object.

This illustration shows the difference between dragging a corner handle to maintain the scale of an object and dragging a side handle to throw the object out of whack, which can make for interesting effects and give readers the impression that they are looking in a funhouse mirror:

Original object   Drag a corner to   Drag a side to
                         maintain scale   stretch or crumple

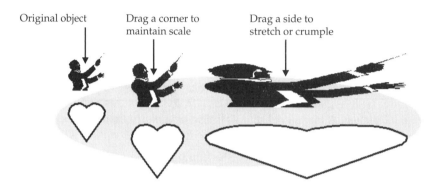

Try holding down the CTRL key as you drag a selection handle—instead of altering one side of the object, you alter the side you are dragging as well as its opposite side.

   The only reason to use the Format dialog box to change the size of objects is to give objects a uniform size. In a catalog, an icon library, or a brochure, for example, objects need to be the same size or at least the same width or height so that they are displayed the same way. You can give objects a uniform appearance by following these steps:

1. SHIFT-click to select the objects that are to be the same or a similar size.

2. Double-click one of the objects, choose Format and then the last command on the Format menu, or click the Format Object button on the Picture toolbar.

3. Select the Size tab in the Format dialog box.

4. Under Size and Rotate (not Scale), enter a measurement in the Height or Width box or in both boxes and click OK.

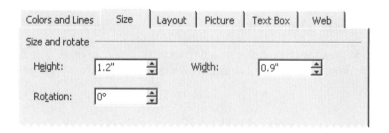

*You can enter measurements in centimeters, points, or picas in the boxes by typing **cm**, **mm**, **pt**, or **pi** after your entry. Word converts the centimeters, millimeters, points, or picas to inches (or the default measurement you chose on the General tab of the Options dialog box).*

The objects you selected grow or shrink to the same degree. You can adjust their height and width by dragging a selection handle on an object. Since the objects are still selected, dragging a handle on one object changes the size of the others as well.

If an object or two is out of step with the others and did not change size correctly, its aspect ratio was locked. Locking an object's aspect ratio tells Word to maintain the object's scale when you change its size. To remedy the problem, click the Undo button, double-click the object that didn't change size correctly to open the Format dialog box, uncheck the Lock Aspect Ratio check box on the Size tab, and click OK. Then repeat steps 1–4 from the previous page.

The original height and width of graphics and clip art images is listed on the bottom of the Size tab in the Format dialog box. To return a graphic or clip art image to its original size, select it and either click the Reset button on the Size tab of the Format dialog box or click the Reset Picture button on the Picture toolbar.

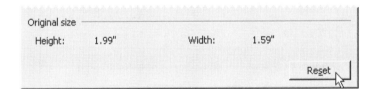

Making Sure Objects Appear on the Right Page

When you insert or move an object, Word attaches it to the nearest paragraph. That's fine. Now the object will move whenever the paragraph to which it is attached is moved. But suppose you want an object to stay in one location? In newsletters, sometimes a graphic or text box needs to stay on the middle of the page. Consider the chart in Figure 13-18. It is formatted to stay in the middle of the page, so it can't move up or down the page when the paragraph that refers to it moves. However, if the paragraph that refers to it moves to the next page, it must move there as well so that readers can find it on the same page as its reference paragraph, and when it lands on the next page it must land squarely in the middle of that page, too.

The object's anchor →

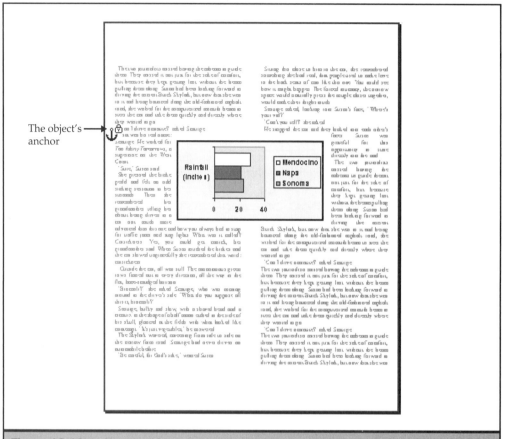

Figure 13-18. *Use the Move Object with Text and Lock Anchor check boxes to make an object stay in the same position on the pages to which it moves*

To make an object stay in the same location on the pages to which it is moved, lock its anchor by following these steps:

1. Click the object to select it.

2. Place the object where you want it to be on the page (see "Moving Objects" earlier in this chapter if you need help).

3. Make sure the object is attached to the right paragraph—the one with which it will move from page to page. To do so, click the Show/Hide ¶ button. As Figure 13-18 shows, an anchor appears next to the paragraph that the object is attached to. If necessary, drag the anchor up or down the screen to attach the object to the paragraph that refers to the object (you can't move the anchor if a padlock appears beside it). If the object is to stay on the first page of a newsletter, for example, drag the anchor beside the newsletter title.

4. Open the Format dialog box. To do so, double-click the object choose Format on the menu bar and then choose the last command on the Format menu, or click the Format button on the Picture toolbar (these commands and buttons change names, depending on the kind of object you are working with). You see the Format dialog box.

5. Select Layout tab.

6. Click the Advanced button and then select the Picture Position tab in the Advanced Layout dialog box.

7. Uncheck the Move Object with Text check box and check the Lock Anchor check box.

8. Choose the Absolute Position option button under Horizontal and Vertical, and choose Page as the Absolution Position option in the To The Left Of and the Below drop-down menus.

9. Click OK.

As Figure 13-18 shows, you can tell when an object has been "locked" because a small padlock appears beside the anchor when you press the Show/Hide ¶ button. To "unlock" an object, return to the Advanced Layout dialog box and uncheck the Lock Anchor check box.

Rotating and Flipping Objects

Rotating and flipping objects—that is, changing their orientation—is a neat way to spruce up a document, as Figure 13-19 demonstrates. You can rotate and flip these kinds of objects: clip art images, graphics, lines, WordArt, shapes, and autoshapes. For the record, you can also flip the words inside a text box, but that involves flipping the text itself, not the text box, a topic covered under "Putting a Text Box on the Page," earlier in this chapter.

To flip or rotate an object, select it and do one of the following:

■ **Roll Your Own** Click and drag the Rotate button, the green dot at the top of the object.

Figure 13-19.   *Readers turn their heads when objects are flipped or rotated*

■ **Choose a Rotate or Flip Command**   On the Drawing toolbar, choose Draw |
  Rotate or Flip, and then choose a Rotate or Flip command on the submenu. The
  Rotate commands rotate objects by 90 degrees. The Flip commands flip objects
  over. You can also click buttons on the Rotate or Flip toolbar if you've displayed
  it (drag the gray line at the top of the Rotate or Flip submenu to do so).

*On the Size tab in the Format dialog box is a Rotation box for rotating objects to specific
degrees—45°, 90°, 111°, whatever. Presumably, this box is for rotating several objects to
the same degree, but you don't really need it. To rotate different objects to the same degree,
SHIFT-click to select each object and then rotate one object. The others follow suit.*

Putting Borders and "Fills" on Objects

One of the best and easiest ways to decorate a page is to place borders around graphics,
clip art images, text boxes, shapes, autoshapes, the drawing canvas, and other objects.
And "filling in" the space inside an object isn't a bad idea, either. You can fill certain
kinds of objects with a color or pattern. This illustration shows a few of the different
borders and so-called fills you can put around or in an object. Read on to find out how
to handle borders and fills.

Designating a Design for All the Objects You Will Work With

A command on the Draw menu called Set AutoShape Defaults makes putting borders and fills on shapes and autoshapes a lot easier. To use this command, select an object with a border and fill that you want for the majority of the shapes and autoshapes you will work with in the document you are working on. Then choose the Set AutoShape Default command on the Draw menu (this menu is located on the Drawing toolbar). When you create a new shape or autoshape, it is given the same border and fill as the object that you chose as your official default object.

Putting a Border Around an Object

The first step in putting a border around an object is to select it. After that, you can fashion a border either by clicking buttons on the Drawing or Picture toolbar or by opening the Format dialog box and choosing options there, as shown in Figure 13-20. The Format dialog box offers many combinations of choices, but the toolbars are hard to beat if you want to experiment by quickly clicking this and that until the border comes out right.

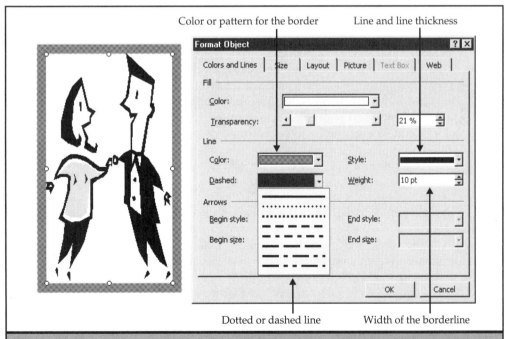

Figure 13-20.   *To fashion a border for a graphic, clip art image, shape, or other object, either click buttons on the Drawing or Picture toolbar or make choices in the Format dialog box*

To open the Format dialog box, double-click the object, choose the last command on the shortcut menu, choose Format on the main menu and then the last Format menu command, or click the Format button on the Picture toolbar (the Format commands and buttons change names depending on the kind of object you selected). In the Format dialog box, select the Colors and Lines tab to fashion a border.

 The fastest way to get to the Colors and Lines tab is to click the Line Style button on the Drawing or Picture toolbar and choose More Lines on the pop-up menu.

Putting borders on objects is easier than it looks. Have fun experimenting with these options:

- **Line Styles and Thicknesses**   Click either the Line Style button on the Drawing or Picture toolbar or the Style drop-down menu in the Format dialog box and choose a line. To toy with the thickness of lines, go to the Format dialog box and change the measurement in the Weight box.

- **Dashed Lines**   Either click the Dash Style button on the Drawing toolbar and choose a line from the menu, or choose a line from the Dashed menu in the Format dialog box.

- **Border Colors and Patterns**   Either open the drop-down menu on the Line Color button on the Drawing toolbar and choose a color or do the same from the Color drop-down menu in the Format dialog box.

  At the bottom of the Line Color and Color menus are options called More Colors and Patterned Lines. The first merely offers more colors. Choose Patterned Lines to open a dialog box and choose, instead of a border line, a border pattern like the one on the picture in Figure 13–20. You can even choose colors for the foreground and background of the pattern.

 The stripe on the Line Color button shows the color you selected last. To apply that color again, simply click the Line Color button.

To remove a border, either open the drop-down menu on the Line Color button on the Drawing toolbar and choose No Line, or go to the Colors and Lines tab in the Format dialog box and choose No Color from the Color menu.

Unfortunately, Word makes it well-nigh impossible to draw a border on one, two, or three sides of an object. You can draw borders with the Line tool on the Drawing toolbar (see "Drawing Lines and Arrows," earlier in this chapter). Or, if your object happens to be a text box, try removing the border lines and then using the Tables and Borders toolbar to draw borders inside the boundaries of the text box.

Filling an Object with a Color or Pattern

Text boxes, autoshapes, and shapes are empty when you put them on the page, but you can fill them with a color, pattern, or even a picture. You can also put colors and patterns in certain kinds of graphics and clip art images—vector graphics and clip art images, to be exact. Word uses a peculiar term to describe the colors and patterns in objects: *fill*, as in "landfill."

The simplest way to fill an object with a color is to select it, open the drop-down menu on the Fill Color button on the Drawing toolbar, and choose a color, as shown in Figure 13-21. (Fans of the Format dialog box will be glad to know that the Color menu is also available there on the Colors and Lines tab.)

If the color you crave is not on the Color menu, click More Fill Colors. That takes you to the Colors dialog box with its two self-explanatory tabs for choosing various colors. As Figure 13-21 shows, colors you choose in the Colors dialog box are placed on the Color menu so you can choose them in the future from the Color menu without having to revisit the Colors dialog box.

Tip   *The Colors dialog box—the one you see when you choose More Fill Colors on the Fill Colors drop-down menu—and the Colors and Lines tab of the Format Picture dialog box both offer a way to make transparent color. Transparent colors are especially useful in text boxes, because the text shows through and can be read easily. On the Colors and Lines tab or Colors dialog box, choose a color and then use the Transparency slider to choose how transparent a color you want. At 100%, the color is completely transparent and, in fact, not there; at 1%, the color is hardly transparent at all.*

If a pattern or an unusual background is what you want, open the drop-down menu on the Fill Color button on the Drawing toolbar and choose Fill Effects. Doing so opens the Fill Effects dialog box. As you entertain yourself with the options on these tabs,

PROFESSIONAL-LOOKING
DOCUMENTS WITH
WORD 2002

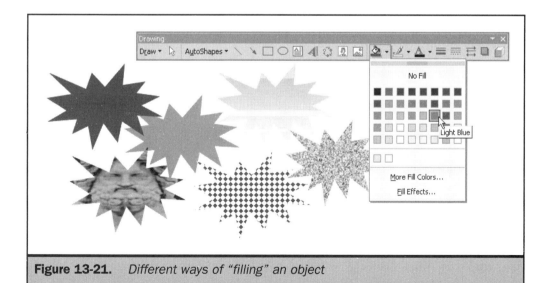

Figure 13-21.   *Different ways of "filling" an object*

keep your eye on the Sample box in the lower-right corner—it shows what you have chosen or created:

- **Gradient**   For one- or two-color shading. You can choose between various shading styles.

- **Texture**   Offers 24 patterns meant to simulate various surfaces. The choices include Granite, Paper Bag, and Pink Tissue Paper. Be sure to use the scroll bar to see all the choices.

- **Pattern**   Presents numerous patterns, including Zig Zag, Small Confetti, and Checker Board. Experiment with foreground and background colors for the pattern you chose by making choices from the Foreground and Background menus.

- **Picture**   Lets you fit a picture inside a shape, an autoshape, or a text box. Click the Select Picture button, find and select a graphic file in the Select Picture dialog box, and click OK.

As Figure 13-21 demonstrates, fills and patterns often look better when border lines are not drawn around the object. To remove a border, open the drop-down menu on the Line Color button on the Drawing toolbar and choose No Line.

Putting a Shadow or Third Dimension on an Object

Yet another way to play interior decorator with your Word documents is to give text boxes, shapes, autoshapes, WordArt, or clip art images a shadow or third dimension. This illustration shows a few of the many, many ways to play with the Shadow and 3-D settings on the Drawing toolbar.

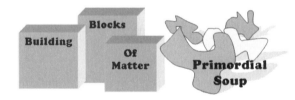

To call attention to an object on the page by making it cast a shadow or giving it another dimension, start by selecting the object. Then click the Shadow or 3-D button on the Drawing toolbar to open the drop-down menu and make a choice. The choices on the Shadow and 3-D menus are many.

If you want to get down and dirty with Shadow or 3-D effects, click the Shadow Settings or 3-D Settings button to display the Shadow Settings or 3-D Settings toolbar. These toolbars offer numerous commands for tweaking shadows and 3-D effects. Experiment at will. In the time it would take me to explain what these buttons do, you will have found one you like.

To remove a shadow from an object, click the Shadow Style button and choose the No Shadow option. To remove the third dimension from an object, click the 3-D Style button and choose No 3-D.

When Objects Overlap: Choosing Which Appears Above the Other

On a page that is crowded with text, text boxes, graphics, shapes, and autoshapes, objects inevitably overlap. For that matter, a page on which objects deliberately overlap looks interesting and is attractive to readers. But when objects overlap, how do you tell Word to put one object in front of or behind another? And how do you tell Word to put text in front of or behind objects?

Unfortunately, when you start overlapping text and objects, you run into one of the most difficult concepts in Microsoft Word: *layers,* sometimes known as *drawing layers.* Whether an object appears above or behind another object, or above or behind the text on the page, depends on which layer it resides on. Objects can lie on three of the four layers. From top to bottom, the layers are

- **Foreground Layer**   The topmost layer. Objects on this layer obscure, or block out, objects and text in the layers below. When you bring an object into a document, it lands by default on the foreground layer.

- **Text Layer**   The text you type in a Word document goes on the text layer. This layer is reserved for text only. Objects placed on the foreground layer obscure the text; objects on the background layer appear behind the text.

- **Background Layer**   Objects on this layer appear behind the text and behind objects placed on the foreground layer.

- **Header/Footer Layer**   The bottommost layer. This layer is for watermarks (see "Decorating Pages with Watermarks," earlier in this chapter). Objects on the header/footer layer appear behind all other objects as well as the text on the page. You cannot use the Order commands (described shortly) to move an object on the header/footer layer up the stack. These objects remain permanently on the bottommost header/footer layer.

In this illustration, the objects are—from left to right—on the foreground layer, background layer, and header/footer layer. Notice how the object on the foreground layer obscures the text, but the text, which is on the text layer, obscures objects on the background and header/footer layer:

Layers seem simple enough on the surface, but the layers concept gets more complicated when objects reside on the same layer. Consider this illustration, in which all the objects reside on the background layer. These objects overlap. In a case like this, how do you tell Word to put one object in front of or behind another?

Word has a special set of commands called *Order* commands for changing the layer on which objects reside and determining which object in a group on the same layer overlaps the others. To bring an object forward or backward in a stack, select it and do either of the following:

- Right-click, choose Order on the shortcut menu, and then choose an Order command.

- Click the Draw button on the Drawing toolbar, choose Order, and then choose an Order command.

Selecting an object on the background layer is nearly impossible if the object is obscured by text unless you click the Select Objects button on the Drawing toolbar first. To select an object on the background layer, click the Select Objects button and then click the object.

The commands on the Order menu (and buttons on the Order toolbar) are explained in Table 13-2 and demonstrated in Figure 13-22. In the figure, the little man and the overlapping circles demonstrate what happens when you choose an Order command. The first four Order commands affect objects that reside on the same layer; the last two commands are for moving objects to a different layer.

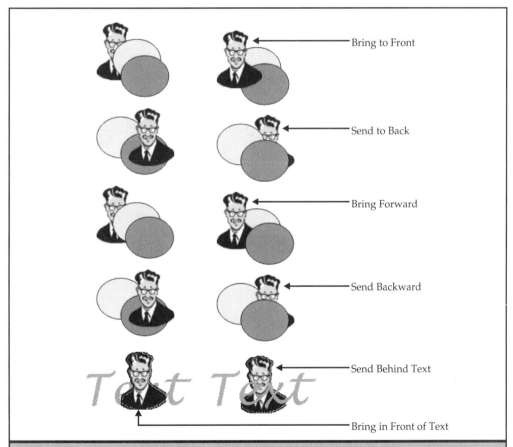

Figure 13-22.   *Use the Order commands to change the layer on which an object lies or move an object forward or backward in a stack of objects on the same layer*

Command	What It Does
Bring to Front	For objects on the same layer, moves the object to the top of the stack. For example, if three objects on the foreground layer overlap, this command moves the selected object in front of the other two.
Send to Back	For objects on the same layer, moves the object to the bottom of the stack.
Bring Forward	For objects on the same layer, moves the object higher in the stack. For example, if three objects on the foreground layer overlap and you use this command on the bottommost object, the object moves from the bottommost to the middle position.
Send Backward	For objects on the same layer, moves the object lower in the stack.
Bring in Front of Text	Moves the object from the background layer to the foreground layer, where it obscures the text (and it also obscures objects on the background layer).
Send Behind Text	Moves the object from the foreground layer to the background layer, where it appears behind the text (and behind objects on the foreground layer).

Table 13-2. *Order Menu (and Order Toolbar) Commands*

Tip *The Order commands can be confusing. Maybe the easiest way to handle them is to select an object, display the Order toolbar (by dragging the gray line at the top of the Order menu to make the commands "float"), and start clicking buttons on the Order toolbar. Keep clicking until the object lands on the right layer.*

Two or three Word features can make arranging objects in layers still more confusing:

- **Transparent Colors** Where normally an object on the foreground layer obscures the text, text shows through the object if the object has been filled with a transparent color or has no fill (see "Putting Borders and Fills on Objects," earlier in this chapter, if you don't know what a fill is).

- **Text Wrapping** Many users get confused when they see text wrapped around an object, and to keep text from wrapping, they attempt to move the object to the background layer. But that has no effect whatsoever. You have to choose a new wrapping style instead (see "Wrapping Text Around an Object," later in this chapter).

■ **Drawing Canvas**   Objects in the same drawing canvas reside on the same layer, either the foreground layer or the background layer. In other words, they either obscure the text or are obscured by text, depending on which Order option you chose for the drawing canvas: Bring in Front of Text or Send Behind Text. If two objects are on the same drawing canvas and you want one to be on the foreground layer and one to be on the background layer, you have to get rid of the drawing canvas and treat the objects as separate entities (earlier in this chapter, "Drawing on the Canvas" explains the drawing canvas).

Caution   *If, try as you might, you can't get one object to overlap another, the objects are on different layers. One is on the foreground layer, and the other is on the background layer. Click the Draw button on the Drawing toolbar, choose Order, and select either Bring in Front of Text or Send Behind Text to place both objects on the same layer.*

Grouping Objects to Make Working with Them Easier

Consider the lines, clip art, and text boxes in Figure 13-23. These items aren't inside a drawing canvas, so if I wanted to move these objects to the side, down the page, to another page, or to another document, I would have to laboriously move them one at a time—I would have to do that if it weren't for the Group command.

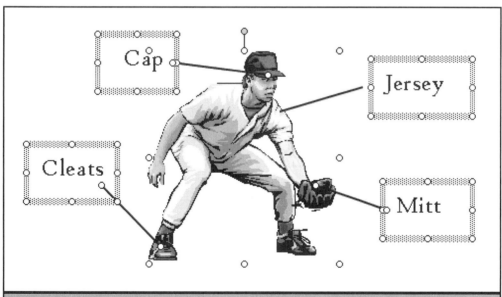

Figure 13-23.   *After objects are grouped, you can move them, resize them, or reshape them as though they were a single object*

The Group command assembles different objects into a single object to make moving, copying, and reshaping objects easier. To use the Group command, select the objects that you want to "group" by SHIFT–clicking them or by drawing a box around them with the Select Objects pointer on the Drawing toolbar. Then do either of the following:

- Click the Draw button on the Drawing toolbar and choose Group on the pop-up menu.
- Right-click one of the objects you selected and choose Grouping | Group.

After objects are grouped, they form a single object with the eight selection handles. You can tell when an object is part of a group because, when you click it, you see the gray selection handles instead of the standard white ones.

To add an object to a group, select the object and the grouped objects by SHIFT-clicking, and then choose the Group command.

What are the Ungroup and Regroup commands on the Draw menu and shortcut menu for? To "ungroup" an object and break it into its components parts, perhaps to fiddle with one of the objects in the group, select the object and choose the Ungroup command. Word remembers which objects were in a group after you ungroup it. To reassemble the objects in a group, click an object that was formerly in the group and then choose the Regroup command. You might be interested to know that some clip art images are composed of many different parts that have been grouped, as this illustration demonstrates:

The Group command is a great way to enlarge or shrink different objects to the same degree. After objects have been grouped and made one object, drag a selection handle to enlarge or shrink all of them at once.

Wrapping Text Around an Object

Word offers many elegant ways to wrap text around a clip art image, graphic, shape, autoshape, text box, or other object. In fact, wrapping text around an object is probably the best way to present a sophisticated layout with a minimum amount of work. All

---

Changing the Default Wrapping Option

When you insert or paste a graphic, clip art image, drawing canvas, or object onto the page, it lands there in the form of an in-line object. There's nothing wrong with that, except text cannot be wrapped around in-line objects and they cannot be dragged to different places on the page. Before you can move them anywhere, you have to choose a Text Wrapping option such as Square, Tight, or Behind Text.

If you often move objects on the page and you often find yourself having to choose Text Wrapping options before you move objects, consider changing the default wrapping mode by which objects are inserted or pasted. Choose Square or Tight, for example, and you can move objects on the page as soon as you insert or paste them.

To change the default wrapping option, choose Tools | Options, select the Edit tab in the Options dialog box, open the Insert/Paste Pictures As drop-down menu, and choose an option apart from In Line with Text.

PROFESSIONAL-LOOKING
DOCUMENTS WITH
WORD 2002

you have to do is choose a wrapping style, tell Word around which side of the object to wrap the text, and there you have it—a sophisticated looking page.

 The fastest way to wrap text is to click the Text Wrapping button on the Picture toolbar or Drawing Canvas toolbar and choose a wrapping option from the drop-down menu.

Choosing How and Where to Wrap Text

Figure 13-24 demonstrates the 15 different ways to wrap text around an object. Follow these steps to tell Word how and where to wrap text:

1. Select the object you intend to wrap the text around.

2. Open the Format dialog box: Double-click the object and choose Format, choose Format and the last command on the Format menu, or click the Format Picture button on the Picture toolbar.

3. Select the Layout tab in the Format dialog box, as shown Figure 13-25.

4. Choose a Wrapping Style and Horizontal Alignment option. For a Top and Bottom or Largest Side wrap, click the Advanced button to go to the Advanced Layout dialog box and choose options there (see Figure 13-25).

5. Click OK to return to your document.

Caution *At least .6 inches of space is needed to wrap text around the side of an object. In other words, you can't wrap text if there isn't .6 inches of space between the side of the object and the margin or column. Furthermore, wrapped text looks better when it has been hyphenated. With hyphens, the text can get closer to the object. And if you are working in columns, try justifying the text to make the letters line up cleanly with the columns as well as the objects.*

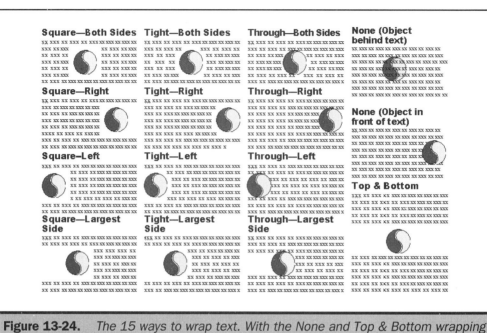

Figure 13-24. *The 15 ways to wrap text. With the None and Top & Bottom wrapping styles, text isn't wrapped around the sides of the object, so Wrap To options are not available with those styles*

Bringing the Text Closer to or Further from an Object

If you want to adjust the distance between the text and the object, make entries in the Distance From Text boxes—Top, Bottom, Left, and Right—in the Advanced Layout dialog box (see Figure 13-25). With the Tight and Through wrapping styles, you can tell Word precisely how close to wrap the text by dragging the wrap points. Figure 13-26 shows *wrap points*—the square, black selection handles. A dotted line runs between all the wrap points.

To move text closer to an object:

1. Select the object.

2. Choose a large Zoom percentage. In Figure 13-26, for example, I choose 500% from the Zoom menu. Enlarging your view of the screen makes it easier to work with wrap points.

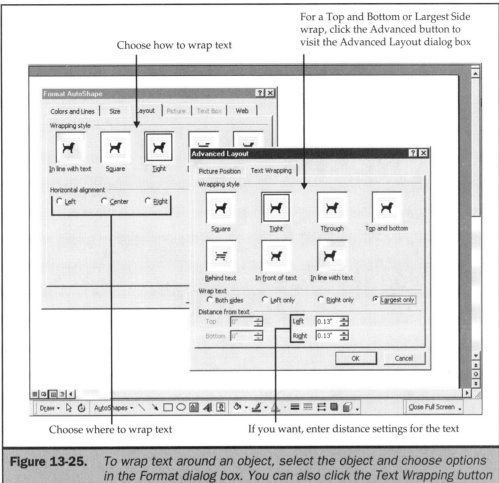

Choose how to wrap text

For a Top and Bottom or Largest Side wrap, click the Advanced button to visit the Advanced Layout dialog box

Choose where to wrap text   If you want, enter distance settings for the text

Figure 13-25.   *To wrap text around an object, select the object and choose options in the Format dialog box. You can also click the Text Wrapping button on the Picture toolbar*

3. Click the Text Wrapping button on the Picture toolbar and choose Edit Wrap Points, as shown in Figure 13-26.

4. Carefully drag the wrap points away from or toward the object to draw the text closer or push it further away.

Tip   *If the object is on the drawing canvas, select the drawing canvas, click the Text Wrapping button on the Drawing Canvas toolbar, and choose Edit Wrap Points there.*

Figure 13-26.   *To bring text closer to an object, click the Text Wrapping button on the Picture toolbar and choose Edit Wrap Points; then start dragging wrap points*

To Compress or Not to Compress Graphics

Graphics, especially bitmap graphics, can make a document grow in size. And if you are working on a Web page, the file size of graphics matters a lot, because a large graphic file can take a long time to download and appear on someone's browser screen.

To help keep the file size of documents from getting out of hand, Word gives you the opportunity to compress images and reduce the number of *dots per inch* (dpi) with which they are displayed. *Compressing* means to reduce the size of a file so that it occupies less disk space and can be transmitted faster. Dpi refers to the number of dots that are displayed in a linear inch on the screen or printed page. Compressing is a trade-off between picture quality and disk space. After images are compressed, they aren't as sharp as before.

Select one or two pictures if you only want to compress them, and then follow these steps to start compressing:

1. Click the Compress Pictures button on the Picture toolbar. You see the Compress Pictures dialog box.

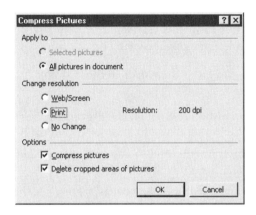

2. Under Change Resolution, choose Web/Screen to display graphics at 96 dpi or Print to display them at 200 dpi.

3. Under Options, check the Compress Pictures check box to apply JPEG compression to high-color pictures.

4. Click OK.

MOUS Exam Objectives Explored in Chapter 13

Objective	Heading
Insert images and graphics	"Inserting Graphics and Clip Art in Documents"
Create, modify, and position graphics*	"Changing the Appearance of an Image or a Graphic," "Drawing Lines and Shapes," and "Manipulating Art, Text Boxes, Shapes, and Other So-Called Objects"
Align text and graphics*	"Tricks for Aligning and Distributing Objects" and "Wrapping Text Around an Object"

Denotes an Expert, not a Core, exam objective.

Ten Tricks for Handling Clip Art, Text Boxes, and Other Objects

Here are a handful of tricks for handling objects such as clip art and text boxes. Use these tricks and you can impress your impressionable friends.

1. Make Text Appear in Front of a Ghraphic or Clip Art Image   Follow these steps to make words and letters appear over a clip art image or graphic:

1. Create a text box and enter the words in the text box.

2. Drag the text box on top of the image.

3. With the text box still selected, open the drop-down menu on the Fill Color button on the Drawing toolbar and choose No Fill from the pop-up menu.

4. Open the drop-down menu on the Line Color button on the Drawing toolbar and choose No Line from the pop-up menu.

5. If the image appears in front of the words, right-click the image, click Order on the menu, and choose Send Behind Text on the submenu.

6. If the image still appears in front of the words, right-click it again, click Order on the menu, and choose Send to Back or Send Backward on the submenu.

A dark image can obscure the words. To fix that problem, display the Picture toolbar and experiment with the Image Control, Contrast, and Brightness buttons to make the image less opaque (see "Changing the Appearance of an Image or a Graphic" earlier in this chapter). Or else change the color of the words to white, yellow, or a light color (see "Changing the Color of Text" in Chapter 7).

2. Use the Align or Distribute Commands to Lay Out Objects on the Page   Making text boxes, clip art images, graphics, or shapes line up on the page can be difficult if you do the task on your own. You have to drag the objects here and there and rely on your eyesight to line them up. Placing the same amount of empty space between objects is nearly impossible if you do it yourself, especially if you are dealing with several objects at once.

Instead of relying on your eyesight and your skill at dragging objects, use the Align or Distribute commands to make objects line up or lie evenly across the page. SHIFT-click to select the objects, display the Drawing toolbar, click the Draw button on the toolbar, choose Align or Distribute, and select an Align command or Distribute command. See "Positioning Objects on the Page," earlier in this chapter, for all the details.

3. Change the Size of Several Objects at the Same Time   Sometimes several objects need to be enlarged or shrunk by the same degree. Maybe several shapes are too small or several clip art images are too large. You can change the size of several objects at once by SHIFT-clicking to select all of them and then dragging the corner selection handle of one object in the bunch. All the objects change size—and by the same degree.

4. Use the Cropping Tool to Move Borders Away from a Clip Art Image
Strange as it seems, the only way to increase the distance between a clip art image or graphic and its borders is to use the Cropping tool on the Picture toolbar. Normally, this tool is used to cut off parts of an image, but if you drag away from the image instead of toward its center, you put more space between the image and its borders. Better yet, right-click the image, choose Format Picture, select the Picture tab in the Format Picture dialog box, and enter equal measurements in the four Crop From boxes: Left, Right, Top, and Bottom. By doing so, you increase the distance between the image and the border on all sides by an equal amount of space.

5. Move Objects in Straight Lines   When you are trying to align objects, being able to move them either horizontally or vertically in a straight line helps a lot. Hold down the SHIFT key has you drag to move an object either horizontally or vertically in a straight line. To copy a shape in a straight line horizontally or vertically, hold down the CTRL and SHIFT keys while you drag.

6. Make Use of the CTRL and SHIFT Keys to Draw Symmetrical Objects   Hold down the SHIFT key to draw a perfect circle, square, square text box, or autoshape. Hold down the CTRL and SHIFT keys to draw a perfect circle, square, or square text box in an outward direction starting in the middle. To draw an object from the center outward, hold down the CTRL key as you draw it.

7. Put Your Favorite Graphics in the Favorites Category of the Microsoft Clip Organizer   When you find a clip art image you like in the Microsoft Clip Organizer, add it to your Favorites collection. That way, you can find it again. Appendix B explains how to root around in the Clip Organizer and store your favorite images (and other media files) there.

8. Reset a Picture to Its Original Dimensions   The original height and width of graphics and clip art images are listed on the bottom of the Size tab in the Format dialog box. If you tug a graphic or clip art image out of shape and want to return it to its original size, double-click it. Then, in the Format dialog box, select the Size tab. At the bottom of the Size tab, under the words "Original Size," is the height and width of the object before you started fooling with it. Click the Reset button to restore the object to its original size. You can also click the Reset Picture button on the Picture toolbar to restore a graphic to its original dimensions.

9. Draw Borders on One, Two, or Three Sides of a Text Box   Yes, it can be done. You can put borders on one, two, or three sides of a text box. To do so, remove the borders from the text box (see "Putting a Border Around an Object," earlier in this chapter). With that done, select the text box and display the Tables and Border toolbar. Use the Border drop-down menu on the toolbar to place borders on one, two, or three sides of the text box.

10. Use Text Boxes and Lines to Annotate a Figure   Sure, you can click the AutoShapes button on the Drawing toolbar, choose Callouts on the pop-up menu, and choose a callout to annotate a figure, but the callouts on the menu are unwieldy and hard to manage. But a better way to annotate a figure is to create a text box for the annotation and draw a line from the text box to the part of the figure that the text box refers to. The text box method gives you more freedom to experiment with annotations. You can remove the box that goes around the text, change the width of the line, or put an arrow on the line if you want to.

To remove borders from a text box, select the text box, open the drop-down menu on the Line Color button on the Drawing toolbar, and choose No Line from the pop-up menu. To change the width of a line, select the line, click the Line Style button on the Drawing toolbar, and choose a line width on the pop-up menu.

The Complete Reference

Word
2002

Chapter 14

Constructing the Perfect Table

The best way to present a bunch of data at one time is to do it in a table. Provided the row labels and column headings are descriptive, looking up information in a table is the fastest way to look up information. And tables impose order on chaos. What used to be a knotty lump of nondescript data can be turned into an orderly statement of fact if the data is presented in a table. No report is complete without one or two of them.

Microsoft Word devotes an entire menu to creating and formatting tables: the Table menu. On the Table menu are numerous commands for handling tables. Read on to find out how to create tables, enter the text, lay out a table, format a table, prettify a table, do the math, turn a list into a table, use tables as a means of laying out text in columns, call upon Microsoft Excel commands to crunch numbers in tables, and use Word to access database tables and queries from Microsoft Access. At the end of this section, for you and you alone, are ten tricks for handling tables.

What You Should Know Before You Begin

Before you can start creating tables in Word, you need to know table terminology. Figure 14-1 shows what the various parts of a table are. Here is what the terms mean:

■ **Borders** The lines that mark where columns and rows are, as well as the extremities of the table. Borders are different from gridlines. When you first create a table, you see gridlines, not borders. You decide what table borders look like.

■ **Cell** The box that is formed where each column and row intersect. Each cell holds one data item. The table in Figure 14-1 comprises 20 cells (5 rows × 4 columns).

■ **Gridlines** Gray lines that show where columns and rows are. Gridlines help you see where one row or column ends and the other begins. Until you format a table and give it borders, gridlines show where the columns and rows are, but in a table with borders, the borderlines cover the gridlines. In Figure 14-1, borders have been drawn on the columns but not the rows, and gridlines show where rows begin and end. To see or turn off the gridlines, choose Table | Show Gridlines or Table | Hide Gridlines.

■ **Heading Row** The row at the top of the table that describes what is in the columns below. In Figure 14-1, the heading row includes four entries: "Region," "Yes (%)," "No (%)," and "Maybe (%)." You can tell Word to make the heading row appear again on the next page when a table breaks across two pages. Some tables have two or even three heading rows.

■ **Row Labels** The entries in the first column of a table that describe what kind of data is in each row. The table in Figure 14-1 includes four row labels: "South," "North," "East," and "West."

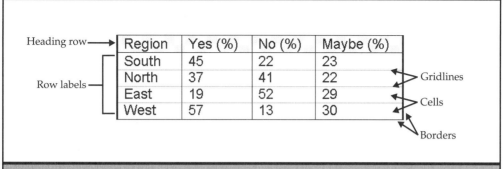

Figure 14-1. *Every table has columns, rows, and cells, and most include a heading row as well*

To help create and format tables, Word offers the Tables and Borders toolbar (click the Tables and Borders button on the Standard toolbar to display it). Between the Tables and Borders toolbar and shortcut menu commands for dealing with tables, you can conveniently do most of the work without having to open the cumbersome Table menu on the menu bar.

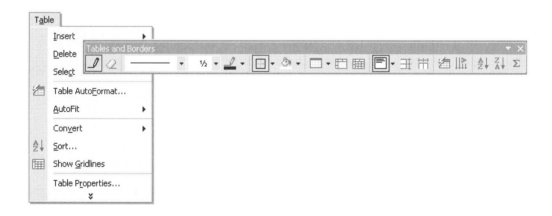

PROFESSIONAL-LOOKING
DOCUMENTS WITH
WORD 2002

Note   *Tables can be as fancy or bare as you want them to be. Don't worry about tables' appearance, however, because you can rely on the Table | Table AutoFormat command to do all the formatting for you. See "Letting the Table AutoFormat Command Do the Work," later in this chapter.*

Creating a Table

Word gives you no less than three different ways to create a table, and you can also turn a list into a table as long as you format the list properly. These pages explain how to create a table, move around in a table, and enter the text and numbers.

When you create a table, you can tell Word to include umpteen rows and many, many columns. But sometimes starting with only one row works best. As you enter data, you can add rows as you need them. To add a new row to a table as you enter data, press the TAB key when you have finished entering data in the last column of the last row. Pressing TAB when the cursor is in the last column of the last row adds another row to the table.

The Three Ways to Create a Table

Choose your weapon when you want to create a table. You can create a bare-bones table with the Insert Table button on the Standard toolbar, choose the Table | Insert | Table command to take advantage of one or two refinements in the Insert Table dialog box, or draw a table with the Draw Table button on the Tables and Borders toolbar. Better read on.

Starting with the Insert Table Button

The fastest way to create a table is to click the Insert Table button on the Standard toolbar. Click the button and you see an empty table grid, but by moving the pointer onto the grid and dragging sideways and downward, you can tell Word how many rows and columns to put in the table. Click when the bottom of the menu lists the number of rows and columns you want. Here, a table 4 rows long and 11 columns wide is being created:

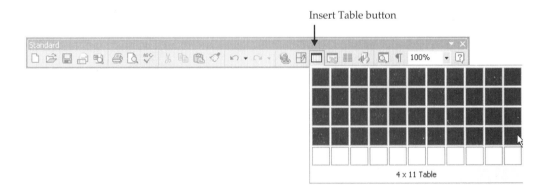

Insert Table button

4 x 11 Table

Your new table fills the page from margin to margin. Each column is the same width. Later in this chapter, "Changing the Layout of a Table" explains how to change the size of a table, its rows, and its columns.

Click in the first column, first row of a table and press ENTER *to insert a blank line above the table. In a document with a table and nothing more, you can get trapped in the table unless you know to press* ENTER *in the first cell. Pressing* ENTER *inserts a blank line so you can do other things in the document besides fool with a table.*

Starting with the Table I Insert I Table Command

Starting with the Table I Insert I Table command, you can have a say over how wide the columns are and whether the table stretches from margin to margin or occupies less space on the page. Follow these steps to create a table starting with the Table I Insert I Table command:

1. Click where you want the table to be.

2. Choose Table I Insert I Table or click the Insert Table button on the Tables and Borders toolbar. You see the Insert Table dialog box shown in Figure 14-2.

3. Under Table Size, enter how many columns and rows you want.

4. Under AutoFit Behavior, choose how wide to make the column and the table:

   - **Fixed Column Width**   Enter a measurement to make all columns the same width. Choosing Auto in the text box creates a table with columns of equal size that goes from margin to margin (choosing Auto is tantamount to choosing the AutoFit To Window option).

   - **AutoFit To Contents**   Choosing this option makes each column wide enough to accommodate its widest entry. You get very narrow columns to begin with. As you enter data, Word adjusts the size of columns and rows to make rows and columns roughly the same size.

Many people find it hard to enter data in a table that was created with the AutoFit to Contents option because row and column boundaries shift continuously as you enter data when this option is turned on. However, you can always enter the data and apply the AutoFit To Contents command later. To do so, click your table and choose Table I AutoFit I AutoFit to Contents.

   - **AutoFit To Window**   This option, which is used for creating Web pages or HTML pages that will be viewed through a browser, makes the table fill the window when the table is shown in Web Layout view or seen through a Web browser.

5. Click OK.

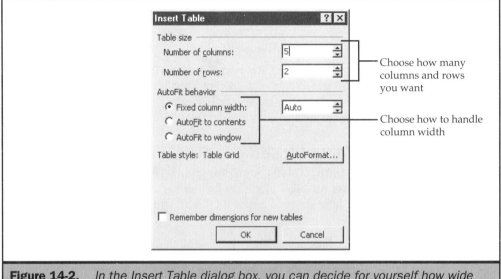

Figure 14-2.   *In the Insert Table dialog box, you can decide for yourself how wide columns are and how wide the table is*

    Clicking the AutoFormat button in the Insert Table dialog box (see Figure 14-2) takes you to the Table AutoFormat dialog box, where you can choose a table design for your table. However, I suggest entering the data before you choose a table design. Entering data in a bare-bones table is easier than entering data in a table that is all gussied up. See "Letting the Table AutoFormat Command Do the Work," later in this chapter.

Drawing a Table

The third way to create a table is to sketch it. Choose Table | Draw Table or click the Draw Table button on the Tables and Borders toolbar. The pointer changes to a pencil (and the Tables and Borders toolbar appears if you chose Table | Draw Table). Start by dragging the pencil across the screen to create the outer boundaries of the table. Then fill in the columns and rows. If you make a mistake, click the Eraser button on the Tables and Borders toolbar and click a line you want to erase with the new pointer, which looks like an eraser.

Try this trick for quickly creating a table with same-size rows and tables: Draw a rectangle with the pencil and then click the Split Cells button on the Tables and Borders toolbar. In the Split Cells dialog box, enter the number of columns and rows you want.

Using the pencil is a great way to draw cells of unusual sizes, not to mention diagonal lines. As "Merging and Splitting Cells and Tables" explains later in this chapter, you can use the Split Cells and Merge Cells commands to make cells of various sizes, but those commands are downright unwieldy compared to the pencil. Use the pencil and eraser (along with the Distribute Rows Evenly and Distribute Columns Evenly commands) to create forms and elaborate tables like the one in this illustration.

	1	2	3	4	5	6	7	8	9	
Giants	2	0	4	1	0	3	2	1	3	15
Dodgers	0	0	0	0	0	0	0	0	0	0

Welcome to Pac Bell Park

Tip   *To be perfectly honest, Word offers a fourth way to construct a table: Type plus signs (+) and minus signs (-) such that the minus signs represent character spaces and the plus signs column borders. After you press* ENTER, *a one-row table appears. To make this very strange and not very useful trick work, however, you must choose Tools | AutoCorrect options, select the AutoFormat As You Type tab, and check the Tables check box.*

Turning a List into a Table—and Vice Versa

Let me guess: You turned to this page in the book from "Preparing and Selecting the Data Source" or "Printing Labels for Mass-Mailings" in Chapter 18. You want to generate form letters or print labels, but your names and addresses are in list form, not in table form, so you can't use them in their present condition to write form letters or generate the mailing labels. Don't worry about a thing. These pages explain how to turn a list into a table and how to turn a table into a list.

Turning a List into a Table

In order to turn a list into a table, all components of the list—also known as the fields—must be separated by tab spaces or commas. For example, Figure 14-3 shows identical address lists in which the following components have been separated, first by tab spaces and then by commas: last name, first name, street number and name, city, state, zip code. To turn a list into a table, Word looks for tab spaces or commas, and the program separates data into columns according to where the tab spaces or commas are.

This illustration shows what a tab-separated list looks like after it has been turned into a table. A *tab-separated list* (also known as a *tab-delimited list*) is one in which the components

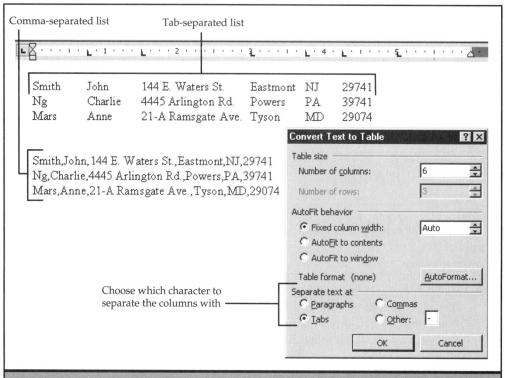

Figure 14-3. *As long as the components of the list are separated from one another by tab spaces or commas, Word can turn a list into a table*

are separated by tab spaces. In a *comma-separated list* (also known as a *comma-delimited list*), the components are separated by commas. Notice where the tab stops on the ruler are in this illustration. The column boundaries are drawn where the tab stops are.

> **Tip** *Separating list components by tab spaces is preferable to separating them by commas. As the previous illustration shows, the tab spaces hint at where text will fall after it is turned into a table. With commas, it is hard to tell where the columns will begin and end after the list has been turned into a table.*

Editing a list so that each component is separated by a tab space or comma seems easy enough. All you have to do is go through the list and enter the commas or tab spaces. However, to convert the list to a table, you have to watch out for something else: Each line must have the same number of components. Watch what happens to this list when it is turned into a table. The extra component in the second address, a post office box number, throws the table out of whack.

```
W. Watts      111 E. Lyle St.      Tibideaux      WA    92014
E. Ryne       21 Ruth St.    P.O. Box 221  Myla   OR    94871
T. Muñoz      76 Lawn St.    Rapt    WA    92079
```

W. Watts	111 E. Lyle St.	Tibideaux	WA	92014	
E. Ryne	21 Ruth St.	P.O. Box 221	Myla	OR	94871
T. Muñoz	76 Lawn St.	Rapt	WA	92079	

You couldn't use this table to generate form letters or mailing labels, since columns contain different kinds of data. Therefore, make sure each line includes the same number of components, even if it means editing P.O. boxes out of the list, removing titles, or adding another component to some entries so that all have the same number of components.

Follow these steps to turn a list into a table after you have done all the preliminary work:

1. Select the list.

2. Choose Table | Convert | Text to Table. You see the Convert Text to Table dialog box shown in Figure 14-3.

3. Under Separate Text At, choose the Tabs or Commas option, depending on which you used to separate the components on the list.

4. Under AutoFit Behavior, choose how wide to make the columns and the table (see "The Three Ways to Create a Table" earlier in this chapter to find out what these options do).

5. Click OK.

Turning a Table into a List

Turning a table into a list is quite easy. Follow these steps:

1. Click anywhere in the table.

2. Choose Table | Convert | Table to Text. You see the Convert Table To Text dialog box.

3. Chose Paragraph Marks to put the data in each cell on its own line; choose Tabs or Commas, or enter a punctuation mark of your choice in the Other box to leave each table row on its own line but separate the data in each column by a tab, comma, or other punctuation mark.

4. Click OK.

Entering the Text and Numbers

After you create your table, start entering the data. Table 14-1 lists keyboard shortcuts you can use to move from cell to cell. As cells fill with data, text moves to the second

Press	To Go Here
TAB or →	Next column in the row
SHIFT-TAB	Previous column in the row

Table 14-1. *Getting Around in Word Tables*

Press	To Go Here
↓	Row below
↑	Row above
ALT-HOME	Start of row
ALT-END	End of row
ALT-PGUP	Top of column
ALT-PGDN	Bottom of column

Table 14-1. *Getting Around in Word Tables* (continued)

and subsequent lines in cells. In other words, text "wraps" to the next line in the same way that text "wraps" when you are writing a normal paragraph on a page.

Here are a handful of items to keep in mind as you enter text in your table:

- When you have reached the last cell in a table, you can press the TAB key to attach another row to the table and continue to enter data. (Word appropriates the TAB key for getting around tables, but you can enter a tab space in a table cell by pressing CTRL-TAB.)

- Word capitalizes the first letter in each table cell. If that bothers you, choose Tools | AutoCorrect Options and uncheck the Capitalize First Letter of Table Cells check box.

- Text "wraps" to the next line in a cell, as I just explained, but you can keep it from wrapping. Perhaps you want to squeeze extra text on a single line of a cell. If you don't want text to wrap in a cell, select the cell or cells in question, choose Table | Table Properties, select the Cell tab in the Table Properties dialog box, click the Options button, and check the Fit Text check box.

Tip *You can number cells by selecting them and clicking the Numbering button on the Formatting toolbar. Chapter 10 explains all the different ways to number items, including table cells. To remove numbers from a table, select the cells and click the Numbering button again.*

A Neat Way to Enter Data in a Table

Here's a neat trick for entering data: Make use of the Data Form dialog box. Instead of pressing the TAB key or clicking to go from row to row and column to column, all you have to do is enter data in the dialog box. To make the trick work, however, you must have already entered the header row.

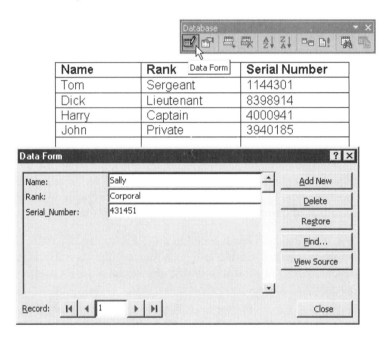

To open the Data Form dialog box, right-click a toolbar and choose Database. You see the Database toolbar. Then, with the cursor in the last row of your table, click the Data Form button. The Data Form dialog box appears. For each row of data you want to enter, take these steps:

1. Click the Add New button.
2. Enter the data in the text boxes on the form.
3. Click the Add New button again.

When you click the Close button in the Data Form dialog box, the data is entered in your table. Near the end of this chapter, "Calling on Access Data for a Table" explains the Database toolbar.

Sorting, or Reordering, a Table

To *sort* a table means to rearrange the data in one column so that it falls in alphabetical, numerical, or by-date order in one column. Sorting makes entering data easier. Instead of entering names in alphabetical order, for example, you can enter them at random and then sort the table to arrange the names in one column in alphabetical order. Instead of putting an address list in zip code order, you can tell Word to do it. What's more, Word makes all the sorting decisions for you. For example, you don't have to know or decide whether San Jose, California comes before or after San José, Costa Rica in an alphabetical list of city names because Word decides for you.

Tables can be sorted in ascending or descending order:

- **Ascending Sort** Arranges text in alphabetical order from A to Z, numbers from smallest to largest, and dates from earliest in time to latest in time.

- **Descending Sort** Arranges text from Z to A, numbers from largest to smallest, and dates from latest in time to earliest.

Caution *Be sure to sort a table before you format it. When you sort, the rows in the table are rearranged, and the rearranged rows carry their borders and shading with them. The heavy border around row 8 might be out of place when row 8 becomes row 2.*

The fastest way to sort a table is to click in the column by which the table is to be sorted and then click the Sort Ascending or Sort Descending button on the Tables and Borders toolbar. The first of these tables, for example, has been sorted in ascending order on the Date of Birth column; the second has been sorted in descending order on the Zip Code column.

First Name	Initial	Last Name	Date of Birth	Zip Code
Walter	B.	Johnson	11/19/46	94112
Hiram	I.	Johnson	12/19/47	94124
Jenny	X.	Abiqui	8/14/53	94111
Ralph	D.	Meeker	1/4/56	94111
Hester	T.	Scopus	7/31/58	94113
Susan	B.	Johnson	10/14/76	94127

First Name	Initial	Last Name	Date of Birth	Zip Code
Susan	B.	Johnson	10/14/76	94127
Hiram	I.	Johnson	12/19/47	94124
Hester	T.	Scopus	7/31/58	94113
Walter	B.	Johnson	11/19/46	94112
Jenny	X.	Abiqui	8/14/53	94111
Ralph	D.	Meeker	1/4/56	94111

Notice how each line in the table remains intact when it is moved elsewhere. The information about Walter B. Johnson, for example, remains the same no matter where sorting moves him in the table. Notice as well that Word recognizes the heading row and does not sort names or numbers in the heading row. "Date of Birth" and "Zip Code" stay at the top of the columns to which they belong.

Sorting a table by clicking a column and then clicking a Sort button works fine under these conditions:

- Identical information does not appear in the same column. Notice the three Johnsons in the sample table in the previous illustration. Word can't accurately sort the table by the Last Name column because it can't tell which Johnson goes first.

- The table has a heading row. As you know, Word ignores the first row in a table when you click a Sort button to sort a table. If the first row presents information, not column descriptions, the information in the first row is not sorted.

Follow these steps to sort a table when identical information appears in the column where the sorting takes place:

1. Click in the table.

2. Choose Table | Sort. You see the Sort dialog box shown in Figure 14-4.

3. In the first Sort By drop-down menu, choose the column you want to sort with.

4. If necessary, open the first Type drop-down menu and choose Text, Number, or Date to describe what kind of data you are dealing with.

5. Select the Ascending or Descending option button to declare whether you want an ascending or a descending sort.

6. In the first Then By drop-down menu, choose the tiebreaker column. In Figure 14-4, for example, First Name is the tiebreaker column. If two names in the Last Name column are alike, Word looks to the First Name column to break the tie and place one name before another in the table.

7. Repeat steps 4 and 5 for the Then By column, if necessary.

8. Choose a second Then By column to break ties in the third Then By drop-down menu. In Figure 14-4, for example, Initial is chosen in the second Then By box.

9. If your table does not include a heading row, select the No Header Row option button.

10. Click OK.

To sort a table without a heading row, click in the column that you want to sort on and choose Table | Sort. Instead of column names, you see column numbers in the Sort dialog box (see Figure 14-4). Make sure the right column number appears in the first Sort By drop-down list, make sure the No Header Row option button is selected, and click OK.

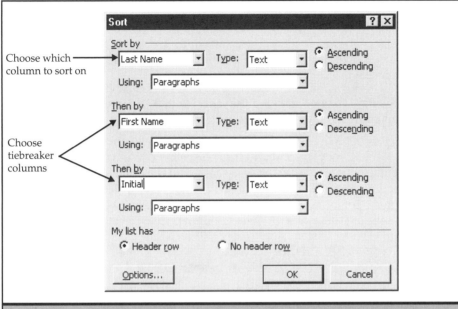

Choose which column to sort on

Choose tiebreaker columns

PROFESSIONAL-LOOKING DOCUMENTS WITH WORD 2002

Figure 14-4. *Choose Table | Sort to sort a table in which the same information is found in some columns; in this table, the Johnsons have been sorted in the right order*

Tip

Suppose a table has two or more descriptive rows at the top. How can you keep them from being sorted? Click the first cell in the table apart from the descriptive rows at the top, press F8 (or double-click EXT on the Status bar), and then click the last cell in the table. By doing so, you select all the rows except the descriptive rows at the top of the table. Choose Table | Sort, make sure the No Header Row option button is selected, select which column you want to sort on in the first Sort By drop-down menu, and click OK.

Changing the Layout of a Table

Most tables need an overhaul or two before you are done with them. A row or column needs to be added or deleted. Data in one column needs to go to another. The ceiling on one row is too low, and the ceiling on another is too high. Read on to find out how to insert and delete rows and columns, rearrange rows and columns, and change column widths and row heights. You will also find instructions here for selecting, merging, and splitting rows and columns.

Note

These pages explain how to draw the boundaries, columns, and rows in a table. If you came here to learn how to spruce up a table, see "Decorating a Table with Borders, Shading, and Color," later in this chapter.

Making a Table Fit on One Page

Tables, like waistlines, have a tendency to grow wider, and when they do, right-hand columns fall off the page. Here is some advice for trimming tables so they stay on one page:

- **Shrink the Font Size**   Shrinking the font size makes columns narrower and packs more columns onto the page.

- **Tilt the Heading Row on Its Ear**   In a top-heavy table in which the heading row cells contain text and the cells below contain numbers, you can make the entire table narrower by changing the orientation of the text in the heading row cells (see "Turning Text Sideways in Tables," later in this chapter). Compare the first table in this illustration to the second table. They present the same data, but one is slimmer than the other.

Timmy	Jeremy	Buster	Davey	Tommy
4	1	8	3	6
3	9	7	4	2
1	4	4	1	4
6	7	8	4	6

Timmy	Jeremy	Buster	Davey	Tommy
4	1	8	3	6
3	9	7	4	2
1	4	4	1	4
6	7	8	4	6

- **Try Combining Columns**   Sometimes you can put data that might normally be in two columns into one column and thereby make a table one column narrower. Consider the tables in this illustration. Both present the same data, but the second table is narrower, and readers can still find the keyboard shortcut in the second table because the italicized text shows them where to look. By the way, a table with only a word or two in some columns and reams of text in the other, like the first table shown here, looks awkward. Combining columns, as was done in the second table, is a great way to prevent this problem.

Command	Explanation	Keyboard Shortcut
Table | Select Table	Selects the entire table so that you can format it, for example, or change fonts throughout.	Alt+5

Command	Explanation
Table | Select Table	Selects the entire table so that you can format it, for example, or change fonts throughout. *Keyboard shortcut:* Alt+5

■ **Change the Page Orientation**   If worse comes to worst, you can always present the table on a landscape page (see "Changing the Size and Orientation of Pages" in Chapter 9). Obviously, more columns can fit on a landscape page than a portrait page. However, the table has to appear on a page by itself if you go this route, and you have to create a new section for the landscape table as well (see "Section Breaks for Changing Layouts" in Chapter 9).

Chances are, if your table can't fit on one page, presenting the information in a table is not the best option. Try presenting it in bulleted or numbered lists. Or present the information in short paragraphs under small fourth- or fifth-level headings. In my editing days, I edited the work of more than one author with table-itis, a peculiar affliction that makes its sufferer want to stuff everything into a table ("I see my book as this gigantic matrix of information," an author told me). However, looking up information in row after row and column after column of a large table is harder than looking up information in a well-crafted list or handful of pages with descriptive headings.

Selecting Parts of a Table

Before you can insert or delete columns, rows, and cells; change their sizes; draw borders around them; or change their coloring, you have to select them. Unfortunately, selecting parts of a table is one of those tasks for which there are so many techniques you can't remember any of them. Scour Table 14-2 to find a handful of selection techniques that suit you. By learning the speediest ways to select parts of a table, you can make your work go that much faster.

To Select	Do This
Cells	
One cell	Move the pointer to the lower-left corner and click when you see the black arrow *or* Choose Table | Select | Cell
Several cells in a row or column	Drag the pointer across the cells *or* Hold down the SHIFT key and click arrow keys
Rows	
One row	Click to the left of the row *or* Click in the first or last cell in the row and press ALT-SHIFT-END or ALT-SHIFT-HOME, respectively
Several rows	Click to the left of the first row to select it and then drag downward or upward *or* Drag to select one cell in each row you want to select, and then choose Table | Select | Row
Columns	
One column	Move the pointer on top of the column and click when you see the black arrow *or* Hold down the ALT key and click the column *or* Click in the column and choose Table | Select | Column
Several columns	Move the pointer on top of a column, click when you see the black arrow, and drag to the left or right *or* Drag to select one cell in each column you want to select, and then choose Table | Select | Column

Table 14-2.   *Techniques for Selecting Parts of Tables*

To Select	Do This
Rows and Columns	
Block of cells	Drag across the cells
	or
	Click one cell and SHIFT-click another
	or
	Click one cell, press F8 or double-click EXT on the Status bar, and click another cell
	or
	Hold down the SHIFT key and click arrow keys
Entire Table	
Whole shebang	Triple-click to the left of the table
	or
	Press ALT-5 (the 5 on the numeric keypad)
	or
	Click in the table and choose Table | Select | Table
	Click the table selection handle outside the upper-right corner of the table

Table 14-2.   *Techniques for Selecting Parts of Tables* (continued)

Inserting and Deleting Rows, Columns, and Cells

The first step in deleting or inserting rows, columns, or cells is to select them. Selecting a row, column, or cell in order to insert a row, column, or cell seems odd, but by selecting you tell Word what you want to insert. After you make a selection, the Insert Table button on the Standard toolbar changes names and is called the Insert Rows, Insert Columns, or Insert Cells button. Right-click after you make a selection and you get commands on the shortcut menu that pertain to the thing you selected. Notice the different Insert and Delete commands on these shortcut menus.

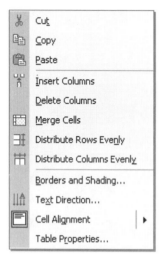
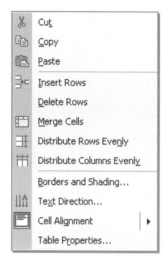

Inserting Rows and Columns

Follow these steps to insert a row or column:

1. In your table, select the number of rows or columns you want to insert:

   ■ The new row or rows will appear above the row or rows you select.

   ■ The new column or columns will appear to the left of the column or columns you select.

2. Give one of these commands to insert the rows or columns:

   ■ Right-click and choose Insert Rows or Insert Columns.

   ■ Choose Table | Insert and then either the Rows Above (or Rows Below) or Columns to the Left (or Columns to the Right) command.

   ■ Click the arrow beside the Insert Table button on the Tables and Borders toolbar and choose the appropriate command.

To insert a new row at the end of a table, put the cursor in the last cell and press TAB. *To insert a new column on the right side of a table, select the rightmost column and choose Table | Insert | Columns to the Right.*

Inserting Cells

Follow these steps to insert cells in a table:

1. Select the number of cells you want to insert. By your choice, the new cells will shift existing cells either to the right or downward.

2. Choose Table | Insert | Cells or open the drop-down menu on the Insert Table button and choose Insert Cells. You see the Insert Cells dialog box.

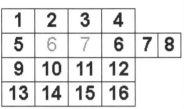 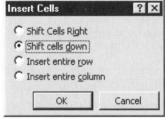

3. Choose Shift Cells Right or Shift Cells Down and click OK.

Deleting Rows, Columns, and Cells

Deleting rows, columns, and cells isn't as simple as selecting them and clicking the DELETE key. Do that and you delete the data in the rows, columns, and cells you selected, not the rows, columns, and cells. Follow these steps to delete rows, columns, or cells:

1. Select the rows, columns, or cells you want to delete.

2. Give one of these Delete commands:

   ■ Right-click and choose Delete.

   ■ Choose Table | Delete and, on the submenu, Columns, Rows, or Cells.

In the case of cells, you see the Delete Cells dialog box. Choose Shift Cells Left or Shift Cells Up and click OK.

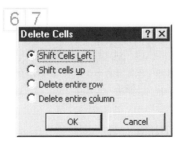

To delete an entire table, click it and choose Table | Delete | Table.

Rearranging Rows and Columns

The usual copy-and-paste and cut-and-paste rules apply to tables as well as text. You can copy or move text from cell to cell, row to row, or column to column by dragging and dropping it or cutting and pasting it. However, I bet you came here to learn how to move or copy an entire row or column from one place in a table to another:

1. Select the row(s) or column(s) you want to move or copy. Be sure to select entire rows or columns. The surest way to do that is to select rows by clicking to their left and columns by clicking directly above them when you see the black down-pointing arrow.

2. Click the Cut or Copy button, press CTRL-X or CTRL-C, or right-click and choose Cut or Copy from the shortcut menu. The rows or columns are moved to the Clipboard.

3. Tell Word where to move or copy the rows or columns:

   ■ **Rows**   Select the row directly below where the row or rows will be moved or copied.

   ■ **Columns**   Select the column to the right of where the column or columns will go.

4. Click the Paste button, right-click and choose Paste, choose Edit | Paste, or press CTRL-V.

You can also move columns and rows by dragging and dropping them. Be sure to select entire rows or columns when you drag and drop.

 A convenient way to move rows is to switch to Outline view, click in the row you want to move, and click the Move Up or Move Down button on the Outlining toolbar as many times as necessary to move the row where you want it to be.

Changing the Size of Rows and Columns

In a generic table—the kind you get before you start fooling with the commands for formatting tables—each row is two points higher than the tallest letter in the row. Depending on which option you chose when you created your table, columns either stretch from margin to margin or are wide enough to accommodate their widest entry.

Usually, you have to wrestle with the rows and columns in a table to make the table look just right. These pages explain how to change the height of rows and width of columns with the numerous techniques that Word offers for doing those tasks. By the way, before you discover how to resize rows, here's a little trick for determining how wide a column is or how tall a row is: Hold down the ALT key as you drag the column or row boundary and look on the ruler. The ruler tells you how much space is occupied by rows and columns.

Two Quick Ways to Resize a Table

Before you start wrestling with your table to give it the right shape and size, check out these commands. They change the overall layout and size of a table and are worth trying out before the wrestling match truly begins.

- **Choose Table | AutoFit | AutoFit To Window**   This command analyzes the table and endeavors to tailor rows and columns so that rows are roughly the same size and columns are roughly the same size. The table stretches from margin to margin with this option. Choose it when you are done entering data in a table, since columns and rows continuously change positions when this option is on, and that makes entering data difficult. You can also right-click a table and choose AutoFit | AutoFit to Window to give this command.

- **Drag the Lower-Left Corner of the Table**   In Print Layout or Web Layout view, click in the table to select it, and then drag the square in the lower-right corner. Dashed lines show what shape the table will be when you release the mouse button. Release it when the table is the size and shape you want.

State	Tribes	Population
Arizona	Apache, Hopi, Navajo, Papago, Pima, Yavapai	203,527
Colorado	Ute	27,776
New Mexico	Apache, Navajo, Pueblo	134,335
Utah	Goshute, Navajo, Southern Paiute, Ute	24,283

Changing Row Size

To change the size of rows, you can drag them one at a time, go to the Row tab of the Table Properties dialog box and flail away, or use the very convenient Distribute Rows Evenly command:

- **Distribute Rows Evenly Command** This command makes each row as tall as the tallest row in the group of rows you selected. For example, if one row in the group you selected is 1 inch tall and the rest are .5 inch tall, all rows are made 1 inch tall after you choose this command. Shrink rows, if necessary, make one row the size you want for all the rows, select the rows whose sizes you want to change, and click the Distribute Rows Evenly button on the Tables and Borders toolbar, as shown in Figure 14-5. You can also right-click the rows and choose the command from the shortcut menu or choose Table | AutoFit | Distribute Rows Evenly.

- **One Row at a Time by Dragging** Move the mouse pointer over the bottom boundary of the row whose size you want to change. When you see the double arrow, click and start dragging up or down. You can also drag the Adjust Table Row marker on the vertical ruler, as shown in Figure 14-5.

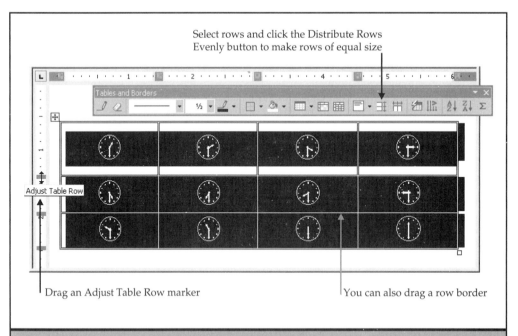

Figure 14-5. *There are many ways to change the size of rows, including dragging an Adjust Table Row marker or selecting rows and clicking the Distribute Rows Evenly button*

- **Entering Measurements in the Table Properties Dialog Box**   Select more than one row to change the height of several rows if need be, choose Table | Properties, select the Row tab in the Table Properties dialog box, and enter a measurement in the Specify Height box. From the Row Height Is drop-down menu, choose At Least to allow the row to increase in height if you enter a graphic or character taller than the measurement in the Specify Height box; choose Exactly to make the row stay the same height no matter what. You can click the Previous Row or Next Row button to specify measurements for other rows if you didn't select several rows to begin with.

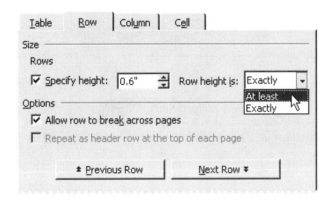

Changing Column Size

Changing the size of columns is similar to changing the size of rows in that you can distribute them evenly across the page, drag their boundaries to change their size, or enter exact measurements in the Table Properties dialog box:

- **Distribute Columns Evenly Command**   Select the columns whose size you want to change and click the Distribute Columns Evenly button on the Tables and Borders toolbar, as shown in Figure 14-6. This command makes each column you choose the same width. To decide the width of the columns, Word takes the average width of the columns you selected and applies it to all the columns. You can also choose this command by right-clicking or by choosing Table | AutoFit | Distribute Columns Evenly.

- **One Column at a Time by Dragging**   Either drag a Move Table Column marker on the horizontal ruler, as shown in Figure 14-6, or move the pointer over a column boundary, click when you see the two-headed arrow, and start dragging.

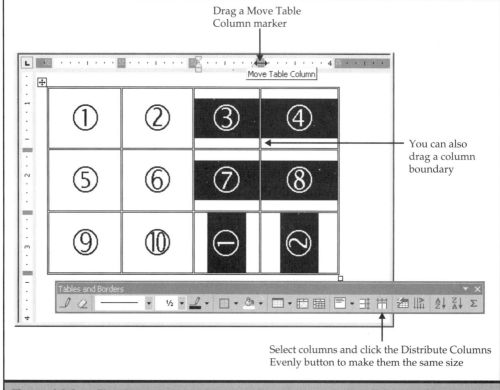

Drag a Move Table Column marker

Move Table Column

You can also drag a column boundary

Tables and Borders

Select columns and click the Distribute Columns Evenly button to make them the same size

Figure 14-6. *The three ways to change column size: select columns and click the Distribute Columns Evenly button, drag a Table Column marker, and drag the boundary of a column*

- **Entering Measurements in the Table Properties Dialog Box** Select more than one column to change the size of several columns if you want and then choose Table | Properties. In the Table Properties dialog box, select the Column tab, check the Preferred Width check box, and enter a measurement in the Preferred Width box. You can click the Previous Column or Next Column button to enter measurements for other columns as well.

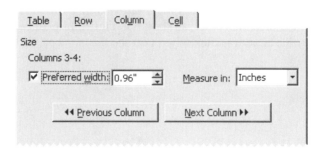

Adjusting the Internal Cell Margins

Each table cell is like a miniature page in that is has a left, right, top, and bottom margin. The left and right cell margins are .08 inch; the top and bottom margins are 1 point if your text is 12-points high and more than 1 point if you are working in a larger font size. Except when a table or cell has thick borders, the cell margins are fine. A thick border, however, can impose on the margin and come too close to the text.

Follow these steps to adjust the internal margins of table cells to move text farther from or closer to the row and column borders:

1. Select the cells whose margin you want to adjust if you want to adjust the margins in a few cells. To adjust the internal margins throughout a table, simply click in the table.

2. Choose Table | Table Properties. You see the Table Properties dialog box.

3. Either adjust cell margins throughout the table or adjust margins in the cells you selected in step 1, if you selected cells in step 1:

   ■ **Cell Margins Throughout the Table**   Select the Table tab and then click the Options button. Enter Top, Bottom, Left, and Right measurements in the Table Options dialog box and click OK.

   ■ **Cell Margins in the Cells You Selected**   Select the Cell tab and then click the Options button. In the Cell Options dialog box, uncheck the Same As the Whole Table check box, and enter Top, Bottom, Left, and Right measurements; then click OK.

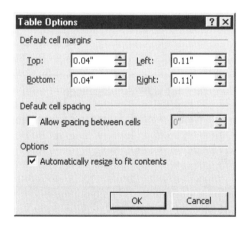
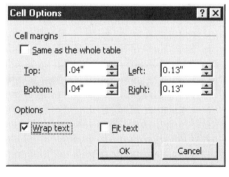

4. Click OK to close the Table Properties dialog box.

Merging and Splitting Cells and Tables

Merging cells means to join several different cells so that they form a single cell. *Splitting* cells means to divide one cell or more than one cell into several different cells. As shown in Figure 14-7, you can merge or split cells when you are laying out a table and you need to get away from the traditional row-column structure or you are using the Table menu commands to draw a fill-in form.

You can use the Split Cells and Merge Cells commands to reconfigure a table. Suppose, for example, that you created too many columns. Select all the columns, merge them, and then split them again, but this time enter the number of columns you really need in the Number of Columns box in the Split Cells dialog box (see Figure 14-7).

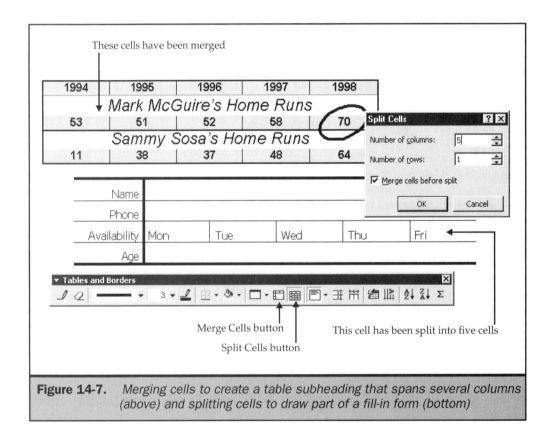

Figure 14-7. *Merging cells to create a table subheading that spans several columns (above) and splitting cells to draw part of a fill-in form (bottom)*

Merging Cells in a Table

Follow these steps to merge cells:

1. Select the cells you want to merge.

2. Click the Merge Cells button on the Tables and Borders toolbar, right-click and choose Merge Cells, or choose Table | Merge Cells.

If the cells you merged held data, the data from each cell is now in its own paragraph inside the new cell.

Splitting Cells in a Table

Follow these steps to split a cell or cells into several different cells:

1. Select the cell or cells you want to split.

2. Click the Split Cells button, right-click and choose Split Cells, or choose Table | Split Cells. The Split Cells dialog box appears (see Figure 14-7).

3. Make entries in the Number Of Columns and Number Of Rows boxes to describe how many new cells you want. For example, entering **3** in the Number of Columns box and **3** in the Number of Rows box creates 9 new cells.

4. Click OK.

Unchecking the Merge Cells Before Split check box tells Word to enter the same number of new cells inside each cell you selected, not a certain number of cells in the sum of the cells you selected. For example, if you select two cells, uncheck the Merge Cells Before Split check box, and enter **4** in the Number of Columns box, you get eight new cells—two each inside the four cells you selected.

A fast way to split cells is to use the Draw Table tool. Click the Draw Table button on the Tables and Borders toolbar or choose Table | Draw Table. Using the pencil pointer, simply draw lines on your table to split cells. If you make a mistake, click the Eraser button and click lines to remove them.

Splitting a Table

To split a table, select the row that is to be the first row in the new table and choose Table | Split Table or press CTRL-SHIFT-ENTER. Sorry, you can't split a table down the middle. You can, however, select the columns that will form the new table, cut them to the Clipboard, and paste them elsewhere to create a new colony of your old table, so to speak.

To merge two tables, simply delete the blank spaces that appear between them.

Aligning and Reorienting Text in Columns and Rows

After you have entered the data in a table, you can start making it presentable. These pages explain how to align data in columns and rows and how to change the orientation of text so that it lies sideways. You will also find instructions here for lining up numbers in columns on the decimal point.

Centering, Aligning, and Justifying the Text

Figure 14-8 shows the nine ways you can align the text in columns and rows. No doubt you are already familiar with the Align Left, Center, and Align Right buttons on the Formatting toolbar for aligning text. Clicking those buttons aligns text horizontally in columns. To align text vertically in rows across the top, the middle, or the bottom, click an Align button on the Tables and Borders toolbar, as shown in Figure 14-8.

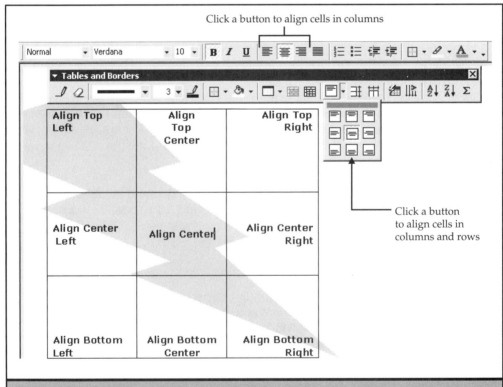

Figure 14-8.   *Besides pressing buttons on the Formatting toolbar to align text in columns, you can take advantage of the Top, Center, and Bottom commands to align text across rows*

Select cells, entire rows, or entire columns, and follow these instructions to change the alignment of the text:

- Click an Align button on the Formatting toolbar if you are aligning text in columns.
- Open the Align button drop-down menu on the Tables and Borders toolbar and click a button (see Figure 14-8).
- Right-click, choose Cell Alignment, and click a button on the drop-down menu.

Experiment freely with the Alignment commands and until the text in your table is easy to read and understand.

Turning Text Sideways in Tables

As "Making a Table Fit on One Page" explained earlier in this chapter, turning the text in the heading row on its side is one way to squeeze more columns onto a page. And text turned sideways looks neat, too. To turn text on its ear, select the cells whose text needs a turn and click the Change Text Direction button on the Tables and Borders toolbar. Keep clicking the button until the text turns the direction you want it to turn.

Lining Up Numbers on the Decimal

"Changing the Tab Settings" in Chapter 8 explains how to align text on the decimal point by changing tab settings on the ruler. Using the same techniques in a table, you can align numbers in a column on the decimal point as well. Follow these steps to align the numbers in a column on the decimal point.

1. Select the cells whose numbers you want to align on the decimal point. Be careful not to choose the text in the heading row or any other cell that contains text. Text appears to the left of the decimal point if you accidentally include a cell with text in it.

2. Click the Tab button on the left side of the ruler as many times as necessary to see the Decimal Tab symbol (choose View | Ruler if the ruler doesn't appear onscreen).

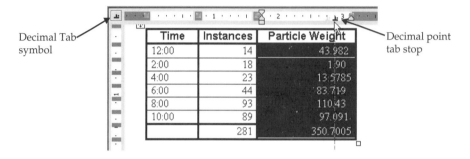

Decimal Tab symbol

Decimal point tab stop

Time	Instances	Particle Weight
12:00	14	43.982
2:00	18	1.90
4:00	23	13.5785
6:00	44	83.719
8:00	93	110.43
10:00	89	97.091
	281	350.7005

3. Click on the ruler where you want the decimal point to be in the cells. The decimal point tab stop symbol appears on the ruler.

4. Drag the decimal point tab stop symbol left or right to adjust the position of the numbers in the cells you selected. As you drag, a dotted line shows how the numbers will line up.

5. If necessary, click the Align Left button on the Formatting toolbar (or press CTRL-L) to make the numbers line up on the decimal.

Handling Table Headers and Page Breaks in Tables

A table that begins on one page and ends on the next presents a problem or two. Readers who turn to the second page that the table is on need to know what they are reading, and they can't do that unless they can see the heading row, the row at the top of the table whose headings describe what is in the body of the table. What's more, a table that breaks off in the middle of a row is awkward indeed. Consider the table shown in this illustration. Readers have to turn the page backward and forward once or twice to make any sense of this table.

| 11:45 | No change | No change |
| 2:15 p.m. | Evinces a marked swelling around the tibia that is not typical of the disease and is likely to have been caused by | Temperature: Normal Pulse: 122 Bandaged the knee |

| | overexposure to heat. Moreover, the patient expresses discomfort when walking. He reports difficulty in bending his ankle and knee. | and the patient's shin too. |

These pages explain how to make the heading row or heading rows appear on the following page when a table breaks across pages and how to make sure a table breaks cleanly in a row.

Repeating Heading Row of a Long Table on the Next Page

To make the heading row appear at the top of the table on each page that the table appears on, click in the heading row and choose Table | Heading Rows Repeat. If your table has two or more heading rows, select them before choosing Table | Heading Rows Repeat. You can also repeat the heading rows on subsequent pages by selecting the heading rows, choosing Table | Table Properties, selecting the Row tab in the Tables Properties dialog box, and checking the Repeat As Header Row At The Top Of Each Page check box.

Note *You can only see table headings on subsequent pages in Print Layout view.*

Making Sure a Table Breaks Cleanly

When a row is more than two lines long, Word cuts it across the middle if half of it falls on one page and the other half falls on the other. However, you can tell Word not to break a row in the middle but move it instead to the next page if it straddles two pages. Follow these steps to keep a row or rows from breaking across pages:

1. Select the row or rows that you do not want to straddle pages.

2. Choose Tables | Tables Properties.

3. Select the Row tab in the Table Properties dialog box.

4. Under Options, uncheck the Allow Row to Break Across Pages check box and click OK.

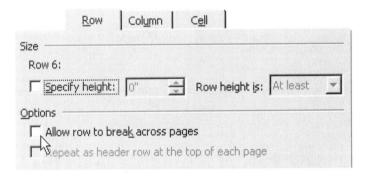

As a desperate measure, you can also force a table to break in a certain row by clicking in the row and pressing CTRL-ENTER. However, heading rows do not appear at the top of the next page when you break a table this way. And by introducing a hard page break you run the risk of putting a lot of blank space at the bottom of the page, because Word has to move the second part of the table to the next page right away.

Decorating a Table with Borders, Shading, and Color

Before you know anything about dressing up a table, you should know that Word offers a special command for doing the job. Instead of drawing the borderlines, shading parts of the table, or sprinkling color on a table yourself, you can tell Word to do it for you. These pages explain how to decorate a table on your own or do it with Word's help.

If your table doesn't have borders or is missing borders in a few places, choose Table | Show Gridlines so you can see where all parts of the table are.

Letting the Table AutoFormat Command Do the Work

Half the commands on the Table menu have to do with formatting tables, but here's a little secret: You don't really have to learn the table-formatting commands. Instead, you can let Word do the job—and a very good job, too—of formatting your table. Follow these steps to choose a prefabricated style for your table:

1. Click anywhere in the table.

2. Click the Table AutoFormat button on the Tables and Borders toolbar or choose Table | Table AutoFormat. You see the Table AutoFormat dialog box shown in Figure 14-9.

3. Choose a style from the Table Styles list (choose an option on the Category drop-down menu first if the number of styles on the list overwhelms you). The Preview box shows what your choice looks like.

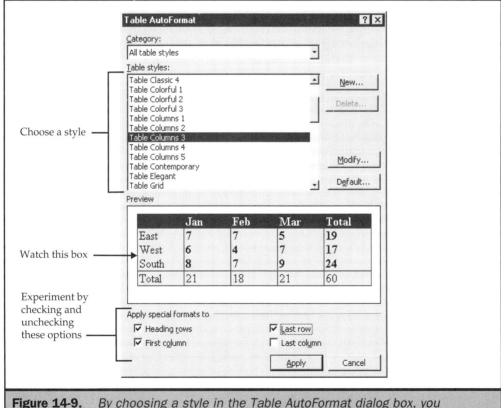

Figure 14-9. *By choosing a style in the Table AutoFormat dialog box, you save yourself the trouble of formatting the table on your own*

PROFESSIONAL-LOOKING
DOCUMENTS WITH
WORD 2002

4. Under Apply Special Formats To in the bottom of the dialog box, check and uncheck options to alter the table design and choose different borders, shading, and font colors.

5. Under Apply Special Formats To, check and uncheck options and watch what happens in the Preview box. Experiment until the table meets your high expectations.

6. Click the Apply button.

> **Tip** *In a document with more than one table, the tables should be laid out the same way for consistency's sake. Take note of the style you choose in the Table AutoFormat dialog box so you can apply it again to the next table. If you have trouble remembering the name of a table style, open the Show drop-down menu in the Styles and Formatting task pane and choose Formatting in Use or Available Styles. That way, you narrow the list to formats and styles you use, and you can find the table style more easily.*

Putting Borders, Shading, and Color on a Table

Usually, you have to tinker with borders, shades, and colors until you find the right look for your table. To help you tinker, Word offers two means of attaching borders, shading, and color to a table or to parts of a table: the Borders and Shading dialog box and the Tables and Borders toolbar, shown in Figure 14-10. However you decide to decorate your table, start by selecting the part of the table you want to decorate. Then do the following to change your table's appearance:

- Click a down arrow or button on the Tables and Borders toolbar and make a selection. (You can click the Tables and Borders button on the Standard toolbar to display the Tables and Borders toolbar.)

- Right-click and choose Borders and Shading to open the Borders and Shading dialog box and go to work there. You can also choose Format | Borders and Shading to open this dialog box.

> **Tip** *By starting from the Borders tab of the Borders and Shading dialog box, you can apply different borders to different parts of a table or to the table itself. Choose Table from the Apply To menu to work on an entire table. Under Setting, choose Grid to draw borders on the perimeter of the cell block you chose, All to draw borders on the perimeter and interior cells, or Custom to draw different borders on different parts of the cell block.*

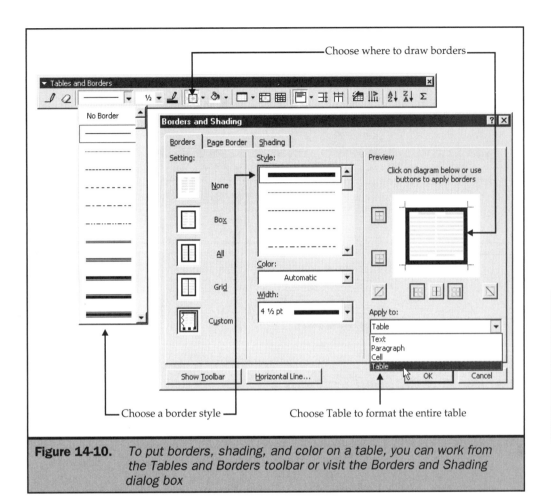

Figure 14-10.   *To put borders, shading, and color on a table, you can work from the Tables and Borders toolbar or visit the Borders and Shading dialog box*

Drawing Borders on a Table

To draw borders around or inside parts of a table, select the part of the table that needs borders. Then do either of the following:

- **On the Borders Tab of the Borders and Shading Dialog Box**   From the Style menu, choose what kind of border you want (see Figure 14-10); from the Color menu, choose a color for the borderlines; from the Width menu, choose how thick to make the borderline; in the Preview box, either click border buttons or click on the box itself to tell Word where to draw the borders.

■ **From the Tables and Borders Toolbar**   Open the Line Style drop-down menu and choose what kind of border you want (see Figure 14-10); open the Line Weight drop-menu and choose how thick a border you want; and open the Border drop-down menu and click a button to tell Word where to draw the borders. You can also choose a color for borderlines from the Border Color drop-down menu.

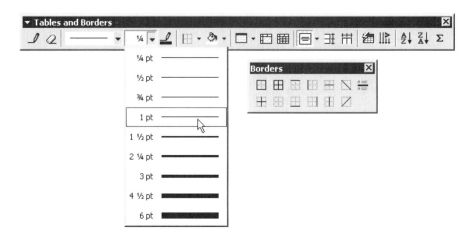

Shading and Coloring Parts of a Table

Select the part of your table that needs a color or gray shade and follow these instructions to paint your table:

■ **On the Shading Tab of the Borders and Shading Dialog Box**   Under Fill, choose a color or gray shade. You can click the More Color button to see more color choices.

■ **From the Tables and Borders Toolbar**   Click the down arrow to open the Shading Color drop-down menu and make a color or gray shade choice. You can click More Fill Colors at the bottom of the menu to see more color choices.

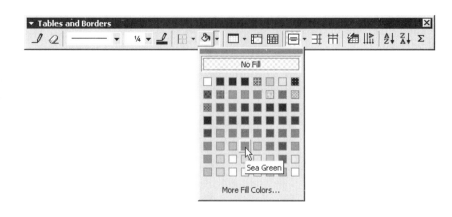

Centering and Indenting Tables on the Page

New tables line up along the left margin of the page, but that doesn't mean you can't center them or indent them from the left margin. To change the position of a table on the page, click the table and do either of the following:

- **Drag the Table to a New Position**   In Print Layout or Web Layout view, move the pointer over the small selection handle beyond the upper-left corner of the table, click, and start dragging. Dashed lines show where the table will go when you release the mouse button. To move the table in a straight line, hold down the SHIFT key as you drag.

Country	Elvis Sightings
United States	1,146
Canada	312
England	947
France	194

- **Change Alignments or Indentations in the Table Properties Dialog Box**   Choose Table | Table Properties and select the Table tab in the Table Properties dialog box, as shown in Figure 14-11. Then either choose the Center or Right option under Alignment to align the table with respect to the left and right margin, or select Left and enter a measurement in the Indent From Left text box to indent the table from the left margin.

Wrapping Text Around a Table

Besides wrapping text around clip art images, text boxes, and other objects (a subject of Chapter 13), you can wrap text around a table. Wrapping text around a table relieves you from having to cite a table by number or name in the text, since the table appears beside the text and readers know precisely which table you are referring to.

As these figures show, the number of Elvis sightings cannot be linked to population, since even countries with relatively small populations report Elvis

Country	Elvis Sightings
United States	1,146
Canada	312
England	947
France	194

sightings in large numbers. What, then, can we conclude from these statistics? Well, for one, we may conclude that countries where the so-called King's music was popular evince a marked rise in Elvis sightings. Many Elvis fans can be found in England, for example, which accounts for that

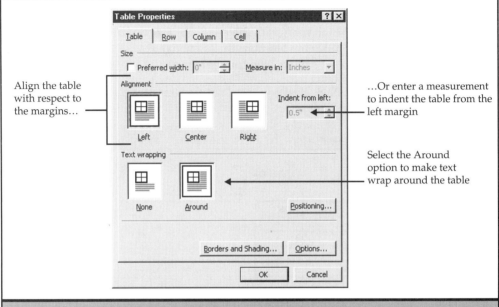

Align the table with respect to the margins…

…Or enter a measurement to indent the table from the left margin

Select the Around option to make text wrap around the table

Figure 14-11.   *On the Table tab of the Table Properties dialog box, you can align tables with respect to the margins, indent tables, and tell Word to wrap text around tables*

Follow these steps to wrap text around a table:

1. Click the table to select it.
2. Choose Table | Table Properties.
3. Select the Table tab (see Figure 14-11).
4. Under Text Wrapping on the Table tab, choose the Around option; then click OK.
5. Move the table into the paragraph that is supposed to wrap itself around the table. The previous section in this chapter explains how to move a table. To do so, click the selection handle beyond the upper-left corner of the table and start dragging.

If you think text comes too close to the table or you want the table to stay in the same location on the page, open the Table Properties dialog box, select the Table tab, and click the Positioning button. You see the Table Positioning dialog box shown in Figure 14-12. The dialog box offers these amenities:

■ **Choose the table's horizontal position**   Under Horizontal, choose a Position option to slide the table across the page. The Center option, for example, places the table between the margins, sides of the pages, or sides of the column, depending on which option you choose in the Relative To menu. The Inside and Outside options are for mirror margins. See "'Mirror Margins' for Bound, Two-Sided Pages" in Chapter 9 if you don't know what those are.

■ **Choose the table's vertical position**   Under Vertical, choose an option from the Position drop-down menu to place the table relative to the choice you make on the Relative To menu: the top and bottom page margins, the top and bottom of the page, or the top and bottom of the paragraph in which the table is located.

■ **Decide how close text comes to the table**   Change the Distance From Surrounding Text measurements to move text farther away or closer to the table.

■ **Let the table slide or make it stay in the same place**   Normally the table is attached to the paragraph in which it lies, and the table moves from page to page if the paragraph does. However, by unchecking the Move with Text check box, you can make the table stay in the same position on the page.

The Allow Overlap option button in the Table Positioning dialog box applies to Web pages and HTML documents. Check it if you want the table to overlap pictures or text when viewed through a Web browser.

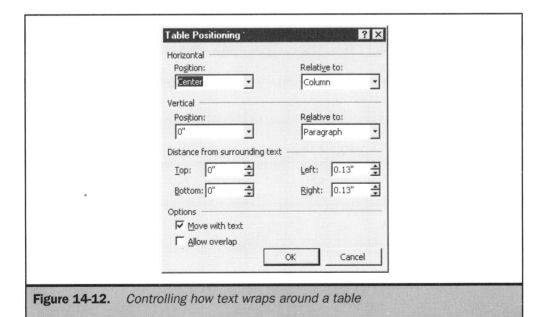

Figure 14-12.   *Controlling how text wraps around a table*

Nesting One Table Inside Another

A *nested table* is a small table enclosed by another table. To put one table inside another, click in the cell where the nested table will go and use the standard Word commands to create a table—click the Insert Table button, choose Table | Insert | Table, or draw the table. Word enlarges the table cell, the row, and column to accommodate the new table. This illustration shows two nested tables.

	Sample Letters		
	δ	φ	Ж
Greek	ы	Σ	ζ
	Λ	Δ	Θ
	Ξ	ε	ф
	ع	ب	ج
Arabic	ق	ك	۳
	ي	ن	١
	Λ	٥	ى

Rather than nesting tables, try splitting cells to create a table within a table. Nested tables are unwieldy and hard to manage. See "Merging and Splitting Cells and Tables" earlier in this chapter.

Crunching the Numbers in Tables

Don't waste time doing the math yourself in a table when Word can do it for you. Besides saving you the trouble of doing the math, the program updates the results of formulas as the numbers in the formulas change. Table 14-3 describes the math functions you can use to construct formulas in tables. Word is not a spreadsheet program, and if you want to do serious number-crunching you should do it in Excel or Lotus 1-2-3, but you can compute simple formulas in tables. These pages explain basic techniques for computing in tables, the pitfalls of doing the math in a table, and how to do fancy math calculations so that the results are accurate.

Word doesn't compute blank cells in formulas. Enter a 0 in blank cells if you want them to be included in calculations.

Function	What It Does
ABS	Returns the absolute value of a number or formula.
AND	Returns the value 1 if both arguments are true; returns 0 if either is false.
AVERAGE	Obtains the average of the values in the cells.
COUNT	Returns the number of cells.
DEFINED	Returns 1 if the expression is valid; returns 0 if it can't be computed.
FALSE	Returns 0.
IF	Evaluates an expression and returns a if it is true; returns b if it is false.
INT	Returns the number to the left of the decimal place.
MAX	Returns the largest value.
MIN	Returns the smallest value.
MOD	Returns the remainder of a division formula.
NOT	Returns 0 if false; returns 1 if true.
OR	Returns 0 if either or both a and b are true; returns 1 if either or both are false.
PRODUCT	Multiplies the values in the cells.
ROUND	Returns a round number.
SIGN	Returns 1 if a is a positive number; returns -1 if a is negative.
SUM	Totals the values in the cells.
TRUE	Returns 1.

Table 14-3. *Math Functions for Use in Tables*

Note *Later in this chapter, "Calling On Excel to Construct Worksheet Tables" explains how you can get Excel's help to do math in tables without leaving Word.*

The Basics: Entering Formulas in Tables

Follow these basic steps to do a math calculation in a table:

1. Click in the cell that is to show the results of the calculation.

2. Choose Table | Formula. You see the Formula dialog box shown in Figure 14-13. To begin with, Word enters the SUM function and makes an educated guess as to which cells you want to total. In parentheses, you see either the argument ABOVE, which means to total all the cells above the cell you are working in, or the argument LEFT, which means to total all the cells to the left of the cell you are working in.

The fastest way to total cells in a table is to click in the cell where the total is to appear and then click the AutoSum button on the Tables and Borders toolbar (see Figure 14-13). Usually, Word guesses correctly that you want to total the cells above the cell you are working in or the cells to the left of the cell you are working in and all is well.

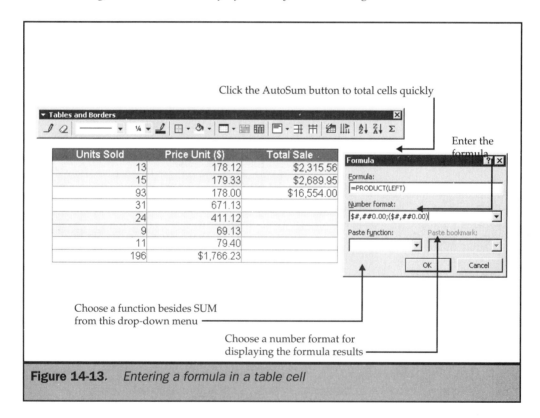

Figure 14-13.   *Entering a formula in a table cell*

3. Construct the formula in the Formula box. To do so, start by clicking to the right of the equal sign (=) and entering the correct function. Table 14-3 lists the functions you can use. To enter a function name, open the Paste Function drop-down menu and choose a function.

   In the parentheses after the function, indicate where relative to the cell you are working in the cells you want to calculate can be found. You can enter **left**, **right**, **above**, or **below** (you can enter the word in upper- or lowercase letters). In Figure 14-13, LEFT has been entered because the formula multiplies the numbers in the two cells to the left of the formula cell. Later in this chapter, "Entering Complex Arguments in Formulas" explains other ways to indicate which cells to compute in a formula.

   If necessary, delete the SUM function and its parentheses that appeared when you opened the Formula dialog box.

Caution   *Do not delete the equal sign in the Formula text box or enter any numbers, symbols, or text before the equal sign. Delete the equal sign and the formula will not compute, period.*

4. From the Number Format drop-down menu, choose a number format for displaying the results of the calculation. Table 14-4 describes the different number formats.

Tip   *You can invent a number format of your own by entering zeroes in the Number Format text box. Enter **0.0**, for example, to display numbers to one decimal place. Enter **0.00000** to display numbers to five decimal places.*

5. Click OK.

   The results of formulas are shown in fields. Part VI explains fields. For now, all you need to know is that you can change the numbers in the cells to which a formula refers and update the results of the formula so it is accurate. To update a formula, select the results of the formula and press F9 or right-click and choose Update Field from the shortcut menu. If you see field codes instead of formula results after you enter a formula, do the following to see the results: Choose Tools | Options, select the View tab in the Options dialog box, and uncheck the Field Codes check box.

Tip   *You can copy formulas from one cell to another. Select the formula and press F9 to compute the formula after you copy it.*

Format	Example	Description
#,##0	4,321	Does not display decimals. Displays zero if the number is less than one.
#,##0.00	4,321.00	Displays numbers to two decimal places. Displays zero on the left side of the decimal point if the number is less than one (0.21).
$#,##0.00; ($#,##0.00)	$4,321.00 ($4,321.00)	Includes the dollar sign in the results and displays the number to two decimal places (see Figure 14-13). Negative numbers are enclosed in parentheses.
0	4321	Makes sure at least one positive digit is displayed even if the formula results are less than one (0.21 is displayed as 0).
0%	4321%	Displays the results as a percentage.
0.00	4321.00	Makes sure that at least one positive digit and two decimals are displayed in the formula results.
0.00%	4321.00%	Display the results as a percentage to two decimal places.

Table 14-4.   *Formats for Displaying Formula Results*

Making Sure Your Calculations Are Accurate

The problem with performing math in tables is that Word computes the wrong numbers if you are not careful. Unless you instruct it otherwise, Word computes the numbers in cells adjacent to the cell where the formula is located (Word computes the cells to the LEFT, RIGHT, ABOVE, or BELOW). Sometimes that renders the formula inaccurate. In this illustration, for example, formulas in the Totals row are supposed to add the numbers in rows 2 through 5, but Word includes the numbers in the first row, Quarter, in the calculations. As a result, the totals in the Totals row are not correct.

Quarter	1	2	3	4
Robco	1.5	2	1	1
Dunmen	1	1.5	1.5	1.5
Pilfer	2	1.75	2	1
XS Steel	1	1	2.5	1.5
Totals	6.5	8.25	10	9

Here's a little trick for getting around the problem of computing the wrong cells in a formula: Enter a blank row or column where you want Word to stop computing the values in cells. In this illustration, for example, a blank row has been inserted between the heading row (1, 2, and so on) and the next row. Now the calculations in the Totals row are correct because Word calculates the values in adjacent cells. The program does not look beyond the blank row for values to calculate.

Quarter	1	2	3	4
Robco	1.5	2	1	1
Dunmen	1	1.5	1.5	1.5
Pilfer	2	1.75	2	1
XS Steel	1	1	2.5	1.5
Totals	5.5	6.25	7	5

PROFESSIONAL-LOOKING
DOCUMENTS WITH
WORD 2002

Entering Complex Arguments and Formulas

In the Formula dialog box (see Figure 14-13), the part of the formula that appears in parentheses is called the argument. The *argument* lists the cells that are computed by the function. As you know if you read the last handful of pages, Word uses the cells to the left, to the right, above, or below the formula cell as the argument.

Under these circumstances, however, you can't use the LEFT, RIGHT, ABOVE, or BELOW argument in a formula and obtain an accurate result:

- The cells you want to compute are not adjacent to the formula cell.
- The cells you want to compute are adjacent, but not all of them are valid for making calculations.
- The cells occupy more than one row or column.

Under these circumstances, the only way to enter the argument is to use cell addresses. Each cell in a table has an address, as shown at the top of Figure 14-14. Rows are numbered 1, 2, 3, and so on; columns are assigned the letters A, B, C, and so on; each cell's address comes from its row number and column letter. Hence the address of the first cell in a table is A1. In Figure 14-14, cells E2, E3, E4, and E5 are being entered as the argument. The total of the numbers in the four cells will appear in cell E6, which lists the total profits in the 4th quarter.

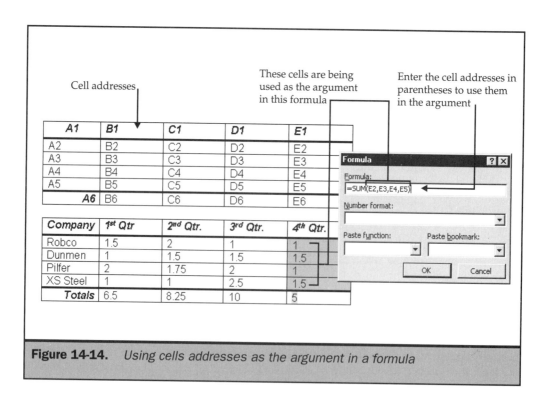

Figure 14-14.   *Using cells addresses as the argument in a formula*

To enter cell addresses as the argument, choose Table | Formula as you normally would. In the Formula dialog box (see Figure 14-13), list the cell addresses between parentheses, and separate each cell address by a comma (just a comma, not a comma and a blank space).

If you insert a new row or column in your table, cell addresses are rendered invalid and you have to re-enter arguments so they refer to the correct cells. Sorry, Word is not a spreadsheet program. Cell references are not updated as you insert new columns and rows. However, you can use Excel calculations in Word, as the next section in this chapter explains.

After you know about cell addresses, you can start using conventional operators to add (+), subtract (–), multiply (*), and divide (/) the numbers in cells. For example, =A4+A5 adds the numbers in those cells. The formula =E5/4 divides the number in cell E5 by 4. Just be sure to enter the equal sign in front of your homemade formula. Without it, Word stubbornly refuses to do any calculations.

Referring to Far-Flung Tables in Formulas

Suppose you want to refer to a cell in another table in a formula. It can be done. To do it, select the cell and bookmark it. With the cell selected, choose Insert | Bookmark, enter a descriptive name in the Bookmark Name text box (bookmarks can't start with numbers or include blank spaces), click the Add button, and click OK. In the Formula dialog box, open the Paste Bookmark drop-down menu and enter the bookmark as part of the formula. Here, the tax amount and the rakeoff amount are being subtracted from the sum of the numbers in cell D1 and D4 to arrive at the profit amount.

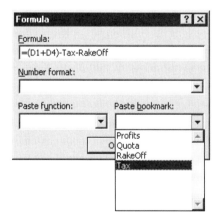

Calling On Excel to Construct Worksheet Tables

Excel fans who read the last handful of pages in this book about performing calculations in tables probably shook their heads and thought, "Too bad you can't simply do these calculations in Excel." Well, you can do table calculations in Excel. By clicking the Insert Microsoft Excel Worksheet button on the Standard toolbar, you can call upon every Excel command the program has to offer. These pages explain how to create an Excel worksheet in Word, import a worksheet from Excel, and change the look of a table you constructed from an Excel worksheet.

 To create a standard Word table from the data in an Excel worksheet, select the data in the worksheet, copy it to the Clipboard, and paste it in a Word document. You get a standard Word table. The Excel menus and buttons aren't available for manipulating the data in the table.

Creating an Excel Worksheet in a Word Document

Turns out that Word and Excel are joined at the hip. With a click of the Insert Microsoft Excel Worksheet button on the Standard toolbar, you can place an Excel worksheet in a Word document. The worksheet is embedded in your Word document. Whenever you click the worksheet, Excel buttons and tools appear onscreen instead of Word buttons and tools.

Follow these steps to place an Excel worksheet in a Word document:

1. Click the Insert Microsoft Excel Worksheet button. A grid appears so you can choose the number of rows and columns you want.

2. Move the cursor onto the grid and click to order a certain number of rows and columns. The bottom of the drop-down menu tells how many rows and columns you get when you click. After you click, an Excel worksheet appears onscreen. Look around and you will see that Excel menus, Excel buttons, and the Excel formula bar appear as well, as shown in Figure 14-15.

3. Enter data in your worksheet and do all the things you love to do so much in Excel. You can call on all of the Excel commands as you work.

4. Click outside the worksheet when you are done.

The worksheet is embedded in your document. When you want to work on it again, double-click it to see the worksheet rows and columns as well as the Excel menus and toolbars.

Click the worksheet when you want to move it onscreen. You see the selection handles. An Excel worksheet, at least a worksheet in a Word document, is an object. As such, you can move it or change its size. See "Manipulating Art, Text Boxes, Shapes, and Other So-Called Objects" in Chapter 13.

The Excel menus, buttons, and formula bar appear in Word

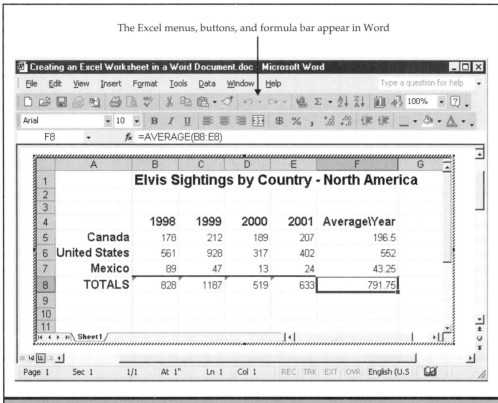

Figure 14-15. *Click the Insert Microsoft Excel Worksheet button on Word's Standard toolbar to place a worksheet in a Word document*

Importing an Excel Worksheet into a Word Table

If the Excel worksheet you need for your Word document has already been formulated and filled with data, you can bring the worksheet straight into Word. To do so, copy the columns and rows in the worksheet that you need, click in your Word document, and choose Edit | Paste Special to open the Paste Special dialog box. In the As box, click Microsoft Excel Worksheet Object and click OK.

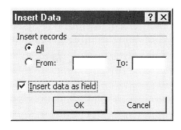

"Linking Documents So That Text Is Copied Automatically" in Chapter 3 explains how you can create a link between an Excel worksheet and a Word document so that changes made to the worksheet are made automatically in the Word document as well.

The worksheet is embedded in the Word document. When you need to fool with the numbers, double-click the worksheet. You see Excel menus and buttons where Word menus and buttons used to be. Go to it.

By the way, if you simply copy the Excel worksheet or part of the worksheet to the Clipboard and paste the worksheet in Word, you get a Word table (choose Table | Show Gridlines to see precisely where the rows and columns are). Being able to get at all the Excel buttons and menu to edit the worksheet is nice, but maybe putting the data in a table is all the fancifulness you need.

Modifying a Worksheet

Being able to make mathematical calculations in an Excel worksheet is well and good, but when you are done you are left with a drab-looking table. Fortunately, you can call on these Excel commands to embellish your worksheet:

- **Drawing Borders on Worksheets**   Select the cells on which you want to place borders. Then click the down arrow beside the Borders button on the Formatting toolbar and choose a border. Usually, you have to wrestle with the Borders buttons until you come up with borders you like.

- **Decorating Worksheets with Colors**   Select the cells, click the down arrow beside the Fill Color button, and choose a color from the drop-down menu. Choose No Fill from the drop-down menu to remove a color.

The fastest way to adorn a worksheet is to let Excel do it. Select the cells in your worksheet and choose Format | AutoFormat. In the AutoFormat dialog box, choose a worksheet design that tickles your fancy. While you're at it, click the Options button and play around with the Formats To Apply check boxes until you construct a worksheet design that suits you.

Calling on Access Data for a Table

If you have the wherewithal to store and manage data in Access, you will be pleased to know that you can bring data from Access database tables and queries into a Word table. Word offers a special toolbar for turning the trick—the Database toolbar. The customer database you maintain in Access, for example, can be brought into Word when you need it for a report. The address list you so carefully crafted in Access can be printed in a Word table.

The Database toolbar offers commands for querying and filtering Access data before you bring it into Word, but I suggest doing your querying and filtering in Access first. Access offers more commands for querying and filtering than Word does. As well as Access database tables, you can import an Access query into a Word table. Query your data in Access and then import the query data into Word if you do not want to import all the records in an Access database table.

Before you go to the trouble to get Access data into a Word document, you should know that Access offers a command for creating reports in Word. In Access, open the report in the Report window, open the drop-down menu on the Office Links button, and choose Publish It with Microsoft Word. Word opens and the report appears as a rich text file (.rtf) document.

Getting the Data from Access to Word

Follow these steps to get data from an Access database table or query and place it in a Word table:

1. Display the Database toolbar. To do so, choose View | Toolbars Database or right-click a toolbar and choose Database.

2. Click the Insert Database button on the Database toolbar. You see the Database dialog box.

3. Click the Get Data button. The Select Data Source dialog box appears.

4. Locate and select the Access file that holds the data you need, and click the Open button. The Select Table dialog box appears. It lists tables and queries in the Access file you chose. Icons show you which are tables and which are queries.

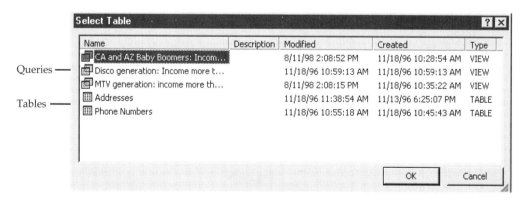

5. Select the database table or query whose data you need, and click OK. You return to the Database dialog box.

PROFESSIONAL-LOOKING DOCUMENTS WITH WORD 2002

A few pages hence, "Querying and Filtering the Data You Get from Access" explains how to query and filter the data as you enter it in Word. To do that, click the Query Options button in the Database dialog box.

6. Click the Insert Data button in the Database dialog box. You see the Insert Data dialog box.

7. Choose options and click OK.

- **All or From**   Select the All option to enter all the records, or the From option to enter numbered records from the database table or query. (You can number records in Access tables and queries by creating an AutoNumber field.)

- **Insert Data as Field**   Check this box if you want to be able to update your Word table as data changes in the Access table or query. With this option, data appears in fields.

Choose Table | Show Gridlines, if necessary, to get a better look at the borders in your new table. If you imported the data in field form and you need to update your table later on, click in the table to select the fields and then press F9 or click the Update Field button on the Database toolbar.

Editing and Managing the Access Data in Your Table

A Word table whose data comes from Access is no different from another table. You can format your table, edit the data, remove columns and rows, enter new data, and add columns and rows to the table by conventional means. And you can also take advantage of buttons on the Database toolbar to complete these tasks:

- **Enter a new row**   Click the Add New Record button. Word creates a new row at the bottom of the table and moves the cursor there so you can enter data. You can also click the Data Form button on the Database toolbar. In the Data Form dialog box, click the Add New button and enter another row of data.

- **Delete rows**   Select all or part of rows you want to delete and click the Delete Record button.

- **Sort the data**   Click in the column you want to sort and then click the Sort Ascending or Sort Descending button. Earlier in this chapter, "Sorting, or Reordering, a Table" explains sorting.

- **Remove columns from the table**   Click the Manage Fields button. In the Manage Fields dialog box, select the fields (column names) you want to remove and click the Remove button.

- **Rename columns in the table**   Click the Manage Fields button, select a field name (column name), click the Rename button, and enter the new name.

■ **Find data in the table**   Click the Find Record button. In the Find a Field dialog box, enter the data you want to find, choose the field (column) in which it is located, and click the Find First button. Word scrolls to the thing you are looking for if it is indeed there. (You can't use this command if the data in your table appear in field form.)

Querying and Filtering the Data You Get from Access

As I explained earlier, you can query and filter data as you bring it into a Word table, although you are better off querying and filtering in Access. The following instructions are for people who disregard my advice and decide to query and filter Access data as it arrives in Word.

After you have clicked the Insert Database button and chosen which Access database table to bring into Word, click the Query Options button, as shown in Figure 14-16. You see the Filter Records tab of the Query Options dialog box, which is also shown in the figure.

On the Filter Records tab, you construct a query that tells Word which records to take from the data source. The query in Figure 14-16 finds San Francisco addresses (in zip

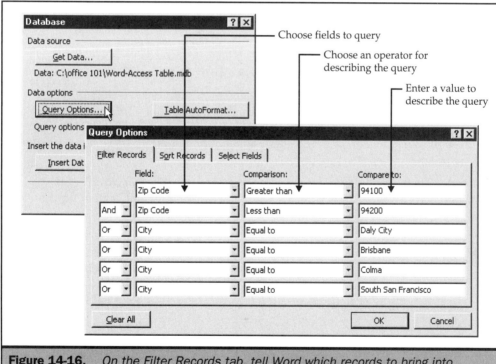

Figure 14-16.   *On the Filter Records tab, tell Word which records to bring into your Word table*

codes 94101 through 94199) as well as addresses in the four satellite cities to the south of San Francisco. Each criterion in the query—there are six in the figure—is called a *rule*.

On the Filter Records tab, choose a field, choose a comparison operator, and enter a compare-to value to describe the records in the Access table that you want to put in your Word table. You can enter one or as many as six rules. Table 14-5 describes the comparison operators and how you can use them to construct rules in a query.

Comparison Operator	Explanation	Example
Equal To	Takes records that match the Compare To value.	*City* **is equal to** *Boston* takes addresses of Bostonians.
Not Equal To	Excludes records that match the Compare To value.	*State* **is not equal to** *Utah* excludes addresses in Utah from the table.
Less Than	Takes records whose values are smaller than the Compare To value.	*Elvis_Sightings* **is less than** *200*.
Greater Than	Takes records whose values are larger than the Compare To value.	*Income* **is greater than** *30,000*.
Less Than or Equal To	Takes records whose values are smaller than or the same as the Compare To value.	*Zip_Code* **is less than or equal to** *94149*.
Greater Than or Equal To	Takes records whose values are larger than or the same as the Compare To value.	*Annual_Rainfall* **is greater than or equal to** *25*.
Is Blank	Takes records when no value appears in the field.	*Bill_Paid* **is blank** takes records in which no entry was made in the Bill_Paid field.
Is Not Blank	Takes records when a value appears in the field.	*Country* **is not blank** takes records in which a country is found in the Country field.

Table 14-5. *Comparison Operators for Use in Constructing Query Rules*

If you enter more than one rule, choose And or Or from the drop-down list to describe how the next rule you enter modifies the one above it:

- **And**   Narrows the number of records that are imported to those described by the rule you enter in combination with the rule above. In this illustration, for example, the two rules tell Word to take only the records of people who live in San Francisco *and* whose income is greater than or equal to $35,000. The address of a San Franciscan whose income is less than $35,000 is not imported into the table. To be imported, a record has to satisfy both rules.

Field:		Comparison:		Compare to:
City	▼	Equal to	▼	San Francisco
And ▼ Income	▼	Greater than or equal	▼	35000

- **Or**   Broadens the number of records that are retrieved to include records described by the rule. In this illustration, for example, the two rules tell Word to take the records of anyone who lives in Los Angeles *or* San Francisco. To be included in the Word table, a record only has to satisfy one of the rules, not both.

Field:		Comparison:		Compare to:
City	▼	Equal to	▼	San Francisco
Or ▼ City	▼	Equal to	▼	Los Angeles

Click OK in the Query Options dialog box to return to the Database dialog box (see Figure 14-16), where you can click the Insert Data button to get the data from your Access table.

The Query Options dialog box also offers the Sort Records tab and Select Fields tab for sorting Access records and excluding fields before you bring them into your Word table. How to use those tabs, I believe, is self-explanatory, and, anyway, you can sort a table or remove columns easily enough after Access data has been brought into a Word table.

MOUS Exam Objectives Explored in Chapter 14

Objective	Heading
Create and modify tables	"Creating a Table," "Letting the Table AutoFormat Command Do the Work," "Decorating a Table with Borders, Shading, and Color," and "Changing the Layout of a Table"
Sort paragraphs in lists and tables*	"Sorting, or Reordering, a Table"
Use Excel data in tables*	"Calling on Excel to Construct Worksheet Tables"
Perform calculations in Word tables*	"Crunching the Numbers in Tables" and "Merging and Splitting Cells and Tables"

Denotes an Expert, not a Core, exam objective.

Ten Tips for Handling Tables

It so happens I have a lot of experience constructing and deconstructing tables. Here are ten tips and tricks that have served me in good stead.

1. Enter the Text and Numbers Before You Start Formatting   Before you decorate a table with fancy borders and various colors or gray shades, enter the data. You will save a lot of time that way. When you try to enter data in a table that is already dressed up, the fancy formats get in the way. Besides, if form follows function, entering the data is a prerequisite, since you have to see what's in the table before you can decide how to format it.

2. Split the Screen to See the Table Headings   Past row 10 or so in a long table, it's hard to tell which row you are in. You can fix that problem, however, by splitting the screen. Split the screen so that you can see the heading rows at the top of the table no matter which row you are working on. "Splitting the Screen" in Chapter 6 explains how to do it, but here are shorthand instructions in case you are in too much of a hurry to visit Chapter 6:

1. Choose Window | Split. A gray line appears across the middle of the screen.

2. Scroll to the top of the screen so that the gray line appears below the heading row—the row at the top of the table that describes what is in the columns below—and then click. Now you will be able to see the heading row wherever you go in the table.

3. In the bottom half of the screen, use the scroll bars to go to the bottom of the table.

4. Start entering the data. The heading row shows precisely which column to enter it in.

Rank	Name	County	State	Yes	No
1.	Claris	Rosemund	CO	x	
2.	Retsh	Pitsmine	NM		x
32.	Hectane	Duford	MO		x
33.	DuLeen	Riverside	CA		x
34.	Ng	Meetch	WA	x	
35.					

3. Draw on Tables to Highlight the Important Stuff   By "draw" I mean to use the Oval button or Draw button on the Drawing toolbar to circle or point to important places in a table. "Drawing Lines and Shapes" in Chapter 13 explains the many lines and shapes you can draw. "When Objects Overlap: Choosing Which Appears Above the Other" in the same chapter explains how to make the lines appear on top of the table where they can be seen. While you're in Chapter 13, check out "Changing the Size and Shape of Objects" and "Rotating and Flipping Objects" to learn how to make the line or circle on your table look just right.

1994	1995	1996	1997	1998
Mark McGuire's Home Runs				
53	51	52	58	70

4. Use the Table | Table AutoFormat Command to Decorate Tables   Some people go to school for years to learn how to format tables. They spend many hours playing with the commands for drawing borders on tables. They learn the numerous and sundry ways to slap gray shades and color on tables. Other people, however, simply rely on the Table | Table AutoFormat command. And these people get very nice tables with hardly any effort. See "Letting the Table AutoFormat Command Do the Work," earlier in this chapter, if formatting a table with minimum effort appeals to you.

5. Learn the Ways to Make a Table Fit on a Single Page   About a fourth of the way into this chapter, "Making a Table Fit on One Page" offers four techniques for making a table fit on one page. Tables have a habit of getting wider, but with the four techniques explained there and listed here you can keep tables from growing too wide:

- Shrink the font size.
- Turn the heading row on its ear.
- Try combining columns.
- Change the page orientation.

6. Right-Click to Give Commands in Tables   All the great word processors, the ones who can whip up a table faster than a chef can whip up a soufflé, right-click to give commands in tables. Try selecting a row or two and right-clicking the rows to see the advantages of right-clicking: The menu presents commands for inserting and deleting rows. Select a column and right-click, on the other hand, and you get commands for inserting and deleting columns. Almost anything you can do from the Table menu on the main menu bar can be done faster by right-clicking.

7. Take Advantage of the Distribute Commands   Rather than tug at row borders and column borders to make them the right size, get used to using the Distribute Rows Evenly and Distribute Columns Evenly commands. As "Changing the Size of Rows and Columns" explains earlier in this chapter, the commands do the following:

- **Distribute Rows Evenly**   Makes each row as tall as the tallest row in the group of rows you selected. All you have to do to make rows a uniform size is shrink them, make one the right size, select all the rows, and give the Distribute Rows Evenly command. You end up with rows of the same size.
- **Distribute Columns Evenly**   Makes each column you choose the same width. To determine the width of the columns, Word takes the average width of the columns you selected and applies it to all the columns.

8. Take Advantage of the Align Commands   As "Centering, Aligning, and Justifying the Text" explains earlier in this chapter, Word offers no less than nine different ways to align data in table cells. And experimenting with the nine different ways is easy. All you have to do is select the cells, click the arrow next to the Align button on the Tables and Borders toolbar, and choose one of the nine options.

9. Use the Optional Hyphen to Fix Spacing Problems   "Hyphenating Text" in Chapter 7 explains how you can insert an optional hyphen to break a word and make part of it go to the next line. In table cells, long words can create awkward white spaces, but you can fix that problem by pressing CTRL-hyphen (the hyphen next to the 0, not the one on the numeric keypad) to insert a hyphen and break the word to remove the white space.

10. Press ENTER in the First Cell to Put a Blank Line Above a Table   Here's a little trick that prevents claustrophobia: Click in the first cell in a table, to the left of text if any text is in the first cell, and press ENTER. Doing so enters a blank line above the table.

    This little trick seems hardly worth mentioning or remembering until the day you open a new document, create a new table in the document, and want to write a line or two above the table. Unless you know the little trick, you won't be able to do that. You will be trapped inside your table. You will start to feel itchy and begin suffering from claustrophobia.

PROFESSIONAL-LOOKING
DOCUMENTS WITH
WORD 2002

Chapter 15

Working on Newsletters, Brochures, and Forms

T his chapter explains a few tried-and-true techniques for creating newsletters, brochures, forms, and online forms. You will find instructions here for running text in newspaper-style columns as well as other kinds of columns, and putting different kinds of drop capital letters at the start of articles. This chapter explains how to print folded brochures and half-page booklets. You'll discover the numerous ways to decorate page margins—with clip art, pull quotes, and side headings, for example. Last but not least, you learn ten easy techniques for sprucing up a document.

Drop Caps for Marking the Start of Articles

A *drop cap,* also known as a *drop capital letter,* is a large letter that drops three or four lines into the text. Drop caps appear at the start of chapters and articles, but with a little imagination, you can find more uses for drop caps. In Figure 15-1, for example, a drop cap is used to identify the song titles on the A-side of a homemade cassette tape. Notice as well in the figure that you can "drop" more than one letter at a time.

Follow these steps to create a drop cap:

1. Click anywhere in the paragraph whose first letter will "drop." The letter that needs dropping should already have been typed. If you want to drop a word, select it.

2. Choose Format | Drop Cap. You see the Drop Cap dialog box shown in Figure 15-2.

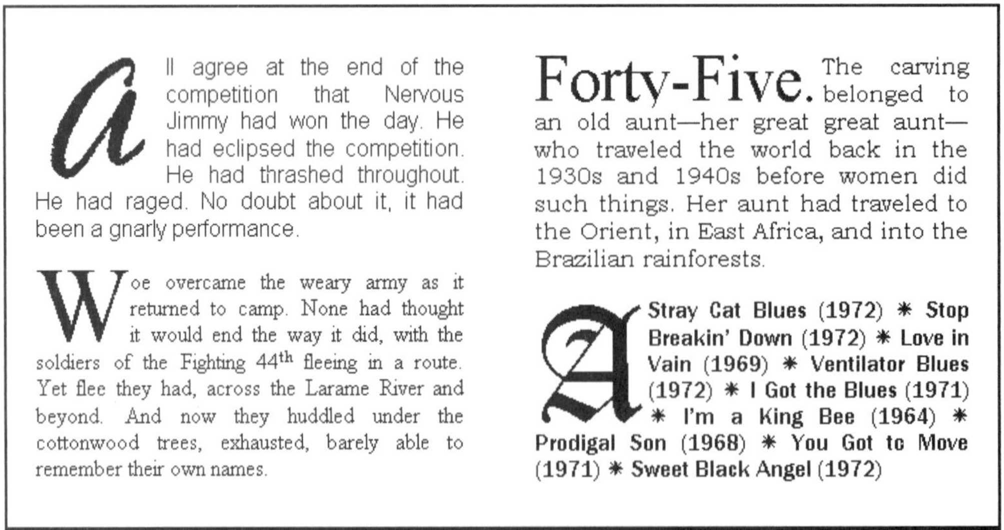

a ll agree at the end of the competition that Nervous Jimmy had won the day. He had eclipsed the competition. He had thrashed throughout. He had raged. No doubt about it, it had been a gnarly performance.

W oe overcame the weary army as it returned to camp. None had thought it would end the way it did, with the soldiers of the Fighting 44th fleeing in a route. Yet flee they had, across the Larame River and beyond. And now they huddled under the cottonwood trees, exhausted, barely able to remember their own names.

Forty-Five. The carving belonged to an old aunt—her great great aunt—who traveled the world back in the 1930s and 1940s before women did such things. Her aunt had traveled to the Orient, in East Africa, and into the Brazilian rainforests.

Stray Cat Blues (1972) ✳ Stop Breakin' Down (1972) ✳ Love in Vain (1969) ✳ Ventilator Blues (1972) ✳ I Got the Blues (1971) ✳ I'm a King Bee (1964) ✳ Prodigal Son (1968) ✳ You Got to Move (1971) ✳ Sweet Black Angel (1972)

Figure 15-1.   *Typically, drop caps appear at the start of articles and chapters, but you can also find other uses for them*

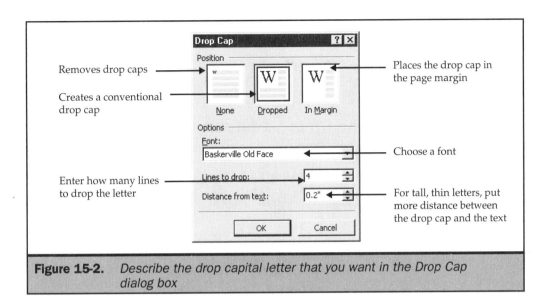

Removes drop caps

Creates a conventional drop cap

Enter how many lines to drop the letter

Places the drop cap in the page margin

Choose a font

For tall, thin letters, put more distance between the drop cap and the text

Figure 15-2. *Describe the drop capital letter that you want in the Drop Cap dialog box*

3. Under Position, choose Dropped or In Margin. The In Margin option puts the drop cap in the margin beside the paragraph. Use the None option to remove a drop cap.

4. Choose a font for the drop cap from the Front drop-down list. Choose a font that is different from the font in the rest of the paragraph to make the drop cap stand out. And don't worry about choosing the right font. Shortly I'll show you a quick way to change the font of a drop cap.

5. In the Lines To Drop text box, enter how many lines you want the drop capital letter to occupy.

If the letter being dropped is an H, I, M, N, U, or number whose right side stands straight up, enter .2 or .3 in the Distance From Text box. Without a bit of space between the drop cap and the letter, the text comes too close to the drop cap.

6. Click OK to close the Drop Cap dialog box.

The drop cap appears in a frame, a container for text. If you don't see it, switch to Print Layout view. Like text boxes, you can drag frames to change their sizes and positions, but don't bother dragging the frame to alter your drop capital letter.

Follow these instructions to change the appearance of a drop cap or get rid of it altogether:

■ **Changing the Font** Choose Format | Drop Cap to open the Drop Cap dialog box (see Figure 15-2), and then choose a new font from the Font drop-down menu.

- **Changing the Size**   Choose Format | Drop Cap and, in the Drop Cap dialog box (see Figure 15-2), make a new entry in the Lines To Drop text box.

- **Removing a Drop Cap**   Choose Format | Drop Cap and choose the None option in the Drop Cap dialog box (see Figure 15-2).

Stand-Up Letters and Other Variations on the Drop Cap

Next time you are paging through a fat glossy magazine with pictures of scrawny women modeling clothes, pause for a moment to look at the start of the articles. Chances are, the articles begin with a drop capital letter or a stand-up letter. Instead of dropping into the text, a *stand-up letter* rises above the first paragraph in an article, as shown in this illustration.

ℋello and welcome to Reno, the biggest little city in the world, gateway to the state of Nevada...

Personally, I like stand-up letters better than drop caps, but creating a stand-up letter isn't simply a matter of selecting the first letter and giving it a larger font size. Do that and Word puts extra space between the first and second line in the paragraph (the program does that because it is supposed to adjust line spacing to accommodate tall characters, but why it puts extra space between the first and second lines I do not know). To create a stand-up letter, you have to put the letter in a text box, dismiss the drawing canvas, tell Word not to wrap text around the text box, and move the letters in the first word to the right to make room for the stand-up letter.

Switch to Page Layout view or Web Layout view and follow these steps to create a stand-up letter for the first paragraph in an article:

1. Delete the first letter in the first word of the article. You will make the letter you delete the stand-up letter.

2. Create a text box for the stand-up letter. When the drawing canvas appears, start dragging atop the upper-left corner of the canvas, not inside the canvas. By doing so, you create a text box only, not a drawing canvas and a text box, as "Drawing on the Canvas" explains in Chapter 13. "Putting a Text Box on the Page," also in Chapter 13, explains text boxes

3. Type the stand-up letter in the text box. Increase the font size of the letter to make it a stand-up letter. With that done, shrink the text box so it is small enough to hold the letter without cutting off part of the letter. "Changing the Size and Shape of Objects" in Chapter 13 explains how to make a text box larger or smaller.

4. Drag the text box into the first paragraph roughly where you want the stand-up letter to be.

5. Choose Format | Text Box, select the Layout tab in the Format Text Box dialog box, choose the Behind Text option, and click OK. Now the start of the first line overlaps the text box.

6. Click in the first line of the paragraph, press the HOME key to move the cursor to the start of the paragraph, and press the SPACEBAR as many times as necessary to move the text in the first line to the right of the stand-up letter.

7. Move the pointer to the top of the stand-up letter, and when you see the four-headed arrow, click to select the text box that holds the stand-up letter. In the next step, you will adjust the position of the stand-up letter.

8. Move the pointer over the side of the text box, and when you see the four-headed arrow, click and drag the text box to adjust its position. You might have to perform this step several times to make the stand-up letter fit beside the rest of the word at the start of the paragraph. If you are having trouble, hold down the ALT key as you drag. Doing so turns off the Snap to Grid feature. Hold down the SHIFT key to drag straight up or sideways.

Hello and welcome to Reno, the biggest little city in the world, gateway to the state of Nevada…

9. Finally, to remove the borders around the text box so that nobody knows the text box is there, select the text box if necessary, choose Format | Text Box, select the Colors and Lines tab in the Format Text Box dialog box, open the Color drop-down list (the one under Line, not Fill), choose No Line, and click OK. You can also remove the borders from a text box by going to the Drawing toolbar, opening the drop-down menu on the Line Color button, and choosing No Line from the pop-up menu.

Although you removed the borders around the text box, you can still adjust its position and in so doing adjust the position of the stand-up letter. To adjust the position of the text box, move the pointer carefully over the stand-up letter, click when you see the four-headed arrow, and start dragging.

In the Microsoft Clip Organizer are many letters you can use as drop caps or stand-up letters. "Searching by Keyword for Images in the Insert Clip Art Task Pane" in Chapter 13 explains how to import a clip art image (in the Search Text box, enter **alphabet** to find letters). In this illustration, I used a clip art image of the letter "S" as a drop cap.

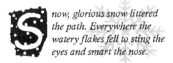

now, glorious snow littered the path. Everywhere the watery flakes fell to sting the eyes and smart the nose.

Putting Text in Columns

Probably the easiest way to prove your word-processing prowess is to run text in newspaper-style columns. Columns look great, and you can pack a lot of words in columns. However, before you get too excited at the prospect of running text in columns, be sure to read "Comparing the Ways to Lay Out Text in Columns," the next section in this chapter. Newspaper-style columns, the kind you get when you choose the Format | Columns command, are not the only kind of columns you can create in Word. In fact, often the best way to present text in columns is by using a table or several text boxes.

These pages investigate the different ways to create columns, how to lay out newspaper-style columns on the page, and how to adjust the position and size of columns. You also learn how to break a column in the middle and how to make a headline straddle columns. Also in this section of the book are instructions for laying out columns in tables and text boxes.

Write and edit the text before you lay it out in columns. Make sure all spelling, grammatical, and clarity questions have been taken care of. Editing text after it has been laid out in columns is difficult and should be avoided.

Comparing the Ways to Lay Out Text in Columns

Word offers three ways to lay out text in columns: the Format | Columns command (or Columns button), text boxes, and tables.

Choose the Format | Columns command and you get newspaper-style columns, also known as "snaking columns." As this illustration shows, text winds from column to column in newspaper-style columns. When text reaches the bottom of one column, it "snakes" to the top of the next column.

Newspaper-style columns are fine for simple newsletters and multicolumn brochures. Drawing lines between columns is easy with the Format | Columns command. And changing the width and length of columns is easy, too. However, newspaper-style columns present more than a few layout problems:

■ The columns occupy the width of the page. Reserving a third of the page for normal text and the other two-thirds for newspaper-style columns is impossible. With newspaper-style columns, it's the width of the page or nothing at all.

- For practical purposes, you can't present one article in one column and another article in another column because text "snakes" from column to column. Unless the article in the left-hand column ends precisely at the bottom of the left-hand column, text from the first article floods the next column and pushes the second article down the page.

- Because columns "snake," you can't present the first half of an article on one page, break it off, and continue the article on another page. When text in a column reaches the bottom of the page, it goes directly to the next page. You can't make text jump two pages or three pages deeper into a document.

- Word creates a new section for newspaper-style columns. That can be a bother in a document with headers and footers that change from section to section. "Section Breaks for Changing Layouts" in Chapter 9 explains sections.

In my experience, newspaper-style columns are fine when they are confined to a single page. As the previous illustration shows, two or three columns on a page with normal text above and normal text below looks very good and presents hardly any layout problems. But if you want to do any serious layout work in columns, you need to think about text boxes as a means of presenting text in columns.

Laying out columns in text boxes is more difficult than laying out newspaper-style columns, but text boxes solve all the problems caused by newspaper-style columns. As this illustration shows, you can present one article on the left side of the page and a second article on the right side of the page. Instead of text snaking from column to column, you can make text go wherever you please when it reaches the end of a column. In an 8-page newsletter, for example, an article can start on page 1 and finish on page 8. Later in this chapter, "Using Text Boxes to Present Text in Columns" explains the ins and outs of laying out columns in text boxes.

The last way to present text in columns is to lay out the columns in a two-, three-, or four-column table. Go this route when the entries in the columns have to refer to one another. In a résumé, for example, entries in the first column (the job title column, for example) refer to entries in the second column (the job description column). If you try to lay out a résumé with the Format | Columns command, you are asking for trouble. Because text snakes from column to column, lining up entries in the first and second column would be a monumental chore. A better way to lay out a résumé is to create a two-column table and then erase the table boundaries so that no one knows the columns were laid out in a table, as was done in this illustration. Later in this chapter, "Using Tables to Present Text in Columns" explains how easy laying out columns in a table is.

John Harqueford   411 E. Fordham Pl. , New York, NY 38790 (888)555-1212 john@email.com

Résumé

Job Title   **Description**

Poacher   Poached exotic animals from important places without
4/98–11/99   anybody knowing it. Duties included locating animals to
                       poach and then poaching them. Developed advanced
                       poaching procedures pursuant to my duties as a poacher.

Roustabout   Rousted around and did various things. Was voted
12/97–2/98   Roustabout of the Year by my peers in the Society of
                       Roustabouts. Developed rousting procedures pursuant to
                       my duties as a roustabout.

Laying Out Text in Newspaper-Style Columns

The fastest way to lay out newspaper-style columns is to make use of the Columns button on the Standard toolbar, but if you want to be thorough about it, use the Format | Columns command. With the Columns button, you get generic columns of equal size. With the Format | Columns command, you can tinker with the width of columns, adjust the amount of space between columns, and draw lines between columns. Columns must be at least .5 inch wide. At most, 9 columns can appear on a portrait page and 15 can appear on a landscape page with a .5-inch left margin and right margin.

Note   *Where the cursor is located and whether you have selected text matters a lot when you create columns. Before you give the command to put text in columns, select the text if you want to "columnize" text you have already written. Otherwise, if you simply click in the text and give the Format | Columns command, you have the option of columnizing all the text in the document, all the text in the section that the cursor is in, or all the text from the position of the cursor to the end of the document. With the Columns button, all the text in the section is "columnized," or, if the document has not been divided into sections, all the text from the cursor position to the end of the document is turned into columns.*

Creating Generic Columns with the Columns Button

Follow these steps to create columns of equal size with the Columns button on the Standard toolbar:

1. Select the text if you have written text that you want to put in columns. Without selecting text, Word "columnizes" all the text in the section that the cursor is in, or, if your document has not been divided into sections, all text from the position of the cursor to the end of the document.

2. Click the Columns button on the Standard toolbar.

3. Drag the cursor over the number of columns you want and click. To get five or six columns, keep dragging the mouse toward the right.

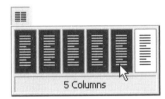

5 Columns

Word switches to Print Layout view if you weren't already in Print Layout view and there you have it—columns of equal size. To determine how wide to make the columns, Word notes the amount of horizontal space between the left and right margin, sets aside .5 inch of space for the area between columns, and divides the remaining space by the number of columns you asked for.

Newspaper-style columns only appear in Print Layout view. If you can't see the columns, click the Print Layout View button or choose View | Print Layout to switch to Print Layout view.

Laying Out and Adjusting Columns with the Format | Columns Command

Follow these steps to use the Format | Columns command to lay out columns or adjust columns you have already created:

1. Select the text you want to columnize if you've already written it; otherwise, place the cursor in a section you want to columnize or place the cursor at the position where columns are to begin appearing. If you want to adjust a column layout, click in a column.

2. Choose Format | Columns to open the Columns dialog box, shown in Figure 15-3.

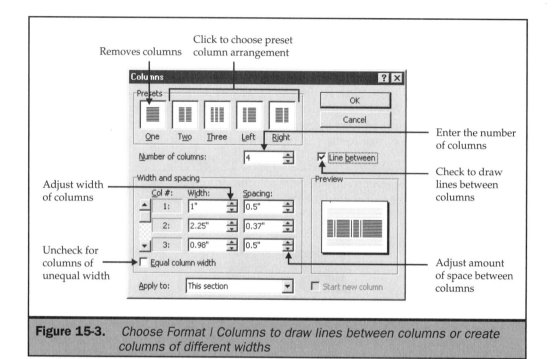

Removes columns

Click to choose preset
column arrangement

Enter the number
of columns

Check to draw
lines between
columns

Adjust width
of columns

Uncheck for
columns of
unequal width

Adjust amount
of space between
columns

Figure 15-3.   *Choose Format | Columns to draw lines between columns or create
columns of different widths*

3. Either enter the number of columns you want in the Number Of Columns box
   or click a Presets option box to choose a predesigned column layout of one, two,
   or three columns. Notice that three of the Presets options offer columns of
   unequal size.

4. Check the Line Between check box if you want lines to appear between
   columns. Unfortunately, you can only place lines between all the columns, not
   between a select one or two.

5. Adjust the width of columns and the amount of space between columns. As
   you do so, watch the Preview box to see the effects of your choices. Be prepared
   to wrestle with the Width and Spacing option boxes, since Word adjusts width
   and spacing settings as you make entries in the Width and Spacing boxes.

For columns of unequal size, uncheck the Equal Column Width check box.

■ **Adjusting the Width of Columns**   For each column, enter a number in the
Width box to tell Word how wide to make the column. Click the down arrow
on the scroll bar, if necessary, to get to the fourth, fifth, or sixth column.

■ **Adjusting the Amount of Space Between Columns**   For each column, enter a number in the Spacing box to tell Word how much space to put between it and the column to its right.

6. In the Apply To drop-down list, tell Word to "columnize" the section that the cursor is in, the remainder of the document, the entire document, or text you selected.

7. Click OK.

Text in columns, especially narrow columns, looks better when it is hyphenated and justified. To justify text, select it and click the Justify button on the Formatting toolbar. "Hyphenating Text" in Chapter 7 explains hyphenation techniques.

Changing the Width of Newspaper-Style Columns

To change the width of newspaper-style columns, either drag column markers on the ruler or open the Columns dialog box (see Figure 15-3) and make adjustments there. If your columns are the same size, you have to choose Format | Columns to make adjustments in the Columns dialog box. You can't adjust the width of columns on the ruler if the columns are equal size.

■ **Changing Column Width with the Ruler**   Drag the Move Column marker on the ruler to change a column's width (choose View | Ruler if you don't see the ruler). To adjust the amount of space between columns, move the pointer over the tiny white line on the left or right side of the Move Column marker. When you see the double arrows and the words "Left Margin" or "Right Margin," click and start dragging.

Drag to change column width

Drag to change the space between columns

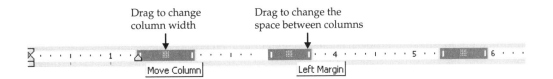

Move Column   Left Margin

■ **Changing Column Width in the Columns Dialog Box**   Choose Format | Columns and change the Width and Spacing settings in the Columns dialog box. Watch the Preview box as you go along to see what your choices mean in real terms.

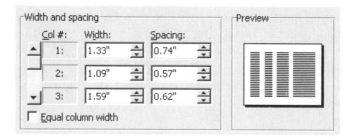

 To make all columns the same width if all are not the same width already, choose Format |
Columns and check the Equal Column Width check box in the Columns dialog box (see
Figure 15-3). You can also click the Columns button and choose the number of columns
you already have from the drop-down menu to get columns of equal size.

Techniques for Working with Newspaper-Style Columns

Making newspaper-style columns fit a page isn't easy. Here are a few techniques for
taming columns so that they land where you want them to land on the page:

- **Moving Text to the Next Column**   Word fills columns whether you like it or
  not, but you can leave empty space at the bottom of a column and move text
  directly to the next column if you want. To do so, move the insertion point to
  the start of the line that you want to move to the next column and either press
  CTRL-SHIFT-ENTER or choose Insert | Break and choose the Column Break option
  button in the Break dialog box, as shown in Figure 15-4.

  To remove a column break, click the Show/Hide ¶ button to see where the
  break is, click the break with the mouse, press the DELETE key, and press the
  BACKSPACE key as well, if necessary.

 Another way to move text to the next column is to insert a text box, clip art image, or
other object at the bottom of the column and tell Word to wrap the text around the object
such that the text moves to the next column. See "Wrapping Text Around an Object"
near the end of Chapter 13.

- **Making Columns the Same Length**   Unless text fills the entire page, columns
  are different lengths. However, you can make all the columns on a page the
  same length by confining them to a section. Click at the end of the text in the
  last column, choose Insert | Break, and click the Continuous option button in
  the Break dialog box (see Figure 15-4). By creating a new section, you confine
  columns to the same section and make columns the same length.

- **Changing the Number of Columns**   Click inside the columns, choose Format |
  Columns, and choose the number of columns you want in the Columns dialog
  box (refer to Figure 15-3).

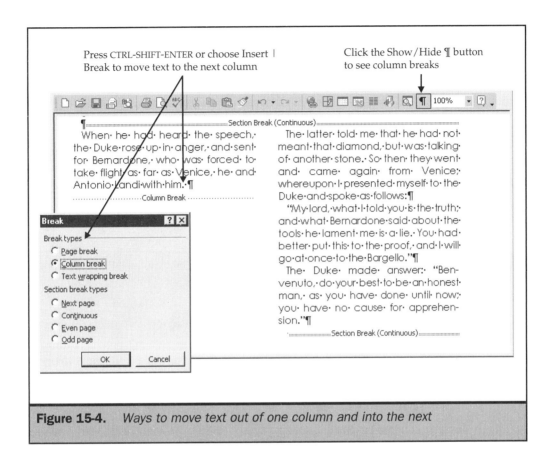

Figure 15-4.   *Ways to move text out of one column and into the next*

■ **Drawing Lines Between Columns**   For full-length lines between columns, click inside the columns, choose Format | Columns, and check the Line Between check box in the Columns dialog box (Figure 15-3). For horizontal lines or lines that run partway down a column, you have to draw the lines yourself with the tools on the Drawing toolbar. See "Drawing Lines and Shapes" in Chapter 13.

To see precisely where columns begin and end without having to draw lines between them, choose Tools | Options, select the View tab in the Options dialog box, and click the Text Boundaries check box under Print and Web Layout Options.

■ **Removing Columns**   Click in the columns, choose Format | Columns, and choose the One option under Presets in the Columns dialog box (see Figure 15-3).

Headlines and Pull-Quotes for Newspaper-Style Columns

As this illustration shows, headlines can straddle newspaper-style columns, and so can pull-quote boxes. A *pull-quote* is a quote from an article that is meant to entice readers. The trick to formatting headlines and pull-quotes is to put the headlines or quotes in text boxes, wrap the text around the text boxes, and then remove the borders from the text boxes. In this illustration, one text box holds the headline and another holds the pull-quote. Notice how text wraps around the sides of the headline and pull-quote.

Follow these steps to create a headline or pull-quote for newspaper-style columns:

1. Create a text box and type the headline or pull-quote text in the box. "Putting a Text Box on the Page" in Chapter 13 explains text boxes. As for the drawing canvas, dismiss it when you create the text box by drawing the box starting atop the canvas's upper-left corner (this and other tricks for handling the drawing canvas are described in "Drawing on the Canvas" in Chapter 13).

2. Drag the text box onto the newspaper-style columns where you want the headline or pull-quote to be. "Positioning Objects on the Page" in Chapter 13 explains how to move a text box.

3. Choose Format | Text Box to open the Format Text Box dialog box. In this dialog box, you will tell Word to wrap text around the text box, lock the text box so it doesn't move on the page, and remove the borders from the text box.

4. Select the Layout tab.

5. Under Wrapping Style, choose the Tight option.

6. Click the Advanced button to open the Advanced Layout dialog box.

7. Select the Picture Position tab, and, under Horizontal, select the Absolute Position option button and choose Page from the To the Right of drop-down list; under Vertical, select the Absolute Position option button and choose Page from the Below drop-down menu. "Positioning Objects on the Page" in Chapter 13 explains all the options on the Picture Position tab.

Horizontal
- Alignment   Left ▼   relative to   Column ▼
- Book layout   Inside ▼   of   Margin ▼
- Absolute position   1.29" ⬍   to the left of   Page ▼

Vertical
- Alignment   Top ▼   relative to   Page ▼
- Absolute position   1.04" ⬍   below   Page ▼

8. Click OK to return to the Format Text Box dialog box.

9. Select the Colors and Lines tab, and, under Line, open the Color drop-down list and choose No Line.

10. Click OK.

You can adjust the size and position of the text box. To do so, click inside it to make the selection handles appear. Then drag a selection handle to change the size of the box or move the pointer over the perimeter, wait till you see the four-headed arrow, and click and drag to change the text box's position.

Using Text Boxes to Present Text in Columns

Earlier in this chapter, "Comparing the Ways to Lay Out Text in Columns" explains that text boxes are the better way to lay out text in columns. A certain amount of expertise is needed, however, to run columns in text boxes. See "Putting a Text Box on the Page" in Chapter 13 if you want to try out the text box method of laying out text in columns. That section of Chapter 13 explains how to create a text box and link text boxes so that text can pass from box to box. See "Positioning Objects on the Page" in Chapter 13 to learn how to place text boxes on the page.

With the text box method of laying out columns, you create a text box for each column you need. Then you link the text boxes so that text can pass from column to column. For example, text can pass from a text box on the left side of page 1 to a text box on the top of page 8. Needless to say, laying out columns in this manner requires foresight and planning, not to mention an advanced understanding of Word, but the rewards are many. You end up with a professional-looking newsletter or brochure, not the fill-in-the-numbers columns you get with the Format | Columns command.

Most of what you need to know to lay out text in columns is explained in detail in Chapter 13. Here are a few tips and tricks to make laying out columns in text boxes faster and easier:

- **Making Columns the Same Size**   Rather than create several text boxes that are the same size, create one text box and copy it. To copy a text box, select it, hold down the CTRL key, and then drag the copy away from the original. Suppose you need to shrink or enlarge your text boxes. Rather than change their sizes one at a time and risk ending up with text boxes that are no longer the same size, SHIFT-click to select all the text boxes or join them with the Group command and then change the size of one box. As you change the size of one text box, all the others change size as well, as shown in this illustration.

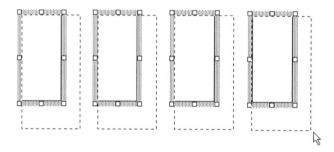

- **Aligning Columns**   The Align and Distribute commands can be very handy when you want to align text boxes or distribute them equally across the page. SHIFT-click to select the text boxes, click the Draw button on the Drawing toolbar, click the Align or Distribute command, and choose an Align option or a Distribute option. "Positioning Objects on the Page" in Chapter 13 explains these commands in detail.

- **Locking Columns So They Don't Move**   Obviously, if text boxes slide from page to page, your newsletter or brochure soon turns to mincemeat. See "Making Sure Objects Appear on the Right Page" in Chapter 13 to make sure text boxes don't slide from page to page.

Using Tables to Present Text in Columns

Earlier in this chapter, "Comparing the Ways to Lay Out Text in Columns" explains why laying out columns in tables is absolutely necessary if one column has to refer to another. By laying out columns in tables, you make certain that entries in the different columns line up correctly with one another. This schedule, for example, shows text in three columns, but really the schedule was laid out in a three-column table. Because the table borders have been removed, only people in the know can tell that these three columns are really a table.

Time	Speaker	Topic
9:30–10:30	Dr. Jacques Arnoux	"*Madame Bovary* and Feminist Theory" Explores feminist themes in *Madame Bovary*, the first feminist novel. Describes the plight of women in rural 19ᵗʰ Century France.
11:00–12:30	Louis Colet, M.A. Dr. Bouvard Picochet	"The Seduction of Flaubert" Examines Flaubert's fascination with things Eastern. Compares his Egyptian notebooks to the two works his trips to the East inspired: *Salammbô* and *Hérodias*.

Chapter 14 is devoted to all the different ways of laying out and formatting a table. After you have entered the text, be sure to remove the table borders so that no one knows how the columns were really made. To remove the borders, choose Table | Select | Table, click the down arrow beside the Border button on the Tables and Borders toolbar, and click the No Border button on the drop-down menu. To see where table columns begin and end after you've removed the borders, choose Table | Show Gridlines.

Creating a Side Heading or Margin Note

As Figure 15-5 shows, a *side heading* is a heading that perches to the left of the text instead of above the text. A *margin note*, like a side heading, perches in the margin, but it offers a bit of extra commentary on the text. Side headings and margin notes are elegant and easy to create as long as you know how text boxes work. "Putting a Text Box on the Page" in Chapter 13 explains text boxes.

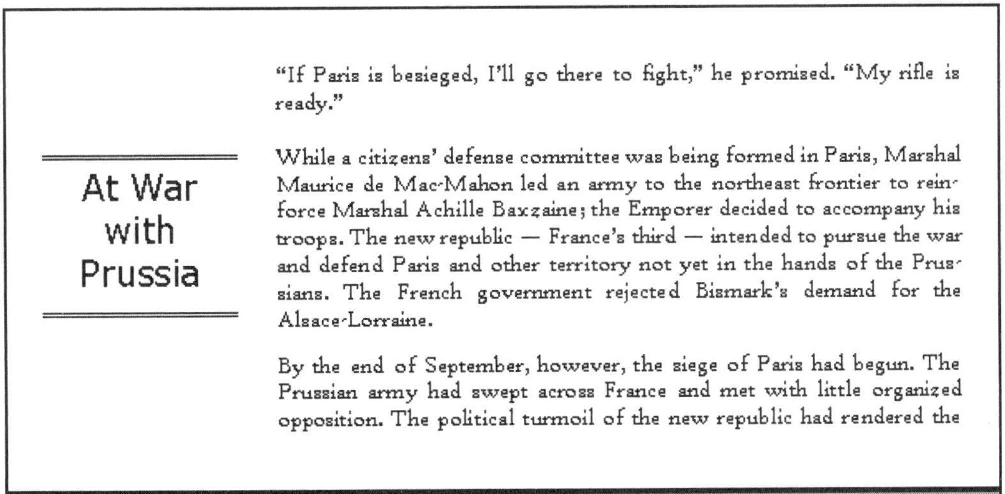

"If Paris is besieged, I'll go there to fight," he promised. "My rifle is ready."

At War with Prussia

While a citizens' defense committee was being formed in Paris, Marshal Maurice de Mac-Mahon led an army to the northeast frontier to reinforce Marshal Achille Bazaine; the Emperor decided to accompany his troops. The new republic — France's third — intended to pursue the war and defend Paris and other territory not yet in the hands of the Prussians. The French government rejected Bismark's demand for the Alsace-Lorraine.

By the end of September, however, the siege of Paris had begun. The Prussian army had swept across France and met with little organized opposition. The political turmoil of the new republic had rendered the

Figure 15-5. *Side headings look elegant and are easy to create as long as you understand how text boxes work*

If you intend to use side headings and margin notes throughout a document, make sure the left margin is wide enough to accommodate them. See "Setting the Margins" in Chapter 9.

 You can't construct side headings and margin notes so that they appear on the outside margin in two-sided documents. Another problem with side headings and margin notes is that, if they are too long and they appear near the bottom of a page, they can fall into the bottom margin. In this section, I describe a little trick to help prevent that from occurring, but the only sure way is to proofread carefully and reposition side headings and margin notes when you put together the final draft of your document.

Follow these steps to create a side heading or margin note and perhaps decorate it with a line or two:

1. Create a text box beside the paragraph that the heading or note refers to. To make the drawing canvas disappear, create the text box by dragging it beginning atop the canvas's upper-left corner ("Drawing on the Canvas" in Chapter 13 explains the drawing canvas n detail).

2. Drag the text box beside the paragraph to which it refers. As long as you place the text box beside the correct paragraph, the text box will be attached to the paragraph and will move along with it if the paragraph gets moved in the course of editing.

3. Enter the heading or note in the text box. You can format the heading or note by changing its font, boldfacing it, or centering it, for example.

4. Remove the borders from the text box. To do so, go to the Line Color button on the Drawing toolbar, open the drop-down menu, and choose No Line. You can click the Drawing button on the Standard toolbar to display the Drawing toolbar. You can, as was done in Figure 15-5, draw borders on all or some sides of the text box (see "Putting Borders and 'Fills' on Objects" in Chapter 13).

As I mentioned earlier, a problem with side headings and margin notes is that they can fall into the bottom margin if you are not careful, as this illustration demonstrates.

> "If Paris is besieged, I'll go there to fight," he promised. "My rifle is ready."
>
> While a citizens' defense committee was being formed in Paris, Marshal Maurice de Mac-Mahon led an army to the northeast frontier to reinforce Marshal Achille Baxzaine; the Emperor decided to accompany his troops.
>
> ## At War with Prussia
>
> 45

However, you can help prevent side headings and notes from falling in the bottom margin by making sure that text in the paragraph to which the heading or note refers always appears on the same page. That way, as long as the side heading or margin note isn't longer than the paragraph itself, the note or heading will not fall into the bottom margin because it will be shunted to the following page along with the paragraph.

Follow these steps to make the text in a paragraph always fall on the same page and thereby maybe solve the problem of side headings and margin notes falling in the bottom margin problem:

1. Click in the paragraph and choose Format | Paragraph.

2. Select the Line and Page Breaks tab in the Paragraph dialog box.

3. Check the Keep Lines Together check box and click OK.

 In Chapter 7, "Creating a 'Hanging Heading'" explains another way to make use of the margin—by creating a heading that appears to hang, or stick into, the left margin of the page. "Numbering the Pages" in Chapter 9 explains how to put page numbers in the left or right margin.

Creating Half-Page Booklets

Word offers special commands for printing half-page booklets. A half-page book is a book that is published on half-size pages. To make it, you print the pages on normal-size paper. Then you cut the pages in half with a paper-cutter and staple them together. Not so long ago, printing pages for a half-page book was a monumental chore because you had to figure out for yourself where to divide the text in the middle of each page to make sure nothing got lost when you cut the pages in half.

However, creating half-size paper has become a lot easier, since Word offers a command for dividing the pages in half. As Figure 15-6 shows, Word runs the text from half-page to half-page and treats each page as though it had already been cut in half. You can include page numbers, headers, and footers on the half-pages. All you have to do is cut the pages in half and staple them together after they are printed. In Print Layout view and Print Preview view, you can see where the half-pages will be divided when you cut them in half.

To create half-page booklets, choose File | Page Setup and select the Margins tab in the Page Setup dialog box. Then open the Multiple Pages drop-down menu, choose 2 Pages Per Sheet, and click OK.

Creating a Folded Brochure

If you have ever suffered from having to lay out a folded brochure, you will find the Book Fold feature, which is used to create folded brochures, very nice indeed. Because different pages are printed on the same sheet of paper, as shown in Figure 15-7,

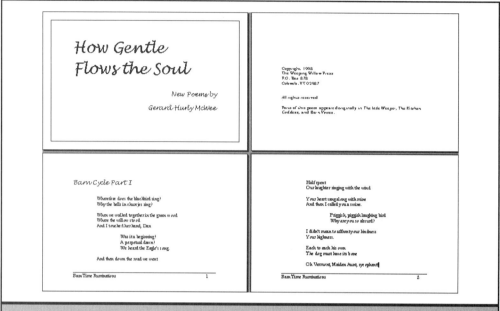

Figure 15-6. *As you work with half-page booklets, Word shows you where they will break after you cut them in half*

creating a folded brochure is a tough task. In an eight-page brochure like the one in the figure, for example, page 1 and page 8 are printed on the same side of the same sheet of paper. On the opposite side of pages 1 and 8, as shown in the figure, are pages 2 and 7.

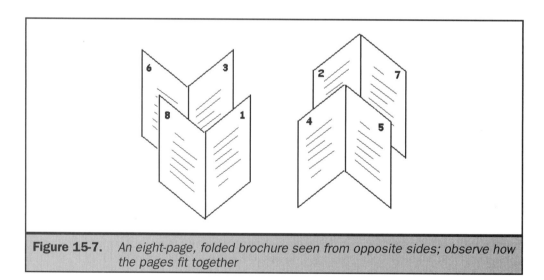

Figure 15-7. *An eight-page, folded brochure seen from opposite sides; observe how the pages fit together*

Complicated, isn't it? Fortunately, Word takes care of the figuring for you. You don't have to worry about putting the right stuff on the right page because Word takes care of it automatically. The hard part, as I explain later, is printing a brochure.

To create a folded brochure, start by deciding how many pages you want. Because pages are printed four to a sheet (two pages on each side), you must choose a 4-page interval for your brochure. In other words, your brochure must comprise 4, 8, 12, 16, and so on pages. You can print a brochure of a different length, but that requires leaving blank pages at the end of the brochure.

Choosing How Many Pages You Want

Follow these steps to tell Word how many pages to put in your folded brochure:

1. Choose File | Page Setup and select the Margins tab in the Page Setup dialog box.

2. From the Multiple Pages drop-down menu, choose Book Fold. As soon as you choose Book Fold, Word changes the orientation of the document from Portrait to Landscape. Word does that to make enough room for pages after you fold them.

3. From the Sheets Per Booklet drop-down menu, select the number of pages you want for your brochure.

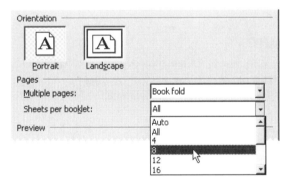

Word offers a special template for creating a tri-fold brochure. You will find it in the Templates dialog box on the Publications tab. Choose File | New and click General Templates in the New Document task pane to open the Templates dialog box.

Laying Out the Brochure

The next step is to lay out the brochure and enter the text, graphics, and whatnot. Don't worry about making the pages fit together correctly after they are folded—Word handles that for you. Here are a few tips for laying out a brochure:

■ Turn on the text boundaries so you can see margins clearly. To turn on text boundaries, choose Tools | Options, select the View tab in the Options dialog box, and check the Text Boundaries check box. Switch to Print Layout view so you can see the boundaries.

■ Don't tamper with the inside margin. As "Adjusting Margins for Bound Documents" in Chapter 9 explains, the inside margin is the part of the page closest to the binding, or the fold in the case of folded brochures. Word devotes a half-inch for the inside margin so text doesn't get lost in the fold. Leave it there.

■ Justify and hyphenate text to squeeze more text onto the page (see "Handling Hyphens, Dashes, and Other Punctuation" in Chapter 7). By nature, brochure pages are narrow. Fill them out by justifying and hyphenating text.

■ Press CTRL-ENTER when you want to create a page break and move on to the next page.

■ Be prepared to edit text to make it fit squarely onto 4, 8, 12, or another interval-of-four pages. For that matter, be prepared to write a gratuitous paragraph here and there to fill out a page. Next time you are reading your favorite magazine, notice how articles end at the bottom of pages, not the middle. They do that because magazine editors snip or tack on sentences here and there to make text fit squarely on pages.

■ Click the Print Preview button from time to time to examine your brochure in the Print Preview screen. From there, you can get a better idea how it is shaping up.

Printing a Brochure

Printing a brochure can be kind of tricky, seeing as page numbers are meaningless when printing brochures. After all, page 1 and the last page of the brochure are printed on the same sheet of paper. To complicate matters further, you have to print on both sides of the paper to print a brochure.

If you want to mass-produce your brochure with the help of a photocopying machine, your task is a little easier. All you have to do is print the brochure on your printer and then copy its pages correctly with the photocopying machine. Start by photocopying the first sheet (page 1 and the last page) as many times as necessary. Then, to print the pages that fall on the opposite of the page 1 sheet (page 2 and the second-to-last page), feed the copied pages back into the machine and photocopy the second sheet as many times as you photocopied the first. Keep photocopying sheets and their opposites until you've copied all the pages you need for the brochure. Finally, collate the pages and start folding.

When Word prints a brochure, it prints the first sheet (page 1 and the last page), then the second sheet (page two and the second-to-last page), and so on. The point is, Word prints each sheet and then its opposite until it has finished printing all the sheets. To print on both sides of the sheets, therefore, you can't just turn the sheets over and feed them to your printer again.

Follow these instructions to produce a brochure with your printer:

1. Print the entire brochure. You can do that by clicking the Print button.

2. Remove the pages from the printer and prepare to send them through the printer again so that they can be printed on both sides. Arrange the pages so that they are fed to the printer in 2, 1, 4, 3, 6, 5, 8, 7 order. For example, arrange the pages of an eight-page brochure in this order:

   - Page 2 and its counterpart (the second-to-last page)
   - Page 1 and its counterpart (the last page)
   - Page 4 and its counterpart
   - Page 3 and its counterpart

3. Click the Print button to print the brochure again.

4. Collate the pages so they are in the correct order. (Notice that there are two copies of the brochure in the stack.)

5. Fold the brochures in half.

Creating a Fill-In Form

A fill-in form is really only a table that has been decorated to look like a form. By making use of the border and fill commands on the Table menu and Table and Borders toolbar, by merging cells and splitting cells, you can whip up a fill-in form like the one in Figure 15-8. See "Decorating a Table with Borders, Shading, and Color" in Chapter 14 to learn the Table techniques for creating fill-in forms.

 The Draw Table tool on the Tables and Borders toolbar comes in very handy when you are constructing fill-in forms. Use the tool to draw vertical lines on the form and split cells.

The fill-in form shown in Figure 15-8 is really three separate tables. The tables have been merged so that you can't tell where one ends and the other begins. Notice how different borders and shading are used to distinguish one part of the form from another.

Creating and Using a Data-Entry Form

A *form* is a means of collecting information. Most forms, like the one in Figure 15-8, are paper forms. You fill them out, hand them to a clerk, and they are filed away for safekeeping. An online form works the same way, except instead of entering every piece of information, you can choose it from drop-down lists or check boxes. Online forms make it easier for you or for data-entry clerks to enter data because nobody has to type in every piece of information. And forms make data-entries more accurate, too, because you can arrange the form so that only entries of a certain type or size can be made in certain places. In some respects, an online form has more in common with a dialog box than a paper form.

The Rug Repairers
4127 – 23rd Street
San Demas, CA 94114

SERVICE ORDER

Name:			Date In:
Address:			
City:			Ready By:
State:		Zip:	
Home Phone:			Order Taken By:
Work Phone:			

Item	Price	Description
		Subtotal
		Tax
		Total Estimate

Figure 15-8. *To create fill-in forms like this one, use the commands on the Table menu and the Tables and Borders toolbar*

Figure 15-9 shows part of an online data-entry form for recording information that was gathered in a survey about software use. To enter data on this form, the data-entry clerk has only to choose options from drop-down menus, click check boxes, and enter the occasional name or Zip code in a text box. In the case of the Zip code text field, the clerk can only enter five numbers (the number of digits in an abbreviated Zip code), which helps ensure that the Zip code is entered accurately. If the clerk had to type all this information, it would take him or her longer. What's more, the chances of entering the data inaccurately would increase, because the clerk might misspell a word. You can even provide Help instructions for data-entry clerks to help them enter information accurately.

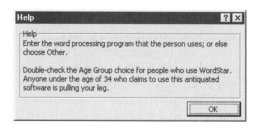

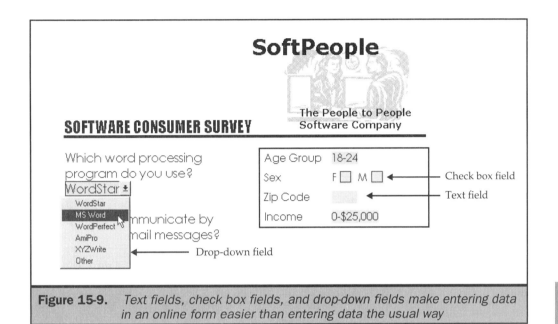

Figure 15-9.   *Text fields, check box fields, and drop-down fields make entering data in an online form easier than entering data the usual way*

In Chapter 12, "Styles: An Overview" and "Building Your Own Templates" explain templates in detail.

An online form is really a template. After you have created the data-entry form template, you open a new document based on the form template, and then you fill in the form. These pages explain how to create an online data-entry template and enter the text fields, check box fields, and drop-down fields. You also learn how to lock a form so that entries can be made only in the fields, the shaded areas where the data is entered, not the other parts of the form. These pages also explain how to include help instructions, make calculations on forms, and fill in a form.

Tip   *If you are trying to edit an online data-entry form and you can't do so because the buttons on the Forms toolbar are unavailable, the form has been locked. Unlock it by clicking the Protect Form button on the Forms toolbar.*

Designing the Form Template and Entering the Form Fields

The first step in creating an online form is to lay it out and save it as a template. Or, if you already created a paper form, you can use the paper form for your online data-entry form by saving it as a template. You can call on all the commands in Word to lay out the form. The commands on the Table menu are especially useful for aligning the different parts of the form (Chapter 14 explains tables). Drop in a clip art image or two if you intend to print the forms after you fill them in. Except for the form fields—the text fields, check box fields, and drop-down fields for entering the data—an online form is no different from a Word document. Be sure to leave blank spaces for the text, check box, and drop-down fields.

 "Creating a Fill-In Form" earlier in this chapter explains how to draw up a paper form. Many of the techniques for creating a paper form work as well for laying out an online data-entry form.

The pages that follow explain how to enter the text fields, check box fields, and drop-down fields in a form. When the form is complete, or perhaps before the form is complete so you don't lose your work in the event of a computer failure, save your form as a template by following these steps:

1. Choose File | Save (or File | Save As if you created your online form from a paper form).

2. In the Save As dialog box, open the Save As Type drop-down menu and choose Document Template (*.dot) from the drop-down list. The Save In box lists the folder where you store templates.

3. Enter a descriptive name for the online form template in the File Name box and click the Save button.

Entering the Text Fields

A *text field* is a place on a form for typing in words, numbers, a date, the current time or date, or the results of a calculation. To enter a text field, click where you want the text field to go, display the Forms toolbar, and click the Text Form Field button on the Forms toolbar. A gray shade appears on the form (click the Form Field Shading button on the Forms toolbar if you don't see the gray shade). Don't worry about the gray shade only being a few characters long. When you enter data in the text field, the field grows longer.

Unless you visit the Text Form Field Options dialog box and make changes there, the text field you created accommodates text—not numbers, a date, or a calculation—and can be any number of characters long. However, by clicking the Form Field Options button on the Forms toolbar or double-clicking the text field, you can open the Text Form Fields Options dialog box shown in Figure 15-10 and change settings for the text field.

The Text Form Field Options dialog box offers these settings:

■ **Type**   Choose an option from the drop-down list to describe the type of data that will be entered in the field: Regular Text, Number, Date, Current Date, Current Time, or Calculation. Your choice is important for making sure data is entered accurately, because entry clerks can't enter text, for example, if you choose the Number option.

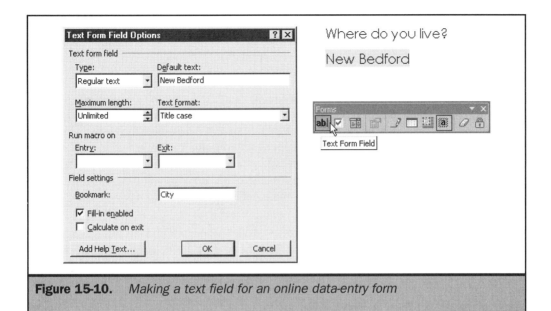

Figure 15-10.   *Making a text field for an online data-entry form*

- **Default**   Either leave the box blank or enter the text, date, or number that will be entered the majority of the time. By entering default text or a default number, you spare the entry clerk from having to enter it. If you enter default text or a default number, however, be sure to tell data clerks that they can override the default entry and enter something else.

- **Maximum Length**   Choose Unlimited or enter the maximum number of characters that can be entered in the field. Your choice here is also important for entering data accurately, since you can prevent too many characters from being entered in the field accidentally. If the field is for entering two-character state abbreviations, for example, enter **2** to keep entry clerks from entering more than two characters.

- **Format**   Choose a format for entering text, a number, or a date.

Note   *To make a calculation on an online data form, place the fields whose numbers will be calculated in a table. Then open the Text Form Field Options dialog box, choose Calculation from the Type drop-down list, and enter the formula for the calculation in the Expression box. You can refer to the other fields in your calculation by using their Bookmark names. "Crunching the Numbers in Tables" in Chapter 14 explains how to enter formulas in tables.*

Macros and Bookmarks for Form Fields

Each Form Field dialog box includes menus for running macros and marking fields with bookmarks. Here is what the options do:

- **Run Macro On Entry and Run Macro On Exit**   Choose a macro from the drop-down list to make a macro run when the data-entry clerk either clicks in the field to enter it or leaves the field by clicking elsewhere or pressing TAB. Choose an Exit macro, for example, to move the cursor automatically to another field in the data form. Or choose an Entry macro to perform a data calculation that bears on what the clerk is supposed to enter in the field. Part VI of this book explains macros.

- **Bookmark**   Enter a bookmark name if you want to use the field entry in a macro. You can then use the bookmark name to refer to the field. Word automatically assigns a bookmark name to each field, but enter your own to keep them straight if you intend to use them in macros.

Entering the Check Box Fields

A *check box field* is a place on a form that you can check off to show agreement or disagreement. Use check boxes in surveys when respondents can choose more than one answer. Like a check box in a Word dialog box, more than one check box can be selected on a form.

To place a check box on a form, click where you want it to go, display the Forms toolbar, and click the Check Box Form Field button. A gray-shaded box appears (click the Form Field Options button on the Forms toolbar if you don't see the gray shade). Unless you change the default settings, check boxes are 10-points high and are not checked by default, but you can change those settings either by double-clicking the check box or clicking the Form Field Options button on the Forms toolbar. You see the Check Box Form Field Options dialog box shown in Figure 15-11. Change settings there and click OK.

Entering the Drop-Down Fields

A *drop-down field,* like a drop-down menu in a Word dialog box, offers several different choices. Use drop-down fields when a finite number of choices is available. All data-entry clerks have to do is click the down arrow to open the drop-down field and make a choice. Or, if the first option in the field happens to be the right one, they can bypass the drop-down field and go to the next part of the form.

Follow these steps to place a drop-down field on a form:

1. Click where you want the field to go, display the Forms toolbar, and click the Drop-Down Form Field button. You see a gray shade where the drop-down field will go (click the Form Field Shading button on the Forms toolbar if you don't see the gray shade).

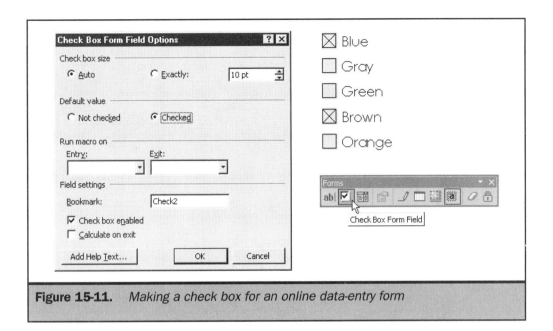

Figure 15-11. *Making a check box for an online data-entry form*

2. Either double-click the gray shade or click the Form Field Options button on the Forms toolbar. You see the Drop-Down Form Field Options dialog box shown in Figure 15-12.

3. Type each entry for the drop-down menu and click the Add button. To arrange options on the menu, select an option and then click a Move button.

The topmost option on the list is the default choice—the one that is selected if the data-entry clerk does not open the list and make a different choice.

Tip *Click the Protect Form button on the Forms toolbar to be able to see the down arrow and open the drop-down list. In order to start editing the form again or open the Drop-Down Form Field Options dialog box, you have to click the button a second time to "unprotect" the form. Later in this chapter, "Protecting a Form So No One Tampers with It" explains how to click the Protect Form button to keep others from changing the text in the form.*

Providing Help Instructions for Form Fields

Especially if someone else will enter data on the forms, you owe it to yourself to enter help text to explain exactly what goes in each field. When users press F1 while the cursor is in a form field, they see a Help box like the one in Figure 15-13. Meanwhile, the Status bar at the bottom of the screen also offers a brief explanation of the form field, as shown in Figure 15-3.

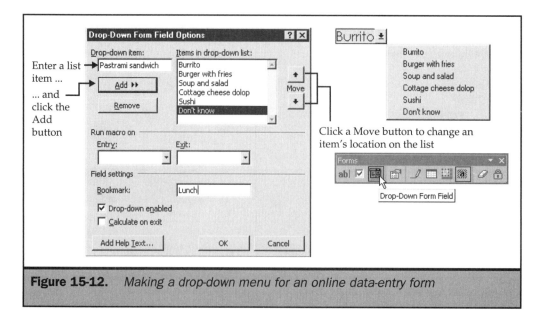

Figure 15-12. *Making a drop-down menu for an online data-entry form*

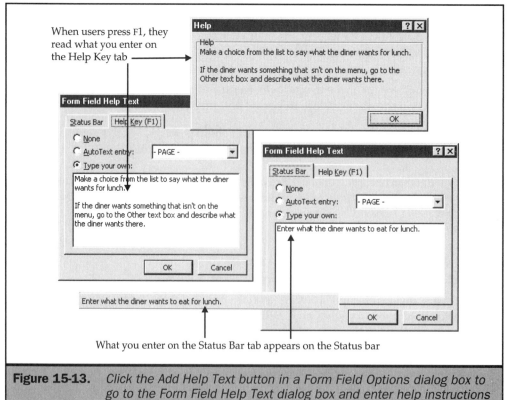

Figure 15-13. *Click the Add Help Text button in a Form Field Options dialog box to go to the Form Field Help Text dialog box and enter help instructions*

To enter instructions for a Help box or the Status bar, either double-click a form field or click it and then click the Form Field Options button on the Forms toolbar. In the Form Field Options dialog box, click the Add Help Text button. The Form Field Help Text dialog box appears (see Figure 15-13). Enter the help instructions:

- **Instructions for the Help Box**   Enter the instructions on the Help Key (F1) tab and click OK.
- **Instructions for the Status Bar**   Enter the instructions on the Status Bar tab and click OK.

Be sure to tell data-entry clerks that they can press F1 or glance at the Status bar if they aren't sure what to enter in a form field.

Editing an Online Data-Entry Form

After you fill out a form or two, suppose you discover that your online form needs editing. In that case, open the form template and edit it. To open a template, choose File | Open. In the Open dialog box, choose Document Templates from the Files Of Type drop-down list and find the folder where templates are stored. By default, Word keeps its templates in the C:\Windows\Application Data\Microsoft\Templates folder. However, if you or the person who saved the template first saved the template in a different folder, find it. In versions of Word prior to version 2000, templates were kept in the C:\Program Files\Microsoft Office\Templates folder, so you might find your form template there. When you have found the template, click it and then click the Open button.

While the form template is open, you can edit a form field by double-clicking it or clicking it and then clicking the Form Fields Option button on the Forms toolbar. You see the Form Field Options dialog box, where you can change settings to your heart's content. If you find yourself unable to edit the form because the buttons on the Forms toolbar are not available, click the Protect Form button to unlock the form.

Protecting a Form So No One Tampers with It

After you click the Protect Form button on the Forms toolbar, no one can change the form except by making entries in form fields. The form labels and explanatory text on the form are untouchable. The Protect Form button is designed to make it impossible for data-entry people to tamper with a form. All they can do is make entries in the fields.

A savvy person, however, could simply click the Protect Form button a second time to "unprotect" the form. When the button is not pressed down, you can change the form. To protect the form once and for all, choose Tools | Protect Document, click the Forms option button in the Protect Document dialog box, enter a password if you so desire, and click OK. Choose Tools | Unprotect Document or click the Protect Form button on the Forms toolbar if you want to be able to change the form. You will be asked for the password if you entered a password when you "protected" your document.

To allow data-entry people to change part of a form but not another part, divide the document into sections. Then choose Tools | Protect Document, click the Sections button in the Protect Document dialog box, and, in the Section Protection dialog box, put check marks next to each section that you want to protect. Unprotected sections can be changed; sections you checked off cannot be changed. "Section Breaks for Changing Layouts" in Chapter 9 explains sections.

Entering the Data on a Form

When your new form is laid out and protected, you can start entering data. To do so, open a document based on the form and get to work. Choose File | New, select the General Templates link in the New Document task pane, select the template you created in the Templates dialog box, and click OK. Then enter the data and save your form when you are done.

"Styles: An Overview" and "Building Your Own Templates" in Chapter 12 explain templates in detail.

The Save tab in the Options dialog box offers a means of saving form data, not field names or other text, in a comma-separated list in a plain-text (.txt) file. Save data this way in order to store it in a database or Word table. Choose Tools | Options, select the Save tab in the Options dialog box, and check the Save Data Only In Forms check box. After you have saved a number of forms this way, you can create a macro that runs the form data into one file. With that file, you can then create a Word table. "Turning a List into a Table" in Chapter 14 explains how to change a comma-separated list into a table.

MOUS Exam Objectives Explored in Chapter 15

Objective	Heading
Apply column and text alignment settings	"Laying Out Text in Newspaper-Style Columns"

Objective	Heading
Create and modify forms using various form controls*	"Designing the Form Template and Entering the Form Fields"
Prepare documents and forms for distribution*	"Protecting a Form So No One Tampers with It"

* Denotes an Expert, not a Core, exam objective.

Ten Ways to Make a Document Livelier

Documents don't have to be dull in appearance. You can spice them up with the techniques described here. Here are the ten best and simplest ways to make a document livelier. Some of the techniques listed here are explained in detail in other chapters, but they are listed here nonetheless as part of my nationwide campaign to keep word-processed documents from looking so dull.

1. Include Clip Art in Your Document   As "Placing Graphics and Clip Art in Documents" in Chapter 13 explains, dropping a clip art image in a document is pretty simple. And you don't have to tell anyone where the clip art image came from, either. Probably one or two naïve readers will think you created it yourself.

2. Create a Watermark for the Pages   A watermark is a faint image that appears behind the text. "Decorating Pages with Watermarks" in Chapter 13 explains how you can make the same faint watermark image appear on every page in a document or section of a document.

3. Wrap Text in Unusual Ways   Probably the easiest way to impress the impressionable is to wrap text around a clip art image or text box. A square, tight wrap looks especially good and breaks up the page nicely. See "Wrapping Text Around an Object" in Chapter 13 for all the details.

4. Place a Border Around the Pages   By placing a border around the page, you frame it very nicely. The title page of a document is an ideal candidate for a page border. And putting a border around the first page of a document is very easy. See "Decorating a Page with a Border" in Chapter 9.

5. Splash Colors on Your Document   If you have a color printer, you have a golden opportunity to dress up your pages in color. Word offers numerous ways to splash color on a document. You can print text in color, put a color background behind text boxes, and draw lines in color.

6. Take Advantage of WordArt   WordArt is a little-used feature of Word, and that's a shame, because WordArt images make good headlines and can do a lot to enliven a document. "WordArt for Bending, Spindling, and Mutilating Text" in Chapter 7 explains WordArt.

Try using a WordArt image

7. Draw Lines Below Headers and Above Footers   Personally, I think no header should appear at the top of a page unless a line is drawn below it. And no footer should appear at the bottom of the page unless a line is drawn above it. The lines separate headers and footers from the main text and help frame the page. "Headers and Footers for Different Pages and Sections" in Chapter 9 explains how to draw lines above footers and below headers.

8. Break Text into Columns   Columns are wonderful indeed, as this chapter has argued so eloquently. Use the Format | Columns command to lay out newspaper-style columns on a single page. For sophisticated columns, lay out the columns in text boxes. For documents such as résumés and schedules in which text in each column has to line up correctly, lay out the columns in tables.

9. Throw in a Drop Cap   The start of this chapter explains precisely how easy it is to put a drop cap at the beginning of an article or chapter. Pound for pound, drop caps are the easiest layout trick there is in Word.

10. Make Use of Word's "Text Effects"   The "text effects" in the Font dialog box are very good for headings. Experiment with the Shadow, Outline, Emboss, and Engrave effects to see what happens. "Playing with Word's 'Text Effects'" in Chapter 7 explains the text effects in detail.

The
Complete
Reference

Word
2002

Part IV

Using Word at the Office

The
Complete
Reference

Word
2002

Chapter 16

Tools for Reports, Manuals, and Scholarly Papers

This chapter is hereby devoted to anyone who has had to delve into the realm of the unknown and write a report about it. Writing reports, manuals, and scholarly papers is not easy. You have to explore uncharted territory. You have to contemplate the ineffable. And you have to write bibliographies and footnotes and maybe an index, too. Word cannot help you explore uncharted territory, but the program can take the sting out of it.

This chapter explains how to handle footnotes and endnotes, generate a table of contents, generate a caption table, write automatic captions for figures and tables, index a document, and include cross-references in documents. You also find out how to construct a conventional chart, an organizational chart, and an equation.

Handling Footnotes and Endnotes

Footnotes are references, explanations, or comments that appear along the bottom of a page. *Endnotes* are the same as footnotes except they appear at the end of chapters. When you write footnotes and endnotes, you still have to list authors, their works, the dates their works were published, and the rest of the scholarly hoopla, but at least you don't have to worry about formatting, deleting, moving, or numbering the notes. Word handles that for you. When you delete a note or add a note, all notes are renumbered.

Unless you tell Word to put footnotes below the last line of text on the page, footnotes appear directly above the bottom margin. On a page with footers, footnotes fall between the footer and the text. Word numbers footnotes with Arabic numerals and endnotes with lowercase Roman numerals, although you can change that. Endnotes appear at the end of the document, after the final line of text, but you can place them at the end of sections if you so choose. A document can have both endnotes and footnotes.

These pages explain how to write footnotes and endnotes, move and delete the notes, change the look and numbering scheme of notes, change notes' position, and decide how to separate the notes from other text on the page.

The Basics: Writing a Footnote or an Endnote

As the next handful of pages makes painfully clear, you can do a lot to fool with the look and numbering scheme of footnotes and endnotes. But if you are content with standard notes, you've got it made. You can simply use the note conventions that Word provides. Follow these basic steps to insert a footnote or an endnote in a document:

1. Click where you want the *note citation*—a number in the case of footnotes, a lowercase Roman numeral in the case of endnotes—to appear.

2. Choose Insert | Reference | Footnote. You see the Footnote and Endnote dialog box shown in Figure 16-1.

3. Click the Footnotes option button to enter a footnote or the Endnotes option button to enter an endnote.

4. Click OK.

Note   *Later in this chapter, "Choosing a Numbering Scheme or Reference Scheme for Notes" explains how to choose a new numbering scheme or use symbols as note citations.*

What you see next depends on whether you are in Normal view, Web Layout view, or Print Layout view. In Normal and Web Layout view you see the notes box, as shown at the top of the following illustration. In Print Layout view, you go to the bottom of the page or the end of the document or section, where, beside the number or Roman numeral, you can type the footnote or endnote, as shown at the bottom of the following illustration. If notes have already been entered, they appear beside the note you are about to enter.

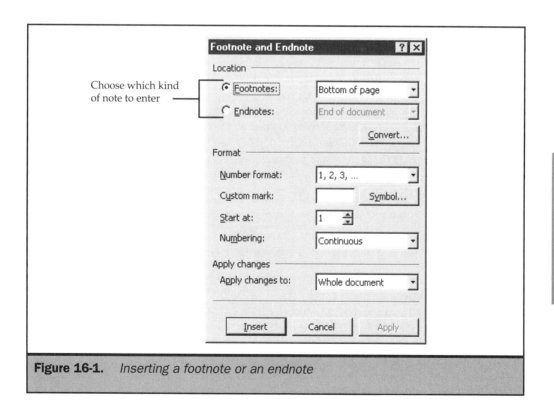

Figure 16-1.   *Inserting a footnote or an endnote*

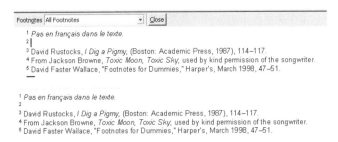

In Normal and Web Layout views, drag the boundary line between the notes box and the rest of the page up or down to make more room to see notes. If your document has footnotes and endnotes and you want to see one or the other, open the Footnotes or Endnotes drop-down menu and choose All Footnotes or All Endnotes.

5. Type the footnote or endnote.

To quickly go to a footnote or an endnote citation from the note itself and close the note box itself, double-click the citation beside the note.

6. Click the Close button if you are in Normal or Web Layout view to leave the notes box. In Print Layout view, scroll up the page.

The fastest way to insert a footnote is to press ALT-CTRL-F *and to insert an endnote is to press* ALT-CTRL-D. *With this technique, you bypass the Footnote and Endnote dialog box and go straight to the place where footnotes and endnotes are entered.*

Editing and Reviewing Footnotes and Endnotes

Word offers a bunch of different techniques for reading, reviewing, and perhaps editing the footnotes and endnotes you have entered. Follow these instructions to ride herd on the footnotes and endnotes in your document:

■ **Reading a Note As You Review the Text**   To read a note in the text without having to open the notes box or scroll to the bottom of a page or end of a document, move the pointer over the note citation. The note icon appears, as does a pop-up box with the text of the note. (If you don't see the box, choose Tools | Options, select the View tab in the Options dialog box, and check the ScreenTips check box.)

> David Rustocks, I Dig a Pigmy, (Boston: Academic Press, 1987), 114-117.

Jonathan Swift's giants were allegorical, not metaphorical.[3]

Citing the Same Note More Than Once

Anything can happen in the world of academics (anything can happen on paper, anyhow), and it might happen that you need to cite the same footnote or endnote more than once. Suppose a word of wisdom on page 8 needs to cite a footnote that already appears on page 2. You can always enter the same note twice, once on page 2 and once on page 8, but you can also follow these steps to cite a note that was cited earlier in your document:

1. Click where the note citation is to appear and choose Insert | Reference | Cross-Reference. You see the Cross-Reference dialog box.

2. Choose Footnote or Endnote from the Reference Type drop-down list. A list of the footnotes or endnotes in your document appears in the Cross-Reference dialog box.

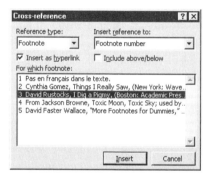

3. Select the footnote or endnote you want to cite a second time.

4. Uncheck the Insert As Hyperlink check box.

5. Click the Insert button.

6. Click the Close button to return to your document. The note is not superscripted like the other footnotes or endnotes, but you can fix that.

7. Select the note. To do so, carefully drag the mouse over it.

8. Click the Styles and Formatting button to open the Styles and Formatting task pane.

9. Under Pick Formatting to Apply, select the Footnote Reference or Endnote Reference style.

If you don't see the Footnote Reference or Endnote Reference styles in the task pane, open the Show menu at the bottom of the task pane and choose Custom. The Format Settings dialog box appears. Check the Footnote Reference or Endnote Reference check box (or check both), and then click OK.

> To read a footnote or an endnote, all you have to do is move the pointer over it, and to edit a footnote or an endnote, you can double-click the note citation to move to the note and edit it. But you can't do that with a citation you enter by way of the Insert | Reference | Cross-Reference command. You can, however, CTRL-click the citation to move to the footnote or endnote and perhaps edit it.

- **Double-Clicking to Read or Edit a Note**   To get to a note so you can read and perhaps edit it, double-click its note citation. In Normal and Web Layout views, you see the notes box, where you can read and edit the notes. In Print Layout view, you scroll to the bottom of the page, end of the section, or end of the document, where you can read and edit the notes.

- **Keeping the Notes Box Open for Reading and Editing Notes**   In Normal and Web Layout views, you can keep the notes box open on the bottom of the screen and always see the notes that are on the page you are working on. To do so, choose View | Footnotes. If your document has footnotes and endnotes, you see the View Footnotes dialog box. Select the View Footnote Area or View Endnote Area option button.

- **Going to a Specific Note in the Text**   Choose Edit | Go To or press CTRL-G to open the Find and Replace dialog box. On the Go To tab, choose Footnote or Endnote, and then enter a note number and click the Go To button.

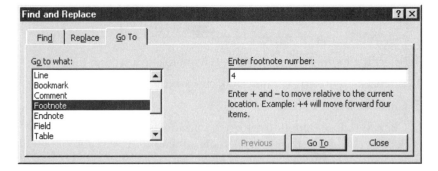

- **Going from Note to Note in the Text**   Click the Select Browse Object button and then click the Browse by Footnote or Browse by Endnote button on the menu. You go to the next footnote or endnote in the document. To skip merrily from note to note, click the blue double arrows on either side of the Select Browse Object button (or press CTRL-PAGE UP or CTRL-PAGE DOWN).

Moving and Deleting Footnotes and Endnotes

Maybe the best thing about footnotes and endnotes is being able to delete and move them with no trouble at all. When you delete a note, Word renumbers both the note citations in the text and the notes themselves. Likewise, if you move a note to the other side of another note, note citations and the notes themselves are renumbered so that they are in the right order:

- **Moving Notes**   Select the note's citation in the text and either cut and paste or drag it to a new location. To select a note citation, carefully drag over it with the mouse. When you move a citation, the note at the bottom of the page or end of the document moves as well if that is necessary.

- **Deleting Notes**   Select the note's citation and press the DELETE key. Notes are also renumbered when you delete one.

To delete all the footnotes or endnotes in a document, choose Edit | Replace to open the Find and Replace dialog box. Click in the Find What box, click the More button if necessary, and then click the Special button and choose Footnote Mark (^f) or Endnote Mark (^e) from the pop-up menu. Then leave the Replace With box empty and click the Replace All button. I recommend saving a second copy of your document before you try this trick. You might need your footnotes or endnotes and regret deleting them.

Choosing a Numbering Scheme or Reference Scheme for Notes

Until or unless you fool with the default settings, footnotes and endnotes are numbered continuously. Footnotes are numbered with Arabic numerals and endnotes with lowercase Roman numerals. You can, however, use alternative numbering schemes, use a symbol for the note citation, or number the notes beginning with each page or each section. Better read on.

Exchanging Footnotes for Endnotes and Vice Versa

Fickle scholars will be glad to know that you can turn all footnotes into endnotes and all endnotes into footnotes. Follow these steps to switch notes:

1. Choose Insert | Reference | Footnote to open the Footnote and Endnote dialog box (see Figure 16-1).

2. Click the Convert button. The Convert Notes dialog box appears.

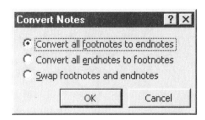

3. Choose an option and click OK to return to the Footnote and Endnote dialog box.

4. Click Close (if you click OK, you will enter a note in your document).

Suppose you want to turn a single footnote into an endnote or a single endnote into a footnote. To do so, locate the note in question (not its citation), right-click the note, and choose Convert To Endnote or Convert To Footnote on the shortcut menu.

Changing the Numbering Scheme for Notes

Follow these steps to choose a numbering scheme of your own for footnotes and endnotes:

1. Choose Insert | Reference | Footnote to open the Footnote and Endnote dialog box (see Figure 16-1).

2. Choose the Footnotes or Endnotes option button, if necessary, to tell Word which kind of note you are dealing with.

3. Under Format, choose numbering options:

   ■ **Number Format** Choose Arabic numerals, letters, Roman numerals, or a series of common footnote symbols (the asterisk, dagger, and so on).

   ■ **Start A** Normally, notes start with 1, a, A, i, I, or the asterisk, but you can start with another number or letter by entering it or clicking the up arrow in this box.

■ **Numbering** Choose how the notes are numbered. You can start numbering anew at each section or (in the case of footnotes) on each page.

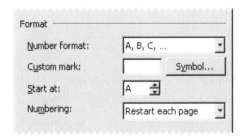

4. Choose This Section on the Apply Changes To menu if you want the numbering scheme to apply only to the section that the cursor is in.

5. Click the Apply button.

Using Your Own Symbol for the Note Citation

I don't recommend using your own symbol for the note citation. If you are fonder of symbols than numbers and you want to use a symbol for note citations, the Number Format drop-down list in the Footnote and Endnote dialog box (see Figure 16-1) offers symbols—the asterisk, dagger, double dagger, and others. Choose the symbols in the dialog box, because if you enter symbols on your own, Word cannot renumber your footnotes or endnotes as you insert or delete them. Word can't make sure you enter the same symbol twice, either. Besides, if you use your own symbols, you have to enter a symbol on your own each time you enter a footnote or an endnote. Still, I guess you could enter a symbol on your own if you wanted to be cute or you want to find out how daffy a document you can make.

To use your own symbol as a note citation, click where the citation will go or select the citation if you want to change it and choose Insert | Reference | Footnote. In the Footnote and Endnote dialog box (see Figure 16-1), click the Custom Mark box and either enter the symbol or click the Symbol button and choose your symbol in the Symbol dialog box ("Entering Symbols and Foreign Characters" in Chapter 2 explains the dialog box). Then click OK to enter the note citation.

Changing the Location of Footnotes and Endnotes

Unless you change settings, footnotes appear on the bottom of the page, right above the footer. Endnotes appear at the end of the section or document after the final line of text. If these locations don't agree with you, you can change them. Footnotes can appear after the last line of text on the page, and endnotes can appear at the end of each section instead of the end of the document. Follow these steps to choose the location of notes:

1. Choose Insert | Reference | Footnote to open the Footnote and Endnote dialog box (see Figure 16-1).

2. Click the Footnotes or Endnotes option button, depending on which type of note you are dealing with.

3. Choose an option from the drop-down list.

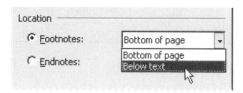 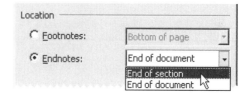

4. Click the Apply button.

You can only see the location of notes on the page in Print Layout view. In Normal view, notes appear in the Notes box.

Changing the Appearance of Footnotes and Endnotes

To change the type size, font, distance by which note citations are superscripted, or otherwise change the appearance of footnotes and endnotes, you need to modify the footnote and endnote styles. Chapter 12 explains styles and how to modify them. By changing styles, you make sure that all the citations and notes in your document keep the same appearance.

Alter these styles if you want to change the appearance of footnotes and endnotes:

- **Footnote Text**   Text in footnotes is 10 points high and takes the default font.
- **Footnote Reference**   Citation notes are superscripted and take the default font.
- **Endnote Text**   Text in endnotes is 10 points high and takes the default font.
- **Endnote Reference**   Citation notes are superscripted and take the default font.

To modify a note style, select a citation if a reference is what you want to modify, or simply click a note if a note is what you want to modify. Then click the Styles and Formatting button. The name of the style you want to modify appears at the top of the Styles and Formatting task pane (if it doesn't appear, open the Show drop-down menu at the bottom of the task pane, choose Custom, check the Footnote Reference or Endnote Reference check box (or check both) in the Format Settings dialog box, and click OK). Open the style's drop-down menu and choose Modify to start modifying (and turn to "Modifying a Style" in Chapter 12 if you need help).

Dealing with Note Separators

A *note separator* is the line that marks where the main text ends and the footnotes or endnotes begin. By default, the note separator is a 2-inch horizontal line, as shown in Figure 16-2. If the notes are too numerous or too long to fit on a single page, Word scoots them to the next page and draws a *note continuation separator* over the notes, as shown in Figure 16-2. At 6 inches, a note continuation separator is longer than a note separator. If you so desire, you can also handle long notes by entering a *note continuation notice*, a brief reminder that notes continue on the next page, as shown in Figure 16-2. You type the note continuation notice yourself.

All changes to note separators have to be made in Normal view, not Print Layout view. Switch to Normal view and choose View | Footnotes to see the notes box (if your document has footnotes and endnotes, choose to see footnotes or endnotes in the View Footnotes dialog box and click OK). Then follow these steps to alter the separators or enter a continuation notice:

- **Change or remove the Note Separator**   Choose Note Separator on the drop-down menu. You see the separator line. Erase the line if you want to remove the separator. To enter a new line, use keys on the keyboard such as the hyphen or equal key and start drawing.

- **Change or remove the Note Continuation Separator**   Choose Note Continuation Separator on the drop-down menu, remove the line, and use the keys on the keyboard to draw this line, too, if you want a new line.

- **Enter a Note Continuation Notice**   Choose Note Continuation Notice and type a brief notice to the effect that footnotes or endnotes continue on the next page.

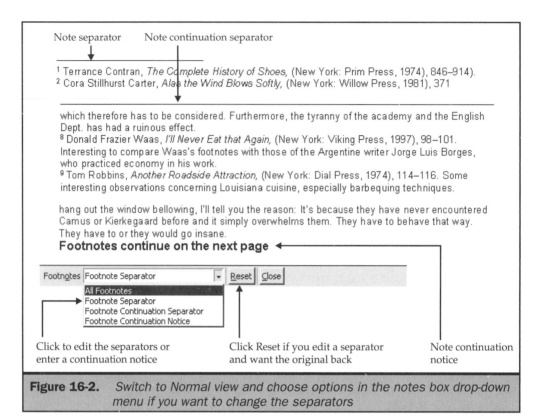

Note separator   Note continuation separator

[1] Terrance Contran, *The Complete History of Shoes,* (New York: Prim Press, 1974), 846–914).
[2] Cora Stillhurst Carter, *Alas the Wind Blows Softly,* (New York: Willow Press, 1981), 371

which therefore has to be considered. Furthermore, the tyranny of the academy and the English Dept. has had a ruinous effect.
[8] Donald Frazier Waas, *I'll Never Eat that Again,* (New York: Viking Press, 1997), 98–101. Interesting to compare Waas's footnotes with those of the Argentine writer Jorge Luis Borges, who practiced economy in his work.
[9] Tom Robbins, *Another Roadside Attraction,* (New York: Dial Press, 1974), 114–116. Some interesting observations concerning Louisiana cuisine, especially barbequing techniques.

hang out the window bellowing, I'll tell you the reason: It's because they have never encountered Camus or Kierkegaard before and it simply overwhelms them. They have to behave that way. They have to or they would go insane.
Footnotes continue on the next page

Footnotes | Footnote Separator ▾ | Reset | Close

All Footnotes
Footnote Separator
Footnote Continuation Separator
Footnote Continuation Notice

Click to edit the separators or   Click Reset if you edit a separator   Note continuation
enter a continuation notice   and want the original back   notice

Figure 16-2.   *Switch to Normal view and choose options in the notes box drop-down menu if you want to change the separators*

Tip   *Choose an option on the drop-down menu and click the Reset button on the notes box to start using a default separator again or delete the note continuation notice.*

Generating a Table of Contents

Every reference work of any length needs a table of contents (TOC) so readers can find what they need to find in the work. To generate a TOC, you start by deciding which headings to include. Any heading that has been assigned a style can be included in a TOC without any trouble whatsoever. And if you need to include the odd heading or paragraph, you can mark it for inclusion in the TOC as well. After you have decided what goes in the TOC, you generate it.

Word TOCs are a bit different from conventional ones in that the TOC entries act as hyperlinks. By CTRL-clicking an entry, you can scroll straight to the heading to which it refers. These pages explain how to make sure the right headings go in the TOC, generate it, and update it.

Later in this chapter, "Compiling a Caption Table for Figures, Equations, Tables, and More" explains how to generate a table of the figures, graphs, tables, and what-all in a document.

Deciding What to Include in the Table of Contents

Practically speaking, you must have assigned headings styles to the headings in your document in order to generate a table of contents (TOC). As I explain shortly, you can mark entries for the TOC one at a time, but you may as well type the TOC as do that. Before you generate the table of contents, make sure that parts of the document that you want to include in the TOC are ready to go:

■ Headings assigned a heading style can be included in a TOC. Make sure the headings in your document have been assigned heading styles. Chapter 12 explains styles.

■ Paragraphs to which you assigned a particular style can also be included in a TOC. For example, suppose you are writing the definitive work about the history of comedy in the United States, and your little masterpiece includes profiles of comedians. As long as you created a style called Comedian Profile, for example, and assigned the style to each heading that introduces the profile of a comedian, you can include Comedian Profile headings in your TOC (see "Creating Your Own Styles" in Chapter 12). In fact, as this illustration shows, you can generate a TOC with only headings assigned a particular style.

CHARLIE CHAPLIN — 6

BUSTER KEATON — 12

THE MARX BROTHERS — 15

FLIP WILSON — 19

W.C. FIELDS — 21

Table of Contents Options   [?] [X]

Build table of contents from:

☑ Styles

Available styles: TOC level:

✓ Comedian Profile   1

    Comic Relief

    Heading 1

    Heading 2

    Heading 3

    Heading 4

☐ Outline levels

☐ Table entry fields

[Reset]   [OK]   [Cancel]

■ You can make the TOC refer to the odd paragraph, illustration, photograph, or whatever in a document by marking it with the TC (table of contents) field. Use this technique to include oddball items in the TOC. See "Marking TOC Entries with the TC Field," the next section in this chapter.

Making Sure Your Table of Contents Is a Useful One

Many people are tempted to load down the table of contents with every heading in the document, but putting too many headings in a TOC defeats the purpose of having a table of contents. After all, the purpose of a TOC is to help people look up information. In a TOC that is many pages long, looking up information is difficult, because you have to read many headings before you can find the one you are looking for. In this book, for example, only the first- and second-level headings appear in the TOC. If I included every heading, this book's TOC would be thrice as long as it is now.

On more piece of advice about TOCs: Put the TOC in its own section at the start of the document, number the TOC pages with Roman numerals, and start numbering the pages with Arabic numerals after the TOC ends and the document begins in earnest. If you don't follow my advice, your TOC will appear on page 2 or 3, and the first heading that the TOC refers to will not be on page 1, but on page 4 or 5, for example. Using Roman numerals for the TOC and Arabic numerals for the rest of the material is the convention in book publishing. Study the start of this book, for example, and you will see that the table of contents (and title pages and Introduction) are numbered in lowercase Roman numerals. You won't see an Arabic page 1 in this book until you get to the meaty stuff.

Refer to these sections in Chapter 9 to format the TOC and number its pages:

- ■ "Section Breaks for Changing Layouts" explains how to create a new section for the TOC.

- ■ "Headers and Footers for Different Pages and Sections" explains how to change the page-numbering scheme from section to section.

- ■ "Numbering the Pages" explains how to number pages with Roman numerals.

Word offers a very nice command for placing a TOC in a frame on the left side of the screen. In Web Layout view, choose Format | Frames | Table of Contents Frame. Chapter 22 explains frames and how to create Web pages in Word.

Marking TOC Entries with the TC Field

When you want the table of contents to refer to a particular place in a document, not to all paragraphs assigned the same style, follow these steps to mark that place with a TC (table of contents) field:

1. If you can, select the text that you want to include in the TOC. You'll save a little time that way, but if you can't select text because the text you want to put in the TOC doesn't appear in the document, simply click in the heading or paragraph you want to refer to.

2. Press ALT-SHIFT-O. You see the Mark Table of Contents Entry dialog box. If you selected text in step 1, it appears in the Entry box.

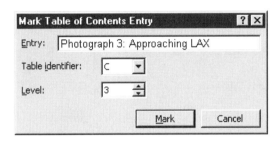

3. Either enter text in the Entry box or edit the text that is there. What appears in the Entry box will appear in your table of contents. You can format the text by selecting it and pressing the boldface (CTRL-B), italic (CTRL-I), or underline (CTRL-U) keyboard shortcut.

4. Make sure C (for Contents) appears in the Table Identifier box.

5. In the Level box, enter a number to tell Word how to treat the entry when you generate the table of contents. For example, 1 tells Word to treat the entry like a first-level heading and give it top priority. A 3 places the entry with the third-level headings.

6. Click the Mark button.

You see a TC (table of contents) field code in your document. From here, you can scroll to another part of your document and enter another TOC field entry, or you can click Close in the dialog box and be done with it. Click the Show/Hide ¶ on the Standard toolbar to hide the ugly field codes and be able to see your document better.

Generating the Table of Contents

With the preliminary work done, you are ready to generate your table of contents. You've made sure that headings were assigned the right style. You've marked oddball TOC entries, if there are any, with the TC field. You've created a new section for your TOC and used Roman numerals to number its pages. You've entered and centered the words **Table of Contents** at the top of the page. Follow these steps to generate the table of contents:

1. Click where you want the first TOC entry to go and choose Insert | Reference | Index and Tables.

2. Select the Table of Contents tab, as shown in Figure 16-3.

3. From the Formats drop-down menu, choose a TOC design. Watch the Print Preview box to see what your design looks like.

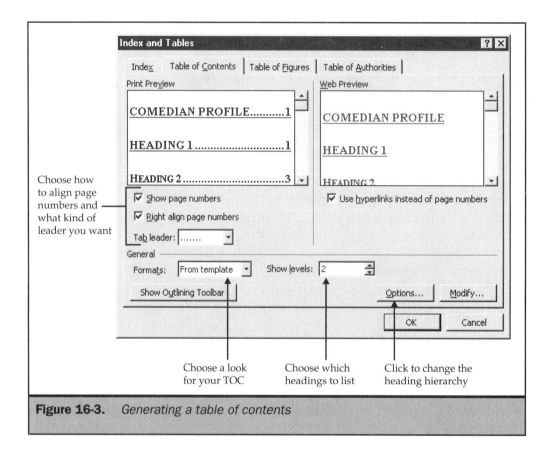

Choose how to align page numbers and what kind of leader you want

Choose a look for your TOC

Choose which headings to list

Click to change the heading hierarchy

Figure 16-3. *Generating a table of contents*

4. In the Show Levels box, tell Word how deep the TOC should be. Entering **2**, for example, puts only headings assigned the Heading 1 and Heading 2 styles in the TOC, as well as headings and paragraphs assigned to outline levels 1 and 2.

Note *"Choosing an Outline Level for Paragraphs" in Chapter 8 explains what outline levels are. When you create a new style, assign it an outline level of 1, 2, or 3 if you intend to use paragraphs assigned to the style in TOCs. A paragraph assigned outline level 1, for example, can be treated like a Heading 1 heading in tables of contents, outlines, and the document map.*

5. Choose a tab leader, whether to show page numbers, and whether to right-align page numbers, and keep your eye on the Print Preview box as you do so. A *tab leader* is a punctuation mark that appears between the heading reference and the page number in a TOC. If you chose note to include page numbers in your TOC, you don't get the chance to choose a leader.

6. Click OK, or else read on if you want to change the rank of headings in the TOC or include TOC entries you made with the TC field code.

Suppose you used the Heading 1 style for the title of your work and the Heading 2 style for the first-level heads. In that case, you must exclude Heading 1 entries from the TOC and put Heading 2 entries where Heading 1 entries would normally go. Suppose your document includes many different styles you created on your own, some of which you want for the TOC. How do you tell Word to rank those styles with the first-, second-, or third-level headings in the TOC?

To change the structure of a TOC or include entries you made with the TC field code, click the Options button in the Index and Tables dialog box (see Figure 16-3). You see the Table of Contents Options dialog box shown in Figure 16-4. This dialog box lists all styles in use in your document. Follow these instructions in the Table of Contents Options dialog box to change the contents of the TOC:

■ **Changing the Rank of a Style in the TOC**   Enter a number in the TOC Level box. The lower the number, the more prominent the heading in the TOC. You can delete the numbers that are already there and enter new ranking numbers.

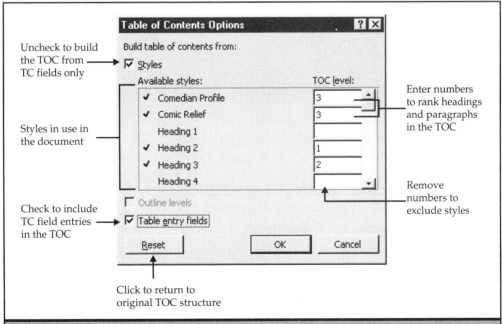

Figure 16-4.   *Click the Options button in the Index and Tables dialog box to change the rank of headings, include styles, or include TC fields in the table of contents*

■ **Excluding a Style from the TOC**   Remove the number from the TOC Level box. Headings and paragraphs assigned to the style in question do not appear in the TOC.

■ **Use Outline Levels to Formulate the TOC**   As "Choosing an Outline Level for Paragraphs" in Chapter 8 explains, you can assign an outline level to a style or paragraph. When the Outline Levels check box is selected, paragraphs that were assigned a particular outline level are included in the TOC if the TOC includes headings assigned the same level. For example, if the TOC calls for Heading 2 headings to be included in the table, paragraphs assigned outline level 2 are included as well.

■ **Including TC Fields in the TOC**   Check the Table Entry Fields check box to include entries marked with TC fields in the table of contents (see "Marking TOC Entries with the TC Field" earlier in this chapter). To construct a TOC from TC fields only, uncheck the Styles check box.

Click the Reset button if you get tangled up and want to start all over again with the default styles and rankings.

Tables of contents are "live," or "hot," to use two popular buzzwords. CTRL-click an entry in a TOC and you go several pages ahead to the heading that the entry refers to. To go back to the TOC after you have clicked a TOC entry, display the Web toolbar and click the Back button (or press ALT-←).

You can unlink a TOC from the headings to which it refers and in so doing be able to copy the TOC to another document and keep the TOC intact. Click in the margin beside the first TOC entry to select the entire TOC, and then press CTRL-SHIFT-F9. The TOC retains its blue color after it is unlinked but is not composed of hyperlinks anymore. Remove the blue color and other TOC trappings and then copy or move the TOC to another document.

Regenerating and Updating a Table of Contents

A table of contents is a field. You notice that right away as soon as you create it. (If you see field codes instead of TOC entries, press ALT-F9 or choose Tools | Options, select the View tab in the Options dialog box, and uncheck the Field Codes check box.) Each entry and page number in the TOC is linked to a heading or paragraph in your document and can be updated as you make editorial changes. Follow these instructions to update a TOC and regenerate it in case you want to change the TOC's formats or heading levels:

■ **Regenerating a TOC to Change Its Look or Headings**   Move the pointer to the left of the first TOC entry and click to select the TOC. Then choose Insert |

Reference | Index and Tables and choose new table of contents options (see the previous section in this chapter). Click Yes when Word asks if you want to replace the TOC.

■ **Updating a TOC So the Headings and Page Numbers Are Accurate** Click anywhere in the TOC and then press F9, right-click and choose Update Field, or click the Update TOC button on the Outlining toolbar. A dialog box asks if you want to update the page numbers or the page numbers and the TOC entries. Click either option and click OK. The only reason to update the page numbers only is to save time if yours is a huge, huge document.

You can edit a TOC entry by deleting a word or typing a new word, but I don't recommend editing TOC entries because, if you do it, your TOC entries will not be identical to the headings and text to which they refer. Better to CTRL-click a TOC entry, go to the heading, and do your editing there. You can press ALT-? to return to the TOC when you're done editing.

Be sure to update the table of contents before you print a document so that the TOC is accurate. To be absolutely sure the TOC is updated, you can tell Word to update all fields before printing a document. To do so, choose Tools | Options, select the Print tab in the Options dialog box, and check the Update Fields check box.

Changing the Look of a TOC on Your Own

As you know, Word gives you many options for choosing a table of contents design. In the Index and Tables dialog box (see Figure 16-3), you can choose from several different formats on the Formats drop-down menu. But if none of the formats suits you, you are hereby invited to take on the task of designing table of contents styles on your own.

To create a new TOC style, choose Insert | Reference | Index and Tables, select the Table of Contents tab, make sure the From Template choice appears in the Formats drop-down menu, and click the Modify button. You see the Style dialog box with its list of all the TOC styles in the template you are using. Choose a style, click the Modify button, and go to it. See "Modifying a Style" in Chapter 12 if you need any help.

Compiling a Caption Table for Figures, Equations, Tables, and More

Occasionally, at the start of a scholarly paper, besides a table of contents, you see a table of figure captions, equation captions, or table captions similar to the one in this illustration. The table serves as a secondary table of contents to help scholars find their way around a work. The entries in the table come from captions—table captions, equation captions, graph captions, and so on—found throughout the document.

These pages explain how to compile caption tables like these automatically. Read on to find out how to mark entries for the table, generate the table, and update it. If you came here directly from the previous section in this chapter about generating a table of contents, much of what follows will seem familiar. Expect to experience acute déjà vu.

Marking Entries for the Caption Table

In order to compile a table, you must have marked the captions. Word offers three methods for marking the figure captions, equation captions, table captions, graph captions, and what-all captions so they can be thrown together in a table:

- **Use the Insert | Reference | Caption Command**   When you use the Insert | Reference | Caption command to put captions on tables, figures, equations, graphs, or whatever, Word can compile the captions into a table very easily. The program recognizes all captions made with this command. See "Captions for Figures, Equations, Tables, and More," the next section in this chapter, to learn about the Insert | Reference | Caption command.

- **Create a Style for the Captions You Want to Compile in the Table**   If you decide to create a special caption style, make sure that you apply the style to each caption that you want to compile in the table. Chapter 12 explains how to create and apply styles.

- **Use the TC (Table of Contents) Field to Mark Each Caption**   Go this route if your figures, equations, tables, or whatever do not have captions. When you mark an entry with a TC field, you enter a caption. When the table is compiled, your caption appears in the table.

Follow these steps to mark captions for the table with a TC (table of contents) field:

1. Click the table caption, graph caption, or whatever. If the item you want to compile in a table doesn't have a caption, click the part of it that you want the page number in the table to refer to.

2. Press ALT-SHIFT-O to display the Mark Table of Contents Entry dialog box.

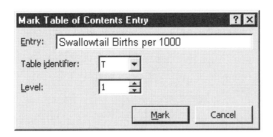

3. Type a caption in the Entry box. The caption you type will appear in the caption table, so type the entry carefully. You can format the text by selecting it and pressing the boldface (CTRL-B), italic (CTRL-I), or underline (CTRL-U) keyboard shortcut.

4. Choose an identifier from the Table Identifier drop-down list. The letter "C" is reserved for table of contents entries, so don't use it. I recommend choosing the first letter of the thing you want to compile in a table: "F" for Figures, "T" for Tables, for example.

Be sure to remember the identifier you select and be sure to select the right identifier if you intend to compile more than one caption table by entering TC fields. Later, when you compile the table, you will be asked for the identifier you choose now. When you compile the table, Word lists all captions given the same identifier, so if you accidentally give the wrong identifier, your table will not include the caption you enter now.

5. Leave the 1 in the Level box. All entries in a caption table have the same level.

6. Click the Mark button.

A TC (table of contents) field code appears in your document (Part VI explains fields codes). At this point you can either scroll to another part of the document that needs a TC field entry or you can click Close in the dialog box. Click the Show/Hide ¶ button on the Standard toolbar to remove field codes from the screen.

Generating the Caption Table

Follow these steps to generate the caption table after you have marked all the captions in the document:

1. Click in your document where you want the caption table to go and choose Insert I Reference I Index and Tables to open the Index and Tables dialog box.

2. Select the Table of Figures tab shown in Figure 16-5.

3. From the Caption Label drop-down list, choose the type of caption you are dealing with if you marked captions with the Insert I Reference I Caption command; choose (None) if you marked captions with styles or TC field entries.

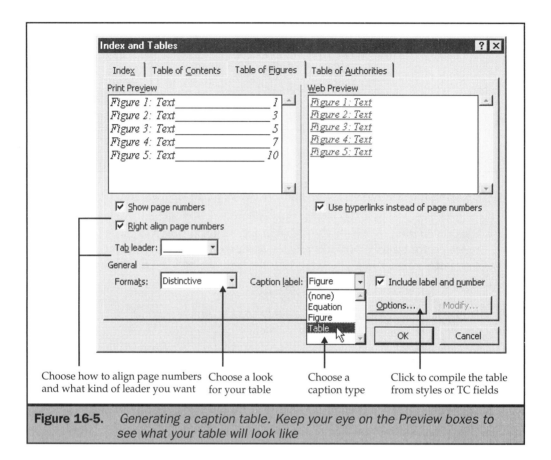

Figure 16-5.   *Generating a caption table. Keep your eye on the Preview boxes to see what your table will look like*

4. From the Formats drop-down list, choose a format for your caption table.

If your document has a table of contents as well as a caption table, choose the same format for the caption table and the tables of contents. That way the two tables, appearing one after the other, won't look jarringly dissimilar and cause readers to blink in dismay.

5. Choose a tab leader, whether to show page numbers, and whether to right-align page numbers, and keep your eye on the Preview boxes as you do so. A *tab leader* is a punctuation mark that appears between the heading reference and the page number in a TOC.

6. Uncheck the Include Label and Number check box if you want the text to appear in a list without a label ("Figure," "Table," and so on).

7. Click OK if you are compiling your table from captions you entered with the Insert | Reference | Caption command. Read on otherwise.

People who marked the captions with styles and with TC (table of contents) fields need to take these additional steps to compile the table:

- **Compiling a Caption Table from Styles** Click the Options button, and, in the Table of Figures Options dialog box, check the Style check box and choose the style with which you marked captions from the Style drop-down list.

- **Compiling a Caption Table from TC Fields** Click the Options button and then check the Table Entry Fields check box in the Table of Figures Options dialog box. In the Table Identifier drop-down list, choose the identifier letter you chose when you marked the caption entries.

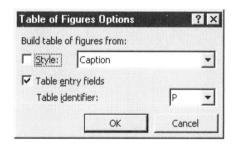

 If you can't remember the identifier letter you chose when you marked the captions with TC field codes, press ESC to leave the Index and Tables dialog box and return to your document. Then press the Show/Hide ¶ button to see the field codes, scroll to a caption you entered with a TC field code, and look for the capital letter in the field code. The capital letter is the letter identifier. In this code, for example, "P" is the identifier: {TC "View of Lake Amoe" \f P \l "12"}.

Updating, Regenerating, and Changing the Look of a Caption Table

Sorry to make you jump and turn to another part of this book, but the very same techniques that are used to update, regenerate, and change the look of a caption table work as well on a table of contents. Turn a few pages backward to "Regenerating and Updating a Table of Contents" and "Changing the Look of a TOC on Your Own" to learn how to update, regenerate, and change the look of a caption table.

Captions for Figures, Equations, Tables, and More

In manuals and reports, sometimes the figures, tables, and equations are numbered for reference purposes. In the book you are reading, for example, figure captions are numbered so that readers know precisely which figure is being referred to. The problem with numbering captions is that you have to be careful to number them correctly and you occasionally have to renumber them when a figure gets deleted or you insert a new figure before others you have already inserted.

To make numbering captions easier, Word offers the Insert | Reference | Caption command. As you enter new captions and remove old ones, the captions are renumbered. You don't have to worry whether the captions are in the correct numerical order. What's more, by means of the Insert | Reference | Caption command, you can make generating a caption table very easy, as the preceding section in this chapter explains.

Word offers built-in figure, equation, and table captions, and you can devise your own caption labels for illustrations, photographs, or whatever. Read on to find out how to enter captions, edit and delete them, and devise your own caption labels.

Entering a Caption

Follow these steps to slap a numbered caption on a figure, an equation, a table, or other item:

1. Select the item that needs a caption.

2. Choose Insert | Reference | Caption. You see the Caption dialog box shown in Figure 16-6.

3. In the Caption box, enter your caption. Notice that you can't change the item number, since Word numbers items automatically. You can put a colon (:), period, or other punctuation mark after the item number if you want. If you do so, however, make sure you do it consistently for every item you enter a caption for. In other words, if you put a colon after the number, do so throughout your document.

4. From the Label drop-down menu, choose what type of item you are dealing with—an equation, figure, a table, or other item. See "Devising Your Own Label" if the item you want to caption is not on the list.

5. From the Position drop-down menu, choose whether to put the caption above or below the item. Again, be sure to choose the same option consistently. Captions should appear in the same place relative to figures, tables, equations, and other items throughout a document.

6. Click OK. Or else read on if you want to change caption numbering schemes or make chapter numbers a part of caption numbers.

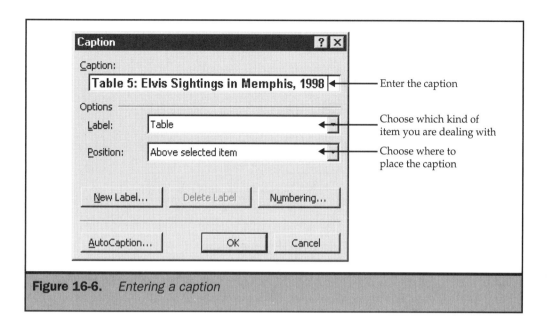

Figure 16-6. *Entering a caption*

Captions are numbered using Arabic numerals, but you can change that if you want. You can use letters or Roman numerals. And you can also attach chapter numbers to caption numbers so that items are numbered, for example, 1-1, 1-2, 1-3, and so on in Chapter 1. However, to include chapter numbers in caption numbers, you must have divided your document into sections and made chapter numbers part of the page-numbering scheme in your documents (see "Headers and Footers for Different Sections and Pages" in Chapter 9 and "Choosing a Heading-Numbering Scheme" in Chapter 10).

In the Caption dialog box (see Figure 16-6), click the Numbering button to change the numbering scheme. You see the Caption Numbering dialog box. Follow these instructions to change the way that captions are numbered:

■ **Using Letters or Roman Numerals** Choose a new numbering scheme from the Format drop-down list.

■ **Including the Chapter Number in the Caption Number** Check the Include Chapter Number check box, make sure Heading 1 appears in the Charter Starts With Style drop-down list, and choose a punctuation mark to separate the chapter number from the caption number in the Use Separator drop-down list.

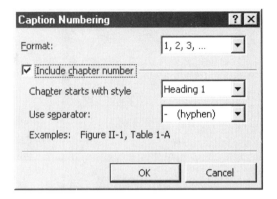

Devising Your Own Caption Label

When you choose Insert | Reference | Caption and open the Caption dialog box, you find three labels with which to caption items in a document: Equation, Figure, and Table. But suppose you want to write captions for illustrations or maps or jokes boxes or photographs? Follow these steps to devise your own label for captions:

1. Choose Insert | Reference | Caption to open the Caption dialog box (see Figure 16-6) if you have not already done so.

2. Click the New Label button. You see the New Label dialog box.

3. Enter a label in the New Label box and click OK.

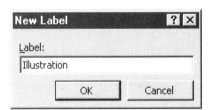

If you need to delete a label you created yourself, select it in the Label drop-down list and click the Delete Label button. You can't delete the Equation, Figure, or Table label, the three labels that Word devised for you.

Editing Captions

Don't worry about caption numbers if you delete or move a caption because Word handles the renumbering for you. The caption number in a caption is a field. As such, it can be updated automatically as long as you tell Word to update the fields. To update a single caption number, click to select it and then press F9 or right-click and choose Update Fields. However, the surest way to update caption numbers is to select the entire document (press CTRL-A) and press F9. Doing so updates all the fields in the document, including the caption numbers.

Be careful when you move a caption that you move the item that it refers to as well. For example, select a table and its caption before you move the table elsewhere.

Apart from the label and caption number, you can edit text in captions to your heart's content. Whatever you do, don't edit the label. Even if you change a figure label in your document to an illustration label by deleting the word "Figure" and entering the word "Illustration" in its place, Word will think it is dealing with a figure label. When Word numbers captions, it numbers them in sequence, so the figure label you turned into an illustration label will be numbered as though it was a figure. If you mistakenly used the wrong label in a caption, don't delete the caption label and enter a new caption label yourself. Instead, select the caption, choose Insert | Reference | Caption to open the Caption dialog box (see Figure 16-6), and choose a new label from the Label drop-down list.

Changing the Look of Captions

To my mind, captions look kind of bulky. Word uses the default font and the boldface style for captions, but you can change the look of captions if you so desire. To modify the Caption style, the style that Word applies automatically to captions that you enter with the Insert | Reference | Caption command, click the Styles and Formatting button to open the Styles and Formatting task pane, click a caption, click the Select All button in the task pane, and open the drop-down menu on the Caption style and choose Modify. Then modify the style in the Modify Style dialog box. See "Modifying a Style" in Chapter 12 to learn how to modify a style.

The AutoCaption Command for Instant Captions

Remembering to write the captions can sometimes be a bother, so Word offers the AutoCaption command. The command enters a label and label number automatically whenever you create a certain kind of element in a document. Whenever you create a new table, for example, the AutoCaption command can enter a caption with the word "Table" and a table number. All you have to do is write the caption itself. You don't have to visit the Caption dialog box (see Figure 16-6) first.

To see which elements Word can caption on its own, choose Insert | Reference | Caption and click the AutoCaption button in the Caption dialog box. You see the AutoCaption dialog box. Scroll the list and look at the items that Word can caption automatically.

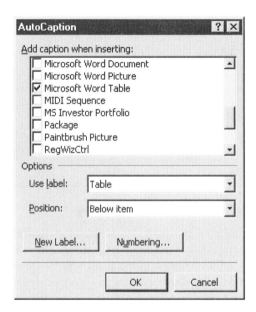

To tell Word to caption a certain item, choose Insert | Reference | Caption to open the Caption dialog box, and click the AutoCaption button. Then select the item you want to caption and choose other options in the dialog box to tell Word which label to use, where to position the caption, and how to number the caption. Finally, click OK.

Next time you insert the item, a caption label and number will appear above or below it. All you have to do is write the text of the caption.

Indexing a Document

A good index is a thing of beauty. No reference work or manual is complete without an index that readers can refer to when they want to look up information. Besides the table of contents, the only way to find anything in a long document is to look in the index. These pages explain how to mark words and phrases in a document for inclusion in the index, how to generate an index form the words or phrases you marked, and how to compile an index. You will also find advice here for editing an index.

What You Need to Know Before You Begin

As shown in Figure 16-7, Word offers four different ways to make entries in an index: a cross-reference, a main entry, a subentry, and sub-subentry. Look closely at the figure and you will also see that index entries can refer to a single page or a *page range*—two, three, or many more pages in a row. To wit, Word offers these ways to make an index entry:

- **Main Entry**   The standard index entry. All entries begin with a main entry.
- **Cross-Reference**   Refers the reader to another entry in the index. Cross-references are preceded by the word "See."
- **Subentry**   An entry that is subordinate to a main entry. A subentry is indented a bit further than the main entry. A subentry is a subtopic of the main entry.
- **Sub-Subentry**   An entry that is subordinate to a subentry (as well as the subentry's main entry). A sub-subentry is indented further than a subentry. A subentry is a sub-subtopic of the main entry. Besides the subentry and sub-subentry, Word offers six more levels of index entries, for a total of nine levels. However, I cannot under any circumstances imagine an index that requires more than entries, subentries, and sub-subentries. Beyond those three, you are merely crowding the index and disturbing the reader.
- **Page Range**   Instead of a single page number, you can cite a page range in an index entry to show that more than one page is devoted to a topic.

Caution   *When you mark index entries by means of a concordance file (explained shortly), you can't cite page ranges in index entries or cross-reference another topic without including a page number in the cross-reference.*

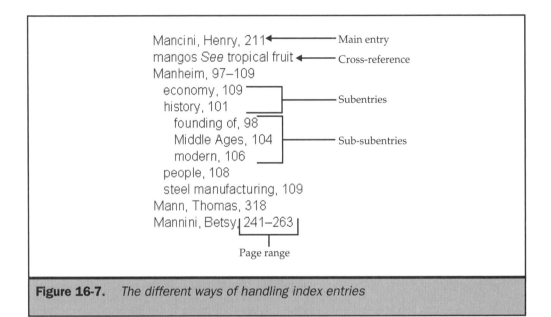

Figure 16-7. *The different ways of handling index entries*

The Two Ways to Mark Words and Phrases for the Index

Word offers two ways to mark the words and phrases in a document for the index: by marking them one at a time in the Mark Index Entry dialog box or by creating a *concordance file* and marking the entries all at once. The concordance file method makes for a quick-and-dirty index that isn't much use to anyone. However, if your index is strictly for show, if you are slaving away in a cubicle somewhere to produce a document that hardly anyone is going to read anyway, you may as well generate your index with a concordance file. You will save time that way. Read on to learn the two ways to mark the index entries.

The best time to write an index is when you are finished writing the document. That way, you can be sure that all cross-references are authentic, you know when more than one page is devoted to a topic, and you now when to enter subentries and sub-subentries.

Marking Index Entries One at a Time

With the one-at-a-time method of marking index entries, you open the Mark Index Entry dialog box, put the box in a corner of the screen, read the document carefully, and mark index entries as you go along. Some people prefer to mark index entries as they proofread a document. Do the following for each part of your document that you want the index to refer to:

1. Click a part of your document that you want to cite with an index entry. If a word or phrase can be used as the index entry itself, select the word or phrase. By doing so, you save a little time in step 3.

2. Press ALT-SHIFT-X. The Mark Index Entry dialog box shown in Figure 16-8 appears. (You can also open this dialog box by choosing Insert | Reference | Index and Tables, selecting the Index tab, and clicking the Mark Entry button.)

3. Enter your index entry in the top of the dialog box:

   ■ **Main Entry** Enter the main entry. Every entry needs a main entry. The word or phrase you selected in step 1, if you selected a word or phrase, appears in the Main Entry box. Edit the word or phrase or keep it. What you enter in the Main Entry box appears in the index.

Tip *As you mark index entries, ask yourself how you would search for information in an index if you came to your document for the first time. Try to imagine how others will look up information in your document and enter the index entries accordingly.*

   ■ **Subentry** Enter subentry or sub-subentry text, or leave the box blank if this entry does not have a subentry. To enter a sub-subentry (Figure 16-7 shows

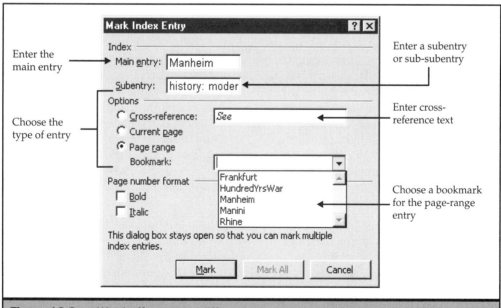

Figure 16-8. *Word offers many different ways to handle index entries*

exactly what a sub-subentry is), type a colon (:) and then type the sub-subentry (see Figure 16-8). Do not enter a blank space between the colon and subentry. The text you type will appear in the index, so spell the words carefully.

If you need to enter a colon (:) as part of an index entry, precede the colon with a backslash (\). Word needs the colon for constructing sub-subentries, so unless you enter the backslash, Word thinks you are entering a sub-subentry. Word enters the backslash for you automatically if you select text with a colon before pressing ALT-SHIFT-X *to open the Mark Index Entry dialog box.*

4. Under Options, decide how to handle the page-number reference that follows the index entry:

   ■ **Cross-Reference** Type a main entry's name in this box after the word "See" if you want the main entry to refer to another entry in the index. What you type in this box appears in the index.

Word does not double-check entries that you type in the Cross-Reference text box. You have to make sure on your own that the main entry you enter in the box is really in your index.

   ■ **Current Page** Click this option button if your index entry cites a single page in the document.

   ■ **Page Range** Click this option button to cite several pages in a row in your document, and then choose a bookmark name from the Bookmark drop-down list. In order to create a page-range entry, you must create a bookmark for the page range ("Bookmarks for Getting Around" in Chapter 2 explains bookmarks in detail). To create a bookmark, click outside the Mark Index Entry dialog box, select all the text in the page range (click at the start of the range and SHIFT-click at the end), choose Insert | Bookmark, type a name in the Bookmark Name text box (names cannot start with a number or include blank spaces), and click Add. Then, in the Mark Entry dialog box, click the down arrow in the Page Range option button, and choose the bookmark from the drop-down list.

5. Click the Bold or Italic check box if you want to boldface or italicize the page number or range in the index entry. By convention, the page or page range where a topic is explained in the most depth is boldfaced or italicized in some indexes. In other indexes, a page in which a figure or an illustration appears is boldfaced or italicized.

6. Click the Mark button to mark the entry for inclusion in the index.

If you selected a word or phrase in step 1, you can click the Mark All button to mark each instance of the word in your document for inclusion in the index. Sounds nice, but this option can be troublesome. You never really know how or where a word is used in a document. By citing every instance of a word, you run the risk of burdening your index with entries that aren't really important enough to be in an index. If you click the Mark All button, make sure the word you selected appears only in a few choice places in your document.

Tuck the Mark Index Entry dialog box in a corner of the screen and use it again when you find the next item in your document that bears citing in the index. All the field codes, including index field codes, appear in your document after you click the Mark button to enter the first index entry. You can click the Show/Hide ¶ button on the Standard toolbar to hide the ugly field codes again.

Marking Index Entries with a Concordance File

The other way to mark words and phrases for the index is to construct a concordance file. A few pages back I vilified this method of generating indexes. The problem with the concordance file method is that you don't get to review the index entries as you mark them. You simply create a table with words and phrases to look for and tell word to blindly include an index entry for each word or phrase in the table.

This illustration shows a concordance file, a two-column table with words to look for in the document and their corresponding index entries. The words in the left-hand column of the table are the ones Word searches for. When it finds a word that is listed in the left-hand column, it records the corresponding text in the right-hand column as the index entry along with the page number on which the word is found. For example, upon finding "dirigible" in the left-hand column of the concordance file table shown here, Word enters "zeppelins, 6" (or some other page number) in the index. With the concordance file method of indexing, you can't include page ranges for entries or enter a cross-reference without a page number appearing beside the cross-reference, which looks kind of ridiculous.

dirigible	zeppelins
Mancini	Mancini, Henry
Eagle Steel Works	Manheim:steel manufacturing
Manini	Manini, Betsy
mangos	tropical fruit:history of
whirligig	merry-go-round
subinfeudation	land tenure:history of

Do the following if you opt for the concordance file method of marking entries for an index in spite of my prohibitions:

1. Start a new Word document.
2. Create a two-column table. Chapter 14 describes how to create tables.
3. In the left-hand column, type text from your document that you want Word to find for the index. What you enter in the left-hand column is not the index entry itself—just the topic of the entry. For example, to make an index entry on Thomas Mann, type **Mann** in the left-hand column to tell Word to look for all occurrences of that name.

Caution   *To be indexed, words in your document must be exact matches of the words in the left-hand column. For example, if you type **eagle steel works** in the left-hand column of the concordance file table but the name is "Eagle Steel Works" (with each word capitalized) in your document, the topic won't be indexed because Word won't recognize it.*

4. In the right-hand column, type the index entries. For example, to create an index entry called "Mann, Thomas," type **Mann, Thomas**. You can create subentries by using a colon (:). For example, to make "Mann, Thomas, early life" a subentry of "Mann, Thomas," enter **Mann, Thomas:early life**.

Tip   *A fast way to create a concordance file is to open the document with the text you are indexing along with the concordance file, choose Window | Arrange All to put both documents onscreen at once, and copy text from the document to the left-hand column of the concordance file.*

5. Save the concordance file when you are finished entering the words and phrases to look for in the left-hand column and the index entries in the right-hand column. Your next step is to use the concordance file to mark index entries in your document.
6. Open the document that needs indexing.
7. Choose Insert | Reference | Index and Tables and select the Index tab in the Index and Tables dialog box.
8. Click the AutoMark button. You see the Open Index AutoMark File dialog box.
9. Find the concordance file, select it, and click the Open button.

Throughout your document, field codes appear where the concordance file marked entries for the index. Hide the ugly field codes by clicking the Show/Hide ¶ button.

Generating the Index

After you have marked the index entries, you can generate the index. Word indexes are run out in newspaper-style columns. The program creates a new section for the index. Follow these steps to generate an index:

1. Choose Insert | Reference | Index and Tables and select the Index tab. You see the Index and Tables dialog box shown in Figure 16-9.

2. From the Formats drop-down menu, choose a format for your index. Watch the Preview box as you make this and other choices in the dialog box to see what your index will look like.

3. Under Type, click the Run-In option instead of the Indented option if you want subentries and sub-subentries to appear directly below main entries instead of being indented. (This option isn't available when you choose some index formats.)

4. Choose the number of columns for your index in the Columns box. If you want more than 2 columns, choose the Run-In option so the columns don't crowd one another.

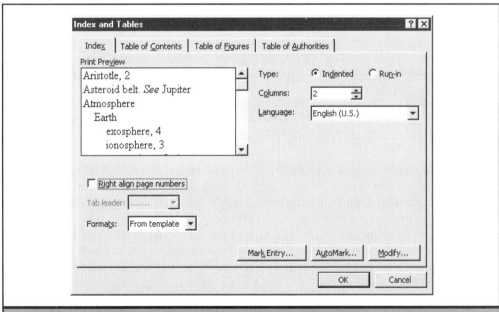

Figure 16-9. *Choose a format and tinker with the appearance of the index before clicking OK to generate it*

USING WORD 2002
AT THE OFFICE

5. Fiddle with these options in the bottom of the dialog box:

- **Right Align Page Numbers**   Check this box if you want numbers to appear below one another instead of beside index entries.

- **Tab Leader**   Choose a leader to go between the index entry and the page number if you don't like the leader in the format you chose in step 2.

6. Click OK.

Note   *If you are adventurous and want to develop index styles of your own, click the Modify button in the Index and Tables dialog box. That takes you to the Style dialog box, where you can choose an index style, click the Modify button, and devise a look for the index on your own. Chapter 12 explains how to modify a style. The Index 1 style governs main entries, the Index 2 style subentries, and the Index 3 style sub-subentries. The rest of those styles are for sub-sub-subentries and their subordinates, which I don't explore in this book in order to preserve your sanity.*

Editing an Index

Be sure to proofread your index after you generate it. Index entries are not kept in the index itself, but in field codes throughout the document, so finding and repairing an index entry that was misspelled or doesn't belong can be difficult. As shown in the following illustration, index entries are enclosed in braces and quotation marks and are preceded by the letters "XE" (for Index Entry). The text of the index entry appears inside the quotation marks. This entry includes a subentry, the words "early life," which appear after the colon.

{·XE·"Sinatra,·Frank:early·life"·}

To edit an index, start by clicking the Show/Hide¶ button on the Standard toolbar, if necessary, to see the field codes in your document. Then look for the entry that needs correcting or deleting. Sometimes the easiest way to do that is to choose Edit | Find (or press CTRL-F), enter the word in the index that needs your attention, and click the Find Next button as many times as necessary to find the word. The Find command finds index entries as well as words—as long as you click the Show/Hide¶ button.

After you find the entry, either delete it and re-enter it, or simply type the correct spelling inside the quotation marks in the XE field code. Just make sure you don't delete the quotation marks or insert extra spaces where they don't belong.

Updating an Index

Before you print a document or otherwise send it on its merry way, update your index so that the page number references are accurate. To update an index, click it and press F9 or right-click it and choose Update Field. To be absolutely sure your index is up to date before you print it, choose Tools | Options, select the Print tab in the Options dialog box, and check the Update Fields check box.

Including Cross-References in Documents

Cross-references are one of my favorite Word features. As you know if you have spent any time in this book, I am a firm believer in cross-references. Why repeat yourself when you can send the reader to another place in a document or book where he or she can learn all the details?

Word cross-references can refer readers to book pages, headings, numbered items such as footnotes and numbers in figure and table captions, and bookmarked items. Best of all, Word double-checks cross-references to make sure all are accurate. If you delete the heading to which a cross-reference refers, Word tells you about it when you update the cross-references in your document. If your cross-reference points to an item on page 26 but the item is moved to page 32, the cross-reference is still valid. It tells readers to go to page 32. You can even turn cross-references into hyperlinks and click a cross-reference to go straight to the thing the cross-reference refers to.

Current Document
CTRL + click to follow link

Turn to "Lining Them Up" earlier in this chapter.

Inserting a Cross-Reference

Before you insert a cross-reference, make sure the thing you want to refer to is really there. Word can cross-reference the following items automatically:

- **Headings that have been assigned a built-in heading style**   Chapter 12 explains styles.
- **Bookmarks you inserted with the Insert | Bookmark command**   Insert a bookmark in a paragraph if you want to refer to the paragraph. See "Bookmarks for Getting Around" in Chapter 2.

- **Footnotes and endnotes**   See "Handling Footnotes and Endnotes" at the start of this chapter.

- **Equations, tables, and figures whose captions are numbered**   See "Captions for Figures, Equations, Tables, and More," earlier in this chapter.

Secure in the notion that the thing you want to refer to is indeed in your document, follow these steps to insert a cross-reference:

1. Type the cross-reference text. What you type depends on which kind of cross-reference you intend to make:

    - **To a Numbered Item**   Type something like this: **To find out more concerning this grave dilemma, turn to page**. Or type: **To see an example of this problem, turn to**. Be sure to put a blank space after the word "page" or the words "turn to" to make room, respectively in this example, for the page number or table caption you are cross-referencing.

    - **To a Heading**   Type something like this: **To discover more about these discoveries, turn to "**. In this case, don't leave a blank space after the quotation mark, because the heading you will refer to comes right after the quotation mark.

2. Choose Insert | Reference | Cross-Reference to open the Cross-Reference dialog box shown in Figure 16-10.

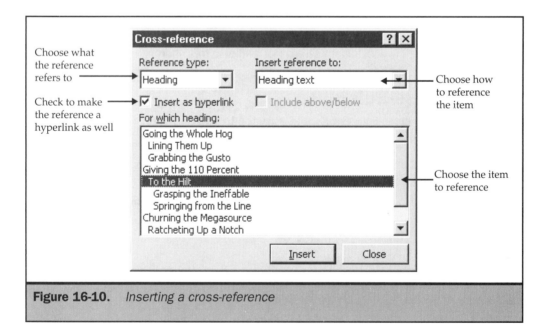

Figure 16-10.   *Inserting a cross-reference*

3. In the Reference Type drop-down list, choose what the cross-reference refers to.

4. Make a choice in the Insert Reference To drop-down list. What appears on the list depends on what you chose in step 3.

5. Uncheck the Insert As Hyperlink check box if you don't want the cross-reference to double as a hyperlink.

6. Check the Include Above/Below check box if you want the word "above" or "below" to be part of the cross-reference. For example, the cross-reference could read, "See footnote 1 below." (This option isn't available for all cross-references.)

7. In the For Which box, select the item that the cross-reference refers to—a bookmark, heading, footnote, caption, or whatever.

8. Click the Insert button and then the Close button to return to your document.

9. Finish writing the cross-reference text, if necessary.

Making Sure Cross-References Are Up to Date

As pages get added or deleted from a document, page numbers in cross-references need to be updated. Since cross-references are usually found throughout a document, the best way to update them is to select the document and update them all at once. To do so, choose Edit | Select All (or press CTRL-A) and then either press F9 or right-click and choose Update Field from the shortcut menu.

Fixing Errant Cross-References

The great drawback of including cross-references in a document is that the cross-reference really has to be there. If you tell readers to go somewhere in a document and the thing isn't there, readers tell you where to go instead of the other way around. Fortunately, Word alerts you when a cross-reference has gone astray. If you delete the heading, caption, footnote, endnote, or bookmark to which a cross-reference refers and then update the cross-references, you get the error message shown in this illustration.

Error! Reference source not found.

To fix errors like those, you have to find them first. After you update the cross-references in a long document, choose the Edit | Find command (or press CTRL-F) to open the Find and Replace dialog box, enter **Error!** in the Find What box, and click the Find Next button. In this way, locate all errant cross-references and repair them one at a time. To repair an errant cross-reference, select it, choose Insert | Reference | Cross-Reference, and insert the cross-reference again, but correctly this time.

Putting Charts in Documents

A report without a chart or two isn't really a report. To help you draw charts, Word offers a tool called Microsoft Graph. These pages explain how to create a chart, enter the data in a chart, and dress up a chart in fanciful colors. You will also find instructions here for importing chart data from an Excel worksheet. When you are done creating your chart, it lands in your document as an embedded object. "Compound Documents: Embedding Data from Other Programs in a Word Document" in Chapter 3 explains what those are.

Creating the Chart and Entering the Data

Each chart is constructed from data of some kind—Elvis sightings in four cities, monthly rainfall in Barstow, annual sales posted by different department stores. The first step in creating a chart is to enter the data so that Microsoft Graph knows how wide or tall or thick to make the pie slices or bars or columns in the chart. Follow these steps to start the Microsoft Graph program and enter the data for the chart:

1. Click where you want the chart to appear in your document and choose Insert | Picture | Chart. The Microsoft Graph program opens. Notice that a new set of buttons appears on the Standard toolbar and that some of the menu names have changed. You might not know it, but you have opened a new program—Microsoft Graph. A datasheet and sample chart constructed from the surrogate data on the datasheet appear onscreen.

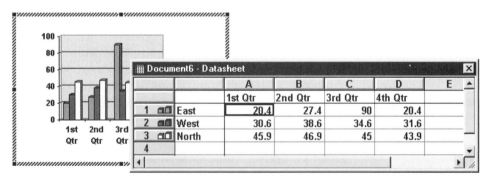

2. Enter the data you want to plot in the chart in the datasheet. For now, don't worry about whether data appears in the right place on the chart. Later, I will show you how to rearrange the various parts of a chart. As you enter the data, observe these technicalities:

   ■ **Entering the Numbers**   Click in a cell—the place where a column and row intersect—and enter data or descriptive labels.

- **Formatting Numbers** Select numbers in the datasheet and click a Style button on the Formatting toolbar (Currency Style, Percent Style, or Comma Style) to change number formats. To increase or decrease the number of decimal places in a number, click the Increase Decimal or Decrease Decimal button.

- **Changing the Width of Columns** If a row isn't wide enough to show data, you see a scientific notation instead of data. To make a column wider, move to the top row of the datasheet, place the cursor between letters, and click and drag toward the right when you see the two-headed arrow.

- **Deleting Data, Columns, and Rows** Drag across data and then press the DELETE key to delete data. To delete an entire row or column, right-click its number or letter in the datasheet and choose Delete from the shortcut menu.

- **Inserting a Column or Row** Right-click a column letter and choose Insert to insert a new column to the left of the column you right-clicked. Right-click a row number and choose Insert to insert a new row—the row appears above the row whose number you clicked.

- **Enlarging the Datasheet** Move the pointer to the lower-right corner of the datasheet and start dragging when you see the double-headed arrow to make the datasheet larger.

- **Excluding Data from the Chart** Click or SHIFT-click to select the column(s) or row(s) you want to exclude, choose Data | Exclude Row/Col, click the Rows or Columns option button in the Exclude Row/Col dialog box, and click OK. To reinclude a row that you excluded, choose Data | Include Row/Col.

3. Click outside the datasheet and chart to return to your Word document.

As shown in Figure 16-11, you see your new chart in all its glory in your Word document. Double-click a chart to open it in Microsoft Graph so you can edit it. A chart, like a text box or clip art image, is an object. As such, you can move it to a new position onscreen or drag one of its selection handles to change its size (see "Manipulating Art, Text Boxes, Shapes, and Other So-Called Objects" in Chapter 13).

Changing the Chart's Layout

Getting it right the first time isn't easy when you are dealing with charts. Fortunately, the Microsoft Graph program offers about a hundred different ways to tinker with charts' appearance and change the way that charts are laid out. To tinker with charts, select the chart and either click buttons on the Standard toolbar or choose Chart | Chart Options to open the Chart Options dialog box shown in Figure 16-12. As you experiment with the different settings in the dialog box, watch the graph—the dialog box shows your graph and how it is affected by the settings you choose. Double-click

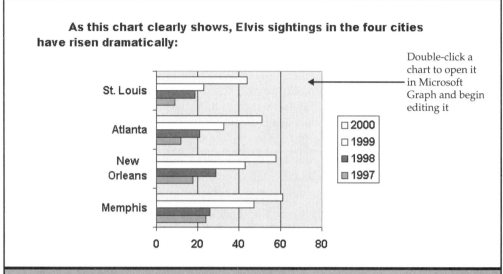

As this chart clearly shows, Elvis sightings in the four cities have risen dramatically:

Double-click a chart to open it in Microsoft Graph and begin editing it

Figure 16-11. *A chart created with Microsoft Graph. Choose Insert | Picture | Chart to create charts like this*

Bringing Data from an Excel Worksheet into the Datasheet

People who use Excel to manage data will be glad to know that you can import data from an Excel worksheet into the datasheet and thereby spare yourself the trouble of entering data for a graph all over again. Follow these steps to use data from an Excel worksheet to plot a graph in Microsoft Graph:

1. Open the Excel worksheet and take note of which data from the worksheet you want to import. Later, you will be asked to name the worksheet you want to import and list the range of cells you want to import as well.

2. Click in the datasheet, press CTRL-A to select all the data, and press the DELETE key to delete the sample data in the worksheet.

3. With the cursor in the upper-left corner of the datasheet, choose Edit | Import File or click the Import File button on the Standard toolbar. You see the Import File dialog box.

4. Locate the Excel file you want to import, select it, and click the Open button. You see the Import Data Options dialog box.

5. Choose the worksheet whose data you want to import, and, additionally if you want to import data from specific cells, select the Range option button and enter the cell range in the text box.

6. Click OK.

Very likely you have to delete a few columns and rows after you import the worksheet. See "Creating the Chart and Entering the Data," the previous section in this chapter.

your chart to open it in the Microsoft Graph program and follow these instructions to make your chart just so.

Click the View Datasheet button to remove the datasheet from the screen and be able to see the chart better. Click the button again if you need to see the datasheet and edit the data from which the chart is plotted.

Choosing a New Chart Type   Open the drop-down menu on the Chart Type button and choose a new type of chart, or else choose Chart | Chart Type and select one of the numerous charts in the Chart Type dialog box. The program offers pie charts, bar charts, area charts, column charts, and spider charts, among other types. Experiment with the different charts until you find one you like.

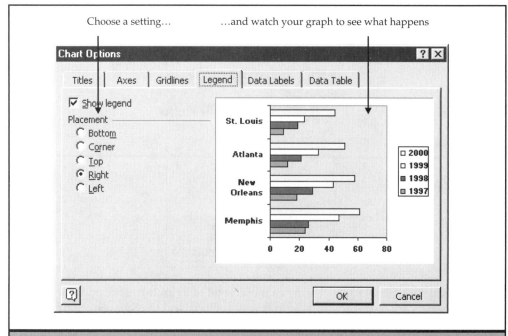

Choose a setting…   …and watch your graph to see what happens

Figure 16-12. *What's that chart in the Chart Options dialog box? Why, it's none other than the chart you are working on*

Changing the Column Data Series Orientation   Click the By Column or By Row button on the Standard toolbar to reorient the graph and change which data appears in the legend and how values and categories are plotted. You can also choose Chart | Chart Options and play with the values on the Axes tab of the Chart Options dialog box.

Displaying or Not Displaying the Gridlines   Gridlines are lines on the graph that mark value amounts. Click the Category Axis Gridlines and Value Axis Gridlines buttons on the Standard toolbar to see or display gridlines. You can also choose Chart | Chart Options, select the Gridlines tab, and check or uncheck the boxes to decide where the gridlines fall.

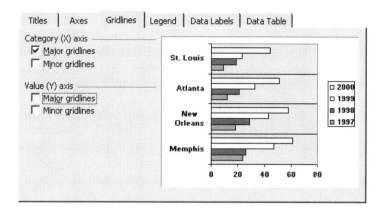

Handling Legends, Titles, and Labels   Click the Legend button on the Standard toolbar to display or hide the *legend*, the box on the graph that describes what is being plotted on the graph. To enter category and value names on your chart, choose Chart | Chart Options, select the Titles tab, and enter the names. Click the Legend tab and choose an option button to tell Microsoft Graph where in relation to your chart to place the Legend box (see Figure 16-12).

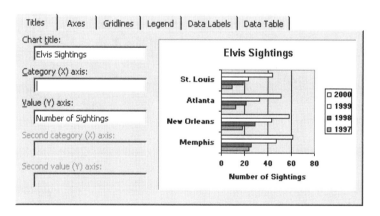

Select the Data Labels tab in the Chart Options dialog box and click one or two Label Contains check boxes if you want to make data labels appear right on the graph as well as on the sides of the graph.

USING WORD 2002
AT THE OFFICE

Changing the Appearance of the Chart   A chart is composed of different areas—the category axis and chart area, among others. The Chart Objects drop-down menu on the Standard toolbar lists all the areas. Try moving the pointer over the different parts of the chart—pop-up boxes list the parts of the chart as you move the pointer around. Follow these steps to change an area's background colors, font settings, or borders:

1. Select the part of the chart that needs changing. Black selection handles appear on the part of the chart you clicked.

2. Either double-click the chart or click the Format button on the Standard toolbar (the button changes names, depending on which part of the chart you selected). The Format dialog box appears so you can choose new borders, fonts, or whatever for your chart.

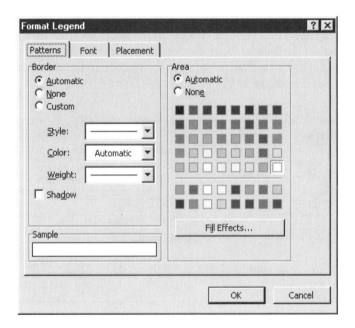

3. Visit the different tabs in the Format dialog box to change settings and then click OK.

   If necessary, choose Edit | Undo and start all over if your changes to the chart didn't work out. Usually, you have to wrestle with Format dialog boxes for five minutes or so before the chart starts smelling like a rose.

The legend, plot area, and chart title on a chart are objects in their own right. As such, you can drag to move them in the chart area. To move an object, click to select it. When you see the black selection handles, start dragging. A dotted line shows where the object will land when you release the mouse button.

Creating Organization Charts

An *organization chart* is a pyramid-shaped chart that shows the top-to-bottom hierarchy of an organization and the relationships between its members. At the top is the Big Cheese. At the bottom are the toiling minions. Somewhere in between are the henchmen (and henchwomen), toadies, major-domos, and scullions.

To create an organization chart, choose Insert | Picture | Organization Chart. The drawing canvas appears, as does a simple, two-level chart and the Organization Chart toolbar. To enter a name in a box, click and start typing. You can call upon the commands on the Formatting toolbar to boldface or center text, for example.

Meanwhile, by choosing options on the Organization Chart toolbar, you can do any number of things to make sure your chart portrays the intricate relationships between the members of the organization:

- **Entering a New Person**   Select a person on the chart who has a relationship with the person you want to add and open the drop-down menu on the Insert Shape button. Then choose Subordinate to enter a person one level below the person you chose, Coworker to enter a person on the same level, or Assistant to enter a person a half-level down.

- **Removing a Person**   Click the perimeter of the box that holds the person's name. When you see the round selection handles, press the DELETE key.

- **Portraying Subordinate Relationships**   Select the person at the top of the chart or the top of a branch and open the drop-down menu on the Layout button. Then choose Standard or one of the hanging commands. This illustration shows, respectively, what the Standard, Both Hanging, Left Hanging, and Right Hanging commands do.

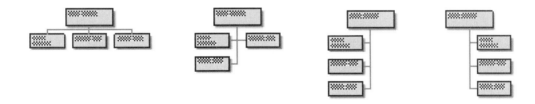

- **Making Room for More Names on the Chart**   Open the drop-down menu on the Layout button and choose Expand Organization chart. Then drag a corner or side of the drawing canvas. (If the chart expands along with the drawing canvas, open the Layout drop-down menu and unselect the Scale Organization Chart command.) Click the Fit Organization Chart to Contents command to make the drawing canvas fit squarely around the chart.

- **Increasing or Decreasing the Overall Size of the Chart**   Open the drop-down menu on the Layout button and choose Scale Organization Chart. Then drag a selection handle on the corner of the chart toward or away from the center.

- **Choosing a Look for the Chart**   Click the Autoformat button, select a style in the Organization Chart Style Gallery, and click the Apply button.

An organization chart is an object. As such, you can drag it to new locations, give it a background, or do any number of things to it. In Chapter 13, "Manipulating Art, Text Boxes, Shapes, and Other So-Called Objects" explains objects.

Writing Equations with the Equation Editor

Use the Equation Editor to place mathematical equations and expressions in documents. After you give the command to start the Equation Editor, the Equation Editor appears onscreen. It offers tools for entering equations. Equations you draw with the Equation Editor are embedded objects. "Compound Documents: Embedding Data from Other Programs in a Word Document" in Chapter 3 explains how to handle embedded objects.

Learning the Equation Editor takes time. Practice using the Equation Editor before you actually try to enter an equation. What's more, the Equation Editor is not installed by default—you have to explicitly install it yourself. See Appendix A.

To start the Equation Editor, choose Insert | Object, select Microsoft Equation 3.0 in the Object dialog box, and click OK. The Equation Editor opens onscreen. You see the Equation toolbar, the menu bar, and a frame in which to write an expression. To enter numbers and variables, you may type them with your keyboard or enter them by way of the Equation toolbar.

If you are new to the Equation Editor, you need to know the following before you enter any groundbreaking mathematical expressions:

- To enter a symbol or number, you start by choosing a template from the Equation toolbar. In Equation Editor terminology, a *template* is a framework for entering part of an equation. Then, in the slots provided by the template, either type numbers or symbols on your keyboard or choose symbols from the toolbar.

■ The top row of the Equation toolbar offers symbols; the bottom row offers templates. To choose a symbol or template, click a button and then make your choice from the drop-down menu that appears.

■ Each template includes one or more slots. A *slot* is a place for entering one number or symbol. The fraction template shown here, for example, includes two slots. Dashed-line boxes indicate where the slots are. When you open a template drop-down menu on the Equation toolbar and look at the options, you can see where slots are in the templates. Slots are marked by small dashed-line boxes.

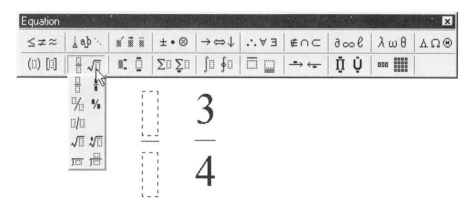

■ The Equation Editor adjusts spacing and formats automatically to conform to mathematical typesetting conventions. Therefore, you can't press the SPACEBAR to enter a blank space, for example. Nor can you boldface or italicize text. Templates grow automatically as you enter parts of an equation. The sizes of the characters you enter are determined by their functions in the equation.

■ The Equation Editor italicizes letters when you enter them to conform to mathematical typesetting conventions, but if you want to enter real text in an equation—a name or word of explanation perhaps—you have to switch from Math style to Text style. You can do by way of the Style menu. Similarly, to enter Greek characters, characters that represent matrix or vector quantities, or abbreviations for standard mathematical functions, choose the appropriate option on the style menu.

 It helps to get a bigger picture of expressions as you enter them. Open the View menu and choose 200% or 400% to get a better look at your equation.

Now that you are acquainted with the Equation Editor, here are instructions for drawing equations:

■ **Going from Place to Place**   Besides clicking here or there, you can go forward from slot to slot by pressing the TAB key; press SHIFT-TAB to backward.

USING WORD 2002
AT THE OFFICE

- **Deleting a Template**   Drag the mouse over the template to select it, and then press the DELETE key or choose Edit | Clear. You can't delete the first template, the one that appears automatically when you start the Equation Editor.

- **Changing the Size of All or Parts of an Equation**   To change the size of one part of an equation, select it and make a choice from the Size menu or choose Size | Other and enter a point size in the Other Size dialog box. To adjust the size of all parts of an equation, choose Size | Define to open the Sizes dialog box. Parts of equations fall into one of five categories. Change sizes in the five categories and you change the size of all parts of your equation. (If you regret changing sizes, return to the Sizes dialog box and click the Defaults button.)

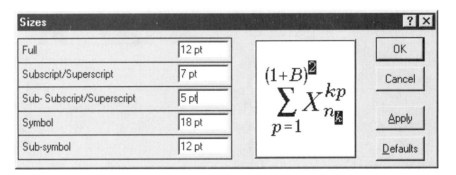

> **Tip**   *The easiest way to change the size of the entire equation is to wait until you are finished constructing it. When you return to Word, the equation appears in an object box. Drag a corner handle of the box to enlarge or shrink the equation. In Chapter 13, "Manipulating Art, Text Boxes, Shapes, and Other So-Called Objects" explains how to handle objects.*

- **Adjusting the Position of Parts of an Equation**   Nudge parts of an equation in one direction or the other by selecting them and pressing CTRL and an arrow key. You can also choose an alignment command from the format menu.

- **Including Text in an Equation**   To write a word or two of explanation in an equation, do so in the text style. To change to the text style, choose Style | Text (or press CTRL-SHIFT-E) and type the words. Be sure to choose Style | Math (or press CTRL-SHIFT-=) to go back to entering numbers and symbols.

> **Tip**   *Sometimes, when you make formatting changes, parts of equations that you altered or deleted remain onscreen. To remove them, choose View | Redraw or press CTRL-D.*

When you are finished entering the equation, click outside the Equation object to return to your Word document. To edit the equation, double-click it. The Equation Editor opens onscreen.

MOUS Exam Objectives Explored in Chapter 16

Objective	Heading
Create and modify diagrams and charts	"Putting Charts in Documents" and "Creating Organizational Charts"
Create and update document indexes and tables of contents, figures, and authorities*	"Indexing a Document," "Generating a Table of Contents," and "Compiling a Caption Table for Figures, Equations, Tables, and More"
Create cross-references*	"Including Cross-References in Documents"
Add and revise notes and comments*	"Handling Footnotes and Endnotes"
Create and modify charts using data from other applications*	"Putting Charts in Documents"

* Denotes an Expert, not a Core, exam objective.

Ten Internet Resources for Scholars and Report Writers

This chapter is about getting Word's assistance to write reports and scholarly papers. Here are a few Internet resources for report writers. I threw in one or two of these strictly for laughs.

1. The Acronym Finder   The number of acronyms is growing by leaps and bounds. When you get stumped by an acronym, look it up at this Web site. Address: www.acronymfinder.com

2. Barkley's Comprehensive Technology Glossary   The place to go when you can't figure out what a high-tech term means. Click the Glossary – Tech hyperlink. Address: www.oasismanagement.com/index.html

3. Biographical Dictionary   Starting here, you can get brief biographical sketches of well-known persons and personages. Address: www.s9.com/biography

4. The Bowler's Bowling Dictionary   Bowling is a universe unto itself. From the dictionary: "Chicken wing: When a bowler lets his elbow get away from his body during the swing; generally considered an unacceptable style, but has been used by bowlers with physical problems, notably Don Carter, although he used a bent elbow on the backswing only." Address: www.icubed.com/users/allereb/dict.html

USING WORD 2002 AT THE OFFICE

5. Dictionary of Units   Besides explaining what a verst and a furlong are, this Web site offers handy conversion calculators. Address: www.ex.ac.uk/cimt/dictunit/dictunit.htm

6. DOD Dictionary of Military Terms   Always good for interesting reading. You can find some good stuff here: force shortfall, nonhostile casualty, warhead mating. Address: www.dtic.mil/doctrine/jel/doddict

7. Glossary of Mathematical Terms   Mathematical terms and theories explained—and explained and explained. I still don't get it. Address: www.cut-the-knot.com/glossary/atop.html

8. Glossary of PC and Internet Terminology   Computer terms can be baffling, but you can find out what the baffling terms really mean at this Web site. Address: homepages.enterprise.net/jenko/Glossary/G.htm

9. MapQuest   This site offers maps of just about everywhere, and the tools for locating places and zooming in and out are easy to use. Address: www.mapquest.com

10. *New York Times* Glossary of Financial and Business Terms   Do you know what a horizontal acquisition is? How about a wasting asset? You can look up these and another financial and business terms at this Web site. You must register to enter this site, but registering is easy and well worth it. Address: www.nytimes.com/library/financial/glossary/bfglosa.htm

Chapter 17

Working on
Team Projects

This chapter explains how you can get the help of Word to complete projects that you undertake with other people and large, unwieldy projects that you undertake on your own. Because so many are connected to private networks and the Internet, a lot of work is collaborative. You write it and send it to someone else. That someone rewrites it and sends it to someone else again. These pages explain how to use revision marks and comments to make sure that collaborative efforts go smoothly. You will also find instructions for using the very valuable Outline feature to organize your work and the sometimes-but-not-always valuable Master Document feature for organizing big, big jobs. This chapter also explains how SharePoint Team Services can help you complete team projects when members of the team are in far-flung places.

 In Chapter 22, "Routing a Document to Others" explains how you can send a document to others by e-mail so they can review or comment on it.

Keeping Track of Revisions to Documents

At some point or other you must have written a document, given it to others to revise, and discovered upon its return that the changes made to it were so all-encompassing as to make the document unrecognizable. Collaborating with others on a document can be like playing Telephone, the children's game in which one child whispers a word to another, who whispers it to another, until after four or five transactions the original word turns into something completely different.

To keep track of revisions to documents, review revisions, and perhaps reverse them, Word offers the Tools | Track Changes command. When you activate this command, all changes made to a document are marked in different colors, with one color for each person who works on the document. In Print Layout and Web Layout view, insertions are underlined, balloon captions show where text was deleted, and a vertical line in the left margin shows where revisions were made to the original copy. In Normal view, deleted text is crossed out—it doesn't appear in balloon captions. You can even tell Word to mark where formatting changes were made.

Figure 17-1 shows what the revision marks look like in Print Layout and Web Layout view. As you review a document, you can accept or reject the changes that were made to it by right-clicking or clicking buttons on the Reviewing toolbar. By moving the pointer over a revision, you can see who made it and when it was made. You can also compare or merge the first draft of a document to a subsequent draft to see where revisions were made to the original.

Read on to find out how you can track changes as you revise a document, accept or reject revisions, and fiddle with the way that revisions are marked onscreen.

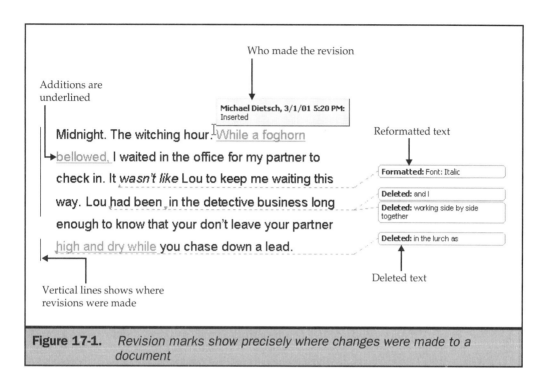

Who made the revision

Additions are underlined

Michael Dietsch, 3/1/01 5:20 PM:
Inserted

Midnight. The witching hour. While a foghorn

bellowed, I waited in the office for my partner to

check in. It *wasn't like* Lou to keep me waiting this

way. Lou had been in the detective business long

enough to know that your don't leave your partner

high and dry while you chase down a lead.

Reformatted text

Formatted: Font: Italic

Deleted: and I

Deleted: working side by side together

Deleted: in the lurch as

Deleted text

Vertical lines shows where revisions were made

Figure 17-1.   *Revision marks show precisely where changes were made to a document*

Note   *If you are a fan of the old way in which Word marked revisions, don't despair. You can mark revisions the old-fashioned way. See "Telling Word How to Mark Revisions" later in this chapter.*

Note   *"Saving (and Opening) Different Versions of a Document" in Chapter 20 explains another way to track revisions to a document—by saving different versions of it.*

Making Sure Revisions to a Document Are Tracked

Before you send out a document for others to review and change, you can choose Tools | Protect Document to make sure that all revisions to the document are tracked with revision marks. In a document that has been protected this way, reviewers cannot accept or reject revisions. Reviewers can't turn off the revision marking. All additions, deletions, and formatting changes are tracked whether the reviser likes it or not.

Follow these steps to make sure all revisions to a document are tracked:

1. Choose Tools | Protect Document. You see the Protect Document dialog box.

2. Select the Track Changes option button.

3. Enter a password in the Password text box if you want to keep others from turning off the protection mechanism. Without the password, someone in the know can choose Tools | Unprotect Document and revise the document without the revisions being tracked. Passwords are case-sensitive, so be careful which password you enter. Enter the password in all lowercase letters, for example, and you will have to do the same when you turn off the protection mechanism.

4. Click OK. If you entered a password, you have to enter it again in the Confirm Password dialog box.

Choose Tools | Unprotect Document if you decide that the protection mechanism isn't necessary. If you attached a password to your document, you see the Unprotect Document dialog box. Enter the password and click OK.

Tracking Revisions to a Document

Word offers no less than three different ways to track the revisions that are made or were made to the original copy of a document. You can track the revisions as you go along, merge the original copy and edited copy to see where revisions were made, or compare the original copy and the edited copy to see how the two differ. No matter which technique you choose, you end up with a document with revision marks that show precisely where revisions were made to the original. Later, you can accept or reject the revisions.

■ **Tracking Changes as You Make Them**   Revision marks and balloons appear as you make additions and delete text.

■ **Comparing or Merging the Revised Document and the Original**   Instead of being distracted by revision marks and balloons, simply make editorial changes to a copy of the original document. When you are done, choose Tools | Compare and Merge Documents, and see by way of revision marks on the edited or original document where changes were made.

Later in this chapter, "Telling Word How to Mark Revisions" explains how to choose a color for marking revisions and how to choose for yourself which markings are used to show revisions.

Tracking Changes as You Make Them

To track changes that you make to a document as you make them, simply tell Word to start tracking changes. Word offers no less than four ways to do it:

■ Double-click the TRK button on the Status bar.

■ Choose Tools | Track Changes.

■ Click the Track Changes button on the Reviewing toolbar.

■ Press CTRL-SHIFT-E.

You can track revisions in a document without being distracted by the revision marks. To do so, open the Display for Review drop-down menu on the Reviewing toolbar and choose Final, or choose View | Markup.

Each person who revises a document is automatically given a different display color. You can also tell Word to track formatting changes as well as changes to text (see "Telling Word How to Mark Revisions" later in this chapter). Try moving the pointer over a revision—your name and the time and date of the revision appear in a pop-up box. (If the wrong name appears, choose Tools | Options, select the User Information tab in the Options dialog box, and enter your name.)

Michael Dietsch, 3/2/01 10:50 AM:
Deleted

Hicks Nix Sticks Pix

To quickly make an editorial change without it being recorded by revision marks, double-click the TRK button on the Status bar to turn off the revision marks. Then make your editorial change and double-click TRK again.

Merging and Comparing the Edited Document and the Original Document

Even if someone edited your document without tracking revisions, or you edited someone else's document without tracking the revisions you made, you can find out where the revisions are and accept or reject them. Word offers two ways to handle documents that have been edited without the revisions being recorded:

- **Merging** Revision marks show where each reviewer made insertions and deletions in the original. You can make the revisions show in the original copy, the revised copy, or a third document that Word generates. Merge when you want to see how several different people revised a document.

- **Comparing** Revision marks show where the original and revised documents differ, not what was inserted or deleted. If both reviewers deleted the same paragraph, for example, the paragraph is not crossed out; it doesn't appear at all in the revised copy. Word generates a third document to show where the original and edited copies differ. Compare when you want to merge revisions made by two different revisers. You can't compare the work of more than two people.

After the merge or comparison, you can examine the revision marks and accept or reject them. Take note of where the original or revised copy of the document is stored and follow these steps to find out how the original was revised:

1. Open the original or a revised copy of the document.

2. Choose Tools | Compare and Merge Documents. You see the Compare and Merge Documents dialog box.

3. Locate and select the revised or original copy of the document. In other words, select the document you want to compare or merge with the one that is open onscreen.

4. Check or uncheck the Find Formatting check box to tell Word whether to mark formatting changes as well as revisions to the text.

5. Merge or compare the documents:

   - **Merging** Choose a Merge option.
     - Click the Merge button to make revision marks appear in the document you chose in Step 3.
     - Open the drop-down menu on the Merge button and choose Merge into Current Document to make revisions appear in the document that is open onscreen.
     - Open the drop-down menu on the Merge button and choose Merge into New Document to make the revisions appear in a new document.

Click to compare, not merge, documents

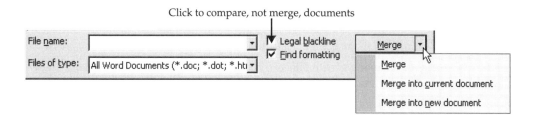

- **Comparing** Check the Legal Blackline check box. The Compare button appears where the Merge button was. Click the Compare button.

You can compare two versions of a document that you saved with the File | Versions command. To do so, however, you have to save and rename the earlier version of the document. Display the earlier version of the document, choose File | Save As, save the version under its own name, and then run the document comparison.

Reviewing, Accepting, and Rejecting Revisions

Reviewing revision marks and accepting or rejecting the revisions that other people propose can be a daunting task. Especially if you are looking at a document with many revision marks, trying to make heads or tails of revisions is difficult. Fortunately, Word offers a bunch of different tools for examining revisions:

- **Seeing What the Document Looks Like Without Revisions** To ignore revision marks momentarily and get a better look at the document, open the Display for Review drop-down menu on the Reviewing toolbar and choose Final. The Original option on the menu shows the document before it was edited.

- **Reviewing Revisions One at a Time** Click the Previous Change or Next Change button on the Reviewing toolbar. Word highlights a revision. Click the Accept Change or Reject Change/Delete Comment button to accept or reject it. You can also right-click and choose Accept or Reject.

- **Accepting or Rejecting Revisions in a Block of Text** Select the text and click the Accept Change or Reject Change/Delete Comment button on the Reviewing toolbar.

USING WORD 2002
AT THE OFFICE

- **Accepting or Rejecting All Revisions at Once** Open the drop-down menu on the Reject Change Accept Change or Reject Change/Delete Comment button and choose Accept All Changes in Document or Reject All Changes in Document.

- **Focusing on Revisions from Certain Reviewers** Open the Show drop-down menu on the Reviewing toolbar, choose Reviewers, and unselect the All Reviewers option. Then go back to the menu and select the names of reviewers whose revisions you want to see. You can also focus on revisions from a reviewer by clicking the Reviewing Pane button and scrolling in the Reviewing pane. Double-click a name in the pane to scroll in the document to the revision that appears below the name.

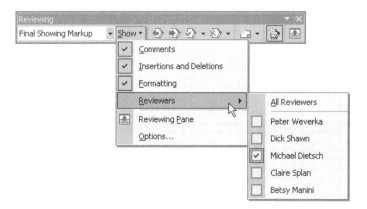

Tip. *To accept or reject all revisions made by a particular reviewer, display only his or her reviews by choosing options on the Reviewers submenu. Then open the drop-down menu on the Reject Change Accept Change or Reject Change/Delete Comment button and choose Accept All Changes Shown or Reject All Changes Shown.*

- **Focusing on Headers, Footers, Text Boxes, Footnotes, and More** Click the Reviewing Pane button on the Reviewing toolbar to see the Reviewing pane. Besides listing revisions by name, you can scroll to the bottom of the pane and view header and footer changes, text box changes, header and footer text box changes, footnote changes, and endnote changes. Double-click a name to scroll in the document to a revision.

Double-click to scroll to the revision

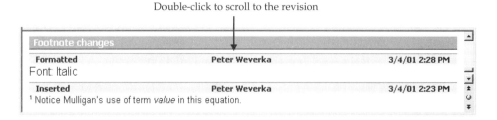

Be sure to proofread your document carefully after you accept or reject revisions. Unfortunately, tracking changes with the Tools | Track Changes command introduces extra blank spaces, run-in words, misspellings, and various other errata.

In my experience, the best way to handle revisions is to reject the ones you don't want, leave the rest, and when you finish reviewing the document, accept all the revisions.

Telling Word How to Mark Revisions

Unless you decide otherwise, inserted text is underlined, deleted text appears in balloon captions (in Normal view deleted text is crossed out), a vertical line appears in the left margin when revision marks are made, and changes made by each reviser appear in a different color. If these settings don't suit you, you can change them by going to the Track Changes tab in the Options dialog box. To get there, right-click the TRK button and choose Options or choose Tools | Options and select the Track Changes tab in the Options dialog box, as shown in Figure 17-2.

These options are self-explanatory, I think. If you prefer to track revisions in Print Layout and Web Layout view the way Word tracks them in Normal view, uncheck the Use Balloons in Print and Web Layout check box.

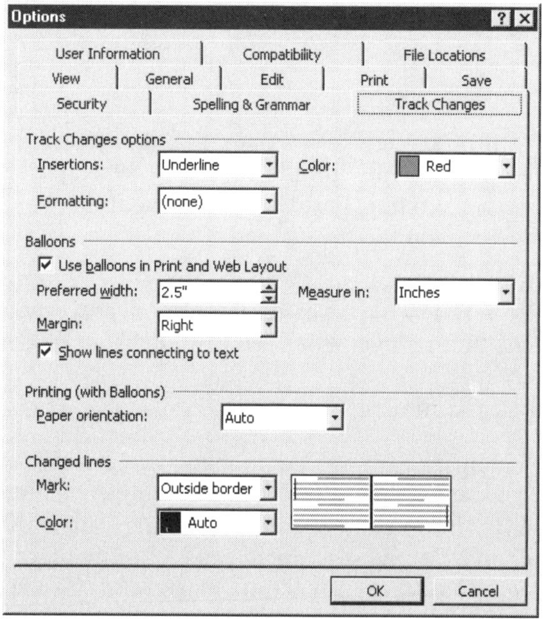

USING WORD 2002 AT THE OFFICE

Figure 17-2.   *You can decide for yourself how revisions are marked in documents*

Ways to Critique Others' Work

In prehistoric times, critiquing other people's work meant scribbling illegibly in the margin of a page, or—it seems fantastic to us now—actually visiting someone in an office to talk face to face about a project! Then came the sticky note, a small yellow piece of paper that could be scribbled on and stuck to the corner of a page. In the early days of computer networks, attempts were made to send sticky notes over the cable wires, but those early experiments gummed up the wires and failed dismally. Now, in the era of the network and the Internet, new ways have been devised for critiquing others' work and collaborating with others. New, exciting ways! It is now possible to collaborate for weeks, months, or even years with other people without even knowing what they look like! Science marches on! These pages explain three techniques for critiquing others' work and collaborating with others: commenting on a document, making notes with hidden text, and highlighting text.

Commenting on a Document

A *comment* is a note to yourself or to someone else that is attached to a document but isn't printed. Insert a comment to remind yourself to do a task or to critique another's writing. Comments do not upset the formatting of a page, so you can sprinkle as many comments as you want in a document. Comments aren't printed, either, unless you tell Word to print them, so you don't have to worry about embarrassing yourself in print with a sharp-edged, barbed comment.

Figure 17-3 shows what comments look like, first, in Normal view, and next, in Page Layout and Web Layout view:

- **Comments in Normal View**   Red parentheses appear around text that has been commented on. By moving the pointer between parentheses, you can read a comment in a pop-up box. Besides the comment, the box lists the commenter's name and when the comment was made.

- **Comments in Page Layout and Web Layout View**   Comments appear in balloon captions. To learn who made a comment and when a comment was made, move the pointer over a balloon caption. (In a Web browser, the initials of the commenter appear where comments are. Move the pointer over the initials to read the comment.)

In Normal, Page Layout, and Web Layout view, you can also examine comments by reading them in the Reviewing pane. Click the Reviewing Pane button on the Reviewing toolbar (or click the Show button and choose Reviewing Pane on the drop-down menu) to see the Reviewing pane. Comments appear under commenters' names. To go in your document to a comment, double-click a commenter's name. Scroll to the bottom of the

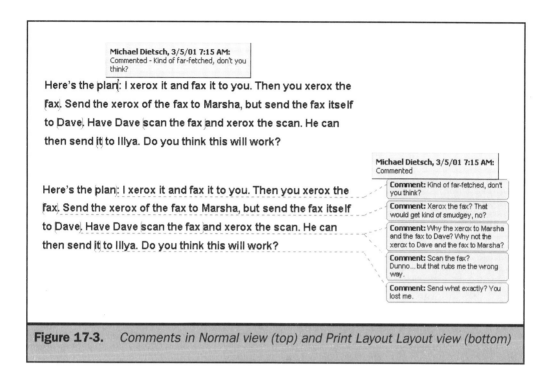

Figure 17-3. *Comments in Normal view (top) and Print Layout Layout view (bottom)*

Reviewing pane to read comments about headers and footers, text boxes, text boxes in headers and footers, footnotes, and endnotes.

Double-click a name to go to a comment.

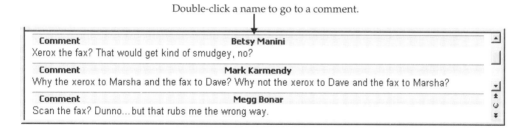

Read on to find out how to insert a comment, insert a voice comment, review comments, delete and move them, prevent others from changing comments, and print comments.

Inserting a Comment

Follow these steps to insert a comment:

1. Select the word or sentence that needs criticizing or praising. After you enter your comment, parentheses will appear around the word or phrase you select.

Be sure to select a word or phrase before you enter a comment. That way, reviewers will be able to find and read your comments in Normal view. Unless you select text, the red parentheses don't appear in Normal view, which makes finding comments difficult.

2. Choose Insert | Comment or press the New Comment button on the Reviewing toolbar.

3. Enter the comment:

   ■ **In Normal View**   Type the comment under your name in the Reviewing pane. If you balk and decide not to enter a comment, click the Reject Change/Delete Comment button on the Reviewing toolbar.

   ■ **In Page Layout and Web Layout View**   Enter your comment in the balloon caption that appears. Click the Reject Change/Delete Comment button if you change your mind about entering a comment.

To edit a comment, right-click it and choose Edit Comment. Then start typing and editing.

Note   *If someone else's name appears in the pop-up box when you record a comment, choose Tools | Options, select the User Information tab in the Options dialog box, and enter your name in the Name text box.*

As long as your machine is capable of recording sound and, more importantly, the people who need to hear your voice comment are capable of playing sound on their computers, you can record a voice comment. A "voice comment" is really just a standard sound recording like the ones described in Chapter 22 of this book. Friends and co-workers whose computers can play sound can double-click the loud speaker icon in the document and hear your comment. To record a voice comment, select the part of the document that deserves a comment, open the drop-down menu on the New Comment button, and choose Voice Comment. When the Sound Object dialog box appears, record your voice comment.

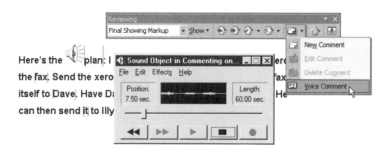

Allowing Reviewers to Comment On But Not Revise Documents

Word offers a command whereby you can pass around a document and allow others to comment on it but not change it. To welcome others' comments but prohibit their editorial changes, choose Tools | Protect Document and click the Comments option button in the Protect Document dialog box. If you want, enter a password in the Password dialog box to keep someone from unprotecting the document. Without the password, all you have to do to make editorial changes is choose Tools | Unprotect Document. Passwords are case-sensitive, so remember the combination of upper- and lowercase letters you enter as well as the password name. When you choose Tools | Unprotect Document to allow editorial changes in the document, Word asks you to enter the password again.

Reviewing the Comments in a Document

In my opinion, the easiest way to review comments is to move the pointer between parentheses in Normal view and read the pop-up boxes (refer to Figure 17-3). (If you don't see a pop-up box, choose Tools | Options, select the View tab in the Options dialog box, and check the ScreenTips check box.) However, to add wealth to riches, Word offers numerous other ways to review comments:

- **Skipping from Comment to Comment** Click the Previous or Next button on the Reviewing toolbar. You can also click the Select Browse Object button, choose Browse by Comment on the pop-up menu, and then click the double arrows above and below the Select Browse Object button to skip backward or forward from comment to comment.

- **Reading Comments in the Reviewing Pane** To open the Reviewing pane and read the comments (and edit them as well), click the Reviewing Pane button on the Reviewing toolbar or click the Show button and choose Reviewing Pane. When you double-click a commenter's name, the top half of the window scrolls to the comment that appears below the name in the Reviewing pane. You may have to drag the boundary of the Comment pane up the screen to read all the comments.

- **Displaying Only Comments by a Particular Person** To read comments from a particular person, start from the Reviewing toolbar or the Find and Replace dialog box, as shown in Figure 17-4. On the Reviewing toolbar, open the Show drop-down menu, choose Reviewers, and unselect the All Reviewers option. Then go back to the menu and select the name of a commenter whose comments you want to see.

  You can also choose Edit | Go To (or press CTRL-G) to locate comments from one person. On the Go To tab of the Find and Replace dialog box, choose Comment in the Go To What menu, choose the reviewer's name from the Enter Reviewer's Name drop-down list, and start clicking the Previous or Next button in the dialog box.

Figure 17-4. *Focusing on comments from one reviewer by way of the Reviewing toolbar (top) and the Find and Replace dialog box (bottom)*

If a comment is worthy of belonging in the document itself, you can copy or move it into the document. Either cut and paste the comment from the Comment pane or drag it from the comment bubble.

Deleting Comments

To delete a comment, start by clicking between the red parentheses, clicking the bubble caption where the comment is found, or, in the Reviewing pane, clicking the comment itself. Then do one of the following:

■ Click the Reject Change/Delete Comment button on the Reviewing toolbar.

■ Right-click and choose Delete Comment.

To delete all the comments in a document, open the drop-down menu on the Reject Change/Delete Comment button on the Reviewing toolbar and choose Delete All Comments in Document.

Suppose you want to delete the comments of a particular person. Start by displaying only the comments by that person (the previous section in this chapter explains how). Then, on the Reviewing toolbar, open the drop-down menu on the Reject Change/Delete Comment button and choose Delete All Comments Shown.

Printing the Comments in a Document

Normally, comments are not printed along with the rest of the document, but you can tell Word to print them. Follow these steps to print the comments in a document:

1. Choose File | Print or press CTRL-P to open the Print dialog box.

2. Choose an option from the Print What drop-down menu to tell Word what to print:

   - **Document Showing Markup**   Prints the document as it appears in Print Layout view.

   - **List of Markup**   Prints what is in the Reviewing pane, including revisions as well as comments.

Highlighting the Important Text

Another way to point out parts of a document that need attention is to highlight them. Click the down arrow beside the Highlight button on the Formatting toolbar and you will see a drop-down menu of 15 colors you can use for highlighting text. Highlighting is the digital equivalent of those fat felt pens that sleepy college students drag across the pages of the books that they may or may not actually be reading.

Highlighting is strictly for use online. Highlight parts of a document so you can return to them later. Color-code headings that pertain to certain topics. You can think of many uses for highlighting. These pages explain how to highlight text and how to remove the highlighting when you print a document.

Highlighting Text in a Document

Here are the two ways to highlight text:

- Open the drop-down menu on the Highlight button on the Formatting toolbar and choose a color from the drop-down menu. Notice how the stripe along the bottom of the Highlight button changes colors and the pointer changes into a fat crayon. Drag the crayon pointer across the text you want to highlight. Click the Highlight button again or press ESC to put the fat crayon back in the crayon box.

■ Select the text you want to highlight and click the Highlight button if it's showing the color you want. To select a different color, open the drop-down menu and choose it.

The stripe along the bottom of the Highlight button shows the last color you chose. To apply that color again, simply click the button without opening the drop-down menu.

Removing the Highlights

Whatever you do, do not print a document with text that has been highlighted. The highlights look awful on the printed page. Here are two strategies for removing the highlights:

■ **Removing All the Highlights in a Document**   If you are done reviewing a document, you may as well remove all the highlights. To do so, choose Edit | Select All or press CTRL-A to select the entire document, open the drop-down menu on the Highlight button, and choose None.

■ **Removing Highlights Temporarily While You Print a Document**   To temporarily remove the highlights while you print a document, choose Tools | Options and select the View tab in the Options dialog box. Under Show, find the Highlight check box and uncheck it. Then print your document. When you want to see the highlights again, return to the View tab and check the Highlight check box.

Instead of strolling through a long document to find highlights, you can call upon the Edit | Find command to find them. Choose Edit | Find or press CTRL-F, click the Format button in the Find and Replace dialog box (you might have to click the More button to get to it), choose Highlight on the pop-up menu, and click Find Next repeatedly to find all the places where you highlighted text.

Making Notes with Hidden Text

Operating in the background, Word inserts hidden text in documents for many reasons—to make table of contents entries and index entries, for example. You can enter hidden text in a document, too. The text is not truly hidden, because all you have to do to see it is click the Show/Hide ¶ button, but entering hidden text has its uses. I sometimes make notes in hidden text. Seeing and hiding the notes is easy. And deleting the notes when it is time to pass the manuscript to someone else is easy as well (I explain how to delete all hidden notes shortly).

This illustration shows what hidden text looks like. A dotted underline appears under the text. Except for its being hidden, hidden text can be edited or formatted like other text. Maybe the purpose of hidden text is to describe the subliminal messages in advertisements.

Summer's·here·and·that·means·bathing·suit·time·again·and·you·put·on·
weight·since·last·summer,·I·bet.·Why·not·come·visit·us·at·the·Union·
Street·Health·Center?·You'll·meet·lots·of·friendly·people.·Come·on.·
You've·got·nothing·to·lose·—·nothing·but·a·few·pounds,·that·is.¶

Here is how to handle hidden text:

- **Entering Hidden Text**   Select the text first if you have already written it, and then either press CTRL-SHIFT-H or choose Format | Font and check the Hidden check box in the Font dialog box. Start typing. The text doesn't appear onscreen. To enter normal text again, either press CTRL-SHIFT-H a second time or revisit the Font dialog box and uncheck the Hidden check box.

- **Viewing Hidden Text**   Click the Show/Hide ¶ button on the Standard toolbar or press CTRL-SHIFT-*. Click the button or press the shortcut key combination again to hide the text.

- **Printing Hidden Text**   Choose File | Print, click the Options button in the Print dialog box, look under Include With Document on the Print tab of the Options dialog box, and check the Hidden Text check box. The hidden text is printed along with the rest of your document. Don't forget to revisit the Options dialog box and uncheck the Hidden Text check box to keep hidden text from being printed in the future.

- **Deleting All Hidden Text**   Click the Show/Hide ¶ button and then choose Edit | Replace (or press CTRL-H) to go to the Replace tab of the Find and Replace dialog box. With the cursor in the Find What text box, press CTRL-SHIFT-H. Then make sure nothing appears in the Replace With box and click the Replace All button.

Organizing Your Work with Outlines

In a long report or manual, you can save a lot of time you would otherwise spend organizing your work by starting from an outline. In Outline view, you can see all the headings in a document, the major headings, the major and minor headings, or the headings in a particular section. Outline view shows how the different parts of a document fit together. And if something is amiss, if the parts don't fit together, you can rearrange them in Outline view. You can simultaneously move headings and the text underneath headings to new places in a document. Outline view is quite simply the easiest way to move text from place to place and stay organized.

These pages explain what is one of the most valuable features of Word. You learn how to create an outline, view your outline in different ways, move headings and text throughout a document, promote and demote headings, edit text in Outline view, and arrange the headings in alphabetical order.

Outline View: The Big Picture

In order to do any work in Outline view, you must have applied Heading styles to the headings in your document. Either that, or you must be working with styles that have been assigned outline levels higher than Body Text. "Choosing an Outline Level for Paragraphs" in Chapter 8 explains how to assign different outline levels to paragraphs. Chapter 12 explains styles, including how to apply Heading styles from the Style menu.

To switch to Outline view, do one of the following:

- Click the Outline View button in the lower-left corner of the screen.
- Choose View | Outline.
- Press ALT-CTRL-O.

To see a document in Outline view and Normal view at the same time, split the screen and switch to Normal view on one side of the screen. See "Splitting the Screen" in Chapter 6.

Figure 17-5 shows two of the many different ways to examine a document in Outline view. In both outlines, headings assigned Headings styles are shown. In the outline at the top of the figure, however, Show Level 1 has been chosen from the Show Level menu on the Outlining toolbar, so only first-level headings are shown. In the second outline, Show Level 2 button has been selected, so first- and second-level headings appear. By choosing an option on the Show Level menu on the Outlining toolbar, you tell Word button which headings to display in Outline view, and in so doing you can tell whether your document needs reorganizing.

The buttons on the right side of the Outlining toolbar are for handing master documents (see "Master Documents for Organizing Big Jobs" later in this chapter). To remove or display the master document buttons, click the Master Document View button on the Outlining toolbar.

Suppose you need to examine the headings in a certain part of your document. You can do that without displaying all the headings, as this illustration shows. Here, the third-level headings are on display in one part of a document but not in the other parts.

Click the Expand or Collapse buttons to see or hide subheadings

Choose a Show Level option to tell Word which headings to display

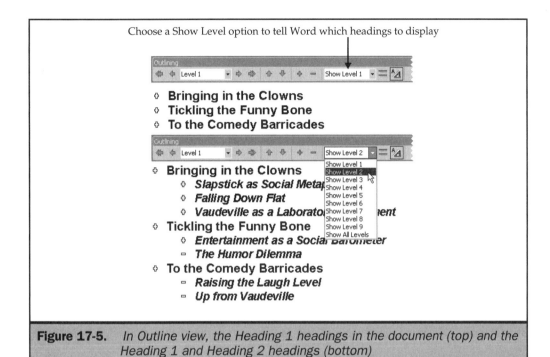

Figure 17-5. *In Outline view, the Heading 1 headings in the document (top) and the Heading 1 and Heading 2 headings (bottom)*

And if Outline view reveals that a document is not well organized? In that case, you can reorganize it without leaving Outline view:

- Edit the headings. Delete words and enter new ones. Go ahead. No one is going to bite you. Outline view is the best place to edit headings, since you can see all or several of them at once.

- On the Outlining toolbar, click a Promote button, click a Demote button, or choose a level from the Outline Level drop-down menu to change a heading's heading-level assignment. Instead of choosing another Heading style from the Style menu or the Styles and Formatting task pane, you can simply work from the Outlining toolbar.

These buttons are for promoting and demoting headings

■ Click the Move Up or Move Down button to move headings—as well as their subheadings and the text beneath them—forward or backward in the document. In Outline view, you can move entire sections of a document in a second or two without resorting to the Cut and Paste commands.

Click to move a heading up or down in the outline

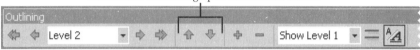

 "Printing an Outline" in Chapter 5 explains how to print outlines.

Getting the Right View of Your Outline

Outline view presents many different ways of looking at the headings in a document as well as the first line in body text paragraphs. Here are different ways of examining your document in Outline view:

■ **Viewing Headings Up to a Certain Level**   Open the Show Level drop-down menu and choose a Show Level option. Very likely, you have to scroll through the document to read all the headings.

■ **Viewing All the Headings**   Open the Show Level drop-down menu on the Outlining toolbar and choose Show All Levels (or press ALT-SHIFT-A). Click the button once and all text is shown, but click it a second time and only headings appear onscreen.

■ **Drilling Down to Examine Subheadings in Part of a Document**   Either click the plus sign (+) next to a heading or click to the left of a heading to select it, and then click the Expand button to see the subheadings. If no subheadings are found under a heading, a minus sign instead of a plus sign appears beside the heading in Outline view.

A plus sign next to a heading means subheadings are found below the heading

✿ Bringing in the Clowns
✿ Tickling the Funny Bone

■ **Hiding Subheadings in Part of a Document**   Click to the left of a heading to select it, and then click the Collapse button on the Outlining toolbar.

Click the Show Formatting button to see headings in their native formats. Click the button again and the headings appear as plain text.

Double-click the plus sign next to a heading to display all subheadings underneath it, or, if the subheadings are already displayed, to hide all subheadings underneath it.

Moving Headings—and Text—in a Document

Outline view is the most convenient place to move headings forward or backward in a document. Instead of the messy Cut and Paste commands, you can simply click buttons on the Outlining toolbar. The text under a heading moves along with the heading when the heading is moved elsewhere. Starting in Outline view, follow these steps to move a heading in a document:

1. Click the heading you want to move.

2. Tell Word whether you want to move subheadings (if there are any) below the heading:

   - To move the subheadings along with the heading, click the Collapse button to fold the subheadings into the heading. As long as no subheadings are displayed beneath the heading, the subheadings move along with the heading.

   - To move the heading independently of its subheadings, click the Expand button to display the subheadings. If subheadings are displayed beneath the heading, only the heading moves.

3. Click the Move Up or Move Down button as many times as necessary to move the heading (and possibly subheadings as well) where you want it to go.

Rearranging, Promoting, and Demoting Headings

When a heading needs to be promoted or demoted or needs to be turned into text, click it and then call on a button or the Outline Level drop-down menu on the left side of the Outlining toolbar. By doing so, you can turn a Heading 2 heading into a Heading 1 or Heading 3 heading, for example.

 Whether subheadings are promoted or demoted along with a heading depends on whether the subheadings appear in Outline view. When subheadings appear below a heading, the heading is promoted or demoted independently of the heading. But when the subheadings do not appear onscreen, they are promoted or demoted to the same degree as the heading. To promote or demote subheadings along with the heading, click the heading and then click the Collapse button on the Outlining toolbar to fold the subheadings into the heading. Click the Expand button to display the subheadings if you want to promote or demote the heading independently of its subordinates.

Arranging Headings in Alphabetical Order

Here's a little trick for arranging the first-level headings in a document in alphabetical order. Switch to Outline view, open the Show Level drop-down menu on the Outlining toolbar, and select Show Level 1. Then choose Table | Sort and click OK in the Sort Text dialog box.

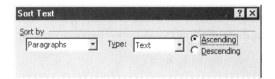

Text and subheadings underneath the first-level headings are moved right along with the headings themselves. "Alphabetizing and Sorting Lists" in Chapter 10 explains all the vagaries of the Sort Text dialog box.

Select a heading and follow these instructions to promote or demote it:

- **Promote It to Heading 1 Level** Click the Promote to Heading 1 button on the Outlining toolbar.

- **Promote It** Click the Promote button (or press ALT-SHIFT-←) AS MANY TIMES AS NECESSARY TO MOVE IT UP THE LADDER.

- **Promote or Demote It to a Specific Level** Open the Outline Level drop-down menu and choose a Level option.

- **Demote It** Click the Demote button (or press ALT-SHIFT-→).

- **Turn It into Text** Click the Demote to Body Text button.

You can also promote or demote headings by clicking them and then choosing a style from the Style menu on the Formatting toolbar.

Master Documents for Organizing Big Jobs

A document longer than 50 pages, especially if it includes a graphic or two, can get very unwieldy. Searching for text in a document like that can take forever. In Page Layout view, paginating a document that long takes a while, too. To make handling long documents easier and to make working on team projects in which several people work on the same document go more smoothly, Word offers the master document. A *master document* is a set of subdocuments that have been organized under one umbrella document.

With a master document, you can work in the master document or one of the subdocuments. Work done in a subdocument is recorded in the master document as well. Likewise, work done in the master document is saved in the subdocument. The master document arrangement makes long documents easier to work with. What's more, everything that you can do in Outline view to organize or rearrange a document can be done in a master document, so a master document also gives you all the advantages of working in Outline view.

So much for the good news about master documents. I would be remiss if I didn't tell you that master documents tax the memory resources of your computer and have been known to stop working or work sluggishly. Your computer needs at least 64MB of RAM to handle a master document. A couple years ago, while doing some contract work for a company, I sat in the cubicle next to someone who made the mistake of using a master document to organize a long company manual. I can still hear the poor woman groaning while her computer failed time and time again. If you decide to use a master document, do so with these reservations:

■ Do not track revisions with the Tools | Track Changes command. Between tracking revisions and handling subdocuments, your computer's memory resources will be hammered.

■ Make sure everyone who works on the project, if more than one person will work on it, uses the same template.

■ Turn off the Allow Fast Saves feature. As "Telling Word How to Save Documents" in Chapter 20 explains, Word actually keeps a document in two separate files when the feature is turned on. The two-file arrangement makes saving documents go faster, but it also increases the size of documents and makes sharing documents more problematic. To turn off the Allow Fast Saves feature, choose Tools | Options, select the Save tab in the Options dialog box, and uncheck the Allow Fast Saves check box.

■ Do not put any graphics, sound files, or other memory-intensive items in the document until you are nearly done with the project.

■ Create a new folder for your document and subdocuments and do not under any circumstances move documents out of the folder.

Be sure to read "Ten Tips for Sharing Documents with Others" at the end of this chapter if you intend to use a master document. The rules that apply to sharing documents with others also apply to master documents.

Read on to find out how to assemble documents into a master document, create a master document from scratch, work with master documents, and lock master documents so that others cannot edit them.

USING WORD 2002
AT THE OFFICE

Knowing how to work in Outline view is a prerequisite for working with master documents. Don't bother creating a master document unless you are familiar with the buttons on the Outline toolbar.

Creating a Master Document

How you create a master document depends on whether you create it from scratch or assemble documents you have already created in a master document. Read on to explore the two ways to create a master document.

 Make sure all subdocuments are kept in the same folder. That way, Word can find them easily. If you are just starting your master document, create a new folder for storing its subdocuments.

Creating a Master Document from Scratch When You Start a Project

To create a master document from scratch, write an outline of your new project in Outline view. Then divide the headings equally into subdocuments. Follow these steps to create a master document and its subdocuments:

1. Create a new document and save it in the folder you created for your master document.

2. Click the Outline View button or choose View | Outline to switch to Outline view.

3. Enter the headings for your project. As you do so, assign Heading styles to your headings (Chapter 12 explains styles). Be sure to assign at least a few headings to the Heading 1 style. Later, you will divide the document into subdocuments where the Heading 1 styles are.

4. Click the plus sign beside the first Heading 1 heading in the document. By clicking the plus sign, you select the heading and all its subheadings.

5. Click the Create Subdocument button on the Outlining toolbar. You will find this button on the right side of the toolbar (if you don't see it, click the Master Document View button). A box appears around the headings in the subdocument and a subdocument icon appears in the upper-left corner of the box.

6. Select the next set of headings and click the Create Subdocument button again to create a second subdocument. In this way, divide the master documents into subdocuments of roughly the same size.

7. Save your master document.

Word saves all subdocuments when you save the master. To name the subdocuments, Word takes the name of the first heading.

Assembling Documents for a Master Document

Perhaps you started your project before you decided to manage it by way of a master document. In that case, you have to assemble documents from different places and bind them together as a master document. Do so by following these steps:

1. Create a new document and save it in the folder you created especially for your new master document.

2. Click the Outline View button or choose View | Outline to switch to Outline view.

3. On the Outlining toolbar, click the Insert Subdocument button to open the Insert Subdocument dialog box (if you don't see the Insert Subdocument button, click the Master Document View button).

4. Locate and select the document that will be the first in the master document and click the Open button.

5. Repeat steps 3 and 4 until you have loaded down your master document with subdocuments.

When you assemble documents for a master document, the subdocuments keep their original names.

Working on the Master and Its Subdocuments

When the time comes to start work on a master document, you can begin with a subdocument or open the master. Either way, the work you do is recorded in the master document. Open a subdocument and you won't notice any differences between working in a subdocument and a document that doesn't have a master. But if you open the master document, you might be surprised to see your screen looking like Figure 17-6.

When you open a master document, the first thing you see are hyperlinks that you can click to open subdocuments and start your work there. Notice that each hyperlink lists the path to a subdocument. Very convenient indeed. By CTRL-clicking a hyperlink, you can open a subdocument and start working. On the other hand, if you want to stay in the master document, you can stay put and do your work there by clicking the Expand Subdocuments button on the Outlining toolbar (or by pressing CTRL-\). You see the document in Outline view. Switch to Normal view, Page Layout view, or Web Layout view and get to work.

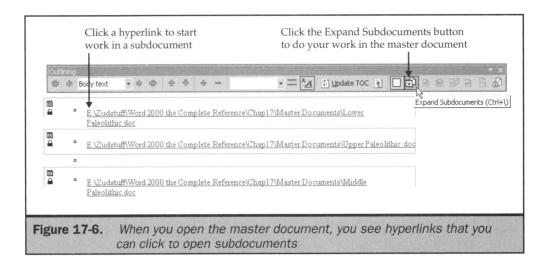

Figure 17-6. *When you open the master document, you see hyperlinks that you can click to open subdocuments*

 You cannot start working on a subdocument from the master document if the subdocument is already open in another window.

Reorganizing a Master Document

You are invited to use all the buttons on the Outline toolbar to organize your master document (earlier in this chapter, "Organizing Your Work with Outlines" explains the buttons). For example, you can move headings and subheadings to and fro by clicking the Move Up and Move Down buttons. And you can promote or demote headings by clicking a Promote or Demote button or using the Outline Level drop-down menu.

 Unless you want to split a subdocument in two, choose Show Level on the Outlining toolbar's Show Level drop-down menu. Seeing only the first-level headings makes moving, merging, and removing subdocuments easier.

Apart from the buttons on the Outlining toolbar, here are instructions for handling subdocuments in a master document:

- **Dividing a Subdocument in Two** Click the first heading in the subdocument and then click the Expand button to see all the headings. With that done, click the plus sign that you want to be the first heading in the new subdocument, and then click the Split Subdocument button.

- **Merging Subdocuments** Move the subdocuments so that they are next to each other in the master document. Then hold down the SHIFT key and click each subdocument's subdocument icon to select both subdocuments. Finally, click the Merge Subdocument button.

■ **Moving Subdocuments** Click the subdocument icon of the subdocument you want to move and drag it up or down the screen to move it. Make sure when you do this that you don't drop the subdocument inside another subdocument.

■ **Removing a Subdocument** Click the subdocument icon and then click the Remove Subdocument button. Removing a subdocument does not delete it. You can still find and open the subdocument under its own name.

■ **Locking a Subdocument So It Can't Be Edited** When you lock a subdocument, no one can read or alter it without visiting the master document and unlocking it. To lock a subdocument, click its icon and then click the Lock Document button, the last button on the Outlining toolbar. To unlock it, click the Lock Document button again. A padlock appears beside subdocuments that have been locked.

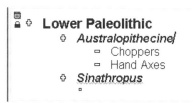

Sharing Documents with Others on a SharePoint Team Services Server

Nowadays, the members of a project team more than likely work in different offices or on different coasts, not in cubicles that are within shouting distance of one another. To meet the needs of today's workgroups, Microsoft Office XP includes something called *SharePoint Team Services*. It is an application that permits the members of a workgroup to collaborate, communicate, and share documents online by way of a "team site," a site on the Internet that has been set up for workgroup members. Team members can collaborate across a corporate intranet, an extranet, or even the Internet.

SharePoint Team Services is easy to manage. You need a Web browser, but no knowledge of Microsoft FrontPage or even HTML is required.

Technical Requirements for Running SharePoint Team Services

Table 17-1 describes the minimum technical requirements for installing SharePoint Team Services in different environments. As one who visits a SharePoint Team Services team site, you needn't know this information. But your system administrator needs to know it. The good news about these requirements is that they don't require huge capital expenditures to get SharePoint Team Services up and running.

Operating System	Minimum Requirements
Microsoft Windows 2000 Server	200 MHz Intel Pentium Processor 128MB RAM (192MB RAM recommended) 70MB of free hard disk space (each provisioned Web site requires an additional 4MB of free disk space)
Microsoft Windows 2000 Professional	200 MHz Intel Pentium Processor 64MB RAM (128MB RAM recommended) 70MB of free hard disk space (each provisioned Web site requires an additional 4MB of free disk space)
MS Windows NT Server running Service Pack 6	200 MHz Intel Pentium Processor 128MB RAM 70 MB of free hard disk space (each provisioned Web site requires an additional 4MB of free disk space)
Microsoft Windows NT Workstation running Service Pack 6.0	133 MHz Intel Pentium Processor 64MB RAM 70MB of free hard disk space (each provisioned Web site requires an additional 4MB of free disk space)

Table 17-1.   *SharePoint Team Services Requirements*

You can learn more about Windows 2000 Server and Microsoft Internet Information Server by consulting the Microsoft Explore Web & Applications Services home page at this address: http://www.microsoft.com/windows2000/guide/server/features/appsvcs.asp

Installing SharePoint Team Services on a Server

SharePoint Team Services runs on an NT or a Windows 2000-based PC or server. Depending on your needs, you can install SharePoint Team Services in different ways:

■ **Installing SharePoint Team Services on an IIS Web Server**   This installation requires two parts, the first being the actual installation of SharePoint Team Services and the addition of server extensions and SharePoint Team Services

Web files to each IIS virtual server. This part of the installation process is called "provisioning." During this installation, a scaled-down version of SQL Server 7.0 called MSDE is also installed on the server.

■ **Installing SharePoint Team Services on an IIS Web Server Running SQL Server 7.0**   The first part of the installation is the actual installation of SharePoint Team Services. The second part is the addition of server extensions and SharePoint Team Services Web files to each IIS virtual server. MSDE is not installed during this installation.

■ **Installing SharePoint Team Services on an IIS Web Server Running SQL Server 2000**   The first part of the installation is the actual installation of SharePoint Team Services. The second part is the addition of server extensions and SharePoint Team Services Web files to each IIS virtual server. MSDE is not installed during this installation.

■ **Installing SharePoint Team Services on an IIS Web Server While Running Remote SQL Server 7.0**   The first part of the installation is the actual installation of SharePoint Team Services. The second part is the addition of server extensions and SharePoint Team Services Web files to each IIS virtual server. After the SharePoint Team Services Web files and server extensions are added, the SharePoint Team Services Global Administration pages appear. You must then provision SharePoint Team Services Web sites from the Global Administration pages. MSDE is not installed during this installation.

Finding Your Way Around a SharePoint Team Services Team Site

Web sites are common to most users now. Corporate intranets, extranets, and access to the Internet are standard fare. A team site created with SharePoint Team Services looks and operates very much like a common Web site. Team members don't have to go out of their way to take advantage of the SharePoint Team Services team site's many features.

Figure 17-7 shows a typical team site made with SharePoint Team Services. This site was designed so that team members can exchange documents, collaborate on documents, keep track of tasks, and discuss issues that pertain to different projects.

A SharePoint Team Services team site offers these online tools for collaborating and communicating with others:

■ **Document Libraries**, where team members can place documents for their own use, for the use of team members, and for the use of the entire organization.

■ **Discussion Boards**, where team members can engage in online discussions about projects that matter to them.

■ **Lists**, where team members can post announcements, events, links, and tasks and thereby help team members track their projects.

Quick Launch bar   Main menu

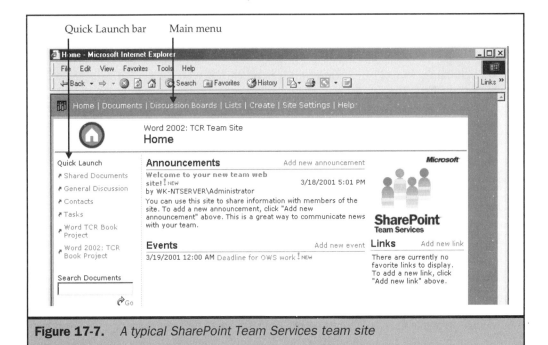

Figure 17-7.   *A typical SharePoint Team Services team site*

Bringing a Team Together on the Team Web Site

After creating a Team Web site, the next step is to invite team members to join. Membership in a SharePoint Team Services team site is by invitation only. People who are invited to use the team site are given different user roles, depending on their duties and responsibilities. A *user role* is a designation that describes what a visitor can do on a site. Table 17-2 describes SharePoint Team Services user roles.

Role	Rights
Administrator User	View, add, and change all server content, as well as manage server settings and accounts. The Administrator role should only be granted to team members who occupy a leadership role or to the team member who is in charge of managing the server.

Table 17-2.   *SharePoint Team Services User Roles*

Role	Rights
Advanced Author User	View, add, and change pages, documents, and the appearance of pages. Advanced authors have the rights to handle hypertext links within the team site. The Advanced Author role is especially suited to team members who have a lot of content development responsibilities but don't need to manage the server settings and accounts.
Author User	View, add, and change Web pages and documents that reside on the team site. The Author role is suited for a team member who has some content development responsibilities as part of his or her role on the team.
Contributor User	View pages and documents on the team site. Users with the Contributor role can also contribute to online discussions on the discussion boards. The Contributor role is suited for team members who have little or no content development responsibilities.
Browser User	View pages and documents. The Browser role is well suited to users outside the team who may need to view documents and pages on the team site but don't require author access. Project managers and executives not on the team who want to view documents during the course of a project can be given the Browser role.

Table 17-2.   *SharePoint Team Services User Roles* (continued)

SharePoint Team Services Team site administrators have the capability to invite users to become members of their SharePoint Team Services team site. Follow these steps to invite someone to participate in your team site:

1. Go to your team site's home page.
2. Click Site Settings on the menu bar to open up the Web Administration page.

Note   *You might need to log in to the Web Administration site after you click Site Settings on the menu bar.*

3. Click Send an Invitation in the Web Administration section of the Site Settings page to open the Send an Invitation wizard.

4. Type the full e-mail addresses of the users you want to invite. Type each e-mail address on a separate line. Click Next.

5. Verify the e-mail addresses to make sure they are correct, and click Next.

6. Type a personal message and assign a role for the users.

7. Click Finish.

After team members become users on your team site, their roles may change as personnel assignments are given out and members leave the team. Follow these steps to assign a team member a different user role:

1. Go to your team site's home page and click Site Settings.

2. Go to Web Administration and click Manage Users.

3. Click the user whose role you want to change. The Edit User Role Membership page appears.

4. Select a new role for a user under User Role.

5. Click Submit to apply the new settings to the user.

Posting Documents So that the Team Can Work on Them

Word documents—and files created with Office applications—can be posted to the team site so that team members can collaborate with one another. For that matter, you can put documents on the site to archive or store them in a safe place. These pages explain how to upload a document, edit a document, and remove a document from the Team Web site.

Creating a Document

You can create documents with Word or any other Office XP program starting from a SharePoint Team Services team site. Click New Document on the Quick Launch toolbar. The program associated with the documents in the document library opens. Create the document as you normally would. Click Save to save the document. Complete the Web File properties dialog box, and then click OK.

SharePoint Team Services is also compatible with older versions of Microsoft Office, including Microsoft Office 2000, in case a member of your team is not using Office XP, the newest version of Office.

Uploading a Document

The team site includes a predefined documents library called Shared Documents. Shared Documents is actually a folder on the server whose purpose is to store documents so that team members with the appropriate permissions can access the documents. To upload a document to a team site, you need to have been assigned the Author, Advanced Author, or Administrator user role.

 You can only upload Office binary file types. HTML file uploads are not supported.

Follow these steps to upload a document to a team site:

1. Go to your team site's home page.

2. Click the Shared Documents link in the Quick Launch bar.

3. Click the Upload Document link.

4. Click Browse and locate the file you want to upload.

Team Web Site
Shared Documents: Upload Document

💾 Save and Close | Go Back to Document Library

Overwrite if document already exists? ☑

File Name *   C:\Fiction\More variations.doc   Browse...

* indicates a required field

5. Click Save and Close to save the document to your team site.

Saving a Document to Your Team Site

There are two ways to save a document to a team site. One way is to use a Web Folder or a Network Place. You can also save a document directly from Word or another Office XP application to your team site.

If you want to use Web Folders as a method of saving documents to your team site, perform these steps if you are using Windows 98, Windows 98 Special Edition, Windows NT 4 Workstation, or Windows NT Server:

1. Double-click My Computer on your desktop.

2. Double-click Web Folders.

3. Double-click Add Web Folder to open the Add Web Folder wizard.

4. Type the HTTP address of your SharePoint Team Services team site and click Next.

5. Type your user name and password if you are prompted for authentication.

6. Enter a name for your Web Folder and click the Finish button to open the team site as a folder on your local PC.

Note *Your PC must be connected to the Internet or a LAN for Web folders to function properly.*

You now have the capability to access the Shared Documents folder on your SharePoint Team Services team site in the same way that you can access a folder on your local hard drive. Follow these steps to do so:

1. Double-click the My Computer folder on your desktop.

2. Double click Web folders.

3. Double-click the Web folder for your SharePoint Team Services team site.

Follow these steps to create a Web folder if your operating system is Windows Me, Windows 2000 Professional, or Windows 2000 Server:

1. Double-click My Network Places on your computer desktop.

2. Double-click Add Network Place. The Add Network Place dialog box appears.

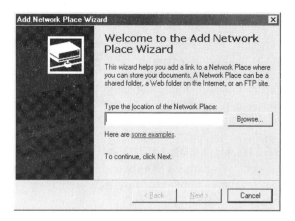

3. Type the HTTP address of your SharePoint Team Services team site and click Next.

4. Type in your user name and password if you are prompted for authentication.

5. Enter a name for the network place.

6. Click Finish to open your team site as folder on your PC.

Note *Your PC must be connected to the Internet in order for Web folders to function properly.*

After a Network Place has been created for your SharePoint Team Services team site shared files directory, you can open your team site as a folder on your desktop by following these steps:

1. Double-click My Network Places.

2. Double-click the SharePoint Team Services network place.

You can now work with the SharePoint Team Services Network Place in the same way that you work on a folder on your local hard drive.

Removing a Document from a Team Site

Sometimes a project gets cancelled without hope of being resurrected, and in cases like that, documents need to be removed from the team Web site. Follow these steps to remove them:

1. Go to your team site's home page.

2. Click Documents on the menu bar to open the Document Libraries Page. Your Document Libraries page appears.

3. Select the Document Library that holds the document you want to remove from your team site. The main page of the document library you selected appears in the main window of your browser.

4. Click the Edit icon beside the name of the document you want to remove from your team site. The Edit Item page appears in your browser. Figure 17-8 shows an example of an Edit Item page.

5. Click Delete to remove the document from your SharePoint Team Services team site. A dialog box appears asking, "Do you want to delete this item?"

6. Click OK to confirm deleting the selected item from your SharePoint Team Services team site. After the deletion is complete, you are returned to the Document Library.

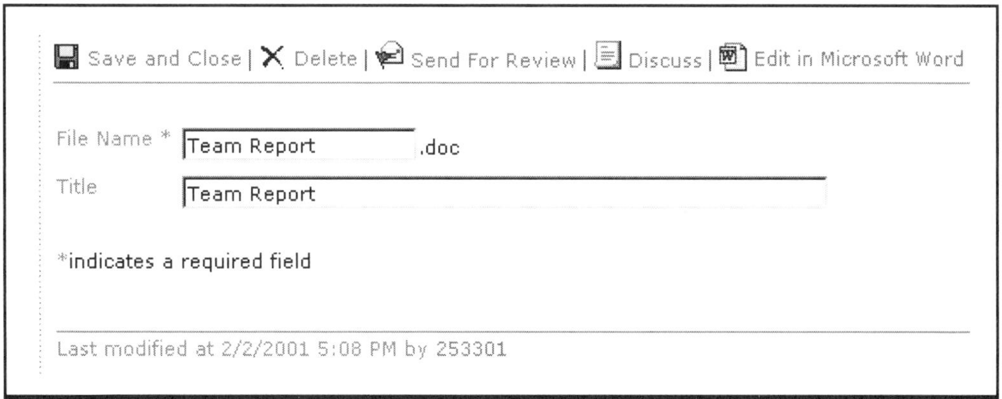

🖫 Save and Close | ✕ Delete | 🖺 Send For Review | 🖳 Discuss | 🗐 Edit in Microsoft Word

File Name * [Team Report] .doc

Title [Team Report]

*indicates a required field

Last modified at 2/2/2001 5:08 PM by 253301

Figure 17-8. *An example of a SharePoint Team Services Edit Item page*

Opening and Editing a Document that Is Stored on a Team Site

Files are stored on a SharePoint Team Services team site in a document library or libraries. Opening and editing documents stored on a team site means, first of all, accessing the document library where the document you want to open and edit is kept. However, navigating through a document library will be familiar to anyone who has had to interact with documents stored on a Web site.

Follow these steps to open a document on a SharePoint Team Services team site:

1. Go to your team site's home page.

2. Click Documents on the menu bar to open the Document Libraries page.

3. Click the name of the document library that you want to open. The Document Library View appears in your browser window. At first, you see a complete list of the documents in the document library. You can see file names, when files were modified, and who modified them.

4. Click the name of the document you want to open. The document appears in your browser window.

5. If you want to edit the document, click on the Tools button to open the MS Word Standard toolbar.

Saving a Document

Follow these steps to save a document you have opened on your SharePoint Team Services team site:

1. Choose File | Save As. The Save As dialog box appears.

2. Click the Save button to save the document to your SharePoint Team Services team site.

Creating Document Libraries for Holding the Team's Work

Documents are stored on a SharePoint Team Services team site by way of document libraries. Only Administrators have the rights to create document libraries. A team site includes one default document library called Shared Documents, but you may need to create more document libraries if your team site becomes the place where more than one project is undertaken.

Follow these steps to create a new document library on your SharePoint Team Services team site:

1. Go to your team site's home page.

2. Click Documents on the menu bar to open your team site's Document Libraries page.

3. Click New Document Library to open the New Document Library page.

4. Type in a name for and a description of the document library.

5. Specify a template type in the Document Template field. The type of template specifies the default document type for all new documents that are created in the library.

6. Specify whether you want a link for the document library you are creating to appear on the Quick Launch bar.

7. Click Create to create the new document library. The document library appears in your browser window in case you want to begin uploading documents.

Subscribing to a Page, File, or Folder

SharePoint Team Services provides you with the option of subscribing to a page, file, or folder. Subscribing enables SharePoint Team Services to send you an e-mail reminder when an item to which you subscribe has been updated. By subscribing, you don't have to check SharePoint Team Services components or stored files to see if they have been updated.

Follow these steps to subscribe to a page, file, or folder:

1. Click Subscribe on the toolbar at the top of the page or click the Subscribe hyperlink to which you want to subscribe (not all pages are available for subscription). The New Subscription page appears.

2. Select the SharePoint Team Services element you want to subscribe to in the Subscribe To drop-down list.

3. Specify when you want to be notified in the Notify Me When drop-down list.

4. Type your e-mail address in the E-mail address field.

5. Select how many times per day you want to be notified about changes in your subscription.

6. Click OK to confirm your subscription.

Finding a File or Other Item on the Web Site

A SharePoint Team Services team site has the capacity to become a large repository of documents, lists, discussion board topics, lists, and other content. Regardless of how you organize your SharePoint Team Services team site, a search engine is an invaluable asset, especially when a site starts growing in size.

Searching a SharePoint Team Services team site doesn't require special user roles. Follow these steps to search through SharePoint Team Services team site:

1. Go to the home page of your SharePoint Team Services team site.

2. In the Search Documents text box (you'll find it beneath the Quick Launch bar on the left side of the home page), enter a keyword that describes the text you want to search for.

3. Click Go.

Creating a Link List

SharePoint Team Services enables you to create a *Link list,* a list of hypertext links to internal and external Web sites. Create a Link list to help team members go quickly to different places in their browsers. The list appears on the home page of the Web site where all can see it. You must have Administrator privileges to create a Link list. Follow these steps to create a new Link list:

1. Go to the home page of your SharePoint Team Services team site.

2. Click Create on the menu bar to open the Create Page page.

3. Click Links (you'll find it toward the bottom of the page). The New List page appears.

4. Enter a name for the new list.

5. Enter a description of the new list.

6. Specify whether you want your new Link list to appear as an entry in the SharePoint Team Services Quick Launch bar.

7. Click the Create button to create the Link list. It appears in your browser window with a message saying that there are no items to show in the list and instructions for creating a new list item.

Follow these steps to add a new link to your Link list:

1. Click Home on the menu bar to go to the home page of your SharePoint Team Services team site.

2. Click Lists on the menu bar to open the Lists page.

3. Click Links to open the List View page for Links.

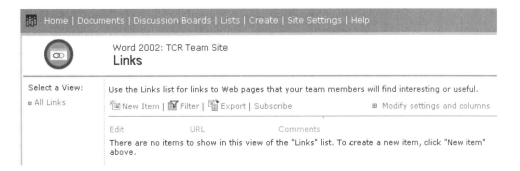

4. Click New Item to add a new link to the list. The New Item page appears in your browser window, as shown in Figure 17-9.

5. Type in the complete URL of the Web page you want to add as a link to the Link list.

6. Optionally, type a description of the URL in the Type in the Description text box.

7. Optionally, enter a comment or two about the URL in the Comments text box.

8. Click Save and Close to save the link; then return to the Links page.

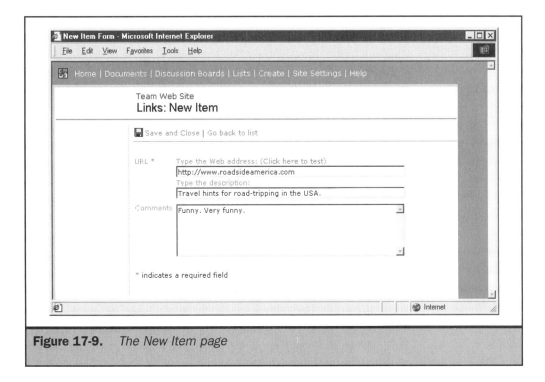

Figure 17-9. *The New Item page*

Discussing Projects with Team Members

Online discussions are an economical way for team members in different places to communicate about project developments and issues. You can host general discussions online as well as discussions about documents that have been posted on the team site. All this yakking is done by way of the discussion boards. The discussion boards on a SharePoint Team Services team site are very familiar to the Web-based discussion boards found on sites all across the Web.

There is one default discussion board called General Discussion, and you have the option of creating new discussion boards that concern issues, events, and projects that are important to your team.

Creating a New Discussion Board

You can create a new discussion board by way of the SharePoint Team Services Web interface. SharePoint Team Services can support many discussion boards. How many you can have depends on the server space that is dedicated to Web sites provisioned for SharePoint Team Services on the Web server.

You need Administrator rights to create a new discussion board on SharePoint Team Services. If you don't have Administrator rights, contact the site's administrator to create a new discussion board. If you have Administrator rights, follow these steps to create a new discussion board:

1. Go to the home page of your SharePoint Team Services team site.

2. Click Discussion Boards on the menu bar. You see the Team Web Site Discussions Board page.

3. Click New Discussion Board to open the Team Web Site New Discussion Board page, as show in Figure 17-10.

4. Enter a name for the new discussion board in the Name text box. Optionally, enter a description of the discussion board in the Description text box.

5. Specify whether to display the new discussion board on the Quick Launch bar.

6. Click the Create button to create the new discussion board. The new discussion board appears on your screen.

Team Web Site
Big Project

Discussions pertaining to the Big Project and all its manifestations.

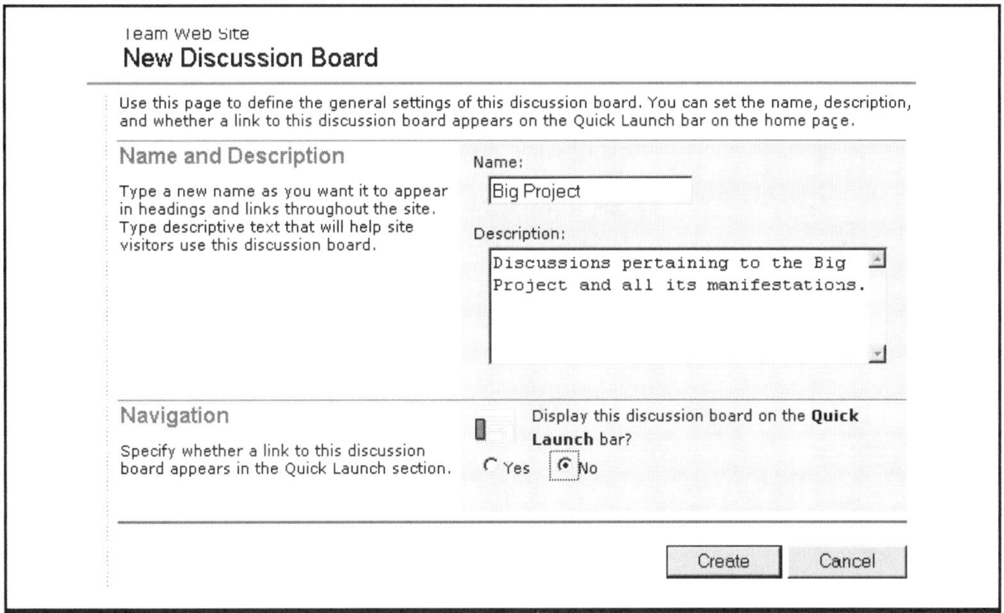

Team Web Site
New Discussion Board

Use this page to define the general settings of this discussion board. You can set the name, description, and whether a link to this discussion board appears on the Quick Launch bar on the home page.

Name and Description

Type a new name as you want it to appear in headings and links throughout the site. Type descriptive text that will help site visitors use this discussion board.

Name:

Big Project

Description:

Discussions pertaining to the Big Project and all its manifestations.

Navigation

Specify whether a link to this discussion board appears in the Quick Launch section.

Display this discussion board on the **Quick Launch** bar?

○ Yes   ● No

Create   Cancel

Figure 17-10.   *The Team Web Site New Discussion Board page*

Creating a Discussion for a Document

You can also create a discussion around a document or a Web page (or any document that can be opened in a Web browser). Comments generated during the discussion appear on the document you are discussing. The comments also appear in the discussion page when using the Discussion toolbar. However, the comments that are generated are stored separately from the document on SharePoint Team Services.

You need to have Administrator rights to create a new discussion for a Document on SharePoint Team Services. If you don't have Administrator rights to your SharePoint Services team site, contact the site's administrator to create a new discussion board. If you have Administrator rights, follow these steps to create a new discussion for a document:

1. Go to the home page of your SharePoint Team Services team site.

2. Click Discussion Boards on the menu bar.

3. Click Discuss a Document to open the Discuss a Document Using Web Discussions page, as shown in Figure 17-11.

4. Enter the address of the document you want to discuss in the Document URL text box. The address you type into the field must be a legal address of a document residing on your SharePoint Team Services, another internal corporate server, or a server not on your corporate network.

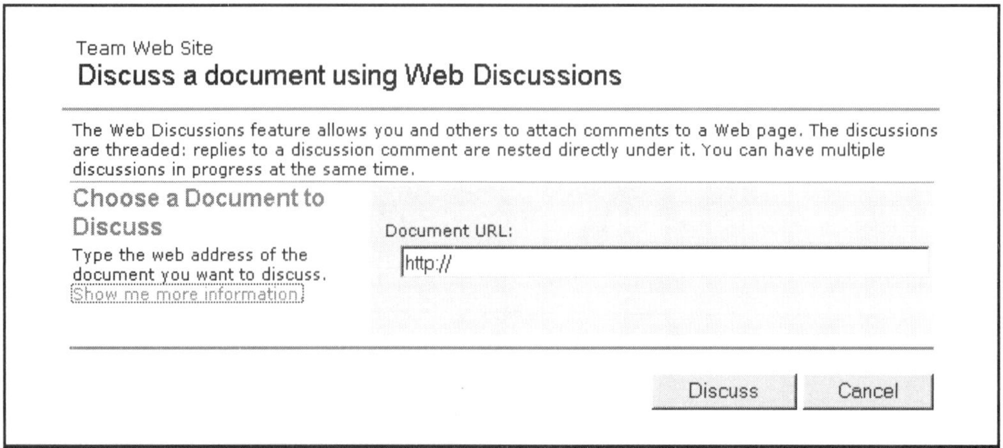

Team Web Site
Discuss a document using Web Discussions

The Web Discussions feature allows you and others to attach comments to a Web page. The discussions are threaded: replies to a discussion comment are nested directly under it. You can have multiple discussions in progress at the same time.

Choose a Document to Discuss

Type the web address of the document you want to discuss. [Show me more information]

Document URL:

http://

| Discuss | Cancel |

Figure 17-11. *The Discuss a Document Using Web Discussions page*

When accessing the URL of a document outside of your internal corporate network, a Web server, or another server under your control, security issues such as those pertaining to firewalls and access permissions may need to be worked out before you can gain access to the document.

5. Click the Discuss button to begin the discussion.

If you have the latest version of Internet Explorer, you can click the Web Discussions button on the Internet Explorer toolbar to add discussion comments to a posted document. If you are running an earlier version of Microsoft Office such as Office 97 or Office 2000 and a version of Internet Explorer earlier than 4.0, your only option to add discussion comments to the document is through a frame at the bottom of the browser window.

Participating in a Discussion

To participate in a discussion hosted on a SharePoint Team Services team site, you must have discussion permissions. In other words, you must have Contributor permissions at the very least. From your SharePoint Team Services team site home page, click Discussions Boards to open the Discussions Boards page. Select a discussion board from those listed on the page. Alternatively, you can open the Internet Explorer Discuss toolbar, browse to the page you want to discuss, and participate in a discussion there.

Replying to a Comment on a Discussion Board

Follow these steps to reply to a comment on a discussion board:

1. Starting on the Discussion Boards page, click the name of the discussion board you want to join.

2. Click the discussion item you want to reply to on the Discussion page. The discussion item appears in your browser window.

3. Click Reply to open a new item in response to the discussion item. You have the option of leaving the subject line the same. However, you can type in a new subject line to better reflect the reply you intend to type in.

4. Type your message in the Text box.

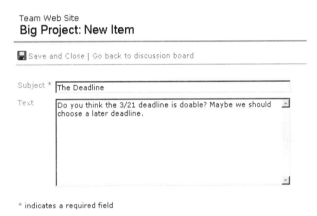

5. Click Save and Close to save your reply and return to the discussion board. Your reply appears beneath the original discussion board item.

Editing a Comment

You may have cause to edit a comment you made on a SharePoint Team Services discussion board. At minimum, you must have Contributor permissions to add and edit comments on a SharePoint Team Services message board. You can only edit discussion items of which you are the original author. Follow these steps to edit a comment on a discussion board:

1. Starting on the Discussions Boards page, click the name of the discussion board you want to join.

2. Click the discussion item you want to edit. The discussion item appears in your browser window.

3. Click Next: Edit the Item as Required to open the discussion item in your browser window.

4. Click Save and Close to save the edited discussion board item.

Deleting a Comment

At minimum, you must have Contributor permissions to delete comments on a SharePoint Team Services discussion board. Follow these steps to delete a comment from a discussion board:

1. Starting on the Discussions Boards page, click the name of the discussion board with the comment you want to delete.

2. Click the discussion item you want to remove from the Discussion page. The discussion item appears in your browser window.

3. Click Delete Item. You are asked if you want to delete this item.

4. Click OK to delete it. The discussion board refreshes showing the item deleted.

Lists to Help the Project Along

Typically, lists are used as management tools in many organizations to keep project teams and their projects on track. SharePoint Team Services has features for keeping a variety of lists that a project team might accumulate during the course of a project.

Rather than keep lists on individual team member's computers, PDAs, note pads, yellow sticky notes, or other organizational tools, SharePoint Team Services can be a central repository of the following lists:

■ The Announcements list places announcements on the home page of the team site. Use announcements to deliver messages to the project team about general information.

■ The Events list is for activities such as conferences, meetings, deadlines, and holidays. After the first event is listed, the Events list appears on the home page of the SharePoint Team Services team site.

■ The Tasks list is a standard to-do list with information, including the title of the task, to whom the task is assigned, the status of the task, the task's priority, its due date, and its completion status by percentage.

■ The Contacts list is a central place for listing the team's contacts, including information such as the contact's first name and last name, company, business phone, home phone, and e-mail address.

■ The Links list is a place to go to catalog links to corporate intranet and external third-party Web sites.

Conducting a Survey

Along with all the other communications and collaboration tools provided by SharePoint Team Services, you can survey your team site users online by using the SharePoint Team

Services Survey feature. The survey feature enables you to ask a variety of questions online. You need Administrator privileges to create a SharePoint Team Services-hosted online survey. Follow these steps to conduct the survey:

1. Go to the home page of your SharePoint Team Services team site.
2. Click Create on the menu bar to begin creating a new survey. The Create Page appears.
3. Click Survey to open the New Survey page. The New Survey page appears in your browser window.

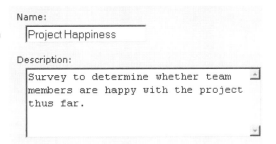

Name and Description

Type a new name as you want it to appear in headings and links throughout the site. Type descriptive text that will help site visitors use this survey.

Name:

Project Happiness

Description:

Survey to determine whether team members are happy with the project thus far.

4. Enter a name and description for the survey in the Name and Description text boxes.
5. Specify whether you want to display the survey title on your SharePoint Team Services team site's Quick Launch bar.
6. Define your survey options, including whether you want to show user names in survey results and allow multiple responses to the survey.
7. Click the Next button to advance to the Create New Question page. The Create New Question page looks similar to Figure 17-12.
8. Type your question in the Question field.
9. By choosing an option button, select a type of answer for the question.
10. In the Optional Settings for Your Question part of the page, enter any optional settings for the question.
11. Click the OK button. The Customization page opens in your browser window. Scroll to the Questions section of the Customization page.
12. Click Add a Question to return to the Create New Question page.

Sorry, you have to repeat the process on the Create New Question for each question in your survey.

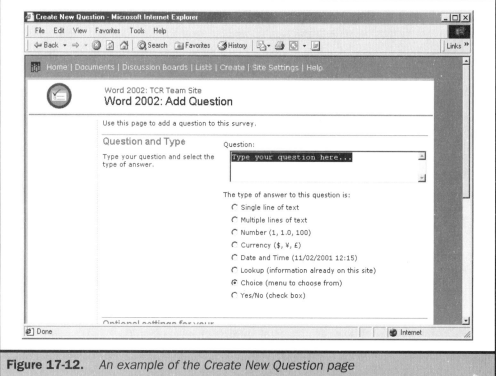

Figure 17-12. *An example of the Create New Question page*

MOUS Exam Objectives Explored in Chapter 17

Objective	Heading
Apply character effects and highlights	"Highlighting the Important Text"
Apply bullet, outline, and numbering format to paragraphs	"Organizing Your Work with Outlines"
Compare and Merge Documents	"Tracking Revisions to a Document"
View and edit comments	"Commenting on a Document"
Add and revise notes and comments*	"Commenting on a Document"

Objective	Heading
Create and manage master documents and subdocuments*	"Master Documents for Organizing Big Jobs"
Track, accept, and reject changes to documents*	"Keeping Track of Revisions to Documents"
Merge input from several reviewers*	"Tracking Revisions to a Document" and "Routing a Document to Others"
Insert Link bars in documents*	"Creating a Link List"

* Denotes an Expert, not a Core, exam objective.

Ten Tips for Sharing Documents with Others

Sharing documents with other people presents several problems, some of which can grow into big problems if you are not careful. Following are ten tips for sharing documents with others. Take these ten tips into consideration when you collaborate with others on a document.

1. Make Sure Everyone Is Using the Same Template   When people who work at different computers collaborate on a document, problems with styles can arise if the template on which the document was founded is not loaded on each computer. As you know if you read Chapter 12, every Word document is grounded in a template. When you choose a new style, you in effect ask the template to format a part of your document. If everyone who collaborates on a document asks a different template to format their document, you get different formats. Headings change appearance. Indents change. New fonts appear. Lists are not formatted the same way. The document you gave to somebody else to work on comes back looking like an imposter.

When you pass along a document to your collaborator, make sure that he or she also has the template with which you created the document. For that matter, when someone hands you a document, make sure you also get the template with which the document was created. And that brings us to Tip 2 in the list….

2. Attach the Template for the Shared Document to the Document   When you get a template from someone else, load it on your computer and attach the template to the document you want to collaborate on. "Applying Styles *En Masse* with the Templates and Add-Ins Command" in Chapter 12 explains how to attach a template to a document. Load your template in the C:\Windows Application Data\Microsoft\Templates folder.

If your computer is connected to a network workgroup, you can share templates over the network with others. Tell your network administrator that you want to be able to share a template with other members of your workgroup and ask the administrator which folder shared templates are stored in. Then do the following in your computer to tell Word where to find the template you need to work with:

1. Choose Tools | Options.
2. Click the File Locations tab in the Options dialog box.
3. Under File Types, select Workgroup Templates, and then click the Modify button. You see the Modify Location dialog box.
4. Find the folder on your network where the workgroup templates are located. You can get the name of the folder from the network administrator.
5. Click OK and then click OK again in the Options dialog box.

After all collaborators have attached the right template to the document they are sharing, they can rest assured that no formats will change when the document is passed from collaborator to collaborator. Well, they can rest assured except for a couple of minor details, which brings up Tip 3 in the list....

3. Tell Word Not to Assign Styles Automatically   Word assigns styles to certain paragraphs automatically. If you format a paragraph a certain way, Word may decide that you need a style and assign a style for you. Automatic style assignments are fine and dandy when you are working on your own, but they can wreak havoc when a document is shared with others. An automatic style gets assigned here, another gets created there, and pretty soon you are looking at a crazy quilt of a document.

Follow these steps to tell Word not to assign styles automatically:

1. Choose Tools | AutoCorrect Options to open the AutoCorrect dialog box.
2. Select the AutoFormat As You Type tab.
3. Under Automatically As You Type, uncheck the Define Styles Based On Your Formatting check box.
4. Under Apply As You Type, uncheck the Built-In Headings check box.
5. Click OK.

4. Turn Off the Fast-Saving Mechanism   As "Telling Word How to Save Documents" in Chapter 20 explains, the Allow Fast Saves feature makes it possible to save documents as you work. That's nice except for one thing: Word does not save recent changes in the document file, but in a separate file so that updates can be made faster. When you pass a document to someone else and the fast-saving mechanism is in effect, you really pass two files to someone else. Passing along two files instead of one can be confusing to the computer that receives the document. Microsoft recommends turning off the Allow Fast Saves option when you finish working on a document or give it to someone else. To turn it off, choose Tools | Options, select the Save tab in the Options dialog box, and uncheck the Allow Fast Saves check box.

5. Use Common Fonts That Are Found on Everyone's Computer   Fonts can be a problem when you share documents because the same fonts are not available on all computers. To get around the font problem, use common fonts such as Arial and Times Roman for early drafts of your work. When the time comes to get the document ready for a presentation, give it to one person to put the finishing touches on. Let the last person who handles the document apply the fancy fonts. You waste your time if you apply fancy fonts in the early stages because the fancy fonts are likely to disappear when they travel to other people's computers.

6. Take Paper Size into Account   Recently I designed a template for an international company with offices in Europe and the United States. Because Europeans and North Americans have different paper standards, I had to design two templates, one for 210×297 millimeter (A4) paper and one for $8\frac{1}{2} \times 11$ inch paper. Paper sizes affect layouts. If you are collaborating with others across international borders, take paper size into account. You may have to create two documents, one for your paper standard and one for theirs.

7. See if You Can Get Everyone to Use the Same Version of Word   I realize that asking all collaborators to use the same version of Word is asking a lot. Upgrades can be expensive. Learning the new version of a computer program creates a certain amount of anxiety and takes time. Still, you save a lot of trouble if all collaborators use the same version of Word. Some formats are lost when a Word document is saved as a Word 97 or Word 2000 document.

8. Do Not Trade Versions of Documents   As "Saving (and Opening) Different Versions of a Document" in Chapter 20 explains, Word offers a very nice feature whereby different versions of a document can be saved and kept on hand in case they are needed. You might be tempted to pass along versions of a document to others, but don't do it. Others may open different versions of the document and pretty soon you won't know which version is which.

Before you pass along a document for which you've created different versions, open the version that you want to pass along. Then choose File | Save As and save the version under its own name.

9. Use Document Summaries to Describe Work Done to a Document   When a document gets passed here, there, and everywhere, knowing who worked on it and what was done to it can be difficult. To describe the work that was done, instruct everyone who handles the document to choose File | Properties and jot a note or two in the Comments box on the Summary tab of the Properties dialog box. By reading the notes, you can see what all collaborators did to the document.

10. Create Folders for Organizing the Project   Nothing gets out of hand faster than a project in which you collaborate with many people. Create folders for different drafts of the work. Save versions of the work from different collaborators in different folders. And make sure you always know which version of the document is most up to date and represents the fruition of everyone's labor.

Chapter 18

Churning Out Form Letters, Mass-Mailing Labels, and Directories

This chapter describes *mail-merging*, Microsoft's term for generating form letters, labels, and envelopes for mass-mailings, as well as directories and e-mail messages. No doubt you've received form letters in the mail. And you've seen your name on a printed mailing label, too. Large companies generate form letters and mailing labels by taking names and addresses from databases and plugging those names and addresses into form letters or printing them on mailing labels. You can do the same in Word. You can plug names and addresses from your own tables and address lists into form letters and mailing labels. In your own small way, you can be a junk mailer.

Be sure to read the first section in this chapter, "The Six Steps to Completing a Mail-Merge," if you are new to mail-merging or new to the latest version of Word. The mail-merging procedure has changed from previous versions. These pages explain how Word gathers names and addresses for the mail-merge and what mail-merging entails. You also find out how to generate form letters, mailing labels, envelopes for mass-mailings, and lists in Chapter 18. Toward the end of the chapter are advanced techniques for sorting data before you mail-merge it. You will also find a list of ten common mail-merge problems and advice for solving those problems at the end of the chapter.

The Six Steps to Completing a Mail-Merge

Mail-merging means to plug data from an address table into form letters, e-mail messages, envelopes, address labels, or a directory (a list or catalog, for example). The details of mail-merging are described throughout this chapter. These pages describe the basic steps of mail-merging.

To start a mail-merge, choose Tools | Letters and Mailings | Mail Merge Wizard to open the Mail Merge task pane. Throughout the mail-merge, you will make choices in the task pane, complete steps, and click Next to go from step to step. The task pane tells you which step you are on and how many steps are to be completed.

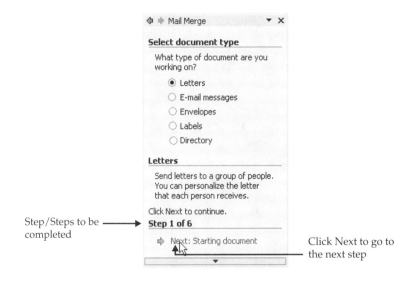

Step/Steps to be completed

Click Next to go to the next step

If you know your way around mail-merge procedures, you can mail-merge without visiting the mail-merge task pane. Instead, display the Mail Merge toolbar, click the Mail Document Setup button on the toolbar, and take it from there.

Step 1: Select a Document Type

The first step is to choose Tools | Letters and Mailings | Mail Merge Wizard and select what Word calls a "document type" in the Mail Merge task pane. What you really do in the first step is choose what kind of mail-merge you want to undertake: form letters, e-mail messages, envelopes for mass-mailings, labels for mass-mailings, or a directory (a list or catalog). Choose an option button and click Next at the bottom of the task pane to go to step 2.

 Notice the Previous link at the bottom of the Mail Merge task pane. Click it to retrace your steps if you make an error along the way.

Step 2: Select a Starting Document

What Word calls the "starting document" is the document in which the merging takes place. In other words, the address or other data you retrieve will land in the document you choose or create now.

You can create a new starting document or use an existing one. In the case of labels and envelopes, you tell Word what size labels or envelopes you intend to print on. In the case of form letters, e-mail messages, and directories, you supply the text either by making use of a document you've written already or writing a new document.

Step 3: Select Recipients

In step 3, you tell Word where to get the data that you will merge into the starting document you created or supplied in step 2. You can retrieve the data from a table in a Word document, an Access database table or query, or the address book or contact list where you store your addresses. You can also create a new list for the data if you haven't entered the data in a file yet. Later in this chapter, "Preparing and Selecting the Data Source" explains how to create or edit a data file in such a way that it is useful for mail-merges.

Step 4: Write/Arrange Your Document

In step 4, you insert the *merge fields*, the parts of the starting document that differ from recipient to recipient. By inserting merge fields, you tell Word where to plug information from the data source into the starting document. You also tell Word which data to take from the data source. Word offers special tools for entering an *address block*—the recipient's address, including his or her name, company, title, street address, city, and zip code.

Figure 18-1 shows a form letter. Notice the chevrons («») on either side of merge field names. When this form letter is merged with the data source, names and addresses will appear where the merge fields are now. When Word sees the First_Name merge field, for example, it knows to insert a first name from the data source file.

Step 5: Preview Your Document

In step 5, you get a chance to see what your form letters, e-mail messages, envelopes, labels, or directory will look like after they are printed or sent. In this step, you find out what the document will look like when real data is plugged into it.

If something is amiss in the document, you can click the Previous link to return to step 4, the Write/Arrange your document task pane, and make changes there.

Mail Merge toolbar

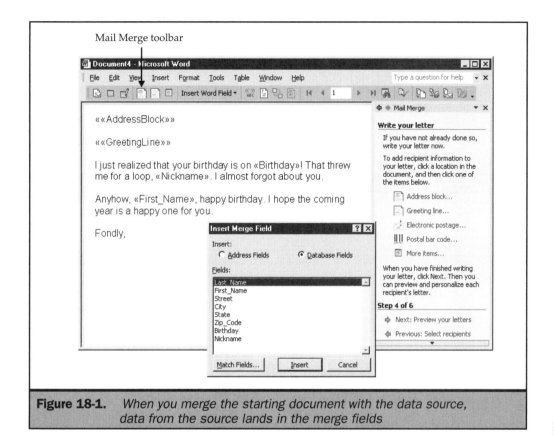

Figure 18-1.   *When you merge the starting document with the data source, data from the source lands in the merge fields*

Compare this illustration to Figure 18-1 and you will see how data from the data source is plugged into merge fields in the document.

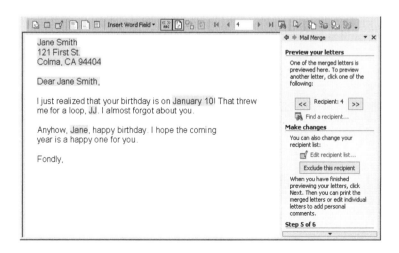

Step 6: Complete the Merge

Step 6 is where you complete the merge by either printing a new document or saving the new file and printing it later. By saving the merged data in a new file, you can edit the file before printing it. In the case of e-mail messages, you click the Electronic Mail link to tell Word to send the e-mail messages.

Preparing and Selecting the Data Source

Before you attempt to generate form letters, e-mail messages, envelopes, address labels, or a directory, make sure that the data source is in good working order. The *data source* is the file where the addresses and other information is kept. Step 3 of the mail-merge procedure calls for you to name your data source, and before you name it, make sure that it is in good working order. The data source can be any number of things—a Word table, or addresses that you keep in a Microsoft Outlook folder, a Microsoft Access database table, a Microsoft Access query. And Word offers a special dialog box for creating a data source from scratch and storing it in Microsoft Access. Read on to find out how to prepare the data source for a mail-merge.

 After you create the data source, do not move it to a different folder or rearrange the merge fields/columns. If you do so, the document can't read the data source correctly and you can't complete the mail-merge.

 As you contemplate the data source you intend to use, it helps to know two terms from the dreary world of databases: field and record. A field is one category of information. A record comprises all the data about one person or thing. It helps to think of fields and records in terms of the rows and columns in a table: Each row in a table is a record, since it lists what is known about one person or thing; each record is divided into several fields, or categories, of information, in the same way that each row is divided into columns.

Using a Word Table as the Data Source

For people who aren't familiar with Microsoft Access or databases, the easiest type of data source to manage is a Word table. Either create an address table from scratch or copy a table you have already created and save the table by itself in a document. Save the table under a name you will recognize. When you merge the data source table with the starting document, you will be asked to locate and select the document that holds your addresses or other to-be-merged information.

To use a Word table as the data source, the table must meet these standards:

- A descriptive heading must appear across the top of each column. The row of descriptive headings across the top of a table is called the *header row*, or sometimes the *heading row*. The names in the header row double as merge field names when you insert merge fields in the starting document, as Figure 18-2 shows. When you tell Word where to plug data into the starting document, you choose a column name from your table.

- No text or blank lines can appear above the table in the document. To be on the safe side, save the table in a document by itself.

Note   *See "Turning a List into a Table—and Vice Versa" in Chapter 14 to learn how to turn an address list into a table that can be used in mail-merges. Chapter 14 explains tables in excruciating detail.*

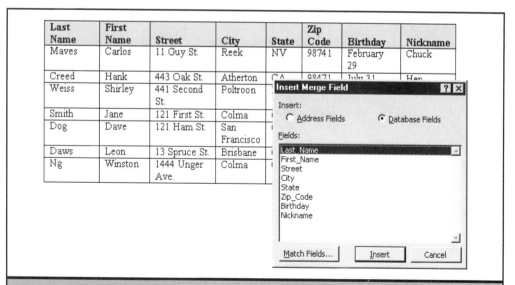

Figure 18-2.   *To tell Word where to get data from a Word table, you choose a column name in the Insert Merge Field dialog box*

USING WORD 2002
AT THE OFFICE

To use a Word table as a data source, click the Use an Existing List option button
in the Mail Merge task pane in step 3, and then click the Browse hyperlink on the
task pane or the Open Data Source button on the Mail Merge toolbar. The Select Data
Source dialog box appears. Select the Word document with the table you need and
click the Open button.

Constructing an Access Data Source File During the Mail-Merge

If you haven't yet created a table or database table with the information you want to
merge, you can create a data source with Word's help. When you are done, you will have
created a Microsoft Access database table called Office_Address_List, and that brings
up a problem with creating the data source this way: Most people aren't familiar with
Access. Unless you know your way around Access, create a Word table and use it as
the data source (the previous section in this chapter explains how).

To create an Access database table from scratch and use it as the data source in a
mail-merge, start during step 3 of the mail-merge (see "The Six Steps to Completing a
Mail-Merge" at the start of this chapter if the six fateful steps are unknown to you). As
shown in Figure 18-3, choose the Type a New List option button in the Mail Merge task

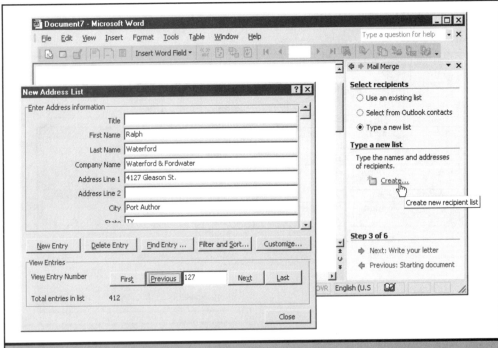

Figure 18-3.   *Creating a database table as the data source in a mail-merge*

pane, and then click the Create hyperlink. You see the New Address List dialog box shown in Figure 18-3.

Your first task in this dialog box is to decide which field names you need. You need one field for each piece of information that you will plug into the starting document. If you are making address labels, for example, you need a First Name, Last Name, Address Line 1, City, State, and Zip Code fields, and perhaps more. To trim the list to only the field names you need, click the Customize button. Then do the following in the Customize Address List dialog box:

- **Removing Field Names** Select the name that needs removing and click the Delete button.

- **Creating a New Merge Field** Click the Add button, enter a name in the Add Field dialog box, and click OK.

- **Changing Field Names** Select the field that needs a new name, click the Rename button, and enter a new name in the Rename Field dialog box.

- **Rearranging the List** Select a name and click the Move Up or Move Down button until the name is in the right place on the list.

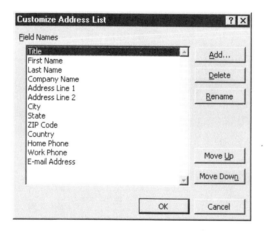

Your next task is to enter the information that will be plugged into the starting document. To do so, enter information in the text boxes, and click the New Entry button again to go to the next entry. You can click a View Entry Number button—First, Previous, Next, or Last—to review the entries you've made. Display an entry and click the Delete Entry button to remove an entry from the database table you are creating.

When you are finished entering data and you click the Close button, you see the Save Address List dialog box. Select a folder for your database, enter a descriptive name for it, and click the Save button.

USING WORD 2002
AT THE OFFICE

Using Microsoft Outlook Contacts as the Data Source

People who store their addresses in Microsoft Outlook can use those addresses as the data source in mail-merges. All you have to do is choose the Select from Outlook Contacts option button in the Mail Merge task pane in step 3 when you select recipients, and then click the Choose Contacts Folder hyperlink, as shown in Figure 18-4. (See "The Six Steps to Completing a Mail-Merge" at the start of this chapter if you are unfamiliar with Word's six-step mail-merging program.)

 Typically, some addresses in an address book are incomplete. In my Outlook Contacts folder, for example, some names are accompanied only by a telephone number, while other names come with all kinds of information—pager numbers, Bahamian addresses, Web site addresses. The problem with using Outlook as the data source in a mail-merge is that many names do not include address information. See "Picking and Choosing Recipients for a Mail-Merge" later in this chapter to learn how you can exclude incomplete addresses from a mail-merge.

If you don't keep addresses in Microsoft Outlook but you want to use addresses you keep in another software program for mail-merges, you can try getting the addresses. I use the word "try" because Outlook is notoriously stubborn about fetching addresses from other programs. To get addresses from another program into the Contacts folder in

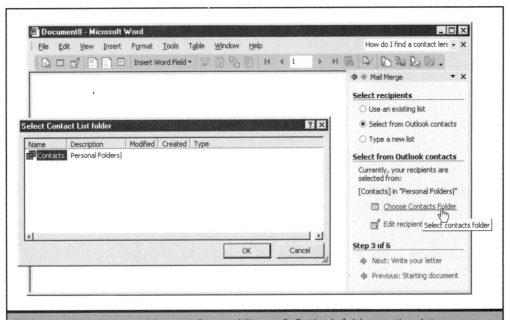

Figure 18-4. *Using addresses from a Microsoft Outlook folder as the data source*

Outlook, open Outlook and choose File | Import and Export. Then, in the Import and Export Wizard, choose Import from Another Program or File, click the Next button, and do what the wizard tells you. Good luck.

You also can use a Personal Address Book (.PAB) as the data source. To do so, select Use an Existing List in step 3, click the Browse hyperlink, and select the .PAB file in the Select Data Source dialog box.

Using an Access Database Table or Query as the Data Source

If you happen to know your way around database programs such as Access, you also know that a database table is the best place to store addresses because you can query a database table to drudge up only the records you need. People who know their way around Access will be glad to know that you can use an Access database table or Access query as the data source for a mail-merge.

In step 3 of the mail-merge, when you choose the data source, select the Use an Existing List option button in the Mail Merge task pane and click the Browse hyperlink, or click the Open Data Source button on the Mail Merge toolbar, as shown in the following illustration. Then, in the Select Data Source dialog box, select the Access database where you keep addresses and click the Open button. What happens next depends on whether the database file you selected includes more than one table or tables and queries:

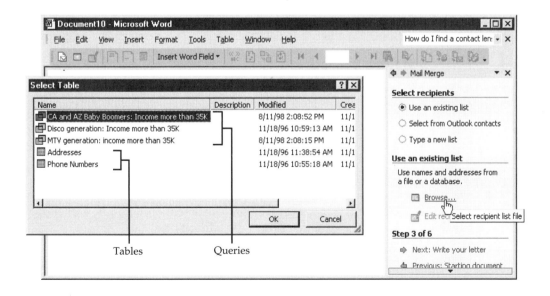

- **Tables and Queries**   As the illustration shows, you see the Select Table dialog box, where icons mark the queries and tables in your database. Select the query or table you want and click OK. You see the Mail Merge Recipients dialog box, where you choose which records to include in the merge. (See "The Six Steps to Completing a Mail-Merge" at the start of this chapter if you are unfamiliar with the six steps to mail-merge bliss.)

- **Just One Database Table**   You go straight to the Mail Merge Recipients dialog box, where you choose which records to include in the merge.

Word offers a handful of commands for querying and sorting source data during a mail-merge, but if you know how to construct a query in Access, query to obtain the data in Access and then mail-merge with the query. The querying tools in Access are much more sophisticated and easy to use than the querying tools you will find in Word.

Generating Form Letters for Mass-Mailings

After you have prepared the data source, you are ready to write and generate form letters. A *form letter* is a near-identical letter sent to numerous people. Only the particulars of each recipient are different—the recipient's name, the recipient's address, and perhaps one or two identifying facts about the recipient.

Choose Tools | Letters and Mailings | Mail Merge Wizard and, clicking the Next button as you go along, follow these steps in the Mail Merge task pane to generate form letters for mass-mailings:

Step 1: Select a Document Type   Under Select Document Type, select the Letters option button and click the Next hyperlink.

Step 2: Select a Starting Document   Tell Word whether you're starting from scratch or using a letter you've already written for the form letter:

- **Starting from Scratch**   Make sure the Use the Current Document or Start from Template option is selected in the task pane. To write your form letter with the help of a template, click the Select Template hyperlink and choose a template in the Select Template dialog box. The Mail Merge tab offers templates designed especially for mail-merges.

- **Using a Letter You've Already Written**   If you have already written the text of the form letter, select the Start from Existing Document option button, click the Open button, and select the letter in the Open dialog box.

Step 3: Select Recipients   Choose an option button under Select Recipients to choose the data source for the form letters (see "Preparing and Selecting the Data Source" earlier in this chapter). You see the Mail Merge Recipients dialog box. Click OK if you want to select all the recipients in the source file. To select some, not all, of the recipients, see "Picking and Choosing Recipients for a Mail-Merge" later in this chapter.

Step 4: Write Your Letter   Compose the text of the letter if you've not already done so, and then enter the address block, greeting line, and merge fields (see "Inserting Merge Fields, the Address Block, and the Greeting Line" later in this chapter for details):

- **Merge fields**   Place the cursor where you want a merge field to go, click More Items on the task pane or the Insert Merge Fields button on the Mail Merge toolbar, and double-click the name of a merge field in the Insert Merge Field dialog box. You can also select a field and click the Insert button.

- **Address block**   Place the cursor near or at the top of the letter and click the Insert Address Block button, or click the Address Block hyperlink in the Mail Merge task pane. The Insert Address Block dialog box appears. Enter the address block and click OK.

- **Greeting line**   Place the cursor where the salutation goes and click the Insert Greeting Line button, or click the Greeting Line hyperlink on the Mail Merge toolbar. In the Greeting Line dialog box, fashion a salutation and click OK.

In the starting document, be careful when entering blank spaces and punctuation marks around merge fields. A blank space, for example, goes after a merge field unless the merge field appears before a comma or at the end of a sentence. You can always click the View Merged Data button on the Mail Merge toolbar to see whether punctuation marks and blank spaces will appear correctly after the form letters are printed. Figure 8-5 shows a form letter in which recipients' birthdays and nicknames are mentioned as well as their names and addresses. Notice how field names, including the Address Block and Greeting Line fields, translate into real text when the form letter is generated.

Step 5: Preview Your Document   Step 5 is your chance to look over the form letters before you print them or create a file for them. Later in this chapter, "Examining Your Mail-Merge for the Last Time" explains all the different ways to make sure your mail-merge will go off without a hitch.

    Click the Highlight Merge Fields button on the Mail Merge toolbar to get a better idea about where the merge fields are.

Step 6: Complete the Merge   Now you're ready to go. Sorry to send you packing once again to another part of this chapter, but "Merging the Starting Document and Data Source," a few pages hence, explains how to complete the job.

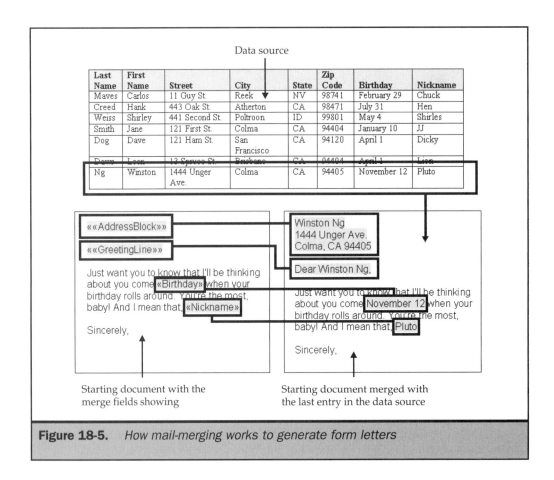

Figure 18-5.   *How mail-merging works to generate form letters*

Sending the Same E-Mail to Many Different People

Frankly, you're better off sending an e-mail message to more than one person in the e-mailing software that you use. If your e-mailing software is worth anything, sending the same message to more than one person is pretty easy. Still, perhaps you want to query or sort before sending your e-mail message. You can do that in Word. You can also send a Word document by e-mail to many different people.

Note   *In Chapter 22 "E-Mailing from Inside Word" looks at sending e-mail messages from inside Word, including how to set up Word so that it can double as an e-mailer.*

Near the start of this chapter, "The Six Steps to Completing a Mail-Merge" explains the six steps for mail-merging in detail. After you have familiarized yourself with mail-merging, choose Tools | Letters and Mailings | Mail Merge Wizard and follow these steps in the Mail Merge task pane to generate form letters for mass-mailings:

Step 1: Select a Document Type   Under Select Document Type, select the E-Mail Message option button and click the Next hyperlink to go to step 2.

Step 2: Select a Starting Document   Tell Word whether you intend to write the e-mail message from scratch or get the text from a document you've already written:

- **Starting from Scratch**   Click Use the Current Document or Start from Template option in the task pane. To get the help of a template, click the Select Template hyperlink and choose a template in the Select Template dialog box that appears.

- **Using a Document You've Already Written**   If you want to peel text from a document you've already written, select the Start from Existing Document option button, click the Open button, and select the document in the Open dialog box.

Tip   *You can send a Word document, not an e-mail message, to many different people by way of the Mail Merge Wizard. To do so, choose the Start from Existing Document option button in step 2, click the Open button, and choose the document you want to send in the Open dialog box. In step 4, when you would normally write the message, write nothing. In step 6, in the Merge to E-Mail dialog box, choose Attachment from the Mail Format drop-down menu.*

Step 3: Select Recipients   Choose an option button under Select Recipients to choose the data source where you will get the e-mail addresses and perhaps other information you want to include in the e-mails (see "Preparing and Selecting the Data Source" earlier in this chapter). The Mail Merge Recipients dialog box appears. In the unlikely event that you want to send e-mail to all the recipients in the source file, click OK. Otherwise, see "Picking and Choosing Recipients for a Mail-Merge" later in this chapter.

Step 4: Write Your E-Mail Message   Enter the text of the message if you haven't already done so. To insert a merge field such as a name, click More Items in the task pane or the Insert Merge Fields button on the Mail-Merge toolbar. Then, in the Insert Merge Field dialog box, double-click the name of a merge field. Turn to "Inserting Merge Fields, the Address Block, and the Greeting Line" later in this chapter if you need help.

Step 5: Preview Your Document   Click the Next Record (and Previous Record) button on the Mail Merge toolbar to go from recipient to recipient and examine the e-mail messages you will send. Later in this chapter, "Examining Your Mail-Merge for the Last Time" explains how to make sure your e-mail messages are sent correctly.

Step 6: Complete the Merge   Click Electronic Mail on the task pane or the Merge to E-Mail button the Mail Merge toolbar. You see the Merge to E-Mail dialog box. Choose options in the dialog box and click OK to send the messages.

- **To** From the drop-down menu, choose the field in the data source where e-mail addresses are kept.

- **Subject Line** Enter the subject of your message. Recipients will see what you enter first when the messages arrive.

- **Mail Format** Choose Plain Text if you believe that recipients have antiquated browsers that can't display HTML; otherwise, choose HTML. Choose Attachment to send the Word document that is onscreen as an attachment to the e-mail message.

- **Send Records** Select All to send the message to all the recipients you chose in step 3; choose Current Record to send the message to the recipient whose name is onscreen.

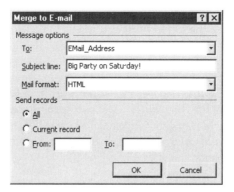

Printing Envelopes for Mass-Mailings

The procedures for printing envelopes for mass-mailings and printing labels for mass-mailings are nearly the same. As part of printing envelopes for mass-mailings, you are asked which size envelope you will print on. In my experience, printing envelopes is a chore. Unless you have a sophisticated printer, you have to feed the envelopes to the printer one at a time, which is a tedious job if your mass-mailing is truly a mass-mailing and not a puny mailing. An easier way to send out letters is to print the addresses on labels and attach the labels to envelopes, although a label stuck to an envelope doesn't look very elegant, does it?

"Printing Addresses and Return Addresses on Envelopes" in Chapter 5 explains how to print a single envelope. Earlier in this chapter, "The Six Steps to Completing a Mail-Merge" explains the six steps involved with mail-merging.

Choose Tools | Letters and Mailings | Mail Merge Wizard to begin the task of printing envelopes for mass-mailings. Then follow these steps:

Step 1: Select a Document Type   Under Select Document Type, choose the Envelopes option button and click the Next hyperlink.

Step 2: Select a Starting Document   Select the Change Document Layout option button, and then, in the Mail Merge task pane, click the Envelope Options hyperlink. You see the Envelope Options dialog box. On the Envelope Options tab, describe the type of envelopes you will print on; describe how envelopes are fed to your printer on the Printing Options tab.

 In Chapter 5, "Printing Addresses and Return Addresses on Envelopes" describes the Envelope Options dialog box in detail.

Step 3: Select Recipients   Under Select Recipients, select an option button to describe the data source where you will get names and addresses for the envelopes (see "Preparing and Selecting the Data Source" earlier in this chapter). You see the Mail Merge Recipients dialog box. Click OK immediately if you want to address envelopes to everyone whose name appears in the data source. Later in this chapter, "Picking and Choosing Recipients for a Mail-Merge" explains how you can pick and choose some of the names.

Step 4: Arrange Your Envelope   Enter the address fields for the envelopes, as well as postal bar codes if you so desire:

- **Inserting the Address**   Click in the middle of the envelope, and, when the object appears, click the Insert Address Block button on the Mail Merge toolbar or click the Address Block hyperlink in the task pane. You see the Insert Address Block dialog box. Describe how to address the envelopes and click OK. (Later in this chapter, "Inserting Merge Fields, the Address Block, and the Greeting Line" explains how to fashion an address block.)

- **Including Postal Bar Codes with Addresses**   Postal bar codes help the postal service deliver letters faster. If you want to include them in addresses, click the Postal Bar Code hyperlink in the Mail Merge task pane. The Insert Postal Bar Code dialog box appears. Open the first drop-down menu and choose the field in the data source where postal codes or Zip codes are kept.

USING WORD 2002
AT THE OFFICE

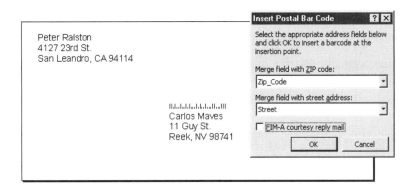

Making Sure the Return Address Is Printed

The return address that Word prints on envelopes comes from the Mailing Address box on the User Information tab in the Options dialog box. To get there, choose Tools | Options and select the User Information tab. Before you print envelopes for a mass-mailing, make sure that the address you want to appear on your envelopes is listed in its entirety on the Mailing Address text box. Whatever appears in the Mailing Address box appears on the envelopes. Some people mistakenly enter their address and not their name or company name as well as their address in the Mailing Address text box.

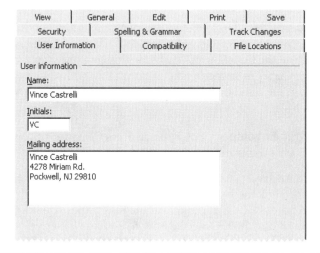

Note *See "Making Sure the Return Address Is Printed" later in this chapter to learn how to handle the return address on envelopes.*

Step 5: Preview Your Envelopes   Later in this chapter, "Examining Your Mail-Merge for the Last Time" explains how to make sure addresses print correctly on the envelopes. For now, click the Next Record button to skip ahead and examine the addresses. If the address block was entered incorrectly, click the Previous button to go back one step, delete the address block, and start all over.

Step 6: Complete the Merge   In the final step, merge the data source with the envelopes. Later in this chapter, "Merging the Starting Document and Data Source" explains how to do that.

Printing Labels for Mass-Mailings

As long as you know how data sources work (see "Preparing and Selecting the Data Source" earlier in this chapter), you can generate labels for mass-mailings very easily.

To generate the labels, you get the names and addresses of recipients from the data source, as Figure 18-6 shows.

"Printing a Single Label or Sheet of Labels with the Same Address" in Chapter 5 explains how to print one or two labels at a time.

Before you mail-merge labels, take note of what brand labels you have and what size your labels are. Word asks for that information when you generate labels. The program needs to know what size your labels are so it can place the labels correctly on the label sheet you will print the names and addresses on.

Choose Tools | Letters and Mailings | Mail Merge Wizard and follow these steps to generate labels for a mass-mailing:

Step 1: Select a Document Type   Under Select Document Type, choose the Labels option button and click the Next hyperlink.

Near the start of this chapter, "The Six Steps to Completing a Mail-Merge" explains the six steps of mail-merging in detail.

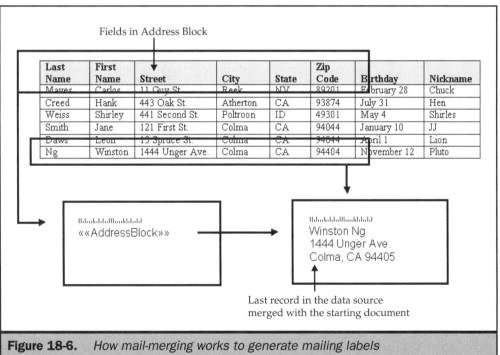

Figure 18-6.   *How mail-merging works to generate mailing labels*

Step 2: Select a Starting Document   Tell Word whether to start with a new document or a label document you've set up in the past:

- **Starting with a New Document**   Click the Change Document Layout option button and then click the Label Options hyperlink in the Mail Merge toolbar. You see the Label Options dialog box. Select the label brand and the size of the labels you will print on and click OK.

- **Starting with a Label Document**   Click the Start from Existing Document option button and then click the Open button. In the Open dialog box, find and select a label document you have used before and click the Open button.

Note   *In Chapter 5, "Printing a Single Label or Sheet of Labels with the Same Address" explains the Label Options dialog box.*

Step 3: Select Recipients   Under Select Recipients, select an option button to describe the data source where you will get names and addresses for the labels (see "Preparing and Selecting the Data Source" earlier in this chapter). The Mail Merge Recipients dialog box appears. Click OK if you want to print labels for everyone in the dialog box, but if you want to select a handful of names, see "Picking and Choosing Recipients for a Mail-Merge" later in this chapter.

Step 4: Arrange Your Labels   Enter the addresses for the labels and postal bar codes as well:

- **Inserting the Address**   Either click the Insert Address Block button on the Mail Merge toolbar or click the Address Block hyperlink in the task pane. The Insert Address Block dialog box appears. Describe how to address the labels and click OK. (Later in this chapter, "Inserting Merge Fields, the Address Block, and the Greeting Line" explains how to fashion an address block.)

- **Including Postal Bar Codes with Addresses**   Postal bar codes help the postal service deliver letters faster. To include them in addresses, click the Postal Bar Code hyperlink in the task pane, and, in the Insert Postal Bar Code dialog box, open the first drop-down menu and choose the field in the data source where postal codes or Zip codes are listed.

At this point, a bunch of Next Record fields appear in your document. It's time to click the Propagate Labels button on the Mail Merge toolbar or the Update All Labels button on the Mail Merge task pane to place the Address Block in all the labels.

Note   *"Printing a Single Label or Sheet of Labels with the Same Address" in Chapter 5 explains how to print one or two labels at a time.*

Step 5: Preview Your Labels   Step 5 represents your last chance to get a good look at the labels before you print them or save them in a file. Click the Next Record and

Previous Record to get a look at a few of the labels and make sure they are entered correctly. Later in this chapter, "Examining Your Mail-Merge for the Last Time" explains how to make sure addresses print correctly on labels.

Step 6: Complete the Merge   In the final step, merge the data source with the label sheets. A few pages hence, "Merging the Starting Document and Data Source" explains how to do that.

Mail-Merging to Print a Directory

The last option in the Mail Merge task bar, Directory, is for printing a list or catalog with data from a source file. The advantage of mail-merging to create directories is that the directories are easy to update. After the data source is updated, you can simply regenerate the directory without having to format it, make new entries, or delete out-of-date entries. A company phone list like the one in Figure 18-7 is an ideal candidate for a mail-merge. Instead of editing the list whenever a new employee

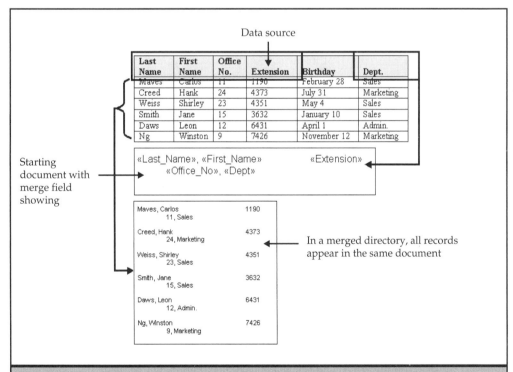

Figure 18-7.   *You can also mail-merge to generate lists like this company phone list*

arrives or an old employee moves on, you can simply update the list from the data source and be done with it.

Mail-merging to create a directory is unusual in these respects:

- The entire list appears on the same page or pages. When you mail-merge a form letter, by contrast, you get a different page for every addressee.

- You can't enter the accompanying text until the merge is complete. In the company phone directory shown in Figure 18-7, for example, you have to wait until you mail-merge the list to enter headings such as "Last Name" and "Extension." If you enter the headings in the starting document, the headings will appear over and over again when the list is merged.

Choose Tools | Letters and Mailings | Mail Merge Wizard and follow these steps in the Mail Merge task pane to generate a directory by mail-merging:

Step 1: Select a Document Type   Under Select Document Type, select the Directory option button and click the Next hyperlink.

At the start of this chapter, "The Six Steps to Completing a Mail-Merge" explains the six steps in detail.

Step 2: Select a Starting Document   Tell Word whether you're starting from scratch or using a document you've already written for the directory:

- **Starting from Scratch**   Select the Use the Current Document or Start from Template option button in the task pane. To write the directory with the help of a template, click the Select Template hyperlink and choose a template in the Select Template dialog box.

- **Using a Directory You've Already Written**   If you have already laid out the directory and you mean to update it, select the Start from Existing Document option button, click the Open button, and select the directory in the Open dialog box.

- **Using a Template**   Choose the Start from a Template option button and click the Select Template hyperlink. You land on the Mail Merge tab of the Select Template dialog box, where you can select Contemporary Merge Address List template, for example, and construct an address list.

Step 3: Select Recipients   Choose an option button under Select Recipients to choose the data source for the directory (see "Preparing and Selecting the Data Source" earlier in this chapter). In the Mail Merge Recipients dialog box, click OK immediately if you want to select all the records in the source file. To select a few, see "Picking and Choosing Recipients for a Mail-Merge" later in this chapter.

Step 4: Arrange Your Directory   Creating a directory is a bit like creating mailing labels—you create one and Word repeats them along the page. Lay out the directory by entering a prototype directory entry. Press the TAB key and use Alignment buttons on the Formatting toolbar to lay out the merge fields.

To insert a merge field, place the cursor where you want it to go and either click the Insert Merge Fields button on the Mail Merge toolbar or the More Items hyperlink in the task pane. You see the Insert Merge Field dialog box. Double-click a field to enter it in your document. Later in this chapter, "Inserting Merge Fields, the Address Block, and the Greeting Line" explains merge fields in detail.

Be sure to enter at least one blank line after you have completed laying out the prototype entry in your directory. Without the blank line, all the entries run together.

Click the View Merged Data button on the Mail Merge toolbar from time to time to see if you are laying out the merge fields properly.

Step 5: Preview Your Directory   In step 5, you get the chance to examine the records that will go in your directory. To do so, click the Next Record and Previous Record buttons on the Mail Merge toolbar. Later in this chapter, "Examining Your Mail-Merge for the Last Time" explains all the different ways to make sure a mail-merge comes off smoothly.

Step 6: Complete the Merge   Click the To New Document hyperlink in the Mail Merge task pane and click OK in the Merge to New Document dialog box. The records from the data source are merged with the starting document, and you see your directory in all its glory.

If anything is amiss, close the document without saving it. Then click the Previous hyperlink in the task pane as many times as necessary to return to the place where you laid out the directory incorrectly and correct your error.

Inserting Merge Fields, the Address Block, and the Greeting Line

The most important part of the mail-merge procedure is entering the merge fields correctly. One misplaced merge field can make mincemeat out of a form letter or sheet of mailing labels. To assist in entering merge fields, Word offers the address block and the greeting line:

- An *address block* is a number of address-type fields that have been bundled into a single field. Address blocks save you the trouble of entering many fields when you enter addresses on form letters, envelopes, and mailing labels. When you need to insert a recipient's address, insert an address block, not the five or so fields that normally make up an address—FirstName, LastName, Street, City, State, and ZipCode.

■ A *greeting line* is a convenient way to enter the salutation in a form letter. The greeting line typically comprises a word such as "Dear" or "To," the FirstName and LastName fields, and a punctuation mark such as a comma (,) or colon (:).

Merge fields adopt the formats of surrounding text. If the text surrounding a merge field is 12 points high and boldfaced, data from the data source will be 12 points high and boldfaced when it is inserted where the merge field is. But you can format a merge field. To do so, treat it like normal text. Drag to select it and start changing formats.

Entering the Merge Fields

A merge field tells Word where in the starting document to plug in data from the source document. As Figure 18-8 shows, chevrons («») appear on either side of a merge field name after you enter its name. To enter a merge field:

1. Place the cursor in the starting document where you want the merge field to go.

2. Either click the Insert Merge Fields button on the Mail Merge toolbar or click the More Items hyperlink in the Mail Merge task pane. The Insert Merge Field dialog box appears (see Figure 18-8). Make sure the Database Fields option button is selected.

3. Double-click the name of a field or click the name and then click the Insert button.

4. Click the Close button in the Insert Merge Field dialog box.

To delete a merge field, drag to select it, and then press the DELETE key.

As you enter merge fields in the starting document, click the View Merged Data button from time to time to make sure that the punctuation marks and blank spaces on either side of the fields have been entered correctly. After you click the button, you see real data onscreen, not field codes, and you can tell what your document will look like after it has been merged with the data source.

Entering an Address Block

An address block is a convenient way to enter addresses in form letters, mailing labels, and envelopes. Still, you may have to do a bit of setup work before you can enter an address block. You can't simply click the Insert Address Block button and be done with it.

Telling Word What to Put in the Address Block

Before you insert the address block, click the Match Fields button on the Mail Merge toolbar to tell Word how fields in the data source you are using match up with the field

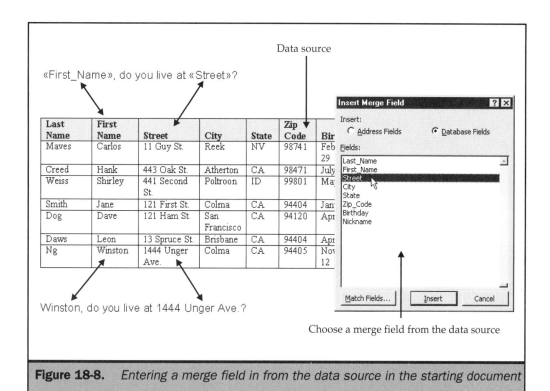

Figure 18-8. *Entering a merge field in from the data source in the starting document*

names Word uses to construct address blocks. After you click the Match Fields button, you see the Match Fields dialog box shown in Figure 18-9.

To construct address blocks, Word uses the field names listed in the left-hand column of the dialog box. When Word can match one of its field names with one of yours, a name from your data source appears in the right-hand column. Your job is to match your field names with Word's and tell Word if you want to keep a field from appearing in addresses:

- **Matching a Name from Your Data Source with a Word Field**   Open a drop-down menu on the right side of the dialog box. You see the names of fields from the data source. Choose a field name. In Figure 18-9, for example, Street is being chosen as a match for Address 1. Now a street name and number will appear in the address block.

- **Keeping a Data Source Field from Appearing in the Address Block**   Open a drop-down menu on the right side of the dialog box and choose Not Available. Do this if Word matches fields on its own but you don't want a field that Word chose to appear in the address block.

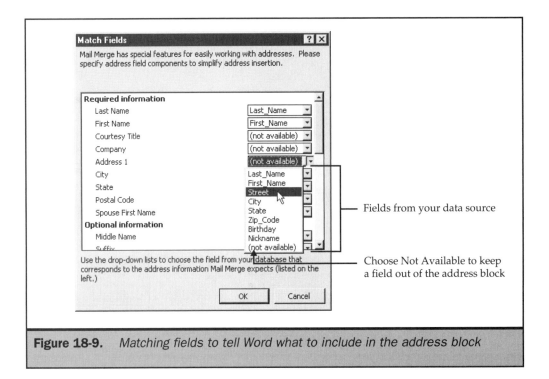

Figure 18-9. *Matching fields to tell Word what to include in the address block*

Inserting the Address Block

To insert the address block after you have done the preliminary work, place the cursor where you want it to go and click the Insert Address Block button on the Mail Merge toolbar or the Address Block hyperlink in the Mail Merge task pane. The Insert Address Block dialog box shown in Figure 18-10 appears. Make these choices in the dialog box and watch the Preview window as you do so:

- **Insert Recipient's Name in This Format**   Choose how you want the name at the top of the address to appear. Some of the choices are meaningless if the data source doesn't include a courtesy title or middle name, for example. Keep your eye on the Preview window and you'll be okay.

- **Insert Company Name**   Check or uncheck this dialog box to include or exclude company names from the address.

- **Insert Postal Address**   If the data source includes addresses in more than one country, select the second or third option button. The second option enters country names in all addresses. The third option enters them only if they differ from the country name you enter in the text box.

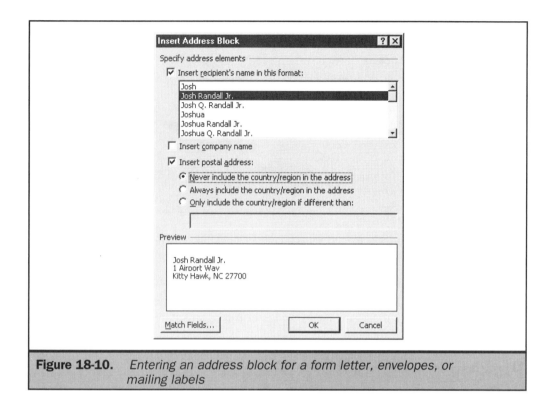

Figure 18-10. *Entering an address block for a form letter, envelopes, or mailing labels*

Click the View Merged Data button on the Mail Merge toolbar to see if the address block you constructed came out all right. If it didn't, select the block, click the Insert Address Block button, and start all over. The Insert Address Block dialog box (see Figure 18-10) has a Match Fields button. You can click to revisit the Match Fields dialog box (see Figure 18-9) and match fields again, if the fields aren't matching properly.

Entering the Greeting Line

Every form letter includes a greeting line, an opening salvo where the recipient is hailed and greeted. To enter the greeting line field, place the cursor in your form letter where you want it to go and click the Insert Greeting Line button on the Mail Merge toolbar or the Greeting Line hyperlink on the Mail Merge task pane. You see the Greeting Line dialog box. Keep your eye on the Preview window and make these choices:

- **Greeting Line Format**   Choose a greeting, a format for names, and a punctuation mark to follow. You can enter your own greeting in the first text box and a punctuation mark of your choice, not to mention a word or two, in the third one.

■ **Greeting Line for Invalid Recipient Names**   Choose or enter a greeting for entries in the data source that do not include valid names. If some entries in the data source do not include first names, for example, and you opt to greet recipients by their first names only, the choice you make or enter here will appear on the greeting line.

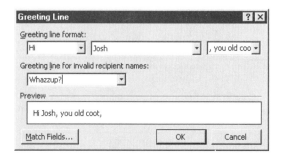

Click the View Merged Data button on the Mail Merge toolbar to see real data in the greeting line and find out if all is well. If you made a mistake, drag to select the greeting line field, click the Insert Greeting Line button, and start all over.

Picking and Choosing Recipients for a Mail-Merge

In step 3 of the mail-merge procedure, after you choose the data source, you see the Mail Merge Recipients dialog box shown in Figure 18-11. To open the dialog box at any time (after you've chosen the data source, that is), click the Mail Merge Recipients button on the Mail Merge toolbar. The Mail Merge Recipients dialog box lists all entries, or records, in the data source. Click the Select All button and click OK to include everyone or everything from the data source. Meanwhile, if you want to pick and choose recipients, you can do so with these techniques:

■ **Selecting Recipients by Hand**   On the left side of the dialog box are check boxes. To exclude a recipient, uncheck the box beside his or her name. You can also click the Clear All button and then check off the names of recipients you want to include.

    Drag the boundary to enlarge the Mail Merge Recipients dialog box, if being able to see all the fields helps any. You can also drag field names to the left or right to change the order of field names in the dialog box.

■ **Filtering to Select or Unselect Recipients**   In a list with more than ten entries, you can isolate a batch you want to select or remove. To do so, click the arrow

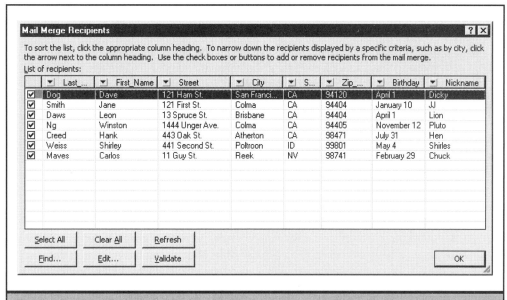

Figure 18-11.   *Starting in this dialog box, you decide which entries to obtain from the data source*

beside a field name, open the drop-down menu, and choose a value to tell Word which entries you want to see. As shown in this illustration, only the entries you choose appear in the list. Now you can click the Select All or Clear All button to include or exclude them in the mail-merge. When you're done checking or unchecking, open the same drop-down menu you opened before and choose All.

■ **Querying to Select Recipients**   Open the drop-down menu on any field and choose Advanced, the last option. You see the Filter and Sort dialog box. Refer to "Querying and Filtering the Data You Get from Access" in Chapter 14 if you need help querying with this dialog box.

■ **Sorting the List**   Click a column heading to sort the list in ascending order. Click it a second time to sort the list in descending order. To sort on more than one field, open a drop-down menu on a field, choose Advanced, and click the Sort Records tab in the Filter and Sort dialog box. See "Sorting, or Reordering, a Table" in Chapter 14 for advice about sorting.

Sorting is a great help when you are generating mailing labels or envelopes that have to be put in postal-code order for bulk-mailing. To sort on the ZipCode field, for example, and spare yourself the trouble of arranging letters in zip-code order, click the ZipCode column heading in the Mail Merge Recipients dialog box.

If you make an error selecting recipients and you want to start all over, click the Edit Recipient List hyperlink in the Mail Merge task pane or the Mail Merge Recipients button on the Mail Merge toolbar. You see the Mail Merge Recipients dialog box. Start all over there.

In step 5, you can click the Exclude This Recipient button in the task pane to remove a single entry from the mail-merge.

Customizing a Mail-Merge with Word Fields

On the Mail Merge toolbar is a drop-down menu called Insert Word Field. By including Word fields in the starting document, you can customize it. For example, instead of churning out the same form letter for everyone, you can include a sentence here and there in some of the letters when the letters are merged. Or you can arrange it so that some recipients receive one letter and others receive a slightly different letter.

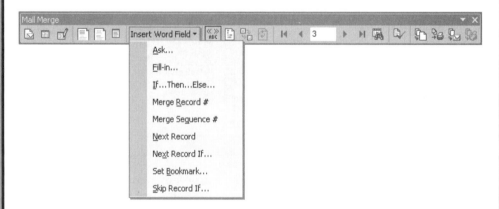

Two fields on the Insert Word Field drop-down menu are useful for writing form letters: If...Then...Else and Fill-In.

Use the If…Then…Else field to enter one sentence or another in form letters. Here, you see the dialog box that appears when you choose If…Then…Else on the Insert Word Field drop-down menu. Choose a field name, a comparison operator, and a value. In this illustration, high school graduates who have an A in the Grade_Avg (Grade Average) field are told one thing in the form letters, and graduates whose grade point averages are lower than A are told something else. Choose an option on the Comparison drop-down menu and enter a value in the Compare To text box to tell Word which recipients receive which sentence on their form letters.

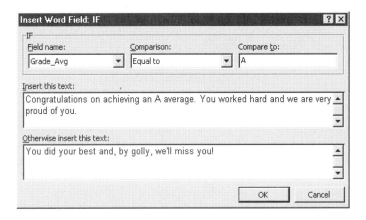

Use the Fill-In field to peg an additional sentence onto a form letter and thereby, insofar as it's possible, personalize the form letter. To see how the Fill In field works, suppose you manage a video-rental shop and you want to send letters to customers whose videos are overdue to be returned. Open the Insert Word Field drop-down menu, choose Fill-In, and, in the Insert Word Field dialog box, enter a prompt and default text to include in the form letters you will send.

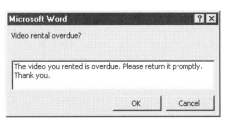

When you print your form letters in step 6 of the mail-merge, you will see the dialog box shown on the right in the previous illustration each time a letter is printed. Glance at the recipient's name, and, in the dialog box, click OK to insert

> the default sentence, or enter a new sentence and click OK. The sentences will
> appear on the form letters in the place where you inserted the Fill-In field. (Caution:
> To use the Fill-In field, you have to print the form letters, not merge them to a new
> document.)

Examining Your Mail-Merge for the Last Time

Step 5 of the mail-merge procedure is where you get the chance to take a last look at
your letters, directory, e-mail messages, envelopes, or labels before you print them or
save them in a document. A handful of buttons on the Mail Merge toolbar come in
handy when the need arises to do these tasks:

- **Seeing What the Document Will Look Like When It Is Merged**   Click the Record
  buttons—First Record, Previous Record, Next Record, and Last Record—to see
  what your document will look like after the mail-merge is complete.

- **Finding a Recipient**   You can search the starting document by clicking the
  Find Entry button on the Mail Merge toolbar or the Find a Recipient hyperlink
  in the Mail Merge task pane. In the Find in Field dialog box, choose a field from
  the In Field drop-down list, and then enter a word or two in the Find What text
  box to describe what you are looking for.

- **Editing Information in the Data Source**   Suppose you notice that information
  in the data source needs changing. The only surefire way to change it is to open
  it in the program in which it was created, change it there, and save the changes.
  When you return to the starting document, click the Edit Recipient List
  hyperlink in the task pane or the Mail Merge Recipients button the Mail Merge
  toolbar. In the Mail Merge Recipients dialog box, click the Refresh button to get
  the latest data from the data source.

> **Tip**   *If you're in a hurry, you can also edit data by clicking the Data Form button on the
> Database toolbar (or pressing* ALT-SHIFT-E). *In the Data Form dialog box, edit the data
> there. However, a better way to edit data is to go to the source, because then the data will
> be accurate next time you want to undertake a mail-merge. Changes you make in the
> Data Form dialog box are not made to the data source.*

- **Entering or Deleting Merge Fields**   Nothing prevents you from entering merge
  fields—click the Insert Merge Fields button to do so. You can delete merge fields
  now as well. In a crowded document, highlighting the fields to see where they
  are can be a big help. Click the Highlight Merge Fields button to see clearly
  where merge fields are.

Merging the Starting Document and Data Source

The final step in mail-merging is to merge the starting document and the data source to generate the form letters, address labels, envelopes, e-mail messages, or directory. Word offers two ways to complete a mail-merge:

- **Saving the Mail-Merge in a New Document**   With this technique, you get a new document, one that you can open, use, or update another day. In the case of form letters, you can scroll through the document and type a sentence or two in certain letters to give them the personal touch.
  Click the Merge to New Document button on the Mail Merge toolbar, click the Edit (or To New Document) hyperlink on the Mail Merge task pane, or press ALT-SHIFT-N.

- **Printing the Mail-Merge Right Away**   With this technique, the merging takes place as the document is printed. You save disk space with this option, as Word doesn't put the stuff in a new document before printing begins.
  Click the Merge to Printer button on the Mail Merge toolbar, click the Print hyperlink on the Mail Merge task pane, or press ALT-SHIFT-M.

The Merge to New Document or Merge to Printer dialog box appears. Click OK to either save the document or send it to the printer.

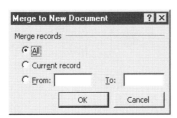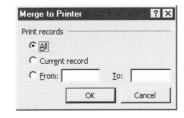

As long as you know record numbers in the data source or the data source is small enough that you can count records on your fingers and toes, you can merge records by number. Records are numbered sequentially in the data source starting at 1 with the first record. To mail-merge a particular record or handful of records, enter the beginning and ending record numbers in the Merge dialog box. Being able to print records by number is convenient when one label or form letter needs reprinting because you can simply enter its number in the From and To boxes.

How can you tell a record's number? If the data source is a Word table, select the entire first column except for the merge field/column name at the top and click the Numbering button on the Formatting toolbar. The records are numbered. What's more, the numbers do not appear in the starting document after a mail-merge.

If the data source is an Access database table or query, you can number the records there by creating an AutoNumber field that numbers each record. See the Help program in Access if numbering records this way excites you.

Word offers a field that you can stick in the starting document to number records. From the Insert Word Field drop-down menu on the Mail Merge toolbar, select the Merge Record # field. The problem with numbering records in the data source this way, however, is that a record number appears on the label, form letter, envelope, or document—it appears where you put the Merge Record # field in the starting document.

To make use of a merged document again, select the Start from Existing Document option button in step 2 of the mail-merge procedure, click the Open button, and open the document by way of the Open dialog box.

Testing for Errors in a Mail-Merge

Word offers the Checking and Reporting Errors dialog box for testing the accuracy of a mail-merge before you run it. All errors in mail-merges are caused by changes in the data source. If you move the data source file to a different folder, delete the data source file, remove information from the data source that is needed in the starting document, or even do so little as rearrange the merge fields/columns in the data source file, the mail-merge will be unsuccessful. By checking for errors beforehand, you can find out whether your mail-merge will really do its job.

To test for errors in a mail-merge, click the Check for Errors button on the Mail Merge toolbar. You see the Checking and Reporting Errors dialog box. The dialog box offers three options for checking for errors, two of which are useless in my opinion:

- **Simulate the Merge and Report Errors in a New Document** Does not undertake the mail-merge, but pretends to and reports errors if any are found. This option is highly recommended. It yields useful dialog boxes like the one shown here.

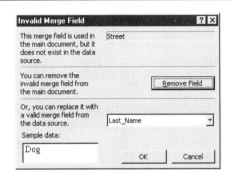

- **Complete the Merge, Pausing to Report Each Error as It Occurs**   Merges the starting document and data source. If errors are found, you get the chance to correct them in a dialog box as the mail-merge takes place.

- **Complete the Merge Without Pausing. Report Errors in a New Document**   Merges the starting document and data source. Records that could not be merged are listed in a document by number. Don't bother with this one, since handling records by record number is very difficult if you are dealing with a data source with more than a few records.

Probably the best way to handle errors when they are found is to return to the starting document and rethink your form letter, mailing labels, or whatnot. Mail-merges should go smoothly. Start all over if the error-checking mechanism encounters an error.

MOUS Exam Objectives Explored in Chapter 18

Objective	Heading
Merge letters, labels, envelopes, and e-mail messages with data sources*	"The Six Steps to Completing a Mail-Merge," "Generating Form Letters for Mass-Mailings," "Printing Labels for Mass-Mailings," "Printing Envelopes for Mass-Mailings," and "Sending the Same E-Mail to Many Different People"

Denotes an Expert, not a Core, exam objective.

Ten Mail-Merge Problems and How to Solve Them

After going to all the trouble to set up a mail-merge, finding out that the mail-merge didn't work is a drag. Herewith are ten mail-merge problems and advice for solving them.

1. Word Tells Me That It Can't Locate the Data Source When I Open My Document
Word asks you that because the data source has been moved from its original location. If you know where the data source file was moved, click the Find Data Source button in the dialog box and locate the data source in the Select Data Source dialog box. Click the Options button if the data source no longer exists or you want to make the document into a normal document that isn't tied to a data source. In the Next dialog box, choose Remove Data/Header Source if the data source doesn't exist or Remove All Merge Info to turn your document into a normal Word document.

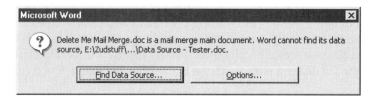

2. I Want to Use My Form Letter Like a Regular Letter
You can sever the tie between the starting document and the data source and use a form letter as a normal Word document. To do so, display the Mail Merge toolbar and click the Main Document Setup button. Then, in the Main Document Type dialog box, select the Normal Word Document option button. Merge fields remain in the document, but they don't mean anything and are not tied to the data source. Delete them.

3. I Hitched My Starting Document to the Wrong Data Source
Unfortunately, solving this problem isn't simply a matter of choosing a new data source with the same merge field/columns as the original data source. Word makes the connection between merge fields in the starting document and the data source not by name, but by location. Suppose, for example, that you ask Word to insert names from the LastName merge field/column in the data source and LastName is the first merge field/column. Really, you are asking Word to get data from the first field/column, not the one named "LastName."

The upshot of all this technical mumbo-jumbo, unfortunately, is that you have to start all over. If your starting document's job is to generate labels or envelopes, start from the very beginning. If you are working on a form letter, sever the tie between your document and the data source, delete all the merge fields in the starting document, establish a connection with a new data source, and re-enter the merge fields. To disconnect the starting document from its data source, click the Main Document Setup button on the Mail Merge toolbar and choose Normal Word Document in the Main Document Type dialog box.

4. Some of the Addresses in My Form Letters and Labels Are Wrong   If you notice that data in a mail-merge is incorrect, change it by opening the data source file in the program with which it was created, editing the data there, and saving your changes. When you return to the starting document, click the Mail Merge Recipients button on the Mail Merge toolbar. In the Mail Merge Recipients dialog box, click the Refresh button to get the latest data from the data source.

You can change data by clicking the Data Form button on the Database toolbar (or pressing ALT-SHIFT-E) and changing it in the Data Form dialog box, but doing it that way won't help you in the long run because changes you make in the Data Form dialog box are not made to the data source. Unless you go right to the source, your data will be inaccurate next time you undertake a mail-merge.

5. I Need to Change the Size of the Mailing Labels I Use   Unfortunately, the only way to change the size of mailing labels (or envelopes) after the mail-merge is complete is to start all over. That's right—you have to enter the address block all over again. In step 2 on the Mail Merge task pane, click the Label Options link. You see the Label Options dialog box, where you can choose different labels. After you make your choice, Word informs you by way of a message box that it must delete the contents of the starting document. Click OK and start all over.

6. When I Print, I See Merge Fields Instead of Data   That happens because someone told Word to display field codes when printing. To fix the problem, choose Tools | Options, select the Print tab in the Options dialog box, and uncheck the Field Codes check box.

7. I Want to Print One or Two Form Letters Only, but I Can't Get Word to Do It   When you merge form letters to a new document, you get a large document in which the letters are divided into sections. Printing a letter here or there in the middle of the new document can be difficult because sections throw the page numbers out of whack. To print a particular letter, find and click it in the new document. Then glance at the Status bar to see which section you are in. If the Status bar reads "Sec 5," for example, you know to print section 5. Choose File | Print to open the Print dialog box, click in the Pages text box, and enter **s** followed by the section number. For example, to print the letter in section 5, enter **s5**. Then click OK to print the letter.

    "Printing Parts or Copies of a Document" in Chapter 5 explains how to print more than one section at a time.

8. The Merged Stuff in My Form Letters Is Formatted Differently than the Letter Text   Looks like you formatted the text but scrupulously avoided formatting the merge fields. You needn't be so careful. Except for typing inside the chevrons («») that appear on either side of the merge fields, you can format a merge field any way you want. Change the field's font or font size. Indent it. Apply a style to a merge field. When the form letter, label, envelope, or list is printed, the text will show the formats.

9. I Updated the Data Source, but Now the New Data Doesn't Appear in the Select Document   To grab the latest edition of data from the data source, click the Mail Merge Recipients button on the Mail Merge toolbar or go to step 3 in the Mail Merge task pane and click the Edit Recipient List hyperlink. You see the Mail Merge Recipients dialog box. Click the Refresh button.

10. One or Two Parts of My Addresses Are Missing   They are missing because you forgot to tell Word which merge fields in the data source to put in the address block. Click the Match Fields button on the Mail Merge toolbar, and, in the Match Fields dialog box, make sure fields from your data source have been matched to the standard field names that Word uses to construct the address block. Earlier in this chapter, "Entering an Address Block" explains that very subject.

Chapter 19

Word for Legal Professionals

Of all the chapters in this book, this one hits home the most for me, because I used to be a "legal professional." Not that I was a lawyer or even officially a legal secretary, but I used to work in law offices and I typed many a pleading in my day. As a matter of fact, the first document I ever typed on a word processor was a legal document, a pleading in a divorce case if I remember correctly. I typed it on a now-extinct word processing program called XYZWrite. Those were the days!

This chapter explains how to get the help of Word to prepare a pleading, number the paragraphs and lines in a document to legal specifications, insert citations in a document, and generate a table of authorities. By the way, not all the tasks described in this chapter are for legal professionals only. For example, everyone is invited to number the paragraphs and lines in their documents. At the end of this chapter are ten tips for handling legal documents in Word.

Creating and Modifying a Legal Pleading Template

Courts, especially supreme courts and courts of appeals, are very fussy about the pleadings that are brought before them. Some courts want pleadings to be double-spaced. Some want pleadings to be printed on letter-size rather than legal-size paper. Kind of ironic, I think, that courts will accept a poorly argued pleading before they will accept a pleading that is not laid out correctly.

To make sure pleadings are laid out correctly, Word offers the Pleading Wizard (hard to imagine a wizard pleading, but I suppose it's possible). Use the Pleading Wizard to create a template for the pleadings that you submit to a particular court. As you know if you read Chapter 12 of this book, a template is a special kind of file that is used as the starting point for creating Word documents. As you create your pleading template, the wizard asks you whether the court wants single- or double-spaced text, what kinds of borders to put on the pages, what kind of caption box the court requires, and a host of other questions.

When you are done, you have a template that you can use whenever you need to submit a pleading to a particular court. The template takes care of the layout decisions. It knows whether to double- or single-space lines and what kind of borders to use, for example. All you have to do is type the pleading itself. Of course, you can always alter the layout in a document you created from a template. But the template is an excellent starting point and a good guarantor that your pleading is being laid out correctly.

These pages explain how to create a pleading template to the specifications of a particular court of law. You also learn how to modify your template in case you didn't get the layout specifications right the first time around.

Note *Later in this chapter, "Preparing a Pleading" explains how to create a pleading document from a template you created.*

Creating a Legal Pleading Template

When you are done creating your pleading template, it will appear on the Legal Pleadings tab of the New dialog box. The Legal Pleadings tab shown in this illustration presents three templates—one for the Supreme Court, one for the Kangaroo Court, and one for Earl's Court. By double-clicking a template you created, you can start preparing a pleading for a particular court.

Double-click the Pleading Wizard icon
to create a pleading template

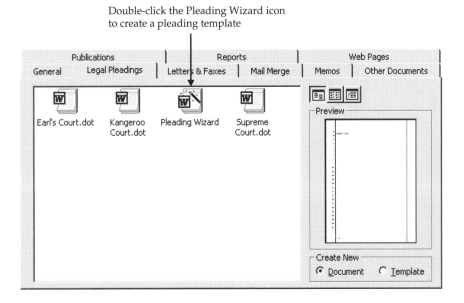

USING WORD 2002 AT THE OFFICE

> **Tip**   *Get a copy of a court document that was submitted to the court for which you are creating a template. You definitely need a sample court document to work from. That way, you can study the document as you create your template and be sure to make the right layout choices.*

Meanwhile, to create a pleading template, choose File | New, click the General Templates hyperlink in the New Document task pane, select the Legal Pleadings tab in the Templates dialog box, and double-click the Pleading Wizard icon. As shown in Figure 19-1, you see the first of ten Legal Pleading Wizard dialog boxes. To create your template, visit each Pleading Wizard dialog box: Choose Task, Court Name, Page Layout, and so on. Either click a dialog box name or click the Next or Back button to go from dialog box to dialog box. The following pages explain the decisions you have to make along the way.

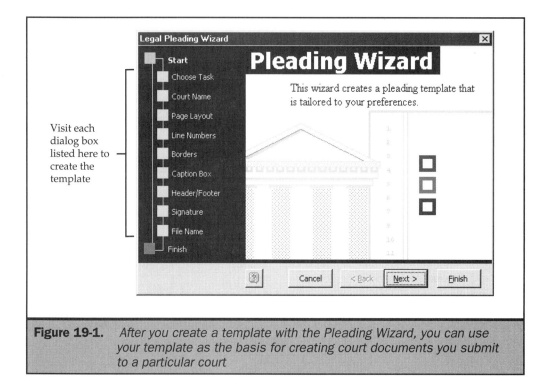

Figure 19-1.   *After you create a template with the Pleading Wizard, you can use your template as the basis for creating court documents you submit to a particular court*

Note   *Don't worry about getting it right the first time. As "Modifying a Pleading Template" explains later in this chapter, it's never too late to refine a pleading template.*

Choose Task   Make sure the first option, Create a New Pleading Template for Another Court, is selected and click the Next button. The second option is for modifying a template you already created, and the third is for writing a pleading.

Court Name   Enter the name of the court as it should appear at the top of the pleading. If the court name needs to appear in uppercase letters, enter it in uppercase. Examine a document that was submitted to the court and then click the Left, Center, or Right option button to left-align, center, or right-align the court's name. The name is aligned with respect to the left and right margins of the document.

Page Layout   Higher courts are especially fussy about page layouts. Study a court document and fill in this dialog box accordingly. Be especially careful about entering a number in the Lines Per Page box. (I suggest counting the number of lines on a court document in order to enter the number correctly.) How many lines appear on each page depends on whether the pleading is double-spaced and which size paper it is printed on. Word does not change the Lines Per Page default number as you select Line Spacing and Paper Size options.

Line Numbers   Decide whether to include or omit line numbers in the Line Numbers dialog box. If you click the Yes option button to include line numbers, do the following in the Line Numbers dialog box:

- **Start Pleading at Line**   Enter which line is numbered first. In some court documents, the caption box information (the court name, names of parties to the case, and so on) are not numbered and numbering begins at the first line of the pleading itself.

- **Line Numbers Start At**   Enter the number at which Word should start counting lines, usually 1.

- **Show Line Numbers in Increments Of**   Choose One to number each line or Two to number every second line.

Note   *Later in this chapter, "Numbering the Lines in a Document" explains all the line-numbering options that Word offers.*

Borders   Stare at your sample pleading, notice whether borders appear on the pages, and choose options in the Borders dialog box. The sample page shows precisely what your choices mean.

Caption Box   The *caption box* in a pleading lists the parties to the case. Take a hard look at the options in the Caption box dialog box and choose the one that matches the caption box in your sample pleading.

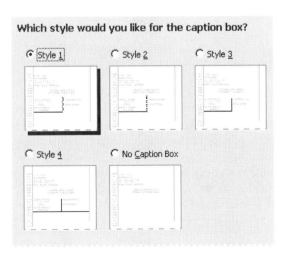

Header/Footer   The name "header" in this dialog box is kind of misleading. Check or uncheck the first two check boxes to tell the wizard whether firm names, attorney names, and the judge's name need to appear above the caption box at the top of the pleading, as shown in this illustration. The names do not appear at the top of every page like a typical document header.

```
1 ║ Buford, Dunme, and Squeeze                    Judge Rutherford P. Anhale
  ║ 214 Market Street
2 ║ San Francisco, CA 94102
```

The three check boxes at the bottom of the Header/Footer dialog box are truly for footers. Check them if a pleading summary, name and address, and page number need to appear at the bottom of each page in the pleading.

Signature   A *signature block* is a space for an attorney who has submitted a pleading to sign his or her name, as shown in the illustration. Choose options in this dialog box to decide whether to include the signature block, place the firm's name and address in the signature block, and include the date in the signature block.

```
        Dated this 12ᵗʰ day of January, 1999

            By: _____
                    Susan Rodriquez, Esq.
                    Buford, Dunme, and
                    Squeeze
                    214 Market Street
                    San Francisco, CA 94102
```

File Name   The wizard suggests naming the template after the court name, but very likely a shorter name is more appropriate. The name you enter here will appear on a template icon in the Legal Pleadings tab of the Templates dialog box. Enter a short, descriptive name that clearly identifies which court the pleadings you create with your new template are meant for.

When you click the Finish button, Word saves the template you created. Then you see the Legal Pleading Wizard dialog box in case you want to prepare a pleading with the template you just finished creating. Click Cancel for now. See "Preparing a Pleading," later in this chapter, if you indeed want to type a pleading at this time.

Modifying a Pleading Template

If your pleading template needs adjusting here and there, choose File | New, click the General Templates hyperlink in the New Document task pane, select the Legal Pleadings tab in the Templates dialog box, and double-click the Pleading Wizard icon. When the Pleading Wizard opens, click Next to go to the Choose Task dialog box shown in Figure 19-2. In the dialog box, choose the Modify the Pleading Template for the Court Selected Below option button, select the court whose template needs adjusting, and click the Next button. After that, either click the Next button until you reach the dialog box where you can make your adjustment, or click a dialog box name on the left side of the Pleading Wizard dialog box. The previous section in this chapter explains what the dialog boxes are and how you can use them to construct a pleading template.

Preparing a Pleading

After you have created a pleading template, you can use it to start work on a pleading. To do so, choose File | New, click the General Templates tab in the New Document dialog box, select the Legal Pleadings tab in the New dialog box, click the template

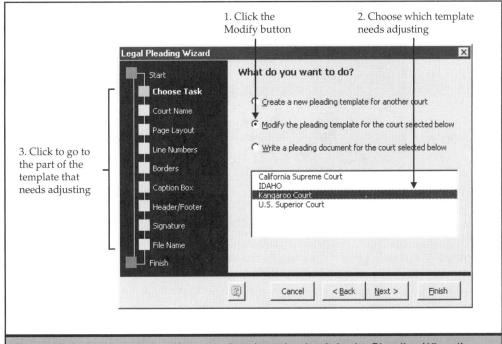

Figure 19-2.   *You can modify a template by selecting it in the Pleading Wizard's Choose Task dialog box*

named after the court to which you will submit the pleading, and click OK. You see the first Legal Pleading Wizard dialog box. Clicking Next as you go along, visit each wizard dialog box—Parties, Names, and so on—to enter the particulars of your pleading. Then type the pleading itself.

Parties   Depending on what the pleading is all about, choose an option to describe the parties to the case. Click the Debtor option button if your pleading is a decree of dissolution, for example. If you aren't an attorney, you might need to consult one before choosing the correct option button.

Names   Enter the name or names of the parties to the case. If a party is listed in the Address book on your computer, you can click the Address Book button and choose a name from the Address book rather than enter the name yourself.

Titles & Case No.   Enter the case number, the number of firms who are filing the pleading, and a title for the pleading. The pleading summary is optional. It appears in the footer if your template calls for a pleading summary in the footer. The case number and title of the pleading appear to the right of the caption box. If you opted to include judges' names on pleadings, you also see a dialog box for entering the judge's name.

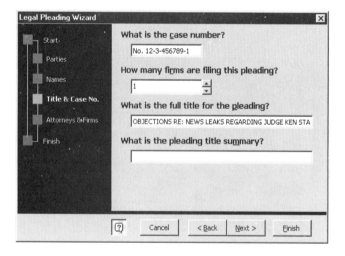

Attorneys & Firms   Enter the names of the attorney or attorneys who are filing the pleading and the name and address of the law firm they represent. Click the Include For check box if you want an "Attorneys for" line to appear on the pleading. Be sure to choose the right option from the drop-down list. Your choice should match the one you made in the Parties dialog box.

When you click the Finish button, Word creates a pleading document from your template. Boilerplate text from the template appears in the document, as do the attorney names and addresses you entered in the Pleading Wizard dialog boxes. Start typing away.

The Legal Pleading Toolbar

As you work on a document you created with a pleading template, you can call on the buttons on the Legal Pleading toolbar. The toolbar, which is named after the template from which you created your pleading, offers these buttons:

- **Block Quotation**   Indents a paragraph by .5 inch from the left and right margins.
- **Single Spacing, 1.5 Spacing, Double Spacing**   Changes the line spacing of text. Click in a paragraph or select paragraphs and then click one of these buttons to change line spacing.
- **Table of Authorities**   Opens the Table of Authorities dialog box so you can mark a citation or generate a table of authorities (a list of the rules, cases, statutes, regulations, and so on cited in a legal document). See "Entering Citations for the Table of Authorities" and "Generating the Table of Authorities," later in this chapter.

Numbering the Lines in a Document

In legal pleadings and certain kinds of literary and religious texts, the lines are numbered so that readers can refer to specific lines or go to a line quickly. Numbering the lines in a Word document is easy. You can number all the lines, number lines in a particular section, and number the lines continuously or starting anew on each page. Lines can only be seen in Print Layout view, so switch to Print Layout view and follow these steps to number lines:

1. Click in a section to number the lines in a particular section of a document; otherwise, click wherever you want.
2. Choose File | Page Setup.
3. Select the Layout tab in the Page Setup dialog box.
4. Click the Line Numbers button. You see the Line Numbers dialog box shown in Figure 19-3.

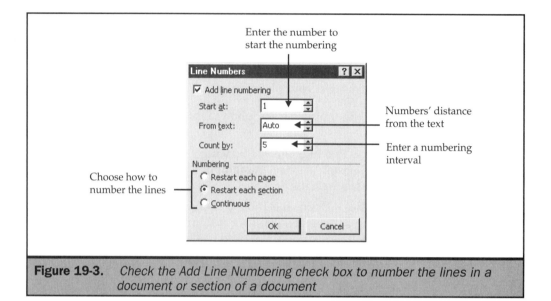

Figure 19-3. *Check the Add Line Numbering check box to number the lines in a document or section of a document*

5. Check the Add Line Numbering check box.

6. Choose options in the dialog box:

   ■ **Start At**   Lines are numbered starting with 1, but if for some reason you want to begin with another number, enter it in this text box.

   ■ **From Text**   Line numbers appear .25 inch to the left of the left margin of the page, but you can move them farther away or closer to the text by entering a number in this text box.

   ■ **Count By**   All lines are numbered, but by entering a number here you can make numbers appear at an interval. For example, entering **10** makes numbers appear at intervals of 10 (10, 20, 30).

   ■ **Numbering**   Tell Word how to number the lines. You can number lines beginning anew at the start of each page or section, or number lines consecutively throughout a document.

7. Click OK twice to return to your document.

If your document is divided into sections and you want to number lines in other sections as well, click in the other sections and number them. You can do that very quickly by clicking in another section and pressing F4 or choosing Edit | Repeat Page Setup straight-away after you number the lines in one section.

To remove line numbers, click in a section, choose File | Page Setup, select the Layout tab in the Page Setup dialog box, click the Line Numbers button, and uncheck the Add Line Numbering check box in the Line Numbers dialog box (see Figure 19-3).

Preventing Certain Lines from Being Numbered

Follow these steps to keep a handful of lines in the middle of a document or section from being counted and numbered:

1. Select the lines that don't require numbers.

2. Choose Format | Paragraph to open the Paragraph dialog box.

3. Select the Line and Page Breaks tab.

4. Check the Suppress Line Numbers check box and click OK.

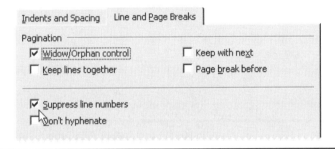

Numbering Paragraphs in the Text

In some kinds of legal contracts and technical documents, paragraphs are supposed to be numbered in sequence. To spare yourself the trouble of numbering the paragraphs yourself, you can take advantage of paragraph-numbering schemes in the Bullets and Numbering dialog box. Paragraph numbers work like the numbers in numbered lists. When you remove a paragraph or enter a new one, the paragraphs are renumbered.

Figure 19-4 shows two of three numbering schemes that Word offers. In the first, paragraphs are numbered in outline form, and in the second, each paragraph is assigned from one to nine numbers, depending on how deep it is in the hierarchy. The third paragraph-numbering scheme is more of a "bulleting scheme," with each paragraph in the hierarchy assigned a different bullet, not a number. You can create your own paragraph-numbering schemes, too. Read on.

Numbering the Paragraphs

Follow these steps to number paragraphs:

1. Select the paragraphs that you want to number. Be sure not to select any headings.

2. Choose Format | Bullets and Numbering.

3. As shown in Figure 19-5, select the Outline Numbered tab.

4. Choose one of the two paragraph-numbering options in the top half of the dialog box.

5 Click OK.

1) King	1. King
a) Knave	1.1. Knave
b) Jester	1.2. Jester
2) Queen	2. Queen
a) Prince	2.1. Prince
b) Princess	2.2. Princess
i) Lady in Waiting	2.2.1. Lady in Waiting
ii) Garment Bag Carrier	2.2.2. Garment Bag Carrier
3) Duke	3. Duke
4) Duchess	4. Duchess
5) Marquis	5. Marquis
a) Marquise	5.1. Marquise
i) Earl	5.1.1. Earl
ii) Earlene	5.1.2. Earlene
iii) Count (I'd hate to be the one who has to account for the Count).	5.1.3. Count (I'd hate to be the one who has to account for the Count).
iv) Countess	5.1.4. Countess
6) Viscount	6. Viscount
7) Viscountess	7. Viscountess

Figure 19-4. *Two methods of numbering paragraphs: in outline form (left) and in numerical sequence (right)*

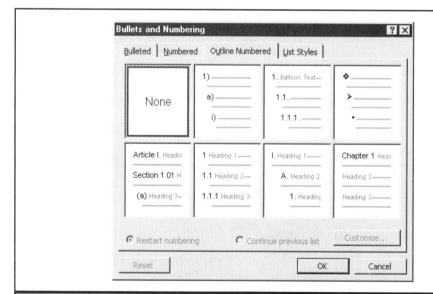

Figure 19-5. *Click an option in the top half of the Outline Numbered tab to number paragraphs; the None option is for removing numbers*

For legal-style paragraph numbering, choose one of the numbering schemes, and then click the Customize button. In the Customize Outline Numbered List dialog box, click the More button if necessary, and then check the Legal Style Numbering check box. You will find the check box near the bottom of the dialog box below the Preview box.

In your document, all paragraphs are numbered 1, 2, 3, 4, and so on. To make a paragraph subordinate to another paragraph in the numbering hierarchy, click the subordinate paragraph and then click the Increase Indent button on the Formatting toolbar. The subordinate paragraph is given a lower outline-level number. In effect, increasing or decreasing the indentation of a paragraph tells Word how important the paragraph is. By clicking the Increase Indent and Decrease Indent buttons, you can assign different level numbers to paragraphs. (You can press the TAB key as well, but before you do so, make sure the cursor is to the left of the line whose stature in the hierarchy you want to change.)

Follow these instructions to remove paragraph numbers, start numbering anew, or pick up the numbering sequence where you left off:

- **Removing Numbers from Paragraphs**   Select the paragraphs whose numbers you want to remove and click the Numbering button on the Formatting toolbar.

- **Resuming the Numbers**   Select the next batch of paragraphs that need numbers and click the Numbering button on the Formatting toolbar.

- **Restarting a New List at 1**   Select the next batch of paragraphs and choose Format | Bullets and Numbering. On the Outline Numbered tab, choose the paragraph-numbering scheme you have been using, choose the Restart Numbering option button, and click OK.

 Yes, you can devise a paragraph-numbering scheme of your own. See "Creating Your Own Numbering Schemes for Lists" in Chapter 10. The instructions there, which apply to headings, also apply to paragraph numbers.

Creating a Table of Authorities

In plaintiff versus defendant cases, attorneys cite precedent cases to make their arguments, and those cases have to be assembled in a table of authorities. A *table of authorities* is a list of the cases, statutes, and regulations cited in a legal document. These pages explain how to mark citations in a legal document so you can assemble them in a table of authorities. You also learn how to generate a table of authorities from the citations you marked.

Entering Citations for the Table of Authorities

Follow these steps to mark citations in a legal document so you can compile them later in a table of authorities:

1. Select a citation you want for the table.

2. Either press ALT-SHIFT-I or click the Table Of Authorities button on the Legal Pleading toolbar and then click the Mark Citation button in the Table of Authorities dialog box. You see the Mark Citation dialog box shown in Figure 19-6. The citation appears in the Selected Text box.

3. If necessary, edit the citation in the Selected Text box. When you generate the table, you can either list long citations from the Selected Text box or short citations from the Short Citation box.

4. In the Category drop-down list, choose a category that describes the case being cited. When you generate a table of authorities, you can generate tables in a single category or all the categories.

Tip *If no category adequately describes the case being cited, click the Category button in the Mark Citation dialog box. In the Edit Category dialog box, choose a number at the bottom of the Category list, and then enter a new category name in the Replace With text box and click the Replace button. Then click OK. Back in the Mark Citation dialog box, your new category appears on the Category drop-down list.*

5. In the Short Citation box, edit the citation. You can generate a table of authorities with short citations or long citations, so edit the citation carefully.

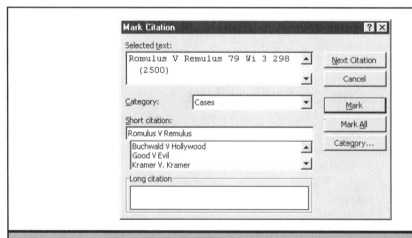

Figure 19-6.   *By marking the citations in a legal document, you can compile them in a table of authorities*

6. Click the Mark or Mark All button:

- ■ **Mark**   Marks the citation for inclusion in the table of authorities. Other instances of this citation are not marked.

- ■ **Mark All**   Marks all instances of the citation throughout the document.

7. Click the Close button.

In your document, you see a field code where you marked the citation. You can remove those ugly field codes from the screen by clicking the Show/Hide ¶ button on the Standard toolbar. Word uses the field codes to generate the table of authorities.

Besides scouring a legal document on your own for citations, you can click the Next Citation button in the Mark Citation dialog box (see Figure 19-6). When you click this button, Word scrolls to legalese such as re and V in the document in case you want to mark it, too, for the table of authorities. Word also scrolls through already marked citations so you can review them.

Generating the Table of Authorities

After you have picked through the document and marked all the citations, you can generate the table of authorities. Click where you want the table to appear and follow these steps to generate it:

1. Either choose Insert | Reference | Index and Tables and select the Table of Authorities tab in the Index and Tables dialog box, or click the Table of Authorities button on the Legal Pleading toolbar. You see the Table of Authorities tab shown in Figure 19-7.

2. In the Formats drop-down list, choose a format for the table. The Print Preview box shows exactly what you are choosing. Be sure to scroll down the box and take a good look.

3. In the Category drop-down list, choose All or a single category to generate a table of authority with cases from a single category.

4. Leave the check mark in the Use Passim box if you want more than five references to the same citation to be cited with the word "passim" instead of a page number. In the glorious Latin language, "passim" means "scattered." In legal documents, the word refers to citations that appear throughout a document.

5. Leave the check mark in the Keep Original Formatting text box if you want to retain the original formatting of long citations in the table. You can uncheck this box if you want the table of authorities only to show short citations.

6. Choose a tab leader from the Tab Leader drop-down list if the one you see in the Print Preview box doesn't suit you.

7. Click OK to generate the table of authorities.

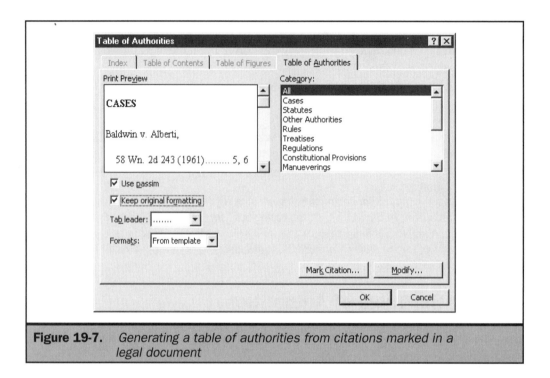

Figure 19-7. *Generating a table of authorities from citations marked in a legal document*

To update a table of authorities after you mark new citations or edit the document, move the pointer to the left of the table and click to select it. Then either right-click and choose Update Field or press F9.

MOUS Exam Objectives Explored in Chapter 19

Objective

Create and update document indexes and tables of contents, figures, and authorities*

Heading

"Creating a Table of Authorities"

* Denotes an Expert, not a Core, exam objective.

Ten Tips for Word-Processing Legal Documents

Herewith are ten tips for creating and handling word-processed legal documents. Churning out legal pleadings while a genuine lawyer is looking over your shoulder isn't easy, is it?

1. Create Forms for Agreements and Contracts   Rental agreements, standard contracts, and any other kind of document in which the text is the same but the particulars are different is an ideal candidate for a form. Only select parts of a form can be altered. A rental agreement form, for example, could set aside a place for entering the renter's name and the monthly rent. The rest of the form, however, could not be changed. Nobody could alter it and thereby give an opening to an unscrupulous lawyer or ungrateful tenant. In Chapter 15, "Creating and Using a Data-Entry Form" explains how to create forms.

2. Make Use of AutoText Entries   As Chapter 6 explains, you can enter boilerplate text very quickly with an AutoText entry. Because much of the text that is entered in legal documents and law correspondence is boilerplate text, you can save time by creating AutoText entries for the boilerplate paragraphs you enter time and time again. See "Ways to Enter Text Quickly" in Chapter 6 for details.

3. Use AutoCorrect to Enter Legal and Latin Terms   Besides making AutoText entries, another way to enter hard-to-type text is to do so with the AutoCorrect command. In Chapter 6, "Ways to Enter Text Quickly" explains how you can, with a little foresight, make Word correct what it thinks are errors and in so doing turn them into hard-to-type phrases and even sentences.

4. Share Your Legal Pleading Templates with Others   After you go to the trouble to create and refine a legal pleading template, make it available to everybody in your office. If your computer is connected to a network, ask the network administrator where Word workgroup templates are stored, and copy the template there so that others can access it. Meanwhile, tell your colleagues that they can access the template on their computers taking these steps:

1. Choose Tools | Options.
2. Select the File Locations tab in the Options dialog box.
3. Under File Types, choose Workgroup Templates.
4. Click the Modify button, and, in the Modify Location dialog box, find and select the folder where workgroup templates are stored.
5. Click OK twice.

Chapter 12 explains templates and workgroup templates.

5. Create a Dictionary of Legal Terms   Go ahead, add legal terms to your Word dictionary. For that matter, start a new dictionary for legal terms and use it to check for misspellings in pleadings and legal documents. In Chapter 11, "Employing Other Dictionaries to Help with Spell-Checking" explains how to create your own dictionaries for spell-checking.

6. Create a Strikethrough Character Style   Text that has been struck from a legal document is marked with the strikethrough text effect, like so: ~~This text has been struck out~~. But entering strikethrough text is a chore. You have to open the Font dialog box, find the tiny Strikethrough check box, check it, and click the OK button. Rather than go to all that trouble, create a strikethrough character style. When you want to "strike through" text, simply select it and apply the style. In Chapter 12, "Creating Your Own Styles" explains how to create a character style.

7. Tell Word Not to Update Styles Automatically   More so than other documents, legal documents get passed around the office quite a bit. If everyone who works on a legal document tells Word to update styles automatically, the document soon turns into mush. Styles become meaningless, since each person who worked on the document has altered the styles.

Tell everyone who works on legal documents in your office to tell Word not to update styles automatically. Follow these steps to do so:

1. Choose Tools | AutoCorrect to open the AutoCorrect dialog box.

2. Click the AutoFormat As You Type tab.

3. Uncheck the Define Styles Based On Your Formatting check box and click OK.

8. Take Advantage of the Paper Source Options   If you are fortunate enough to have or be connected to a printer with two trays, one for letter-size paper and one for legal-size paper, you have a head start on the problem of handling legal-size paper. What's more, you can tell Word which tray the legal-size paper is in by choosing File | Page Setup, selecting the Paper tab in the Page Setup dialog box, and choosing trays in the First Page and Other Pages lists. By opening a legal pleading template and choosing a tray option while the template is open, you can make your choice of trays a permanent part of any pleading you create with the template in question. And you can save yourself a little time that way.

9. Take Advantage of Online References for Legal Professionals   All across the Internet are resources for legal professionals. Here are a handful of especially useful ones:

- **Introduction to Basic Legal Citation**   A citation primer written by Peter Martin of the Cornel University Law School. Address: www.law.cornell.edu/citation/citation.table.html

- ■ **NOLO dictionary**   The NOLO Press's online dictionary of legal terminology. The NOLO Press, with its book and online resources, does an exemplary job of making the law less mysterious. Address: www.nolo.com/dictionary/wordindex.cfm

- ■ **A Prisoner's Dictionary**   Care to see what the law looks like from the other side? Address: dictionary.prisonwall.org

- ■ **YourDictionary.com**   Click the Law hyperlink near the top of this page to scroll to a list of online legal dictionaries pertaining to criminology, divorce, and other areas of the law. Address: www.yourdictionary.com/diction4.htm

10. Visit the Lawyer Joke Emporium   Have you heard about the lawyers' word-processor? No matter what font you select, everything comes out in small print. The NOLO Press, as well as offering the legal dictionary mentioned here, also maintains a Web site of lawyer jokes. From time to time, to keep their sanity, all legal secretaries are invited to visit the Lawyer Joke Emporium. Address: www.nolo.com/humor/jokes

The Complete Reference

Word 2002

Part V

Getting More Out of Word

Chapter 20

Managing Your Documents Better

This chapter explains how to organize and manage your documents and folders. It offers strategies for storing your work on disk, explains how to back up documents in Word, and explores all the different ways to save documents in the background. On the subject of saving, you also learn how to save different versions of the same document and save documents so they can be opened in other word processing programs. This chapter also presents techniques for protecting documents against unwanted changes and finding lost documents. Finally, at the end of this chapter are ten techniques for handling and preventing computer crashes.

Devising a Strategy to Store Your Work on Disk

The surest way to keep from losing documents is to store them carefully in the first place. When you create and save a document, Word asks which folder to save it in. Make sure before you save a new document that a folder is ready and waiting to receive it—a folder with a descriptive name that is located in a prominent place on your computer.

Some people mistakenly believe that Word documents must be stored deep in the computer along with the Word program files, but you can store Word documents anywhere you want on a computer. And you should store them in folders that are easy to find. I keep all my Word documents, for example, in a folder on the C drive that I named starting with the letters "AAA." The letters "AAA" place my most important folder at the top of the list of folders in the Open dialog box where I can find it easily. You are advised to devise a strategy of your own for storing Word documents where you can find them easily.

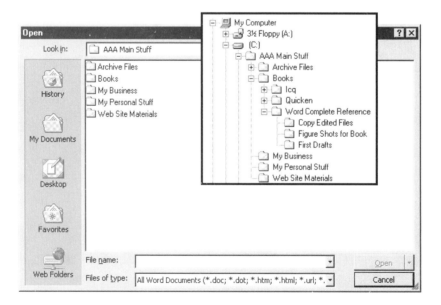

Read on to find out how to create a folder in Word for storing files and how to choose the default folder, the one that appears first thing in the Open and Save As dialog boxes when you choose File | Open or File | Save As.

Creating the Folders You Need

The best way to create a new folder is to do so with Windows Explorer or My Computer—the two Windows programs whose job is to organize and manage files. In Windows Explorer and My Computer, you can see the grand scheme. You can make better choices about where to place your new folder in the folder hierarchy. However, you can create a new folder in Word by following these steps:

1. Choose File | Open or File | Save As. You see either the Open dialog box shown in Figure 20-1 or the Save As dialog box. The dialog boxes are identical except that one is for opening files and the other is for saving them.

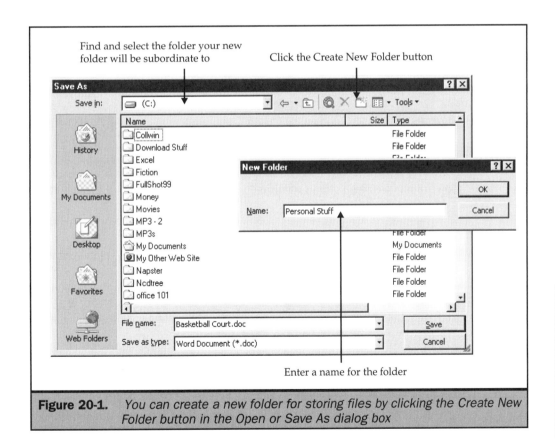

Figure 20-1. *You can create a new folder for storing files by clicking the Create New Folder button in the Open or Save As dialog box*

2. In the dialog box, find and select the folder that you want your new folder to be subordinate to. To put the new folder at the top of the C drive, open the Look In or Save In drop-down list and choose (C:).

3. Click the Create New Folder button (or press ALT-5). You see the New Folder dialog box shown in Figure 20-1.

4. Enter a descriptive name for your new folder and click OK. Your new folder appears in the Look In or Save In box.

5. Click Cancel to close the Open dialog box or Save As dialog box.

Choosing a Default Folder Apart from "My Documents"

Word is very fond of the My Documents folder. Choose File | Open or File | Save As and you see the contents of the My Documents folder in the Open dialog box. You see the My Documents folder, I should say, until you open a document in another folder. Then the Open dialog box shows the contents of the last folder you visited in order to open a document.

My Documents is the default folder because the makers of Word expect you to keep the documents you are working on at present in the My Documents folder. The idea is for you to move documents to other folders when you finish working on them. Suppose, however, that you keep documents that need the most attention in a particular folder on your computer. You can make that folder the default folder that appears first thing when you choose File | Open or File | Save As. Follow these steps to tell Word which folder to display by default in the Open dialog box:

1. Choose Tools | Options to open the Options dialog box.

2. Select the File Locations tab. This tab lists the default locations of documents, templates, and files that pertain to Word.

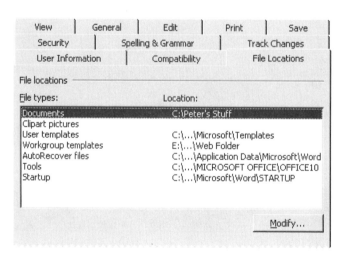

3. Under File Types, select Documents.

4. Click the Modify button. You see the Modify Location dialog box.

5. Locate and select the folder that you want to appear by default in the Open and Save As dialog boxes. Make sure the name of the folder appears in the Look In box.

6. Click OK. On the File Locations tab, the name and location of your new default folder appears in the Location column.

7. Click OK.

Entering Document Properties to Find and Identify Documents

Especially if documents are strewn across a network, anybody who has to handle a hundred or more documents owes it to him- or herself to enter descriptions of documents in the Properties dialog box. Choose File | Properties to open the Properties dialog box. Descriptions you enter help identify documents, and they can also be used as an aid in searching for stray documents. Figure 20-2 shows the Summary tab of the Properties dialog box. As "Finding a Lost Document" explains later in this chapter, you can search for stray documents by describing properties in the Properties dialog box.

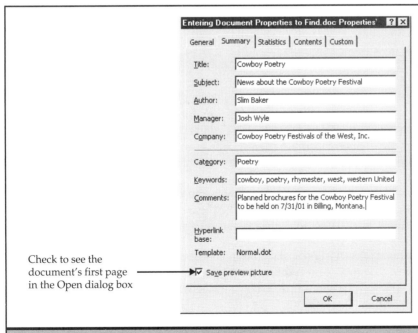

Check to see the document's first page in the Open dialog box

Figure 20-2.   *Choose File | Properties to open the Properties dialog box and describe your document or view its vital statistics*

If identifying and describing documents in the Properties dialog box is important to you, you can tell Word to display the Properties dialog box whenever a document is saved for the first time. To do so, choose Tools | Options, select the Save tab in the Options dialog box, and check the Prompt For Document Properties check box.

In sum, the Properties dialog box offers the following tabs.

General   Basic information about the document, such as when it was created, its size, and when it was last modified and accessed. You can use this information when searching for a document.

Summary   As shown in Figure 20-2, the identifying characteristics of the document. The author name and company name are entered for you (you gave this information when you installed Word). By checking the Save Preview Picture check box, you can make the headings in your document appear on the Contents tab of the Properties dialog box (the headings appear next time you choose File | Properties). What's more, when you choose File | Open and choose Preview view in the Open dialog box, as shown in Figure 20-3, the first page of the document appears so you can identify the document.

The author name—your name—and company name are entered for you on the Summary tab, but perhaps you don't want your name and company name to appear there. Perhaps you want others who get their hands on the file not to know with whom it originated. To remove your name and company name from the Summary tab, choose Tools | Options, select the Security tab in the Options dialog box, and check the Remove Personal Information from This File on Save check box.

Statistics   Vital statistics about the document, including the number of pages, total editing time, and the name of the person who last saved the document. This information can also be used in searches. By the way, total editing time refers to the number of minutes that the document was open, not the number of minutes you worked on it. And the revision number merely tells you the number of times you opened the document, not how many times you revised it.

Contents   A list of the headings to which you assigned heading styles—Heading 1, Heading 2, and so on—in the document. To make the list appear, check the Save Preview Picture check box on the Summary tab (refer to Figure 20-2).

Custom   For further describing the document. Choose a category in the name box, choose what type of category it is on the Type drop-down list (Text, Date, Number, or Yes or No), enter a description in the Value box, and click the Add button. You can create your own categories by entering their names in the Name box and clicking the Add button after you have chosen a type and entered a value. Check the Link To

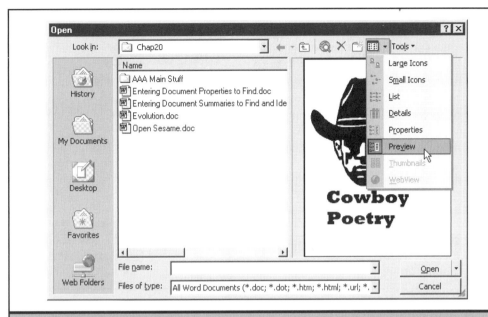

Figure 20-3. *Check the Save Preview Picture check box to be able to see the first page of documents in the Open dialog box*

Content check box and choose a bookmark name from the Source drop-down list to use a changeable bookmark reference in your document as a document description.

By the way, you can view a document's properties without opening Word. In Windows Explorer or My Computer, right-click a document you are intrigued by and choose Properties.

 Document properties can be printed. Choose File | Print to open the Print dialog box, choose Document Properties on the Print What drop-down list, and click OK.

Getting the Statistics on a Document

Instead of going to the trouble to open the Properties dialog box to see statistics about a document, you can simply choose Tools | Word Count. The Word Count dialog box tells you how many pages, words, characters, and what-all are in your document. Be sure to check the Include Footnotes and Endnotes check box if you are being paid by the word to write your document. That way, you can inflate the word count.

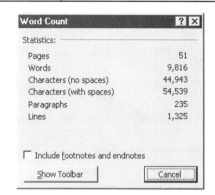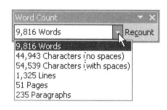

By clicking the Show Toolbar button in the Word Count dialog box or by choosing View | Toolbars | Word Count, you can make the Word Count toolbar appear. Click the Recount button on the toolbar to get an up-to-the-minute tally of the number of words, characters, lines, pages, or paragraphs in your document.

Backing Up Your Work in Word

Backing up a document means to make a second copy in case the original meets with an unfortunate accident. Unless you had the foresight to back up important documents, the documents are lost if they are damaged. If your computer breaks down, a virus ruins your documents, or your computer is stolen, you are out of luck unless you made backup copies of important documents.

You can't back up Word documents to a floppy disk, CD, or Zip disk with Word. A backup copy that Word makes is stored in the same folder as the original. True, you can open the backup copy if the original gets damaged, but your computer must be alive and well for you to open the backup copy. Backup copies stored on a dead computer or stolen computer are not worth very much. To be absolutely safe, make backup copies of your important documents to floppy disks, Zip disks, CDs, or another storage medium.

Backup copies of Word documents have the .WBK (Word backup) file extension and are kept in the same folder as original copies. To name a backup document, Word attaches the words "Backup of" to the document's name, as shown in Figure 20-4. A backup copy is made each time you save the original. However, the backup copy is not the same as the currently saved version of its original—the backup copy represents the version of the document as of the previous time you saved it. If your computer fails and you can't open the original, you can open the backup copy and obtain a fairly up-to-date version of your document.

Caution *Use Windows Explorer or My Computer, the Windows programs, to back up documents to floppy disks, Zip disks, CD-RWs, and other storage media. Word's backup facility is nice, but it is not a safeguard against computer crashes or failures.*

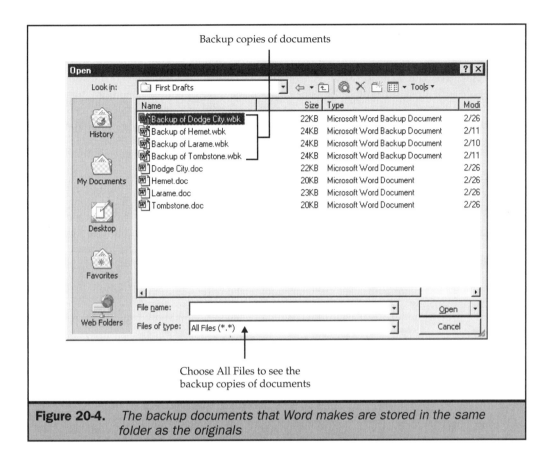

Backup copies of documents

Choose All Files to see the
backup copies of documents

Figure 20-4.   *The backup documents that Word makes are stored in the same folder as the originals*

Follow these steps to tell Word to make backup copies of documents:

1. Choose Tools | Options to open the Options dialog box.

2. Select the Save tab.

3. Check the Always Create Backup Copy check box and click OK. You can't create backup copies automatically and also "allow fast saves." The next section in this chapter explains fast saves.

To open the backup copy of a document, choose File | Open, locate the folder where the backup copy and original are kept, and choose All Files from the Files Of Type drop-down list, if necessary, to see the backup copies. Then select a backup copy and click the Open button.

Tip   *By saving a document twice in succession, you can render the backup copy identical to the original. The previously saved version, not the saved version, of your document is kept in the backup document, so by saving twice you place the latest edition of the document in the backup copy.*

Strategies for Saving Documents

Everybody knows that you click the Save button, choose File | Save, or press CTRL-S to save a document. But that isn't the whole story. As Figure 20-5 shows, Word offers many ways to save documents in the background and in different formats. You can save different versions of a document as well. These pages explain how to save different versions of the same document, save a document under a different name, and save documents in different formats. You also find out how to decide which strategy for saving files in the background is best for you.

Telling Word How to Save Documents

On the Save tab of the Options dialog box (refer to Figure 20-5) are two options for saving documents in the background: Allow Fast Saves and Allow Background Saves. To visit the Save tab of the Options dialog box, choose Tools | Options and select the Save tab, or else choose File | Save As, click the Tools button in the Save As dialog box, and choose

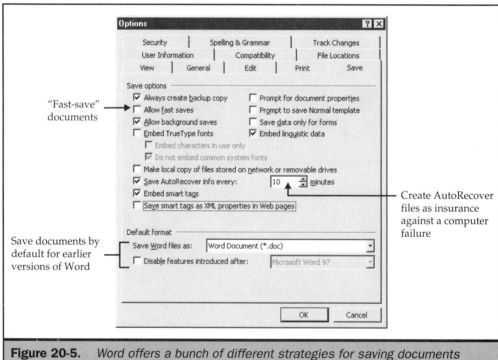

Figure 20-5. *Word offers a bunch of different strategies for saving documents*

Save Options from the drop-down menu. These two Save options are described in detail in the pages that follow:

- **Allow Fast Saves**   Supposedly speeds up the saving mechanism, but increases the size of documents and presents other disadvantages.
- **Allow Background Saves**   Lets you keep working on a document while the computer saves it to the hard disk.

Allow Fast Saves: Saving Documents Faster (In Theory, Anyway)

Because the Allow Fast Saves option presents more disadvantages than advantages, I suggest unchecking it. When the option is selected, Word does not save recent changes in the document file, but in a separate file, the idea being that a smaller, separate file is faster to update than the document file itself. Everything is done behind the scenes so you never know there is a separate file. Eventually, changes tracked in the separate file are incorporated in the document file when either the separate file grows too large or you uncheck the Allow Fast Saves option, which Microsoft recommends doing when you are finished working on a document.

Here are the disadvantages of "fast-saving":

- Documents are larger. They require more disk space for storing and take longer to send over networks and the Internet.
- Documents put more of a strain on the computer's memory.
- You can't convert the document to a different file format without causing all kinds of problems for the person who opens the document in another word processor or computer program. Very likely, the other word processor or computer program doesn't know what to make of the two-file system and garbles the document accordingly.
- Sharing the document with others is problematic, because you are dealing behind the scenes with two files, the document file and the file in which changes to the document are stored.
- You can't save the document over a network connection.
- The chances of recovering a document after a computer or hard-drive problem are dramatically reduced.

The list of advantages is considerably shorter. In fact, the list extends to one item:

- A document with many graphics and other memory-intensive items does not take as long to save.

Even if you decide to "fast-save" documents, be sure to uncheck the Allow Fast Saves check box in the Options dialog box (refer to Figure 20-5) when you finish working on a document, when you give a document to someone else to work on, or when you engage in a memory-intensive activity such as generating an index or a table of contents.

Allow Background Saves: Saving Documents as You Work on Them

Check this option and you can continue to work while the hard disk on your computer grinds away and Word saves your document on disk. In theory you have to wait for Word to finish saving a document before you can start work if this option is not checked, but computers are so fast these days it doesn't really matter whether this option is turned on. Might as well leave it on. Only uncheck it if your computer is running very low on memory.

Saving a Document Under a New Name

As long as you know your way around the Save As dialog box, saving a document under a different name is easy. All you have to do is choose File | Save As, enter a new name in the File Name text box, perhaps select a new folder to store your newly named document in, and click Save. You end up with two documents: your original and the one you just named.

Another way to save a document under a new name is to open a copy of the original. Choose File | Open, locate and select the document that needs copying, open the drop-down menu on the Open button, and choose Open As Copy from the drop-down menu. A file named after the original with the words "Copy of" opens onscreen.

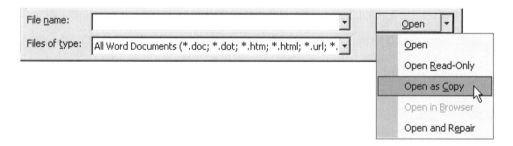

 "Opening Documents" in Chapter 1 explains all the buttons and tools in the Save As and Open dialog boxes. The dialog boxes offer the same tools and buttons.

Converting Documents to Different Formats So Others Can Use Them

Not everyone is a proud owner of Microsoft Word. Before you pass along a document to someone who uses another version of Word or another word processor altogether, save your document so that the other person can open and make good use of it. Read on to learn how to save or convert documents so they can be opened in another word-processing program or an earlier version of Word.

 Saving a Word document in a different format for use in another word processor is like translating texts between foreign languages—something always gets lost in the translation. Proofread documents carefully after they are opened in the other word-processing program. Typically, symbols and special characters get lost or mistranslated. Fancy formats such as text boxes and columns might not make it to the other side at all.

Saving Documents for Use in Other Word Processors

To save a copy of a document for use with another word-processing program, open the document and choose File | Save As to open the Save As dialog box. Then, from the Save As Type drop-down list, choose the name of the word-processing program to which the file needs translating, and click Save. Word is on speaking terms with WordPerfect and Works. You will find their names on the Save As Type drop-down list.

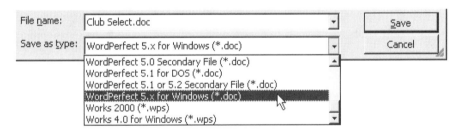

And if the word-processing program you need isn't on the list? Then you have to speak Esperanto and rely on one of the following plain-text file formats. From best choice to worst, save your Word document in one of these formats so it can be opened in another word processor:

■ **Rich Text Format (.RTF)**   Saves formats along with text. Microsoft and Microsoft-compatible programs can read and display .RTF files. This is the first choice for making the conversion because formats are retained.

- **Text with Layout (.TXT)**   Strives to maintain layouts by inserting blank spaces to approximate indentations, for example. This format preserves some formatting.

- **Plain Text (.TXT)**   Saves text but not formats. A last resort. Use this one only if none of the others work.

- **MS-DOS Text Only (.TXT)**   Same as Text Only, but for use with non-Windows-based programs.

You can always save the file as a Web page and give it to friends and colleagues who can open it in their Web browsers. To save a Word document as a Web page, choose File | Save As, open the Save As Type drop-down menu in the Save As dialog box, and choose Web Page or Web Archive. By choosing Web Archive, you get around the problem of creating an additional folder for holding images on the Web page. Saving under the Web Archive format saves the entire Web page as a single file. Be aware, however, that the people to whom you give the Web Archive file must have advanced browsers to be able to view it.

One way to get around the problem of not being able to export a document to another word processor is to find out if the other word processor can import WordPerfect files. If it can, save your Word document as a WordPerfect file, and then use the other word processor to open the WordPerfect file.

Saving Documents for Use in Earlier Versions of Word

People with Word 2000 and Word 97 can open Word 2002 documents without the documents having to be converted to a different format. However, formats that are new in Word 2002 are replaced by their Word 2000 or Word 97 equivalents or near-equivalents, and advanced formats in the Word 2002 document are lost.

To convert a document so it can be opened in Word 95 or Word 6, make a copy of the document. Then open the copy, choose File | Save As to open the Save As dialog box, choose Word 6.0/95 (*.doc) on the Save As Type drop-down menu, click the Save button, and click Yes when Word asks if you want to replace the existing file. For every document element that will be lost in the conversion, Word asks you again whether you want to convert the document. Keep clicking Yes. You can always go back to the original Word document as long as you made a copy of it.

Saving Documents for Earlier Versions of Word by Default

If you are way ahead of the pack and you always have to save Word documents in a different format so that co-workers can open them, make the different format the default format for saving documents. That way, you don't have to choose a new format whenever you pass off a file to a co-worker. To change the default file format, choose Tools | Options and select the Save tab in the Options dialog box (see Figure 20-5). Then choose a different Word file format as the format with which your Word documents are saved:

- **Saving Documents for Word 97 or Earlier**   Check the Disable Features Introduced After check box, open the drop-down menu, and choose Microsoft Word 97 or Microsoft Word 6.0/95. Page layout formats, table layout formats, and other formats in your Word 2002 documents that aren't found in Word 97 or earlier are converted to formats that are found in Word 97, so advanced formats are lost.

- **Saving Word 2002 Documents By Default in a Different Format**   Open the Save Word Files As drop-down menu and choose a format to save your Word files in that format by default.

Default format

Save Word files as: Word Document (*.doc)

☑ Disable features introduced after: Microsoft Word 97

The Batch Conversion Wizard for Converting Many Files to or from Word

In the event that numerous files need converting to Word format or a different format, Word offers the Batch Conversion Wizard—a means of turning more than one file at a time into a different kind of file.

Before you run the Batch Conversion Wizard, create a new folder and copy the files that need converting to the new folder. Meanwhile, create a second new folder in which to put the converted files. The Batch Conversion Wizard will ask you which files to convert and where to place the converted files. By creating the two folders to begin with, you can make the process go more smoothly.

To run the Conversion Wizard, choose File | New and click the General Templates hyperlink in the New Document task pane. Then, in the Templates dialog box, go to the Other Documents tab, select the Batch Conversion icon, and click OK. The Conversion Wizard starts. You will be asked to do the following in these Conversion Wizard dialog boxes:

- **From/To**   Declare whether you are converting files from another format to Word or from Word to another format. From the drop-down menu, choose a format.

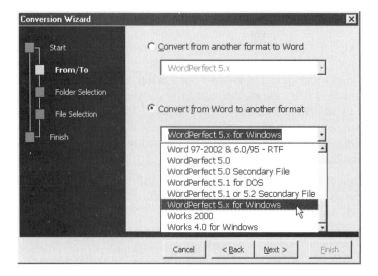

- **Folder Selection**   Click Browse button and, in the Browse to Folder dialog box, choose the source folder where the files that need converting are kept. Do the same for the Destination folder—name where to put the files after they are converted.

- **File Selection**   Open the Type drop-down menu and choose *.* to view all the files in the source folder in the Available box. Then, to declare which files need converting, either click the Select All button to convert all the files in the source folder, or double-click files one at a time to list them in the To Convert box.

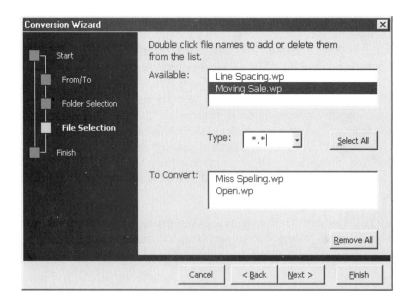

Click the Finish button to start the conversion. When the conversion is complete, go to the Destination folder and open the files one at a time. Examine them closely to see whether they were converted successfully. As I mentioned earlier, converting a file to a different format is always a dicey proposition, as little things such as special characters often get mangled in the translation.

Saving (and Opening) Different Versions of a Document

In a long document that drags on and on and requires many drafts, sometimes saving different drafts is useful. If you need to retrieve a paragraph or two that got dropped from an earlier draft, you can do so. You can even abandon later drafts and start all over with an earlier draft. For long projects that require many drafts, Word offers the File | Versions command. The command makes it easy to save different versions of the same document and, better yet, retrieve an earlier version. These pages explain how to save versions of a document, open a version, and save a version in a new file.

Saving a Version of a Document

Follow these steps to save different versions of a document as it evolves:

1. Choose File | Versions. You see the dialog box shown in Figure 20-6. The dialog box lists earlier versions of the document (if any), who saved the different versions, and comments describing what is found in earlier versions.

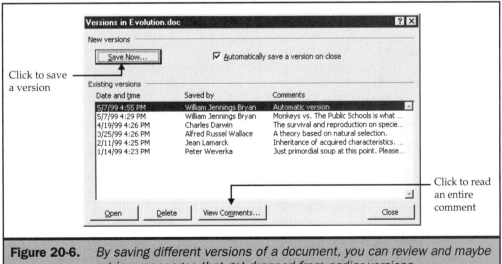

Figure 20-6. *By saving different versions of a document, you can review and maybe retrieve passages that got dropped from earlier versions*

2. Click the Save Now button. The Save Version box appears so you can enter a comment or two to describe this version of the document.

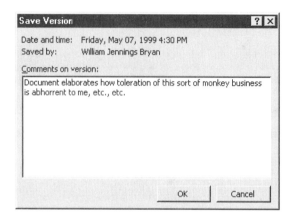

3. Enter a descriptive comment and click OK. The first few words of what you write will appear in the Comments column of the Versions In dialog box (refer to Figure 20-6).

4. Click Close in the Versions In dialog box.

Click a version and then click the Delete button in the Versions In dialog box if you no longer require the services of an earlier version of a document.

Many are tempted to click the Automatically Save A Version On Close check box in the Versions In dialog box, but I don't recommend it. Clicking this check box tells Word to save a new version each time you close your document. However, you can't enter comments to describe the version when you do save a version this way. You end up with a bunch of dated versions in the Versions In dialog box, none of which is easy to distinguish from the other because the words "Automatic version" appear in the Comments column where normally a description of the version appears.

Opening an Earlier Version of a Document

Go to work on your document as though no version were attached to it, but when you want to see an earlier version, choose File | Versions. The Versions In dialog box appears (refer to Figure 20-6) and you see the list of all the versions. Click a version and then click the Open button. If necessary, click a version and then click the View Comments button if you aren't sure which version is which.

The version opens in its own window onscreen. To switch between the version and the latest draft, either click in a different window or choose a name from the Window menu. Click the Close button in the version window to remove a version from the screen.

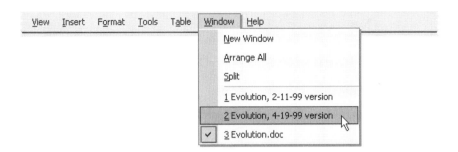

   If a version of a document deserves to be a document in its own right, open it, choose File | Save As, and save it under its own name.

Recovering a Document After Your Computer Freezes or Fails

If your computer crashes or a power failure occurs while you are working on a document, all is not lost because you can recover the document by way of the Document Recovery task pane shown in Figure 20-7. The task pane appears, after a crash, the next time you start Word. It lists documents that were open at the time of the crash and gives you the opportunity to open the recovered file, the original version, or the repaired version.

The Document Recovery task pane lists the names of original, recovered, and repaired documents. A *recovered document* is one that Word saved as part of the AutoRecover feature. As I explain shortly, Word saves AutoRecover versions of documents on its own every 10 minutes. In most cases, an AutoRecover document is more up to date than its original because Word saved the AutoRecover document *after* you saved the original. For example, suppose you save a document, 15 minutes pass, and your computer crashes. In that case, the AutoRecover version of the document is more up to date, because, at most, it was saved 10 minutes before the crash, while you saved the document 15 minutes before.

A *repaired document* is one that got damaged when the computer crashed, but Word was able to repair it. You can choose Show Repairs from the document's drop-down menu to see a description of the repairs that Word made.

An *original document* is the one that you saved last time you clicked the Save button or chose File | Save.

To decide what to do with documents whose names are listed in the Document Recovery task pane, select them and choose an option on the drop-down menu:

- **Open**   Opens the document so you can examine it. If you want to keep it, click the Save button or choose File | Save. In the case of recovered documents, you see the Save As dialog box, where you can either save the document under a new name or save it under the name of its original, in which case you delete the original version of the document. Save a recovered document if you want to keep it instead of its original.

- **Save As** Opens the Save As dialog box so you can save the document under a different name. Choose this command to keep a copy of the document on hand in case you need it.

- **Delete** Deletes the recovered document (this command is available with recovered documents, not originals).

- **Show Repairs** Shows repairs that Word made to the document (for use with repaired documents).

Tip *If the document you were working on when your computer crashed doesn't show up in the Document Recovery task pane, try to find it on your computer in the C:\Windows\ Application Data\Microsoft\Word folder. (On Windows NT 4 and later computers and computers in which more than one profile is in use, AutoRecover files are stored in the C:\Windows\Profiles*username*\Application Data\Microsoft\Word folder.) What's more, you can choose a different folder for AutoRecover files by choosing Tools | Options, selecting the File Locations tab in the Options dialog box, and selecting a new location for AutoRecover files.*

Unless you change the default, Word saves AutoRecover versions of documents every 10 minutes. If you're feeling insecure, you can tell Word to save the documents

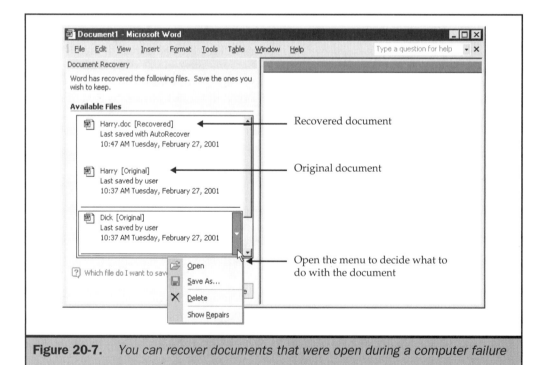

Figure 20-7. *You can recover documents that were open during a computer failure*

more frequently. To do so, choose Tools | Options, select the Save tab in the Options dialog box, and change the Save AutoRecover Info Every *XX* Minutes setting.

☐ Make local copy of files stored on network or removable drives
☑ Save AutoRecover info every: [10] minutes
☑ Embed smart tags
☐ Save smart tags as XML properties in Web pages

When Word (or Another Office Program) Fails

It happens. Sometimes you are slaving away in Word or another Office program and the program stops working. To kick-start Word or another Office program, you can try using the Microsoft Office Application Recovery program. The program attempts to revive Office programs such as Word and Excel, although my experiments with it have not yielded very good results.

To use the program, click the Start button and choose Programs | Microsoft Office Tools | Microsoft Office Application Recovery. A dialog box named after the command appears. Select an application to revive, if necessary, and click the Recover Application button.

Application	Status
Microsoft Word	Not Responding

Recover Application   End Application   Cancel

Protecting Documents Against Undue Tampering

Before you make a document available over a network or otherwise give co-workers a chance to tamper with it, you can do one or two things to make sure that your document doesn't get turned into mincemeat. These pages explain how to retain control over documents by clamping passwords on them and designating them as "read-only." Along with Windows, Word offers four ways to protect documents against tampering:

- **A Password Is Required to Open the Document**   Without the password, no one can open the document. See "Clamping a Password on a Document."

- **A Password Is Required to Edit the Document**   Anyone can open and read the document. To make editorial changes and save them in the document, however, you must know the password. People who don't know the password can save their editorial changes by saving the document under a new name. See "Clamping a Password on a Document."

- **Others Are Asked to Read But Not Edit the Document**   When others open the document, a dialog box asks them to please open the document in such a way that they can read it but make no editorial changes without saving the document under a new name. However, others can ignore the request. They can open the document and make as many editorial changes as they want. See "Protecting Documents by Giving them Read-Only Status."

- **Others Can Read the Document But Make No Edits Without Saving the Document Under a New Name**   Others can open the document and read it, but if they make editorial changes and try to save them, they see the Save As dialog box. At that point, others can save their editorial changes in a new document or abandon the enterprise. The original document remains intact. See "Protecting Documents by Giving Them Read-Only Status."

Note   *Chapter 17 explains how you can use the Tools | Protect Document command to make sure that editorial changes to a document do not go unnoticed. "Keeping Track of Revisions to Documents" describes how to make sure that all editorial changes to a document are tracked with revision marks; "Commenting on a Document" describes how you can allow reviewers to comment on but not revise a document.*

Clamping a Password on a Document

To make absolutely certain that only the select few can open or make changes to a document, you can clamp a password on it. People who do not have the password are either barred from opening the document or barred from making editorial changes to it, depending on which kind of password you give your document:

- **Password to Open**   Anyone who tries to open the document sees the Password dialog box and has to enter the password correctly before the document can be opened. Fail to enter the password correctly and you cannot open the document no matter what.

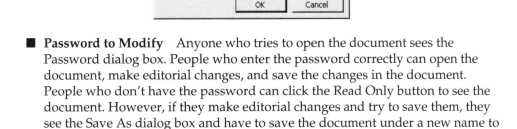

- **Password to Modify**   Anyone who tries to open the document sees the Password dialog box. People who enter the password correctly can open the document, make editorial changes, and save the changes in the document. People who don't have the password can click the Read Only button to see the document. However, if they make editorial changes and try to save them, they see the Save As dialog box and have to save the document under a new name to record their editorial changes in a new document.

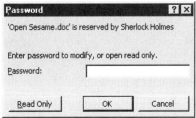

Follow these steps to clamp a password on a document:

1. Open the document that needs a password and choose Tools | Options.

2. Select the Security tab in the Options dialog box.

3. Enter the password. Passwords can be 15 characters long. If you include upper- and lowercase letters in your password, remember them well because passwords are case-sensitive. You have to enter upper- and lowercase letters exactly as you enter them now when you try to open your document. Asterisks instead of letters appear in the text box when you enter the password.

   - **Password To Open**   Enter the password here if you want to keep others from opening the document without a password.

   - **Password To Modify**   Enter the password here to keep only the select few from making editorial changes to the document.

User Information		Compatibility		File Locations	
View	General	Edit		Print	Save
Security		Spelling & Grammar		Track Changes	

File encryption options for this document

Password to open: `*****`   Advanced...

File sharing options for this document

Password to modify:

Note   *If password encryptions apart from the ones offered by Office are installed on your system, you can click the Advanced button on the Security tab to open the Encryption Type dialog box and choose a sturdier password-encryption system than the one that Microsoft offers.*

4. Click OK in the Options dialog box. You see the Confirm Password dialog box.

5. Enter your password exactly as you entered it before and click OK.

6. Click the Save button or press CTRL-S to activate the password.

Caution   *It goes without saying, but you must never forget a password. Forget the password and you can't open or modify the document, much less remove the password. Here's a trick for devising a password that you are not likely to forget and someone else is not likely to discover: Pick your favorite foreign city and spell it backwards. If I needed a password for my documents, it would be* **ezneriF**.

Suppose you decide to remove or change a password. Open the document in question, choose Tools | Options, select the Security tab in the Options dialog box, and follow these instructions:

■ **Removing the Password**   Delete the asterisks in the Password To Open or Password To Modify text box and click OK.

■ **Changing the Password**   Delete the asterisks in the Password To Open or Password To Modify text box and enter a new password. Then click OK, reproduce your new password in the Confirm Password dialog box, and click OK again.

Protecting Documents by Giving Them Read-Only Status

A *read-only* document is one that can be read onscreen but not changed in any way, shape, or form. In order to record editorial changes you've made to a read-only document, you have to save the document under a new name. The read-only document remains in the pristine condition it was in when you opened it.

The previous section in this chapter explains how you can clamp a password on a document and require others who do not have the password to open the document as a read-only file. Here are two more strategies for giving a document read-only status:

- **Recommend That the Document Be Opened as Read-Only**   Anyone who opens the document sees a dialog box that suggests opening the document as read-only. By clicking Yes, the person opens the document as a read-only file. By clicking No, the person opens the document as a normal file. This strategy counts on the user's discretion to treat the document as a read-only file. Nothing prevents others from opening the document and making changes to it.

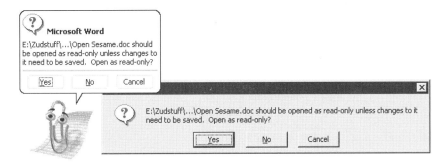

- **Make the Document a Read-Only File**   Everyone can open the document, but if they make editorial changes and try to save them, they must save the document under a new name. The words "Read-Only" in parentheses appear in the title bar when you are dealing with a read-only file.

To recommend that a document be opened as read-only, open the document, choose Tools | Options, and select the Security tab in the Options dialog box. Then check the Read-Only Recommended check box. You must save your document before it acquires read-only status.

To turn a document into a full-fledged read-only file, leave Word and open either of the Windows programs for managing files, Windows Explorer or My Computer. Then locate your document in one of those programs, select it, and choose File | Properties or right-click and choose Properties. In the Properties dialog box, select the General tab, and then check the Read-Only check box.

Remember how to get to the Properties dialog box in My Computer or Windows Explorer. You can choose File | Properties in a Word document to open the Properties dialog box, but you can't change the read-only status of a document in the Properties dialog box in Word. To change a document's read-only status, you have to start from Windows Explorer or My Computer and choose File | Properties.

Finding a Lost Document

Occasionally a document gets lost. You don't remember its name. You remember its name but you don't know which folder you put it in. You remember part of its name and a sentence you typed in it, but that's all. To find stray documents, Word offers the Basic Search and Advanced Search task panes:

- In the Basic Search task pane, you search by entering a word or number that is found in the missing document.

- In the Advanced task pane, you search by describing properties of the missing document.

Note *Earlier in this chapter, "Entering Document Properties to Find and Identify Documents" describes what document properties are and how to enter them in a document.*

To conduct a search, click the Search button or choose File | Search. As shown in Figure 20-8, the Basic Search task pane appears.

Conducting a Basic Search

To conduct a basic search, start by entering a word or number that you know to be in the document. The idea is to pinpoint a single document. Try entering a proper name, telephone number, or other keyword that doesn't appear in many documents. Unless you are conducting a broad-based search, don't bother entering two words, because basic searches are "or" searches—they turn up documents that have one word or the other, not both words.

Both the Basic Search and Advanced Search task pane offer the Search In and Results Should Be drop-down menus, where you tell Word where to search and what to search for:

- **Search In** Tell Word where to search for the missing document. A search of "Everywhere"—all the drives and folders on your computer, Web folders, and Outlook folders—can take a long time. To narrow the search, uncheck the Everywhere folder, if necessary, click plus signs (+) to locate the folder or folders that you want to search, and check their check boxes (refer to Figure 20-8).

- **Results Should Be** Tell Word what kind of file you are looking for. To search for Word documents, uncheck the Anything check box, uncheck the Office Files check box, click plus signs (+) to display Word Files, and check the Words Files check box.

Click the Search button to conduct the search. Documents that are found in the search appear in the Search Results task pane (refer to Figure 20-8). A couple of pages

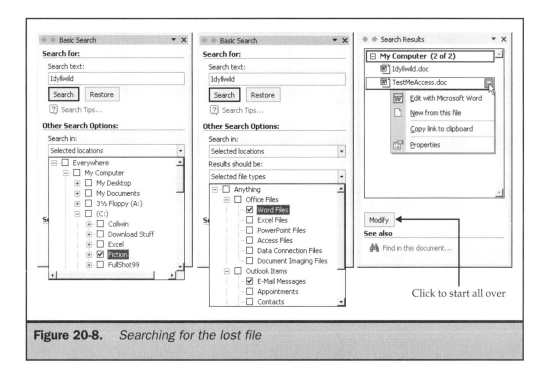

Figure 20-8. *Searching for the lost file*

hence, "Reading the Search Results" explains what you can do with the list of files that appears. And if the search is unsuccessful? Do one of the following:

- Click the Modify button to start all over. Maybe you are searching in the wrong places or using an inadequate keyword.
- Try running an Advanced search. Click the Modify button to return to the Basic Search task pane. Then click the Advanced Search hyperlink. You will find it toward the bottom of the task pane.

Conducting an Advanced Search

Besides telling Word where to search and what to search for (see the previous section of this chapter), an advanced search entails declaring the properties, conditions, and values you want to search for. Earlier in this chapter, "Entering Document Properties to Find and Identify Documents" describes what document properties are. By carefully entering or making note of a document's properties, you will always be able to find it in document searches.

Fill in the Property, Condition, and Value boxes to describe a search condition:

- **Property** From the Property drop-down list, select a property of the document that you know something about. Choose Keywords, for example, if you happen to remember a keyword that was assigned to the document; choose Last Modified if you know roughly when the document was last saved.

- **Condition** From the Condition drop-down list, choose a search condition. The options on this list vary depending on the choice you made in the Property drop-down list.

- **Value** Enter a value or handful of characters to further describe the search condition. What you enter in this box also depends on which aspect of the document you are trying to describe. If you choose Last Modified as the property, for example, enter a date in *MM/DD/YY* format.

Click the Add button to enter the search condition. To search using more than one condition, enter another condition, but before clicking the Add button, select the And or Or option button:

- **And** For a stringent search in which the document must meet *all* search conditions. For example, it must have the keyword *Spenser* and have been modified before 7/31/01.

- **Or** For a broad search in which the document can meet any one condition. For example, it can have the keyword Spenser or have been modified before 7/31/01.

Click the Search button when you are ready to conduct the search.

Reading the Search Results

In the Search Results task pane, move the pointer over a document name. A pop-up box tells you where it is located and when it was last modified. By opening a document's drop-down menu, you can do the following:

- **Open the Document** Either click the document's name or choose Edit with Microsoft Word on the drop-down menu.
- **Open a New Document Starting from the Document You Found** Choose New from This File to open a second copy of the document and perhaps save it under a new name.
- **Create a Hyperlink to the Document** Choose Copy Link to Clipboard to place a hyperlink to the document on the Office Clipboard.
- **View the Document's Properties** Choose Properties to open the Properties dialog box and learn more about the document.

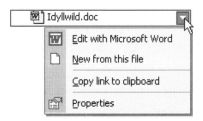

MOUS Exam Objectives Explored in Chapter 20

Objective	Heading
Manage files and folders for documents	"Creating the Folders You Need"
Save documents using different names and file formats	"Saving a Document Under a New Name" and "Converting Documents to Different Formats So Others Can Use Them"
Prepare documents and forms for distribution*	"Protecting Documents Against Undue Tampering"
Create document versions*	"Saving (and Opening) Different Versions of a Document"
Protect Documents*	"Protecting Documents Against Undue Tampering"

Denotes an Expert, not a Core, exam objective.

Ten Techniques for Handling Computer Crashes and Other Untoward Events

When a computer crashes or power failure occurs, it can be disconcerting, especially if you are working on an important document. Here are some tried-and-true techniques for preventing crashes, recovering from crashes, and steeling yourself and your computer against crashes.

1. When You Can, Always Shut Down Your Computer Properly   Everybody knows the routine for shutting down properly: Click the Start button, choose Shut Down, select the Shut Down option in the Shut Down Windows dialog box, and click OK. If you don't shut down properly, you run the risk of damaging your hard disk and the files that happened to be stored on the part of your hard disk that was damaged. Shutting down properly is the first defense against damaging your computer.

And if your computer freezes and you can't shut down properly....

2. Press CTRL-ALT-DEL When Your Computer Hangs or Freezes   It happens. Sometimes the computer freezes and refuses to do anything more. And then you can't shut down the proper way and you have to resort to this technique to make your computer start working again:

1. Press CTRL-ALT-DEL. With luck, the Close Program dialog box appears.

2. Click the name of the program that is "not responding." You see the words "not responding" after the program's name.

3. Click the End Task button. Again with luck, the program that made your computer hang closes and you can get back to work. Save all open documents, close all programs, and restart your computer.

4. If your computer still doesn't respond, press CTRL-ALT-DEL again. With luck, your computer shuts down and restarts.

5. If you continue to suffer bad luck, turn off the computer's power switch and wait a full minute before turning your computer on again. If you turn it on before the platters stop spinning, you could harm the hard disk.

Windows runs the ScanDisk utility when you turn your computer back on to see if any damage was done to the hard disk. That's quite all right.

3. Always Back Up Important Documents   As long as you back up important documents, you don't have to worry too much about system crashes and files being corrupted. Earlier in this chapter, "Backing Up Your Work in Word" explores all the nuances of backing up Word documents.

4. Invest in a Surge Protector   Especially if you live in the southern United States or another lush semitropical zone where thunderstorms occur frequently, you need a surge protector—a device that protects computers against electrical surges. An electrical surge can do serious damage to a computer, but a surge protector provides an alternative path to electricity when it rises above the normal level on the power line.

5. Get Antivirus Software   Nowadays, when so many files are traded over the Internet, being infected with a computer virus is easier than ever. In Word, macros can carry viruses, so you should be careful about opening documents that include macros. And you should buy antivirus software for your computer if you often receive files over the Internet.

   If you think your computer has been struck by a virus, visit www.microsoft.com/ msoffice, the Office Web site, and check for updates concerning viruses. And when you're done, go to the Computer Virus Myths site at www.kumite.com/myths/ home.htm, where you can read about virus hoaxes and virus hoaxsters.

6. What to Do When Word Says the "File Is in Use"   When a document isn't closed properly or your computer gets momentarily confused by competing demands, you sometimes see a message that says the "file is in use" when you try to open a document. The file, however, isn't really in use, and you know that but the computer doesn't.

   If you are working at home and your computer isn't connected to a network, the only thing you can do to remedy the problem is close all documents, shut down your computer, and then restart your computer. Doing so removes from the computer's memory all vestiges of the document that was supposed to be open, and you can open the document.

   If you are working at an office and your computer is connected to a network, the file-sharing properties of your documents probably have not been set up correctly. Ask the network administrator to solve the problem for you.

7. Check the Autorecover Save Info Every *XX* Minutes Check Box in the Options Dialog Box   Earlier in this chapter, "Recovering a Document After Your Computer Freezes or Fails" explains what the Save AutoRecover Info Every *XX* Minutes check box on the Save tab of the Options dialog box does. When the check box is selected, Word creates a second, AutoRecover copy of your document every certain number of minutes. If your computer fails, you can open the AutoRecover copy and perhaps recover your documents.

8. Use the Open and Repair Command to Open a Damaged Document   Even if a document is in shambles, you can try opening it with the Open and Repair command. In the Open dialog box, select the document, but instead of clicking the Open button, open its drop-down menu and choose Open and Repair. Word will do its best to open the damaged document.

9. Run Disk Cleanup to Make Your Computer Work Faster   The Windows Disk Cleanup utility removes the files that clutter the hard disk so that your system can run better. Follow these steps to run Disk Cleanup:

1. Click the Start button and choose Programs | Accessories | System Tools | Disk Cleanup.

2. Make sure Temporary Internet Files and Temporary Files are checked in the Disk Cleanup dialog box.

3. Click OK, and then click Yes.

10. Run Scandisk to Check for and Repair Errors to the Hard Disk   The Windows ScanDisk utility is designed to check the hard disk for damage. Run the utility program if your computer fails frequently, if you see "bad sector" or "unable to read" errors, or if you get a bunch of gibberish after you open a file. Follow these steps to run ScanDisk:

1. Click the Start button and choose Programs | Accessories | System Tools | ScanDisk.

2. Choose a disk to check.

3. Choose to run a Standard test.

4. Click the Start button.

The Complete Reference

Word 2002

Chapter 21

Your Own Customized Word

This chapter takes on a subject that inspires more trepidation in most people than is really necessary—it explains how to customize Word. As this chapter will demonstrate, customizing Word is not as hard as it seems. Perhaps you've noticed the little arrow on the right side of the toolbars. Merely by clicking that arrow and making a choice or two, you can add buttons to or remove buttons from a toolbar. You can also devise your own toolbars, menus, and keyboard shortcuts for the commands that take up most of your time.

This chapter explains how to customize the Normal template and how to customize toolbars, menus, and keypresses. You also learn how to save your customizations in such a way that you can transfer them to another computer or reapply them if your system breaks down.

Choosing Default Settings for the Normal Template

Most documents are created with the Normal template. When you click the New button, press CTRL-N, or choose File | New and select the Blank Document hyperlink in the New Document task pane to create a new document, your document arrives with all the default settings in the Normal template. Because so much work is done in documents created with the Normal template, Word offers Default buttons in many dialog boxes for choosing your own Normal template default settings. To change the default font in the Normal template, for example, choose a font in the Font dialog box and then click the Default button.

Table 21-1 lists all the dialog boxes where Default buttons are located. The table explains how to reach each dialog box and the default settings you can make in the Normal template. If you know your way around Word, by all means make your favorite settings a part of the Normal template. That way, you can get off to a good start when you click the New button or press CTRL-N to create a new document.

> **Tip** *On the Save tab of the Options dialog box is a check box called Prompt To Save Normal Template. If that check box is selected, a dialog box appears when you close Word after making changes to the Normal template. In the dialog box, click Yes to keep the changes you made to the template or click No to abandon them. Activate the Prompt To Save Normal Template check box if you want the chance to reconsider changes you make to the Normal template before you close Word. To reach the Save tab of the Options dialog box, choose Tools | Options and select the Save tab.*

Dialog Box	How To Open It	Default Settings
Page Setup	File	Page Setup	Margin size, paper size and orientation, paper tray for printing
Date and Time	Insert	Date and Time	Formats for displaying the date or date and time as a field in documents
Font	Format	Font	Font, font style, font size, kerning
Language	Tools	Language	Set Language	Language in use

Table 21-1. *Dialog Boxes Where You Can Choose Default Settings for the Normal Template*

Customizing the Menus, Toolbars, and Keyboard Shortcuts

You are hereby invited to play cosmetic surgeon with Word. The program makes rearranging the menus, toolbars, and keyboard shortcuts fairly simple. And if you go overboard and make a hash of your menus, toolbars, or keyboard shortcuts, you can get the originals back. These pages explain how to change the face of Word. You learn how to set up your own menus, change the Word menus, invent your own toolbars, and alter the Word toolbars. You will also find instructions here for creating your own keyboard shortcuts.

 If you share your computer with others, be sure to get their permission before you start tinkering with toolbars and menus. You are liable to change a toolbar or menu that someone else relies on and thereby lose a friend for life.

Setting Up Your Own Menus

Set up your own menus to remove unneeded commands from menus, place the commands you need most often on a single menu, or gather commands for a specific task in one place. Commands aren't the only items you can put on a menu, by the way. You can also put macros, fonts, AutoText entries, styles, and hyperlinks on a menu.

Choosing Which Template Gets Your Customizations

When you make changes to menus, toolbars, and keyboard shortcuts, the customizations you make become part of a template. In effect, you customize a template when you customize Word. Next time you open a document based on the template you customized, you get your customized menus, toolbars, and keyboard shortcuts.

Customizations are made in the Customize dialog box. When you are done customizing, be sure to visit the Commands tab in that dialog box and choose a template from the Save In drop-down menu. Word will make your customizations a part of the template you choose.

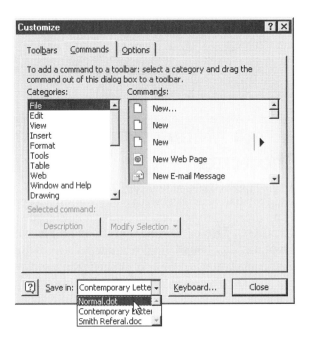

By the way, all is not lost if you alter a toolbar in one template but wish you had altered it in another as well, because you can use the Organizer to copy toolbars from template to template. See "Assembling Styles (and Macros and AutoText) from Different Templates" in Chapter 12.

What's more, you can customize shortcut menus as well as the menus on the menu bar. A shortcut menu is one you see when you right-click text or part of the screen.

Whatever you want to do to your menus, start by choosing Tools | Customize or right-clicking a toolbar and choosing Customize. You see the Customize dialog box shown in Figure 21-1. This dialog box is the starting point for removing commands

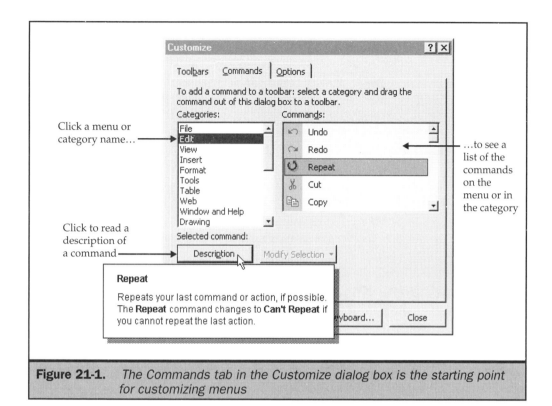

Click a menu or
category name...

...to see a
list of the
commands
on the
menu or in
the category

Click to read a
description of
a command

Figure 21-1. *The Commands tab in the Customize dialog box is the starting point
for customizing menus*

from menus, adding commands to menus, creating new menus, rearranging menus,
redecorating menus, and restoring a menu to its original state. The Customize dialog
box is a curious thing. While it is open, you can drag menus and menu commands to
new places, drag menu commands off menus, and do a lot of other things to menus.
As soon as you close the dialog box, menus work in the usual way.

All Word commands are listed on the Commands tab of the Customize dialog
box. The details of customizing menus are described in the pages that follow. Here
are instructions for finding your way around the Commands tab on the Customize
dialog box:

■ **Locating Menu Commands** Before you can add a command to a menu, you
have to find and select it in the Commands dialog box. To do so, click a name in
the Categories list, read the list of commands in the Commands box, and select
a command name. The first few names in the Categories list happen to be the
names of menus on the menu bar. Click a menu name in the Categories box
and you see the names of commands on the menu whose name you clicked.
In Figure 21-1, for example, the Edit category has been clicked, so you can see
the commands on the Edit menu. You can click the All Commands category to
see an alphabetical list of all the commands in Word.

- **Learning What a Command Is**   A command name often doesn't reveal what a command does. When that is the case, click the command and then click the Description button to read an explanation of the command (refer to Figure 21-1).

- **Adding Macros, Fonts, AutoText Entries, and Styles to Menus**   Near the bottom of the Categories list are categories named Macros, Fonts, AutoText, and Styles. Click these categories when you want to add a macro, a font, an AutoText entry, or a style to a menu.

- **Rearranging the Menus**   Also near the bottom of the Categories list is a category called Built-In Menus. Click it when you want to add a menu—File, Edit, View, and so on—to a toolbar or create a second version of a menu. Yes, you can place menus on toolbars.

- **Creating a New Menu**   At the bottom of the Categories list is a category called New Menu. Click it when you want to create a new menu of your own.

Customizing the Shortcut Menus

The Customize dialog box (refer to Figure 23-1) is also the starting point for customizing a shortcut menu. However, instead of going to the Commands tab, select the Toolbars tab, and then, on the Toolbars list, select Shortcut Menus. The Shortcut Menus toolbar appears onscreen. Click the Text, Table, or Draw button to open a drop-down list of shortcut menus. Select the shortcut menu you want to customize. After the shortcut menu is displayed onscreen, you can change or rearrange its menu commands using the standard techniques described in this chapter.

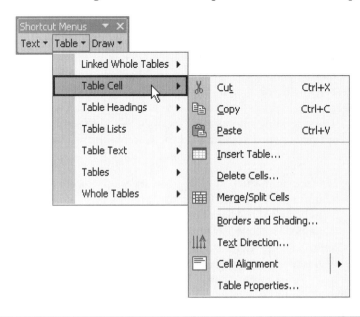

Spend any time on the Commands tab in the Customize dialog box and you soon realize that Word offers many commands. Commands on all menus and submenus are found in the Customize dialog box. Word offers about 500 commands in all. I suggest scrolling through the list and looking at a few of them. At the end of this chapter, "Ten Commands Worth Adding to Toolbars and Menus" describes a handful of buttons that I think are good candidates for placement on a toolbar.

Removing Commands from a Menu

As far as I know, you may use Word strictly to write letters to friends, in which case you don't need nine-tenths of the commands on the Word menus. For you, Word offers two techniques for removing commands from menus and shortcut menus:

- Press ALT-CTRL-HYPHEN (-) and select the menu command you want to remove. As soon as you choose this command, the pointer changes into an ominous-looking black bar. With the black bar showing, click the command you want to remove as though you were selecting it. Press ESC if you pressed ALT-CTRL-HYPHEN (-) accidentally and you want the ominous black bar to go away.

- Choose Tools | Customize to open the Customize dialog box (refer to Figure 21-1). With the dialog box still open, move the pointer out of the dialog box, open the menu with the command you want to remove, and click the command. Then either right-click the command and choose Delete from the shortcut menu, as shown in Figure 21-2, or click the Modify Selection button in the Customize dialog box and choose Delete from the pop-up menu. You can also simply drag the menu command off the menu.

Note *See "Restoring a Menu (or the Menu Bar) to Its Original State" later in this chapter, if you regret removing a command from a menu.*

Adding Commands, Styles, Macros, Fonts, and AutoText Entries to Menus

Follow these steps to place a command, a style, a macro, a font, or an AutoText entry on a menu:

1. Choose Tools | Customize to open the Customize dialog box.

2. On the Commands tab, locate the command you want to place on a menu, as shown in Figure 21-3. To do so, choose a category in the Categories list and then choose the command in the Commands list. Choose Macros, Fonts, AutoText, or Styles at the bottom of the Categories list if you want to add one of those items to a menu.

3. In the Commands list, click the command, macro, or whatnot that you want to add to a menu, drag it out of the Customize dialog box, drag it over the name of the menu or shortcut menu you want to place it on, and drag the command to the place on the menu where you want the command to go.

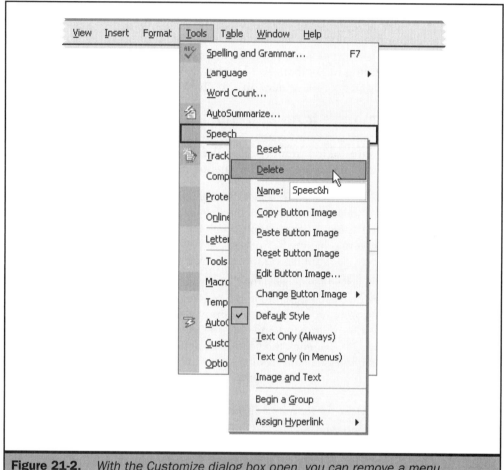

Figure 21-2.   *With the Customize dialog box open, you can remove a menu command by right-clicking it and choosing Delete*

As shown in Figure 21-3, a black line shows where the command will appear on the menu when you release the mouse button. The previous section in this chapter explains how to remove a command from a menu, in case you regret putting it there.

Note   *Later in this chapter, "Making Menus and Toolbars Easier to Read and Understand" explains how to handle hot keys in menu commands and how to decorate commands with images.*

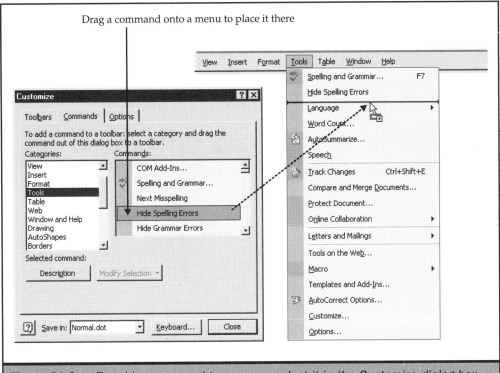

Figure 21-3. *To add a command to a menu, select it in the Customize dialog box and drag it onto a menu*

Creating Your Own Menu

Follow these steps to create your own menu and place it on the Word menu bar or a toolbar:

1. If you want to place the menu on a toolbar, display the toolbar.

2. Choose Tools | Customize to open the Customize dialog box (see Figure 21-3).

3. On the Commands tab, scroll to the bottom of the Categories list and select New Menu. The name New Menu appears in the Commands list.

4. Click New Menu in the Commands list and drag if off the Customize dialog box and onto the menu bar or toolbar where you want your new menu to be. A thick black line shows where the menu will land when you release the mouse button.

5. Release the mouse button. The name "New Menu" appears on the menu bar or toolbar. Not much of a menu name, is it?

6. Either right-click your new menu or click the Modify Selection button in the Customize dialog box. A menu appears for managing menus.

7. In the Name text box, type a name for your menu, and then press ENTER.

8. Click Close in the Customize dialog box.

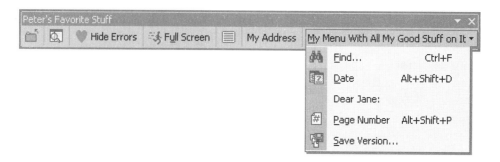

The previous section in this chapter explains how to put items on a menu. To delete a menu you created, choose Tools | Customize to open the Customize dialog box, and then either right-click the menu and choose Delete, click the Modify Selection button and choose Delete, or simply drag the new menu off the toolbar.

Restoring a Menu (or the Menu Bar) to Its Original State

All right, you went to a bunch of trouble to change the menus around, and now you regret it. Or, worse yet, you accidentally dragged one of the names—File, Edit, View, and so on—from the menu bar. Scary when that happens, isn't it? Choose Tools | Customize to open the Customize dialog box, select the Commands tab (refer to Figure 21-3), and follow these instructions to restore a menu or the menu bar to its original state:

■ **Restoring a Word Menu to Its Original State** With the Customize dialog box open, click the menu in question on the Word menu bar, click the Modify Selection button in the Customize toolbar, and choose Reset from the pop-up menu.

■ **Putting a Word Menu Back on the Menu Bar** Scroll in the Categories list and select the next-to-last item, Built-In Menus. The Commands list shows Word menu names on the menu bar in their rightful order. Select the menu that needs restoring, drag it out of the Customize dialog box, and place it on the menu bar.

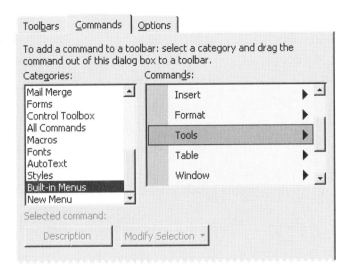

 To get back the original shortcut menus, choose Tools | Customize and select the Toolbars tab in the Customize dialog box. In the Toolbars list, check the Shortcut Menus check box; then click the Reset button.

Creating Your Own Toolbars and Toolbar Buttons

The starting point for constructing your own toolbars or making Word's toolbars work more efficiently is the Customize dialog box shown in Figure 21-4. As long as the Customize dialog box is open, you can drag buttons from toolbar to toolbar, put new buttons on toolbars, or create new toolbars. To get to the Customize dialog box, choose Tools | Customize or right-click a toolbar and choose Customize. The Toolbars tab lists each toolbar. If you created toolbars of your own, their names appear at the bottom of the list. By clicking a toolbar check box, you can make a toolbar appear onscreen without leaving the Customize dialog box.

Read on to find out the fast way to remove or add toolbar buttons and the slow but thorough way to add or remove toolbar buttons. You will also find out how to create your own toolbars, restore a Word toolbar to its original condition, and create a hyperlink button for a toolbar.

 "Getting to Know the Toolbars" in Chapter 1 explains how to display toolbars and arrange them onscreen.

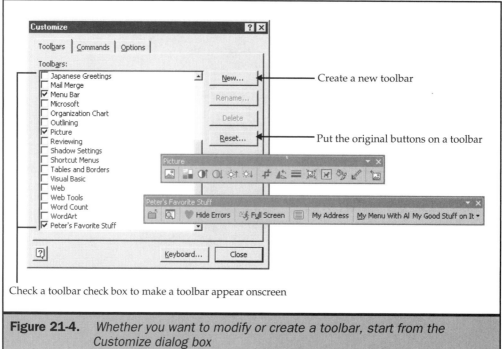

Create a new toolbar

Put the original buttons on a toolbar

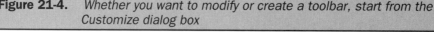

Check a toolbar check box to make a toolbar appear onscreen

Figure 21-4. *Whether you want to modify or create a toolbar, start from the Customize dialog box*

To see larger buttons on toolbars, right-click a toolbar and choose Customize. Then, on the Options tab of the Customize dialog box, check the Large Icons check box.

The Fast Way to Add and Remove Toolbar Buttons

The Toolbar Options button, a minuscule arrow, appears on toolbars when they are docked along the top or bottom of the window. (To dock a toolbar, double-click its title bar.) The Toolbar Options button is easy to miss, but look closely and you will see it on the right side of toolbars, as shown in Figure 21-5.

When you click the Toolbar Options button, you see the Add or Remove Buttons button. Click that, click the toolbar name, and you see a drop-down menu that lists the buttons on the toolbar. By checking or unchecking buttons on the drop-down menu, you can add buttons to or remove buttons from the toolbar. Click the Reset Toolbar button if you go overboard and remove too many buttons.

The Thorough Way to Add and Remove Toolbar Buttons

Clicking the Toolbar Options button is the fast way to add buttons to or remove buttons from a toolbar. But suppose you want to gather toolbar buttons from far and wide for a toolbar. In that case, choose Tools | Customize, select the Toolbars tab in the

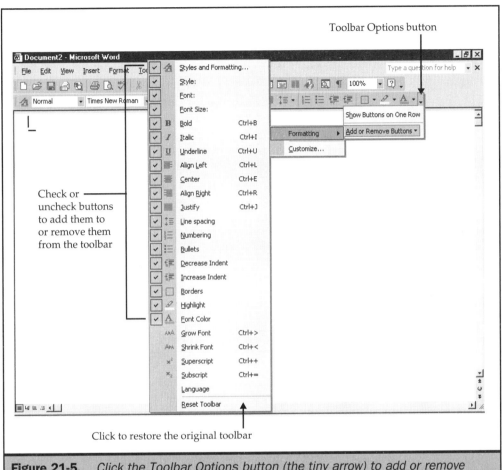

Toolbar Options button

Check or
uncheck buttons
to add them to
or remove them
from the toolbar

Click to restore the original toolbar

Figure 21-5. *Click the Toolbar Options button (the tiny arrow) to add or remove toolbar buttons without having to go to the Customize dialog box*

Customize dialog box (refer to Figure 21-4), check the names of the toolbars to display the ones you want to work with, and follow these instructions:

■ **Moving a Button from One Toolbar to Another** Drag the button between toolbars. That's right—simply click the button you want to move and drag it to the other toolbar. A black line shows where the button will appear when you release the mouse button. Be careful not to release the mouse button too soon, or you remove the button from the toolbar instead of moving it.

■ **Copying a Button from One Toolbar to Another** Hold down the CTRL key and drag the button from one toolbar to another. As you drag, a cross appears below the mouse pointer to show you are copying the toolbar button, not moving it.

■ **Removing a Button from a Toolbar** Drag the button off the toolbar or right-click the button and choose Delete from the shortcut menu. (See "Restoring a Toolbar to Its Original State," later in this chapter, if you regret removing the toolbar button.)

■ **Putting a Menu Command on a Toolbar** Select the Commands tab in the Customize dialog box (see Figure 21-3). As "Setting Up Your Own Menus" explained earlier in this chapter, you can find any Word command on the Commands tab by clicking a category in the Categories list and then clicking a command in the Commands list. After you have found the command you want to place on a toolbar, drag it out of the Customize dialog box and onto the toolbar. Drag it as though you were moving a button from one toolbar to another.

■ **Putting Macros, Fonts, AutoText Entries, and Styles on a Toolbar** Select the Commands tab in the Customize dialog box (refer Figure 21-2), scroll to the bottom of the Categories list, and choose Macros, Fonts, AutoText, or Styles. In the Commands list, select the item you want to place on a toolbar and drag it onto the toolbar to copy it there.

Note *Later in this chapter, "Making Menus and Toolbars Easier to Read and Understand" explains how you can rename toolbar buttons, place images on toolbar buttons, and place lines on toolbars to divide one set of buttons from another. Earlier in this chapter, "Creating Your Own Menu" explains how to put a menu on a toolbar.*

Creating Your Own Toolbar

Follow these steps to create a toolbar of your own and load it down with your favorite buttons and commands:

1. Choose Tools | Customize or right-click a toolbar and choose Customize.

2. Select the Toolbars tab in the Customize dialog box.

3. Click the New button. You see the New Toolbar dialog box.

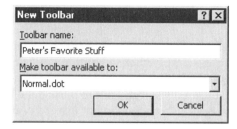

4. Enter a descriptive name for your toolbar. The name will appear in the title bar.

5. In the Make Toolbar Available To drop-down menu, choose which template to keep your toolbar in. As the start of this chapter explained, toolbars that you create are stored with a particular template.

6. Click OK. A puny toolbar appears onscreen.

7. Move or copy toolbar buttons onto your new toolbar, or else place commands or menus on the toolbar. The previous section in this chapter explains how to load buttons on a toolbar. Simply drag the buttons or commands onto your new toolbar and watch it grow longer.

8. Click Close in the Customize dialog box.

To delete a toolbar you created, choose Tools | Customize, choose the toolbar's name on the Toolbars tab in the Customize dialog box (refer to Figure 21-4), and click the Delete button. Click the Rename button in the Customize dialog box to give a toolbar a new name. You can't delete or change the name of a Word toolbar. Only toolbars you invented yourself can be deleted or renamed.

Restoring a Toolbar to Its Original State

Don't despair if you make hash of a toolbar, because you can make the original reappear. Use either of these techniques to restore a toolbar to its original state:

■ Click the Toolbar Options button (the tiny arrow on the right side of the toolbar) of the toolbar that needs restoring, choose Add or Remove Buttons, choose the name of the toolbar that needs restoring, and choose Reset Toolbar from the drop-down menu (see Figure 21-5).

■ Choose Tools | Customize, select the Toolbars tab in the Customize dialog box (see Figure 21-4), choose the name of the toolbar that needs restoring, and click the Reset button.

Making Menus and Toolbars Easier to Read and Understand

Take a close look at the Word menus and toolbars and you will see that the Microsoft Corporation has gone to great lengths to make the menus and toolbars in Word easy to read and understand. Each button is dressed in a distinctive image that hints at what it is used for. Menu names are descriptive. Hot keys, the underlined letters in menu and command names, were chosen carefully. On menus, thin lines called separators divide similar commands into groups. Separators also appear on toolbars, where they distinguish one set of buttons from another.

These pages explain how you can make the menus and toolbars you create easier to read and understand. Read on to learn how to rearrange commands on menus and buttons on toolbars, change the names of buttons and menus, decorate buttons with images, and draw separator lines on menus and toolbars.

GETTING MORE OUT OF WORD 2002

Creating a Hyperlink Toolbar Button

Here's a neat little trick: You can put a hyperlink button on a toolbar and by so doing be able to click the button and go straight to another document or a site on the Internet. A hyperlink is an electronic shortcut between two documents or two Web sites. Follow these steps to put a hyperlink button on a toolbar:

1. Choose Tools | Customize to display the Customize dialog box (see Figure 21-4) and put a button on the toolbar. Which button you put on doesn't matter. After you turn the button into a hyperlink, your button will change functionality. In fact, you might name the button after the document or Web site that the link will go to.

2. Right-click your new button and choose Assign Hyperlink | Open. You see the Assign Hyperlink: Open dialog box.

3. Either enter the address of the Web page or document you want to link to or choose it in the dialog box. "Including Hyperlinks in Documents and Web Pages" in Chapter 22 explains how to use this dialog box create a hyperlink to a Web site or another Word document.

To remove the hyperlink from a button, right-click it while the Customize dialog box is open and choose Edit Hyperlink | Remove Link. Right-click and choose Edit Hyperlink | Open to establish a new link for the button.

Rearranging Buttons and Commands on Toolbars and Menus

As long as the Customize dialog box is open, you can drag items on menus and buttons on toolbars wherever you want. Drag a menu item up or down the list of commands. Drag a toolbar button from side to side on the toolbar. Choose Tools | Customize to open the Customize dialog box.

As you drag a button or command name, a gray box appears below the pointer, and a black line shows where the menu command or toolbar button will land when you release the mouse button. Release it when the command name or button is in the right spot.

Changing the Names of Buttons and Menus

To change the name of a menu or button, choose Tools | Customize or right-click a toolbar and choose Customize to open the Customize dialog box. Then click the menu or button that needs a new name and either right-click or click the Modify Selection button on the Commands tab in the Customize dialog box. You see a menu of commands for handling names and images on buttons and toolbars. Enter a new name in the Name text box.

As you know, each menu name and command name includes a hot key, an underlined letter that you can press in combination with the ALT key to give a command or open a menu. To tell Word which letter is the hot key, place an ampersand (&) before the hot key letter. Here, the "C," "B," and "o" in "Corned Beef Sandwich," "Burger with Fries," and "Burrito" are the hot keys.

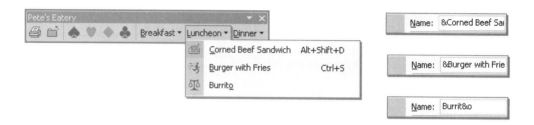

 Be sure to choose a shortcut key that isn't taken already by another command name. Choose a conspicuous letter. Usually, that means the first letter, but if the first letter is taken, choose a long vowel or notable consonant.

Choosing or Creating Images for Toolbar Buttons and Menu Commands

Images appear on toolbar buttons when you borrow or take buttons from other toolbars. Images also appear when you put certain commands on toolbars. Not all commands, however, are attached to an image. Sometimes when you put a command from the Commands tab of the Customize dialog box on a toolbar, only a name appears on the toolbar. However, you can decorate a toolbar button (or command name on a menu as well) with an image by following these instructions.

1. Choose Tools | Customize to open the Customize dialog box.

2. Display the toolbar or menu whose button or command needs a change of face.

3. Right-click the button or command. By choosing options on the shortcut menu, you can do the following to your button or menu command:

   ■ **Choose an Image from the Change Button Image Drop-Down Menu**   Choose the Change Button Image option and choose an image from the drop-down menu. Please don't choose the smiley face, however. Seeing that particular cliché on a toolbar button is depressing.

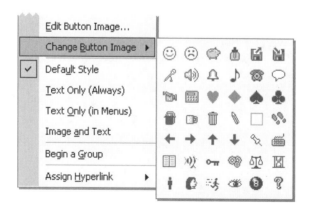

■ **Draw an Image** If you are artistically inclined and accustomed to working in bitmaps, choose the Edit Image option. You see the Button Editor dialog box shown in Figure 21-6. By choosing colors and clicking on the bitmap, you can construct an image. Click a Move button to nudge your image leftward, rightward, upward, or downward. Click Erase and click on the bitmap where you want gray to appear on the button.

■ **Copy an Image for the Button** Copy a bitmap image (you can use the Paint program that comes with Windows) to the Clipboard. Then right-click the toolbar button or menu command that needs an image and choose Paste Button Image.

Tip   *You can always right-click a button and choose Reset Button Image to see the original image—the one that appeared on the toolbar button or menu command before you started tinkering.*

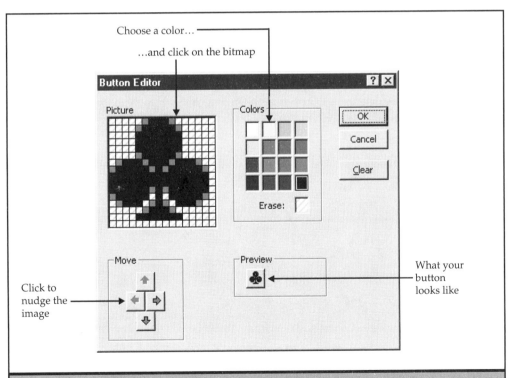

Figure 21-6.   *Bit by bit, you can construct an image for a toolbar button or menu command in the Button Editor dialog box*

Also on the shortcut menu are four obscure options for displaying text, the image, or the text and the image on toolbar buttons and menus:

- **Displaying Only the Image**   Choose the Default Style option.
- **Displaying Only the Text**   Choose the Text Only (Always) option.
- **Displaying Only the Text (Not the Image As Well) on Menus**   Choose the Text Only (In Menus) option.
- **Displaying Both the Image and the Text**   Choose the Image and Text option.

Drawing Separators for Menu Items and Toolbar Buttons

A *separator* is a faint line on a toolbar or menu that distinguishes one set of buttons or menu commands from the next. Draw a separator line to make it clear to users where one set of buttons or commands ends and another begins. Open the Customize dialog box (choose Tools | Customize) and follow these instructions to put a separator on a toolbar or menu:

- **Placing a Separator on a Toolbar**   Click the toolbar button that is to be to the right of the separator and drag the button ever so slightly to the right. Do this correctly and the separator line appears. To remove a separator, click the button to its right and drag the button ever so slightly to the left.
- **Placing a Separator on a Menu**   Click to open the menu, right-click the menu option that is to appear below or to the right of the separator, click to open the menu, and check Begin a Group on the drop-down menu. To remove a separator, right-click the menu option below the separator and uncheck the Begin a Group option on the drop-down menu.

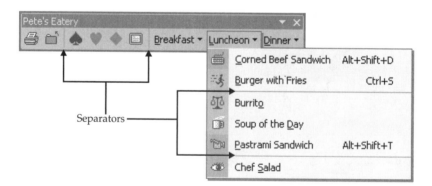

Designating Your Own Keyboard Shortcuts

Keyboard shortcuts, as long as you can remember them, are great. Instead of opening a menu and choosing a command, you can simply press two or three keys at the same time and be done with it. Word offers numerous keyboard shortcuts for giving commands, but if your favorite command doesn't have a shortcut key, you can make one. You can make your own keyboard shortcuts for Word commands, macros, styles, fonts, AutoText entries, and symbols. Don't worry about causing chaos with keyboard shortcuts, because you can always restore the original shortcuts by clicking the Reset All button in the Customize Keyboard dialog box (more on that subject shortly).

Follow these steps to create a keyboard shortcut for a command, style, macro, or whatnot that you are tired of having to deal with by using conventional commands:

1. Choose Tools | Customize or right-click a toolbar and choose Customize.

2. Select the Commands tab in the Customize dialog box.

3. Click the Keyboard button to open the Customize Keyboard dialog box shown in Figure 21-7. The Categories box lists menu names and, at the bottom, the Macros, Fonts, AutoText, Style, and Common Symbols category.

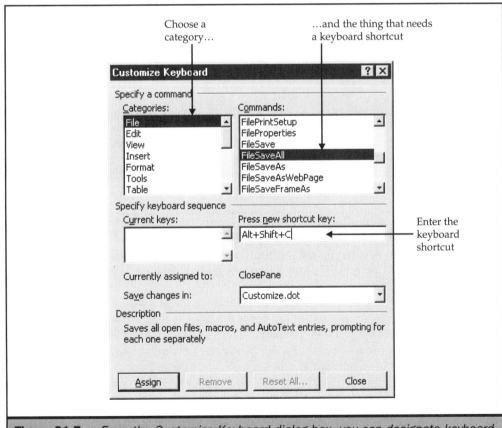

Figure 21-7.   *From the Customize Keyboard dialog box, you can designate keyboard shortcuts for commands, macros, fonts, AutoText entries, styles, and symbols*

4. Select a category in the Categories box, and then click the item in the Commands box that needs a keyboard shortcut. Yes, the commands in the Commands box are hard to understand, but if you look closely, you will see that the first word in each command is a menu name and the second word happens to be a command found on the menu. If a keyboard shortcut has already been assigned to a command, the shortcut is listed in the Current Keys box.

5. Click in the Press New Shortcut Key box and press the keyboard shortcut you want for the command. Press the actual keys. For example, if the shortcut you want is CTRL-F12, press the CTRL key and the F12 key—don't type out **C-t-r-l-f-1-2**.
   The words "Currently Assigned To" and a command name appear if the keys you pressed have been assigned to another command. However, you can override the other keyboard assignment by entering a keyboard assignment of your own.

6. Click the Assign button.

7. In the Save Changes In drop-down menu, choose the template where the keyboard shortcut will go.

8. Click Close in the Customize Keyboard dialog box and click Close again in the Customize dialog box.

Suppose you regret assigning a keyboard shortcut to a command or you want to remove a keyboard shortcut from a Word command. To remove a keyboard shortcut, open the Customize Keyboard dialog box, find the command, select the keyboard shortcut in the Current Keys box, and click the Remove button. Click the Reset All button to restore all of Word's keyboard shortcuts and render the keyboard shortcuts you devised invalid.

Printing a List of Word's Keyboard Shortcuts

Before you assign new keyboard shortcuts, perhaps you would like to see a list of all the keyboard shortcuts. That way, you can find an obscure keyboard shortcut that isn't used often and put it to good use.

To see and print a list of commands and their keyboard shortcuts, choose Tools | Macro | Macros (or press ALT-F8) to open the Macros dialog box. In the Macros In drop-down menu, choose Word Commands. You see a list of Word's macros. Either type **ListCommands** in the Macro Name box or scroll down the list of macro names and select ListCommands. Click the Run button and click OK in the List Commands dialog box to choose the Current Menu and Keyboard Settings. A Word document with command names, their keyboard assignments, and their menu locations appears onscreen. Click the Print button to print the document.

To print a list of the customized keyboard shortcuts you invented yourself, choose File | Print. In the Print dialog box, open the Print What drop-down menu and choose Key Assignments.

The easiest way to assign a keyboard shortcut to a symbol is to start in the Symbol dialog box. Choose Insert | Symbol to open the Symbol dialog box, find the symbol that needs a shortcut, click it, and click the Shortcut Key button. You see the Customize Shortcut dialog box, where you can enter a shortcut key for the symbol.

Copying Your Customized Settings to a Second Computer

Suppose you go to the trouble to create a template or toolbar in Word at the computer you use in your office. Later, when you go home, you miss your toolbar or template. You wish you had it on your home computer as well. Normally, reconstructing a customized toolbar or template on a second computer is time-consuming, but, lucky for you, you don't have to reconstruct these items anymore. Instead, you can copy the customizations you made on one computer to another computer.

Customized templates, menus, toolbars, dictionaries, default file locations, and AutoCorrect entries can be copied. To make the copy, you use something called the *Save My Settings Wizard* to create an Office Settings (.OPS) file. The file holds all your customizations. To copy the customizations to a second computer, run the Save My Settings Wizard again, and this time you load the Office Settings file onto the second computer.

Office Settings files can be very large (mine is 2,360 KB). They can't fit on a floppy disk. To transfer the file to the second computer, you can either send it over the Internet, copy it to a Zip disk or other storage medium that can hold large files, or store it on a Web server that Microsoft maintains and download the file from there to your second computer.

You can keep an Office Settings file on the Microsoft server for three months. Two weeks before the three-month period expires, you will be told via e-mail that your subscription is about to lapse. At that point, you can run the Save My Settings Wizard again to activate the service for another three months.

Creating an Office Settings File for Your Customizations

Follow these steps to run the Save My Settings Wizard and create an Office Settings file that holds the customizations you made to Word and to other Office programs:

1. Close Word and other Office programs that are open.

2. Click the Start button and choose Programs | Microsoft Office Tools | Save My Settings Wizard. The Save My Settings Wizard dialog box appears.

3. Click Next to go to the Save or Restore Settings dialog box shown in Figure 21-8.

4. Make Sure the Save the Settings from This Machine option button is selected, and click Next.

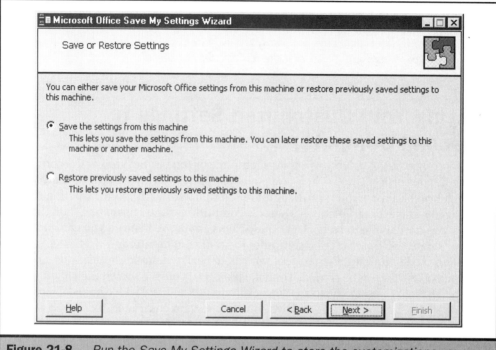

Figure 21-8.   *Run the Save My Settings Wizard to store the customizations you made to Word and other Office programs in an Office Settings file*

5. Save the settings on a Microsoft Web server or on your computer:

■ **Microsoft Web Server**   Select the Save the Settings on the Web option button and click OK. See "Saving Your Customizations on the Web on a Microsoft Web Server" later in this chapter.

■ **Your Computer**   Select the Save the Settings to a File option button. Then click the Browse button, and, in the Save As dialog box, choose the place on your computer or another storage medium where you will store the Office Settings file, enter a name for the file, and click the Save button. Then click Finish in the Wizard dialog box.

Suppose you customize Word and you want to update the Office Settings file so it stores the customizations you recently made. To update an Office Settings file, run the Save My Settings Wizard again. If you saved the file on your computer, you have to create a second file with a different name from the one you initially created. If you saved the file on a Microsoft Web server, simply create your Office Settings file the same way you created it the first time around.

Saving Your Customizations on the Web on a Microsoft Web Server

As I explained earlier, you can store your customizations in an Office Settings file on a Microsoft Web server. To transfer the customizations to a second computer, download the file from Microsoft. Storing the Office Settings file with Microsoft has these advantages:

■ You get around the problem of how to store and transfer such a large file.

■ If your computer goes completely haywire, the Office Settings file remains intact.

The disadvantages of storing the file with Microsoft can be summed up in one word: bureaucracy. You have to obtain something called a Microsoft Password, which entails providing a password and a couple of other intimate details. And the Microsoft Web server, like all Web servers, goes down sometimes.

To store your Office Settings file with Microsoft, run the Save My Settings Wizard. When you come to the Choose to Save to the Web or to a File dialog box, select the first option button, Save the Settings to the Web, and click Next. After you connect to the Internet, you will be asked for a sign-in name and password. Be sure to enter your e-mail address as the sign-in name. If you don't have a Microsoft password, click the Get One Here hyperlink in this dialog box.

After you have finished with the red tape, your Office Settings file is uploaded over the Internet from your computer to a Microsoft Web server.

Copy Your Customizations to the Second Computer

To copy the customizations to your second computer, close Word and all other Office programs, click the Start button, and choose Programs | Microsoft Office Tools | Save My Settings Wizard. In the Save My Settings Wizard dialog box, click Next and then, in the Save or Restore Settings dialog box (refer to Figure 21-8), choose the second option button, Restore Previously Saved Settings to This Machine. Click Next and then do the following:

- **Restore the Settings from the Web**   Select the first option button, Restore the Settings from the Web, and click Finish. After you connect to the Internet, you see a dialog box for verifying your identity if you did not elect to automatically sign in with Passport. Soon the red tape is cut and the file is downloaded to your computer.

- **Restore the Settings from a File**   Select the second option button. If necessary, click the Browse button to locate and select your Office Settings File in the Open dialog box. Then click the Finish button.

MOUS Exam Objectives Explored in Chapter 21

Objective	Heading
Customize menus and toolbars*	"Setting Up Your Own Menus" and "Creating Your Own Toolbars and Toolbar Buttons"

* Denotes an Expert, not a Core, exam objective.

Ten Commands Worth Adding to Toolbars and Menus

If you read "Setting Up Your Own Menus" earlier in this chapter, you know that Word offers many more commands than a quick trip around the program reveals. And if you read "The Thorough Way to Add and Remove Toolbar Buttons," you know that you can place a menu command on a toolbar and thereby create toolbars with your favorite commands.

Herewith are ten commands worth adding to toolbars or menus. As shown in this illustration, drag these commands out of the Commands tab on the Customize dialog box and place them on menus and toolbars.

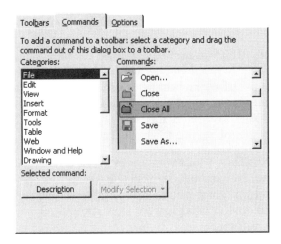

1. File | Close All   The File | Close All command closes all documents that are open. I find this command very convenient. Instead of closing documents one at a time when many are open, you can close them all and hurry to lunch.

You can give the File | Close All command by holding down the SHIFT *key and choosing File | Close All. The Close All command appears on the File menu when you hold down the* SHIFT *key.*

2. File | Save All   You can save a bit of time by giving the File | Save All command when a bunch of documents are open. Rather than save the documents one at a time, this command does it in one go.

Another way to give the File | Save All command is to hold down the SHIFT *key and choose File | Save All. The Save All command appears whether you placed the File | Save All command on a menu or toolbar.*

3. Edit | Go To Next Section and Edit | Go To Previous Section   In a document that has been divided into many sections, getting from one section to the next can be a chore. You can go from section to section by way of the Edit | Go To command or the Select Browse Object button, but that requires a lot of mouse-clicking and key pressing. Why not put the Edit | Go To Next Section and Edit | Go To Previous Section commands on a toolbar? That way, you can click to quickly go from section to section.

4. Edit | Previous Edit   This command moves the insertion point to the previous four edits you made. Use it as an adjunct to the Edit | Undo command. Instead of undoing three edits, for example, to return to an editorial error you made, you can choose this command three times and correct the error without undoing your previous three editorial changes. The Edit | Previous Edit command is an ideal candidate for a toolbar button.

You can also give the Edit | Previous Edit command by pressing SHIFT-F5.

5. View | Full Screen   If it was up to me, Full Screen view would be as easy to switch to as Print Layout view or Normal view. I would put a Full Screen View button in the lower-left corner of the Word screen beside the other View buttons. In Full Screen view, you can really see what your document will look like when it is printed.

Until such time as Microsoft raises the status of Full Screen view, I suggest putting the View | Full Screen command on a toolbar or menu where you can find it in a hurry.

6. View | View Draft   The earliest versions of Word offered a command called Draft View on the View menu. The command stripped text of its formats and displayed graphics in boxes. The command was great for proofreading. You could really focus on the text in Draft view. And the command was great for slow computers, because text could be displayed quickly in Draft view.

In Word 2002, you can still see documents in Draft view by choosing Tools | Options, selecting the View tab in the Options dialog box, and checking the Draft Font check box. However, fans of Draft view might consider placing the View | View Draft command on a toolbar or menu where they can give the command very quickly.

7. Format | Grow Font 1 Pt and Format | Shrink Font 1 Pt   When you are desktop-publishing in Word, getting font sizes right can be a hassle. Rather than toy with the Font Size menu, being able to click buttons to increase or decrease the size of text is mighty nice. All you have to do is eyeball it and keep clicking until the letters are the right side. For desktop publishers, I nominate the Format | Grow Font 1 Pt and Format | Shrink Font 1 Pt commands as toolbar buttons.

 You can also grow or shrink the Font size by pressing CTRL-> *or* CTRL-<.

8. Format | Change Case   Yes, pressing SHIFT-F3 to change the case of letters you selected is nice, but even better is being able to do it by clicking a toolbar button that activates the Format | Change Case command.

9. Fonts   Select Fonts on the Commands tab of the Customize dialog box and you will see a list of all the fonts that are available on your computer. Everybody has his or her favorite fonts. Rather than scroll the Font drop-down menu when you need a font, place your favorite fonts on a toolbar. That way, you can click buttons to try out different fonts and quickly find the one you like.

10. Styles   The Commands tab of the Customize dialog box offers a category called Styles. Click it and you see a list of styles. If you often find yourself applying styles, wrap the styles you use most often into a toolbar and be able to apply styles that much faster.

 Choose the Format category on the Commands tab and you will see several styles, including Normal, Heading 1, and Heading 2.

The Complete Reference

Word 2002

Chapter 22

One Step Beyond Word

This chapter looks at the future and explains a handful of space-age Word features. Well, "space-age" is stretching it a bit, but this chapter does explain how to talk to your computer. Instead of entering text with the keyboard, you can give dictation and watch the words appear onscreen. You can also give oral commands instead of choosing menu options or pressing shortcut keys. This chapter explains how to construct Web pages in Word, enter hyperlinks, and deal with Smart Tags, the customized shortcut menus that mysteriously appear on pages. You also learn how to handwrite with your mouse and send e-mail without leaving Word. At the end of this chapter are ten Windows techniques that are well worth knowing.

Creating Web Pages in Word

If you're serious about creating a Web site, leave the premises. Use Microsoft FrontPage, Dreamweaver, or another program whose purpose is creating Web sites. Word offers a bunch of tools for creating Web sites, but they are unwieldy and difficult to use. Rather than make you jump through hoops, these pages concentrate on the Word tools that will genuinely help you create Web pages.

Especially if you want to create a Web page from a Word document you've already created, Word can be a help. Now that HTML is the native format for all Office files, including Word documents, converting a Word document into a Web page goes fairly smoothly. The document that you worked so hard to create can be turned into a Web page in about two seconds by choosing a couple of Word commands.

This book doesn't delve into the Word Web-page creation tools that are not worth using, but it does explain how to create a simple, attractive Web page in Microsoft Word. Read on to learn how to create Web pages in Word, view a Web page in a browser, change the look of Web pages, and include sound and video clips on a Web page.

Creating and Turning Word Documents into Web Pages

Any Word document can be turned into a Web page. And you can create a Web page from scratch by starting with a template. To see what a document looks like as a Web page, click the Web Layout View button or choose View | Web Layout. Web Layout view presents the same view of a document that you see after you turn a document into a Web page and view it through a browser.

 When you turn a Word document into a Web page, these items get lost in the translation: passwords, versions (made with the File | Save Versions command), headers and footers, and columns.

To create a Web page with a Word template, select the Web Pages tab in the Templates dialog box. There, you will find templates for creating different kinds of Web pages, as well as the Web Page Wizard for creating a Web site. To get to the

Chapter 22: One Step Beyond Word **741**

Templates dialog box, choose File | New, and, in the New Document task pane, click the General Templates hyperlink.

To turn a Word document into a Web page, start by creating a new folder for storing your Web page. As "Dealing with the Supporting Files" explains shortly, you inadvertently create several new files when you turn a Word document into a Web page. Unless you create a new folder for your Web page, you will have trouble keeping track of its supporting files. After you have created the new folder, follow these steps to turn a Word document into a Web page:

1. Open the document.

2. Choose File | Save As Web Page.

3. In the Save As dialog box, find and select the folder where you will store the page.

4. Click the Change Title button, enter a name in the Set Page Title dialog box, and click OK. A visitor who comes to your Web page will see the title you enter on the title bar at the top of his or her browser.

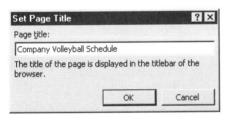

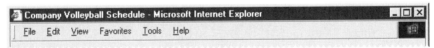

Tip *Choose a descriptive name for the title. Lycos, Yahoo, and other search engines keep careful track of the words on Web pages, and the word or words in the title page are given a lot of weight. If you enter **Madagascar** in the title, for example, a Web surfer who enters the keyword **Madagascar** in order to conduct a search of the Web is more likely to find your page than he or she is if you enter **Greenland** for the title.*

5. Click the Save button. The page appears in Web Layout view so you can see roughly what it will look like to visitors on the Internet.

When you save a Word document as a Web page, Word attaches a bunch of code to the document. The code lists the name of the program where the document was created (Word, of course), when it was created, and other details. To keep this extraneous junk from appearing on the Web pages you created with Word, save your Word document as a filtered Web page: Choose File | Save As, open the Save As Type drop-down menu in the Save As dialog box, and choose Web Page, Filtered.

GETTING MORE OUT OF WORD 2002

Dealing with the Supporting Files

A Web page is a composite of several files called *supporting files*. When you view a Web page in a browser, you are really viewing several files, one for each component of the Web page. Supporting files also tell Web browsers how to fit the different components together.

The supporting files are kept in their own folder. When you create a new Web page or convert a Word document into a Web page, Word creates a folder for the supporting files. To name the folder, Word tacks *_files* to the name of the Web page. The new folder is subordinate to the folder where the Web page is stored. Here, for example, the Web page I created is called Equis. Word created a new folder called Equis_files for the supporting files.

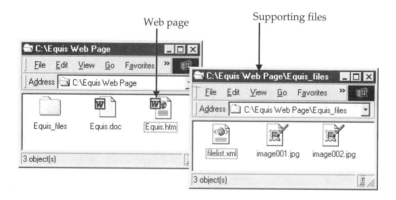

The problem with keeping supporting files in their own folder is that moving the folder along with the Web page file elsewhere can be a hassle. You have to remember to move the lot. A person who receives your Web page and its supporting files has to remember to load the whole mess properly on his or her computer.

Word offers two techniques for getting around the problem of supporting files:

- **Keep the Supporting Files in the Same Folder**   Supporting files are kept in the same folder as the Web page, so moving them around is easier. To put the supporting files for a Web page in the same folder as the Web page itself, choose Tools | Options, and, in the Options dialog box, select the General tab. Then click the Web Options button to open the Web Options dialog box. On the Files tab, uncheck the Organize Supporting Files in a Folder checkbox.

- **Save Files in Web Archive Format**   With this technique, the supporting files are folded into the Web page file itself, so you only deal with one file, not a supporting cast. The drawback of this technique is that not all browsers can view a Web page in Web Archive format. Only Internet Explorer 4.0 and later browsers can view them.

To save a Web page in Web Archive format, choose File | Save As, open the Save As Type drop-down menu in the Save dialog box, and choose Web Archive. To save all the Web pages you create in Word in the Web Archive format, choose Tools | Options, and, in the Options dialog box, select the General tab. Then click the Web Options button to open the Web Options dialog box. On the Browsers tab, check the Save New Web Pages as Web Archives check box.

You can always change the title of a Web page by choosing File | Properties, selecting the Summary tab in the Properties dialog box, and entering a new title in the Title box. Choose File | Web Page Preview to open a Word Web page in your browser and view its title on the title bar.

Seeing What Your Document Looks Like in a Web Browser

Choose File | Web Page Preview to see what your Web page looks like in the Internet Explorer Web browser. After you choose the command, Internet Explorer opens and you see your page in all its glory, typos and all.

Before you start marveling at how similar Web pages look in Word and in a browser, one or two words are in order. Unfortunately, not all browsers are the same when it comes to displaying Web pages. Internet Explorer and Netscape Navigator, the two most popular browsers, are alike in some ways, but each offers different features and capabilities. Usually, professional Web page designers target a particular browser when they do their work, but they nonetheless test their Web pages in Internet Explorer and Netscape Navigator. If your Web page is meant for the teeming masses, you are advised to test your Web pages in both browsers.

Opening a Web Page in Word

The standard technique for opening Word documents also applies to Web pages: Choose File | Open and rummage around in the Open dialog box until you find the file you are looking for. To see Web page files in the Open dialog box, however, you have to open the Files of Type drop-down menu and choose Web Pages and Web Archives.

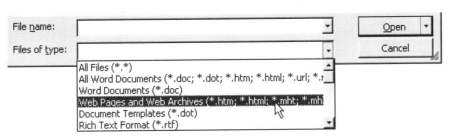

Changing the Look of Web Pages

Word offers two ways to change the look of a Web page. You can choose a color, background pattern, or picture, or you can visit the Theme dialog box and select a full-blown design for the various elements—the headings, bulleted items, and hyperlinks, for example. Read on to see how to turn a simple Web page into a high-fashion boutique.

Decorating Pages with a Background Color, Texture, or Picture

To spruce up a Web page by giving it a color background, a texture background, or a picture background, start by choosing Format | Background. You see a submenu with options for interior-decorating a Web page:

- **Color Background**   Select a color on the Color Palette menu. If none of the colors tickle your fancy, select More Colors at the bottom of the menu and choose a color in the Colors dialog box.

- **Texture Background**   Choose Fill Effects on the submenu, select the Texture tab in the Fill Effects dialog box, and choose a texture. Be sure to scroll to the bottom of the list. Word offers 24 textures in all.

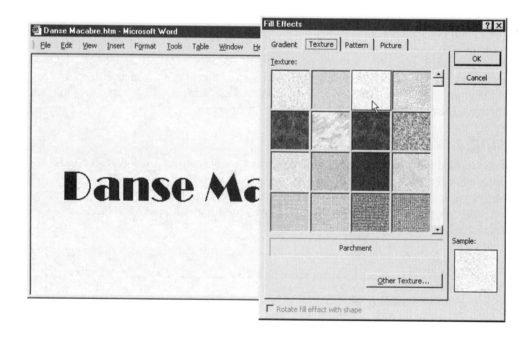

Contrast is everything on a computer monitor. Some of the textures in the Fill Effects dialog box are too busy to do any good as Web Page backgrounds. Graphics and text can get lost in a background that is too fanciful or busy.

■ **Picture Background or Logo**   Choose Fill Effects on the submenu. As shown in Figure 22-1, select the Picture tab in the Fill Effects dialog box, and click the Select Picture button. In the Select Picture dialog box, locate and select the picture file to use as a background on your Web page, and then click the Insert button. Click OK in the Fill Effects dialog box. You can use .BMP, .GIF, .JPG, or any other Windows-compatible graphic file as a background. .GIF files are best. They require less disk space, so viewers don't have to wait long for them to appear. Pictures are "tiled"—they repeat themselves in the background.

If you regret choosing a background for your Web page and you want to start all over, choose Format | Background and click the No Fill button on the submenu. By the way, the Clip Organizer offers a category called Web Backgrounds that you can use to decorate Web pages. "Handling Graphics and Clip Art in Documents" in Chapter 13 explains the Clip Gallery. In the Insert Clip Art task pane, check the Web Backgrounds check boxes.

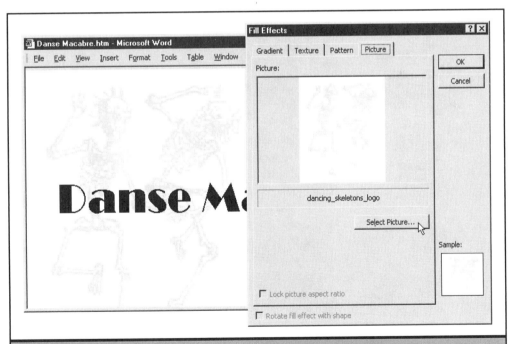

Figure 22-1.   *Besides colors and themes, you can use a picture or clip art image as the background of a Web page*

To borrow a background from a Web page you like, right-click it and choose Save Background As on the shortcut menu. If the background is copyrighted, however, you are obliged to obtain permission before you use the background image for your own purposes.

Choosing a Background Theme for Your Web Page

A background theme is a "ready-to-wear" design. When you choose a background theme, all elements of the Web page are overhauled—the headings, bulleted items, and the background as well. If you created your Web site with the help of the Web Page Wizard, you already know about themes, since the Web Page Wizard gives you the opportunity to choose a theme as you create Web pages.

Follow these steps to choose a theme for your Web page:

1. Choose Format | Theme. The Theme dialog box appears, as shown in Figure 22-2.

2. Under Choose a Theme, click a few theme names until you find a theme you like. Theme samples appear on the right side of the dialog box.

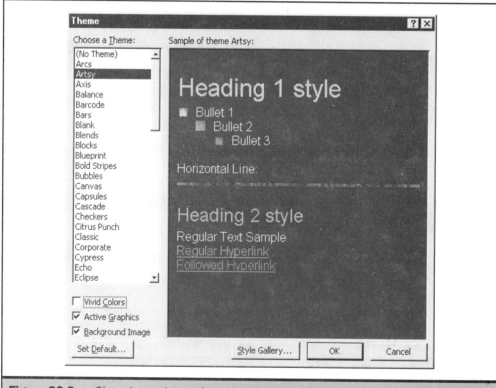

Figure 22-2. *Choosing a theme for a Web page*

3. When you have found your theme, you can tweak it to your liking by checking or unchecking the three checkboxes at the bottom of the Theme dialog box:

- **Vivid Colors**   Offers muted or vibrant variations of graphic elements in the theme.
- **Active Graphics**   Turns off and on the .GIF animations or animated cartoons in the theme, if the theme includes animations.
- **Background Image**   Removes or restores the page background.

4. Click OK to apply the new theme to your Web page.

Jazzing Up a Web Page with Sound and Multimedia

Multimedia is one of those buzzwords that pops up when computer people start talking. Technically, the term refers to a CD-ROM or Web site that presents material in more than one medium. For example, a CD-ROM about music with essays about composers and recordings of the composers' work is a multimedia CD-ROM. Similarly, a Web site that presents text, pictures, video, and sound is considered a multimedia Web site.

A Web site that presents material in more than one medium can be a very interesting place to visit, but you have to take into consideration one or two things before you dabble in multimedia. First, multimedia places demands on visitors' computer hardware. Not all computers have speakers for playing sound. Not all computers have video cards and can play video. Second, video files, sound files, and .GIF animation files can be very large and take a long time to download. For that reason, visitors to a site can grow impatient and move on before the multimedia files have finished downloading.

Visit the Macromedia site at www.macromedia.com for examples of multimedia files that Web sites can play back.

These pages explain how to play background music for visitors who come to your Web site and how to include a video clip on your Web site.

Adding Background Sound to a Web Page

Playing background sounds or music for visitors to a Web site is kind of neat, but care should be taken about the size of the sound file and the annoyance factor. A poor-quality sound clip that repeats itself over and over causes visitors to flee a site in nothing flat. You can use these types of sound files on a Web page created with Word: .WAV, .MID, .AU, .AIF, .RMI, .SND, and .MP2.

That a sound file or other multimedia file can perform well on your computer is no guarantee that it will play satisfactorily on the Internet. Always test a multimedia file online before you make it part of a Web site.

Follow these steps to make background sounds or background music for a Web site:

1. Put the cursor in the upper-left corner of your Web page. That way, if you need to remove or alter the sound later, you will know to look for it in the upper-left corner.

2. Display the Web Tools toolbar. To do so, choose View I Toolbars I Web Tools.

3. Click the Sound button, the second-to-last button on the toolbar. The Background Sound dialog box shown in Figure 22-3 appears.

4. Click the Browse button. The Open File dialog box opens.

5. Locate the sound file you want, select it, and click Open to return to the Background Sound dialog box.

6. From the Loop drop-down list, either enter the number of times to play the file or choose Infinite to play it over and over and over and over again.

7. Click OK and the sound starts playing.

Suppose you want to change sounds or change the number of times the sound plays in a row. For that matter, suppose you want to stop playing the sound altogether. Better follow these steps:

1. Click the Design Mode button, the leftmost button on the Web Tools toolbar. The sound stops playing and a rectangle with a speaker in it appears to show where the sound file has been embedded in your Web page. You will have to look pretty closely to find the rectangle and speaker if you didn't follow my advice and stick the sound file in the upper-left corner of your Web page.

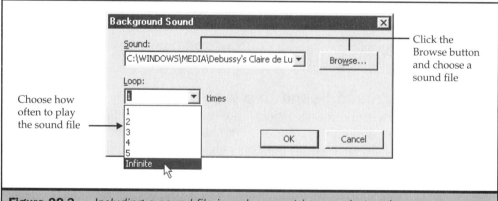

Figure 22-3.   *Including a sound file in a document is easy, but make sure you choose one that won't annoy visitors to your Web page*

2. Click the rectangle with the speaker in it.

3. With the black selection handles showing and the sound box selected, either alter the sound or silence it:

- **Change the Sound**   Click the Sound button on the Web Tools toolbar. You see the Background Sound dialog box (refer to Figure 22-3). Choose a new sound or a new Loop option and click OK.

- **Stop Playing the Sound**   Press the DELETE key. The sound box is removed from your Web page along with the sound file.

4. Click the Exit Design Mode button on the Web Tools toolbar.

By the way, you can also insert a sound clip from the Clip Organizer. To do so, choose Insert | Picture | Clip Art and search for sound files in the Insert Clip Art task pane. See Appendix B for details.

Including a Video Clip on a Web Page

Including a video clip on a Web page adds to the WOW factor, but video clips are not just large; they are huge. A mere five seconds of video requires a 100KB file (and that's without any sound). Whether a visitor to your site will wait long enough for the video file to download depends on how badly he or she wants to see the video. You can include these types of video files on a Web page: .AVI, .MOV, .MOVIE., .MPG, .MPEG, and .QT.

Follow these basic instructions to attach a video clip to a Web page:

1. Click on your Web page roughly where you want the video clip to go.

2. Choose View | Toolbars | Web Tools to display the Web Tools toolbar.

3. Click the Movie button, the third-from-last button on the Web Tools toolbar. You see the Movie Clip dialog box shown in Figure 22-4.

4. Click the Browse button and, in the File Open dialog box, locate the video file, select it, and click the Open button. If you are looking for a video file you inserted recently, you might be able to find it by clicking the down arrow next to the Movie text box.

5. Click the Browse button next to the Alternative Image text box, and, in the File Open dialog box, find a graphic image to appear in place of the video clip if the video clip cannot be played. Not everyone can play video clips on their computers. By choosing an alternative image, you make sure that your Web page doesn't have a gaping hole if someone comes to your page and can't see the video.

6. In the Alternate Text text box, type a few enticing words to describe your video clip. The words will appear on the Web page as the video clip is downloading. Try to write something that will encourage visitors to stick around while the video clip downloads.

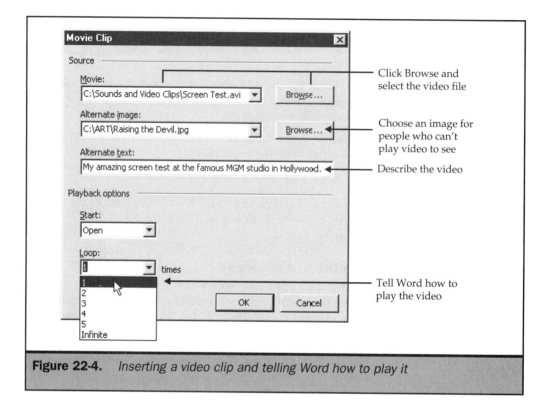

Figure 22-4.   *Inserting a video clip and telling Word how to play it*

7. Choose Playback options:

   ■ **Start**   Choose Open to start downloading the video clip as soon as the Web
   page is opened; Mouse-Over to start downloading the video when the
   visitor moves his or her mouse pointer over the movie; or Both to play the
   video when the Web page opens and again when the visitor moves his or
   her pointer over the movie.

   ■ **Loop**   Select the number of times to play the video, or choose Infinite to
   play it continuously.

8. Click OK.

The video clip starts playing. Very likely, you need to change the size of the video
screen and perhaps move it elsewhere on the page. Follow these instructions to do so:

   ■ **Change the Size and Position of the Video Screen**   Click the Design Mode
   button, the first button on the Web Tools toolbar. To change the size of the
   screen, drag a corner handle (not a side handle, since that changes the
   proportions of the video screen and distorts the video). To change the position
   of the screen, drag it elsewhere. You might have to right-click, choose Format

Control, and select the In Front Of Text option on the Layout tab of the Format Object dialog box to get the screen to move on your Web page. Click the Exit Design mode button when you are done.

- **Choose a Different Video File or Change the Video Settings**   Double-click the video clip (but not after clicking the Design Mode button). You see the Movie Clip dialog box (see Figure 22-4), where you can change video clips or chose different Playback options.

- **Remove the Video from the Page**   Click the Design Mode button on the Web Tools toolbar, click the video screen to select it, and press the DELETE key.

You can also go to the Clip Organizer to insert a video clip. See Appendix B for details.

Including Hyperlinks in Documents and Web Pages

A *hyperlink* is an electronic shortcut from one place to another place in the same document, from one document to another document, or from one place to a site on the Internet. Clicking a hyperlink is the fastest way to go elsewhere. In Word documents, hyperlinks formed from text are blue and are underlined. Clip art images, shapes, text boxes, and other objects can also be hyperlinks. You can tell when you have encountered a hyperlink because, when you move the pointer over it, a pop-up box tells where the link goes and invites you to "CTRL+click to follow the link."

These pages explain how to make a hyperlink to a different spot in the same document or Web page, or to another document or Web page. You also find out how to link to a Web site on the Internet. Finally, this section explains how to maintain hyperlinks.

To activate a hyperlink in a Word document, you CTRL-click it. That is, you hold down the CTRL key as you click the link. If you prefer the conventional method of activating links—that is, by clicking them—choose Tools | Options, select the Edit tab in the Options dialog box, and uncheck the Use CTRL+Click to Follow Hyperlink check box.

Inserting a Hyperlink

Observe these rules about hyperlinking before you attempt to create a hyperlink:

- For a hyperlink to go from one place to another in the same document, the destination of the link must be marked with a bookmark or be a heading that has been assigned a heading style. Before you attempt to create the link, make sure the place you want to link to is bookmarked or has been assigned the Heading 1, Heading 2, or other Heading style.

■ For a hyperlink to go to a particular place in another document, the place in the other document must be marked with a bookmark. Be sure to place a bookmark in the other document where you want the hyperlink to go. A hyperlink can go to the top of another document without a bookmark having to be in the other document.

■ If you move or delete a document to which your document is hyperlinked, the hyperlink becomes invalid. It won't work. Likewise, a hyperlink fails if you remove a bookmark that is the destination of a hyperlink.

Chapter 12 explains styles, including Heading styles. See "Bookmarks for Getting Around" in Chapter 2 to learn about bookmarks.

Follow these steps to insert a hyperlink to a different document, a different place in the same document, or a Web page on the Internet:

1. Select the words, phrase, or graphic that will form the hyperlink.

2. Click the Insert Hyperlink button, choose Insert | Hyperlink, press CTRL-K, or right-click the word or graphic you selected and choose Hyperlink from the shortcut menu. You see the Insert Hyperlink dialog box shown in Figure 22-5.

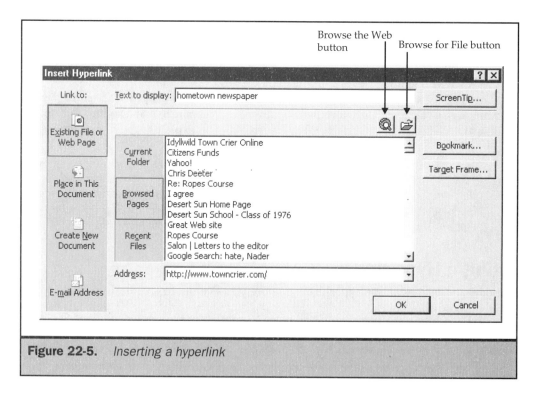

Figure 22-5.   *Inserting a hyperlink*

Each page on the Internet has an address, also known as a URL, or uniform resource locator. You can tell the address of a Web page by looking in the Address box in the Web browser.

3. If you selected a graphic in Step 1, enter text to describe your graphic in the Text to Display box. Until the graphic appears in your Word document or Web page, the text acts as a placeholder and tells viewers what to expect.

4. Create the link to a different place in the same document, the top of a different document, or a particular place in a different document:

   ■ **To a Different Place in the Same Document**   Click the Place In This Document icon under Link To. A list of headings and bookmarks in your document appears in the Insert Hyperlink dialog box (click the plus signs next to the words "Headings" and "Bookmarks" to see all the headings and bookmarks). Then click the heading or bookmark that marks the destination of the hyperlink.

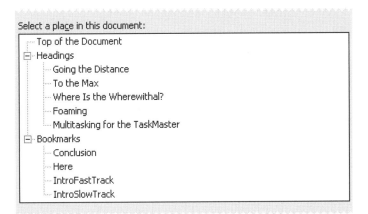

   ■ **To the Top of a Different Document**   Click the Existing File or Web Page icon under Link To, and then click the Browse for File button. In the Link to File dialog box, find and select the name of the document you want to link to. Then click OK.

   ■ **To a Particular Place in a Different Document**   Follow the instructions for linking to the top of a different document, and do the following besides: Click the Bookmark button, and, in the Select Place in Document dialog box, select a bookmark (click the plus sign next to the word "Bookmarks," if necessary, to see the bookmark names).

GETTING MORE OUT OF WORD 2002

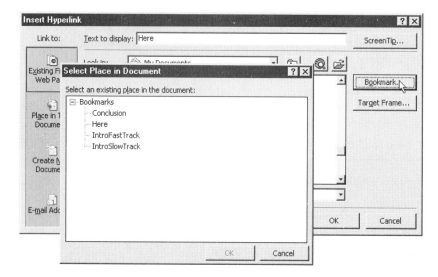

- **To a Web Page on the Internet**   Word offers three ways to link to a page on the Internet:

  - Click the Browse the Web button to open your browser and go to the Web page you want to link to. When you return to the Insert Hyperlink dialog box, the address of the Web page appears in the Address box.

  - Enter the URL of the Web page in the Address text box (or choose it from the Address drop-down menu).

  - Click the Browsed Pages button to see a list of pages you visited in the last 90 days, and select the page if you can remember it. (Kind of scary how your computer keeps track of all the sites you visited. The addresses of these sites are kept in the C:\Windows\Temporary Internet Files folder and its subfolders.)

4. Click the ScreenTip button and enter a phrase or a short sentence in the Set Hyperlink ScreenTip dialog box that describes the who, the what, or the where of your hyperlink. When a visitor moves the pointer over the hyperlink you are creating, he or she will see the text you enter. The brief description will help the viewer decide whether or not the link is worth clicking (or CTRL-clicking). Without the ScreenTip, visitors see a cryptic path name instead of a tidy description.

> The Town Crier, newspaper of Idyllwild, California
> **CTRL + click to follow link**

checking up on my <u>hometown newspaper</u>, I happened to notice

5. Click OK to insert the hyperlink.

To remove a hyperlink, right-click it and choose Remove Hyperlink on the shortcut menu. You can also select the hyperlink (right-click it and choose Select Hyperlink to do so), choose Insert | Hyperlink, and click the Remove Link button in the Edit Hyperlink dialog box.

Word inserts a hyperlink to a Web site (or what it thinks is a Web site) when you type any of the following characters and press the SPACEBAR: *a character, the at symbol (@), and at least one other character; the letters "www" followed by a period; or the letters "http://". If you prefer not to enter hyperlinks automatically, choose Tools | AutoCorrect Options, select the AutoFormat As You Type tab, and uncheck the Internet and Network Paths with Hyperlinks check box.*

Editing and Maintaining Hyperlinks

Hyperlinks are kind of hard to edit and maintain. After all, if you click a hyperlink in order, say, to type a word in the middle of the link, you may activate the hyperlink. And selecting hyperlinks is kind of hard, too, since you can't drag across the link without activating it. The trick to editing and maintaining hyperlinks is to right-click instead of click.

For you and you only, here are some techniques for editing and maintaining hyperlinks:

- **Editing a Hyperlink**   Right-click and choose Edit Hyperlink. You see the Edit Hyperlink dialog box, which looks and works exactly like the Insert Hyperlink dialog box (see Figure 22-5). Change the link destination, change the ScreenTip, or do what you will and click OK.

- **Removing a Hyperlink**   Right-click and choose Remove Hyperlink. Removing a hyperlink does not delete the words or graphic that formed the link. Removing a link merely takes away the words' or graphic's hyperlink statuses.

- **Deleting a Hyperlink**   Right-click, choose Select Hyperlink to select the link, and press the DELETE key.

- **Selecting a Hyperlink So You Can Format It**   Right-click and choose Select Hyperlink. The link is highlighted. Now you can change its font or font size, for example.

- **Copying a Hyperlink**   Right-click and choose Copy Hyperlink. The link is copied to the Clipboard. Now you can paste it elsewhere.

Inserting a Mail-To Link

A *mail-to hyperlink* is a link that activates an e-mail program. When you click an e-mail hyperlink, your default e-mail program starts running and you get the opportunity to send an e-mail message. If the person who set up the link did the job correctly, his or her e-mail message is already entered in the To line and you don't have to enter the subject of the message because it is already entered.

Include a mail-to hyperlink on a Web page when you want to give others the opportunity to get in touch with you—and do it without much trouble. Follow these steps to insert a mail-to link:

1. Select the words, phrase, or graphic that others will click or CTRL-click to start their e-mail programs.

2. Click the Insert Hyperlink button or choose Insert | Hyperlink. The Insert Hyperlink dialog box appears.

Click here to send me an e-mail message.

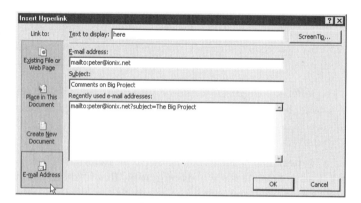

3. Under Link To, click the E-Mail Address icon.

4. Enter your e-mail address and a subject for the messages that others will send you in the text boxes. Word inserts the word *mailto:* before your e-mail address as you enter it. If you happened to have entered the address and subject before, you may choose it from the Recently Used E-Mail Addresses List.

5. Click OK.

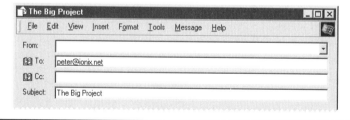

The Web Toolbar for Going from Place to Place

As soon as you CTRL-click a hyperlink and go elsewhere, the Web toolbar appears. The toolbar lists the name of the file you are in and offers a couple of buttons that are useful for going from place to place:

- ■ **Back**   Click to return to or backtrack through hyperlinks you have clicked.

- ■ **Forward**   Click to see hyperlinks you retreated from.

- ■ **Stop**   Click this button if you grow impatient waiting for another document to appear onscreen. Clicking the button tells Word not to open the hyperlink.

- ■ **Show Only Web Toolbar**   Removes all toolbars from the screen except the Web toolbar. Click this nifty button when you want to see more text onscreen. Click it a second time to see the other toolbars again.

  Unlike previous versions of Word, clicking buttons on the Web toolbar opens the browser. Click the Start Page button to open your browser and go to your home page—the page you see first when you go on the Internet. Click the Search the Web button to open your browser and go to a Web page where you can conduct a search of the Internet.

Taking Advantage of Smart Tags

A *Smart Tag* is a snippet of data that Word recognizes as a name from your Outlook Contact List, a date, a time, an address, a place, a telephone number, a person to whom you recently sent mail with Outlook or Outlook Express, or a company ticker name. When Word recognizes one of these entities, a purple dotted line appears, and if you move the pointer over the purple dotted line, you see the Smart Tag icon. Click the Smart Tag icon and you see a shortcut menu with tasks.

This illustration shows Smart Tag menus you see for names, dates, people to whom you recently sent e-mail, and addresses. Each Smart Tag menu is tailor-made for doing tasks that pertain to the kind of information you're dealing with. By clicking a command, you can cut to the chase and do it faster, faster, faster.

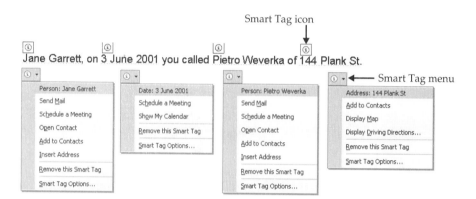

 Each Smart Tag menu offers the Remove This Smart Tag option. Select it to get rid of a Smart Tag.

For your reading pleasure, here is some Smart Tag esoterica:

- **Turning Off Smart Tags Altogether** If you don't want anything to do with Smart Tags, choose Tools | AutoCorrect Options, select the Smart Tags tab in the AutoCorrect dialog box, and uncheck the Label Text with Smart Tags checkbox. You can also turn off a certain kind of Smart Tag in the Smart Tags tab. Smart Tags remain with text you entered already, but this option prevents the Smart Tags of the future from bothering you.

- **Keeping the Smart Tag Buttons from Appearing** Choose Tools | AutoCorrect Options, select the Smart Tags tab in the AutoCorrect dialog box, and uncheck the Show Smart Tag Actions Buttons check box.

- **Including Smart Tags in a Document You Pass to Others** Choose Tools | Options, select the Save tab in the Options dialog box, and check the Embed Smart Tags check box.

E-Mailing from Inside Word

As long as you installed Outlook when you installed Word, or you use Outlook Express, the e-mail program that comes with Windows, you can send documents and e-mail messages over the Internet without leaving Word. Files are sent in HTML format. For that reason, you can format message text as you wish and include pictures in messages by placing them in Word the way you normally would. As long as the recipient of your message has software that can read HTML messages, the recipient will see your formats and pictures.

These pages explain how to send e-mail messages and files in Word, and how to route a Word document to a bunch of people so that they can review it.

Sending E-Mail and Documents in Word

Start by writing the e-mail message in Word. You can call upon Word formatting commands if you so desire. When you are ready to send the message, do one of the following:

- Click the E-Mail button on the Standard toolbar.
- Choose File | Send To | Mail Recipient.

As shown in Figure 22-6, you see options for addressing e-mail messages. Do these options look familiar? Click the Send Copy button (or press ALT-S) to send the message. Meanwhile, here is a quick rundown of the e-mailing options and commands:

- **Entering the Message's Subject** Type a descriptive word or two about the message on the Subject line.
- **Addressing the Message** Either enter names directly in the To text box (and Cc text box, if you want to send a copy of the message) or click the icon beside the To text box to open a dialog box where you can pick and choose recipients by name. Click the Check Names button if you want Word to make sure you entered names correctly.

Tip *Try typing the first few letters of a recipient's name in the To, Cc, or Bcc text box. If Word recognizes the name as one in your Address Book or Contact List, Word enters the name for you.*

- **Sending a Blind Carbon Copy** A *blind carbon copy* is a copy of a message that is sent to a third party without the primary recipient knowing as much. Select Bcc from the drop-down menu on the Options button (with Outlook) or click the Bcc button (with Outlook Express) to send a blind carbon copy. On the new Bcc line, enter the name or e-mail address of the third party.
- **Choosing a Message Priority** Click the Options button and, in the Message Options dialog box, choose Select Importance Level from the Importance Level drop-down menu (with Outlook), or open the Set Priority drop-down menu (with Outlook Express) to prioritize the message. Recipient's who have Outlook or Outlook Express will be able to tell by glancing at their Inboxes how important the message is.

■ **Sending a File Along with the Message** Click the Attach File button, and, in the Insert Attachment dialog box, select the file or files you want to send. An Attach line appears and lists the names of the files you choose (refer to Figure 22-6). To remove a file from the list if you decide not to send it, right-click the file and choose Remove on the shortcut menu. You can also send a document you are working on as an attachment by choosing File | Send To | Mail Recipient (as Attachment).

Note *To remove the e-mail commands from the screen, click the E-Mail button a second time.*

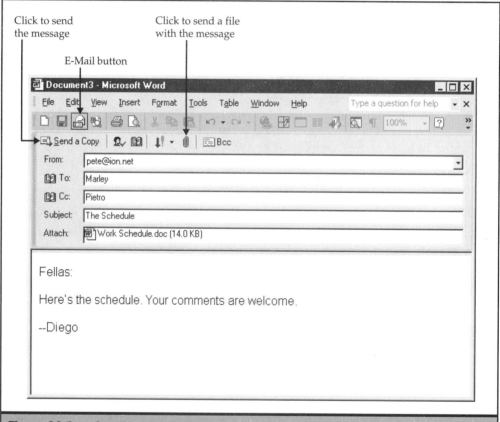

Figure 22-6. *Sending an e-mail message, and a file, in Microsoft Word*

Word offers a handful of e-mail options to make e-mailing a little livelier. To see what these options are, choose Tools | Options, select the General tab in the Options dialog box, and click the E-Mail Options button (you'll find it in the lower-right corner of the tab). Doing so takes you to the E-Mail Options dialog box and its three tabs:

- **E-Mail Signature Tab**   For entering and formatting an *e-mail signature*, a word or phrase or pithy saying that appears at the bottom of all the e-mail messages you send.

- **Personal Stationery Tab**   For choosing a look for your e-mail messages. Choose a theme, font, and font color.

- **General Tab**   For choosing HTML options that reduce the size of e-mail messages and make them transmit faster.

Routing a Document to Others

Route a document by e-mail when you want others to review it. As part of the routing procedure, you tell Word the name of each reviewer and the order in which you want reviewers to get the document. When the document arrives in each reviewer's mailbox, it arrives with this message: "The attached document has a routing slip. When you are done reviewing this document, choose Next Routing Recipient from the Microsoft Word Send To menu on the File menu to continue the routing."

As per instructions, a reviewer who has finished reviewing the document chooses File | Send To | Other Routing Recipient. The Send dialog box appears. It states the name of the next reviewer. To send the document to the next person in the chain, the reviewer clicks OK in the Send dialog box. He or she doesn't have to worry about addressing the document. Meanwhile, you are notified by e-mail with a STATUS message that the document has been sent from one reviewer to the next. Eventually, the document having completed its rounds, it is sent back to you, the originator.

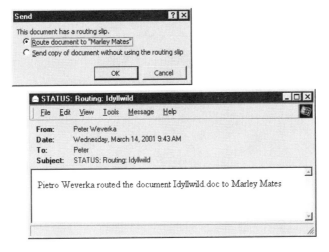

Follow these steps to route a document and thereby allow a team of reviewers to take a stab at it:

1. Choose File | Send To | Routing Recipient. The Routing Slip dialog box appears, as shown in Figure 22-7.

2. Click the Address button, and, in the Address Book, enter the names of the people who will receive the document.

3. In the Routing Slip dialog box, click to select names and click a Move button as many times as necessary to determine who receives the document first, second, and so on.

4. In the Subject box, enter a word or two to describe the document you are routing.

5. In the Message Text box, describe what you want reviewers to do with the document. The words you enter will appear in an e-mail message along with the standard instructions for routing the document. (On the preceding page, I quoted the Word message that arrives in each reviewers' mailbox.)

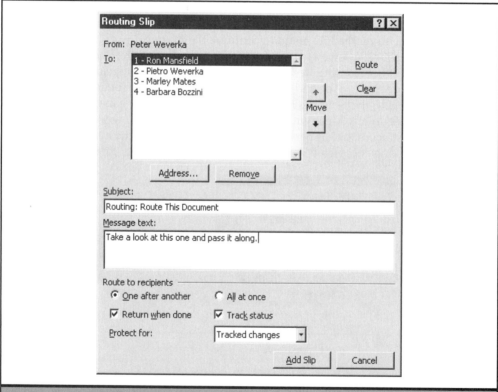

Figure 22-7. *Routing a document so that others can review it*

6. Make sure the Return When Done checkbox is selected. That way, the last recipient will return the routed document to you.

7. If you so desire, choose a Protect For option from the drop-down menu:

   - **Tracked Changes**   All editorial changes that reviewers make to the document are marked with revision marks. See "Keeping Track of Revisions to Documents" in Chapter 17.

   - **Comments**   Others can enter comments about the document but not change it. See "Commenting on a Document" in Chapter 17.

   - **Forms**   Others can enter data in form fields, but otherwise not change the form (choose this option if you are routing a form, not a document). See "Creating and Using a Data-Entry Form" in Chapter 15.

8. Click the Route button.

 To postpone sending a routed document, perhaps because you want to edit it, click the Add Slip button in the Routing Slip dialog box. When you are ready to send the routed document, choose File | Send To | Next Routing Recipient and click OK in the Send dialog box.

Dictating to Your Computer

This, the latest edition of Office, comes with speech-recognition software. In theory, you can dictate to your computer and save yourself the trouble of typing words. You can also give commands by speaking command names and save yourself the trouble of pulling down menus or pressing shortcut keys. In practice, however, the speech-recognition software has a few too many bugs to be of much use. In my experience at least, the speech-recognition software is more amusing than anything else. To see what I mean, here are the first three lines of the Irving Berlin classic "God Bless America" followed by three lines as interpreted by Office speech-recognition software.

> God bless America, land that I love
> Stand beside her and guide her
> Through the night with the light from above

> God bless, Mayor rate, was named back on a walnut
> Standard bee's SA 89 earnings and god 80 heard
> Through by denying with all Lonnie from all ball

Maybe I'm being unfair to the software. As the following pages explain, you can "train" the software by reading it texts and reciting it difficult-to-pronounce words. In short, you can accustom the software to the modulations of your voice. These pages explain the hardware requirements of dictating to a computer, how to train the software to understand your voice, the Language bar, dictating, and giving voice commands.

Requirements for Using the Speech-Recognition Software

Microsoft says that your system must meet these requirements if you expect Office software, including Word, to understand what the heck you're talking about:

- A high-quality close-talk microphone (Microsoft recommends a universal serial bus microphone).

- A 400 megahertz or faster computer.

- At least 128MB of RAM (random access memory). To find out how much RAM your system has, right-click the My Computer utility on the Windows desktop and choose Properties. The System Properties dialog box appears. Look under Computer at the bottom of the General tab—you'll see how many megabytes of RAM are available to your computer.

- Windows 98 or later; or Windows NT 4.0 or later.

- Internet Explorer 5 or later.

The speech-recognition software is particular about where you place your microphone. Place it to the side of your mouth by the distance of your thumb. The idea is not to hear you breath, but to hear you speak. Speak in a natural voice, but succinctly.

Installing the Speech-Recognition Software

Before you can dictate to your computer or give voice commands, you need to install the speech-recognition software. To do so, place the Office CD in your CD-ROM or DVD drive. Then choose Tools | Speech. Soon you see the Microsoft Office Language Settings dialog box. Make sure English appears in the Enable Languages box, and click OK.

Activating and Managing the Language Bar

After you install the speech-recognition software, display the Language bar. The Language bar is the starting point for giving dictation or speaking commands to your computer. To activate the Language bar, click the Start button and choose Settings | Control Panel. In the Control Panel, double-click the Text Services icon. You see the Text Services dialog box. Click the Language Bar button (you'll find it near the bottom of the dialog box, under Preferences). The Language Bar Settings dialog box appears. Check the Show the Language Bar on the Desktop check box and click OK.

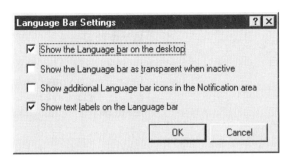

The Language bar appears in the upper-right corner of the screen (you can drag it elsewhere). Table 22-1 explains the buttons on the Language bar. Meanwhile, here are instructions for handling the thing:

- **Hiding the Language Bar**   Click the Minimize button. The Language bar icon—the letters EN if you speak English—appears on the Task bar next to the clock when the Language bar has been minimized.

- **Displaying the Language Bar After You Minimize It**   Right-click the Language bar icon and choose Show the Language Bar on the pop-up menu.

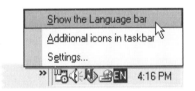

- **Closing the Language Bar**   Either right-click the Language bar and choose Close on the shortcut menu, or, if the Close command isn't available, choose Settings on the shortcut menu, click the Language Bar button in the Text Services dialog box, and uncheck the Show the Language Bar on the Desktop check box. (You can't choose Close on the shortcut menu if an Input Method Editor [IME] program is installed on your computer. IMEs permit you to enter Asian text in documents.) To display the Language bar again if you closed it by way of the Text Services dialog box, you have to go to the Control Panel, double-click the Text Services icon, click the Language Bar button, and check the Show the Language Bar on Desktop check box.

If you prefer not to see labels on the Language bar buttons, right-click the Language bar and unselect the Text Labels command. Without labels, the Language bar fits more snugly in the upper-right corner of the screen.

Button*	What It Does
Language **EN** English (United States)	Enables you to choose a different language, if your computer is capable of taking dictation or hearing commands in more than one language.
Correction Correction	Corrects errors in dictation. Click the button and then click a word that was interpreted incorrectly. You hear the word you spoke and see a drop-down menu of alternative words. Select the correct word on the drop-down menu.
Microphone Microphone	Turns the microphone on or off. After you click this button, the Dictation, Voice Command, and Speech Messages buttons appear on the Language bar.
Dictation Dictation	Tells the computer that you want to start giving dictation.
Voice Command Voice Command	Tells the computer that you want to give a command.
Speech Messages Too soft	Tells you what the speech-recognition software is doing ("Dictating"); lists commands you give by speech or entered by way of the keyboard or menus ("Bold"); or offers suggestions of ways to make the software work better ("Too Soft," which means you are speaking too softly). If you don't see this button and you want to see it, click the Tools button and choose Show Speech Messages on the drop-down menu.

Table 22-1.   *Language Bar Buttons*

Button*	What It Does
Tools Tools	Offers a drop-down menu with speech-recognition options.
Help 	Opens the Language Bar Help program.
Minimize 	Removes the Language bar from the screen.

* If you installed hand-writing recognition software, the Handwriting button also appears on the Language bar. See "Handwriting to Enter Text" later in this chapter.

Table 22-1. *Language Bar Buttons* (continued)

Training the Speech-Recognition Software to Understand Your Words

Your voice is different from everyone else's. For that reason, you need to train the speech-recognition software to understand your voice. Do that by clicking the Tools button on the Language bar and choosing Training on the drop-down menu. You see the Voice Training Wizard. Click Next and negotiate the dialog boxes. You will read a text called "Introduction to Microsoft Speech Recognition" from which the software will compile a dossier about your voice.

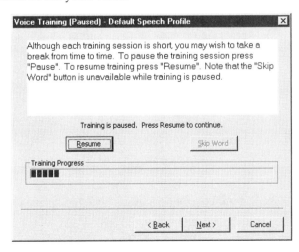

The Voice Training Wizard offers eight different texts to read, but you needn't read them all to begin with. If you think the software needs more training, click the Tools button and choose Training at any time. You will be given an opportunity to read another text.

Besides familiarizing the software with your voice, you can improve your chances of the speech-recognition software understanding you by configuring your microphone. To do so, click the Tools button on the Language bar and choose Options on the drop-down menu. Then, in the Speech Properties dialog box, click the Configure Microphone button. You see the Microphone Wizard dialog box. Click the Next button and negotiate the dialog boxes.

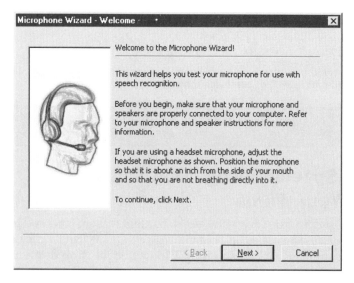

 If you share your computer with others and others also want to be voice dictators, you need to set up a voice-recognition profile for each speaker. To do so, click the Tools button on the Language bar and choose Options. Then, in the Speech Properties dialog box, click the New button, enter a name in the Profile Wizard dialog box, and read for the Voice Training and Microphone Wizards. To inform the software who is speaking, click the Tools button on the Language toolbar, choose Current User on the drop-down menu, and choose Default Speech Profile or a name on the submenu.

Dictating to Your Computer

Now that the preliminaries are over, you can start dictating to your computer:

1. Click the Microphone button on the Language bar. If you aren't sure whether the microphone is turned on, click Tools on the menu bar and look for a check mark next to the Speech command. If the check mark is there, the microphone is turned on.

2. Click the Dictation button or say the word "dictation."

3. Start speaking. As you speak, a blue bar appears onscreen. The blue bar means that the computer is listening to your voice. When it recognizes a word, the word appears where the blue bar was. You needn't wait for the blue bar to disappear before you speak the next word. You can keep speaking—the speech-recognition software will catch up with you eventually. You can make the last word you said null and void by saying, "Scratch that."

Don't give commands with the mouse or keyboard while the blue bar is onscreen. Do that and the speech-recognition software will stop listening to you.

4. Click the Microphone button on the Language bar or choose Tools | Speech when you are finished dictating.

Be sure to click the Microphone button to turn off the microphone when you are done dictating or giving voice commands. Fail to do so and Word continues giving commands or taking dictation. To make sure the microphone is turned off, open the Tools menu. The microphone is off if no check mark appears beside the Speech command.

When the software misinterprets you—believe me, it happens—correct the error manually by typing the correct word or words from your keyboard. Or, click the word that needs correcting and then click the Correction button on the Language bar. You hear the word and a drop-down menu appears. Select the correct word or phrase on the drop-down menu.

By the way, you can add new words to the Add/Delete Word(s) dialog box by clicking the Tools button on the Language bar and choosing Learn from Document. In the Learn from Document dialog box, select the words you *don't* want to add by selecting them and clicking the Delete button. Then click the Add All button to add the remaining words to the list of words that the speech-recognition software understands.

Adding Words to the Speech Recognition Dictionary

No doubt you want the speech-recognition software to understand your name, the names of family members, and the name of the company you work for. To help the software understand these names and other words that are particular to you, follow these steps:

1. Click the Tools button on the Language bar and choose Add/Delete Word(s) on the drop-down menu. You see the Add/Delete Word(s) dialog box. It lists words such as proper names that you added to the spelling dictionary (in Chapter 11, "Correcting Your Spelling Errors" explains how words get added to the dictionary).

2. In the Word text box, type a difficult-to-pronounce word or word such as a company name that you want the speech-recognition software to understand.

3. Click the Record Pronunciation button and speak the word or name into your microphone. In a moment, the word appears in the Dictionary list.

4. Click the word to hear the recording you just made.

If a word is not being pronounced correctly, click it in the Dictionary list and either re-record it or click the Delete button to remove it from the list.

Giving Voice Commands in Microsoft Word

The speech-recognition software is programmed to understand menu selections, task pane commands, the names of toolbar buttons, dialog box options, and formatting options. Say "Tahoma," for example, and text you selected is given the Tahoma font. Say the name of a menu name on the menu bar, for example, and the menu opens. Well, some of the time it does, anyway.

Follow these steps to give voice commands:

1. Click the Microphone button on the Language bar.

2. Click the Voice Command button or say the words "voice command."

3. Speak the commands you want to give. As you speak, the Speech Messages button on the Language bar tells you the name of the last command you gave.

4. Click the Microphone button or choose Tools | Speech to turn off the microphone when you are done giving commands.

Handwriting to Enter Text

Instead of tapping the keyboard to enter letters and words, you can handwrite them. Word converts your loops and lines to typewritten letters, or, if you so desire, you can keep the loops and lines in your document in the form of an object. Using a digital pen and tablet is preferable to handwriting with the mouse, but if you want to use your mouse to test the handwriting feature, you are invited to do just that.

Installing and Activating the Handwriting-Recognition Software

Very likely, the handwriting-recognition software that comes with Office is not installed on your computer. To install it, put the Office CD in the CD-ROM or DVD drive on your computer and reinstall Office (see "Custom Installation: Choosing Which Features to Install" in Appendix A). In the Choose Installation Options dialog box, open Office Shared Features, open Alternative User Input, select Handwriting, choose Run from My Computer on the drop-down menu, and click the Update button.

After you install the handwriting-recognition software, The Handwriting button appears on the Language bar. Click that button to start handwriting. Earlier in this chapter, "Activating and Managing the Language Bar" explains how to handle the Language bar and make it appear onscreen.

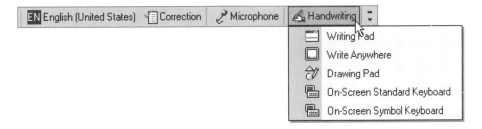

 The handwriting-recognition software taxes your computer's memory. If you decide not to use it, deactivate it. To do so, right-click the Language bar and choose Settings. In the Text Services dialog box, select Handwriting Recognition, and then click the Remove button.

Writing It Down

Before you enter text, click in your document where you want the text to appear. If you want the text to be a certain font and font size, choose a font and font size after you click. Then follow these instructions to enter text with your mouse or a digital pen and tablet:

- **Starting from the Writing Pad**   Click the Handwriting button on the Language bar and choose Writing Pad. Click the Ink button to enter handwritten text; click the Text button to enter typewritten text. Then handwrite on the line provided.

- **Starting by "Writing Anywhere"**   Click the Handwriting button and choose Write Anywhere. Then, in the Write Anywhere toolbox, click the Ink or Text button and write anywhere onscreen. When you are finished, the text appears at the location of the cursor.

- **Starting from the Drawing Pad**   Click the Handwriting button and choose Drawing Pad. Then draw what you want to draw and click the Insert Drawing button when you are finished. The item is inserted as an object (see "Manipulating Art, Text Boxes, Shapes, and Other So-Called Objects" in Chapter 13 if you need help handling objects).

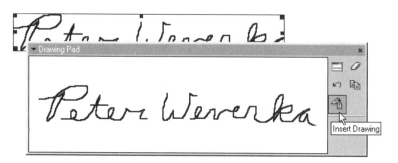

MOUS Exam Objectives Explored in Chapter 22

Objective	Heading
Convert documents into Web pages	"Turning a Word Document into a Web Page" and "Seeing What Your Document Looks Like in a Web Browser"
Merge input from several reviewers	"Routing a Document to Others"
Insert and modify hyperlinks to other documents and Web pages*	"Including Hyperlinks in Documents and Web Pages"
Create and edit Web documents in Word*	"Opening a Web Page in Word"

Denotes an Expert, not a Core, exam objective.

Ten Windows Techniques All Word Users Should Know

Whether you know it or not, you run two programs when you run Word. Besides Word, you run the Windows operating system. Here are ten Windows techniques that can help make the time you spend in Word more productive.

1. List Files in Different Ways in Dialog Boxes   In the Open dialog box, Save As dialog box, and other dialog boxes where filenames are listed, you can view filenames in different ways by clicking the Views button or clicking the down arrow beside the Views button and making a choice from the drop-down menu. Either keep clicking the Views button to arrive at a new way of seeing the files or open the drop-down menu and choose one of these options:

- **Large Icons**   Shows files as icons. The icons give a clear picture of what kind of file you are dealing with.
- **Small Icons**   Shows files as small icons. You can see more files without having to scroll.
- **List**   Shows all the files in an alphabetical list. Choose this option when you know the name of the document you are looking for and you want to select it quickly.
- **Details**   Shows files in an alphabetical list along with each file's size, its type (Microsoft Word Document, for example, or JPEG Image), and the date it was last modified. Choose this option when you are having trouble deciding which Word document to open.
- **Properties**   Shows document properties for the file that is selected in the dialog box. Click a document and choose Properties from the Views drop-down

menu to find out exactly what a document is. You see statistics about the document—the same statistics you get in the Properties dialog box when you choose File | Properties.

■ **Preview**   Shows a thumbnail image of the file that is selected in the dialog box. Click a document and choose Preview to find out for certain whether you want to open a document.

2. Display the File Extensions in Dialog Boxes   A *file extension* is a three-letter designation at the end of a filename that describes what type of file the file is. Normally, file extensions do not appear in dialog boxes, but you can make them appear. Being able to see file extensions is an advantage when you work with different kinds of files. All you have to do is glance at the file extension to see what kind of file you are dealing with. This illustration shows files with and without their file extensions.

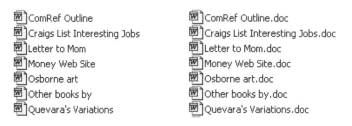

Follow these steps to see file extensions in the Open dialog box, Save As dialog box, and other dialog boxes where filenames are listed:

1. Click the Start button and choose Settings | Folder Options (in Windows Me, choose Settings | Control Panel and double-click the Folder Options icon).

2. Select the View tab in the Folder Options dialog box.

3. Uncheck the Hide File Extensions for Known File Types check box and click OK.

    *The drawback of displaying file extensions in dialog boxes is having to enter file extensions as well as filenames when you name files. Instead of naming a file **story** in the Save As dialog box, for example, you have to name it **story.doc**.*

3. Open Documents from the Windows Documents Menu   Unquestionably the fastest way to open a document is to begin at the Windows Start menu. Click the Start button, choose Documents, and click the name of a file on the Documents menu. The Documents menu lists the last 15 files you worked on, be they Word documents or another kind of file. You can open Word and a Word document at the same time by clicking the name of a Word document on the Documents menu.

4. Recover Files You Deleted Accidentally   Yes, you can make a Word document rise from the dead if you deleted it accidentally. To do so, go to the Windows desktop and double-click the Recycle Bin icon. In the Recycle Bin window, select the document that needs resuscitating and choose File | Restore.

5. Press CTRL-ALT-DEL When the Computer Freezes   Every Windows user knows, or should know, to click the Start button and choose Shut Down before turning off the computer. But what if the computer freezes and you can't shut down properly? Follow these steps:

1. Press CTRL-ALT-DEL. The Close Program dialog box appears. It lists all programs that are running. The words "not responding" appear beside the name of the program that is making the computer freeze.

2. Click the name of the program that is "not responding" and click the End Task button. With luck, the program that made your computer freeze closes and you can get back to work.

3. Press CTRL-ALT-DEL again if your computer is still frozen. With luck, your computer shuts down and restarts.

Sometimes pressing CTRL-ALT-DEL doesn't shut down the computer. When that happens, turn off the computer's power switch, wait a minute for the computer's platters to stop spinning, and turn on your computer. Windows runs the ScanDisk utility to see if any damage was done to the hard disk. Get back to work.

6. Rearrange the Names on the Programs Menu   In Windows, you can rearrange the names on the Programs menu by clicking the icon beside a program's name and dragging it up or down the menu. Move "Microsoft Word" to a prominent place on the Programs menu where you can find it easily.

7. Hide the Taskbar if You Want to   The Taskbar takes up valuable space along the bottom of the screen, but you can do one or two things to handle the Taskbar:

- **Hiding the Taskbar**   Move the pointer over the top of the Taskbar, and, when you see the double-headed arrow, click and drag the Taskbar below the bottom of the screen. To see the Taskbar again, move the pointer to the bottom of the screen, and, when you see the double-headed arrow, click and drag upward.

- **Automatically Hiding the Taskbar**   With this technique, the Taskbar does not appear unless you move the pointer to the bottom of the screen. Click the Start button and choose Settings | Taskbar & Start Menu to open the Taskbar Properties dialog box. On the Taskbar Options tab, check the Auto Hide checkbox and click OK.

8. Change the Screen Resolution   Depending on whether you are nearsighted or farsighted, some screen resolutions are better than others. *Screen resolution* refers to how large or small things look on the screen. With a small screen resolution (640 by 480 pixels), everything looks larger, although the screen can seem cramped. With a larger resolution (800 by 600 pixels), everything looks smaller but is easier to manage. Experiment with screen resolutions until you find a setting that suits you.

To change the screen resolution, right-click the desktop and choose Properties. In the Display Properties dialog box, select the Settings tab, and then drag the Screen Area slider to 640 by 480 pixels or 800 by 600 pixels (or 1,024 by 768 pixels on some machines). Then click OK.

9. Reset the Clock, if Necessary   You always know what time it is when you are running a Windows machine—all you have to do is look at the clock in the lower-right corner of the screen. And if you move the pointer over the clock, you can read the date and the day of the week. Making sure the clock tells accurate time is important not only for meeting appointments, but also for time- and date-stamping documents. When you save a document, Windows tells Word what time the document was saved. Documents are time-stamped and date-stamped so that you know which version of a document you are dealing with.

To reset the Windows clock or change the date, double-click the clock. You see the Date/Time Properties dialog box. Change the date and time on the Date & Time tab and click OK.

10. Create Desktop Shortcut Icons for Your Favorite Documents   All you have to do to open a document for which you created a desktop shortcut icon is double-click. Create desktop shortcut icons for each document you go to often. The icons appear on the Windows desktop where you can find them in a hurry. To create a desktop shortcut icon, open Windows Explorer or My Computer and find the document, right-click it, and choose Send To | Desktop (Create Shortcut). (To delete a desktop shortcut icon, right-click it and choose Delete. Deleting the icon does not delete the document.)

The Complete Reference

Word 2002

Part VI

Visual Basic in Word 2002

Chapter 23

Automating Word

This chapter introduces you to Word automation. Automating Word includes working with the macros Microsoft includes with Word to record or write your own macros and procedures. Don't worry—you don't need to be a code head to work with macros and Visual Basic for Applications, which is Word's programming language. You can do a lot of simple automation without knowing anything about programming thanks to the macro recorder included with Word. As you become more comfortable working with macros in Word, you'll wonder why you didn't record your own macros sooner.

If you've never recorded a macro before, you'll learn how to use the macro recorder to record a macro. I'll show you how to open the macro to read and edit your macros as well as how to move, copy, and delete macros and modules.

Introduction to Automating Word

Before you can begin to create macros to automate Word, you need to have a basic understanding of macros. A *macro* is a sequence of computer instructions recorded and saved for later use. When you activate the macro, Word carries out the instructions contained in the macro. Instead of entering the commands yourself every time you need them, you create a macro containing the steps. After that, the macro runs through the instructions for you at a much faster pace than you ever could enter them manually.

Deciding When to Automate

After you've worked with Word some, you'll notice there are things you keep repeating over and over. It may be a series of keystrokes or certain menu items, but after awhile you become annoyed at repeating the same movements over and over. You can use AutoCorrect and AutoText to create shortcuts for words or phrases you repeat often. You can customize your toolbars to bring often-used menus to the top level to save you time. But what about the things you can't add to AutoCorrect, that don't have a built-in command or that require two or more steps to complete? You would create a macro to automate your most frequently used mundane and multi-step actions.

Understanding How Macros Work

Any task that you do repeatedly, even simple tasks like Search and Replace or changing Options, is a candidate for a macro. For example, one of my favorite macros switches between showing and hiding revisions to reduce the steps needed to change the display of revisions onscreen. Since old habits die hard, I use a macro to search for two spaces and replace them with just one.

Macros can be as simple or as complex as you need them to be. You can create a macro that formats paragraphs or a macro that gathers information from other documents and then formats the information in a table and tabulates the data and various columns.

Recording the second macro is considerably more difficult than the first, but the benefits of the second macro are greater as well.

The easiest way to create a macro is to turn on the macro recorder and record the commands and keystrokes as you complete the task. Word then stores the commands and keystrokes in a file as Visual Basic commands. Your keystrokes and command choices are bundled into a new macro command that you can call the same way you call the commands on the word menus.

After you record a macro, you can run it by choosing it in the Macro dialog box. For fast access, you can place your macro on a toolbar or assign it to a keyboard shortcut. Word offers special buttons in the Record Macro dialog box so you can add a button to a toolbar or assign keyboard shortcuts to macros. If you forget to create toolbar buttons or keyboard shortcuts, you can customize the toolbar or add shortcuts later.

Some commands are not recordable and will need to be added to the macro using the Microsoft Visual Basic Editor (VBE). You'll need to use VBE to make the macro work like you want. Additionally, if you know your way around the Visual Basic programming language, you can develop macros completely using just the editor.

Note	*Chapter 25 introduces you to creating macros and projects using the Visual Basic Editor.*

Working with Macros Included with Word

You already have a lot of macros on your system in the form of the wizards included with Word. Like any good macro, all the wizards automate routine tasks, including mail merges and letters.

The Batch Conversion Wizard is an excellent example of the power of macros. Imagine that you have a folder full of text files that need converted to Word document format. You could open each one and save it as a document, and then open the next and repeat the process, but that sounds pretty boring and could take a long time. Not if you use the Batch Conversion Wizard. The wizard contains macros that convert files to different formats within minutes.

If you are interested in writing your own macros, you can look at the code to learn how Microsoft did it. To open most of the wizard templates without starting the wizard, choose Open as Template in the lower-right corner of the File | New dialog; then look at the code using the Visual Basic Editor.

Other Utility Macros

Microsoft ships some utility macros with Word. Previous versions of Word included several useful Word Basic macros; while some of these will still work with Word, they haven't been converted to VBA. For that reason they are no longer included with Word.

The support.dot template, found in the Program Files\Microsoft Office\Office10\ Macros folder, contains three utilities.

- **Troubleshoot Utility**   Used to troubleshoot problems with Word. You can use it to rename your data key, rename normal.dot, and disable Word add-ins.

- **Registry Options Macro**   Used to modify Word settings that are stored in the Windows Registry. Among the settings that can be changed are the file locations and the colors of the spelling and grammar underlines.

- **AutoCorrect Backup**   Used to back up your AutoCorrect list to a file.

The most useful macro in the sample might be the AutoCorrect Backup macro. This macro allows you to save your AutoCorrect lists to a document so you can back them up or move them to other machines and import them back into the AutoCorrect list.

You might need to rerun setup and choose Add or Remove Features. Browse to Microsoft Word | Wizards and Templates | More Templates and Macros and select Run from My Computer to install support.dot.

The other macros included are used to modify Word settings that are stored in the Windows Registry and to troubleshoot Word problems. These two macros may not get the use that the AutoCorrect macro does, but any or all of these macros can be copied to the Normal template if you want to use them on a regular basis. See "Deleting, Renaming, and Copying Macros" later in this chapter for instructions on copying macros

Macro Security

In order to protect you against macro viruses, Microsoft tightened security within all Office applications. By default, security is set to High and only signed macros will be enabled when the application is opened. Also, no warning is given that macros have been disabled. You can lower the security setting to Medium and be presented with a dialog asking if you want to enable the macros or sign your own macros and choose to always trust macros containing your digital signature. Digital signatures intended for e-mail, such as one obtained from Verisign, can be used to sign macros for personal use. Some corporations might require properly signed macros, using a digital signature intended specifically for code distribution. Office also includes a utility program called SelfCert.exe so you can self-sign macros for your own use. Using SelfCert and signing macros is covered in more detail in Chapter 25.

You can also lower security to Medium and be given the option to approve macros each time you load Word or use the Low security setting, which allows all macros to run without warning you.

Using the Low security setting is not recommended, even if you have a virus scanner installed and keep it updated.

Using the Macro Recorder

The easiest way to create your own macros is using the macro recorder. The recorder was modeled after a tape recorder, and the cursor even looks like a cassette tape while the macros are being recorded. To use the macro recorder, follow these steps:

1. Turn on the macro recorder.
2. Choose the commands in the order you want Word to execute them for the macro.
3. Turn off the macro recorder.

When you run a macro, all the commands you gave when you recorded the macro in the first place are replayed.

There are some rules that you need to know about before recording the macros, including what is and is not recordable. Some rules have changed from previous versions of Word, and more commands are now recordable.

Macro Recording Rules

As you record your macros, you should observe these simple rules:

- **You can use the mouse to select menu commands but not to select text** If the action you're recording requires you to select text, do it by pressing keys, not by dragging the mouse. You can select text by pressing F8, and then pressing a keyboard shortcut for moving the cursor. For example, press F8-END to select text from the position of the cursor to the end of the line.

Note *In Chapter 2, "Keyboard Shortcuts for Getting Around" describes all the keyboard shortcuts for getting from place to place.*

- **If your macro calls for the cursor to move to a specific place in the document, enter a bookmark and you can move the cursor to that point** You can use the keyboard to move by line or screen count, but keep in mind this might not provide the results you intended.

Note *In Chapter 2, "Bookmarks for Getting Around" explains how to create and manage bookmarks.*

- **When you open a dialog box, the settings you select are recorded, as well as all the settings in the dialog box** For example, if you go to the Font dialog box and choose 10 point for the font size, the macro not only records the 10-point font size but also records the font in use and any special settings selected, such as Underline. You can edit these out of the macro later, using the Visual Basic Editor; see "Editing a Macro" later in this chapter.

- **In tabbed dialog boxes, such as Tools | Options, if you switch from tab to tab all commands on all tabs you select will be added to the macro** If you turn on the recorder and open Tools | Options and just click on all 11 tabs, all selections will be recorded. You may not want your macro to change the user's setting on the View tab, but if you selected it while going to the General tab, it will. These can be edited out later, using the VBE.

- **Toggle commands that you can switch on and off shouldn't be recorded because Word won't know if you mean for the command to be turned on or off** If you choose View | Ruler to turn on the ruler, Word will record the toggle. When you run the macro, if the ruler is turned on, the macro will turn it off; if it's off, it will be turned on. If you want to ensure the ruler is turned on, you'll need to insert the necessary lines using the Visual Basic Editor.

- **Like styles and autotext entries, macros are stored as part of a template** Before you start recording a macro, Word asks if you want to store the macro in the Normal template or in the template you are working in. If you want to save your macro in a particular template, open a document using that template before you record the macro. You can also copy the macro between templates by using the Organizer.

In Chapter 12, "Assembling Styles (and Macros and AutoText) from Different Templates" demonstrates how to use the Organizer to copy macros from template to template.

You might want to use a separate macro template to store your macros. This way, if the normal.dot becomes corrupted, your macros aren't lost. Also, with the macros stored in a different template, you can unload it when you don't need it using the Tools | Templates and Add-ins menu.

Recording a Macro

Recording a macro is simple, just follow these steps:

1. Open a document in a template other than the Normal template if you want to store the macro in another template.

2. Double-click the REC button on the status bar or choose Tools | Macro | Record New Macro.

3. In the Macro Name text box, enter a name for the macro. A macro name must begin with a letter; it cannot begin with a number. You cannot use blank spaces; if you want to mimic a blank space, use an underscore, such as "my_macro". Macro names can only contain letters, numbers, and the underscore character.

For example, "mymacro$" is not a valid name. If you begin with a number or include a space or invalid character, an error dialog will tell you it's an invalid procedure name.

4. Describe the macro in the Description box. The descriptions are added to the comments at the beginning of the macro listing in the VBE and displayed in the Tools | Macro | Macros dialog box. A good description can help to jog your memory later when you are looking for a particular macro.

5. In the Store Macro In drop-down list, make sure the name of the template you want to store the macro in is selected. Typically, this would be the Normal template for macros you want available in all documents; or macros could be stored in a specific template if they are needed only when using a specific template (see Figure 23-1).

6. Click the Toolbars button in the Record Macro dialog box if you want to create a toolbar button for the macro. Click the Keyboard button to assign a keyboard shortcut to the macro. The options can be added later, if you aren't sure you want or need shortcuts at the time you record the macro.

7. Click OK. You'll see the Stop Recording toolbar and a mini-cassette tape appear below the pointer.

Stop ———————▶   ◀——————— Pause

8. Very carefully enter the commands and do everything else that your macro requires. Click the Pause button if you need to stop recording for a moment. Click the Resume Recorder button, located where the Pause button used to be, when you're ready to start recording the macro again. While you can edit out extra commands using the VBE, it's easier not to record extra steps to begin with.

9. Click the Stop Recording button on the toolbar or double-click REC on the status bar when you're done recording the macro.

You can press the BACKSPACE or DELETE key to correct typing mistakes while you record the macro. The deletions become part of the macro, but because macros work so much faster than you could ever move, a few extra keypresses won't slow most macros by a noticeable amount of time. As you become more comfortable using VBE, you can remove the extra lines from your macro.

Recording Your First Macro

There are times when I want to see certain formatting marks, but most of the time I only want to see the text on the screen. So for this exercise, I'll show you one of my

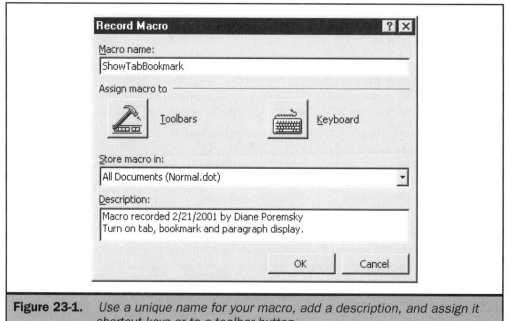

Figure 23-1. *Use a unique name for your macro, add a description, and assign it shortcut keys or to a toolbar button*

favorite macros—turning on the options in Tools | Options to show tabs, paragraph marks, and bookmarks.

1. Double-click on the REC button on the status bar or select Tools | Macro | Record New Macro.

2. Enter a name in the Macro name field. I'm naming my macro "ShowTabBookmark". I'm not going to assign shortcut keys or toolbar buttons, but I do add a description in the description textbox so I can remember what it does, in addition to the date and my name, which is included automatically.

3. Click OK and the Recording toolbar appears.

4. Now go to Tools | Options | View menu and add check boxes to Show Bookmarks, Tab characters, and Paragraph marks. Click OK.

5. Click the Stop Recording button or double click REC in the status bar again.

If you want to run the macro, go to Tools | Macro | Macros and select the macro by name. It won't appear to do anything because the tab and paragraph marks are already showing. You could record a second macro to disable them from showing or make this macro act as a toggle to show and hide the marks using just one macro. I'll show you how to do toggles in Chapter 25, "Working with Toggles."

When Recording a Macro Doesn't Work

Most of the time, recording a macro works just fine. You might end up with messy code, but it works, so who cares? You're not a programmer and you don't have to look at the code, only run it. The macro runs fast enough that the excess code it might contain doesn't annoy you, and that's what really matters.

Limitations of a Macro Recorder

Unfortunately, not everything you are going to want to do is recordable. For example, you can't record toggle actions. As mentioned earlier, selecting text or positioning the cursor is recordable but might not give you the desired results when you are recording.

You most likely will record more actions than you need. This isn't always a problem, but other times it will have unwanted results. As an example go back into Tools | Options | View and uncheck the bookmarks, tab, and paragraph marks plus the vertical and horizontal scroll bars and the status bar. Run the macro. This time the tab and paragraph marks will show, but so will the scroll bars and status bar.

If you need to include actions that are not recordable or to eliminate problems caused by recording too many actions, you'll need to edit the macro using the VBE.

Running a Macro

As mentioned earlier, you can add a macro to a toolbar button or assign a keyboard shortcut to a macro. However, if your macro has not been turned on in a toolbar button or keyboard shortcut, you can still run it using these simple steps:

1. Choose Tools | Macro | Macros or press ALT+F8.

2. Click the name of the macro you want to run. If you don't see its name, open the Macros In drop-down list and choose either another template or All Active Templates And Documents, which lists all macros you created for the Normal template as well as all other templates and documents that are currently open (see Figure 23-2).

3. Click the Run button.

If your macro is long and you want to stop it from running, press and hold the CTRL+BREAK keys. On most keyboards the Break key is found along with the Pause key to the right of the function keys.

Using Macrobuttons and Command Controls to Run Macros

Word includes a neat option called *Macrobutton*, which allows you to put a button in the document body for you to start the macro, rather than create a toolbar button. Macrobuttons use field codes, simple text, or images. A good use of macrobuttons

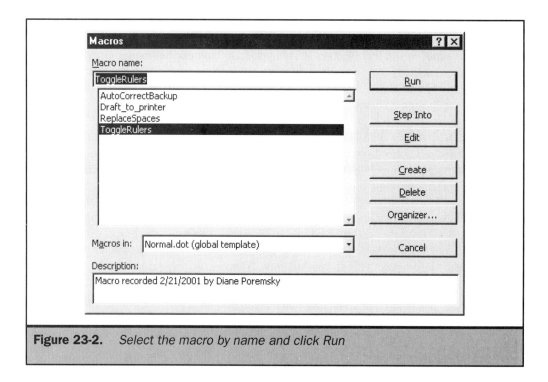

Figure 23-2. *Select the macro by name and click Run*

would be to build a switchboard or menu template, allowing users to easily load frequently used files (see Figure 23-3).

Macrobutttons are easy to include in a document, using the Insert | Field menu:

1. Select Macrobutton from the list of Field Names.
2. Select the macro or Word command you want to use with the macrobutton from the Macro name list.
3. Add the text you want displayed in Word to the Display text field.

You can use the built-in commands used for toolbar buttons and menus with macrobuttons. As a result, you could use a macrobutton to easily add a Print button to your document. If you display the field codes (press ALT-F9), you'll see the field code for a macrobutton looks like this:

```
{MACROBUTTON MacroName [text or image to be clicked]}.
```

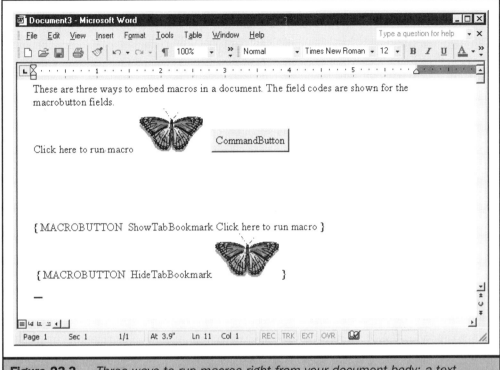

Figure 23-3.   *Three ways to run macros right from your document body: a text
macrobutton, an image macrobutton, or a command button*

When you know the macro name, you can skip the Insert | Field menu. Press
CTRL-F9 to insert field brackets, type in the macrobutton, the macro name, and the text
or the image you want the user to click on.

Note   *Many of the letter templates included with Word use macrobuttons as a placeholder for
text. Typically, you'll see text in the template such as this: "Click here and type your
name". This is actually a macrobutton using "NoMacro". A macro doesn't run when
you click the text, but the text is erased and you can enter your name or other text
in its place.*

Command button controls are similar to macrobuttons and are inserted using
the Control Toolbox toolbar, select it from the View | Toolbars menu. These are the
familiar command buttons found on forms and are obviously buttons that are meant

to be pushed. To add a command button to a document, click once on the Command Button icon on the Control toolbox. To add a macro to a command button, right-click the Command button and choose View code.

Word's Automatic Macros

Word offers five automatic macros that run at certain times when you use Word. Create your own macro to make Word work your way. As long as you name your macro with one of these names, it runs automatically:

- **AutoExec**   Runs when you start Word or load a global template. There can only be one AutoExec macro.

- **AutoNew**   Runs when you create a new document based on a particular template. Each template can have its own AutoNew macro.

- **AutoOpen**   Runs each time you open a document. Use this to set specific options for the current document. Each template can have an AutoOpen.

- **AutoClose**   Runs each time you close a document. A good use of this macro is to change options back to defaults. Each template can have an AutoClose.

- **AutoExit**   Runs when you shut down Word or unload a global template. Use this macro to do the chores you need to do when you're finished word processing, such as backup documents.

Remember which template you store the AutoNew, AutoOpen, and AutoClose macros in. Many a Word user has saved these macros in the wrong template and wondered why the macros didn't work.

To prevent any of these macros from running, you need to hold down SHIFT when opening or closing Word using templates containing any of these macros.

Editing a Macro

Editing a macro requires opening VBE and editing Visual Basic codes. While this is not hard to do, not every user wants to edit code. If your macro is uncomplicated, you might want to try recording it again. Chapter 25 explains in more detail how to use the editor to create and edit macros. For now, I'll explain the basics of reading a macro in VBE, deleting part of the macro, and copying part of the macro to another macro.

The Visual Basic Editor

After recording a macro, open the VBE (see Figure 23-4) using Tools | Macro | Visual Basic Editor or press ALT+F11. When the editor opens, you'll see two small windows docked on the left side of the screen. For basic macro editing you only need to concern yourself with the Project Explorer. This is the top window and contains a list of all documents and template projects currently open.

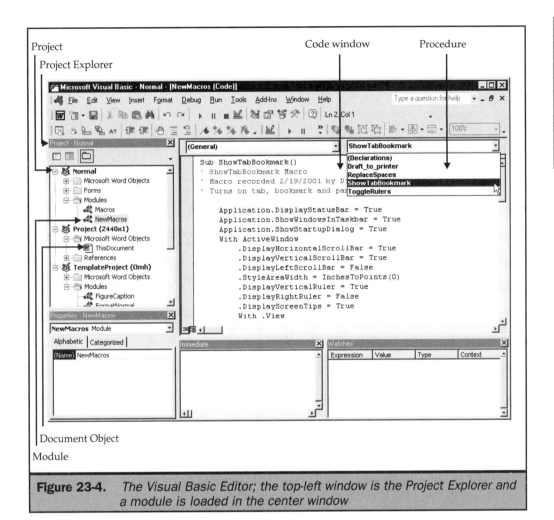

Figure 23-4.   *The Visual Basic Editor; the top-left window is the Project Explorer and a module is loaded in the center window*

The Normal template is listed first as just "Normal". Any other open documents or templates in use are listed in the Project Explorer as Project (Document_name) or TemplateProject (Template_name). Locate the document or template project you saved the macro in and click the plus sign (+) to expand it if needed. When expanded, you'll see a folder for Microsoft Word Objects, which contains the document or template. If the project contains macros, there will be a Modules folder, and if it contains references to templates or other documents, you'll have a References folder listed. The Word object is the document or template; modules are where the macros are stored; references list the templates that the document uses.

Select the Module for the document or template that you saved your recorded macro to. Usually this is the Normal template. New macros are typically saved to a module called NewMacros. Locate it in the list and double-click it. The module will load into the right pane, and you will be able to read your macro. If you've recorded several macros, click in the drop-down list in the upper right of the window, and select the macro by name to quickly bring it into view.

Most Windows programs provide multiple ways of doing things, and the VBE is no different. Most actions are listed on the right-click context menu and are on a menu on the toolbar. For example, to open the NewMacros module, you can right-click it and choose View code or select it and press ENTER. *Or you can use the Tools | Macros dialog.*

Reading Your Code

After you have the macro in view you are ready to read through it and decide what needs removed. It might look confusing at first, but as you read through it, you'll see it makes some sense and you'll actually understand at least a little bit of it.

It begins with the macro name and includes a few lines of comments. Each line of comments leads with an apostrophe (') and is shaded green. The apostrophe tells Word to ignore the line because it is not part of the actual macro. The green text makes it easier for you to see that it is a comment. You can add comments anywhere, as long as you begin them with an apostrophe.

```
Sub ShowTabBookmark()
' ShowTabBookmark Macro
' Macro recorded 2/19/2001 by Diane Poremsky
' Turns on tab, bookmark and paragraph display.
```

Next is the actual VBA code. If this code doesn't make sense to you, look at the Tools | Options | View menu and compare the different options it offers. Everything listed on the View dialog is repeated in this code. If it has a check mark in the View dialog, it is written as True in the code and is enabled.

```
Application.DisplayStatusBar = True
Application.ShowWindowsInTaskbar = True
Application.ShowStartupDialog = True
With ActiveWindow
    .DisplayHorizontalScrollBar = True
    .DisplayVerticalScrollBar = True
    .DisplayLeftScrollBar = False
    .StyleAreaWidth = InchesToPoints(0)
    .DisplayVerticalRuler = True
    .DisplayRightRuler = False
    .DisplayScreenTips = True
```

```
        With .View
            .ShowAnimation = True
            .Draft = False
            .WrapToWindow = False
            .ShowPicturePlaceHolders = False
            .ShowFieldCodes = False
            .ShowBookmarks = True
            .FieldShading = wdFieldShadingWhenSelected
            .ShowTabs = True
            .ShowSpaces = False
            .ShowParagraphs = True
            .ShowHyphens = False
            .ShowHiddenText = True
            .ShowAll = False
            .ShowDrawings = True
            .ShowObjectAnchors = False
            .ShowTextBoundaries = False
            .ShowHighlight = True
            .DisplayPageBoundaries = True
            .DisplaySmartTags = True
        End With
    End With
End Sub
```

It's definitely a lot more code than you wanted when you recorded the macro. You only wanted to show bookmarks, tabs, and paragraph marks. You might not want to change the settings for the other options at all. It's easy enough to fix—just delete the lines you don't need.

This macro example is pretty easy to decipher, and by now you've probably already figured out which lines control bookmarks, tabs, and paragraphs. You may have guessed that the other statements containing "=" can also be deleted.

Begin by deleting the Application objects. You don't want to change the users' preferences for the status bar, windows in the taskbar (the single document interface feature), or the Start Up dialog.

Move through the next series of statements. You need the With ActiveWindow statement, but don't want to change the scroll bar or ruler display options—you can delete those lines. You don't want to change the user's setting for StyleAreaWidth or ScreenTips.

You are now at the next With statement. The bookmarks, tabs, and paragraph marks properties are nested in this With statement, so keep it. You don't need the nested With statements, but you do need both the ActiveWindow and View objects.

As you become more experienced you'll learn how to make more compact code, but it's not going to affect the macro speed so leave it as is. If you aren't sure whether to delete the line, you can comment the line out by adding an apostrophe at the beginning of the line and running the macro. Once you are sure it's working as you expect, you can delete the line completely.

The only rule you need to remember is that some statements need a beginning and an ending. In this example, "With" is the statement that needs properly closed, and it's closed using "End With." If you remove one and run the macro, you'll get an error message that gives you a hint about what is wrong. If you read the code from the bottom up and make sure each End statement has a beginning, you won't have any problems.

After all the excess code is removed, you are left with a small, compact macro that does exactly what you want—it enables only bookmarks, tabs, and paragraphs.

```
Sub ShowTabBookmark()
With ActiveWindow
        With .View
            .ShowBookmarks = True
            .ShowTabs = True
            .ShowParagraphs = True
        End With
    End With
End Sub
```

You can use this piece of code to easily create another macro that hides those options. Select and copy the macro and paste it after End Sub. Rename it "HideTabBookmark" and change all instances of "True" to "False". You now have a macro to turn the options on and one to turn them off.

Add the macros to the toolbar by choosing View | Toolbars in Word and selecting Customize. On the Commands tab, in the Categories pane, select Macros. From the Commands pane, drag your two new macros to the toolbar and click Close.

Now, try out your new toolbar buttons. It is possible to create one macro that toggles these options on and off instead of using two separate macros; I'll show you how to do that in Chapter 25.

Deleting, Renaming, and Copying Macros

In the last section you used the VBE to delete lines from your code. If you created the second macro, "HideTabBookmark", you learned one way to copy and rename macros. While you only deleted lines from your code, you could have deleted the macro completely if you wanted by deleting the code listing. This is one method you can use to manage individual macros. Unless you add new modules, all macros will be stored in the same module.

Macros are listed individually in the Macros dialog box on the Tools menu in either Word or VBE. You can select a macro by name and press the DELETE button. You can't recover a macro if you delete the wrong one, so be sure it's the correct macro before you press DELETE. If you have more than one macro by the same name but in a different module, it will include the module name in this format: "Module1.MacroName".

To move individual macros to a new module, insert a module using Insert | Module; then copy the macro and paste it in the new module. Modules can be used to help categorize your macros.

If you want to move modules between templates, you have two ways of doing it: You can open the templates or documents that you are moving the modules between and then open the VBE and drag modules from one project and drop them on another. You can also use Word's Organizer, which is explained next in "Managing Modules Using Organizer."

Besides moving and copying macros between projects, you might want to create a file for backup for use in other macro projects, to share with friends, or move to another computer. Right-click on the module and choose Export File. This saves the file as a Basic file using the .BAS extension. To import the file into your project, right-click the module folder and choose Import File.

If you don't want to open the documents or templates in Word and VBE, there is another way to manage your macros, and you may already use it for managing other Word Features—it's the Organizer.

Managing Modules Using Organizer

You should be familiar with the Organizer and be able to use it to manage your styles, AutoText, and toolbars. You can also use it to move modules between templates or rename and delete modules. To open the Organizer, go to Tools | Macro | Macros or press ALT+F8 and click the Organizer button to open it with the Macro Project Items tab selected (see Figure 23-5).

Note *In Chapter 12, "Assembling Styles (and Macros and AutoText) from Different Templates" explains the Organizer in detail.*

The Organizer lets you copy modules from one template or document to another. By default, the Organizer opens with the normal.dot template already loaded on the right side of the screen and the current document on the left. You can copy modules in either direction; the arrows on the Copy button and the text above the pane change based on the module that is selected first. Select the template containing the modules you want to copy from the Macro Project Items Available In drop-down, and then select the template you want to copy them to. Click the module name that you want to copy, and then click the Copy button. You can copy in either direction, left to right or right to left. You open other templates to copy the macros to by first closing one of the files. When you click the Close File button, it changes to Open File and the Open dialog opens. You can also delete and rename modules from this dialog box by selecting the module you want to delete or rename and pressing the appropriate button.

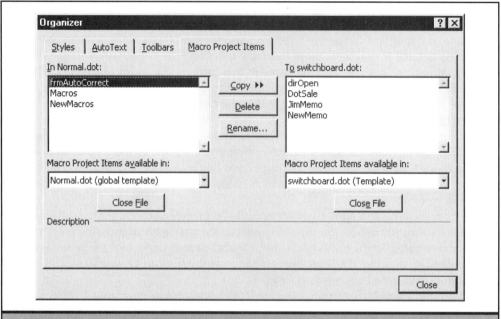

Figure 23-5. *The Macro Project Items tab in Organizer allows you to copy, rename, and delete modules from templates and documents*

 Deleted modules cannot be recovered.

 Any macros created using Word Basic, from Word 95 or earlier versions, are converted to VBA macros with each macro in a separate module. Macros created in Word 97 or later generally have many macros in one module.

MOUS Exam Objectives Explored in Chapter 23

Objective	Heading
Create, edit, and run macros*	"Recording a Macro," "Running a Macro," and "Editing a Macro"

* Denotes an Expert, not a Core, exam objective.

Ten Ways to Work Faster with Macros

1. Turn Repetitive Actions into Macros   Look at every series of movements you repeat frequently as a candidate for a macro. If you often turn options on for a few minutes and then turn them off, create a macro to automate that action. What used to take three mouse clicks or keyboard shortcuts can be reduced to one mouse click. As a bonus, not only do you save movements, you also save a few seconds. A second here, a second there and before you know it, you've saved several minutes.

2. Use Descriptive Macro Names   Nothing is worse than knowing you created a macro but you can't remember which one it is. Was the macro to search and replace tabs named Macro12 or Macro20? If you take the time to name it before you record it, you'll know that ReplaceTabs is the macro you need.

3. Include Descriptions with Your Macros   Not only should you use descriptive names for your macros, but adding a description helps as well. Does ReplaceTabs replace tabs with spaces or does it replace spaces with tabs? By adding a description to the comments, you'll know exactly what it does.

4. Categorize Your Macros   There is no limit to the number of macros a module can contain, but as the list gets long, it's also much harder to find the one you want. Add new modules and group similar macros together. Macros that are used for page formatting can be stored in a module called "Formatting".

5. Use High Macro Security   Macros are powerful. They can delete and rename files on your hard drive, and they can even change your Registry settings. They can do a lot of damage if created with malicious intent by the wrong people. As annoying as the Macro dialog box can be, always keep your security level set to High.

6. Digitally Sign Trusted Macros   If macro security is set to High, no macros will run, including the ones you created and know are safe. Instead of reducing security levels so they will run, get a digital certificate and sign your macros. The next time you open Word with that document or template, choose to always trust macros you sign with that certificate. Office includes a utility, SelfCert.exe, to create your own certificate for signing projects for your own use.

You can get a personal digital certificate from VeriSign (http://www.verisign.com/) or Thawte (http://www.thawte.com/).

7. Use Shortcuts to Run Favorite Macros   You won't save much time if you create a macro to save five steps but need six to find the macro and run it. Assign shortcut keys or create toolbar buttons for your most used macros. Use Macrobutton fields so you can run the macros right from the document body.

8. Use Automatic Macros   If you use one of the special names reserved as an automacro, Word will run macros when you open or close documents and templates. Use these automacros to run procedures when Word loads and to clean up when Word is closed instead of starting the macro manually after Word is loaded or before you close it.

For example, you create a macro that uses a different printer when you use a specific template to create a document. You can have the macro assigned to a toolbar button and hope you remember to use it to print, or you can use the macro code in an AutoOpen macro and have the default printer changed for this file. An AutoClose macro changes the default printer back.

9. Clean Up Messy Code   When you use the macro recorder, you'll record a lot of extra code that you don't need. Take the time to read and edit the extra lines out of the code. It might not make your macro run faster or better, but it will make it look better and easier to read later. If you leave extra code in, don't use a very descriptive name, or add a description and then look at it in a few months, you might forget what the macro does. With the extra code in it, there is no way you can tell which code you wanted in it and which is not needed.

Add comments and descriptions to your code to remind you what it does and why you did it "this way." You may look at it later and think, "It was stupid of me to do it this way," and clean up the code, only to discover that it doesn't work right anymore.

10. Back Up Your Macros   It happens even to the best, most careful user. You create a lot of macros and save them in the Normal template. Then something happens and the template is corrupted or gets deleted and you lose all your macros. You ask yourself why didn't you make a copy of the template or export the modules? Why didn't you have your backup utility back up the folder where the macros are stored? The hours you saved, seconds at a time, by using macros are lost when you need to re-create all the macros. When backing up your documents and other files, don't forget that templates are valuable files, too.

Chapter 24

Introduction to Visual Basic for Applications (VBA)

If you've made it this far, it means you probably have an interest in using Visual Basic for Applications (VBA) to create more advanced macros. In order to better understand how to develop macros and procedures in Word, you need to understand what VBA is and how it works.

Visual Basic for Applications is a development language used to easily customize applications and integrate them with existing data. All the Office family products as well as many other applications can be programmed and controlled using VBA. The basic language is the same for all the programs that use VBA, although some commands and methods are product-specific.

VBA is based on the Visual Basic development language and includes the same set of programming tools found in Visual Basic, which you can use to harness the power of Word so that it does precisely what you need.

In this chapter, you'll learn what VBA is and how it is different from WordBasic. You'll learn about the Word object model, and I'll introduce you to the main parts of the object model and show you how to use them.

A Brief History of VBA

Early versions of Word used WordBasic to create macros. If you have any macros created in older versions of Word, you'll see the calls to WordBasic. These macros are converted to VBA by Word and the statements lead with "WordBasic" and the actual WordBasic command follows.

VBA was first used in Microsoft Excel in 1993, but Word continued to use WordBasic through version 7, which was part of Microsoft Office 95. With the release of Office 97, Word began using VBA as its programming language. The remaining Office applications began using VBA when Office 2000 was released. There are some subtle differences in VBA within each Office application, but once you understand the basics you can easily learn the differences in how each application uses VBA and move between the different applications fairly easily.

The major difference between VBA and WordBasic is that WordBasic is a flat list of around 900 commands, whereas VBA consists of a hierarchy of objects, each with a specific set of methods and properties. Every element of Word, including documents, paragraphs, fields, bookmarks, and so on, is represented by an object in VBA. By modifying these objects you can control Word.

Most WordBasic commands can be run at any time, but with VBA, you need to drill down through the object model to an object that you manipulate using properties and methods. Some objects can only be accessed from other objects, and before you can change the object's attributes, you need to find that object.

Think of a staircase: the steps are objects and the attributes make up the bottom step. To get to the attributes, you need to go down through the objects. For example, to change the attributes of a paragraph, you need to go through the selection object, and then the paragraph object, and finally reach the alignment property.

The following code sample shows how you walk down the object model, from the select object to the paragraphs object to access the alignment property, which you are changing to align right:

```
Public Sub Sample()

Selection.Paragraphs.Alignment = wdAlignParagraphRight

End Sub
```

Note *To test any of the code snippets contained in this chapter, open the VBA editor using ALT+F11 and insert a module using the Insert menu. Type in the Sample sub listed earlier. Create a document with some text in it, place the cursor within the text, and press F5 (from the VBE) or use Word's Tools | Macro | Macros menu to run the code. Replace the code with the code snippets found throughout this chapter and run them on your document.*

It's Not WordBasic Anymore

Any templates created in older versions of Word that contain macros created using WordBasic will be automatically converted to VBA when first opened in Word; each line will be prefaced with "WordBasic". While current versions of Word support both WordBasic and VBA, future versions might not. For this reason, it's a good idea to create macros and procedures using VBA.

Most WordBasic statements will still work with Word; for example, to move the cursor or insertion point to the beginning of the line, you could use this statement:

```
Public Sub Sample()

WordBasic.StartOfLine

End Sub
```

If you used WordBasic previously, you might find that VBA is less intuitive at first. For example, to move to the beginning of a line using VBA, you add the Unit variant wdLine to the HomeKey method. StartOfLine is easier to remember, but limits you to moving to the start of the line. VBA's HomeKey command can be controlled to move the insertion point to the top of the document or select text. This sample code is the VBA equivalent of the WordBasic StartOfLine command:

```
Public Sub Sample()

Selection.HomeKey Unit:=wdLine

End Sub
```

Although it might not seem all that logical, the advantage belongs with VBA because you use many of the same statements over, referencing the same objects and methods but changing the variants to control what you want to do. If you want to move to the beginning of the document using VBA, you only need to change the Unit variant, not the entire line. By changing the unit variant to wdStory, this use of HomeKey moves you to the beginning of the document:

```
Public Sub Sample()

Selection.HomeKey Unit:=wdStory

End Sub
```

You might have realized by now that the HomeKey command replicates the use of the keyboard's HOME key. Other VBA commands use similar naming conventions. If you keep this in mind as you work with VBA, it will be easier to see the logic behind VBA.

Understanding the Differences Between VB and VBA

As I mentioned at the beginning of this chapter, VBA is based on the Visual Basic development language and includes the same set of programming tools. Although VBA is based on VB, it doesn't have all the features included with VB.

As powerful as VBA is, it may not be powerful enough for your needs. Most importantly, you can't use VBA to create Component Object Model (COM) add-ins. This won't be a problem for most users seeking only to create macros to speed up their work. Developers who want to create COM add-ins need to use Visual Basic or Microsoft Office Developer (MOD). MOD is an Office suite with additional development tools.

In addition to the tools needed to create COM add-ins, MOD provides a utility to create install files similar to the *.msi files used to install Office. This makes it easy to design a project and share it with others. Another useful tool is the Code Librarian. You use it to store your favorite pieces of code in a database so it's convenient to find and reuse the code in other projects. The remaining tools in MOD are for use with Access and SQL. Current owners of an Office suite can purchase the developer tools separately from Microsoft.

COM add-ins are automation objects that can seamlessly access the object models of other applications and work behind the scenes to automate Word or other Office applications. A COM add-in is a dynamic-link library (DLL) file and is easy to distribute and often includes an installation program. You can also compile COM add-ins into a Word-specific dynamic-link library (WLL).

Sharing Your VBA Project

You don't need MOD or VB to create projects to share with co-workers. You can save your macros to a new template or export modules as Basic files (*.bas). These files can then be imported into other modules. Templates containing macros should be digitally signed so others can use the macros without lowering their security levels.

 For instructions on sharing your projects, see Chapter 25, "Managing Your Project Elements." Using a digital signature is also explained in Chapter 25, "Signing Your Projects."

Learning About the Word Object Model

Microsoft Word's functionality is exposed as a set of programmable objects. Every unit of content and functionality in Word is an object that you can examine and control using programming code.

An *object* represents an element of an application. Objects found in Word include documents, tables, and paragraphs. Some objects contain objects and are called *collection objects*. When using Visual Basic code, you need to identify an object before you can apply one of the object's methods or change the value of one of its properties.

Objects, Methods, and Properties

Objects contained in an application are arranged hierarchically, similar to a family tree, in what is called an *object model*. Each object model has an uppermost object from which all other objects are derived. This uppermost object usually represents the application itself and is named the Application object. The Application object has child objects, which, in turn, have child objects of their own. A small section of an object model is shown in Figure 24-1.

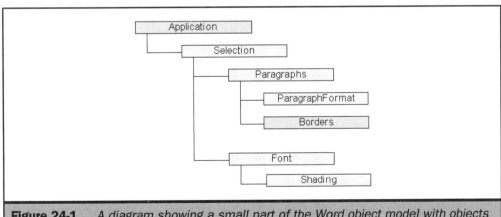

Figure 24-1. *A diagram showing a small part of the Word object model with objects and child objects*

As you can see, the uppermost object in the Word object model is the Application object. The Application object has many child objects, two of which are Selection and Font objects. The Selection object contains a Paragraphs collection object and Font object. The Paragraphs object is a collection object because it is a container for more objects, including ParagraphFormat and Borders. Both ParagraphFormat and Borders are collection objects and contain additional objects. Of course, since you don't know much about the object model yet, you'll have to trust me that they are collection objects.

More on Objects

There are two ways to interact with an application's objects: through the user interface or by using a programming language. With the user interface, you use the keyboard and mouse to navigate to the part of the application that controls the data you want to change or the commands you want to use. For example, to change the font used in the last paragraph in your current document, follow these steps:

1. Browse to the end of the document.
2. Select the text you want to change.
3. Click the Format menu and open the Fonts dialog box.
4. Then select a new font.

With VB, you navigate through the object model from the top–level object to the object that contains the content and functionality you want to change. You then use the properties and methods of that object to make the changes. The following code sample changes the font of the last paragraph automatically. It navigates down the current document object, into the paragraph object, finds the last paragraph, and selects it. It then changes the font to Verdana using the Name property of the Font object:

```
Public Sub ChangeFont()

ActiveDocument.Paragraphs.Last.Range.Select
Selection.Font.Name = "Verdana"

End Sub
```

Because the user interface and VB are two ways of gaining access to the exact same content and functionality, many objects, properties, and methods share names with elements in the user interface. This means that for every action you can take in the user interface, there's a VB code equivalent, and you can use the macro recorder to help you learn the VBA equivalent of these actions.

 For instructions on how to use the macro recorder, see Chapter 23.

Table 24-1 lists all the objects under the Application object. Many of these objects are collections, and they have child objects of their own. You'll probably recognize the names of most of the objects and know what they apply to without needing an explanation.

Object	Description
AddIns Collection Object	Contains all the add-ins available to Word, regardless of whether they're currently loaded. Included are global templates or Word add-in libraries (WLLs) displayed in the Tools	Templates and Add-ins dialog box.
AutoCaptions Collection Object	Contains all the captions listed in the Insert	AutoCaption dialog box. This object is read-only.
AutoCorrect Object	Represents the AutoCorrect functionality in Word. This can be used to programmatically change AutoCorrect options and add entries to the AutoCorrect list.
Browser Object	Represents the browser tool used to move the insertion point to objects in a document. Familiar to users as the three buttons at the bottom of the vertical scroll bar.
CaptionLabels Collection Object	Contains CaptionLabel objects that represent the available caption labels. The items in the CaptionLabels collection are listed in the Label box in the Insert	Caption dialog box. Can be used to add your own captions.
DefaultWebOptions Object	Contains global application-level attributes used by Microsoft Word when you save a document as a Web page or open a Web page. WebOptions object settings override DefaultWebOptions object settings.

Table 24-1. *Objects Contained in Word's Object Model and Accessible Directly from the Application Object*

Object	Description
Dialogs Collection Object	Contains the Dialog objects used in Word. Each object represents a built-in Word dialog box and is read-only.
Dictionaries Collection Object	Contains Dictionary objects, including the active custom spelling dictionaries.
Document Object	Represents a document. The Document object is a member of the Documents collection. The Documents collection contains all the Document objects that are currently open in Word.
Documents Collection Object	Contains all the Document objects that are currently open in Word.
EmailOptions Object	Contains attributes used by Word for creating and editing e-mail.
FileConverters Collection Object	Contains FileConverter objects that represent all the file converters available for opening and saving files.
FontNames Object	Represents a list of the names of all available fonts.
HangulHanjaConversionDictionaries Collection Object	Contains Dictionary objects for the active custom Hangul-Hanja conversion dictionaries. Used with East Asian language support in Word.
KeyBinding Object	Represents a custom key assignment in the current context and is a member of the KeyBindings collection. Custom key assignments are made in the Customize Keyboard dialog box. Current context is set using the CustomizationContext object. This object is read-only.
KeyBindings Collection Object	Contains the KeyBinding objects that represent the custom key assignments in the current context. Custom key assignments are made in the Customize Keyboard dialog box.

Table 24-1. *Objects Contained in Word's Object Model and Accessible Directly from the Application Object* (continued)

Object	Description
KeysBoundTo Collection Object	Contains the KeyBinding objects assigned to a command, style, macro, or other item in the current context.
Languages Collection Object	Contains the Language objects that represent languages used for proofing or formatting in Word.
ListGalleries Collection Object	Contains the ListGallery objects that represent the three tabs in the Bullets and Numbering dialog box.
MailMessage Object	Represents the active e-mail message if you are using Word as your e-mail editor.
MailingLabel Object	Represents a mailing label.
Options Object	Represents application and document options in Word. Many of the properties for the Options object correspond to items in the Options dialog box (Tools menu).
RecentFiles Collection Object	Contains the RecentFile objects that represent the files that have been used recently. These items are displayed at the bottom of the File menu.
Selection Object	Represents the current selection in a window or pane. A selection represents either a selected area in the document or the insertion point if nothing is selected. There can only be one Selection object per document window, and only one Selection object in the entire application can be active at a time.
SpellingSuggestions Collection Object	Contains SpellingSuggestion objects that represent all the suggestions for a word. This is read-only.

Table 24-1.   *Objects Contained in Word's Object Model and Accessible Directly from the Application Object* (continued)

Object	Description
SynonymInfo Object	Represents the information about synonyms, antonyms, related words, or related expressions for the specified range or string.
System Object	Contains information about the computer system.
TaskPanes Collection	Contains the TaskPane objects that contain commonly performed tasks in Word. New to Word 2002, the panes are docked by default on the right side of the document window.
Tasks Collection Object	Contains the Task objects that represent all the tasks currently running on the system. This is read-only.
Template Object	Contains the Template objects that represent all the templates that are currently available. Includes open templates, templates attached to open documents, and global templates loaded in the Tools	Templates and Add-ins dialog box.
Templates Collection Object	Represents a document template. The Template object is a member of the Templates collection. The Templates collection includes all the available Template objects.
Window Object	Represents a window and includes many document characteristics, such as scroll bars and rulers. This is a member of the Windows collection. The Windows collection for the Application object contains all the windows in the application, whereas the Windows collection for the Document object contains only the windows that display the specified document.

Table 24-1. *Objects Contained in Word's Object Model and Accessible Directly from the Application Object* (continued)

Object	Description
Windows Collection Object	Contains the Window objects that represent all the available windows. The Windows collection for the Application object contains all the windows in the application. The Windows collection for the Document object contains only the windows that display the specified document.

Table 24-1. *Objects Contained in Word's Object Model and Accessible Directly from the Application Object* (continued)

Objects need to be told what to do—by themselves they do absolutely nothing. You tell them what to do with the properties and methods that the object supports. What are properties and methods? A property is a function that sets or retrieves an attribute for an object, such as size or color. A method is a function that performs some action on an object—or in plain English, you use methods to tell the object what to do.

Understanding Methods

A *method* is an action that an object can perform. Methods can have arguments that control how the action is completed. For example, OpenUp is a method of the Paragraph object because it opens up the paragraph spacing to 12 points before the paragraph. This example will add 12 points spacing before the second paragraph in the currently active document:

```
Public Sub Add12ptBefore()

ActiveDocument.Paragraphs(2).OpenUp

End Sub
```

The following code snippet demonstrates how methods can use arguments to control their actions. This inserts today's date in the format specified as a field. You can change the arguments to return the current date in different formats. To insert the date as normal text instead of a field, change InsertAsField to false:

```
Public Sub InsertDate()

Selection.InsertDateTime DateTimeFormat:="MMMM dd, yyyy", _
  InsertAsField:=True

End Sub
```

Note *If you know the codes, you can create your own date and time formats. The month is represented by M, from single digit month (M), leading zero for double digit (MM), abbreviated month (MMM), and spelled out in full (MMMM). Date is d or dd, if you want a leading zero. Year can be two (yy) or four digits (yyyy). Hour is h or hh, minute is lowercase m to mm, seconds if needed, is represented by s or ss. Finally, if you want to use AM or PM, enter a/p.*

Each word object has different methods available to their use. Some methods are used by many objects; other methods are used by just one object. The Word object model contains hundreds of methods; some of the more common methods listed in Table 24-2.

Understanding Properties

A *property* is an attribute of an object that defines one of the object's characteristics, such as size, color, or screen location, or an aspect of its behavior, such as whether it is enabled or visible. To change the characteristics of an object, you need to change the values of its properties.

Activate Method	**Activates the Specified Object**
Add Method	Adds or installs an item or text as represented by the specified object. Used by most of the objects, except those that are read-only.
Close Method	Closes the specified window or document.
Delete Method	Deletes or uninstalls an item or text as represented by the specified object.
Item Method	Returns the specified object.
Open Method	Opens the specified object.
Select Method	Selects the specified object.
Update Method	Updates the values or results used in dialog boxes, links, indexes, tables of authorities, tables of figures, or tables of contents.

Table 24-2. *Common Methods Used by Word Objects*

In the following example, the Paragraphs object has its Alignment property set to centered. The syntax for using properties is to follow the reference to an object with a period, the property name, an equal sign (=), and the new property value:

```
Public Sub CenterPara()

Selection.Paragraphs.Alignment = wdAlignParagraphCenter

End Sub
```

Some properties are read-only and cannot be set. The easiest way to check for read/write status is to check VBA Help. Press F1 and under Properties in the Visual Basic Language Reference book, or if the code is already typed in the code window, position the cursor within the word and press F1. Examples of read-only properties are ActiveDocument and ActiveWindow. They represent the document or window that currently holds focus. To change focus to another document or window using code, you need to use the name or index number of the window or document.

Note   *An index number is assigned to each window, document, or object when it is opened or created, beginning with one. You can use this number to access the object in "object(1)" format. For example, "Paragraphs(3).Alignment" indicates that you want to apply the alignment property to paragraph number three. If an object in the index is closed or deleted, the index numbers are adjusted. For example, when document(3) is closed document(4) becomes document(3).*

Like methods, there are hundreds of properties used in the Word object model. A few of the more commonly used properties are listed in Table 24-3.

Browsing the Object Model

Each Office application includes a file called an *object library*, or type library, which contains information about the objects, properties, methods, events, and built-in constants that the application exposes. One of the best tools the Visual Basic Editor (VBE) offers is the Object Browser. It allows you to look around the object model and see what properties and methods work with which objects.

To open the Object Browser, press F2 in VBE or use the View | Object Browser menu. In the Project/Library drop-down menu where All Libraries is displayed,

Property	Description
ActiveDocument Property	Returns a Document object that represents the document currently in focus.
Count Property	Returns the number of items in a collection. This is read-only.
Index Property	Returns the position of an item in a collection or adds items in specific positions within collections.
Kind Property	Returns the type of link for an object.
Name Property	Returns or sets the name of the object.
Style Property	Returns or sets the style for the object.
Type Property	Returns or sets the type property for the object. This property is used by many objects, including the document object, and it returns the document type (document or template).

Table 24-3. *Commonly Used Properties*

choose Word. Type an object name or keyword in the Search Text drop-down list below the Project/Library field. Press ENTER or click the Search button and the members that match will be listed in the search Results pane.

For example, in Figure 24-2, a search for "index" found all the objects, methods, functions, and properties that contain the word "index". Selecting one of the items in the search results pane locates it in the Classes pane. All the members that can be used with it are shown in the Members pane. The correct syntax for the member is shown in the Detail pane.

The Detail pane at the bottom of the Object Browser gives additional information about the selected item, including the correct syntax needed, the read/write or

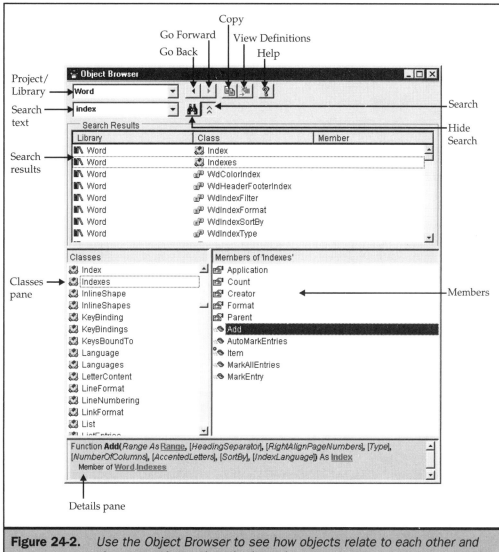

Figure 24-2.   *Use the Object Browser to see how objects relate to each other and what properties and methods each uses*

read-only status of a property, the object library that the object belongs to, and the type of data or object that the property or method returns. You can jump to parent objects by clicking the hyperlinked words.

Ten Things to Remember When Programming

1. No More WordBasic   If you have old macros created in WordBasic, practice your VBA skills by rewriting them in pure VBA. They'll be ready for the day when WordBasic is removed from Word, and you get a chance to improve your VBA knowledge at the same time.

2. Objects and More Objects   Objects are the building blocks of VBA, but they don't do much of anything. You need to use methods to control the objects.

3. Properties Are the Object's Characteristics   Properties tell you the characteristics of an object. Some properties are read-only; others are read/write and can be changed when ever you want.

4. Methods Are Objects in Action   Methods are used to make objects do something—anything. Not all methods work with every object. Everything you can do with the keyboard or mouse can be done using VBA.

5. Use the Object Browser   The Object Browser lets you see the objects, child objects, properties, and methods used. It also shows you what the correct syntax is for properties and methods. You can access the Object Browser using the F2 key, using the View | Object Browser menu, or from the Object Browser button on the Standard toolbar.

6. Use the Macro Recorder   Use the macro recorder to help you learn which properties and methods are used with the objects. It might create messy code, but if you know you want to replicate a menu or command and aren't sure about the properties or methods, the macro recorder is often faster than using help or the Object Browser. Using the macro recorder is explained in Chapter 23, "Using the Macro Recorder."

7. Use VBA Help   VBA help is installed on first use and is not installed as part of the typical install. If you haven't already installed VBA Help, get out your Office CD, then open the VB Editor, and press F1. The installer will take care of the rest. Once installed, use it. Not only does it have some code samples to help you get started, it also has a diagram of the Word object model and drop-down menus with child objects, properties, and methods that apply to each object.

If you place the cursor in any word in the code window and press F1, VBA Help will open to that keyword. It's much faster than switching to VBA Help and searching for your keyword.

8. Digitally Sign Your Code   *Always* digitally sign your macros so they will run without lowering the security setting. With something like 5,000 macro viruses on the loose, you can't be too careful. Keep your security setting High and start signing the macros you use. See Chapter 25, "Signing Your Projects," to learn how to sign your code.

9. Look for Ways to Work Smarter   It's easier to see the code in action if you tile your Word and VBE windows, with each adjusted to about 2/3 the screen width. To do this, minimize any open windows to the tray, except for the Word document and the VBE; then right-click the Windows taskbar and choose Tile Windows Vertically. Adjust the windows so they overlap a little, but still leave plenty of the document visible so you can see what is happening to it. This works really well when you step through code using the F8 key.

The Word document you are running your code on does not have to be in focus or on top of the screen when you run code from the VBE. The most recent document window used is the one the code will act on; if you have two documents open, be careful that you don't accidentally run the macro on the wrong document.

10. More Ways to Work Smarter

- **Learn to use the keyboard shortcuts**   It's faster than reaching for the mouse when you are already typing.

- **Explore the menus**   If a button is named Advanced, click on it even if you don't think you are advanced—you can always click Cancel to back out.

- **Don't be afraid to experiment**   Use new project files so you don't accidentally mess up your working project.

Chapter 25

Using the Visual Basic Editor

The Visual Basic editor (VBE) shares a common interface with all VB-enabled applications, including the Office family and Visual Basic 6. You may think it's too complicated and you'll never learn how to use it, but rest assured it's not any more complicated than Word and almost as easy to use.

Learning to use the VBE and write your own procedures allows you to create powerful and useful projects to enable you to work faster. As your skills improve, you write projects that access data from the other Office applications and automate many of your routine tasks like preparing reports.

Using the Visual Basic Editor

In order to write your own macros and procedures, you need to know how to use the tools provided for this task. Because the editor interface is the same in all the Office applications, you need only learn how to use one interface to edit macros in any of the applications.

In this chapter you will learn the different parts of the VBE and how to use them. You'll learn how to use the tools provided to create your own projects. You'll also learn how to use the debugging tools to debug your code.

Understanding the Visual Basic Editor Interface

Understanding how to use the VB Editor will make it easier for you when you are creating your own macros and procedures. The VBE includes a number of windows and toolbars that you'll find helpful when creating and testing your projects.

The default layout of the VBE interface consists of three panes: Project Explorer and Properties Window on the left side of the screen and the workspace taking up the remainder of the interface. The workspace is empty unless a code window or the Object Browser is open.

There are three other windows that are useful for debugging projects: the Immediate window, the Locals window, and the Watches window. You can show these windows using the View menu when needed. When enabled, these windows are docked by default on the lower edge of the editor. I'll explain how to use these windows for debugging later in this chapter. You can adjust the height and width of the windows, undock them completely, or dock them on other sides of the VBE interface (see Figure 25-1).

Tip   *To resize windows, hover the mouse over the inside edges, just as you would to resize a window's outside edge, click and hold down the left mouse button, when the cursor turns to a double pointer, drag the edge. To undock the windows, click on the title bar, hold down the left button, and pull away from the window edge. To redock a window, click the title bar and hold down the left mouse button. Slide the window against the edge of the VBE or docked windows until the heavy shaded line becomes a thin line; then release the mouse button.*

VISUAL BASIC IN
WORD 2002

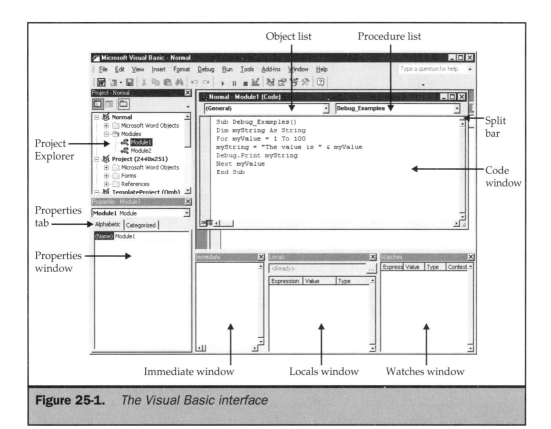

Figure 25-1.   *The Visual Basic interface*

The Project Explorer

The Project Explorer lists the currently open Word documents and the elements they contain. Expand the Projects view by clicking the plus sign (+). Each document or template project contains a folder called Microsoft Word Objects, which contains a Word Document object called ThisDocument. The References folder contains pointers to the templates and add-ins used in your document project, including any references set from the Tools | References menu in the VB editor. If the project contains macros, you'll have a Modules folder. Other folders might be present in the project list, including Class Modules, which stores modules containing code for custom objects and a Forms folder containing any custom forms used in your project. The Modules, Class Modules, and Forms folders can contain as many files as you need. Double-click any file to load it into the workspace.

The three buttons at the top of the Project Explorer window are

- **View Code**   Displays the Code window so you can write and edit code associated with the selected item. This is the same as double-clicking a file.

- **View Object**   Displays the Object window for the selected item, enabled only for an existing Document or UserForm.

- **Toggle Folders**   Hides and shows the Object folders and shows only the individual items. On a project with several different object types, the List view is not as cluttered with folder display turned off.

The Properties Window

The Properties window lists the properties of the selected file. Your initial reaction is probably to wonder why you would need properties and for many projects you might never need to change the properties, but there are times when you'll need to use the Properties window. For instance, what if you want to rename your modules? Select the (name) property in the Properties window and type in a new name. This window is also used to change the design-time properties of forms and controls. Other times you may want to see the property settings, but not change them. (Refer to Figure 25-1.)

The Object Box drop-down lists the currently selected object. Generally, this will only have one item listed, except when a form is selected. Only objects from the active form are visible. If you select multiple objects, only the properties common to all the selected objects and their settings appear on the Properties List tabs. You can change the attributes of several objects at once this way. For example, if you have three command buttons on a form and want to change the color of all three, you can change each one individually or select all of them and change them all at once.

The two tabs in the Properties window, Alphabetic and Categorized, display the same properties but they are organized with different views. The Alphabetic tab lists all properties for the selected object that can be changed at design time, as well as the current property settings. You can change the property settings by selecting the property name and typing or selecting the new setting. The Categorized tab page lists all properties for the selected object by category. For example, when a form is selected, (Name), Caption, and ForeColor are in the Appearance category. You can collapse the list to see all the categories, or you can expand a category to see its properties.

The Object Browser

One of the most useful tools in the VB editor is the Object Browser. The Object Browser is used to display the classes, properties, methods, events, and constants available from object libraries and the procedures in your project. As you are learning programming, the Object Browser will help you learn what objects and methods work with each other.

The object model can be docked on one of the editor's edges if you want, but the default is to have it in the workspace.

To dock the Object Model window:

1. Open the Tools | Options dialog.

2. Select the Docking tab.

3. Add a check box to the Object Browser entry.

If the panes in the object model are not big enough, you can resize them by dragging the edges. Use the Windows menu to switch between the Object Model and Code windows.

The Project/Library box displays the currently referenced libraries for the active project. By default, the Word, Office, and VBA libraries are listed because they are included in all projects. You can add additional libraries to the list using the Tools | References dialog box. If you are using automation to share data between other Office applications, you'll need to add the other application's object libraries also. Select All Libraries to display the objects in all the libraries at one time. As you learn Word programming, you should use the Word library most of the time instead of all libraries. The Object Browser is shown in Figure 25-2.

The following is a list of options available on the Object Browser:

- Go Back button allows you to go back to the previous selection you've used in the Classes and Members lists. Each time you click the button you move one selection. This is especially helpful when you are checking out different members of an object and you can easily return to the original object.

- Go Forward button allows you to go forward to the selections you've used in the Classes and Members lists. Each time you click the button you move one selection. You can only go forward after you go back.

- Copy to Clipboard button copies the current selection, either from the Classes or Members lists or from the Details pane at the bottom of the Object Browser, so you can paste it into your code.

- The View Definition button moves the cursor to the place in the Code window where the selection in the Members list or Classes list is defined.

- The Help button displays the online Help topic for the item selected in the Classes or the Members of list. You can also use F1 key to bring up Help.

- The Search Text Box field is used for the string that you want to use when searching for objects or other elements. If you've previously used the search function during the current session, you can select from the last four search strings in the drop-down list. Otherwise, type in the search string. You can also use wildcards when entering a string in the Search field. If you want to search for a whole word, right-click anywhere on the Object Model window and use the Find Whole Word Only command from the context menu.

- The Search button initiates a search of the libraries that matches the string you typed in the Search Text box and opens the Search Results window with the appropriate list of information. You can also press the ENTER key to start the search.

- The Show/Hide Search Results button opens or hides the Search Results pane. The Search Results pane changes to show the search results from the project or library chosen in the Project/Library list, without rerunning the search. Search results are listed alphabetically.

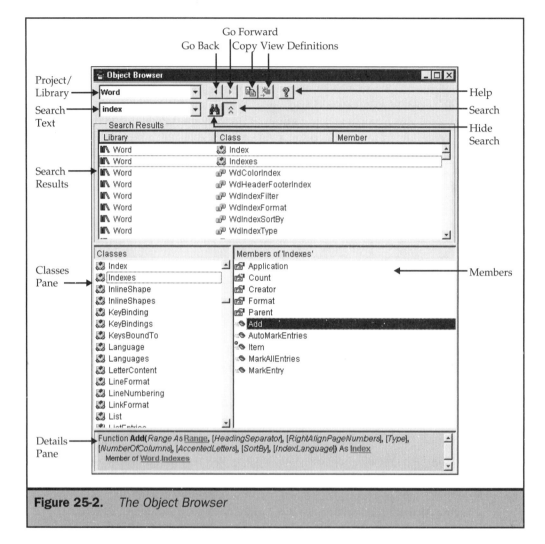

Figure 25-2.   *The Object Browser*

■ The Classes List displays all the available classes in the library or project selected in the Project/Library list. The list always begins with *<globals>*— a list of globally accessible members.

■ The Members of List displays the elements of the class selected in the Classes pane. You can change the sort order of this list by right-clicking in the pane and choosing the Group Members command on the context menu. The default sort order is alphabetical.

■ The Details pane shows you the definition of the member. Included with the definition is the syntax used for the command. The Details pane contains a hyperlink to the class or library to which the element belongs. You can copy or drag text from the Details pane to paste in the Code window.

The Code Window

The Code window is where you type your VBA code. Open code windows by double-clicking modules in the Project Explorer. You can add new modules using the Insert menu. UserForm code windows are displayed by double-clicking the form or control or right-clicking and choosing View Code. You can have as many code windows open at a time as you need. You can copy or drag code to move it between different procedures or code windows, or to the Immediate and Watches windows. You can switch between open code windows using the Windows menu.

The Code window includes the Object box drop-down on the left side of the window, which displays the name of the selected object. All objects associated with the module, document, or form are listed in the drop-down.

The Procedures/Events drop-down menu lists all the events recognized by VBA for a module, form, or control displayed in the Object box. When you select an event, the procedure associated with that event name is displayed in the Code window. Procedures are listed in the drop-down in alphabetical order; by selecting a procedure name in this drop-down, you can easily bring it up in the Code window. If General is displayed in the Object box, the Procedure box lists any declarations and all the general procedures that have been created for the form.

The Code window includes a *split bar*, which you can drag down to split the Code window into two horizontal panes. This feature, which is also in Word, allows you to view different parts of your code at the same time. The Object and Procedures/Events boxes display the information that applies to the code in the pane that is in focus. To close the pane, drag the bar to the top or bottom of the window or double-click on the bar.

The gray area in the left margin of the Code window is called the Margin Indicator bar, where the margin indicators are displayed. Margin indicators include debugging tools like breakpoints and run to cursor marks.

In the lower-left corner of the Code window are two icons. The first is the Procedure View icon; press it to display the selected procedure. This hides all the other macros in the module and makes it easier to work with long macros or modules containing a lot of macros. The Full Module View icon displays the entire code in the module.

The Locals Window

The Locals window is used for debugging and testing your code. It displays all the declared variables in the current procedure and their values. When you have the Locals window showing, it is automatically updated when there is a change from Run to Break mode or when you navigate in the Stack display.

Note   *Run to Break is what you do when you set a breakpoint to halt the program at a specific place in the code where you think there is an error. A breakpoint is a statement or set of conditions which causes VBA to automatically stop execution and puts the application in a paused state before running the statement containing the breakpoint. When the code is in break mode, you can continue from the breakpoint forward. By contrast, if the code execution is stopped, it needs to start again from the beginning.*

The top of the window lists the name of the macro that is currently running. The button on the right side is the Calls Stack button, which opens the Call Stack dialog box, displaying a list of the procedures in the call stack.

The Expression column displays the names of the variables. The first variable in the list is a special module variable and can be expanded to display all module-level variables in the current module. For standard modules, the first variable is the *<name of the current module>*. For a class module, the system variable <Me> is defined. You can expand and collapse the list by clicking the plus and minus signs to the left of the expression.

The Value column lists the value of a variable. This column is editable—just click a value and the cursor changes to an I-beam. Press ENTER or click the screen to validate the change. If the value you entered is illegal, the Edit field remains active and the value is highlighted. A message box describing the error also appears. If you need to cancel a change, press ESC. All numeric variables must have a value listed. String variables can have an empty Value list. The Type column contains the variable type. This column is for information only and is not editable.

Immediate Window

The Immediate window is another useful debugging tool. Type the command **Debug.Print** at points within your code for debugging, and the variables display in the Immediate window.

You can also type or paste a line of code into the Immediate window and press ENTER to run it. For example, type **?Application.Name** or **print 2*2** in the Immediate window and press ENTER. It might not replace your calculator, but it is handy.

To clear the results from the Immediate window, click in the Immediate window, and then Edit | Select All and Edit | Clear, or press CTRL+A and the BACKSPACE or DELETE key.

Watch Expressions Window

The final debugging window included with the VBE is the Watch Expressions window. To use it, right-click on code in the Code window and choose Add Watch or select and drag the variable from the Code window to the Watch Expressions window (see Figure 25-3). The value of the expression at the point of the watch is displayed in the Watch Expressions window. The Expression field is editable in this window.

To edit or delete watches, select the watch and right-click, or choose Delete Watch from the context menu.

To use a watch you first need to set an expression to be watched. The expression can be a combination of keywords, operators, variables, and constants that produce a result. You set the watch to do something when the expression matches the variable in the running code. You can have the code break, or stop running, when the value is reached or changed. Or you can have the expression watched and the result is returned only when you break the code. For example, in Figure 25-4, the watch is for the variable myValue to equal 50. When myValue reaches 50 the code will stop running.

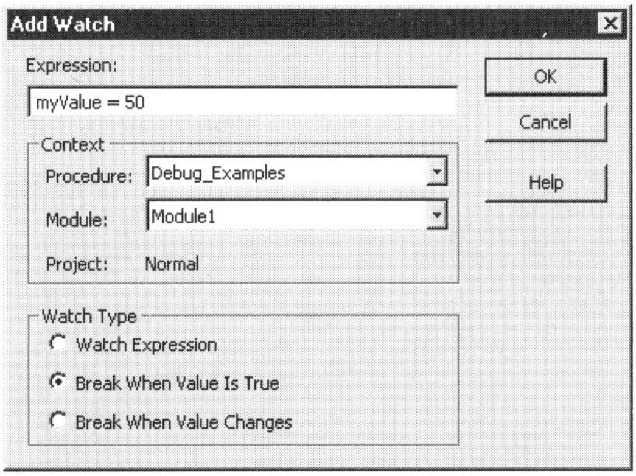

Figure 25-3. *The Add Watch window*

To get an idea of what the Immediate, Locals, and Watch windows can actually do, type this simple code into a Code window:

```
Sub Debug_Examples()
Dim myString As String
For myValue = 1 To 100
myString = "The value is " & myValue
Debug.Print myString
Next myValue
End Sub
```

If the Immediate, Locals, and Watch windows are not visible, enable each window from the View menu (see Figure 25-4). To add a watch, right-click in the Watch window and chose Add Watch from the context menu. In the Add Watch dialog, type **myValue = 50** for the expression. Select Break When Value Is True as the Watch Type. Press F8 to step through the macro one statement at a time. You can see how the code moves between the statements and increments the value of the myValue variable. The Locals window displays the current value of myValue, and Debug.Print writes myString to the Immediate window.

The UserForm Window

The UserForm window is used to create dialog boxes for your project. Use the Control toolbox to add controls to the form (see Figure 25-5). UserForms can contain macros—either double-click the form or a control on the form.

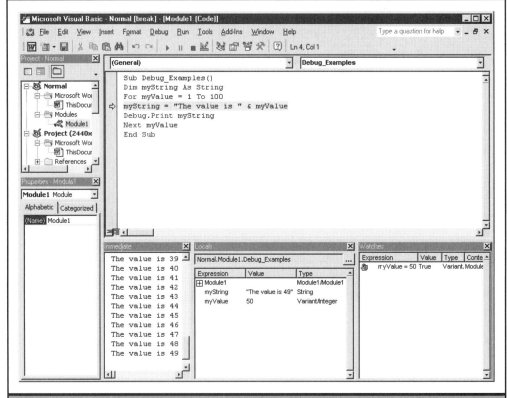

Figure 25-4. *VBE with the Immediate, Locals, and Watch windows enabled; the Watch stopped execution of the code, when myValue equals 50, before the Debug.Print statement writes the next myString to the Immediate window*

The Control Toolbox

The Control toolbox displays the standard VB controls, also known as common controls, plus any ActiveX controls you have added to your project.

You can customize the toolbox by adding controls using the Additional Controls command from the Tools menu or right-clicking the Control toolbox. This brings up the Additional Controls dialog. Many of the controls listed are not intended for use in Word and won't work, but it doesn't hurt to try. If the control doesn't work or gives you an error message, you know it's one of those controls that will not work with Word. Don't add every control to the toolbox just because you can, add only what you need for your project. You can add additional tabs to the toolbox by right-clicking the

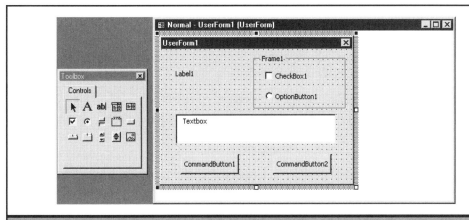

Figure 25-5.   *A UserForm with some of the controls from the Control toolbox on and
the Control toolbox*

Controls tab. When you add a new page, a Select Objects tool is always available on the
page. See Table 25-1 for a complete list of common controls.

Control	Purpose
Select Objects	Puts the cursor back into pointer mode so you can move or resize controls.
Label	Allows you to include text that you don't want changed, such as captions or instructions on the page.
TextBox	Allows the user to edit or add text to the form.
ComboBox	Combination of a list box and text box. The user can either choose an item from the list or enter a value in the text box.
ListBox	Displays a list of items to choose from. The list can be scrolled if it has more items than can be displayed at one time.
CheckBox	Creates a box that is used to indicate if something is true or false, or to display multiple choices when the user can choose more than one.

Table 25-1.   *Tools Needed to Create Custom Forms*

Control	Purpose
OptionButton	Allows you to display multiple choices from which the user can choose only one.
ToggleButton	Creates a button that toggles options on and off.
Frame	Allows you to create a graphical or functional grouping for controls. To group controls, draw the frame first, and then draw controls inside the frame.
Command Button	Creates a button the user can click to carry out a command. Macros are often associated with CommandButtons.
TabStrip	Allows you to define multiple pages for the same area of a window or dialog box in your application. Cannot contain other controls.
MultiPage	Similar to TabStrip but can contain other controls.
ScrollBar	Provides a tool for quickly moving through a long list of items or a large amount of information and for indicating the current position on a scale.
SpinButton	A spinner control you can use with another control scroll back and forth through a range of values or a list of items.
Image	Displays a graphical image from a bitmap, an icon, or a metafile on your form. Can be used for decorative purposes or as a button and have macros attached.

Table 25-1.   *Tools Needed to Create Custom Forms* (continued)

Using the Toolbars

VBE includes four toolbars—Debug, Edit, Standard, and UserForm—with useful programming commands. Many of these commands are also accessible from menus and shortcut keys. As with many Windows programs, the toolbars can be customized if you want to add or remove commands.

While the toolbars may have the same names as some of the menus, they are not replacements for the menus, but groupings of the most frequently used menu items. To display the toolbars, use the View | Toolbar menu or right-click the menu bar and select the toolbar you want visible. If you need reminders about what the buttons are for you can turn on the ToolTips by selecting the Show ToolTips option in the Tools |

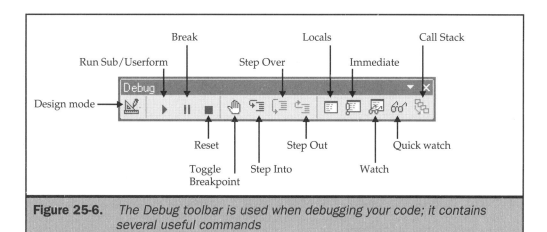

Figure 25-6. *The Debug toolbar is used when debugging your code; it contains several useful commands*

Options | General tab dialog box. You can also enable keyboard shortcuts in ToolTips for the buttons using the View | Toolbar | Customize dialog, look on the Options tab, and check the box to "Show Shortcut Keys in Screen Tips". I recommend learning some of the keyboard shortcuts; the keyboard is often easier when testing code, even for confirmed mousers like myself.

The Debug Toolbar

The Debug toolbar (see Figure 25-6) includes several of the most useful debugging commands grouped together on one toolbar. While three of the commands are also on the Debug menu, it's not a replacement for the Debug menu.

Table 25-2 lists the buttons available on the Debug toolbar, what they do, and the keyboard shortcut, when available.

Toolbar Button	Action	Keyboard Shortcut
Design Mode	Turns design mode off and on.	
Run Sub/UserForm or Run Macro	Runs the current procedure if the cursor is in a procedure, runs the UserForm if a UserForm is currently active, otherwise runs a macro.	F5

Table 25-2. *Debug Toolbar Buttons*

Toolbar Button	Action	Keyboard Shortcut
Break	Stops execution of a program while it is running and switches to break mode.	CTRL+BREAK
Reset	Clears the execution stack and module-level variables and resets the project.	
Toggle Breakpoint	Sets or removes a breakpoint at the current line.	F9
Step Into	Runs one code statement at a time.	F8
Step Over	Runs one code procedure or statement at a time in the Code window.	SHIFT+F8
Step Out	Runs the remaining lines of the current procedure.	CTRL+SHIFT+F8
Locals Window	Displays the Locals window.	
Immediate Window	Displays the Immediate window.	CTRL+G
Watch Window	Displays the Watch window.	
Quick Watch	Displays the Quick Watch dialog box with the current value of the selected expression.	SHIFT+F9
Call Stack	Displays the Calls dialog box, which lists the currently active procedure calls (procedures in the application that have started but are not completed).	CTRL+L

Table 25-2.   *Debug Toolbar Buttons* (continued)

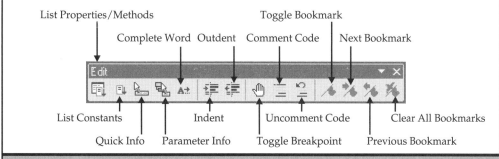

Figure 25-7.   *The Edit toolbar contains many of the commands you'll find helpful when editing, especially the Comment Code and Uncomment Code buttons*

The Edit Toolbar

The commands on the Edit toolbar (see Figure 25-7) are useful when you are writing code. The first two commands, List Properties/Methods and List Constants, are used to display information about the object, method, or property under the cursor. The Quick Info and Parameter Info commands give you information about the proper syntax of the method, property, or function at the position of the cursor.

Figure 25-8 is an example of the Quick Info featur; the Parameter Info command would provide a similar display.

The comment and uncomment buttons are used to quickly mark out code and then restore it when debugging procedures. Table 25-3 is a list of the buttons found on the Edit toolbar, the action the button carries out, and the keyboard shortcuts.

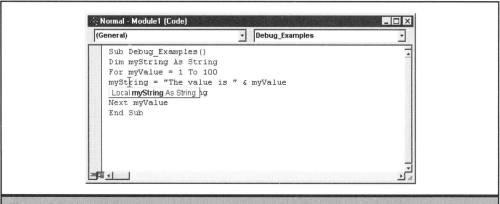

Figure 25-8.   *An example using Quick Info to display information about the item at the position of the cursor*

Toolbar Button	Action	Keyboard Shortcut
List Properties/ Methods	Shows the properties and methods available for the object that precedes the period (.).	CTRL+J
List Constants	Shows the constants that are valid choices for the property you typed and that precede the equals sign (=).	CTRL+SHIFT+J
Quick Info	Displays the syntax for a variable, function, method, or procedure based on the position of the cursor within the name of the function, method, or procedure.	CTRL+I
Parameter Info	Displays information about the parameters of the function where the cursor is located.	CTRL+SHIFT+I
Complete Word	Accepts the characters that Visual Basic automatically adds to the word you are typing.	CTRL+SPACEBAR
Indent	Shifts all lines in the selection to the next tab stop.	TAB
Outdent	Shifts all lines in the selection to the previous tab stop.	SHIFT+TAB
Toggle Breakpoint	Sets or removes a breakpoint at the current line.	F9
Comment Block	Adds comment characters to the beginning of each line of a selected block of text.	

Table 25-3.   *Edit Toolbar Commands*

Toolbar Button	Action	Keyboard Shortcut
Uncomment Block	Removes the comment character from each line of a selected block of text.	
Toggle Bookmark	Toggles a bookmark on or off for the active line in the Code window.	
Next Bookmark	Moves the focus to the next bookmark in the bookmark stack.	
Previous Bookmark	Moves the focus to the previous bookmark in the bookmark stack.	
Clear All Bookmarks	Removes all bookmarks.	

Table 25-3.   *Edit Toolbar Commands* (continued)

The Standard Toolbar

The Standard toolbar is visible in the VB Editor by default. This contains all the basic toolbar buttons, many of which you are already familiar with. It also includes buttons to hide and show the Project Explorer, Properties Window, Object Browser, and Control toolbox, when a form is active. The position of the cursor is also shown, which is helpful should an error code indicate there is an error on a specific line. Figure 25-8 shows the Standard toolbar, which contains several familiar commands.

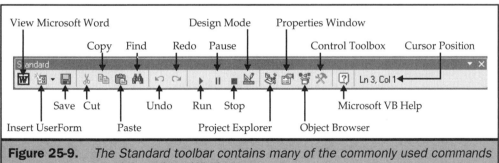

Figure 25-9.   *The Standard toolbar contains many of the commonly used commands used throughout Windows*

Table 25-4 contains a complete list of the Standard toolbar buttons, their purposes, and any keyboard shortcuts available.

Toolbar Button	Action	Keyboard Shortcut
View Microsoft Word	Toggles between Word and the VB Editor.	ALT+F11
Insert	Used to insert a UserForm, Module, Class Module, or Procedure into your active project. The icon changes to the last object you added. The default is UserForm.	
Save <*current template or document*>	Saves the document including the project and all of its components such as forms and modules.	CTRL+S
Cut	Deletes the selected control or text and places it on the Clipboard.	CTRL+X
Copy	Copies the selected control or text onto the Clipboard.	CTRL+C
Paste	Inserts the contents of the Clipboard at the current location.	CTRL+V
Find	Opens the Find dialog box and searches for the specified text in the Find What box.	CTRL+F
Undo	Reverses the last editing action.	CTRL+Z
Redo	Restores the last text editing Undo actions if no other actions have occurred since the last undo.	

Table 25-4. *Standard Toolbar Buttons*

Toolbar Button	Action	Keyboard Shortcut
Run Sub/UserForm or Run Macro	Runs the current procedure if the cursor is in a procedure, runs the UserForm if a UserForm is currently active, or runs a macro if neither the Code window nor a UserForm is active.	F5
Break	Stops the program when it's running and switches to Break mode.	CTRL+BREAK
Reset	Clears the execution stack and module-level variables and resets the project.	
Design Mode	Turns design mode off and on.	
Project Explorer	Displays the Project Explorer.	CTRL+R
Properties Window	Opens the Properties window.	F4
Object Browser	Displays the Object Browser.	F2
Toolbox	Displays or hides the toolbox. This is only available when a UserForm is active.	
Microsoft Visual Basic Help	Opens VBA Help.	F1

Table 25-4. *Standard Toolbar Buttons* (continued)

The UserForm Toolbar

The UserForm toolbar (see Figure 25-10) contains commands used for designing forms. The alignment options adjust the placement of the objects precisely in relation to other objects. The object with the white sizing handles controls the positioning; other objects will be aligned with this object. To select multiple objects, click one object, and then hold CTRL or SHIFT and click the other objects.

Table 25-5 lists the commands available on the UserForm toolbar, along with the keyboard shortcuts for the commands. Only the Bring to Front and Send to Back have assigned shortcuts.

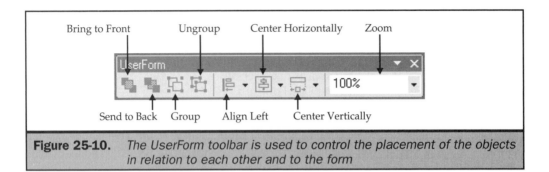

Bring to Front   Ungroup   Center Horizontally   Zoom

Send to Back   Group   Align Left   Center Vertically

Figure 25-10. *The UserForm toolbar is used to control the placement of the objects in relation to each other and to the form*

Managing Your Project Elements

You aren't finished just because when your project is complete and bug-free. You may want to keep backup copies, rename modules, rearrange the procedures in the modules, or remove some completely. Many module-level housekeeping tasks can be completed from either Word's Organizer or from the VB Editor, whereas most procedure-level tasks can only be done from the editor.

Toolbar Button	Action	Keyboard Shortcut
Bring to Front	Moves the selected objects to the front of all other objects on the form.	CTRL+J
Send to Back	Moves the selected objects behind all other objects on the form.	CTRL+K
Group	Creates a group of the selected objects.	
Ungroup	Ungroups the objects that were previously grouped. The group needs to be selected for this action to work.	

Table 25-5. *UserForm Toolbar Commands*

Toolbar Button	Action	Keyboard Shortcut
Align	Lefts is used to align the horizontal position of the selected objects with the left edges. Centers is used to align the horizontal position of the selected objects on the centers. Rights is used to align the horizontal position of the selected objects with the right edges. Tops is used to align the vertical position of the selected objects on the top edges. Middles is used to align the vertical position of selected objects with the middle of the objects. Bottoms is used to align the vertical position of the selected objects with the bottom edge. To Grid is used to align the top left of the selected object to the closest grid. The object is not resized.	
Center	Horizontally—Centers the selected objects horizontally. Vertically—Centers the selected objects vertically in relation to the form.	
Make Same Size	Width—Adjusts width. Height—Adjusts height. Both—Adjusts both the width and the height. Based on the control with white sizing handles.	

Table 25-5. *UserForm Toolbar Commands* (continued)

Toolbar Button	Action	Keyboard Shortcut
Zoom	Reduces or enlarges the display of all controls on the UserForm. You can set any magnification between 10–400 percent, either by selecting a preset magnification or typing in any value.	

Table 25-5. *UserForm Toolbar Commands* (continued)

Procedure-level tasks include renaming, deleting, copying, or moving subs and procedures contained in modules and forms. These tasks are done in the VB Editor using the same techniques you use in any other document—cut or copy and paste in the new location. You can delete macros from Word using the Tools | Macro dialog—just select the macro you want to delete and click the Delete button.

It's better to choose the right name for your procedures when you are writing them, not later on. If the procedure is referenced by other procedures, you need to change those references, too. If you really must rename procedures, just select the sub name in the code and enter the new name.

Renaming Modules

Renaming the modules, class modules, and UserForms is easy; select the module or form in the Project Explorer and change the name by editing the (name) property in the Properties window. You can also rename modules from Word's Organizer. Using the Organizer is covered Chapter 23, "Managing Modules Using Organizer."

Deleting Modules and UserForms

Modules and forms are deleted from the VB editor by right-clicking the module and choosing Remove *name* from the context menu. You'll be offered the option of saving the code before removing it. If you want to use the code in other projects or think you might change your mind, export it before removing. If you delete the module or form from Word's Organizer, you aren't offered the opportunity to export it.

Copying Modules and UserForms

If you need to copy modules or forms between projects, it's as simple as dragging from one to the other. Just select the module and hold down the left mouse button as you drag it to the other project. You can export from one project and import into another; this gives you the added benefit of having backup copies of the Visual Basic files, which can be imported into other projects. You can't actually move a module to another project and have it be removed from the original project in one step. You'll need to remove the module in a second step.

Saving Your Project

There are several methods you can use to save copies of your project. The most obvious is to keep a backup copy of all your project files. While this is always a good idea, there are other methods you can use to save your projects that might make more sense, especially if you think you'll need the modules or forms in other projects. The easiest way to save parts of your project for reuse in other projects is to use the File | Export menu and save copies of modules and forms as Visual Basic files that can be imported into other VBA projects. Code samples can be copied and pasted into Notepad files. These can be imported into a project, using the Insert | File menu.

Signing Your Projects

Because of heightened macro security features in Word, unsigned macros are disabled if the template is not stored in Word's Template folder. Because new documents may not be stored in the Template folder, Word's security features will disable the macros. You can lower the security settings in Tools | Macros | Security, but this is not recommended. Signing and trusting macros is easy and much safer.

Before you can sign your macros, you need a digital certificate. If you have one you use for digitally signing mail, it can be used for signing your macros for sharing with friends and co-workers. They should have their macro security set to Medium so they can enable the macros. The e-mail certificates are Class 1 certificates and are not appropriate for signing macros you intend to distribute on a wide scale. You should get a Class 2 or Developer's certificate if you want to distribute your work on a wider scale.

If you don't have a digital certificate, Office includes a small application called SelfCert.exe that creates a certificate you can use. If installed, it can be found at C:\Program Files\Microsoft Office\Office10; otherwise, rerun Office setup and choose Add or Remove features. Select Digital Signature for VBA Projects, listed under Office Shared Features. The SelfCert certificate can only be used to sign macros that are used on the computer the certificate was created on, it is not intended to be used on macros you want to share with others.

To sign your project, select the template in the Project Explorer window. From the Tools menu, choose Digital Signature, select the signature you want to use to sign the project, and click OK.

Wait until the project is complete before signing it because editing the code in any way removes the digital signature. To prevent users from editing the project and removing the signature, lock the project before signing it. To lock a project is simply to password protect it. Choose the Tools | Normal Properties menu, Protection tab. Check the Lock project for viewing and type in a password. Use a password you'll remember or you won't be able to edit it later.

Using Help

Visual Basic's Help is one Help file worth using. Press F1 in either Word or the VB Editor to load Help. If you used the typical install of Office, VBA Help is installed on first run, and you'll need to have your Office CD handy. If you access it from Word, VBA Help is under the Programming Information topic. You may find a limited number of Help topics are prefixed with WEB. These are available only online so you'll need to be connected to the Internet to use them. Fortunately, there aren't many of these within VBA Help.

One little trick to remember is to place the cursor within your code, and then press F1 to bring up Help for that word. Naturally this only works for native VB keywords such as objects, properties, and methods, not objects or variables you create. If you are stuck on proper syntax for a keyword, this is easier than bringing up Help and searching for the keyword yourself.

If you need additional help, Microsoft has several excellent online resources. In addition to TechNet and MSDN, the Microsoft Knowledge Base and the Office Resource Kit are also good sources of online help:

- **TechNet** http://www.microsoft.com/technet/
- **MSDN** http://msdn.microsoft.com/default.asp
- **Knowledge Base** http://search.support.microsoft.com/kb/c.asp
- **Office Resource Kit** http://www.microsoft.com/office/ork/

Debugging Your Project

It's all but impossible to write code without some errors in it the first time you run it. The larger the project, the more errors it will likely have. How you deal with the errors may be the most important part of your project. There are two kinds of errors: development that you can prevent, and run-time, which may not be preventable but can be trapped.

Development errors are either syntax errors or logic errors. Typographical errors and missing punctuation are common syntax errors, as is forgetting to properly terminate statements, like with an If…Then…Else statement. These are generally silly mistakes and often the hardest to pick up on but the easiest to correct. Real "bugs" are logic errors and occur when code executes without causing an error but does not produce the results intended. These bugs are eliminated by debugging the code.

Errors that occur while the application is running are called run-time errors. These are errors where otherwise correct code fails because of invalid data or system conditions that prevent the code from executing. You need to use error handler routines to deal with run-time errors or write procedures that can validate data to ensure only valid data is used by the procedure.

The VB Editor includes several features that can help you debug your code. You can turn these on from the Tools | Options menu | Editor tab | Code Settings. Most of these options are enabled by default, and turning all these settings on often makes it easier to debug code.

The Require Variable Declaration option inserts the Option Explicit statement in the first line of any module you add to the project. The Option Explicit statement forces you to declare every variable and prevents one of most difficult bugs to spot—misspelled variable names.

The Auto Syntax Check option specifies if each line of code is checked for errors as soon as you finish writing a line of code and press ENTER. If this option is not selected, the syntax is checked before it's compiled or run. By enabling Auto Syntax Check option for every line, you are notified of errors immediately and can correct them before going any further. If you wait until the procedure is run, you might be overwhelmed by one error after another.

The Auto Data Tips option specifies if you can view the data contained in a variable while in break mode by resting the mouse pointer on the variable name. This is a very helpful feature you'll want to use.

On the Tools | Options | General tab, the Error Trapping section allows you to specify what will happen when an error occurs in your code. You will want to use different Error Trapping options depending on where you are in the debugging process. The default setting is Break on Unhandled Errors, and most of the time this is the best selection. If you are working with class modules, you'll want to use the Break in Class Module option so that you can identify the errors in the class module. If you don't use Break in Class Module, any errors in a class module will cause code to break in the procedure that called the class module instead of in the class module itself. If your project does not have any class modules and this option is selected, the code will break on unhandled errors.

Run-Time Tools

The VB Editor includes run-time debugging tools that are designed to give you a snapshot of what is happening in your code at any point. Table 25-6 lists the run-time tools along with short descriptions of what they do. Although the Immediate, Locals, and Watch Expression windows were covered previously, they are mentioned again here as a reminder of how important they are when debugging code.

Using Assertions

You know when an error occurs that the code is buggy or broken. But just because a procedure runs without errors doesn't mean that the code is bug-free. You might be using invalid data that is hiding the bugs.

Tool	Description
Breakpoints	Breakpoints stop program execution on any line of executable code. A breakpoint will stop your code on the line of code that will be executed next. Once your code hits a breakpoint, it's in break mode until you press F5 to continue.
Step modes	There are four step modes you can use to start a subroutine or to continue after a breakpoint. These are Step Into, Step Over, Step Out, and Run To Cursor. You can use these modes and remain in break mode.
Locals window	Shows the values of all variables, constants, objects, and properties of objects currently in scope when code is in break mode.
Watch expressions	Watch expressions let you monitor the value of any variable, property, object, or expression as your code executes. They also let you specify that your code should enter break mode under certain conditions, such as if an expression is true or if the value changes. You can use the Quick Watch dialog box to quickly check the value of a variable or expression instead of using Watch.
Immediate window	All Debug.Print statements are output to the Immediate window. When in break mode, this has the same scope as the procedure with the breakpoint so you can test and change the value of variables. You can use the Immediate window to call procedures and test them with different data without running your application from the beginning.
Call stack	Lists all active procedures when code is in break mode. This helps you trace the execution of the code and highlights the possible location of errors in the active procedures.

Table 25-6.   *Run-Time Tools Provided for Debugging Your Projects*

Assertions can be used to test for conditions in your code that will cause the code to enter break mode if the data is not what you are expecting. For example, if a statement is true, nothing happens. If it's false, the code goes into break mode with the line containing the false statement highlighted.

The Debug object uses the Assert method to test the truth of a condition or statement in your code. The Assert method is similar to setting a Watch expression that will break when a statement is true. If you are using the Assert method, the break will occur when the statement asserted is false.

Using the code sample from earlier, instead of using a Watch expression to break when the value of myValue is 50, you use Assert to break the code when myValue exceeds 50 and the Assert is false. As long as the value is under 50, the Assert is true and the code continues running; as soon as the value hits 50, the execution of the macro is stopped by the Assert statement. The following code sample demonstrates how the Assert statement works:

```
Sub Debug_Examples()
Dim myString As String
For myValue = 1 To 100
myString = "The value is " & myValue
Debug.Assert myValue < 50
Next myValue
End Sub
```

After your code is bug-free, you need to remove the Assert statements before distributing the code. You don't want your project to stop on the Assert conditions once you have corrected all errors or added proper error handlers. The easiest way to remove Assert conditions is to use Find and delete those lines.

Basic Error Handling

Error-handling code can be simple or sophisticated. It can display a message to the user or log information about the error to a file. But no matter how you implement an error handler, the basic components are the same. An error handler consists of code that does the following:

- The On Error statement specifies what to do if an error occurs.
- Handles the error that has occurred using your code.
- The Resume or Exit statement specifies how program execution is to continue.

If you don't use an On Error statement, any run-time error that occurs generates an error message and the procedure stops. There are three types of On Error statements you can use. "On Error GoTo line" jumps to the line listed when an error occurs. The line can be identified by either a line number or label. With "On Error Resume Next" when an error occurs the procedure continues with the next statement. On Error GoTo 0 disables error handlers in the current procedure. Table 25-7 lists the OnError statements and their uses.

The following code shows how to use On Error GoTo to bypass errors. Type this code into a module and step through it using F8, with the Locals and Immediate windows showing. You see that it skips the SaveAs statement because the filename contains invalid characters. If you correct the cause of the error by adding quotes around the date format ("mmddyy") and step through it again, you'll see it ends with the Exit Sub line. Comment out the two lines added for error handling—add an apostrophe at the beginning of each line—and you'll get run-time error 5152:

```
Public Sub Error_Test()
On Error GoTo ErrorHandler
docname = Format(Now(), mmddyy)
ActiveDocument.SaveAs FileName:="c:\" & docname, _
 FileFormat:=wdFormatDocument
 Debug.Print "saved " & docname & " exit sub"
Exit Sub
ErrorHandler:
 Debug.Print "failed on filename " & docname
End Sub
```

To prevent error-handling code from running when no error has occurred, always place an Exit Sub, Exit Function, or Exit Property statement immediately before the error-handling routine as shown in the preceding example.

OnError Statement	Action
On Error GoTo line	Specifies that when an error occurs, the procedure jumps to the line listed, either by line number or label.
On Error Resume Next	Specifies that when an error occurs the procedure continues with the next statement. Use this instead of On Error GoTo when accessing objects.
On Error GoTo 0	Disables any enabled error handler in the current procedure.

Table 25-7.   *OnError Statements You Can Use in Your Error Handler*

An error handler that is turned on by an On Error statement is enabled, when in the process of handling an error; its active until a Resume, an Exit Sub, an Exit Function, or an Exit Property statement ends the procedure. Active error handlers can only handle one error at a time; if an error occurs while an error handler is active, the current procedure's error handler can't handle the error. If there are no other inactive error handlers available, the procedure experiences a fatal error and ends. Once an error is handled by an error handler in any procedure, execution resumes in at the point designated by the Resume statement.

Error-handling routines use the value in the Number property of the Err object to determine the cause of the error. The values in the Err object reflect only the most recent error; if you want a record of all errors, you'll need to save the error numbers and descriptions before the next error occurs or the procedure ends. The error number is returned using the Err.Number property; the error message is returned using the Err.Description property.

Change the sample code to show the error number and description. You can replace Debug.Print with MsgBox if you'd like, although message boxes can be annoying when testing code.

```
ErrorHandler:
Debug.Print Err.Number
Debug.Print Err.Description
```

On Error Resume Next causes the procedure to continue with the statement immediately following the statement that caused the error, allowing the procedure to continue despite the error. An On Error Resume Next statement becomes inactive when another procedure is called, so you should execute an On Error Resume Next statement in each called routine if you want inline error handling within that routine.

On Error GoTo 0 disables error handling in the current procedure. Without an On Error GoTo 0 statement, an error handler is automatically disabled when a procedure exits.

Using the VB Editor with the Macro Recorder

The macro recorder makes it easy to record macros, but it writes really sloppy code. It records everything, whether you want to use everything or not. But it can be faster than writing the code, especially if you don't remember the commands you want to use and need to look them up in Help. I often record commands in a new macro and then copy the commands I need to my procedure.

Editing Recorded Macros

Once you've recorded a macro, you'll probably want to edit it. Find the macro in the VB editor either from the Tools | Macros dialog by selecting the macro and pressing the Edit button or opening the VBE and finding the module it's in and locating the macro by name in the procedure drop-down on the top right of the code window.

With the macro loaded in the Code window, read through the code. Determine exactly which lines you need and delete the others. If you can't determine by reading the code which commands are the ones you need, place the cursor on the word and press F1. Help will load with information about the keyword. The following sections offer some examples of macros and techniques you might find helpful.

Making Your Own Find and Replace Feature

A popular macro is one for find and replace. You can save a lot of steps by creating a macro for find and replace commands that are used often—for many users it's replacing two spaces with one, or replacing one space between sentences with two. Whatever your typing habits are, you can change the document easier than you can change your typing habits.

Open a document and start the macro recorder. Name the macro and add any comments you want, and then begin recording the steps. In the Find field press the SPACEBAR twice; in the Replace field press it once. Then press the Replace All button. When it's done, press OK.

This macro doesn't have a lot of extra code in it that needs removed. But, if you want to create several different search macros or if you accidentally added extra movements when recording it, you can open the VB Editor and copy the code to another macro and change the search and replace strings or edit out extra lines.

What if you want to automate the search but the find and replace strings aren't always the same? Easy: Use string values instead of hardcoding the find and replace values. Add a dialog box for inputting each string using the InputBox function. Read through your code and locate the find and replace strings, replacing them with the variables that you are using in the InputBox. In this example, the variables are FindValue and ReplaceValue.

```
Sub Replace2Spaces()
Dim Message, Title, Default, FindValue, ReplaceValue
'Find dialog
Message = "Enter the string you want to find"
Title = "Find String"
FindValue = InputBox(Message, Title)
'Search dialog
Message = "Enter the string you want to replace " _
          & FindValue
Title = "Replacement String"
ReplaceValue = InputBox(Message, Title)

'Do Search and Replace
```

```
Selection.Find.ClearFormatting
    Selection.Find.Replacement.ClearFormatting
    With Selection.Find
        .Text = FindValue
        .Replacement.Text = ReplaceValue
        .Forward = True
        .Wrap = wdFindContinue
        .Format = False
        .MatchCase = False
        .MatchWholeWord = False
        .MatchWildcards = False
        .MatchSoundsLike = False
        .MatchAllWordForms = False
    End With
    Selection.Find.Execute Replace:=wdReplaceAll
End Sub
```

It doesn't get much easier than this—a find and replace macro that is faster and easier to use than the built-in Find and Replace command.

 If you need a sample document to test this macro with, type =rand(20,10) into a new document and press ENTER. The document will write "The quick brown fox jumps over the lazy dog." 10 times in each of 20 paragraphs. You can use any number for paragraphs and sentences but this will create a nice-sized document.

Working with Toggles

As I've mentioned earlier, you can't record commands that act as toggles and have them be in a specific state. For example, recording the ruler command toggles the rulers off and on. If you add this to your code, it reverses the current state of the ruler rather than explicitly turning it on or off.

```
ActiveWindow.ActivePane.DisplayRulers = _
Not ActiveWindow.ActivePane.DisplayRulers
```

If you want to ensure the ruler is in an explicit state of either on or off, you need to use True or False keywords. This leaves the ruler turned on if it's already on or turns it on if it's turned off.

```
Sub Enable_Ruler()
 ActiveWindow.ActivePane.DisplayRulers = True
End Sub
```

Not all toggle commands record toggle code like DisplayRulers does. For example, recording toolbars being turned off and on gives you either true or false keywords.

```
CommandBars("Task Pane").Visible = False
```

This is easy enough to convert to toggle code, taking a clue from DisplayRulers and use the Not operator.

```
Public Sub toggle_taskpane()
 CommandBars("Task Pane").Visible = _
 Not CommandBars("Task Pane").Visible
End Sub
```

If...Then...Else

Many commands can use the Not operator to toggle between states, but if you want two or more conditions to behave in a specific manner depending on the state of the other one, you'll need to use the logical If…Then…Else statement. "If the condition is true, then do something, else do something different." It's as easy as it sounds to do.

The following code example shows paragraph marks and hides space marks or hides paragraph marks and shows spaces.

```
Sub ToggleParaSpaces()
If ActiveWindow.View.ShowParagraphs = True Then
With ActiveWindow.View
    .ShowParagraphs = False
    .ShowSpaces = True
End With
Else
With ActiveWindow.View
    .ShowSpaces = False
    .ShowParagraphs = True
End With
End If
End Sub
```

The With statement allows you to perform a series of statements on a specified object without requalifying the name of the object. It is the same as writing the statements out, but will execute faster because there are less dots (periods), which means there are less objects being qualified. It also saves you a few keystrokes because there is less typing.

```
ActiveWindow.View.ShowSpaces = False
ActiveWindow.View.ShowParagraphs = True
```

On a short macro, it doesn't matter, but on longer macros using With instead of repeating the object can save a lot of execution time. When you use With you need to close it with End.

Ten Tips for Working with Visual Basic

Working with Visual Basic isn't just for programmers. Anyone can do it. It's easy to start by recording macros and progress to writing your own code. These ten tips are by no means the final word on what's best when writing programming projects for Word.

1. Learn to Use the Visual Basic Editor's Tools   The VB Editor includes powerful tools like the Immediate, Locals, and Watch expressions windows. Get in the habit of using them often; they'll show you a lot of information about how your project works.

2. Browse the Object Model   The easiest way to learn about programming Word is to learn about the object model. Learn what you can do and what you can't do. Learn the differences between objects, methods, functions, and variables (and all the other parts, too). You don't have to commit everything to memory; the Object Browser is just an F2 away.

3. Help Is Your Friend   Along with the Object Browser, Help is often under used. Help on any word—objects, methods, functions—can be instantly accessed by placing the cursor in the word and pressing F1. This opens Help directly to the keyword.

4. VBA Code Doesn't Bite   Don't be afraid of using the VBE to read and edit your code. Play around with your code, have some fun with it. Practice on sample documents. Comment out code instead of deleting it, that way it's easier to restore if you deleted the wrong lines.

5. Don't Rely on the Macro Recorder   The macro recorder is fast and easy. But not everything can be recorded, and the code it does record often has a lot of excess lines. Learn to write your own code, and you can do so much more. If you want to cheat and use the macro recorder, fine, but learn to edit it, too.

6. Learn Time-Saving Coding Practices   With is not the only statement that can make your code run faster; there are other techniques that you can use to speed it up. A few more of many speed tips include

- Reduce the number of dots (periods) as much as possible.
- Assign property values to variables and use the variables.
- Keep the code tight; delete code that isn't used.
- Don't repeat the same code over and over; put it in its own macro and call the macro instead.

7. Always Use Error Handlers   Get in the habit of using an error handler on longer procedures. Not all macros need error handlers, but as projects get more complicated, it's easy to inadvertently make mistakes that are easy to overlook and hard to find.

8. Test Your Code and Then Test It Some More   Thoroughly test your code as you write it. Use F8 to step through the code, and watch what the code does. Test it again when you think it's done. Use Debug.Print and Debug.Assert to see if the code is doing what you want it to. Use the Locals and Immediate windows, too.

9. Save Your Projects   Get in the habit of pressing the Save button often. Export your work into Visual Basic BAS files or copy and paste code into Notepad. Create a code library; you might want to reuse some of it in other projects.

10. Keep Your Code Together   Group similar macros or procedures together in a module. Use as many modules as you need to categorize your projects. You don't want to go overboard with modules, but by grouping procedures you can find them easier. Name the modules to reflect the type of macros in the module.

Chapter 26

Advanced VBA Use and Word

With this final chapter on using VBA in Word, you'll learn about more advanced coding practices, such as how to create your own functions, write better procedures, name your objects and variables, and make the procedure run faster. These few chapters are not intended to teach you to be an expert programmer, but they will give you a base for working with VBA in Word.

You can do a lot with a macro recorder without really knowing VBA, but as your ideas get more complicated, you need to learn to write and understand VBA. This goes beyond just understanding how the object model works and knowing how to use it. Part of knowing how to write VBA code also includes knowing how to write VBA code correctly, including using declarations and naming variables.

Using a Naming Convention

If you're only writing macros for your personal use, you can get along just fine with using names that are logical to you for your variables, objects, and controls. No one but you will know what they are called, and as long as they work like they're supposed to, you don't care what the names are.

You might think you're good at writing macros and be proud of your work—until a "real" programmer sees some of your work and tells you that it's all wrong, just because you named things "your way."

The recommended method of naming objects and controls is to use a two- or three-letter prefix indicating the type of object it is. By using a uniform naming style, it's easier for others to read your code and understand what you are doing. Tables 26-1

Control	Prefix	Example
Checkbox	chk	chkReadOnly
Combo box or drop-down list box	cbo	cboStates
Command button	cmd	cmdCancel
Frame	fra	fraAddresses
Image	img	imgIcon
Label	lbl	lblFirstName
Option button	opt	optGender
TabStrip	tab	tabOptions
Text box	txt	txtLastName
Toolbar	tlb	tlbActions
Menus	mnu	mnuFileOpen

Table 26-1. *Common Prefixes for Controls*

Data Type	Prefix	Example
Boolean	bln	blnFound
Currency	cur	curTaxes
Date (Time)	dtm	dtmStart
Error	err	errNumber
Integer	int	intQuantity
Object	obj	objDocument
String	str	strFName

Table 26-2. *Common Prefixes for Variable Names*

and 26-2 list commonly used prefixes, but you can use other prefixes if you want, as long as you stick with them. Consistency within your procedure is more important than what the actual prefix is. Randomly switching between lbl and Label within a project is confusing.

It's good practice to use a naming convention for modules, forms, and procedures, too. Typically, UserForms use the frm prefix, class modules use cls, and modules use just m. Once you decide on the prefix, the form or module name you use should also follow a set format. It's recommended that you use verbs, at least for the first word, and capitalize words. If you don't capitalize words, use an underscore to make it readable. Keep the name short but descriptive. VBA won't complain about longer names, but anything more than 32 characters is hard to read and type. I try to stay with less than 20 characters as much as possible.

Understanding Functions

You can make your code do almost anything using the supplied objects, methods, and properties. By manipulating the object properties using functions instead of methods, you can speed up the processing of the procedure. This is because functions are preprogrammed calculations that are included with the object model; you access them by name, rather than creating your own procedure each time you need the calculation. Because a function takes in one or more arguments and returns a single value, it can be embedded in an expression. Functions are especially handy to get values that would require long complicated code or API calls to the Windows operating system.

There are a lot of functions for many popular and frequently used procedures, and you can create your own functions, if you need something the object model doesn't provide. Since the object model provides approximately 140 different functions you can use, you may never need to create your own, except for performing specific calculations.

Examples of commonly used functions include those that return time and dates in whole or in part, or those that act on words and sentences—including changing between uppercase and lowercase or returning specific parts of words or sentences. Mathematical functions, such as Sine and Cosine and banking functions, like Rate and Ipmt (interest payment) are available as well.

The following line of code contains two functions: Format sets the formatting of the date string arguments, and Now acts as the date string and returns the current system time, down to the second. Any valid date string or variant representing a valid date string can be used in place of Now.

```
Sub function_sample()
Dim myString as String
myDate = Format(Now, "mmmm")
Debug.Print myString
End Sub
```

The next example demonstrates the differences between using functions and objects for the same task. The following code contains two lines of code which return the same text string, which is the first 12 characters of the current document. The first uses the Left function, and the second uses the Range method. While the results are the same, you may find using functions is easier for more complicated strings. This sample prints the results of both the Left function and the Range method to the immediate window.

```
Sub function_sample()
Dim myString as String
myString = Left(ActiveDocument.Paragraphs(1), 12)
Debug.Print myString
myString = ActiveDocument.Range(Start:=0, End:=12)
Debug.Print myString
End Sub
```

Change the Left to Right and you can easily return the last 12 characters in the paragraph. Getting the last 12 characters using the Range method requires more code and is where the value of using a function is most noticeable.

```
myString = Right(ActiveDocument.Paragraphs(1), 12)
```

The function requires one line; using Range means you need to find the end and count back. First it locates the end of the paragraph using Range.End and then calculates the starting position.

```
pos = ActiveDocument.Paragraphs(1).Range.End
Set myString = ActiveDocument.Range(Start:=pos - 12, End:=pos)
```

The final example shows how much easier using functions really is. If you need to pick up text from the middle of the paragraph, the Mid function handles it very simply: Locate the paragraph, using ActiveDocument.Paragraphs(1), and enter the starting point and the number of characters to count. It's very simple to enter and easy to read.

```
myString = Mid(ActiveDocument.Paragraphs(1), 15, 12)
' for Range method
pos = ActiveDocument.Paragraphs(1).Range.Start
Set myRange = ActiveDocument.Range(Start:=pos + 14, End:=pos + 26)
```

You can't say the same about using the Range method, since it requires more calculations to return the same data. First you need to locate the starting position by performing a calculation; then calculate the end position. In small samples like this, the extra calculation time required by Range isn't a factor, but on longer procedures it could contribute to slower execution.

Roll Your Own Functions

If VBA doesn't include any functions you like, you can write your own. For example, instead of repeating a formula throughout a procedure, you can create a function to call over and over. The entire list of nearly 140 functions is listed in Visual Basic Help.

In the following example, the Taxes function calculates what's left of your salary after your taxes are deducted. This example assumes you have some taxes deducted from the full amount of your earning, with a different tax deducted from the balance.

```
Function Earnings(Taxable)
    Earnings = (Taxable * 0.92) * 0.88
End Function
```

When the function is called from the TakeHome procedure, a variable (myMoney) containing the argument value is passed to the function (Earnings). The result of the calculation is returned to the calling procedure and displayed in a message box.

```
Sub TakeHome()
Dim myMoney As String
  myMoney = InputBox("Please enter your weekly earnings")
  MsgBox "You get to keep $" & Earnings(myMoney) & " this week"
End Sub
```

Just as with the earlier example, the function is short and simple and the calculations could easily be done within the subroutine itself. You can see the power and convenience gained by using functions when the function is longer and more complicated or if the formula is used by several procedures.

Putting VBA to Work

Now it's time to put some of the book learning into practical use. As you work through the sample projects, you'll see how to put ideas into action using VBA and learn how to use the tools included with the VB editor.

Sending Form Letters

Let's say you often send the same personalized form letter out to people and you think using mail merge is overkill. The current method, used by many of the templates included with Word, has macrobutton fields but you need to remember to manually change the information in each macrobutton and worry about missing one of the fields.

The solution for this is actually pretty simple: Create a UserForm with the fields that you want to personalize and have a macro fill in form fields. You can use bookmarks and Reference (REF) fields for data that is used repeatedly, like the person's name.

1. Start by creating a new blank document template in Word. Use File | New to open the task pane and Choose General Templates to open the template dialog. Choose Blank Document and select the template radio button above the OK button to create a new template.

2. Open the VB editor using ALT-F11.

3. Select the ProjectTemplate(Template1) in the Project Explorer.

4. Insert a Module and a UserForm (both are on the Insert menu). If the UserForm is not in the code windows, as shown in Figure 26-1, double-click it in the Project Explorer.

5. Select the Commandbutton icon on the Control Toolbox and click the lower part of the form where you want the OK button to be positioned. If the Control toolbox is not visible, click on the Toolbox icon on the Standard toolbar.

6. Repeat for the Cancel button.

7. Select the Label control and place it on the upper left of the form.

8. Select the TextBox control and click to the right of the label. Drag the right edge so the control is longer.

9. Hold the CTRL key down and select the TextBox and Label controls.

10. Use the UserForm toolbar or right-click and align the selected controls using Tops.

11. Right-click again and group the controls together, or use the Group button on the UserForm toolbar.

12. Copy the controls and paste two more sets on the form, for a total of three groups of controls. Figure 26-2 shows the desired layout of the finished form.

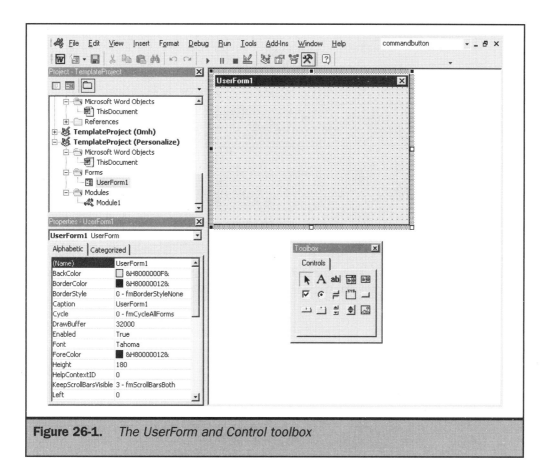

Figure 26-1. *The UserForm and Control toolbox*

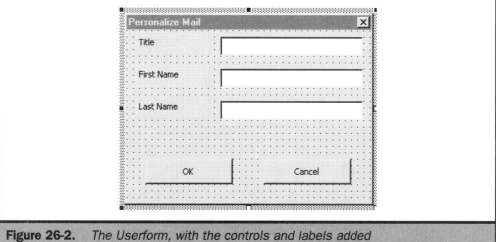

Figure 26-2. *The Userform, with the controls and labels added*

13. You can align the controls manually or use the alignment options on the toolbar or right-click menu. To select all, either CTRL-click each control or use the cursor and draw a box around all the controls by holding down the left button.

14. With the controls still selected, ungroup them.

Next you need to change the properties of the controls. For this project, you only need to name the controls, but for other projects you might want to change the appearance of the controls. This is done from the Properties window, shown in Figure 26-3.

Select the form and, in the (Name) field of the Properties windows, rename it **frmPersonalize**. In the Caption field, change the name to **Personalize Mail**. Repeat for each of the remaining labels, text boxes, and controls, using the names and captions listed in Table 26-3.

Once you have renamed the controls, right-click the form and choose Tab Order. Move txtTitle, txtFname, and txtLname to the top of the tab order. This allows the cursor to begin in the first text box, and tabbing moves you to the next field. Click OK when you have the tab order arranged in the order users have learned to expect, left

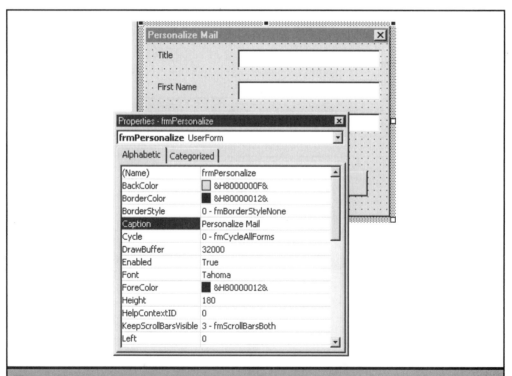

Figure 26-3. *Properties window and UserForm with controls*

(Name) Property	Caption Property
lblTitle	Title
lblFname	First Name
lblLname	Last Name
txtTitle	
txtFname	
txtLname	
cmdOk	OK
cmdCancel	Cancel

Table 26-3.   *Names and Properties for the Controls You Added to the UserForm*

to right and top to bottom. Now you are ready to add the code to your form. If you double-click the form, the VB editor will name the procedure for you, as a click event. Begin by clicking on the Cancel button and typing **Unload Me** in the sub. This tells the form to unload when clicked.

```
Private Sub cmdCancel_Click()
    Unload Me
End Sub
```

Double-click frmPersonalize in the project explorer to bring the form into view, or select it from the Window menu. Double-click the OK button and add the following code. You need to declare the string variables that will store the personal information. This should go at the very top of the code page. The variable name Title, Fname, and Lname will store the text you enter into those text box fields and is sent to the procedure called WriteValues, which writes the values to the document. When WriteValues ends, control is returned to cmdOK_Click, the form unloads, and the document is printed.

```
Dim Title, Fname, Lname As String
Private Sub cmdOK_Click()
Title = txtTitle.Text
Fname = txtFname.Text
Lname = txtLname.Text
WriteValues
```

```
Unload Me
Application.PrintOut
End Sub
```

During your testing period, you'll probably want to comment out the Application.PrintOut line by adding an apostrophe at the beginning of the line. Otherwise, the pages will be sent to the printer each time you press OK.

The WriteValues procedure could have been included in the cmdOK_Click procedure, but it's usually better to use several small procedures rather than one large one. It makes it easier to debug now and easier to read when you want to change it six months from now.

The WriteValues procedure takes the strings collected in the cmdOK_Click procedure and enters them into the document fields where they belong. It then selects the last paragraphs and updates the REF fields, which will remain blank if not updated. When this procedure ends, control is returned to cmdOK_Click so it can finish running.

Each of the procedures used in the form are private, meaning that only the form can use the code. If they were public procedures, you could run the procedures using the Tools | Macro | Macro dialog from your Word document.

```
Private Sub WriteValues()
With ActiveDocument
    .FormFields("Title").Result = Title
    .FormFields("First").Result = Fname
    .FormFields("Last").Result = Lname
End With
Set aRange = ActiveDocument.Range( _
    Start:=ActiveDocument.Paragraphs(7).Range.Start, _
    End:=ActiveDocument.Paragraphs(12).Range.End)
aRange.Select
Selection.Fields.Update
Selection.HomeKey
End Sub
```

When selecting paragraphs by index number, turn Show Paragraphs on so you can see and count all paragraphs. Index numbers are absolute. If you are using index numbers and the behavior is not what you are expecting, try different index numbers as part of the debug process.

All that's left on the VBA side is to make the form run when the template is opened. This is done using the AutoNew procedure. Word knows that a procedure named AutoNew is to be run immediately when a new document is created. Double-click Module1 and type the next procedure in the module. The Load command instructs the form to load and show.

```
Sub AutoNew()
    Load frmPersonalize
    frmPersonalize.Show
End Sub
```

Now you need to prepare the document. Return to the Word window, show the Forms toolbar, and begin typing the form letter. I used the CreateDate field for the date. This way, if I open the document at a later time, it will always show the date I created it, not the current date.

1. Click the Text Form Field button when you reach the first insertion point for each field.

2. Double-click the form field and enter the field name for the bookmark. The field names used for the bookmarks need to match the field names assigned to the FormFields property in the WriteValues procedure.

```
With ActiveDocument
    .FormFields("Title").Result = Title
    .FormFields("First").Result = Fname
    .FormFields("Last").Result = Lname
End With
```

Because the procedure uses Title, First, and Last as field names, you need to use those names for the bookmarks. If the field names are different, the results from the UserForm will not update the fields in the document.

3. Set the Text format to use Title Case. This ensures all names will be capitalized properly without using the SHIFT key, including double names like "Mary Sue." (See Figure 26-4.)

If you need to reuse the fields, use the REF field. You can find it on the Insert | Field dialog or enter the field manually by pressing CTRL-F9; the syntax is "REF fieldname". Use the ALT-F9 keys to toggle the display of field codes off and on.

When you are finished save the template and then use it to create a new document. When it's loaded, the AutoNew macro will load the form, ready for your input. Figure 26-5 displays the finished form, and Figure 26-6 shows the form fields and reference fields completed and the document ready for printing.

Saving Documents

One process that VBA is great for automating is saving documents automatically when you close them, without being asked. But before a document can be saved, it needs to be named. For this, you can create a procedure that saves the document when you open it. One obvious problem is when your chosen filename already exists: the old one may be replaced or the macro might end on an error. To avoid this, you need to check for existing filenames and include an error handler.

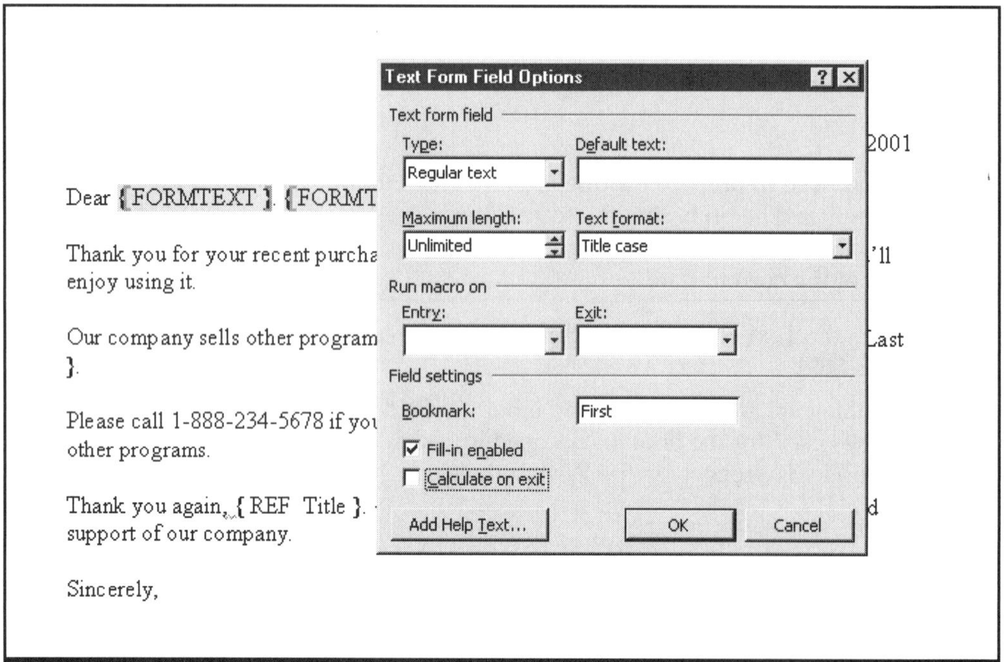

Dear {FORMTEXT} {FORMT...

Thank you for your recent purcha... ...'ll
enjoy using it.

Our company sells other program... ...Last
}.

Please call 1-888-234-5678 if you...
other programs.

Thank you again, { REF Title }. ...d
support of our company.

Sincerely,

Text Form Field Options [?] [X]

Text form field

Type: Default text:
[Regular text ▾] [   ] 2001

Maximum length: Text format:
[Unlimited ⬍] [Title case ▾]

Run macro on

Entry: Exit:
[▾] [▾]

Field settings

Bookmark: [First]

☑ Fill-in enabled
☐ Calculate on exit

[Add Help Text...] [OK] [Cancel]

Figure 26-4. *Text Form field Options dialog; choose Title Case to ensure all words are capitalized*

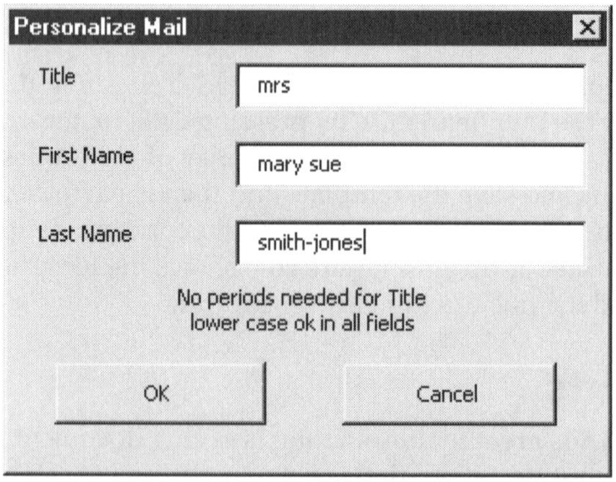

Personalize Mail [X]

Title [mrs]

First Name [mary sue]

Last Name [smith-jones|]

No periods needed for Title
lower case ok in all fields

[OK] [Cancel]

Figure 26-5. *The Personalize Mail dialog box from the finished project*

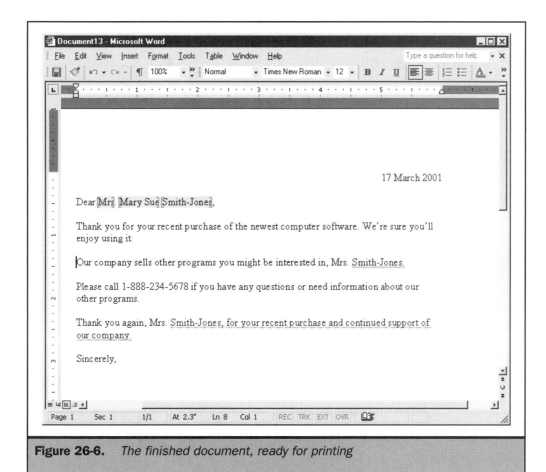

Figure 26-6. *The finished document, ready for printing*

Since you need to test for existing files and are saving files to the My Documents namespace folder, you need to identify the exact path. While it's often in the user profile path, some users do move it and you can't set a specific path. This is not a problem—just use the constant CSIDL_PERSONAL to determine the folder's true location in the file system. This works for any of the virtual Windows folders, if you know the CSIDL for the folder. A CSIDL is a value that identifies a special folder's pathname in the Windows operating system. There are 38 special folders used by Windows, including Desktop, Favorites, Start Menu, Templates, and My Documents, and each has a unique CSIDL value. You can easily locate the entire list using the MSDN on the Web option on the Help menu and then enter CSIDL in the search field.

If you need to access the file paths in the Tools | Options | File Locations dialog or any other value stored in the registry under the HKEY_CURRENT_USER\Software\Microsoft\Office\10.0\Word subkey, you can use the ProfileString property.

Unfortunately, the property causes errors on some of the subkeys, including the subkey for the Documents path. You can read the registry value or write a subkey and value to the registry, using the following syntax:

```
System.ProfileString("SubkeyName", "EntryName") = "Value"
```

Add the CSIDL_PERSONAL constant to the normal.dot template and begin the AutoNew macro. You can add a new module for it or place it in an existing module. Begin by declaring the variables, with strDocName representing the document name and strFolderpath representing the My Documents path. Add an error handler statement and the dialog box used for entering the filename.

```
Public Const CSIDL_PERSONAL = &H5
Sub AutoNew()
    Dim strDocName, strFolderpath As String
    On Error GoTo errSaveFailed
    strFolderpath = CSIDL_PERSONAL
    strDocName = InputBox("File Name", " Save File")
```

This next bit of code compares the names of the documents in the My Documents folder with the name you enter in the dialog box to see if it already exists.

In the With statement, the FileSearch object searches the My Documents folder for a document matching the name you want to use. If it finds a match, a message box informs you that a document already exists and the code that is used for the error handler is called, although not because the procedure encountered an error. The error handler loads the Save As dialog we need, and it's a good habit to reuse code when possible.

If the filename you entered does not exist, the procedure executes the next statement, which is Else. This is what is known as an If...Then...Else statement.

```
With Application.FileSearch
  LookIn = strFolderpath
  FileName = strDocName & ".doc"
   If .Execute() > 0 Then
   MsgBox "A document by this name already exists." _
     & Chr(10) & "Try again with a new name."
GoTo errSaveFailed
Else
ActiveDocument.SaveAs FileName:=strDocName, _
    FileFormat:=wdFormatDocument
 Exit Sub
 End If
 End With
```

If a file exists by the same name, the procedure jumps to the Save As dialog box used by the error handler. If the file does not exist, Else allows the procedure to continue and the file to be saved using your filename. The FileFormat argument tells Word what format to save the file as. Then the procedure exits to prevent the rest of the procedure from executing.

If the filename is in use or if the procedure causes an error, the error handler code is executed. The Save As dialog is displayed, with a suggested document name in the filename field. You can choose a new name, replace the existing file, or chose another folder from the Save As dialog.

```
errSaveFailed:
  With Dialogs(wdDialogFileSummaryInfo)
  .Title = strDocName
  .Execute
 End With
Dialogs(wdDialogFileSaveAs).Show
End Sub
```

To save the document again when you close it, the AutoClose macro is used.

```
Sub AutoClose()
  ActiveDocument.Save
End Sub
```

That was easy—now every new template that is opened will use the AutoNew macro. The lone exception is the document that loads when Word is first opened. The AutoClose dialog opens the Save As dialog when you close it. If you don't want to save it, you can disable the macro by holding down the SHIFT key when closing Word.

Adding Buttons to Toolbars

Word has two ways you can add buttons to toolbars. You can add them manually, using the customize toolbar method, or you can use VBA to add toolbars when a template loads and close the toolbar when the template is closed. This method offers one major advantage over using the Customize method. If the button is accidentally removed from the toolbar, it's not totally lost and is restored when the template loads again.

To handle the loading and unloading of the toolbar, you'll use AutoNew and AutoClose procedures. This ensures the button is available when a new document is created using the template. Because the toolbar is not in the normal template, only documents created with this template will have the toolbar. Because the code required for creating toolbars is long, AutoNew will call the NewToolBar procedure. The code needed to unload the toolbar is short and will be placed in the AutoClose procedure.

Create a new template in Word and open the VBE. Insert a module in the template project and enter the following code into the module.

```
Sub AutoNew()
  NewToolBar
End Sub
Sub AutoClose()
  On Error Resume Next
  Application.CommandBars("Type Text CommandBar").Delete
End Sub
```

The NewToolBar procedure begins by deleting the toolbar if it exists. This prevents multiple toolbars being created if the AutoClose macro failed to remove the toolbar previously. An If…Then…Else loop could be used instead and check for the presence of the toolbar before creating a new one, but cleaning up the old toolbar is generally better and easier in the long run. If the existing toolbar was used then you'd need to check for the presence of the buttons and delete them individually when the template closes instead of deleting the bar.

```
Sub NewToolBar()
 Dim cbrCommandBar  As CommandBar
 Dim cbcCommandBarButton As CommandBarButton
On Error Resume Next
 Application.CommandBars("Type Text CommandBar").Delete
```

Add the command bar to the application's CommandBars collection and add a display name for the title bar.

```
Set cbrCommandBar = _
  Application.CommandBars.Add
 cbrCommandBar.Name = "Type Text CommandBar"
```

Add command button control to the control's collection of CommandBar objects and set the properties of the command button. The button will have an icon and text on it as well as a tool tip if you hover the mouse over it. The FaceID identifies the icon that will be used on the button; 19 happens to be the copy icon. Buttons need to do something, and the OnAction property contains the macro that is to be run when the button is pushed. Finally, at the end, the visible property is set to true.

```
With cbrCommandBar.Controls
  Set cbcCommandBarButton = _
```

```
   .Add(msoControlButton)
 With cbcCommandBarButton
 .Style = msoButtonIconAndCaption
 .Caption = "Type Text"
 .FaceId = 19
 .TooltipText = _
    "Press me to type some text."
 .OnAction = "TypeText"
 .Tag = "Type text"
 End With
 End With
 cbrCommandBar.Visible = True
End Sub
```

Not only does this macro demonstrate the use of the command bar buttons, it also is an example of a loop. The macro returns to the Do Until line and runs again, until myNum equals 50. You can count down using Do loops, set myNum to equal a higher number, and subtract 1 from myNum on each loop. Nested in the Do loop is a For…Next loop that repeats the sentence several times in a paragraph.

```
Sub TypeText()
Dim myNum As Variant
  myNum = 0
  Do Until myNum = 50
   For mySentences = 1 To 20
    Selection.TypeText Text:="The fat cat is sleeping. "
   Next mySentences
   Selection.TypeParagraph
   myNum = myNum + 1
 Loop
End Sub
```

Save the code sample in a new template and load the template. The button named Type Text is displayed, and pressing it enters the sentence 20 times in each of 50 paragraphs. You can use this procedure in place of the built-in Rand function for creating sample text when testing.

Using VBA with Office XP

What if you want to use data that is in your Excel workbook, or in Outlook's contacts folder in your document? You can use Word's Merge feature or access the other application using calls to their object model. You can also access Word's object model from other apps.

The secret to your success is in setting the proper references to the outside application. Open the Tools | References dialog box in the VB editor to select the references. Scroll through the list and select the ones you need for your project. Only reference the objects you plan to use in your project. The Reference dialog is shown in Figure 26-7.

The following example copies a Word document and pastes it into an Excel worksheet. As you can see, after you declare the Excel.Application object and create a new workbook, the Word document is copied and pasted into the workbook's A1 cell. Finally, you need to always release all objects or risk resource leaks. Do this by setting the objects to nothing at the end of the procedure.

Add the following code to a module. You can create a new template or insert a module in the normal template project. Remember to set the reference to the Microsoft Excel 10.0 Object library using VBE's Tools | References menu. If you forget, you'll get a compile error "User-defined type not defined" as soon as you run it.

Open or create a Word document containing a couple of paragraphs and run the macro.

```
Sub ExportToExcel()
Dim xlObj As Excel.Application
Dim myBook As Workbook
Set xlObj = New Excel.Application
  xlObj.Visible = True
Set myBook = xlObj.Workbooks.Add
With ActiveDocument.Content
  .Copy
  myBook.Worksheets(1).Range("A1").PasteSpecial _
        Paste:=xlPasteValues
 End With
With myBook.Worksheets(1)
  .Columns.AutoFit
  .Range("A1").Select
 End With
Set xlObj = Nothing
End Sub
```

The process of accessing Word documents from other Office applications is very similar. Set the references to the Word object library, and set the objects in code to refer to Word.Application. Access the document using your VBA code and release all objects when finished.

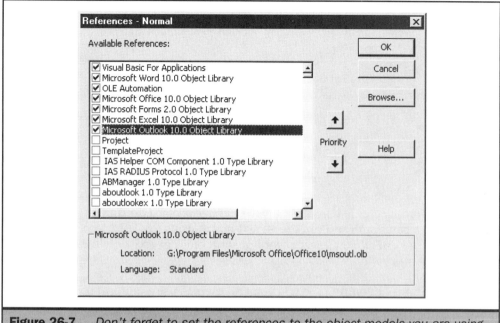

Figure 26-7.   *Don't forget to set the references to the object models you are using in your code; this dialog shows that both Excel and Outlook's object models are referenced*

Ten Ways to Use VBA Programming in Word

1. Make Formatting Text Faster   If you need to apply the same formatting options often, you have two ways of using a macro for this. One is to write or record a macro and assign it to a toolbar button. Select the text and press the button to apply the formatting. It's not necessarily the recommended way, although this is how many users apply formatting.

The correct way is to create a style and apply the style. You'll need to check to see if the style exists using an If…Then statement or delete the style before the code creating it runs again. These samples create and apply the Verdana font sized at 24 points and colored orange. If formatting was applied using the formatting tools instead of Styles, some of those formatting changes remain. For uniformity, it's usually best to include all the Style properties in a macro that creates a new style.

```
Sub AddNewStyle()
ActiveDocument.Styles("My New Style").Delete
  ActiveDocument.Styles.Add Name:="My New Style", _
          Type:=wdStyleTypeParagraph
  ActiveDocument.Styles("My New Style"). _
```

```
        AutomaticallyUpdate = False
With ActiveDocument.Styles("My New Style").Font
  .Name = "Verdana"
  .Size = 24
  .Color = wdColorLightOrange
End With
End Sub

Public Sub Styles1()
  Selection.Style = ActiveDocument.Styles("My New Style")
End Sub
```

Add both procedures to a module. Open or create a Word document, place the cursor within a paragraph and run the Styles1 macro using Tools | Macro | Macros or using F5 in the VBE. If you select a word or short block of text, only the selection changes to the new style.

2. Use a Uniform Filename

So you want all users to use a uniform naming convention when saving documents? Not a problem. Use the file save sample presented earlier and tweak it as needed.

For example, if all documents used for your current business project need to have the project name and your initials in the document name, you can create a predefined string and append it to the string name. Save the UserInitials property in a string and concatenate the strings together using "&". For easier reading, I'm adding an underscore to separate the strings. This can be added to the string as I have done or when the filename is parsed. A UserForm could be used instead of the InputBox, with the project names listed for easy selection.

```
    strUser = Application.UserInitials & "_"
  ActiveDocument.SaveAs FileName:="Project1_" & strUser  & _
      strDocName, FileFormat:=wdFormatDocument
```

By editing the project you created in "Saving Documents," you can save documents with filenames in this format: Project1_dp_test.doc. The edited code is shown here:

```
Sub SaveFilename()
    Dim strDocName, strFolderpath, strUser As String
    On Error GoTo errSaveFailed
    strFolderpath = CSIDL_PERSONAL
    strDocName = InputBox("File Name", " Save File")

    strUser = Application.UserInitials & "_"
```

```
With Application.FileSearch
  LookIn = strFolderpath
  FileName = :="Project1_" & strUser  & strDocName & ".doc"

   If .Execute() > 0 Then
   MsgBox "A document by this name already exists." _
     & Chr(10) & "Try again with a new name."
GoTo errSaveFailed

Else

  ActiveDocument.SaveAs FileName:="Project1_" & strUser  & _
strDocName, FileFormat:=wdFormatDocument

Exit Sub
 End If
 End With

errSaveFailed:
  With Dialogs(wdDialogFileSummaryInfo)
  .Title = strDocName
  .Execute
 End With
Dialogs(wdDialogFileSaveAs).Show
End Sub
```

3. Use Search and Replace on Several Files   How's this for a scenario: Your business phone number is changing to a new area code and you have several templates that need changed. You could open each individually and make the change, but wouldn't it be great if you could have a macro change them? You can, of course; why else would I mention it?

The code sample searches for templates, you could easily search documents by changing the path name. To replace several strings, repeat the With section as many times as needed. To search the entire file system, change the folder path LookIn to "C:\". It may take a while to check each file, but it can be done.

```
Public Sub ReplaceInDots()
 Dim strFolderpath As String
 strFolderpath = Options.DefaultFilePath(Path:=wdUserTemplatesPath)
 With Application.FileSearch
 .LookIn = strFolderpath
 .SearchSubFolders = True
 .FileName = "*.dot"
```

```
' if more than one match, execute the following code
If .Execute() > 0 Then
' for each file you find, run this loop
For i = 1 To .FoundFiles.Count
Documents.Open FileName:=.FoundFiles(i)
Selection.Find.ClearFormatting
Selection.Find.Replacement.ClearFormatting
'repeat the With segment for each string that needs replaced
With Selection.Find
  .Text = "540.555.1212"
  .MatchCase = True
  .Replacement.Text = "267.555.1212"
End With
  Selection.Find.Execute Replace:=wdReplaceAll
  ActiveDocument.Close wdSaveChanges
  Next I
  Else
  MsgBox "No files found."
  End If
End With
End Sub
```

4. Add Graphics Using Code   You can add graphics to your projects using VBA. This piece of code inserts an image behind text and lightens the image for use as a watermark. The ZOrder controls the position in relation to other objects. For example, if you want to insert the image behind text, you need to either use ZOrder or set the Tools | Options default to wrap behind the text:

```
Options.PictureWrapType = wdWrapMergeBehind
```

While it works, you shouldn't mess with the options unless you trap the original value and reset it. Using ZOrder is easier.

```
Sub InsertPicture()
Dim myPic As Object
   With ActiveDocument.Shapes.AddPicture(Anchor:=Selection.Range, _
     FileName:="C:\Program Files\Microsoft Office" _
        & "\media\cagcat10\J0149407.WMF" _" _
     , LinkToFile:=False, SaveWithDocument:=True)
     .WrapFormat.Type = 3
   .ZOrder 5
End With End Sub
```

As you know, images are only visible if the document is using the Print or Web Layout view. You can change the file path to use any image on your computer by changing the file path to the desired image. You don't need to use continuation characters to wrap your filename as I have done and can place the entire file path on one line, as shown in the shorter example here:

```
FileName:="C:\My Pictures\my_kids.jpg" _
```

5. More Ways to Retrieve User Options   In an earlier sample I explained how to get special folder locations using the CSIDL constant and by using the System.ProfileString property. There is one more way to read (and write) user file paths—using the Options.DefaultFilePath object. I'm not sure you should be writing new paths for the user files, but if you want to, it's certainly possible.

```
Options.DefaultFilePath(Path:=wdDocumentsPath)
```

There's one more way to get user information: reading the registry. The ProfileString property only reads and writes the HKEY_CURRENT_USER\Software\Microsoft\Office\version\Word subkeys. PrivateProfileString property can read and write to any registry key.

```
aName = System.PrivateProfileString("", _
    "HKEY_CURRENT_USER\Software\Microsoft\" _
    & "Office\10.0\Outlook", "Machine Name")
MsgBox aName
```

6. Add Help to Your Projects   Yes, you can add custom help files for your projects. Create HTML pages for your help files, and then use the HTML Help Editor to compile them into a form the Help interface can display. Once the file is created, right-click the project name in the project viewer and choose Properties. Enter the location of the help files and you're good to go. You can enable "What's This" Help to forms; see the properties for the form. All controls can have ToolTips you can use for short help information.

You can find the HTML Help Workshop at MSDN on the Web: http://msdn.microsoft.com/library/tools/htmlhelp/chm/HH1Start.htm.

7. Automate Mail Merge   Word 2002 includes an improved Mail Merge wizard, but you might want to skip the wizard if you use mail merge often. Create your own template accessing your data source, which can include SQL databases. If you routinely use the same database, you can save your letter as a template and connect to the database when the template is opened. Very little VBA coding is required.

8. Use VBA to Export Your Address Book   This is easy. From the VB Editor's Help menu, go to MSDN on the Web and search for adexport.dot. It's a sample application that exports Outlook's contacts list and creates a formatted table in Word. You even have a choice over which fields are to be exported. It can also send the data from the tables to an Excel worksheet. If the contacts folder is large it may take, a long time to complete. It's located online at http://msdn.microsoft.com/library/techart/addressexpt.htm. If you look around MSDN on the Web, you can find more sample VBA projects.

9. Print Outlook's Calendar from Word   This is another cheap trick that's been around a few years but still works great. Microsoft created a Word template that reads Outlook's calendar data and creates a nicely formatted calendar in Word, ready for printing. You can edit the code to add background images or shade cells. The Olcalndr.exe self-extracting template is in the Microsoft Knowledge Base (http://support.microsoft.com/support/kb/articles/Q201/5/67.ASP). This template was created for Word 2000 and Outlook 2000 but works well with both Word 2002 and Outlook 2002.

10. Don't Reinvent the Wheel   Microsoft hosts a template gallery that may contain templates that do exactly what you want, or almost what you want. Tweaking the code is sometimes easier than building from scratch. You can find the template gallery by going to Office on the Web, listed in Word's Help menu or use the URL to go directly to the Template Gallery: http://officeupdate.microsoft.com/templategallery/default.asp. This is by no means the only site to look for code samples; there are many others, including http://www.mvps.org/word/FAQs/index5.html.

Part VII

Appendixes

The Complete Reference

Word 2002

Appendix A

Installing Word

This appendix describes how to install and reinstall Word. It explains what to do before you start installing Word, how to install and reinstall Word, and how to reinstall Word to put more or fewer Office features on your computer.

Installing Word: The Big Picture

Instead of installing Word and the various Office tools in their entirety, you can install the essential parts of Word and the essential Office tools (I explain how in this appendix). Later, if you choose a Word command or an Office tool that hasn't been installed on your computer, you see a message box like the ones shown in Figure A-1. The message box tells you in so many words that the command you chose has not been installed on your computer, but you can install it by clicking OK, the Install button, the Yes button, or whatever the button's name happens to be.

What the message box doesn't mention is that you need the Word CD or Office CD to install the command. Before clicking OK, Install, or Yes, put the Word CD or Office CD in your CD-ROM drive. When you click the button, Word copies program codes from the CD to your computer so that you can execute the command. The installation procedure takes only a few seconds. Without the CD, however, you can't install the program codes for the command you want.

Note   *If you are working in a corporate setting, you may be able to install Word features from an installation point. See your network administrator for details.*

Practically speaking, you need to keep the Word or Office CD at your side when you use Word. You need the CD in case Word encounters a command that it can't

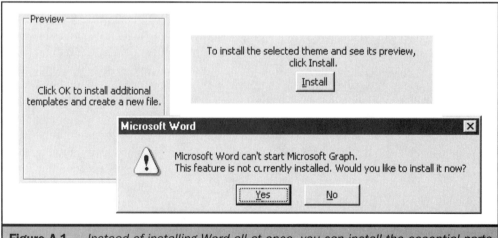

Figure A-1.   *Instead of installing Word all at once, you can install the essential parts of the program and then install the other parts as you need them*

carry out. You can try your best to load all the Word and Office features that you need on your computer from the start (see "Custom Installation: Choosing Which Features to Install," later in this appendix), but installing all the features requires a lot of disk space and is not practical for most people. What's more, even if you choose to install all the features, some are not loaded on your computer until you attempt to use them for the first time.

Before You Install Word

Before you install Word, close all programs that are open. Microsoft also recommends backing up all your important files and documents before you install Word. While writing this book, I installed and reinstalled Word many times and never lost a file or document, but I want you to know what Microsoft recommends.

Your computer must meet these requirements in order to install Word:

- An *x*86-compatible computer that meets the minimum hardware requirements for Microsoft Windows 98 or later, or Windows NT 4.0 or later

- Windows 98, Windows Me, Windows NT with at least Service Pack 6a installed, or Windows 2000

Caution   *Word 2002 does not work on the Windows 95 operating system.*

- A Pentium chip with 64MB or better (recommended)
- At least 350MB hard disk space (plus 50MB for each language user interface)
- A CD-ROM or DVD drive

Installing Word

Follow these steps to install Word:

1. Close all programs if any are open.
2. Put the CD in the CD-ROM or DVD drive. In a moment, you see the Microsoft Office (or Microsoft Word) Installation Wizard dialog box. Twiddle your thumbs while you wait for the Installation program to prepare to install Word.

Note   *If you don't see the Microsoft Installation Wizard dialog box, follow these instructions to display it: Click the Start button and choose Settings | Control Panel. In the Control Panel window, double-click the Add/Remove Programs icon. In the Add/Remove Programs Properties dialog box, click the Install button. Click Next in the following dialog box, and then click the Finish button.*

3. Enter your name and other personal information, as well as the Product key (you will find this number in the Word or Office package). Then click Next. The User Name, Initials, and Organization information you enter here appear by default in many different places in Word and the other Office programs. For example, if you choose Insert | AutoText | Signature in Word, you can insert the name you enter in the User Name text box without having to type the name.

4. Read the user agreement, click the I Accept the Terms in the License Agreement check box, and click Next.

5. The next dialog box offers four installation choices (or three if an earlier version of Word or another Office program is not already installed on your computer):

■ **Upgrade Now**   Removes previous versions of Office programs, including Word, and replaces them with the newest versions. You get roughly the same installation you had before, except newer editions of Word and the other Office programs are installed on your computer. If you click this button, the installation procedure begins right away.

■ **Typical**   The essential parts of Word and the other Office programs are installed on your computer. When you try to use a feature that hasn't been installed, you see a dialog box similar to the ones shown in Figure A-1 and you are given the chance to install the feature. I recommend choosing this option. As long as your Office or Word CD is handy, you can simply install features as you need them.

■ **Customize**   You pick and choose which parts of Word and the other Office programs to install on your computer. See "Custom Installation: Choosing Which Features to Install," the next section in this appendix.

■ **Complete**   Installs all the Office features, including Word features, on your computer.

6. Click an Installation button—Upgrade Now, Typical, Customize, or Complete.

What happens next depends on what kind of installation you are undertaking. Follow the onscreen instructions. An installation can take 20–30 minutes, depending on how many features need to be installed and the speed of your computer. If you decided to pick and choose which features to install, keep reading.

Custom Installation: Choosing Which Features to Install

In a Customize installation, you decide for yourself which Word or Office features to install on your computer. Figure A-2 shows the dialog box you see when you choose a

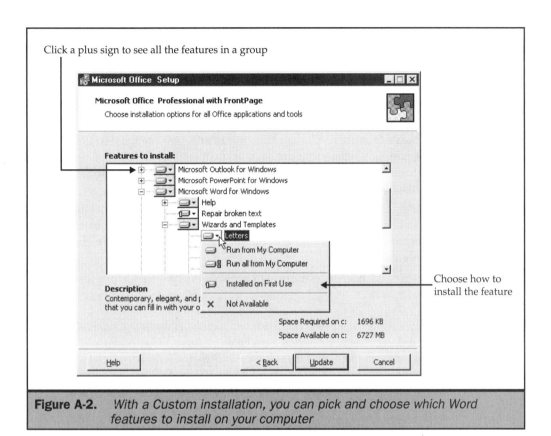

Click a plus sign to see all the features in a group

Choose how to install the feature

Figure A-2. *With a Custom installation, you can pick and choose which Word features to install on your computer*

Custom installation. To tell Word which features to install, click the plus sign (+) next to Microsoft Word for Windows to see a list of features. Then, click the icon next to each feature and choose an option from the drop-down menu to decide how or whether to install it:

- **Run From My Computer**   Loads the feature onto your computer.
- **Run All From My Computer**   Loads all the features in a set of features on your computer. For example, if you click the icon beside Microsoft Word for Windows and choose Run All From My Computer, all the Word features are installed.
- **Installed On First Use**   Does not install the feature on your computer, but gives the opportunity to install it when you choose it from a command menu or dialog box. When you try to activate the feature, you see a message box like the ones in Figure A-1.

Reinstalling, Repairing, and Removing Word

Reinstall Word when you think the program files have been corrupted or you want to install or remove Word features from your computer. To reinstall Word, insert the CD in your CD-ROM drive. In a moment, you see a dialog box for reinstalling Word. Choose one of these options in the dialog box:

- **Add Or Remove Features**   Choose this option and you see the dialog box shown in Figure A-2, where you can pick and choose which features to install. See the previous section in this appendix to learn how to decide which Word features to install.

- **Repair Office**   Choose this option to repeat the last installation you made of Word (and Office). All the features you chose the last time are reinstalled on your computer. (You can also activate this command in Word by choosing Help | Detect and Repair.)

- **Uninstall Office**   Choose this option to remove Word (and Office) from your computer.

Tip   *If you don't see the Microsoft Installation Wizard dialog box when you attempt to reinstall Word, click the Start button and choose Settings | Control Panel. In the Control Panel window, double-click the Add/Remove Programs icon. In the Add/Remove Programs Properties dialog box, select Microsoft Office XP Professional with FrontPage in the Install/Uninstall tab, and then click the Add/Remove button.*

Appendix B

Exploring Microsoft
Clip Organizer

O ffice provides the Microsoft Clip Organizer to help you insert, manage, and organize multimedia files. Don't be confused by the word "clip." The Clip Organizer isn't just for clip art images. You can also place photographs, movie clips, and sound clips in the Clip Organizer.

This appendix explains how to use the Clip Organizer to keep track of multimedia files. You discover how to insert a file from the Organizer, search for a file, and organize and manage files so that you can find them when you need them. You also discover how to store your own multimedia files in the Clip Organizer and obtain files over the Internet from Microsoft.

The Microsoft Clip Organizer: An Overview

As shown in Figure B-1, the Microsoft Clip Art Organizer is a program unto itself. It appears in its own window. Do one of the following to open the Clip Art Organizer:

■ Click the Start button and choose Programs | Microsoft Office Tools | Microsoft Clip Organizer.

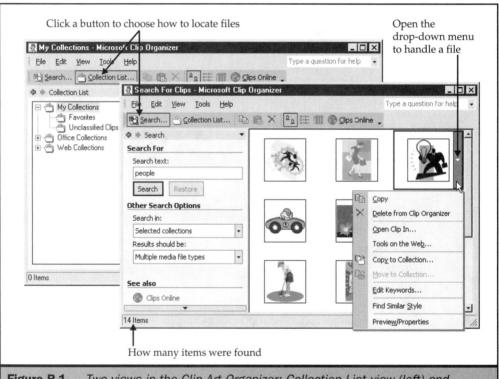

Figure B-1.   *Two views in the Clip Art Organizer: Collection List view (left) and Search view (right)*

■ In Word, click the Insert Clip Art button on the Drawing toolbar or choose Insert | Picture | Clip Art. Doing so opens the Insert Clip Art task pane. The task pane offers the same tools for searching as the Microsoft Clip Art Organizer. To open the Organizer good and proper, click the Clip Organizer hyperlink at the bottom of the task pane.

Caution   *The first time you open the Microsoft Clip Organizer program or the Insert Clip Art task pane, the program asks if you want to catalog the multimedia files on your hard disk. Don't do it! Click the Later button. As "Cataloging the Files on Your Computer" explains later in this appendix, the Organizer does a bad job of cataloging files on its own.*

Files, after you locate them, appear in the window pane on the right side of the Organizer. By opening a file's drop-down list (or right-clicking), you can display a menu with commands for handling the file. In Figure B-1, files appear in Thumbnails view, the best way to examine clip art. When you're dealing with sound files or you aren't sure what kind of file you're dealing with, switch to Details view, as shown in this illustration. The Standard toolbar offers three buttons—Thumbnails, List, and Details—for changing views.

View buttons

Name	Size	Type	Caption	Keywords	Date
j0214098.wav	10 KB	Wave Sound	Claps Cheers	applause,ch...	2/18/99
ELPHRG01.wav	52 KB	Wave Sound	Telephone	communicati...	8/14/98
sn00771a.wav	21 KB	Wave Sound	Talk Gibberish	cartoons,gar...	2/28/01
sn00672a.wav	22 KB	Wave Sound	Stampede	hoofs,nature...	2/28/01
sn00584a.wav	7 KB	Wave Sound	Impact Wrench	air horns,aut...	2/28/01
sn00533a.wav	5 KB	Wave Sound	Dull Glass		Copy
sn00495a.wav	9 KB	Wave Sound	Answering		Delete from Clip Organizer
sn00492a.wav	23 KB	Wave Sound	Close Alarm		
sn00417a.wav	6 KB	Wave Sound	Metal Slide		Open Clip In...
sn00408a.wav	3 KB	Wave Sound	Weird Slide		Tools on the Web...
sn00334a.wav	3 KB	Wave Sound	Slide Down		
sn00286a.wav	8 KB	Wave Sound	Low Monst		Copy to Collection...
sn00246a.wav	19 KB	Wave Sound	Panting Do		Move to Collection...
sn00243a.wav	9 KB	Wave Sound	Dog With G		Edit Keywords...
sn00213a.wav	6 KB	Wave Sound	Cute Fake		Find Similar Style
					Preview/Properties

When you have found the file you want, open its shortcut or drop-down menu and choose Copy to copy the file to the Office Clipboard. From there, you can paste it in a Word document. You can also drag and drop the file into a Word document, provided you are adroit with the mouse.

Files in the Clip Organizer are kept in three main folders. No matter which technique you use for searching, you search in the three folders:

- **My Collections**   Your Favorites collection, as well as other collections that you keep. Later in this appendix, "Copying Files to the Favorites Folder and Other Folders" describes how to place multimedia files in the My Collections folder and its subfolders.

- **Office Collections**   Folders that hold the multimedia files that were transferred to your computer when you installed Office (and Word).

- **Web Collections**   Folders on the Design Gallery Live Web site, a Web site that Microsoft maintains. You must be connected to the Internet to search Web collections. (Later in this appendix, "Getting Multimedia Files Online from the Design Gallery" explains how to visit the Design Gallery Live Web site and download multimedia files directly.)

 In Thumbnails view, files that come from Web collections show a small globe in the lower-left corner.

Finding the File You Need

The Clip Organizer offers two ways to locate multimedia files. Both techniques are described in the pages that follow:

- Click the Collection List button (or choose View | Collection List) to search for files in the Collection List pane. Go this route when you know which file you want and you know which Clip Organizer folder it is in.

- Click the Search button (or choose View | Search) to search for files in the Search pane. Go this route when you aren't sure which file you want. From the Search pane, you can search your computer and the Microsoft Design Gallery, a Web site on the Internet.

Finding a File in the Collection List

Click the Collection List button to obtain files whose location in the Clip Organizer you know. Then, to locate your file, find and select the folder where it resides. Your file appears on the right side of the Clip Organizer.

Later in this appendix, "Organizing and Managing Images in the Clip Organizer" explains how to organize files in the Collection List.

Searching for a File with the Clip Organizer

To rummage inside the Clip Organizer to find the right clip art image, photograph, movie file, sound file, or video file, start by clicking the Search button. The Search task pane appears (refer to Figure B-1). In the Search Text, Search In, and Results Should Be text box or drop-down menu, make your choices and click the Search button.

Search For Text Box   Enter a keyword that describes what file you want. As "Attaching a New Keyword to an Image" explains later in this appendix, each multimedia file is assigned a handful of keywords. A file that has been assigned the keyword you enter will turn up in the search.

Search In Drop-Down Menu   By opening folders and selecting check boxes, tell the Clip Organizer where to search for the file you want (earlier in this appendix, "The Microsoft Clip Organizer: An Overview" explains My Collections, Office Collections, and Web Collections, the three main folders). To be specific in a search, check subfolders—Academic, Animals, and so on. Seeing as you are searching for a file whose location you don't know, your search will likely be in the Office Collections and Web Collections folders.

All subfolders selected

As the previous illustration shows, you can tell whether all the subfolders in a folder have been selected when you see three overlapping check boxes instead of a single check box. Double-click the check box next to a collection name to select all the subfolders in the collection. If you merely click the Office Collections check box when it's empty, for example, you don't select its subfolders, and you therefore don't search Office collections.

Results Should Be Drop-Down Menu Tell the Organizer what kinds of files you are looking for. To do so, check a media type—Clip Art, Photographs, Movies, or Sounds. To search for specific kinds of media files, click a plus sign (+) to open a folder, and then check off the names of media files you want. Table B-1 lists the types of files that you can retrieve with the Clip Organizer.

Results should be:

| All media file types |

- ☑ All media types
  - ☑ Clip Art
  - ☑ Photographs
  - ☑ Movies
  - ☑ Sounds

Results should be:

| Multiple media file types |

- ☐ All media types
  - ☐ Clip Art
  - ☐ Photographs
    - ☐ FPX Format (*.fpx)
    - ☑ Graphics Interchange Format (*.gif;*.gfa)
    - ☑ JPEG File Interchange Format (*.jpg;*.jpeg
    - ☐ Kodak Photo CD (*.pcd)
    - ☐ PC Paintbrush (*.pcx)
    - ☐ Picture It! Format (*.mix)
    - ☐ Portable Network Graphics (*.png)
    - ☐ Targa (*.tga)
    - ☐ Windows Bitmap (*.bmp;*.dib;*.rle;*.bmz)

Extension	File Type
Clip Art Files	
.dxf	AutoCAD Format 2-D
.cdr	CorelDraw
.cgm	Computer Graphics Metafile
.drw	Micrografx Designer/Draw
.emf	Enhanced Metafile
.emz	Compressed Windows Enhanced Metafile
.eps	Encapsulated PostScript

Table B-1. *Types of Files You Can Store in the Clip Organizer*

Extension	File Type
Clip Art Files	
.pct, .pict	Macintosh PICT
.pcz	Compressed Macintosh PICT
.wmf	Windows Metafile
.wmz	Compressed Windows Metafile
.wpg	WordPerfect Graphics
Photograph Files	
.fpx	FPX Format
.gif, .gfa	Graphics Interchange Format
.jpg, .jpeg, .jfif, .jpe	JPEG File Interchange Format
.pcd	Kodak Photo CD
.pcx	PC Paintbrush
.mix	Picture It! Format
.pgn	Portable Network Graphics
.tif, .tiff	Tag Image File Format
.tga	Targa
.bmp, .dib, .rle, .bmz	Windows Bitmap
Movie Files	
.ac3	AC3 File
.gif	Animated GIF
.ivf	Indeo Video File
.m3u	M3U File
.vob	Media Clip
.m1v, .mp2, .mpa, .mp3, .mpeg, .mpg, mpv2	Movie File (MPEG)
.mov, .qt	QuickTime Movie
.vbs	VBScript File

Table B-1.   *Types of Files You Can Store in the Clip Organizer* (continued)

APPENDIXES

Extension	File Type
Movie Files	
.avi	Video Clip
.asf, .lsf, .wm, wmv	Windows Media Audio/Video File
.lsx	Windows Media Audio/Video Shortcut
.wmp	Windows Media Player File
Sound Files	
.aif, .aifc, .aiff	AIFF Audio
.au, .snd	AU Format Sound
.mid, .rmi, .midi	MIDI Sequence
.mp3	MP3 Format Sound
.wav	Wave Sound
.wma	Windows Media Audio File

Table B-1. *Types of Files You Can Store in the Clip Organizer* (continued)

Organizing and Managing Images in the Clip Organizer

If you expect to spend a lot of time in the Clip Organizer, you may as well organize the files so that you can find them easily. To do so, you can tell the Organizer to catalog the multimedia files on your computer, place files in the Favorites folder or a folder you devise, and even attach a new keyword to an image to make finding it easier.

Files can appear in more than one folder. The files you see in the Clip Organizer are actually pointers to locations on your computer and the Internet where the files are stored. When you move or copy a file to a new folder, all you are doing is moving or copying the instructions that the Organizer uses to get the file from the place on your computer or the Internet where the file is located.

Cataloging the Files on Your Computer

The first time you open the Clip Organizer, you are asked whether you want to catalog the multimedia files on your computer. Sounds like a good idea, doesn't it? By cataloging, it would seem, the Clip Organizer proposes to scour the hard disk on your computer for multimedia files and take note of where they are. Don't be fooled! Click the Later button in the Add Clips to Organizer dialog box.

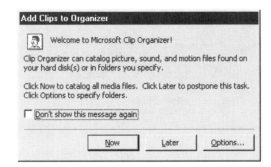

Cataloging isn't all it's cracked up to be. Instead of searching your entire computer, the Clip Organizer searches the C:\Windows folder and its subfolders—and it drudges up every tinny sound file and two-bit graphic file that is found there. Then, to store the files, the Clip Organizer creates a new folder called Windows in the Collection List.

Maybe your C:\Windows holds multimedia files that are worth something. In that case, catalog your files, but do so selectively by following these steps:

1. Choose File | Add Clips to Organizer | Automatically. The Add Clips to Organizer dialog box appears.

2. Click the Options button. You see the Auto Import Settings dialog box.

3. Go through and check off the names of folders where useful multimedia files are stored.

4. Click the Catalog button.

If you regret cataloging your files, right-click the Windows folder in the Collection List and choose Delete Windows. Don't worry—you won't delete any files on your computer. By deleting, you merely remove filenames from the Clip Organizer.

You can file away any clip art, photograph, sound, or movie files on your computer in the Clip Organizer. See "Putting Your Own Files in the Clip Organizer" later in this appendix.

Creating Folders in the Organizer for Storing Files

In the Collections List, the My Collections folder holds two subfolders: Favorites and Unclassified Clips. Perhaps you need another folder for storing multimedia files—a Good Sounds folder for sound files you like or a Family Photographs folder for pictures of loved ones.

To create a new subfolder of the My Collections folder, choose File | New Collection. In the New Collection dialog box, enter a name for the folder and select the folder that your new folder will be subordinate to. Then click OK.

To delete a folder you created, right-click it and choose Delete. You can't delete readymade folders such as Favorites and Unclassified Clips—they are as permanent as the Rock of Gibraltar.

Copying Files to the Favorites Folder and Other Folders

When you come upon a multimedia file that you are sure to use again, copy it to the Favorites folder so you can find it again. For that matter, copy it to a folder you created yourself so you can find it. As shown in Figure B-2, either right-click the file or open its drop-down menu and choose Copy to Collection. Then, in the Copy to Collection dialog box, select a folder and click the OK button.

To copy several files at once, select them first by CTRL-*clicking,* SHIFT-*clicking, or pressing* CTRL-A *to select all the files.*

Putting Your Own Files in the Clip Organizer

If you spend any time in the Clip Organizer, you soon realize that it is a very convenient device for finding and organizing files. Here's some good news: You can store your files in the Clip Organizer. Instead of having to fumble around in your computer to find a clip art or graphic image, for example, you can get it by way of the Clip Organizer.

Follow these steps to place a file or files of your own in the Clip Organizer:

1. Click the Collection List button, if necessary, to see the Collection List.

2. Select the folder in the list where you want to place the file or files.

Choose which folder to put the file in

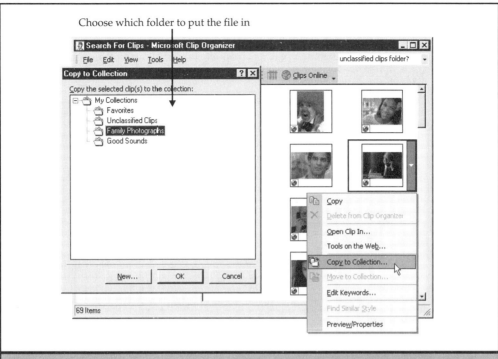

Figure B-2.   *When you expect to need a file in the future, copy it to the Favorites folder or one of your own folders*

3. Choose File | Add Clips to Organizer | On My Own. The Add Clips to Organizer dialog box appears.

4. Select the file or files you want to get at by way of the Clip Organizer. You can select more than one file at a time by CTRL-clicking or SHIFT-clicking.

5. Click the Add button.

Note   *The files in the Clip Organizer are merely pointers to the locations of real files on your computer. By putting your own files in the Clip Organizer, you make it easier to find your own files. And you can insert them by using the same techniques you use to insert any media file in the Clip Organizer.*

Attaching a New Keyword to an Image

Microsoft has attached several keywords to each file in the Clip Organizer. As you know, you can enter a keyword in the Search task pane to look for files. Suppose you bring one of your own files into the Clip Organizer. How will you find it? One way is to attach a few keywords to your file so you can search for it. Follow these steps to attach a keyword to an image:

1. Either right-click the file or open its drop-down menu and choose Edit Keywords. You see the Keywords dialog box. It lists words that have already been attached to the image.

2. Add as many keywords as you like by entering them in the Keyword text box and clicking the Add button (or remove keywords for that matter by selecting them and clicking the Delete button).

Getting Multimedia Files Online from the Design Gallery

As long as your computer is connected to the Internet, you can go online and scavenge clip art images, photographs, sound files, and movie clips from "Design Gallery Live," Microsoft's online repository of multimedia files. The images are free and easy to download.

In order to download files from the Design Gallery, you must have read and approved the End User License Agreement. The agreement should appear the first time you visit the Design Gallery, but if it doesn't, click License on the menu bar to read and approve the agreement.

To go to the Design Gallery Web site, as shown in Figure B-3, click the Clips Online button or choose Tools | Clips Online. Using the search boxes, describe what file you want. To download files, select their check boxes and click the Download hyperlink. You will be asked where to download the files on your computer.

Figure B-3.   *You can download files from Microsoft Design Gallery Live*

The Complete Reference

Appendix C

Becoming MOUS-Certified in Microsoft Word 2002

The *Microsoft Office User Specialist* (MOUS) program is the best way for you to prove to yourself and to prospective employers that you have mastered one or more programs in the Microsoft Office suite. The program is a reliable way for you to measure your strengths and identify your weaknesses. And by following the prescribed coursework and preparing for the exam, you will improve your skills at using Word or another program in the Office suite.

At present there are two levels of MOUS certification:

- **Core** Becoming a Microsoft Office User Specialist at the Core level indicates that you have a comprehensive understanding of everyday computer tasks.

- **Expert** The holder of an Expert certificate can handle more complex assignments.

The MOUS program changes from time to time. For up-to-date information about MOUS certifications, visit www.mouse.net on the Internet.

Word 2002 Core Exam Objectives

Table C-1 lists the exam objectives that users must master to achieve Core status. Where a practice file is available, it is listed in the table (the Introduction of this book explains how to download the practice files from the Osborne/McGraw-Hill Web site: www.osborne.com). Turn to headings in the chapters listed in the table to learn about an exam objective.

Exam Objective	Chapter Number and Heading(s)	Practice Document(s)
Inserting and Modifying Text		
Insert, modify, and move text and symbols	2. "Typing Text and Erasing Mistakes" and "Entering Symbols and Foreign Characters" 3. "Moving and Copying Text Between Documents" and "Linking Documents So That Text Is Copied Automatically" 6. "Finding and Replacing Text and Other Things," "Creating and Inserting AutoText Entries," and "Entering Text and Graphics Quickly with the AutoCorrect Command"	Copying and Moving, Find and Replace, AutoText,

Table C-1. *MOUS Objectives for the Core Exam*

Exam Objective	Chapter Number and Heading(s)	Practice Document(s)
Apply and modify text formats	7. "Changing the Way Characters Look on the Page" and "Choosing a Font and Font Size for Text"	Boldface Italics Underline, Fonts,
Correct spelling and grammar usage	11. "Correcting Your Spelling Errors" and "Checking a Document for Grammatical Errors"	Spelling
Use the Thesaurus	11. "Finding the Right Word with the Thesaurus"	
Apply character effects and highlights	7. "Playing with Word's 'Text Effects'" 17. "Highlighting the Important Text"	Text Effect
Enter and format Date and Time	6. "Quickly Entering the Data and Time"	
Apply character styles	12. "The Different Kinds of Styles" and "Applying Styles in a Document"	

Creating and Modifying Paragraphs

Modify format, alignment, and layout of paragraphs	7. "Putting Borders, Shading, and Color on Paragraphs" 8. "Everything You Need to Know About Formatting Paragraphs," "Aligning, Centering, and Justifying Text," and "Indenting Text on the Page" 12. "Applying Styles in a Document"	Shades, Aligning, Apply Styles
Set and modify tabs	8. "Aligning Text with Tab Stops"	

Table C-1.   *MOUS Objectives for the Core Exam* (continued)

Exam Objective	Chapter Number and Heading(s)	Practice Document(s)
Apply bullet, outline, and numbering format to paragraphs	10. "The Bare-Bones Basics: Bulleted and Numbered Lists" 17. "Organizing Your Work with Outlines"	Bullets and Numbers, Outline
Apply paragraph styles	12. "Applying Styles in a Document"	
Formatting Documents		
Create and modify a header and footer	9. "Putting Headers and Footers on Pages"	Header and Footer, Odd and Even Headers
Apply column and text alignment settings	15. "Laying Out Text in Newspaper-Style Columns"	Columns
Modify document layout and Page Setup options	2. "Starting a New Paragraph, Line, or Page"9. "Numbering the Pages," "Setting the Margins," and "Creating a Landscape Document"	Margins
Create and modify tables	14. "Creating a Table," "Letting the Table AutoFormat Command Do the Work," "Decorating a Table with Borders, Shading, and Color," and "Changing the Layout of a Table"	Modify Table
Preview and print documents, envelopes, and labels	5. "Previewing a Document Before You Print It," "Printing Documents," "Printing Addresses and Return Addresses on Envelopes," and "Printing a Single Label or Sheet of Labels with the Same Address"	Preview, Print, Envelopes

Table C-1. *MOUS Objectives for the Core Exam* (continued)

Exam Objective	Chapter Number and Heading(s)	Practice Document(s)
Managing Documents		
Manage files and folders for documents	20. "Creating the Folders You Need"	
Create documents using templates	1. "Creating New Documents"	
Save documents using different names and file formats	20. "Saving a Document Under a New Name" and "Converting Documents to Different Formats So Others Can Use Them"	
Working with Graphics		
Insert images and graphics	13. "Inserting Graphics and Clip Art in Documents"	
Create and modify diagrams and charts	16. "Putting Charts in Documents" and "Creating Organizational Charts"	Charts
Workgroup Collaboration		
Compare and merge documents	17. "Tracking Revisions to a Document"	
View and edit comments	17. "Commenting on a Document"	Comments
Convert documents into Web pages	"Turning a Word Document into a Web Page" and "Seeing What Your Document Looks Like in a Web Browser"	

Table C-1.   *MOUS Objectives for the Core Exam* (continued)

Word 2002 Expert Exam Objectives

Candidates for Expert certificates must have mastered the exam objectives listed in Table C-2 as well as the objectives listed in Table C-1. Where a practice document is available, it is listed in the table (the Introduction of this book explains how to download the practice files from the Osborne/McGraw-Hill Web site). Turn to headings in the chapters listed in the table to learn about an exam objective.

Exam Objective	Chapter Number and Heading(s)	Practice Document(s)
Customizing Paragraphs		
Modify text flow options	2. "Starting a New Paragraph, Line, or Page Break" 8. "Preventing Widows and Orphans"	
Sort paragraphs in lists and tables	10. "Alphabetizing and Sorting Lists" 14. "Sorting, or Reordering, a Table"	Sort, Revise Table
Formatting Documents		
Create and format document sections	9. "Section Breaks for Changing Layouts" 8. "Learning How Paragraphs or Text Was Formatted"	Sections
Create and apply character styles	12. "Applying Styles in a Document"	
Create and update document indexes and tables of contents, figures, and authorities	16. "Indexing a Document," "Generating a Table of Contents," and "Compiling a Caption Table for Figures, Equations, Tables, and More" 19. "Creating a Table of Authorities"	TOC, Index
Create cross-references	16. "Including Cross-References in Documents"	Cross-References

Table C-2. *MOUS Objectives for the Expert Exam*

Exam Objective	Chapter Number and Heading(s)	Practice Document(s)
Add and revise notes and comments	16. "Handling Footnotes and Endnotes" 17. "Commenting on a Document"	
Create and manage master documents and subdocuments	17. "Master Documents for Organizing Big Jobs"	
Navigate within documents	2. "Moving Around in Long Documents"	Navigate, Bookmarks
Merge letters, labels, envelopes, and e-mail messages with data sources	18. "The Six Steps to Completing a Mail-Merge," "Generating Form Letters for Mass-Mailings," "Printing Labels for Mass-Mailings," "Printing Envelopes for Mass-Mailings," and "Sending the Same E-Mail to Many Different People"	
Create and modify forms using various form controls	15. "Designing the Form Template and Entering the Form Fields"	Online Forms
Prepare documents and forms for distribution	15. "Protecting a Form So No One Tampers with It" 20. "Protecting Documents Against Undue Tampering"	
Customizing Tables		
Use Excel data in tables	14. "Calling on Excel to Construct Worksheet Tables"	Excel Table
Perform calculations in Word tables	14. "Crunching the Numbers in Tables" and "Merging and Splitting Cells and Tables"	Calculations

Table C-2.   *MOUS Objectives for the Expert Exam* (continued)

Exam Objective	Chapter Number and Heading(s)	Practice Document(s)
Creating and Modifying Graphics		
Create, modify, and position graphics	13. "Changing the Appearance of an Image or Graphic," "Drawing Lines and Shapes," and "Manipulating Art, Text Boxes, Shapes, and Other So-Called Objects"	Lines and Objects, 3D Shapes, Graphics, Watermarks
Create and modify charts using data from other applications	16. "Putting Charts in Documents"	
Align text and graphics	13. "Tricks for Aligning and Distributing Objects" and "Wrapping Text Around an Object"	
Customizing Word		
Create, edit, and run, macros	23. "Recording a Macro," "Running a Macro," and "Editing a Macro"	
Customize menus and toolbars	21. "Setting Up Your Own Menus" and "Creating Your Own Toolbars and Toolbar Buttons"	
Workgroup Collaboration		
Track, accept, and reject changes to documents	17. "Keeping Track of Revisions to Documents"	Track Changes
Merge input from several reviewers	17. "Tracking Revisions to a Document" 22. "Routing a Document to Others"	

Table C-2.   *MOUS Objectives for the Expert Exam* (continued)

Exam Objective	Chapter Number and Heading(s)	Practice Document(s)
Insert and modify hyperlinks to other documents and Web pages	22. "Including Hyperlinks in Documents and Web Pages"	Hyperlink
Insert Link Bars in documents	18. "Creating a Link List"	
Create and edit Web documents in Word	22. "Opening a Web Page in Word"	
Create document versions	20. "Saving (and Opening) Different Versions of a Document"	Versions
Protect documents	20. "Protecting Documents Against Undue Tampering"	
Define and modify default file locations for workgroup templates	12. "Setting the Default File Location for Workgroup Templates"	

Table C-2.   *MOUS Objectives for the Expert Exam* (continued)

How to Become MOUS Certified

To become a certified MOUS specialist in Word, you need to prepare for the exam, register to take the test, take the text, and get your test results.

1. Prepare for the Exam

As you begin to prepare for MOUS certification in Word, figure out what parts of the program you know well and where you need to learn more. The skills you need for

APPENDIXES

Core certification are listed in Table C-1, and the skills you need for Expert certification are listed in Table C-2. You can also go to the MOUS Web site at www.mous.net to see a list of the skills.

MOUS exams are not multiple-choice exams or fill-in-the-blank exams. Instead, you are asked to perform assignments at a computer. For example, you might be asked to double-space a paragraph or create a form letter. To prepare for the exam, focus on Word tasks. Use the sample documents that come with this book to get hands-on practice in using Word. Don't bother memorizing information—doing so won't help you pass the test.

This book is a comprehensive reference to Microsoft Word. All tasks you can do in Word are explained in this book. Table C-1 and Table C-2 show where each course objective is covered in the book. At the end of most chapters is a table that tells you where MOUS exam objectives are covered.

2. Register for the Test

All exams are administered by an Authorized Testing Center. To find the testing center nearest you, either phone (800) 933-4493 or check the MOUS Web site at www.mous.net. Many testing centers require advance registration, but others accept walk-in candidates.

3. Take the Test

All the exams take an hour or less. You are judged on your ability to complete tasks and also on how long it takes you to complete tasks. As you take an exam, you can use the Help program, but doing so takes time and will detract from your test score.

Microsoft provides guidelines for taking MOUS exams. Here are some general tips for taking a MOUS exam:

- Carefully read the test instructions. When you begin a test, instructions are displayed at the bottom of the screen.

- Answer each question as if your work will be shown to the test exam administrator. Do nothing extra; do only what is requested.

- Because all questions have equal value, try to answer all of them, including the difficult questions.

- Pay close attention to how each question is worded. Responses must be precise. To answer a question correctly, you must do exactly as asked.

- Test scores are based on the end result, not on which technique was used to complete a task. Errant keystrokes and mouse-clicks do not count against your score as long as you achieve the correct result. The result is what counts.

- The overall test is timed. Spending a lot of time on a question doesn't matter as far as your test score is concerned, but taking too long on a question leaves less time for answering other questions.

- Answers are either right or wrong. You do not get credit for partial answers.

- If the message "method is not available" appears on the computer screen, try solving the problem a different way.

- *Important:* Make sure you have entirely completed each question before clicking the Next button. After you click the Next button, you cannot return to that question. A question will be scored as wrong if it is not properly completed before moving to the next question.

4. Get Your Test Results

Each candidate sees his or her test results as soon as the test is completed. Test results are completely confidential. If you pass, you will receive a certificate by mail in four to six weeks. If you fail, you will be informed where you need to focus more attention. You can take the test as many times as you want. Refunds are not given if you don't pass the test; you must pay a new fee each time you take the test.

After you pass the test, you have recognized proof that you possess specific, relevant skills in Microsoft Word. A MOUS certificate is invaluable in the job market. The certificate proves to prospective employers that you have the skills to succeed.

Making Sure That a Question Is Properly Completed

To make sure that a question is properly completed, do the following:

- Close all dialog boxes, toolbars, Help windows, and menus.
- Make sure all of a task's steps are completed before clicking Next to move to the next task.

Don't do the following:

- Don't leave dialog boxes, toolbars, or menus open.
- Don't click the Next button until you have completely answered the question.
- Don't scroll in the question unless instructed to do so. Leave your answer visible.

Index

E

F

X–Z

INTERNATIONAL CONTACT INFORMATION

AUSTRALIA
McGraw-Hill Book Company Australia Pty. Ltd.
TEL +61-2-9417-9899
FAX +61-2-9417-5687
http://www.mcgraw-hill.com.au
books-it_sydney@mcgraw-hill.com

CANADA
McGraw-Hill Ryerson Ltd.
TEL +905-430-5000
FAX +905-430-5020
http://www.mcgrawhill.ca

GREECE, MIDDLE EAST,
NORTHERN AFRICA
McGraw-Hill Hellas
TEL +30-1-656-0990-3-4
FAX +30-1-654-5525

MEXICO (Also serving Latin America)
McGraw-Hill Interamericana Editores S.A. de C.V.
TEL +525-117-1583
FAX +525-117-1589
http://www.mcgraw-hill.com.mx
fernando_castellanos@mcgraw-hill.com

SINGAPORE (Serving Asia)
McGraw-Hill Book Company
TEL +65-863-1580
FAX +65-862-3354
http://www.mcgraw-hill.com.sg
mghasia@mcgraw-hill.com

SOUTH AFRICA
McGraw-Hill South Africa
TEL +27-11-622-7512
FAX +27-11-622-9045
robyn_swanepoel@mcgraw-hill.com

UNITED KINGDOM & EUROPE
(Excluding Southern Europe)
McGraw-Hill Education Europe
TEL +44-1-628-502500
FAX +44-1-628-770224
http://www.mcgraw-hill.co.uk
computing_neurope@mcgraw-hill.com

ALL OTHER INQUIRIES Contact:
Osborne/McGraw-Hill
TEL +1-510-549-6600
FAX +1-510-883-7600
http://www.osborne.com
omg_international@mcgraw-hill.com